Lecture Notes in Computer Science

Vol. 1: GI-Gesellschaft für Informatik e.V. 3. Jahrestagung, Hamburg, 8.–10. Oktober 1973. Herausgegeben im Auftrag der Gesellschaft für Informatik von W. Brauer. XI, 508 Seiten. 1973. DM 32,–

Vol. 2: GI-Gesellschaft für Informatik e.V. 1. Fachtagung über Automatentheorie und Formale Sprachen, Bonn, 9.–12. Juli 1973. Herausgegeben im Auftrag der Gesellschaft für Informatik von K.-H. Böhling und K. Indermark. VII, 322 Seiten. 1973. DM 26,–

Vol. 3: 5th Conference on Optimization Techniques, Part I. (Series: I.F.I.P. TC7 Optimization Conferences.) Edited by R. Conti and A. Ruberti. XIII, 565 pages. 1973. DM 38,–

Vol. 4: 5th Conference on Optimization Techniques, Part II. (Series: I.F.I.P. TC7 Optimization Conferences.) Edited by R. Conti and A. Ruberti. XIII, 389 pages. 1973. DM 28,–

Vol. 5: International Symposium on Theoretical Programming. Edited by A. Ershov and V. A. Nepomniaschy. VI, 407 pages. 1974. DM 30,–

Vol. 6: B. T. Smith, J. M. Boyle, B. S. Garbow, Y. Ikebe, V. C. Klema, and C. B. Moler, Matrix Eigensystem Routines – EISPACK Guide. X, 387 pages. 1974. DM 28,–

Vol. 7: 3. Fachtagung über Programmiersprachen, Kiel, 5.–7. März 1974. Herausgegeben von B. Schlender und W. Frielinghaus. VI, 225 Seiten. 1974. DM 20,–

Vol. 8: GI-NTG Fachtagung über Struktur und Betrieb von Rechensystemen, Braunschweig, 20.–22. März 1974. Herausgegeben im Auftrag der GI und der NTG von H.-O. Leilich. VI, 340 Seiten. 1974. DM 26,–

Vol. 9: GI-BIFOA Internationale Fachtagung: Informationszentren in Wirtschaft und Verwaltung. Köln, 17./18. Sept. 1973. Herausgegeben im Auftrag der GI und dem BIFOA von P. Schmitz. VI, 259 Seiten. 1974. DM 22,–

Vol. 10: Computing Methods in Applied Sciences and Engineering, Part 1. International Symposium, Versailles, December 17–21, 1973. Edited by R. Glowinski and J. L. Lions. X, 497 pages. 1974. DM 34,–

Vol. 11: Computing Methods in Applied Sciences and Engineering, Part 2. International Symposium, Versailles, December 17–21, 1973. Edited by R. Glowinski and J. L. Lions. X, 434 pages. 1974. DM 30,–

Vol. 12: GFK-GI-GMR Fachtagung Prozessrechner 1974. Karlsruhe, 10.–11. Juni 1974. Herausgegeben von G. Krüger und R. Friehmelt. XI, 620 Seiten. 1974. DM 42,–

Vol. 13: Rechnerstrukturen und Betriebsprogrammierung, Erlangen, 1970. (GI-Gesellschaft für Informatik e.V.) Herausgegeben von W. Händler und P. P. Spies. VII, 333 Seiten. 1974. DM 30,–

Vol. 14: Automata, Languages and Programming – 2nd Colloquium, University of Saarbrücken, July 29–August 2, 1974. Edited by J. Loeckx. VIII, 611 pages. 1974. DM 48,–

Vol. 15: L Systems. Edited by A. Salomaa and G. Rozenberg. VI, 338 pages. 1974. DM 30,–

Vol. 16: Operating Systems, International Symposium, Rocquencourt 1974. Edited by E. Gelenbe and C. Kaiser. VIII, 310 pages. 1974. DM 30,–

Vol. 17: Rechner-Gestützter Unterricht RGU '74, Fachtagung, Hamburg, 12.–14. August 1974, ACU-Arbeitskreis Computer-Unterstützter Unterricht. Herausgegeben im Auftrag der GI von K. Brunnstein, K. Haefner und W. Händler. X, 417 Seiten. 1974. DM 35,–

Vol. 18: K. Jensen and N. Wirth, PASCAL – User Manual and Report. VII, 170 pages. 1974. DM 20,–

Vol. 19: Programming Symposium. Proceeding, Colloque sur la Programmation, Paris, April 9–11, 1974. V, 425 pages. 1974. DM 35,–

Vol. 20: J. Engelfriet, Simple Program Schemes and Formal Languages. VII, 254 pages. 1974. DM 25,–

Vol. 21: Compiler Construction, An Advanced Course. Edited by F. L. Bauer and J. Eickel. XIV. 621 pages. 1974. DM 42,–

Vol. 22: Formal Aspects of Cognitive Processes. Proceedings, Interdisciplinary Conference, Ann Arbor, March 1972. Edited by T. Storer and D. Winter. V, 214 pages. 1975. DM 23,–

Vol. 23: Programming Methodology. 4th Informatik Symposium, IBM Germany Wildbad, September 25–27, 1974. Edited by C. E. Hackl. VI, 501 pages. 1975. DM 39,–

Vol. 24: Parallel Processing. Proceedings of the Sagamore Computer Conference, August 20–23, 1974. Edited by T. Feng. VI, 433 pages. 1975. DM 35,–

Vol. 25: Category Theory Applied to Computation and Control. Proceedings of the First International Symposium, San Francisco, February 25–26, 1974. Edited by E. G. Manes. X, 245 pages. 1975. DM 25,–

Vol. 26: GI-4. Jahrestagung, Berlin, 9.–12. Oktober 1974. Herausgegeben im Auftrag der GI von D. Siefkes. IX, 748 Seiten. 1975. DM 49,–

Vol. 27: Optimization Techniques. IFIP Technical Conference. Novosibirsk, July 1–7, 1974. (Series: I.F.I.P. TC7 Optimization Conferences.) Edited by G. I. Marchuk. VIII, 507 pages. 1975. DM 39,–

Vol. 28: Mathematical Foundations of Computer Science. 3rd Symposium at Jadwisin near Warsaw, June 17–22, 1974. Edited by A Blikle. VIII, 484 pages. 1975. DM 37,–

Lecture Notes in Computer Science

Edited by G. Goos and J. Hartmanis

28

Mathematical Foundations of Computer Science

3rd Symposium at Jadwisin near Warsaw,
June 17–22, 1974

Edited by A. Blikle

Springer-Verlag
Berlin · Heidelberg · New York 1975

Prof. Andrzej Blikle
Computation Centre
Polish Academy of Sciences
P.O. Box 22
Warschau/Polen

Library of Congress Cataloging in Publication Data

Symposium on Mathematical Foundations of Computer Science, 3d, Jadwisin, Poland, 1974.
Mathematical foundations of computer science.

(Lecture notes in computer science ; v. 28)
"Organized by the Computation Center of the Polish Academy of Sciences and sponsored by the International Mathematical Stefan Banach Center in Warsaw."
1. Sequential machine theory—Congresses. 2. Formal languages—Congresses. 3. Programming (Electronic computers)—Congresses. I. Blikle, Andrzej. II. Polska Akademia Nauk. Centrum Obliczeniowe. III. International Mathematical Stefan Banach Center. IV. Title. V. Series.

QA267.5.S4S89 1974 519.4 75-9642

AMS Subject Classifications (1970): 68A05, 68A20, 68A25, 68A30, 68A50
CR Subject Classifications (1974): 3.64, 3.70, 5.22, 5.23, 5.24, 5.27

ISBN 978-3-540-07162-4

Offsetdruck: Julius Beltz, Hemsbach/Bergstr.

PREFACE

These Proceedings are based on the papers presented at the 3rd Symposium on Mathematical Foundations of Computer Science held in Jadwisin near Warsaw, June 17 - 22, 1974. The Symposium was organized by the Computation Center of the Polish Academy of Sciences and sponsored by the International Mathematical Stefan Banach Center in Warsaw.

The Symposium was a continuation of two other international symposia of the same name:

1st Symposium on Mathematical Foundations of Computer Science - - called in short MFCS-72 - held in Jabłonna near Warsaw, August 21 - 27, 1972 and organized by the Computation Center of the Polish Academy of Sciences and the Institute of Computing Machines of the Warsaw University.

2nd Symposium on Mathematical Foundations of Computer Science - - called in short MFCS-73 - held in High Tatras (Czechoslovakia), September 3 - 8, 1973 and organized by the Mathematical Institute of the Slovak Academy of Sciences.

Proceedings of these symposia have been published informally as technical reports and have been distributed only among the participants. The MFCS-73 Proceedings is expected to be republished in the Lecture Notes in Computer Science.

According to an informal agreement of the Polish and Czechoslovak organizers of these symposia, the MFCS symposia are expected to be held every year: every even year in Poland and every odd year in Czechoslovakia. For information about MFCS-75 write to J.Bečvař, Mathematical Institute, Czechoslovak Academy of Sciences, Žitna 25, Prague 1, Czechoslovakia.

Our MFCS-74 Symposium, besides being the 3rd successive MFCS meeting, has also been a closing event of the MFCS Semester, February 1 - June 22, 1974 held in the International Mathematical Stefan Banach Center in Warsaw. Proceeding of this Semester, covering full-time lectures, will be published by the Polish Scientific Publisher and should appear early in 1976.

The organizers wish to express their thanks to all contributors to the scientific program of the Symposium.

Warsaw, October 1974 Andrzej Blikle

ORGANIZING COMMITTEE

A.Blikle (vice chairman)
P.Dembiński (secretary)
B.Konikowska
W.Kwasowiec
J.Małuszyński
A.Mazurkiewicz
Z.Pawlak (chairman)
J.Winkowski

TABLE OF CONTENTS

AUTOMATA THEORY

COMPUTING SYSTEMS

MATHEMATICAL ASPECTS OF APPLICATION METHODOLOGY

THEORY OF PROGRAMS

SEQUENTIAL FUNCTIONS AND GENERALIZED MOORE AND MEALY AUTOMATA

Jiří Bečvář

Mathematical Institute
Czechoslovak Academy of Sciences
Prague

0. INTRODUCTION

In view of the fact of behavioural equivalence between Moore and Mealy automata one uses to choose in developing abstract automata theory one of these two models as the basic one. The treatment of sequential functions also preferably follows one of the two corresponding lines. Our aim in what follows is to provide a technical basis for the possibility of relating systematically results in both directions. The main tool is a simultaneous consideration, for sequential functions, of both their derivatives and M-derivatives (Moore derivatives) and a study of relations between these derivatives and the corresponding operations of closure. Both kinds of derivatives have been separately in use in the literature for a long time under various names and in various contexts (see, for example,[1] and [3]). Thus we restrict ourselves to essentially listing a more or less coherent body of definitions and results (including some classical ones) which appear as relevant to our purpose. They are chosen so as to fit the case of generalized automata.

1. AUTOMATA

Notation: Let S be a set. Then $\mathcal{P}S$ is the power set of S; S^* is the free monoid generated by S; e is the unit in S^* ; $S^+ = S^* - \{e\}$. If $u,v \in S^*$, then $|u|$ is the length of u, $u \subseteq v$ means that u is a prefix of v. For two sets M,N the set of all (total) functions from M to N is denoted $[M \to N]$. The composition of two functions g,h is sometimes written $h \circ g$, with $(h \circ g)(x) = h(g(x))$.

Though we shall not use the adjective "generalized", automata which we consider are in fact generalized automata (see [2]).

A <u>Mealy automaton</u> is a 5-tuple (Q,X,Y,δ,λ); Q, X, and Y are set of states, input alphabet, and output alphabet, respectively; δ: $Q \times X \to Q$ is the transition function, λ: $Q \times X \to Y^*$ is the output function of the automaton.

A <u>Moore automaton</u> is a 5-tuple (Q,X,Y,δ,μ), where Q, X, Y, and δ are as above; $\mu: Q \to Y^*$ is the marking function of the automaton, the output function is defined to be $\lambda = \mu \circ \delta$.

By an <u>automaton</u> we mean either a Mealy or a Moore automaton; in such a case it is sometimes written $(Q,X,Y,\delta,.)$.

In the sequel we use a rigid notation: Q, X, Y, δ, and λ always mean the state set etc. of the automaton, say A, under consideration, and μ the marking function of A - if A is a Moore automaton; the symbol q always means a state of A; x denotes an element of the set X under consideration, u, v, and t are from X^*. If necessary, the symbols Q,... may have the name of the corresponding automaton subscripted (this concerns also symbols φ, ψ, etc. introduced later).

Let A be an automaton. The transition function δ of A is extended to the domain $Q \times X^*$ as follows:

$$\delta(q,e) = q\ , \qquad \delta(q,ux) = \delta(\delta(q,u),x)$$

The output function λ is extended to $\lambda^+: Q \times X^+ \to Y^*$ as follows:

$$\lambda^+(q,ux) = \lambda(\delta(q,u),x)$$

If A is a Moore automaton, λ^+ is further extended to $\lambda^*: Q \times X^* \to Y^*$ as follows:

$$\lambda^*(q,e) = \mu(q)\ , \qquad \lambda^*(q,ux) = \lambda^+(q,ux)$$

(An equivalent definition of λ^* is $\lambda^* = \mu \circ \delta$.) The <u>response function</u> (transducing function) $\varphi: Q \times X^* \to Y^*$ of an (arbitrary) automaton A is defined as follows:

$$\varphi(q,e) = e\ , \qquad \varphi(q,ux) = \varphi(q,u)\,\lambda^+(q,ux)$$

If A is a Moore automaton then, in addition to φ, the <u>M-response function</u> $\psi: Q \times X^* \to Y^*$ is defined as follows:

$$\psi(q,u) = \mu(q)\,\varphi(q,u)$$

One then has

$$\psi(q,e) = \mu(q)\ , \qquad \psi(q,ux) = \psi(q,u)\,\lambda^+(q,ux)$$

$$\psi(q,uv) = \psi(q,u)\,\varphi(\delta(q,u),v)$$

Henceforth we use the notation φ^q for the function $\varphi(q,.)$, and

ψ^q for $\psi(q,.)$.

Equivalence of states $q_1 \in Q_A$, $q_2 \in Q_B$ of automata A, B is defined as follows:

$$q_1 \sim q_2 \Leftrightarrow \varphi_A^{q_1} = \varphi_B^{q_2}$$

Equivalence of automata A, B is defined as follows:

$$A \sim B \Leftrightarrow \{\varphi_A^q : q \in Q_A\} = \{\varphi_B^q : q \in Q_B\}$$

If A, B are Moore automata then, in addition, M-equivalence of states ($q_1 \widetilde{\scriptstyle M} q_2$) and of automata ($A \widetilde{\scriptstyle M} B$) is defined as above, with symbol ψ substituted everywhere for φ .

An (arbitrary) automaton A is reduced if

$$\forall q_1, q_2 \in Q : q_1 \sim q_2 \Rightarrow q_1 = q_2$$

The automaton A is a reduct of the automaton B if A is reduced and $A \sim B$. If A, B are Moore automata then, in addition, the concept of A being M-reduced and of A being an M-reduct of B are defined similarly.

2. SEQUENTIAL FUNCTIONS

A function $f : X^* \to Y^*$ is called

(i) s-function (sequential), if

$$u \sqsubseteq v \Rightarrow f(u) \sqsubseteq f(v)$$

(ii) l-function (length-preserving), if

$$|f(u)| = |u|$$

(iii) e-function (e-preserving), if

$$f(e) = e$$

We use also combined terminology, thus for example an se-function is a function which is both sequential and e-preserving. For any sequence α of the symbols s, l, e, let $[X^* \underset{\alpha}{\to} Y^*]$ denote the set of α-functions from $[X^* \to Y^*]$. (In the sequel, l-functions do not appear explicitly.)

For $f : X^* \to Y^*$ let $g = \gamma(f) : X^* \to Y^*$ be defined as follows:

$$(*) \begin{cases} g(e) = f(e) \\ g(ux) = g(u)f(ux) \end{cases}$$

<u>Proposition 1.</u> Given X, Y, the mapping γ is a bijection $\gamma : [X^* \to Y^*] \to [X^* \xrightarrow{s} Y^*]$. For each s-function $g : X^* \to Y^*$ the function $f = \gamma^{-1}(g)$ is uniquely determined by the equations (*).

$\gamma(f)$ is called the function <u>generated</u> by f ; $\gamma^{-1}(g)$ is called the <u>generating function</u> of the s-function g and will be denoted $[g]$.

For $f \in [X^* \xrightarrow{s} Y^*]$ and $u \in X^*$ the <u>derivative</u> $D_u f$ and the <u>M-derivative</u> (Moore derivative) $D_u^M f$ of f with respect to u are defined as follows ($v \in X^*$):

$D_u f(v)$ = solution of the equation $f(uv) = f(u) D_u f(v)$

$D_u^M f(v) = [f](u) D_u f(v)$

<u>Proposition 2.</u> Let $f \in [X^* \xrightarrow{s} Y^*]$. Then

(a) $D_u f$ is an se-function

(b) $D_u^M f$ is an s-function

(c) $D_e f = f \Leftrightarrow f$ is an se-function

(d) $D_e^M f = f$

The effect of applying meaningfully to an s-function subsequently two of the operations $[.] = \gamma^{-1}$, D_u, and D_v^M is as follows:

<u>Theorem 1.</u> Let $f \in [X^* \xrightarrow{s} Y^*]$. Then

(a) $$[D_u f](v) = \begin{cases} e & \text{if } v = e \\ [f](uv) & \text{if } v \neq e \end{cases}$$

(b) $[D_u^M f](v) = [f](uv)$
(thus $[D_u^M f] = [f] \circ L_u$, where $L_u(v) = uv$)

(c) $D_v(D_u f) = D_v(D_u^M f) = D_{uv} f$

(d) $$(D_v^M(D_u f))(t) = \begin{cases} D_u f(t) & \text{if } v = e \\ D_{uv}^M f(t) & \text{if } v \neq e \end{cases}$$

(e) $D_v^M(D_u^M f) = D_{uv}^M f$

M-derivatives of s-functions have close connection to derivatives of languages. Let $L \subseteq X^*$ be a language. Then the derivative $D_u L$ of L with respect to $u \in X^*$ is

$D_u L = \{ v \in X^* : uv \in L \}$

Now let $\chi_L : X^* \to \{0,1\}$ be the characteristic function of L and let $\sigma_L = \gamma(\chi_L) : X^* \to \{0,1\}^*$ be the s-function generated by χ_L. Then $[\sigma_L] = \chi_L$ and we have

Proposition 3.

(a) $|\sigma_L(u)| = |u| + 1$

(b) $\sigma_{D_u L} = D_u^M \sigma_L$

Derivatives give rise to corresponding concepts of closure which play essential role in questions concerning realizability of functions in automata. For an s-function $f : X^* \to Y^*$ we define three kinds of closure of f:

$D^\bullet f = \{D_u f : u \in X^*\}$ w-closure (weak closure)

$Df = \{f\} \cup D^\bullet f$ closure

$D^M f = \{D_u^M f : u \in X^*\}$ M-closure (Moore closure)

These operations are further extended to sets $F \subseteq [X^* \underset{s}{\to} Y^*]$ by putting $D^\bullet F = \bigcup_{f \in F} D^\bullet f$, and similarly for D, D^M. A set F is called w-closed (closed, M-closed) if $D^\bullet F \subseteq F$ ($DF \subseteq F$, $D^M F \subseteq F$).

For a language $L \subseteq X^*$, let us define $DL = \{D_u L : u \in X^*\}$. Moreover, for a set of languages $\mathbb{L} \subseteq \mathcal{P}X^*$ let $D\mathbb{L} = \bigcup_{K \in \mathbb{L}} DK$. Then by Proposition 3 one gets

$$\{\sigma_K : K \in DL\} = D^M \sigma_L \ , \ \{\sigma_K : K \in D\mathbb{L}\} = D^M\{\sigma_K : K \in \mathbb{L}\}$$

The effect of a repeated application of the operations of closure $D^\bullet$, D, and D^M to a set of s-functions is summarized in the following theorem.

Theorem 2.

(I) $D^\bullet$, D, and D^M are completely additive set functions. Hence they are monotonic with respect to $\subseteq$, and

$D^\bullet(\emptyset) = D(\emptyset) = D^M(\emptyset) = \emptyset$

(II) Let $F \subseteq [X^* \underset{s}{\to} Y^*]$. Then

(a) $F \subseteq D^\bullet F \Leftrightarrow F \subseteq [X^* \underset{se}{\to} Y^*]$

(b) $F \subseteq DF = F \cup D^\bullet F$

(c) $F \subseteq D^M F$

(d) $D^\bullet D^\bullet F = D^\bullet F$, $DDF = DF$, $D^M D^M F = D^M F$

(e) $D^{\bullet}DF = DD^{\bullet}F = D^{\bullet}F$

(f) $D^{\bullet}D^{M}F = D^{\bullet}F$

(g) $D\,D^{M}F = D^{M}DF = D^{M}F \cup D^{\bullet}F = D^{M}F \cup DF$

(III) If G is obtained from F by a finite number of applications of the operations $D^{\bullet}$, D, and D^{M}, then G is one of the sets

$F\ ,\ D^{\bullet}F\ ,\ DF\ ,\ D^{M}F\ ,\ D^{M}D^{\bullet}F\ ,\ D^{M}F \cup DF$

As to the variants of the concept of closed set one has

<u>Proposition 4.</u> Let $F \subseteq [X^* \xrightarrow[s]{} Y^*]$. Then

(a) $D^{\bullet}F = F \Leftrightarrow$ F is w-closed & $F \subseteq [X^* \xrightarrow[se]{} Y^*]$

(b) F is w-closed $\Leftrightarrow$ F is closed $\Leftrightarrow DF = F$

(c) F is M-closed $\Leftrightarrow D^{M}F = F$

3. SEQUENTIAL FUNCTIONS IN AUTOMATA

The basic s-functions which appear in automata are the response functions. We are interested in their derivatives and generating functions. The result - which includes also known facts - is as follows.

<u>Proposition 5.</u>

(I) In an automaton one has

(a) $\{\varphi^q : q \in Q\}$ is a closed set of se-functions

(b) $[\varphi^q](u) = \begin{cases} e & \text{if } u = e \\ \lambda^+(q,u) & \text{if } u \neq e \end{cases}$

(c) $D_u \varphi^q = \varphi^{\delta(q,u)}$

(d) $D_u^M \varphi^q(v) = \begin{cases} \varphi^q(v) & \text{if } u = e \\ \lambda^+(q,u)\varphi^{\delta(q,u)}(v) & \text{if } u \neq e \end{cases}$

(II) In a Moore automaton one has in addition

(e) $\{\psi^q : q \in Q\}$ is an M-closed set of s-functions

(f) $[\psi^q](u) = \lambda^*(q,u)$

(g) $D_u \psi^q = D_u \varphi^q = \varphi^{\delta(q,u)}$

(h) $D_u^M \psi^q = \psi^{\delta(q,u)}$

(i) $D_u^M \varphi^q = \psi^{\delta(q,u)}$ if $u \neq e$

It is in the spirit of this exposition to distinguish two concepts of realizability of functions in automata. As usually, a function f is called realizable in an automaton A if $f = \varphi^q$ for some state q of A. Further, f is called M-realizable in A if A is a Moore automaton and $f = \psi^q$ for some state q of A. A set F of functions is called realizable (M-realizable) in A if each $f \in F$ is realizable (M-realizable) in A.

Using our concepts we then get for example the following variants of familiar results: Let $F \subseteq [X^* \to Y^*]$. Then

(i) F is realizable (M-realizable) in some automaton iff $F \subseteq [X^* \xrightarrow[se]{} Y^*]$ ($F \subseteq [X^* \xrightarrow[s]{} Y^*]$).

(ii) F is realizable (M-realizable) in automaton A iff DF ($D^M F$) is realizable (M-realizable) in A.

Next let us consider closed and M-closed sets of functions. A closed set $F \subseteq [X^* \xrightarrow[se]{} Y^*]$ of se-functions (M-closed set $F \subseteq [X^* \xrightarrow[s]{} Y^*]$ of s-functions) can be converted - in just one way - into the set of states of a reduced Mealy automaton (M-reduced Moore automaton) having the property that $\varphi^f = f$ ($\psi^f = f$) for each state $f \in F$. Namely one has to define

$$(\ast) \quad \begin{cases} \delta(f,x) = D_x f \\ \lambda(f,x) = f(x) \end{cases} \qquad \left(\begin{array}{l} \delta(f,x) = D_x^M f \\ \mu(f) = f(e) \end{array} \right)$$

This construction, if applied especially to the set $\{\varphi^q : q \in Q\}$ of response functions (set $\{\psi^q : q \in Q\}$ of M-response functions) of an automaton A (Moore automaton A), yields a reduct (M-reduct) of A.

Now start again with $G = \{\varphi^q : q \in Q\}$ corresponding to an automaton A, but then first form the M-closure $F = D^M G$. Then F is an M-closed set of s-functions (from II(g) in Theorem 2 it follows that F is also closed), thus one can apply the M-variant of the above construction (right column in ($\ast$)). The resulting Moore automaton B has state set $F \supseteq G$. Taking into account properties of derivatives of response functions one sees that, besides that B is M-reduced, B is equivalent to A. One thus arrives at a description of the behavioural background of the classical procedure for getting a Moore automaton equivalent to a given Mealy automaton. (The Moore automaton resulting in the classical procedure need not be M-reduced. Automata are rather closed (or

M-closed) systems of functions than sets - the set of indices of the system being the state set of the automaton.)

Properties of closed sets of sequential functions or of their various closures may provide motivation for certain considerations concerning automata. Let us give an example.

Let us consider a closed set $F \subseteq [X^* \xrightarrow[s]{} Y^*]$ of s-functions which are not necessarily se-functions. Using the definition of δ and λ in $(\ast)$ (left column) one again gets a Mealy automaton A which has F as the set of states. In A, however, one has now for $f \in F$ not $\varphi^f = f$, but only $\varphi^f = D_e f$. (At the same time one observes that defining a "marking function" $\mu: F \to Y^*$ by $\mu(f) = f(e)$ would not convert A into a Moore automaton, since in A in general $\lambda \neq \mu \circ \delta$.) In A the states which are not se-functions are not reachable from other states, and A is reduced if and only if F consists of se-functions. Though for $f \in F$ the response function φ in A does not at all take into account the (nonempty) values f(e), it may be reasonable to use them, for example if f has deliberately been chosen as the starting state. Then, in addition to the usual response function φ^f corresponding to f, one would define the "σ-response function" (start response function) ω^f: $X^* \to Y^*$ by $\omega^f(u) = f(e)\varphi^f(u)$, thus putting in front of $\varphi^f(u)$ the "starting reaction" $\sigma(f) = f(e)$. This leads to the following definition. (We give only the Mealy variant, the case of Moore automata is similar.)

A <u>start Mealy automaton</u> is a 6-tuple $A = (Q,X,Y,\delta,\lambda,\sigma)$, where $\sigma: Q \to Y^*$ is an additional mapping, the <u>starting function</u>. Besides the usual response function φ we define in A the <u>σ-response function</u> $\omega: Q \times X^* \to Y^*$ as follows

$$\omega(q,u) = \sigma(q)\,\varphi(q,u)$$

(One gets the usual Mealy automaton as a special case when $\sigma(q) = e$ for each state q. Then $\omega = \varphi$.) In A the function ω has obviously different properties than has the M-response function ψ in a Moore automaton. For example, (h) from Proposition 5 does not hold for ω.

REFERENCES

[1] Arbib, M.A. <u>Theories of abstract automata</u>. Prentice - Hall, Inc., Englewood Cliffs 1969

[2] Salomaa, A. <u>Theory of automata</u>. Pergamon Press, Oxford 1969

[3] Ginsburg, S. <u>An introduction to mathematical machine theory</u>. Addison - Wesley Publishing Co., Inc., Reading 1962

MATHEMATICAL METHODS OF THE THEORY OF STOCHASTIC AUTOMATA

A. Bertoni

Gruppo Elettronica e Cibernetica

Istituto di Fisica, Università di Milano

20133 MILANO - Via Viotti, 5 / Italia

INTRODUCTION

The concept of stochastic automata was introduced by Rabin [1], as a mere extension to probabilistic instances of finite state automata concept. Further extension and growth have been studied by Paz, Tura Kainen, Salomaa et al. Moreover, among the many works devoted to this subject, we remember [16] which sums up all the developments reached by the theory up to 1971.

In this work we aim to develop two matters:

1) Showing, along the lines followed in [5], [14], how formal series theory allows to extend to probabilistic cases typical results of non-probabilistic automata theory, in a simple and graceful way (section 1), and how by this way we may produce simple regularity tests for fuzzy events (section 2).
2) Analyzing some decidibility problems related to stochastic automata theory, actually two kinds of problems: the first concerning co-sets of stochastic events (equivalence of stochastic events, of stochastic languages, etc.), the second referring to topological closing of co-sets (isolated cut-point problems) (section 3).

To avoid dull reading, as far as possible, subjects will be discussed through examples, referring to Bibliography about general theory.

§ 1

STOCHASTIC AUTOMATA, WEIGHTED GRAMMARS AND REGULAR FORMAL POWER SERIES

In this section, we set up basic definitions of stochastic automata, of weighted grammars and classes of regular formal power series.

By means of examples we emphasize the correlations, while for general theories, see references.

Let $\Sigma \equiv \{\sigma_1 \dots \sigma_n\}$ be an alphabet, i.e. a finite set of symbols. We introduce the free monoid generated by Σ, written $\langle \Sigma^*, \cdot, \Lambda \rangle$, where Σ^* is the set of all strings of Σ, $\cdot$ is the concatenation operation and Λ is the empty string. We will say $\ell(x)$ the number of symbols in x.

Def. 1 - A probabilistic (stochastic) automaton A_p, is a set $\langle \Pi, A(\sigma_j), \eta_T \rangle$, where

a) Π is a stochastic vector 1xn, i.e. $\Pi \equiv (\Pi_1, .., \Pi_n)$; $\sum_{K=1}^{n} \Pi_K = 1$; $\Pi_K \geq 0$

b) $A(\sigma_j)$ is, for all j, a stochastic matrix, i.e.

$$a_{iK}(\sigma_j) \geq 0 \ ; \quad \sum_{K=1}^{m} a_{iK}(\sigma_j) = 1 \quad (i = 1 \dots n)$$

c) η_T is a nx1 vector with 0 or 1 components.

Let A_p be a given stochastic automaton.

Def. 2 - A stochastic matrix is specified to every $x \in \Sigma^*$:

a) $A(\Lambda) = I$; I is the identity matrix

b) $A(x\sigma_j) = A(x) A(\sigma_j)$

Def. 3 - A stochastic event generated by the automaton A_p is the function $p: \Sigma^* \to [01]$, $p(x) = \Pi A(x) \eta_T$

We observe that the stochastic event is an application $p: \Sigma^* \to [0\,1]$

Def. 4 - A rational number λ is said isolated for the event p if

$$\exists \delta \ (\delta > 0; \ \forall x \ (|p(x) - \lambda| \geq \delta))$$

Note 1 - If we drop the hypothesis that Π is a stochastic vector and $A(\sigma_j)$ a stochastic matrix, we define the set $\langle \Pi, A(\sigma_j), \eta_F \rangle$ as a generalized probabilistic automata.

Note 2 - A probabilistic event can be regarded as a fuzzy set over Σ^* [3] ; the class of probabilistic events results closed with respect to "fuzzy complementation" (if p is a probabilistic event then 1 - p is a probabilistic event, too) [18] ,but not with respect to "fuzzy union and intersection" ($(p \vee q)(x) = \mathrm{Max}\{p(x), q(x)\}$ and $(p \wedge q)(x) = \mathrm{Min}\{p(x), q(x)\}$ may not be probabilistic events) [14].
The class of probabilistic events is, on the contrary, closed with respect to Hadamart product (if p and q are p.e. (p.q) is a p.e.), the linear convex combination (q_i p.e., $\alpha_i \geq 0$, $\sum_{i=1}^{N} \alpha_i = 1 \Rightarrow \sum_{i=1}^{m} \alpha_i q_i$ p.e.) and respect to transposition $(Tp)(x) = p(x_T)$, where: $\Lambda_T = \Lambda$; $(x\sigma_j)_T = \sigma_j x$

Def. 5 - Let A_p be a given probabilistic automaton and λ be a real number; we define stochastic language $T(A_p, \lambda)$ as the set of strings $\{x \mid p(x) > \lambda\}$.

Def. 6 - A context-free grammar, weighted over R is the set $\langle \Sigma, Q, \mathcal{P}, q_0, \omega \rangle$ where:

a) Σ is a finite alphabet of symbols;

b) Q is a finite set (non terminal alphabet);

c) $\mathcal{P}$ is a finite set of productions, a finite subset of $Q \times (Q \cup \Sigma)^*$. We will write: $q_s \rightarrow x$

d) $q_0 \in Q$ is the axiom.

e) ω is an application $\omega : \mathcal{P} \rightarrow R$ $(R = \{\alpha \mid -\infty < \alpha < +\infty\})$
If: $\omega(q_s \rightarrow x) = \alpha$, we will write $q_s \xrightarrow{\alpha} x$
$\omega(q_s \rightarrow x)$ is defined "weight" of the production $q_s \rightarrow x$

Now we assume the set of real numbers as the ring $\langle R, +, \cdot, 0, 1 \rangle$ ("+" and "." are the usual operations). Let Σ be a finite alphabet.

Def. 7 - A formal power series of Σ^* over R is an application

$\varphi : \Sigma^* \to R$. It can be expressed as a formal sum $\sum_{x \in \Sigma^*} \varphi(x) \cdot x$

Let $S(R)$ be the set of formal power series defined over R
From the operations on R some operations are defined on $S(R)$:

(1) Sum of formal power series

$$(\varphi + \psi)(x) = \varphi(x) + \psi(x)$$

(2) **Chauchy** product of formal power series

$$(\varphi \cdot \psi)(x) = \sum_{yz=x} \varphi(y) \cdot \psi(z)$$

(3) Product of formal power series for a real number

$$(\lambda \varphi)(x) = \lambda \varphi(x)$$

Furthermore, only for formal power series with the coefficient $\varphi(\Lambda) = 0$ we introduce the following operation:

(4) Quasi-inversion of formal power series

$$\tilde{\varphi} = \sum_{k \geq 1} \varphi^k$$

The following property holds: $\tilde{\varphi} = \varphi + \varphi \cdot \tilde{\varphi} = \varphi + \tilde{\varphi} \cdot \varphi$

Def. 8 - A formal power series over R is said to be regular iff it belongs to the smallest class containing polynomials, closed with respect to the foregoing operations.

From language theory, it is well known that the class of languages recognized by finite automata coincides with the class of languages generated by right linear grammars, i.e. the set of regular expressions.

Now we can interpretate every (generalized) probabilistic event as a formal power series.

The following theorem holds:

Th. 1 - The class of generalized probabilistic events coincides with the class of regular formal power series.

Let G be a weighted context-free grammar:

Def. 9 - If $p_{\delta_k} \in \mathcal{P}$ and $p = p_{\delta_1} \cdots p_{\delta_k} \cdots p_{\delta_s}$ is a leftmost derivation of the string $x \in \Sigma^*$ from the axiom q_0, i.e. $q_0 \xrightarrow{p_{\delta_1}} \cdots \xrightarrow{p_{\delta_s}} x$ the weight of p is: $\omega(p) = \prod \omega(p_{\delta_k})$

Def. 10 - If $x \in \Sigma^*$, we define $\omega(x) = \sum_{q_0 \xrightarrow{p} x} \omega(p)$

Then, to every weighted context-free grammar with finite ambiguity we can associate a formal series $\omega : \Sigma^* \to R$

An elegant approach to the algebraic description of the weighted grammars is a method introduced by [5]. By this method, we can associate to every weighted grammar G a polinomial system of equations in formal power series variables [5]; [9]; [14]; [10]; [6]; [7].
The existence and unicity of the solutions of this system implies that the solution is the formal series generated from the context-free weighted grammar [5]; [8].

A theorem holds for right-linear weighted grammars:

Th. 2 - The class of formal series generated by right-linear weighted grammars coincides with the class of regular formal series.

§ 2

REGULARITY OF A FORMAL POWER SERIES

Techniques to investigate the regularity of a formal power series $\varphi : \Sigma^* \to R$ are discussed. Sufficient (section A), as well as necessary conditions (section B) are investigated.

A_1 : The case $|\Sigma| = 1$ can be treated with eigenvalue's techniques. The main result follows from the following theorem, permitting an explicit representation of the stochastic events [11]:

Th. Let A be a stochastic matrix. Then:

$$(A^m)_{kj} = \sum_{k=1}^{s} \lambda_k^m \cdot \omega_{khj}(m)$$

where: a) $|\lambda_i| \leq 1$

b) $|\lambda_i| = 1$ implies that λ_i is a root of unity.

ω_{khj} (m) is a polinomial in m of smaller order than the multiplicity of λ_k.

A_2 : The difficulty of relating the eigenvalues of a matrix product AB to the eigenvalues of A and B (with the exception of the commutative case: AB = BA), makes useless the extension of the above approach to the case of formal power series defined over Σ, if $|\Sigma| > 1$. In this case, a known result makes it possible to relate the regularity of a formal power series to the finiteness of the rank of a suitable infinite matrix [18],[14] ,[13] . Let us give more details.

Def. 1 - Given $\varphi : \Sigma^* \rightarrow R$, let $H(\varphi): \Sigma^* \times \Sigma^* \rightarrow R$ be defined in the following way:

$$H_{x,y}(\varphi) = \varphi(xy)$$

H will be called Hankel matrix of the series φ.

Def. 2 - The rank of a matrix H is n if there exists a minor of n order different from 0 and every minor, whose order is greater than n, is 0.

The rank of the matrix H is $+\infty$ iff, for every n, there exists a minor of order n different from 0.

Th. 2 - A formal power series φ is regular iff H (φ) is of a finite rank.

Ex. 1 - Let $\varphi : \{a\}^* \rightarrow [01]$, $(a^n) = 1/\alpha^n$. Every minor of order 2 of the matrix $H(\varphi)$ is:

$$\text{Det}\begin{pmatrix} 1/\alpha^{i+j} & 1/\alpha^{i+k} \\ 1/\alpha^{s+j} & 1/\alpha^{s+k} \end{pmatrix} = 0$$

It follows easily that φ is regular.

Ex. 2 - Let $K = \{0,1,\ldots,k-1\}$ a finite set. Let us consider every string $x = K_{j_1} \ldots K_{j_n} \in K^*$ as the representation of the number α, $0 \leq \alpha < 1$, defined by:

$$\alpha = \sum_{j=1}^{n} \frac{K_{js}}{k^s}$$

Let Σ be a finite alphabet, and $: \varphi : \Sigma^* \to K^*$ an homomorphism from the free monoid $\langle \Sigma^*, \cdot, \Lambda \rangle$ into the free monoid $\langle K^*, \cdot, \Lambda \rangle$.

If we interpret the elements of K as numbers, φ is a formal power series $\varphi : \Sigma^* \to R$.

Every minor of order 3 of the matrix $H(\varphi)$ is:

$$\text{Det}\begin{pmatrix} x_1y_1 & x_1y_2 & x_1y_3 \\ x_2y_1 & x_2y_2 & x_2y_3 \\ x_3y_1 & x_3y_2 & x_3y_3 \end{pmatrix} = 0$$

φ is hence regular. It is easy to build up a probabilistic automaton with 2 states generating the event φ.

B_1 : A useful necessary condition so that $\varphi : \Sigma^* \to [01]$ is a stochastic event, is the following:

$\varphi : \Sigma^* \to [01]$ probabilistic event $\Rightarrow \exists n \forall x \exists \{c_0; c_1; \ldots; c_m\}:$
$: (x, y, z \in \Sigma^*;\ c_k \in R;\ \ P(yx^{n+1}z) = \sum_{j=0}^{n} P(yx^j z)$

Ex. 1 - An application of such condition is the proof that there exist context-free languages which are not stochastic [15].

Proof outline:

Let $\mathcal{L} \equiv \{a^k b a^{k_1} b \ldots a^{k_s} b \mid \exists t\ (t \leq s;\ k = k_1 + \cdots + k_t)\}$

$\mathcal{L}$ is context-free (Ginsburg 1966).

Let $\mathcal{L}$ be stochastic. Then, there exists the event P and a cut-point λ, such that: $\mathcal{L} \equiv \{x \mid P(x) > \lambda\}$

Furthermore (B_1) :

$$\exists\{c_0,\dots,c_m\}\left(P(a^{m+1}u) = \sum_{j=1}^{m} c_j \cdot P(a^j u)\right)$$

Depending on the specific sequence of the signs of $\{c_0,\dots,c_m\}$, on the definition of $\mathcal{L}$ and on the previous property, an u can be chosen such as to bring to the contradiction: $a^{m+1}u \notin \mathcal{L}$, $P(a^{m+1}u) > \lambda$

B_2 : A technique used to prove that a given language is not regular or context-free is the one based on the asynthotic behaviour, by introducing the concept of the asynthotic density of a language [17].

Similar methods are easily extensible to determine non-regularity conditions of formal series. Let us consider some examples:

Ex. 1 - Let φ be a regular formal series with rational coefficients. If the sums $\sum_{\ell(x)=n} \varphi(x)$ converge and $\delta(\varphi) = \sum \varphi(x)$ then $\delta(\varphi)$ is a rational number.

This result comes from the fact that the function generating the succession $S_n = \sum_{\ell(x)=m} \varphi(x)$ is $\Pi \cdot (I - t \sum_{\sigma} A(\sigma))^{-1} \eta_T$ where:

$\langle \Pi, A(\sigma), \eta_T \rangle$ is the probabilistic automaton generating event φ ;

$f(t) = \Pi \cdot (I - t \sum_{\sigma} A(\sigma))^{-1} \eta_T$ is obviously a rational function with rational coefficients;

As, by Abel 's theorem , from $\sum S_n t^m = f(t)$

$\lim_{t \to 1} f(t) = f(1) = \sum_{0}^{\infty} S_m$ follows $\delta(\varphi) = f(1)$

hence the thesis.

Ex. 2 - By using the previous method, we can prove that

$\varphi(x) = \frac{1}{\ell(x)!}$ is not rational.

$$\sum_x \frac{1}{\ell(x)!} = \sum_{K=0}^{\infty} \sum_{\ell(x)=K} \frac{1}{K!} = \sum_{0}^{\infty} \frac{|\Sigma|^K}{K!} = e^{|\Sigma|}$$

$e^{|\Sigma|}$ is not a rational number, hence the thesis follows.

Ex. 3 - Obviously this condition is just necessary, e.g. as follows from the study of $\varphi(a^n) = \frac{1}{n(n+1)} \quad (n \geq 1)$

As $f(t) = \sum_1^{\infty} \varphi(a^n) t^n = 2t - (1-t)\log(1-t)$

φ is not regular (really its generating function cannot be reduced to a rational function).

In spite of this, there is $\sum_1^{\infty} \frac{1}{n(n+1)} = 1$ which is rational.

§ 3

PROBLEMS OF DECIDIBILITY ON EVENTS AND LANGUAGE

Let us assume probabilistic events represented by formal power series with rational coefficients. Some simple predicates on these events are as follows:

(1) - $\forall x(p(x) = q(x))$

(2) - $\exists x(p(x) = q(x))$

(3) - $\exists x(p(x) > q(x))$

where: $x \in \Sigma^*$ $\quad$ $p: \Sigma^* \to [0,1]$ $\quad$ $q: \Sigma^* \to [0,1]$

p, q stochastic events with rational coefficients

While (1)- means the equality of two stochastic events, in (3)- stochastic language $\mathcal{L}_{pq} = \{x \mid p(x) > q(x)\}$ is not empty. Only for events with rational coefficients, [18], we have the following implication:

(2)- undecidable $\Rightarrow$ (3)- undecidable

Now let us extend the problem (1)- to regular formal power series with rational coefficients.

Th. - Let p and q be two regular formal power series with rational coefficients. Then it is decidable if p = q.

Proof outline:

Let $\langle \pi, A(\sigma_j), \eta_T \rangle$ be the automaton generating $\tilde{p}=p(x) - q(x)$, which is regular. If $\otimes$ is the usual Kronecker product:

$$\pi \otimes \pi \cdot \left(I \otimes I - t \cdot \sum_{\sigma_j} A(\sigma_j) \otimes A(\sigma_j)\right)^{-1} \cdot \eta_T = \frac{P(t)}{Q(t)}$$

where P(t) and Q(t) are polynomials, is the generating function of the series: $\sum_0^\infty a_K \cdot t^K$; $a_K = \sum_{\ell(x)=K} \tilde{p}^2(x)$

Hence: $\forall K (a_K = 0) \Leftrightarrow \forall x (\tilde{p}(x) = 0) \Leftrightarrow \forall x (p(x) = q(x)) \Leftrightarrow P(t) = 0$

It follows that problem (1)- is transposed in order to verify if P(t) = 0.

Th. - Problem (2)- is recursively undecidable. Then

$$\mathcal{L} = \phi \qquad\qquad (\ \phi \text{ is the empty set})$$

where $\mathcal{L}$ stochastic language, is undecidable.

Proof outline:

Let p and q be elements belonging to the class defined in § 2. The problem becomes: let $\psi_1 : \Sigma^* \to K^*$ and $\psi_2 : \Sigma^* \to K^*$ be two generic homomorphisms, then is it decidable if

$\exists x (\psi_1(x) = \psi_2(x))$?

This problem (Post correspondence problem) is a typical example of undecidable problems [19], [20] .

Observation:

A different proof of this theorem can be found in [21], where the undecidability of these problems is proved, too:

a) Is stochastic language $\mathcal{L}$ regular?

b) Is stochastic language $\mathcal{L}$ context-free?

c) If p and q are regular formal power series with rational coefficients, then is $p \vee q$ $(p \wedge q)$ a regular series?

We may prove these theorems in the same line as the previous instance. E.g.:

Th. - It is undecidable whether a stochastic language is regular or not.

Proof outline:

Alphabet $\Sigma \cup \tilde{\Sigma}$ $(\Sigma = \{\sigma_1 \dots \sigma_s\}$; $\tilde{\Sigma} = \{\tilde{\sigma}_1 \dots \tilde{\sigma}_s\})$ is given.

If $x \in \Sigma^*$ and $x = \sigma_{j_1} \dots \sigma_{j_n}$, let's write $\tilde{x} = \tilde{\sigma}_{j_1} \dots \tilde{\sigma}_{j_n}$

Let $\chi : \{\Sigma \cup \tilde{\Sigma}\}^* \to \{0;1\}$ be the characteristic function of set $\Sigma^* \tilde{\Sigma}^*$.

Let's assign homomorphisms $\psi_1, \psi_2, \psi_3, \psi_4 : \{\Sigma \cup \tilde{\Sigma}\}^* \to \{K_1, \dots, K_n\}^*$

where:

$\psi_2(\tilde{\sigma}_R) = \psi_1(\sigma_R) = K_R \quad \psi_1(\tilde{\sigma}_R) = \psi_2(\sigma_R) = \psi_3(\tilde{\sigma}_R) = \psi_4(\tilde{\sigma}_R) = \Lambda \quad \psi_3(\sigma_R) = z_R \quad \psi_4(\sigma_R) = y_R$

Function $p : \{\Sigma \cup \tilde{\Sigma}\}^* \to [01]$ defined by $p = \chi \cdot \left(\frac{1}{2} - \frac{(\psi_1 - \psi_2)^2 + (\psi_3 - \psi_4)^2}{8}\right)$

is a stochastic event (as it is a convex arrangement of stochastic events). Let $\frac{1}{2}$ be a cut-point, then we note:

$p(x) = \frac{1}{2} \implies$ a) $\chi(x) \neq 0$ b) $\psi_1(x) = \psi_2(x)$ c) $\psi_3(x) = \psi_4(x)$

a) implies that $x = y\tilde{z}$;

b) implies that $\tilde{y} = \tilde{z}$, i.e. $x = y\tilde{y}$

c) implies that $\psi_3(y) = \psi_4(y)$

Therefore, called $\mathcal{L} = \{x \mid P(x) = \frac{1}{2}\}$ is $\mathcal{L} \equiv \{y\tilde{y} \mid \psi_3(y) = \psi_4(y)\}$

Consequently:

A. Post Correspondence Problem solvable for $\psi_2, \psi_3 \Rightarrow \mathcal{L}$ not regular
(Really, if $\psi_3(\bar{y}) = \psi_4(\bar{y})$ is $\{\mathcal{L} \cap \bar{y}^n \tilde{\bar{y}}^m\} = \{\bar{y}^n \tilde{\bar{y}}^n\}$ not regular)

B. Post Correspondence Problem not solvable for $\psi_3, \psi_4 \Rightarrow \mathcal{L}$ regular
(In this case $\mathcal{L} = \phi$, therefore it is regular).

Undecidability follows.

Another class of decisional problems is related with the concept of "isolated cut-point" [18],[1] .

(4)- Is it possible to find an algorithm to decide if, for each given probabilistic automaton with rational coefficients A and each rational number λ , $0 \leq \lambda \leq 1$, λ is an isolated cut-point for A ?

(5)- Is it possible to decide if a given probabilistic automaton has no isolated cut-points?

Ex. 1 - Let p be an event of type § 2 ; every rational number $0 \leq \lambda < 1$ can be represented in base K, with an infinite string $\ell = K_{\delta_1} \dots K_{\delta_s} \dots$. The language $R_\lambda \equiv \{x \mid x \in K^*;\ \ell = x\, K_{\delta_{s+1}} \dots\}$ is proved regular.
The range of p is $R_p \equiv \{\psi(\sigma_1); \psi(\sigma_2); \dots; \psi(\sigma_n)\}^*$. Then:
λ is an isolated cut-point for p $\Leftrightarrow$ $R_\lambda \cap R_p$ is finite.

Hence, a decisional method exists because it is decidable if the regular expression $R_\lambda \cap R_p$ is finite.

Th. 1 - Problem (4)- is undecidable for 4-states stochastic automata and for $\lambda \neq 0$.

Proof outline:

For every deterministic Turing Machine (TM) a rational probabilistic event is constructed for which $\frac{1}{2}$ is an isolated cutpoint iff TM halts.

The complete proof of this theorem is reported in [25].

The present paper has been sponsered by CNR (Comitato per la Fisica)

BIBLIOGRAPHY

[1] RABIN Probabilistic Automata. Information and Control 6 (1963), 230-245.

[2] TURAKAINEN Generalized Automata and Stochastic Languages Proc. Am. Math. Soc. 21 (1969), 303-309.

[3] ZADEH Fuzzy Sets. Information and Control 8 (1965),338-353

[4] SALOMAA Probabilistic and weighted grammars. Information and Control 15 (1969), 529-544.

[5] CHOMSKY, SCHUETZENBERGER The algebraic theory of context-free languages. Comp. Prog. and Formal Systems (1963).

[6] BLIKLE, MAZURKIEWICZ An algebraic approach to theory of programs, algorithms, languages and recursiveness. Summer school on Math. Found. of Comp. sc. Warsaw - Jablonna (1972).

[7] SHAMIR Algebraic, rational and context-free power series on noncommuting variables. Alg. Theory of Mach., Lang. and Semigroups Academic Press (1968)

[8] GATTO, MANDRIOLI Equilavenza tra grammatiche, sistemi di equazioni in variabili di serie formali. Convegno AICA, Pisa, 1-3 Marzo 1973.

[9] BERTONI Equations of formal power series over non commutative semirings. Proc. of Symp. MFCS - High Tatras (1973) 185-190.

[10] STANAT A homomorphism theorem for weighted context-free grammars. Jour. Comp. Syst. Science (1972).

[11] FRECHET Recherches theoretiques modernes sur le calcul des probabilités. Gauthiers-Villars, Paris (1938).

[12] SCHUETZENBERGER On definition of a family of Automata. Information and Control 4 (1961) 245-270.

[13] CARLYLE-PAZ Realization by stochastic finite automata (1972).

[14] FLIESS Automates Stochastiques Automata, Lang. and Programming (1972).

[15] NASU-HONDA Context-free but not stochastic language Information and Control 18 (1971) 233-236.

[16] COBHAM Uniform tag sequences. Math. Syst. Theory (1972) 164-192.

[17] BERSTEL Sur la densité asympotique des languages formels Automata, languages and programming, North Holland (1972) 345-358.

[18] PAZ Introduction to probabilistic automata. Academic Press New York (1971).

[19] POST A variant of a recursively unsolvable problem. Bull. Am. Math. Soc. 52 (1946) 264-268.

[20] HOPCROFT, ULLMAN Formal languages and their relation to automata . Addison Wesley Publishing Co. (1969).

[21] NASU, HONDA Mappings induced by PGSM mappings and some recursively unsolvable problems of finite probabilistic automata. Information and Control 15 (1969) 250-273.

[22] PAZ Fuzzy star function J. Comp. System Science 1 (1967) 371-389.

[23] BERTONI Grammatiche context-free su spazi metrici compatti. Calcolo 1 (1974) 155-170.

[24] BERTONI Complexity problems related to the approximation of prob. languages by deterministic machines. Automata, lang. and programming, North Holland (1972), 507-516.

[25] BERTONI The solution of problems relative to probabilistic automata in the frame of formal languages theory. To appear at the 4th Annual Meeting GI 74 Berlin

ON THE QUASI-CONTROLLABILITY OF AUTOMATA

L. Beyga
Institute of Control Engineering
Technical University of Poznan

At first the basic definitions will be introduced. Here an automaton is the ordered triple (S,Σ,M), where S is a non-empty finite set of states, Σ - is a non-empty finite set of input symbols, $M:S\times\Sigma \longrightarrow S$ - is a next state function. The set Σ together with the operation of juxtaposition generates the set I, named an input semigroup. The function M can be extended to the domain $S\times I$ in the following manner:

$$M(s,x\sigma) = M(M(s,x),\sigma) \quad \text{where } s\in S \;,\; \sigma\in\Sigma \;,\; x\in I \;.$$

For every $x\in I$ symbol $|x|$ denotes the lenght of x, i.e. if

$$x = \sigma_1\sigma_2.....\sigma_l \;, \text{ where } \sigma_1,\sigma_2,......,\sigma_l\in\Sigma \;, \text{ then } |x| = l \;.$$

An element $\sigma\in\Sigma$ implies mapping

$$f_\sigma : S \longrightarrow S \;, \text{ where } f_\sigma(s) = M(s,\sigma) \;.$$

The set of all such mappings - denoted by J - together with the operation of superposition, is a set of generators of some semigroup F. For the sequence

$$J^1, J^2, ..., J^i, ...$$

let τ and T be minimal non-negative integers such that

$$J^{\tau+1} = J^{\tau+T+1} \;.$$

Numbers τ , T are the characteristic numbers of given automaton A.

An automaton A = (S,Σ,M) is said to be asynchronous if and only if for every $f \in J$ we have $f \equiv f^2$. If in general for every $f \in J$ we have $f^k \equiv f^{k+1}$ then we say that given automaton is k-asynchronous.

A permutation automaton is an automaton with J to be a set of permutations of S.

The next definition is taken from [1]. The automaton A = (S,Σ,M) is said to be quasi-controllable if and only if there exists such a natural number k, that for every function f F there exists an element $x \in I$ with lenght equal to k , and for every $s \in S$ we have f(s) = M(s,x). It is also know from [1] , that the automaton A is quasi-controllable if and only if T = 1 and $F^2 = F$. From the above result it follows that the problem when the automaton is quasi-controllable is equivalent to the problem when T=1 and F^2=F.

<u>Theorem 1</u>. <u>For given automaton</u> A <u>the characteristic number</u> T <u>equals</u> 1 <u>if and only if there exists such a natural number</u> p <u>that</u> $J^p \subseteq J^{p+1}$.

<u>Proof</u>. Let p be natural number with $J^{\tau+1} = J^{p+p'}$. From that and our assumption it follows that:

$$J^{\tau+2} = J^{p+p'+1} \supseteq J^{p+p'} = J^{\tau+1} \text{ . Similarly :}$$

$$J^{\tau+3} \supseteq J^{\tau+2}, \ldots\ldots, J^{\tau+i+1} \supseteq J^{\tau+i}, \ldots\ldots, J^{\tau+T+1} \supseteq J^{\tau+T} \text{ . But:}$$

$$J^{\tau+T+1} = J^{\tau+1} \text{ and hence: } J^{\tau+1} = J^{\tau+2} = \ldots\ldots = J^{\tau+T} \text{ , and } T=1 \text{ .}$$

Otherwise if T=1 then $J^{\tau+1} = J^{\tau+2}$ and a number p is equal say $\tau+1$.

Theorem 1 is a special case of a general theorem proved independently in [2] : if $J^l \subseteq J^{l+p}$, where l,p are natural numbers, then p is a multiple of T.

<u>Theorem 2</u>. $F^2 = F$ <u>if and only if</u> $J \subseteq F^2$.

<u>Proof</u>. The proof follows from the simple following fact:

$$F^2 = F \cdot F = (J^1 \cup J^2 \cup \ldots\ldots \cup J^{\tau+T}) \cdot (J^1 \cup J^2 \cup \ldots\ldots \cup J^{\tau+T}) =$$

$$= J^2 \cup J^3 \cup \ldots\ldots \cup J^{\tau+T} .$$

From Theorem 1 and Theorem 2 follows an algorithm for determining of quasi-controllability of automata.

Algorithm. Find a set J. Take p succesivly equal to 1,2,3,..... and and compute J^{p+1}. Verify if $J^p \subseteq J^{p+1}$ and if $J \subseteq (J^2 \cup J^3 \cup \ldots\ldots \cup J^{p+1})$. If for some numbers p_1 and p_2 we have

$$J^{p_1} \subseteq J^{p_1+1} \quad \text{and} \quad J \subseteq (J^2 \cup J^3 \cup \ldots\ldots \cup J^{p_2+1}) ,$$

respectively, then given automaton is quasi-controllable. If for some pair p,T of numbers p,T we have

$$J^{p+1} = J^{p+T+1}$$

and there do not exist $p_1 \leqslant p$ and $p_2 \leqslant p$ as above then given automaton is not quasi-controllable.

If we assume that an automaton A is asynchronous then for every f J we have $f \equiv f^2$. It implies that $J \subseteq J^2$ and from the above algorithm we obtain that every asynchronous automaton is quasi-controllable.

In general k-asynchronous automata with $k \geqslant 2$ are not quasi-controllable.

Every permutation automaton has a semigroup F such that $F^2 = F$. Hence the permutation automaton is quasi-controllable if and only if there exists a natural number p with $J^p \subseteq J^{p+1}$.

REFERENCES

[1] GRZYMALA-BUSSE,J.W. Subautomata of finite automata associated with the change of operating time. in Polish , Rep.46, Technical University of Poznan,1972.

[2] GRZYMALA-BUSSE,J.W. On the finite non-annul semigroups. presented for publication .

MODELS FOR ANALYSIS OF RACES IN SEQUENTIAL NETWORKS*

J.A. Brzozowski
University of Waterloo
Waterloo, Ontario, Canada

M. Yoeli
Technion
Haifa, Israel

ABSTRACT

Two models for the analysis of races in asynchronous sequential networks constructed with gates are described. The first model is a modification and a formalization of intuitively clear concepts. The second model is applicable, if the delays associated with the gates do not differ too widely from each other. A new concept of internal state is required in this model; namely, in addition to the values of gate outputs, one must also know the previous history of the race, in order to predict the next state.

1 Introduction

This paper is concerned with the analysis of races in asynchronous sequential networks constructed with gates. We assume that the network has n external binary inputs $x_1,\ldots,x_n$, and consists of s gates $G_1,\ldots,G_s$. For gate G_j, the output is y_j and the gate performs a Boolean function f_j of the n+s variables $x_1,\ldots,x_n,y_1,\ldots,y_s$. The ordered s-tuple $(y_1,\ldots,y_s)$ represents the present gate-state of the network. For j = 1,...,s, let

$$Y_j = f_j(x_1,\ldots,x_n,y_1,\ldots,y_s).$$

The ordered s-tuple $(Y_1,\ldots,Y_s)$ represents the present excitation of the network.

Specifically we consider the following problem. Suppose that the network finds itself in some total state (x,y), where $x \in \{0,1\}^n$ is an input state, and $y \in \{0,1\}^s$ is the present gate-state. Assuming that the input x will not change, what will be the possible behavior of the network, as far as the gate-state is concerned? We do not need a separate notion of network output since we tacitly assume that each gate output is an external output of the network.

This problem corresponds to the familiar problem of finding the behavior of a network from its excitation table. However, many texts on switching theory erroneously associate state variables with feedback loops rather than gates. In this respect, our point of view is very closely related to that of Muller [MU,MI] who associates a variable with each gate. However, we incorporate a simplifying assumption that

* This work was supported by the National Research Council of Canada under Grant A-1617.

two gate outputs cannot change at precisely the same instant, but that either one gate or the other must "win the race". We call this model the general single-winner model (GSW). The formal definition of the model is given in Section 2.

In Section 3 we show that, under certain conditions, the GSW model is not realistic. In Section 4 we define a new model, applicable to networks in which all the gate delays are approximately equal. One of the consequences of this model is a new concept of internal state.

Logical OR, AND, and complementation is denoted by $x+y$, xy, and x', respectively. Δ_i denotes the delay associated with gate G_i.

2 The General Single-Winner Model (GSW)

Consider a gate G_i. If its output y_i differs from its excitation Y_i, we say that G_i is unstable. A condition where two or more gates are unstable is called a race. We assume that any one of the unstable gates can win the race, but that no ties are possible. The model can be easily generalized to allow ties. However, the single-winner condition appears realistic, and leads to a simpler model. If gate G_i wins the race, the network goes to a new gate-state with variable y_i changed. The excitation is recomputed using the new state and the process repeats. The model implicitly assumes that the delays associated with the gates are "inertial", in the following sense. Suppose gates G_i and G_j are racing and G_i wins the race. If G_j is stable in the new state (i.e. if $y_j = Y_j$), the fact that G_j was temporarily excited is ignored.

More formally, for each $x \in \{0,1\}^n$ define a binary relation R_x on $\{0,1\}^s$ as follows. Let (x,y) be some total state of the network and Y the corresponding excitation state. If $y = Y$, then yR_xy. Otherwise, consider each i such that $y_i \neq Y_i$. Then $yR_xy^{(i)}$, where

$$y \quad = (y_1,\dots,y_{i-1},y_i,y_{i+1},\dots,y_s), \text{ and}$$

$$y^{(i)} = (y_1,\dots,y_{i-1},y_i',y_{i+1},\dots,y_s).$$

For example, if $y = 110$ and $Y = 011$, then $110R_x010$, and $110R_x111$.

To interpret this model consider the relation diagram for R_x. The nodes of this diagram correspond to elements of $\{0,1\}^s$ and, for nodes y and $\bar{y}$, a directed edge is drawn from y to $\bar{y}$ iff $yR_x\bar{y}$. If yR_xy, then the total state (x,y) is stable, and no change will take place (unless the input changes). Otherwise, follow all directed paths in the relation diagram for R_x, starting with node y. Any such path must reach a cycle after a finite number of steps. Starting from y, if we reach more than one cycle we have a critical race. If only one cycle can be reached, and this cycle is of length greater than 1, we have an oscillation. If only one cycle can be reached and this cycle is of length 1, the corresponding node gives the unique stable state that the network will reach from y.

As an example, consider the network of Fig.1, where the gates are NAND gates, for the input x = 011. Then

$$Y_1 = 1, \quad Y_2 = (y_1 y_3)', \quad Y_3 = y_2'.$$

Figure 2 shows the part of the relation diagram that is relevant to the initial state y = 011. In each node, the unstable variables are underlined. A label on an edge gives the number of the variable that is assumed to be changing. According to Fig.2, the network of Fig.1 has a critical race here.

3 Difficulties with the GSW Model

We want a mathematical model that is independent of the actual magnitudes of the delays associated with the gates. This is because the gate delays are not precisely known, may vary from gate to gate (even for gates of the same type), may vary with time, etc. We will now show that the GSW model is, in a sense, "too independent" of the gate delay magnitudes, and can be unreasonable.

We begin by re-examining the analysis of Fig.2. Starting with 011, if $\Delta_1 > \Delta_3$, variable y_3 wins the race, and the final outcome is the stable state 110. On the other hand, if $\Delta_1 < \Delta_3$ the network reaches the unstable state 111 first, with y_2 and y_3 now racing. Suppose, in the original race, y_1 and y_3 both become unstable at the same time. After time Δ_1, y_1 changes and becomes stable. Also around this time, y_2 becomes unstable. Now, if y_2 wins the second race, variable y_3 will have been unstable for a total of $\Delta_1 + \Delta_2$ units of time. This implies that $\Delta_3 > \Delta_1 + \Delta_2$. Under the assumption that all three NAND gates have the same type of realization, it may be reasonable to assume that the gate delays are (very) approximately equal to some nominal value Δ. In order for $\Delta_3 > \Delta_1 + \Delta_2$ to be true we would have Δ_3 about twice as big as Δ_1 (or Δ_2). If this possibility is excluded, then variable y_3 must win the second race. Now the outcome for the starting state 011 is the unique stable state 110. Under these conditions, the original race is not critical.

If it is not justified to assume that no delay exceeds the sum of two other delays, it should certainly be reasonable to assume that no delay exceeds the sum of k other delays, for some large enough k. We illustrate this with a more complex example. A commercially available integrated-circuit JK flip-flop SN74H76 [TI] consists of 8 NAND gates and its logic diagram corresponds to the following equations:

$$Y_1 = (PK¢y_8)' \quad , \quad Y_2 = (CJ¢y_7)'$$
$$Y_3 = (Cy_1y_4)' \quad , \quad Y_4 = (Py_2y_3)'$$
$$Y_5 = (y_1y_3)' \quad , \quad Y_6 = (y_2y_4)'$$
$$Y_7 = (Cy_5y_8)' \quad , \quad Y_8 = (Py_6y_7)',$$

where P, C, J, K and ¢ are inputs. Consider the input state P = 1, C = 1, J = 0, K = 1, ¢ = 1 and the gate-state y_a = 10011110 (which is used in the actual operation of the network). One can verify that the network first reaches state y_b = 11011011, without any races. In y_b the variables y_1 and y_7 race. According to the GSW model, the race is critical because it can lead to stable states y_c = 01101101 and y_d = 11100110. However, the only way to reach y_d is to have the variables change in the following order: 1, 3, 4, 6, 8, 1, 5. During the first five changes, gate 7 is unstable all the time. Thus a critical race will occur only if

$$\Delta_7 > \Delta_1 + \Delta_3 + \Delta_4 + \Delta_6 + \Delta_8.$$

This is certainly unreasonable, if all the NAND gates are similar. In the next section we define a model which avoids such difficulties, but corresponds to k = 2, i.e. no delay is larger than the sum of two other delays. These concepts could be generalized to other values of k.

4 The Almost-Equal-Delays Model (AED)

Call a total state (x,y) of a network primary iff there exists an input $\bar{x}$ such that $(\bar{x},y)$ is stable. We will consider only primary total states as starting states, since we want to avoid total states which are not reachable during the normal operation of the network. We assume that first the network is stable in $(\bar{x},y)$; then the input changes to x, and we wish to find out what happens next. From here on we assume that the input remains fixed at x.

For any total state (x,y), define $u_x(y)$ (or simply u(y), if x is understood) to be

$$u(y) = \{i \in S | y_i \neq Y_i\},$$

where $S = \{1,2,\ldots,s\}$. Let P(S) be the set of all subsets of S and let $V = \{0,1\}^s \times P(S)$. We shall be interested in a certain subset T of V. It turns out to be convenient to define T inductively, and to define a relation R on T at the same time. In general, R depends on the total state (x,y).

Let $(x,\hat{y})$ be primary. Define T and R corresponding to $(x,\hat{y})$ as follows:

<u>Basis</u>: $\langle\hat{y},u(\hat{y})\rangle \in T$.

<u>Induction Step</u>: Given $\langle y,v\rangle \in T$,

1) If $v = \phi$, then $\langle y,v \rangle \; R \; \langle y,v \rangle$.

2) If $v \neq \phi$, for each $i \in v$ compute

$$w_i = (v-\{i\}) \cap u(y^{(i)}).$$

(a) If $w_i = \phi$, then

$$\langle y^{(i)}, uy(^{(i)}) \rangle \in T \text{ and } \langle y,v \rangle \; R \; \langle y^{(i)}, u(y^{(i)}) \rangle.$$

(b) If $w_i \neq \phi$, then

$$\langle y^{(i)}, w_i \rangle \in T \text{ and } \langle y,v \rangle \; R \; \langle y^{(i)}, w_i \rangle.$$

The relation diagram of the relation R on T is now interpreted like the relation diagram of R_x in the GSW model. Starting with $\langle \hat{y}, u(\hat{y}) \rangle$ we must reach a cycle along each path. If only one cycle is reached and it is of length 1, a unique stable state is reached. Otherwise, the network can have ciritical races and oscillations as before.

Fig.3 shows the analysis of the network of Fig.1 in the AED model. This should be compared with Fig.2. In the AED model, the race is not critical.

The proper concept of internal state in the AED model is the pair $\langle y,v \rangle$, not just the s-tuple y of gate outputs. In fact, a network may have the same gate-state with different race histories. This is illustrated by the network with two AND gates and two NOR gates whose excitation equations are:

$$Y_1 = xy_3,$$
$$Y_2 = xy_4,$$
$$Y_3 = (y_1+y_4)',$$
$$Y_4 = (y_2+y_3)'.$$

One verifies that $x = 0$, $y = 0001$ is a stable total state. Hence, the total state $x = 1$, $y = 0001$ is primary. In the relation diagram for R, corresponding to this initial total state, the 4-tuple 0000 appears twice. Of course, in both cases, the unstable variables are the same (y_3 and y_4). However, in the first case y_3 must win, whereas in the second, variable y_4 has priority.

For a further discussion and applications of these concepts see [B & Y], where these models are used to explain the behavior of complex, commercially available flip-flops, such as master-slave and edge-sensitive types.

References

[B & Y] BRZOZOWSKI, J.A.; YOELI, M. Digital Networks. Prentice-Hall, Inc. — in preparation.

[MI] MILLER, R.E. Switching Theory, Vol.2, John Wiley and Sons, Inc., New York, 1965.

[MU] MULLER, D.E. Lecture Notes on Asynchronous Circuit Theory. Digital Computer Laboratory, University of Illinois, Spring 1961.

[TI] TEXAS INSTRUMENTS STAFF. The TTL Data Book for Design Engineers. Texas Instruments Inc., 1973.

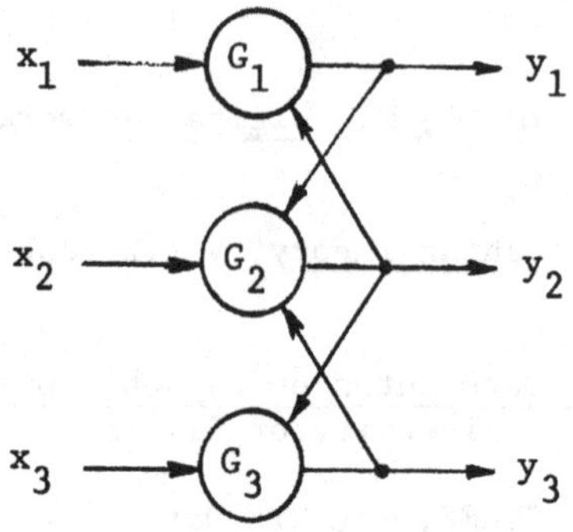

Fig.1 Network N

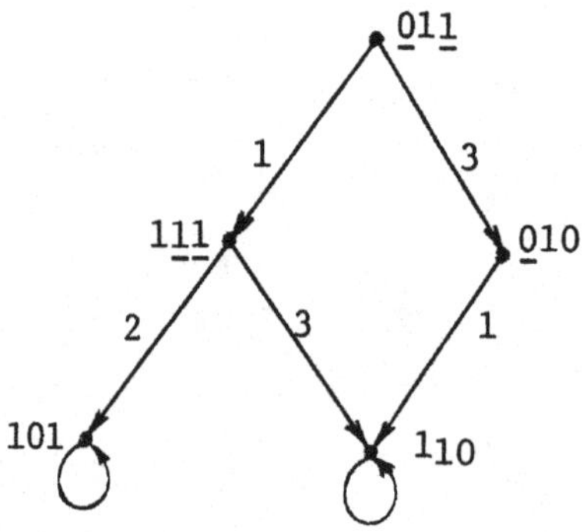

Fig.2 GSW analysis of a race in N

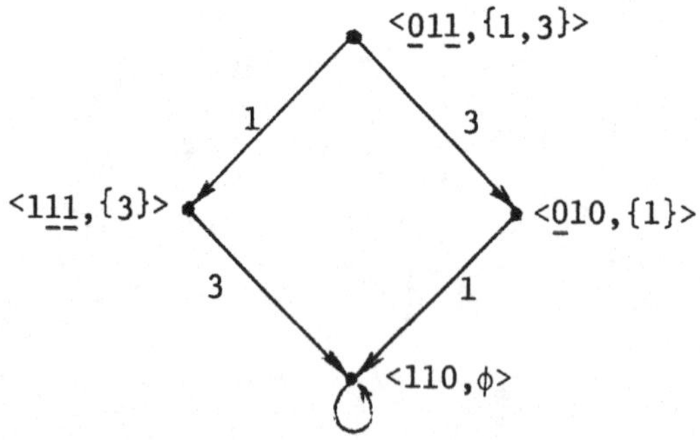

Fig.3 AED analysis of the same race of N

FACTORIZATIONS, CONGRUENCES, AND THE DECOMPOSITION OF AUTOMATA AND SYSTEMS

by J. A. Goguen,** J. W. Thatcher,† E. G. Wagner† and J. B. Wright†

Conditions for the parallel decomposition of a number of types of automata and other systems are well-known and go back some distance in the literature (Birkhoff [1], Büchi-Wright [2], Thatcher [3], Yeh [4], Gallaire-Harrison [5], Hartmanis-Stearns [6], Sipusic [7], for example). We give a general theorem which includes all these, plus many many more. Interestingly enough, the proof of the general theorem is simpler than that of many special cases, assuming as we do that the reader is familiar with the necessary preliminary mathematics (for which see Goguen-Thatcher-Wagner-Wright [8], MacLane-Birkhoff [9] or MacLane [10]). Moreover, the proof involves features of significant interest in other contexts as well.

1. Initial Factorizations

An object A is initial in a category $\underline{\underline{C}}$ iff for each B in $\underline{\underline{C}}$, there is a unique morphism $f:A \to B$ in $\underline{\underline{C}}$. Dually, A is terminal in $\underline{\underline{C}}$ iff for each B in $\underline{\underline{C}}$, there is a unique $f:B \to A$ in $\underline{\underline{C}}$. Objects A,A' are isomorphic in $\underline{\underline{C}}$ iff there are morphisms $f:A \to A'$, $g:A' \to A$ in $\underline{\underline{C}}$ such that* $fg=1_A$ and $gf=1_{A'}$.

Proposition 1. If A,A' are both initial [or both terminal] in category C, then the unique morphism $A \to A'$ is an isomorphism. Moreover, any object isomorphic to an initial [or terminal] object is initial [or terminal].

One particular use of initiality is to set up a special category in which something we are interested in characterizing appears as an initial (or terminal) object. The present example illustrates this point.

Consider the category $\underline{\underline{Set}}$ of sets. Here the term "factorization" is used in the conventional way; a pair of functions $<f_0,f_1>$ is a factorization of a function f iff their composite $f_0\ f_1$ is f. Some factorizations are of particular

---

*We write composition in the "diagramatic" order, $A \xrightarrow{f} A' \xrightarrow{g} A = A \xrightarrow{fg} A$.

**Computer Science Department, UCLA, Los Angeles, CA. 90024
†IBM Watson Research Center, Yorktown Heights, N. Y. 10598

interest. In $\underline{\underline{Set}}$ every function $f:A \to B$ has a factorization $A \overset{e}{\to} Q \overset{m}{\to} B$ where e is a surjection and m is an injection; such factorizations are unique up to isomorphism in the category of factorizations of f to be described below. The left factor, $e:A \to Q$, is called the quotient of f and the right factor $m:Q \to B$ is called the image of f. The present development characterizes the surjective-injective factorizations as initial factorizations through injections (equivalently, as terminal factorizations through surjections); and in fact the surjections are characterized as being the left factors of such initial factorizations.

For the formal development, let $\underline{\underline{C}}$ be a category and $f:A \to B$ a morphism in $\underline{\underline{C}}$. Define the (special) category $\underline{\underline{Fac}}(f)$ to have objects $\langle f_0, f_1 \rangle$ which are pairs of morphisms of $\underline{\underline{C}}$ such that $f_0 f_1 = f$. A morphism from $\langle f_0, f_1 \rangle$ to $\langle f_0', f_1' \rangle$ is a morphism[1] $g: f_0\partial_1 \to f_0'\partial_1$ of $\underline{\underline{C}}$ such that

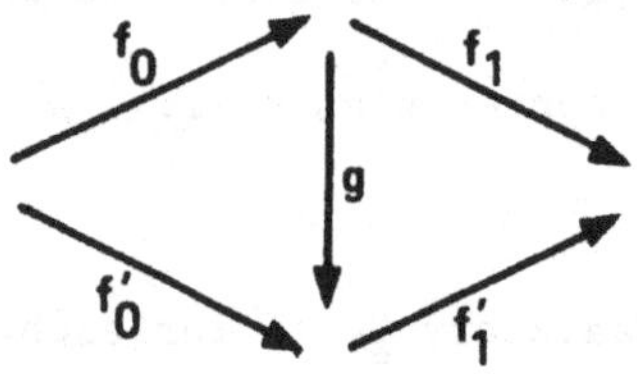

commutes in $\underline{\underline{C}}$. Given also $g':\langle f_0', f_1' \rangle \to \langle f_0'', f_1'' \rangle$, gg' is a morphism from $\langle f_0, f_1 \rangle$ to $\langle f_0'', f_1'' \rangle$ since, as can be seen from the diagram,

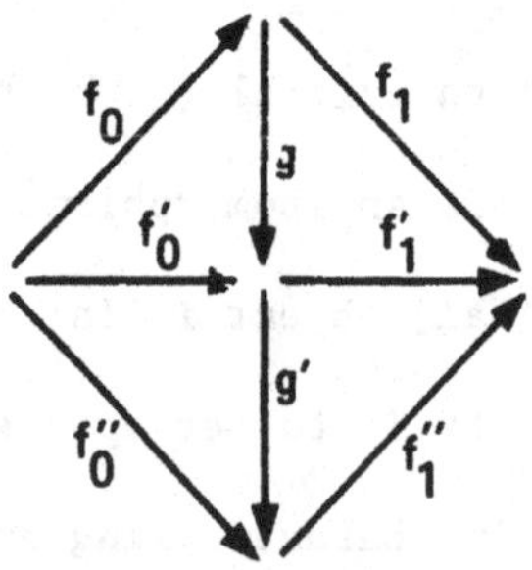

[1] If $f:A \to B$ is a morphism of $\underline{\underline{C}}$, $f\partial_0 = A$ is the source of f, and $f\partial_1 = B$ is its target.

$f_0gg' = f_0'g = f_0''$ and $gg'f_1 = gf_1' = f_1$. $1_{f_0\partial_1}: \langle f_0,f_1\rangle \to \langle f_0,f_1\rangle$ is the identity for $\langle f_0,f_1\rangle$ in $\mathbf{Fac}(f)$.

$\langle f,1_A\rangle$ is terminal in $\mathbf{Fac}(f)$ and $\langle 1_A,f\rangle$ is initial. Checking the latter assertion, we have $f_0:\langle 1_A,f\rangle \to \langle f_0,f_1\rangle$ in $\mathbf{Fac}(f)$ because $1_Af_0 = f_0$ and $f_0f_1 = f$.

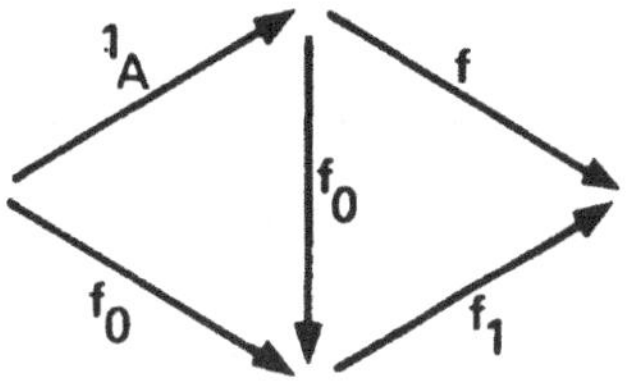

Trivally, if h: $\langle 1_A,f\rangle \to \langle f_0,f_1\rangle$ then $h = 1_Ah = f_0$.

The most interesting factorizations arise from restricting allowable right (or, dually left) factors and morphisms between factorizations. Still keeping $\mathbf{C}$ fixed, define $\mathbf{Fac}$ $(f,\mathbf{R})$ to be the subcategory of $\mathbf{Fac}(f)$ in which the right factors and morphisms are taken from a *strict*[2] subcategory $\mathbf{R}$ of $\mathbf{C}$. From the argument above and the fact that $\mathbf{R}$ is strict, we still have that $\langle f,1_A\rangle$ is terminal. Moreover, if $f \in \mathbf{R}$ then $\langle 1_A,f\rangle$ is initial; but for $f \in \mathbf{C}$ and not in $\mathbf{R}$, things become more interesting. We say that an initial object in $\mathbf{Fac}(f, \mathbf{R})$ is an *initial (right)* $\mathbf{R}$*-factorization* of f, and if every morphism of $\mathbf{C}$ has an initial $\mathbf{R}$-factorization we say that $\langle \mathbf{C}, \mathbf{R}\rangle$ is an *initial factorization situation*.

---

[2]A subcategory $\mathbf{R}$ of $\mathbf{C}$ is *strict* iff $|\mathbf{R}| = |\mathbf{C}|$, where $|\mathbf{X}|$ denotes the class of objects of the category $\mathbf{X}$.

The importance of initiality here (as is often the case) lies in Proposition 1, that initial objects are isomorphic, and that anything isomorphic to an initial object is initial. This means that if $A \overset{\ell}{\to} Q \overset{r}{\to} B$ and $A \overset{\ell'}{\to} Q' \overset{r'}{\to} B$ are both initial then there is an isomorphism in $\underline{\underline{C}}$, $h: Q \to Q'$ such that $\ell h = \ell'$ and $hr' = r$, in particular Q and Q' (called the <u>center objects</u> of the factorizations) are isomorphic in $\underline{\underline{C}}$. Reliance on Proposition 1 will be clear in the following key property of initial factorization situations.

<u>Proposition 2</u>. If $\langle \underline{\underline{C}},\underline{\underline{R}}\rangle$ is an initial factorization situation and $\langle \ell,r\rangle$ is an initial $\underline{\underline{R}}$-factorization then $\langle \ell,r'\rangle$ is initial for all r' in $\underline{\underline{R}}$ for which $\ell r'$ is defined.

<u>Proof</u>. Let $\langle k,s\rangle$ be an initial factorization of $\ell r'$, and let $a: \langle k,s\rangle \to \langle \ell,r'\rangle$ be the unique morphism guaranteed by $\langle k,s\rangle$ being initial.

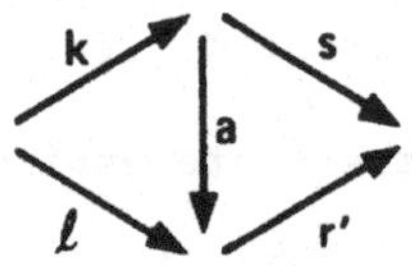

Since $ka = \ell$, we see that $kar = \ell r$. But $\langle \ell,r\rangle$ being initial gives a unique $b: \langle \ell,r\rangle \to \langle k,ar\rangle$.

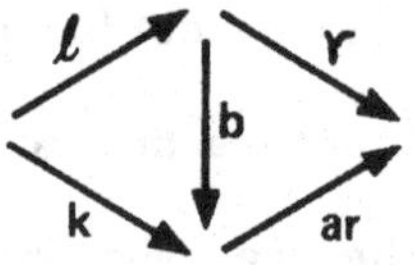

Putting the previous two diagrams together we see by uniqueness that ba is an identity.

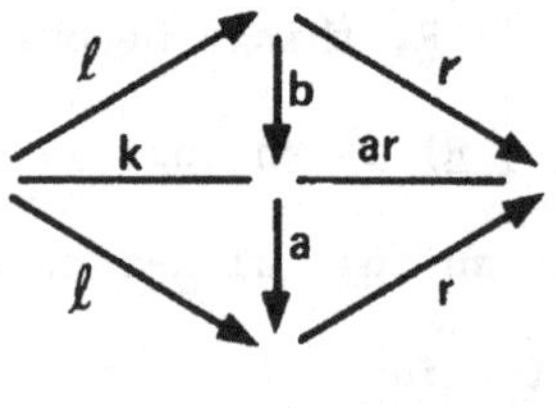

Since $ar' = s$, premultiplication by b shows that $r' = bs$. So we have a similar situation for the initial factorization $\langle k,s\rangle$ showing that ab is also the identity and $a: \langle k,s\rangle \to \langle \ell,r'\rangle$ is an isomorphism so by Proposition 1, $\langle \ell,r'\rangle$ is also initial. □

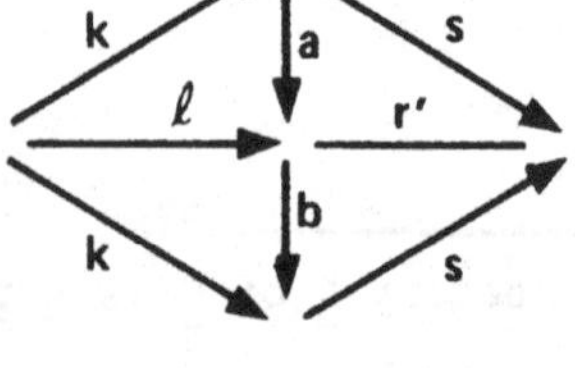

This result has more profound implications than would seem to be the case; particularly, there are quite interesting applications to factorizations in theories.

Assume now that $\langle \mathbf{C}, \mathbf{R} \rangle$ is an initial factorization situation (as $\langle \mathbf{Set}, \mathbf{Set}_{inj} \rangle$ is) and define the class $\underset{\sim}{L}$ to be all those morphisms which occurr as left factors in initial $\mathbf{R}$-factorizations ($\underset{\sim}{L}$ is not necessarily a subcategory). Because of the initial factorization situation, every morphism of $\mathbf{C}$ has an $\underset{\sim}{L}$-$\mathbf{R}$ factorization, and being initial, any two such factorizations of the same morphism are uniquely isomorphic. This often leads us to speak of <u>the</u> $\underset{\sim}{L}$-$\mathbf{R}$ factorization of a morphism f.

The left factors of initial $\mathbf{R}$-factorizations enjoy some properties that are useful in the next Section.

<u>Proposition 3</u>. If h is an isomorphism and $\ell \in \underset{\sim}{L}$, then $h\ell$ and ℓh are in $\underset{\sim}{L}$ if either is defined. If $r \in \mathbf{R}$ is also a left factor, then r is an isomorphism.

<u>Proof</u>. First, $\ell \in \underset{\sim}{L}$ says (Proposition 2) that $\langle \ell, 1 \rangle$ is initial. But $h: \langle \ell, 1 \rangle \to \langle \ell h, h^{-1} \rangle$ is an isomorphism, so (Proposition 1) $\langle \ell h, h^{-1} \rangle$ is initial and $\ell h \in \underset{\sim}{L}$. That $h\ell \in \underset{\sim}{L}$ is a bit more complicated, but we leave that proof to the reader. For the last assertion, we have already observed that $r \in \mathbf{R}$ means $\langle 1, r \rangle$ is initial and $r \in \underset{\sim}{L}$ means (Proposition 2) that $\langle r, 1 \rangle$ is initial. Thus (Proposition 1) there is an isomorphism $r': \langle r, 1 \rangle \to \langle 1, r \rangle$; i.e., $r'r = 1$ and $rr' = 1$; i.e., r is an isomorphism.□

This entire development dualizes by choosing a strict subcategory $\mathbf{L}$ of $\mathbf{C}$ and taking <u>terminal</u> factorizations in $\mathbf{Fac}(\mathbf{L}, f)$, the subcategory of $\mathbf{Fac}(f)$ in which left factors and morphisms are taken from $\mathbf{L}$. This dual version will be applied in the next Sections.

2. The Lattice of Quotients

The structure of an object is often revealed in the structure of closely associated objects. In the familiar case of universal algebra, (see Birkhoff [1] or [11]) the subalgebras, and the quotient algebras modulo congruences, of an algebra X form quosets[3] — actually lattices — which tell a lot about how X is put together. We generalize these ideas to the abstract concept of quotients in a category (the dual would be subobjects). In the next Section we prove a sometimes useful (and well-known) criterion for product decomposition of an algebra. One application is the decomposition of automata (see [2], [3], [6]). Part of the interest of the present material is the far reaching generalization of this result obtained with no extra effort.

The basic situation consists of an object X in a category $\underline{\underline{C}}$, and a subcategory $\underline{\underline{E}}$ of $\underline{\underline{C}}$ containing only epics[4.] from $\underline{\underline{C}}$. A <u>quotient</u> of X is defined to be just a morphism $q:X \to Q$ in $\underline{\underline{E}}$; and a morphism $q \to q'$ of quotients of X is a morphism $g:Q \to Q'$ in $\underline{\underline{C}}$, such that

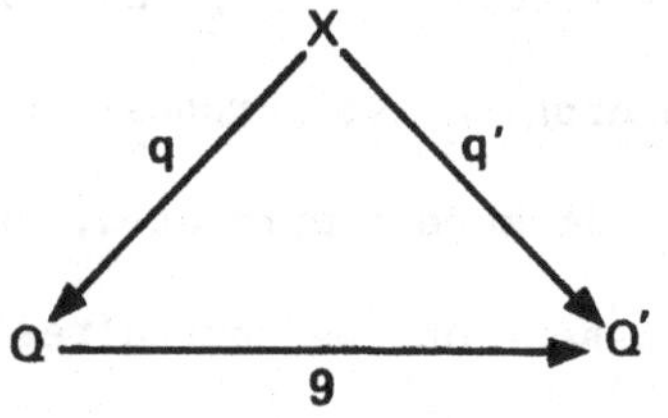

3. "Quoset" is short for "<u>quasiordered set</u>", which is a set Q with a binary relation ≤ which is both reflexive and transitive (but not necessarily antisymmetric). Quosets are in bijective correspondence with small categories such that for each pair A,B of objects, there is at most one morphism A → B (see Goguen-Thatcher-Wagner-Wright [8]).

4. A morphsim $q:X \to Q$ is <u>epic</u> in a category $\underline{\underline{C}}$ iff $qa = qb$ implies $a = b$ (whenever qa and qb are defined in $\underline{\underline{C}}$). For example, in $\underline{\underline{C}}=\underline{\underline{Set}}$, the epics are the surjections.

commutes in $\underline{\underline{C}}$. The reader should verify that this gives rise to a category, denoted $\underline{\underline{Q}}(X)$; identities are identities in $\underline{\underline{C}}$, and composition is composition in $\underline{\underline{C}}$. Because the quotients are epic, there is a unique $g:q \to q'$, if any; thus if $g:q \to q'$ and $g':q' \to q$, then $q \cong q'$.

But $\underline{\underline{Q}}(X)$ is unnecessarily large for most purposes. If $\underline{\underline{C}}$ is $\underline{\underline{Set}}$ and $\underline{\underline{E}}$ is the epics (i.e., the surjections), then $\underline{\underline{Q}}(X)$ (for $X \neq \phi$) is just not a set; the problem is that there are unsetlingly many copies of each "actual quotient" of X (say, as specified by the equivalence relations on X; or equivalently, the partitions of X).

The way around this is to "skeletize" $\underline{\underline{Q}}(X)$; i.e., to regard isomorphic quotients of X as equal (see MacLane [10]). Let $\underset{\sim}{Q}(X)$ denote the resulting category; hereafter, the reader will be unable to tell whether "quotient" means element of $\underline{\underline{Q}}(X)$ or of $\underset{\sim}{Q}(X)$; generally, it won/t matter. Note that $\underset{\sim}{Q}(X)$ will often be small, even when $\underline{\underline{Q}}(X)$ isn't. For example, with $\underline{\underline{Set}}$ above. Note also that $\underset{\sim}{Q}(X)$ will be a poset, rather than a quoset, since the anti-symmetry law will now be satisfied (isomorphic subjects are equal).

We now show that a limited degree of completeness in $\underline{\underline{C}}$ implies completeness of $\underset{\sim}{Q}(X)$.

Proposition 4. If $\underline{\underline{C}}$ has products[5.], if $\underline{\underline{E}}$ is a strict subcategory of eqics in $\underline{\underline{C}}$ such that $<\underline{\underline{C}},\underline{\underline{E}}>$ is a terminal factorization situation, and if $X\varepsilon|\underline{\underline{C}}|$, then $\underset{\sim}{Q}_1(X)$ has products,

Proof. Consider a family $<e_i:X \to Q_i|i\varepsilon I>$ of objects in $\underline{\underline{Q}}(X)$, and let er be a terminal $\underline{\underline{E}}$-factorization of the target tuple $[e_i]:X \to \Pi_i Q_i$. (Thus e_i and $e:X \to Q$ lie in $\underline{\underline{E}}$). We will show that $e = \Pi_i e_i$ in $\underline{\underline{Q}}(X)$. Let $p_j:\Pi_i Q_i \to Q_j$ be the projections of the product in $\underline{\underline{C}}$; then $(er)p_j = e_j$. Let $e':X \to Q'$ in $\underline{\underline{Q}}(X)$, with $q_j:Q' \to Q_j$ (in $\underline{\underline{E}}$) such that $e'q_i = e_j$. We must show there is a unique $u:Q' \to Q$ (in $\underline{\underline{E}}$) such that $e'u = e$. First note u is unique if it exists (since e' is epic). Now let $q = [q_j]:Q' \to \Pi_i Q_i$ then $qp_j = q_j$. Furthermore $e'q = [e_i]$, since $(e'g)p_j = e'q_j = e_j = [e_i]p_j$. But $e'q = [e_i]$ is an $\underline{\underline{E}}$-factorization, so there is a (unique) $u:Q' \to Q$ such that $e'u = e$ (and $ur = q$).□

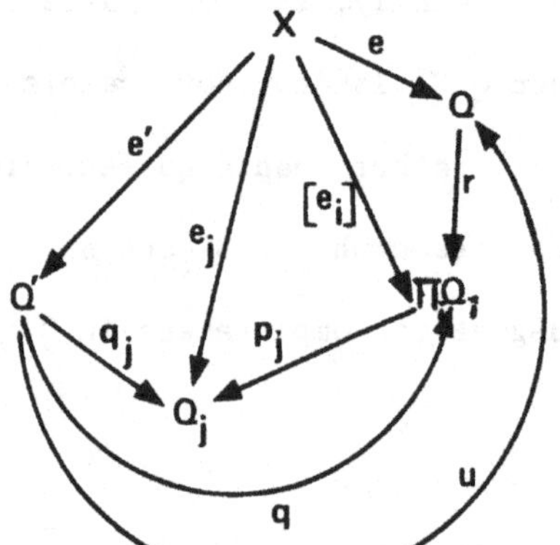

[5.] A category $\underline{\underline{C}}$ has products iff for each family $<A_i|i\varepsilon I>$ of objects of $\underline{\underline{C}}$ (where I is a set), there is an object A of $\underline{\underline{C}}$ (called the product object) and a family $<p_i:A \to A_i|i\varepsilon I>$ of morphisms in $\underline{\underline{C}}$ (called the projections of the product) such that for any other family $<q_i:B \to A_i|i\varepsilon I>$, with common source B, in $\underline{\underline{C}}$, there exists a unique morphism $q:B \to A$ such that

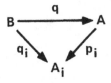

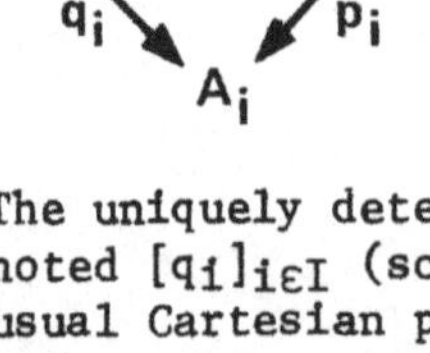

commutes in $\underline{\underline{C}}$ for all $i\varepsilon I$. The uniquely determined q is called the target tupling of the q_i, and is denoted $[q_i]_{i\varepsilon I}$ (sometimes just $[q_i]$). In $\underline{\underline{Set}}$, the product object A is the usual Cartesian product $\Pi_{i\varepsilon I} A_i$, and this notation, $\Pi_i A_i$, is generally used for products in any category $\underline{\underline{C}}$.

Corollary 5. If C has products, if $\underline{\underline{E}} \subseteq \underline{\underline{C}}$ is a terminal factorization subcategory of epics, and if $X \varepsilon |\underline{\underline{C}}|$ such that $\underset{\sim}{Q}(X)$ is small, then $\underset{\sim}{Q}(X)$ is a complete lattice.

Proof. Products in $\underline{\underline{Q}}(X)$ will give products in $\underset{\sim}{Q}(X)$, which will be order suprema since $\underset{\sim}{Q}(X)$ is a poset[6.]. But then $\underset{\sim}{Q}(X)$ is a complete lattice since a poset with all suprema also has all infima.□

This result applies to a number of significant situations. For example, let $\underline{\underline{C}}$ be $\underline{\underline{Alg}}_{\Sigma}$, the category of all Σ-algebras for Σ an operator domain (see [8]); and let $\underline{\underline{E}}$ be the surjective Σ-homomorphisms. Certainly these are all epic (though not conversely for the general case of varieties of Σ-algebras), and the existence of images gives terminal $\underline{\underline{E}}$-factorizations. The other hypotheses are trivial, and we get the lattice $\underset{\sim}{Q}(X)$ of quotients of (or congruences on) the Σ-algebra X. This also holds for $\underline{\underline{C}}$ the category rings, or groups, or automata, etc., and the reader will easily find many other examples, many of them presumably not already treated in the literature by "ordinary" methods; e.g., linear topological machines.

3. Product Decompositions

In this section, we continue the assumptions of Proposition 4, but we make a little more use of the properties of terminal factorization situations to obtain a very general result giving necessary and sufficient conditions for an object to have a product representation. A quotient $X \to Q$ is trivial iff it is an isomorphism, i.e. iff it is (a representative of) the minimum element $\bot$ of $\underset{\sim}{Q}(X)$. Let $\underset{\sim}{M}$ denote the class of right factors for the factorization situation $\langle \underline{\underline{C}},\underline{\underline{E}} \rangle$. A nontrivial product representation of an

[6.] A poset is an antisymmetric quoset. The reader can check that products in a poset (or quoset) are just least upper bounds.

object X in $\underline{\underline{C}}$ is a morphism $h:X \to X_1 \times X_2$ in $\underset{\sim}{M}$ such that neither hp_1 nor hp_2 lie in $\underset{\sim}{M}$ (where p_i are the projections).

Theorem 6. If $\underline{\underline{C}}$ has binary products, $\underline{\underline{E}}$ contains only epics, and $<\underline{\underline{C}},\underline{\underline{E}}>$ is a terminal factorization situation, then $X\varepsilon|\underline{\underline{C}}|$ has a non-trivial product representation iff there are non-trivial quotients q_1, q_2 such that $q_1 \wedge q_2 = \perp$ (in $\underset{\sim}{Q}(X)$).

Proof. First suppose given q_1, q_2 as above, and let em = $[q, q_2]$ be a terminal $\underline{\underline{E}}$-factorization of $[q_1, q_2]$ which is hereafter denoted h.

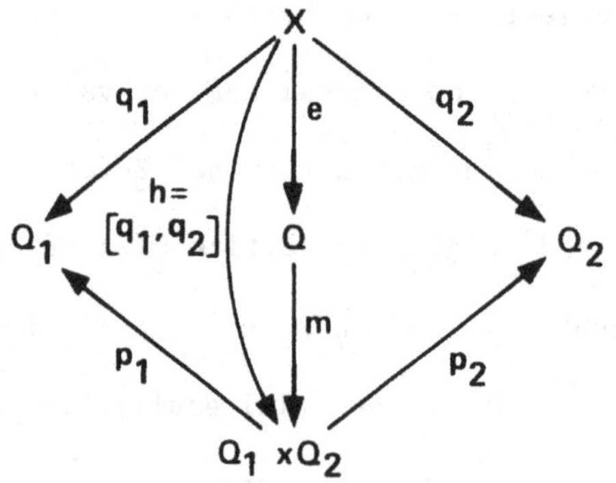

But $e = q_1 \wedge q_2$, and is thus as isomorphism. By Proposition 3, h = em is also a right factor, and therefore $h\varepsilon\underset{\sim}{M}$, as required. Now suppose that $q_i = hp_i\varepsilon\underset{\sim}{M}$, then $q_i\varepsilon\underline{\underline{E}}\cap\underset{\sim}{M}$, and so (by Proposition 3 again) q_i is an isomorphism; contradiction.

Conversely, suppose we have a non-trivial product representation of X; i.e. $h\varepsilon M$ but $hp_i\not\varepsilon\underset{\sim}{M}$ for i = 1,2. Let $<q_i, m_i>$ be a terminal $\underline{\underline{E}}$-factorization of hp_i; let $q:X \to Q$ be a lower bound for $\{q_1,q_2\}$, i.e., assume there are $f_i:Q \to Q_i$ such that $q_i = qf_i$ (we want to show q is an isomorphism); let $C:Q \to X_1 \times X_2$ be $[f_1m_2, f_2m_2]$; and let c = em be a terminal $\underline{\underline{E}}$-factorization of C.

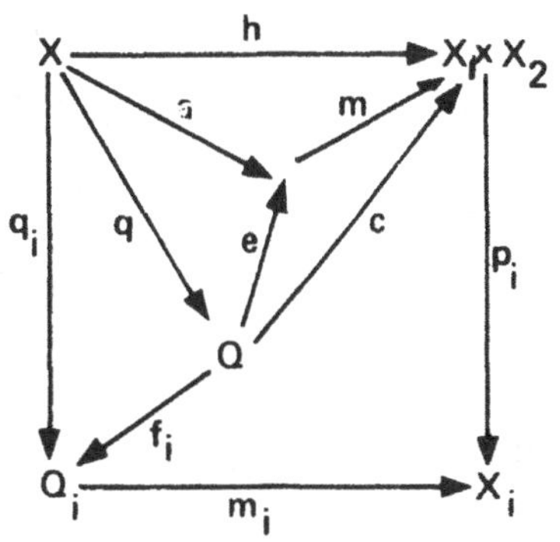

Now <qe, m> and <1,h> are isomorphic $\underline{\underline{E}}$-factorizations of h; let the isomorphism be a, with $ab = 1_X$. Then qe = a, so $q(eb) = ab = 1_X$. Therefore q is a retraction[7.], but was assumed epic; thus q is an isomorphism. That is, $q_1 \wedge q_2 = \bot$, as desired.

Finally, we have to show that the q_i's are non-trivial. If q_i is a right factor (by Proposition 3 again, using $m_i \varepsilon \underset{\sim}{M}$), contradicting the hypothesis. Thus neither q_i is trivial.□

Note that the result for non-trivial representation by a product over an index set I iff there are $\langle q_i | i\varepsilon I\rangle$ with $_{i\varepsilon I}q_i = \bot$ has just the same proof (but needs the additional hypothesis of products over I).

Returning to $\underline{\underline{C}} = \underline{\underline{Ag}}_\Sigma$ and $\underline{\underline{E}}$ = surjective Σ-homomorphisms, we get a classical result of "general algebra" (Birkhoff [1]). Note that our proof is not really harder than that of the special case, but out result is much more general. It is often the case that a formulation of a result in categorical terms exposes the essential ideas clearly, and gives a much broader result; this has also happened in the minimal realization theory of automata and systems (see Goguen [12], Arbib-Manes [13]).

---

7. A morphism $f:A \to B$ is a <u>retraction</u> in $\underline{\underline{C}}$ iff there is some g in $\underline{\underline{C}}$ such that $fg = 1_B$. They property about to be used is that if f is both a retraction and an epic, then it is an isomorphism.

A very special case of the above result is familiar in automation theory as the "parallel decomposition" theorem (see Büchi-Wright [2], Thatcher [3], Hartmanis-Stearns [6]). Just let[8] $\Sigma_1 = X$ and $\Sigma_n = \phi$ for $n \neq 1$. The interpretation is that non-trivial product representation is "non-trivial simulation by a parallel connection of automata," quotients have been viewed (somewhat misguidedly) in our opinion, as "state-preserving partitions" of automata.

8. Σ_n is the set of n-ary operation symbols for Σ-algebras.

References

[1] Birkhoff, G., Lattice Theory, Amer. Math. Soc. Colloq. Pub. 25, New York (1948); revised edition (1960).

[2] Büchi, R. and Wright, J.B., "Mathematical Theory of Automata," unpublished unpublished notes, University of Michigan (1960).

[3] Thatcher, J., "Notes on Mathematical Automata Theory," University of Michigan Technical Note 03105-26-T (1963).

[4] Yeh, R., "A study of general systems using automata theory", Cybernetica 13 No. 3 (1970) 180-194.

[5] Gallaire, H. and Harrison, M., "Decomposition of linear sequential machines," Math. Sys. Th. 3 (1969) 246-287.

[6] Hartmanis, J. and Stearns, R.E., Algebraic Structure Theory of Sequential Machines, Prentice-Hall, New Jersey (1966).

[7] Sipusic, T., "Two Automata Decomposition Theorems Generalized to Machines in a Closed Monoidal Category," Quarterly Report No. 35, Institute for Computer Research, the University of Chicago, Section IID (1972).

[8] Goguen, J.A., Thatcher, J.W., Wagner, E.G., and Wright, J.B., "A junction between computer science and category theory, I: basic concepts and examples (part 1)", Report RC 4526, IBM Watson Research Center, New York (1973).

[9] MacLane, S. and Birkhoff, G., Algebra, MacMillan, New York (1967).

[10] MacLane, S., Category Theory for the Working Mathematician, Springer-Verlag, New York (1971).

[11] Birkhoff, G., "On the structure of abstract algebras", Proc. of the Cambridge Phil. Soc. 31 (1935) 433-454.

[12] Goguen, J.A., "Minimal realization of machines in closed categories" Bull. of the Amer. Math. Soc. 78 No. 5 (1972) 777-783.

[13] Arbib, M.A., and Manes, E.G., "Foundations of system theory: decompressible systems" Automatica (May 1974).

ON THE PERIODIC SUM AND EXTENSIONS OF FINITE AUTOMATA

Jerzy W. GRZYMALA-BUSSE
Institute of Control Engineering
Technical University of Poznan

In this paper we consider some properties of the periodic sum of finite automata associated with isomorphisms and disconnected extensions of finite automata.

First we quote a few definitions from [2-7].

A finite automaton (or briefly automaton) is a triple (S, Σ, M), where S is a finite nonempty state set, Σ is a finite nonempty input set, and $M: S \times \Sigma \longrightarrow S$ is a transition function.

The set of all finite sequences of elements from Σ will be denoted by I.

The transition function M can be extended to domain $S \times I$ as follows: if $M(s,x)$ is defined, then

$$M(s,x\sigma)=M(M(s,x),\sigma),$$

where $s \in S$, $\sigma \in \Sigma$, and $x \in I$.

An automaton $A=(S,\Sigma,M)$ is connected if and only if for each pair (s,s') of states of A there exist a state sequence $s=s_0$, s_1, ..., $s_{n-1}=s'$ and an input sequence x_0, x_1, ..., x_{n-2} such that either $M(s_i,x_i)=s_{i+1}$ or $M(s_{i+1},x_i)=s_i$, where $i=0,1,\ldots,n-2$.

Let $A=(S,\Sigma,M)$ and $A'=(S',\Sigma,M')$ be finite automata. A one to one function f of S onto S' will be called an <u>isomorphism</u> if and only if for each $s\in S$ and $\sigma\in\Sigma$ we have

$$M'(f(s),\sigma)=f(M(s,\sigma)).$$

The set of all isomorphisms of A onto A' will be denoted by $Is(A\longrightarrow A')$. An isomorphism for which $A=A'$ is an <u>automorphism</u>. The set of all automorphisms of the automaton A, together with the operation of superposition, forms a group, denoted by $G(A)$.

Let T be a positive integer. A <u>strictly periodic automaton</u> (or briefly <u>periodic automaton</u>) V is a triple (S^+,Σ,M^+), where S^+ is a sequence $S_0^+,S_1^+,\dots,S_{T-1}^+$ of finite nonempty state sets, Σ is a finite nonempty input set, M^+ is a sequence $M_0^+,M_1^+,\dots,M_{T-1}^+$ of transition functions, where $M_t^+\colon S_t^+\times\Sigma\longrightarrow S_{t+1\,(\mathrm{mod}\ T)}^+$, and $t=0,1,\dots,T-1$. The number T is said to be a <u>period</u> of V.

A <u>fixed analog</u> V^* of the periodic automaton $V=(S^+,\Sigma,M^+)$ is an automaton (S^*,Σ,M^*), where $S=S_0^+\cup S_1^+\cup\dots\cup S_{T-1}^+$ and $M^*\colon S^*\times\Sigma\longrightarrow S^*$ is a transition function defined for all $s\in S_t^+$, $\sigma\in\Sigma$, and $t=0,1,\dots,T-1$ as follows

$$M^*(s,\sigma)=M_t^+(s,\sigma).$$

A <u>periodic representation</u> of the automaton A is a periodic automaton V such that the fixed analog V^* of V and the automaton A have the same state sets, input sets, and transition functions. The periodic representation of A with the maximal period will be called <u>maximal</u>.

Let $A^0=(S^0,\Sigma,M^0)$, $A^1=(S^1,\Sigma,M^1)$, ..., $A^{T-1}=(S^{T-1},\Sigma,M^{T-1})$ be automata. Let $\psi_0\colon S^0\longrightarrow S^1$, $\psi_1\colon S^1\longrightarrow S^2$, ..., $\psi_{T-1}\colon S^{T-1}\longrightarrow S^0$ be one to one and onto functions. Then a <u>periodic sum of automata</u> $A^0, A^1,\dots,A^{T-1}$, <u>associated with functions</u> $\psi_0,\psi_1,\dots,\psi_{T-1}$, is a periodic automaton $V=(S^+,\Sigma,M^+)$ with period T, where S^+ is a sequence $S^0, S^1, \ldots, S^{T-1}$ and M^+ is a sequence $M_0^+, M_1^+, \ldots, M_{T-1}^+$, where for all $s \in S^t$, $\sigma \in \Sigma$, and $t=0,1,\ldots,T-1$ we have

$$M_t^+(s, \sigma) = \psi_t M^t(s, \sigma).$$

This is denoted

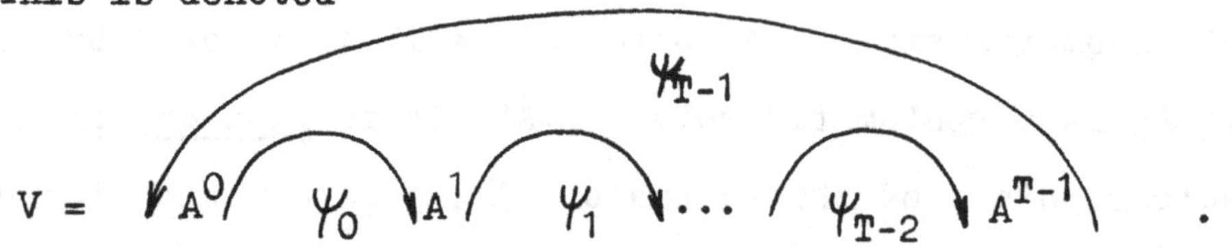
V =
ψ_{T-1}
A^0
ψ_0
A^1
ψ_1
...
ψ_{T-2}
A^{T-1}

Let $A^0, A^1, \ldots, A^{T-1}$ be mutually isomorphic automata and let g^t be an isomorphism between A^0 and A^t for $t=0,1,\ldots,T-1$. Then the periodic sum of $A^0, A^1, \ldots, A^{T-1}$, associated with functions ψ_0, ψ_1, ..., ψ_{T-1} will be called an <u>extension of the automaton</u> A^0, <u>associated with isomorphisms</u> $g^0, g^1, \ldots, g^{T-1}$, if and only if

$$\psi_t = g^{t+1 \pmod T}(g^t)^{-1}$$

for $t=0,1,\ldots,T-1$.

Let $V^1=(S^+, \Sigma, M^+)$ and $V^2=(S^-, \Sigma, M^-)$ be periodic automata with the same period T. Then a one to one function f defined as the sequence of functions: f_0 of S_0^+ onto S_1^- , f_1 of S_1^+ onto S_2^- , ..., f_{T-1} of S_{T-1}^+ onto S_0^- such that

$$M^-_{t+1 \pmod T}(f_t(s), \sigma) = f_{t+1 \pmod T}(M_t^+(s, \sigma))$$

for all $s \in S_t^+$, $\sigma \in \Sigma$, and $t=0,1,\ldots,T-1$ will be called a <u>(T+1)-adic isomorphism</u> or a <u>polyadic isomorphism</u>.

A one to one function g defined as the sequence of functions: g_0 of S_0^+ onto S_0^- , g_1 of S_1^+ onto S_1^- ,..., g_{T-1} of S_{T-1}^+ onto S_{T-1}^- such that

$$M_t^-(g_t(s), \sigma) = g_{t+1 \pmod T}(M_t^+(s, \sigma))$$

for all $s \in S_t^+$, $\sigma \in \Sigma$, and $t=0,1,\ldots,T-1$ will be called an <u>ordinary isomorphism</u> or just an <u>isomorphism</u>.

We have the following properties of periodic sum of automata, associated with isomorphisms.

Proposition 1. Let A *be an automaton, let* T *be a positive integer, and let* $A^0, A^1, \ldots, A^{T-1}$ *be automata isomorphic to* A . *Let* $\mathcal{A}$ *be a set of all nonisomorphic automata of the type*

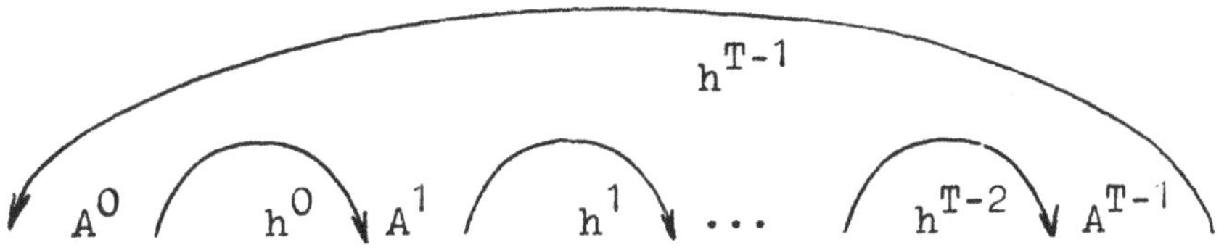

,

where $h^0 \in Is(A^0 \longrightarrow A^1)$, $h^1 \in Is(A^1 \longrightarrow A^2)$,..., $h^{T-1} \in Is(A^{T-1} \longrightarrow A^0)$. *Then*

$$|\mathcal{A}| \leqslant |G(A)| ,$$

where $|X|$ denotes the cardinality of the set X .

Proof. For arbitrary fixed $h^0 \in Is(A^0 \longrightarrow A^1)$, $h^1 \in Is(A^1 \longrightarrow A^2)$, ..., $h^{T-2} \in Is(A^{T-2} \longrightarrow A^{T-1})$ let $\mathcal{L}$ be a set of all automata of the type

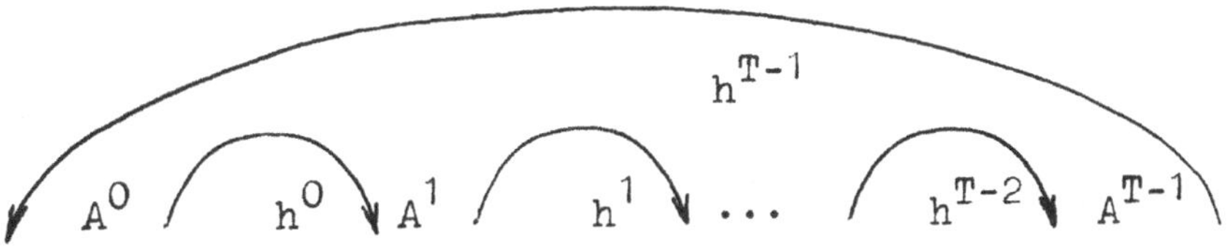

,

where $h^{T-1} \in Is(A^{T-1} \longrightarrow A^0)$.

For arbitrary fixed h^{T-1} in $Is(A^{T-1} \longrightarrow A^0)$ we have

$$Is(A^{T-1} \longrightarrow A^0) = G(A^{T-1})h^{T-1} = h^{T-1}G(A^0),$$

as follows from [1] , and hence

$$|\mathcal{L}| \leqslant |G(A)| .$$

Let

$V =$ 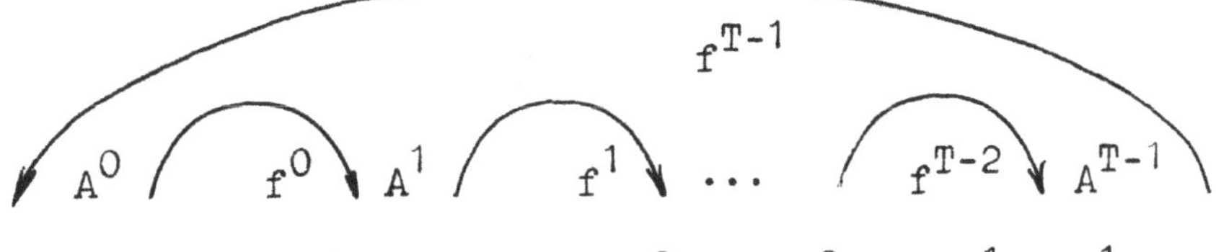

be arbitrary member of $\mathcal{A}$, i.e. $f^0 \in Is(A^0 \longrightarrow A^1)$, $f^1 \in Is(A^1 \longrightarrow A^2)$,..., $f^{T-1} \in Is(A^{T-1} \longrightarrow A^0)$.

Furthermore, let k_0 be a fixed member of $G(A^0)$, and let

$$k_1 = f^0 k_0 (h^0)^{-1} ,$$
$$\cdots\cdots\cdots$$
$$k_{T-1} = f^{T-2} k_{T-2} (h^{T-2})^{-1}$$
$$= f^{T-2} \cdots f^0 k_0 (h^0)^{-1} \cdots (h^{T-2})^{-1} .$$

In the set $\mathcal{L}$ there exists a member

W = 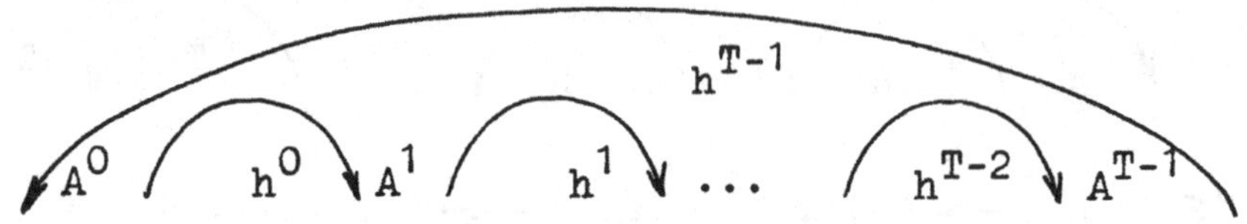

indicated by such a function h^{T-1} that the condition

$$k_0 = f^{T-1} \cdots f^0 k_0 (h^0)^{-1} \cdots (h^{T-1})^{-1}$$

is satisfied.

For the rest of the proof we note that the sequence of functions $k_0, k_1, \ldots, k_{T-1}$ is an isomorphism between W and V .

For the sake of simplicity, the following result will be stated for two periodic automata with periods equal to 2 .

Proposition 2. Let A^1 , A^2 , B^1 , B^2 *be mutually isomorphic automata, and let* $h^1 \in Is(A^1 \to A^2)$, $h^2 \in Is(A^2 \to A^1)$, $h^3 \in Is(B^1 \to B^2)$, and $h^4 \in Is(B^2 \to B^1)$. *Then the automaton equal to the union of irreducible automata*

V= 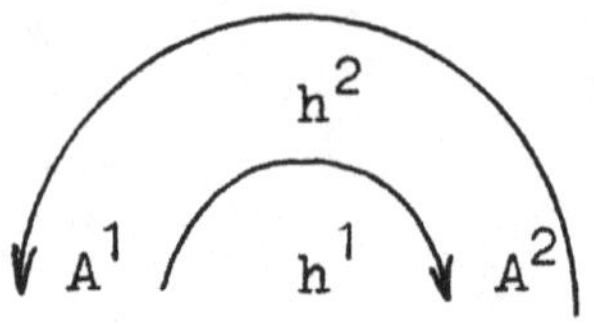

and

W= 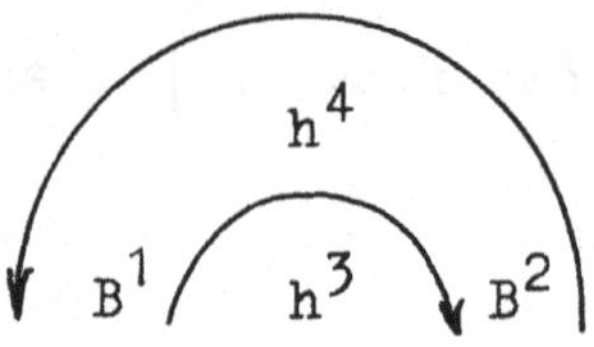

is reducible if and only if there exist $f^1 \in Is(A^1 \to B^1)$ *and* $f^2 \in Is(B^2 \to A^2)$ *such that*

$$h^2 f^2 h^3 f^1 = (f^1)^{-1} h^4 (f^2)^{-1} h^1 = id. \; .$$

Proof. The proof follows from the fact that the union of irreducible automata V and W is reducible if and only if there exists

$f^1 \in Is(A^1 \longrightarrow B^1)$ and $f^2 \in Is(B^2 \longrightarrow A^2)$ such that all automata

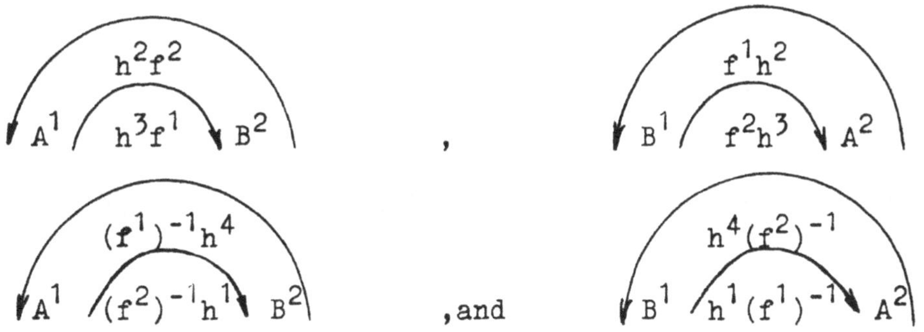

are reducible and 3-adically isomorphic.

Now we discuss the question: when the union of connected and irreducible automata is reducible? Again for the sake of simplicity, the answer will be given for the reducibility to ordinary automata. This result is an expansion of the corresponding remark in [6] .

Proposition 3. *Let* $\mathcal{A}$ *be a set of connected irreducible periodic automata with the same period* T. *The union of all automata in* $\mathcal{A}$ *is reducible to an ordinary automaton equal to the union of connected subautomata whose maximal periodic representations have periods* D_1 , $D_2, \dots, D_n$ *if and only if on the set* $\mathcal{A}$ *there exists a partition* π *such that members of* π *have exactly* $\gcd(T,D_1)$, $\gcd(T,D_2)$, ..., $\gcd(T,D_n)$ *mutually (T+1)-adically isomorphic automata from* $\mathcal{A}$.

REFERENCES

[1] BAVEL,Z.: *Structure and transition-preserving function of finite automata*. J. Assoc. Comput. Mach. 15, 1 (1968), 135-158.

[2] FLECK,A.C.: *Isomorphism groups of automata*. J. Assoc. Comput. Mach. 9, 4 (1962), 469-476.

[3] GILL,A.: *Time-varying sequential machines*. J. Franklin Inst. 276, 6 (1963), 519-539.

[4] GRZYMALA-BUSSE,J.W.: *Automorphisms of polyadic automata*. J. Assoc. Comput. Mach. 16, 2 (1969), 208-219. Err.:646.

[5] _____ : *On the periodic representations and the reduci-*

bility of periodic automata. J. Assoc. Comput. Mach. 16, 3 (1969), 432-441. Err.: 17, 4 (1970), 739.

[6] ______ : Periodic representations and T-partitionable equivalents of sequential machines. IEEE Trans. Computers C-20, 2 (1971), 190-198.

[7] WEEG,G.P.: The structure of an automaton and its operation-preserving transformation group. J. Assoc. Comput. Mach. 9, 3 (1962), 345-349.

FINITE BRANCHING AUTOMATA:
AUTOMATA THEORY MOTIVATED BY PROBLEM SOLVING

Ivan M. Havel
Institute of Information Theory and Automation
Czechoslovak Academy of Sciences
180 76 Prague, Czechoslovakia

Finite automata were historically developed as abstract models of discrete finite-state devices that change their internal states in response to inputs. Here we take another point of view which comes from the theory of problem solving in artificial and human intelligence. In problem solving, the main interest is concerned with state-space search methods (cf. NILSSON [1]). In principal, one looks for a sequence of elementary operators, leading from a given initial state to one of the goal states in a particular problem domain. Let us call any such sequence a "plan" (it serves as a prescription how to achieve the goal). Consider the following example. A maze consists of nine rooms, some of them connected by a door according to Fig. 1(a).

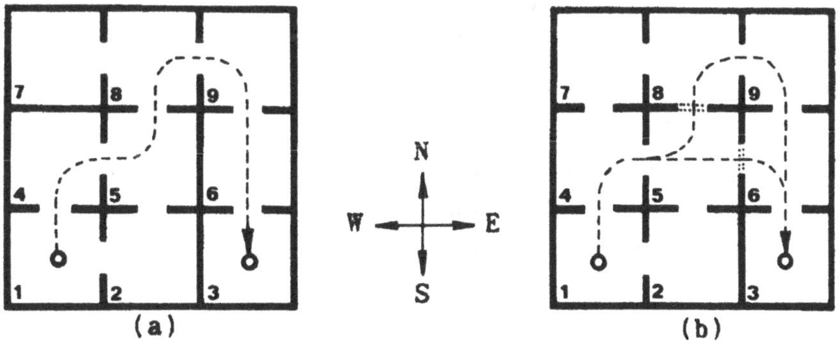

Fig. 1. The maze. (a) simple plan; (b) branching plan

An intelligent robot with a complete knowledge of the maze is initially in room 1 and its task is to move into room 3. In each room it may decide to move east, north, west, or south, provided there is a door in the chosen direction. There are thus four elementary operators, which we denote E, N, W, and S. To make a plan means just to make all the decisions in advance. One such plan, the sequence NENESS, is indicated in Fig. 1(a); another possible plan is ENNESS. The corresponding state space consists of nine different locations of the robot. The concept of a finite automaton[1] (with $\Sigma = \{E,N,W,S\}$ and δ a partial function) is a natural and obvious abstraction of such a state space. The set of all plans is just the regular language recognized by the automaton -- and this seems to be all in which one field can contribute to the other.

However, there exists a radical generalization of the concept of a plan which is important in problem solving (cf. ŠTĚPÁNKOVÁ and HAVEL [2], FIKES, HART, and NILSSON [3]) and quite appealing from automata-theoretic point of view. It is the case of so called "branching" or "conditional" plans: roughly speaking, a lack of prior information about a particular state makes it necessary to consider two or more outgoing operators in parallel, thus yielding a plan consisting of a set of sequences instead of a single sequence.

Let us illustrate this case by our example of the robot in the maze. Consider the maze as above, except that the robot has a gap in its knowledge: it knows that there is a door from room 5 either to room 6 or to room 8 -- but does not know which of these two possibilities really holds or will hold in proper time (Fig. 1(b)). To be able to make an advance plan even now, the robot has to take both cases into account. This yields, e.g., a plan of the form indicated in Fig. 1(b):

$$\mathrm{NE}\left\langle\begin{array}{l}\mathrm{NESS}\\ \mathrm{ES}\end{array}\right.$$

or, written as a set, {NENESS, NEES}. Another possible plan is {ENNESS, ENES}. A similar situation may arise when the goal state itself is ambiguous. For instance the maze from Fig. 1(a), if the goal were to get a reward which is placed either in room 3 or in room 9, would yield plans {NENE, NENESS} and {ENNE, ENNESS}.

Such a generalization of the concept of a plan, which comes out naturally from the logical approach of [2], explains the idea behind the new model called "finite branching automaton". The difference from

---

[1] A finite automaton is a quintuple $\mathcal{A} := \langle Q, \Sigma, \delta, q_0, F\rangle$ where Q is a finite nonempty set (of states), Σ an alphabet, $\delta : Q \times \Sigma \to Q$, $q_0 \in Q$, $F \subseteq Q$. We extend δ to $\delta : Q \times \Sigma^* \to Q$ and define $T(\mathcal{A}) := \{ w \in \Sigma^* \mid \delta(q_0, w) \in F \}$. $L \subseteq \Sigma^*$ is regular iff $L = T(\mathcal{A})$ for some finite automaton $\mathcal{A}$. (Σ^* is the free monoid generated by Σ , with identity Λ .)

conventional finite automata lays mainly in the form of acceptance: instead of strings the new device accepts languages, and thus instead of languages it recognizes families of languages (we make an obvious distinction between "accepting" and "recognizing"). The detailed treatment of finite branching automata, including formal proofs of all results mentioned below without proofs, can be found in HAVEL [4].

Definition 1. A finite branching automaton is a quintuple

$$\mathcal{B} := \langle Q, \Sigma, \delta, q_0, B \rangle ,$$

where $\langle Q, \Sigma, \delta, q_0 \rangle$ is an ordinary finite automaton (without the set of final states) and $B := \langle B_0, B_1 \rangle$ is a pair of subsets of $Q \times 2^{\Sigma}$ (the transient and the terminal branching relations).

We shall use the following notation:

$$\mathcal{L}(\Sigma) := 2^{\Sigma^*} - \{\emptyset\}$$

(2^A is the set of subsets of A). For $L \subseteq \Sigma^*$ we define

$$\mathrm{Pref}(L) := \{u \in \Sigma^* \mid uv \in L \text{ for some } v \in \Sigma^*\} ,$$

$$\mathrm{Fst}(L) := \mathrm{Pref}(L) \cap \Sigma ,$$

$$\partial_w L := \{v \in \Sigma^* \mid wv \in L\} ,$$

where $w \in \Sigma^*$. Any subset $X \subseteq \mathcal{L}(\Sigma)$ is called a family (of languages).

Definition 2. A language $L \in \mathcal{L}(\Sigma)$ is accepted by a finite branching automaton $\langle Q, \Sigma, \delta, q_0, B \rangle$ iff for each $w \in \mathrm{Pref}(L) - L$

$$(\delta(q_0, w), \mathrm{Fst}(\partial_w L)) \in B_0 ,$$

and for each $w \in L$

$$(\delta(q_0, w), \mathrm{Fst}(\partial_w L)) \in B_1 .$$

We denote $T(\mathcal{B})$ the family of all languages accepted by $\mathcal{B}$.

Definition 3. A family $X \subseteq \mathcal{L}(\Sigma)$ is recognizable iff $X = T(\mathcal{B})$ for some finite branching automaton $\mathcal{B}$.

Example. Fig. 2 illustrates a finite branching automaton $\mathcal{B}$ with

$B_0 = \{(q_0, \{a\}), (q_0, \{a,b\}), (q_0, \{c\}), (q_1, \{a,b,c\}), (q_2, \{a,b\}), (q_2, \{c\})\}$;

$B_1 = \{(q_1, \emptyset), (q_1, \{a,c\}), (q_1, \{c\}), (q_2, \{b\}), (q_2, \{c\})\}$.

(In Fig. 2 white and black dots bind edges corresponding to B_0 and B_1, respectively. The dot in the circle for q_1 means $(q_1, \emptyset) \in B_1$.)

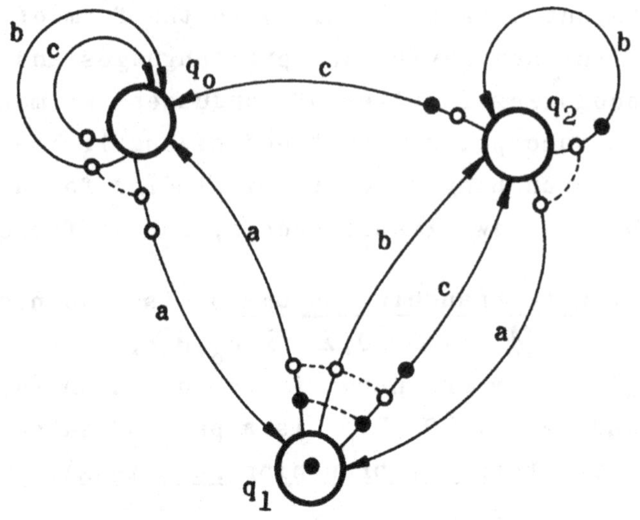

Fig. 2. State graph of a branching automaton

The following are examples of languages accepted by $\mathcal{B}$:

$$L_1 = \{a, acb^nca\} \cup \{acb^i \mid 0 \leq i \leq n\}, \quad (n \geq 0) ;$$

$$L_2 = b^*a \ ;$$

$$L_3 = ca \cup cac(a \cup bb^*) \ .$$

Given an ordinary finite automaton $\mathcal{A} = \langle Q, \Sigma, \delta, q_0, F \rangle$, there are two natural ways of viewing it as a special case of a finite branching automaton. We can build $\mathcal{B}$ such that $T(\mathcal{B}) = \{\{u\} \mid u \in T(\mathcal{A})\}$, as well as $\mathcal{B}'$ such that $T(\mathcal{B}') = \{T(\mathcal{A})\}$ (except when $T(\mathcal{A}) = \emptyset$). Thus every (nonempty) regular language can be accepted by a finite branching automaton. However, there are also nonregular languages acceptable by finite branching automata. In fact, we have

<u>Theorem 1.</u> $\mathcal{L}(\Sigma)$ is recognizable.

According to this theorem any family $X \subseteq \mathcal{L}(\Sigma)$ is a subset of some recognizable family (namely of $\mathcal{L}(\Sigma)$). Let us call X <u>strong</u> iff $\mathcal{L}(\Sigma)$ is the only recognizable family containing X as a subfamily. The following fact gives a negative answer to a problem posed in [4]:

<u>Fact</u> (A.Pirická). There is no finite strong family.

To show this let X be finite. There exists $w = a_1 \ldots a_{k-1} \in \Sigma^*(k \geq 1)$ such that $\{w\} \notin X$. Define $\mathcal{B}_w := \langle Q, \Sigma, \delta, q_0, B \rangle$ where

$$Q = \{q_0, q_1, \ldots, q_k\},$$

$$\delta(q_i, a) = \begin{cases} q_{i+1} & \text{if } i \neq k \text{ and } a = a_i \\ q_k & \text{otherwise}, \end{cases}$$

$$B_0 = Q \times 2^{\Sigma} \quad \text{and} \quad B_1 = B_0 - \{(q_{k-1}, \emptyset)\}.$$

Then $X_w := T(\mathcal{B}_w) = \mathcal{L}(\Sigma) - \{w\}$, i.e., $X \subseteq X_w \subsetneq \mathcal{L}(\Sigma)$ where X_w is recognizable.

From the fact that finite branching automata can accept very "complex" languages one should not conclude that there are also very "complex" recognizable families. Some of the following results give an evidence against such a conclusion by demonstrating that a number of mutually "similar" languages necessarily belong to the same family.

Definition 4. For every $u \in \Sigma^*$ we define a binary replacement operator R_u as follows. For each $L_1, L_2 \subseteq \Sigma^*$,

$$R_u(L_1, L_2) := (L_1 - u\Sigma^*) \cup uL_2 .$$

We shall be particularly interested in a special application of the replacement operator, namely $R_u(L_1, \partial_u L_2)$. In problem solving this has the meaning of "jumping" from one plan to another. The result of such composition of plans should yield again a genuine plan.

Definition 5. A family $X \subseteq \mathcal{L}(\Sigma)$ has the replacement property iff for each $u \in \Sigma^*$ and each $L_1, L_2 \in X$, if $u \in Pref(L_1) \cap Pref(L_2)$ then

$$R_u(L_1, \partial_u L_2) \in X .$$

Note that any family closed under union and intersection with regular sets has the replacement property.

Theorem 2. Every recognizable family has the replacement property.

Using the finiteness of Q we obtain the following two theorems.

Theorem 3. For every recognizable family X there exists a constant $n \geq 1$ such that for any $L \in X$ and any $K \subseteq Pref(L)$, if $|K| > n$ then there exist two distinct strings $u, v \in K$ such that

$$R_u(L,\partial_v L) \in X$$

and

$$R_v(L,\partial_u L) \in X .$$

The second theorem is an analogy of known "pumping lemma" for conventional finite automata.

<u>Theorem 4.</u> For every recognizable family X there exists a constant $n \geq 1$ such that for any $L \in X$ if L contains a string w of length $lg(w)>n$, then there are three languages L_1, L_2, L_3 and two strings u, v such that

(i) uv is a prefix of w ;

(ii) $L = L_1 \cup uL_2 \cup uvL_3$;

(iii) for every $m \geq 0$

$$L_1 \cup \bigcup_{i=0}^{m-1} uv^i L_2 \cup uv^m L_3 \in X .$$

Next we shall establish the necessary and sufficient conditions for a family to be recognizable.

<u>Definition 6.</u> Let $X \subseteq \mathcal{L}(\Sigma)$ and $w \in \Sigma^*$. We define

$$\partial_w X := \{\partial_w L \mid L \in X\} - \{\emptyset\} ;$$

$$\mathcal{D}(X) := \{\partial_w X \mid w \in \Sigma^*\} .$$

We shall call the family $\partial_w X$ the <u>derivative of X (with resp. to w)</u>.

The following theorem gives the necessary (but not sufficient!) condition for recognizability.

<u>Theorem 5.</u> If X is a recognizable family then $\mathcal{D}(X)$ is finite.

As a corollary, for any recognizable family X the union $\bigcup_{L \in X} L$ is regular. Thus, in particular, a singleton $\{L\}$ is recognizable iff L is a nonempty regular language.

Observe that for $X = \{\{aa,b\},\{ab\}\}$ we have $\mathcal{D}(X) = \{X,\{\{a\},\{b\}\},\{\Lambda\},\emptyset\}$, i.e. finite, but X has not the replacement property.

<u>Definition 7.</u> Let $X \subseteq \mathcal{L}(\Sigma)$ and $L \in \mathcal{L}(\Sigma)$. We say that L is <u>compatible with X</u> iff for each $w \in \Sigma^*$ there is a language $L_w \in X$

such that

$$\text{(i)} \quad w \in L \text{ iff } w \in L_w ,$$

and

$$\text{(ii)} \quad \mathrm{Fst}(\partial_w L) = \mathrm{Fst}(\partial_w L_w) .$$

The family of all languages compatible with X will be denoted $C(X)$. While it can be easily seen that $X \subseteq C(X)$ and $C(X) = CC(X)$, it is not true, in general, that $X = C(X)$. In fact this equality takes part in the desired characterization theorem:

Theorem 6. A family $X \subseteq \mathcal{L}(\Sigma)$ is recognizable iff $X = C(X)$ and $\mathcal{D}(X)$ is finite.

The property $X = C(X)$ coincides with the replacement property for finite X, but in general it is strictly stronger as the following example shows.

Example. Let X_{fin} be the family of all finite nonempty languages. Clearly X_{fin} has the replacement property (and, moreover, $\mathcal{D}(X_{fin}) = \{X_{fin}\}$ is a singleton), but $C(X_{fin}) = \mathcal{L}(\Sigma) \neq X_{fin}$. (This is, in general, true for any family $X \neq \mathcal{L}(\Sigma)$ containing X_{fin} and closed under union, intersection with regular sets, derivative of languages, and concatenation.)

This yields a negative answer to another problem mentioned in [4].

Up to now we were primarily concerned with the internal structure of the recognizable families. To keep the habit from automata theory we shall investigate some operations on recognizable families.

Theorem 7. The class of all recognizable families (over a fixed alphabet) is closed under intersection but not under union and not under complement.

As for concatenation there are two distinct natural definitions: strong concatenation

$$X_1.X_2 := \{L_1L_2 \mid L_1 \in X_1, L_2 \in X_2\} ,$$

and weak concatenation

$$X_1 \circ X_2 := \{ \bigcup_{v \in L_1} vF(v) \mid L_1 \in X_1 \text{ and } F \text{ is a function } L_1 \to X_2\}.$$

Theorem 8. The class of recognizable families is not closed under strong concatenation.

The weak concatenation is somewhat more appealing from the intuitive point of view. In problem solving it corresponds to the chaining of plans in the following manner: Let X_1 and X_2 be the sets of plans for goals G_1 and G_2, resp. Then to obtain a plan realizing first G_1 and then G_2, one can just take any $L_1 \in X_1$ and concatenate each $v \in L_1$ with some $L_2 \in X_2$. Doing it in all possible ways yields precisely $X_1 \circ X_2$.

Open problem. If X_1 and X_2 are recognizable, is $X_1 \circ X_2$ also recognizable?

In order to obtain one more positive result we observe that

$$\partial_u C(X) = C(\partial_u X)$$

and thus if $\mathcal{D}(X)$ is finite then $\mathcal{D}(C(X))$ is also finite. Hence

Theorem 9. If X_1 and X_2 are recognizable then $C(X_1 \cup X_2)$ is also recognizable.

Open problem. Give an algebraic characterization of recognizable families (an analogy of Kleene's theorem for regular languages).

Besides the results reported here there is a great variety of interesting research topics related to finite branching automata and recognizable families. Let us just mention problems concerning the decidability questions (KARPIŃSKI [5]), nondeterministic and infinitary variants of branching automata, a decomposition theory, algebraic and topological properties of recognizable families and, of course, questions related to the original motivation.

Acknowledgement. I am grateful to participants of the MFCS '74 meeting in Jadwisin, especially to M. Karpiński, A. Pirická, J. Brzozowski, and J. Bečvář for their interest in this work and their stimulating remarks.

REFERENCES

[1] NILSSON,N.J. Problem solving methods in artificial intelligence. McGraw-Hill Book Co., New York 1971.

[2] ŠTĚPÁNKOVÁ,O.; HAVEL,I.M. Some results concerning the situation calculus. Proc.Symp. MFCS'73, High Tatras, 1973, pp.321-326.

[3] FIKES,R.E.; HART,P.E.; NILSSON,N.J. Some new directions in robot problem solving. In: Machine Intelligence 7 (B.Meltzer and D.Michie, ed.), Edinburgh University Press, 1972.

[4] HAVEL,I.M. Finite branching automata. Kybernetika 10(1974), pp. 281-302.

[5] KARPIŃSKI,M. (research in progress).

ON CONFIGURATIONS IN CELLULAR AUTOMATA

Peter Mikulecký
Institute of Applied Mathematics
Faculty of Natural Sciences
Komenský University
816 31 Bratislava, Czechoslovakia

ABSTRACT.

For the class of d-dimensional cellular automata, two general decision questions concerning the existence and recognizability of certain general "qualitative" properties of configurations in these automata are formulated. The problems can be stated as follows:

1. Given a general property of configurations, does a configuration with this property exist in a cellular automaton ?

2. Given a configuration in a cellular automaton, can we recognize certain (given) property of this configuration ?

Some particular questions of both types are investigated and a review of known results and open questions in the area is presented.

PRELIMINARIES.

By a <u>d-dimensional cellular automaton</u> we shall understand a quintuple $A=(V,Z^d,X,q_0,f)$ where V is a finite non-empty set of <u>states</u> (the state alphabet of A), d is a positive integer (the dimension of A), X is a p-tuple ($p \geq 1$ is an integer) of distinct d-tuples of integers, called the neighbourhood index of A, q_0 in V is the quiescent state of A, and f is a mapping of a subset of V^p to V (the local transformation of A). f is supposed to satisfy $f(q_0, q_0, \ldots, q_0) = q_0$. Elements of Z^d are called cells and they are represented simply by d-tuples of integers. Z is the set of all integers.

The definitions we use are due to Yaku[8] and Codd[3]. There are some papers with different definitions of the same subject (compare, e.g., [1], [9], or [5]).

A configuration in A is a recursive function c: $Z^d \longrightarrow V$. The image c(i) of i from Z^d is the state of the cell i. A configuration c is said to be with finite support if the set sup(c) is finite, where $\sup(c) = \{i \in Z^d \mid c(i) \neq q_0\}$ is called the support of the configuration c. We define a mapping N_X: $Z^d \longrightarrow (Z^d)^p$ as follows: if $X = (x_0, x_1, \ldots, x_{p-1})$ and $i \in Z^d$, then $N_X(i) = (i+x_0, i+x_1, \ldots, i+x_{p-1})$ where $i+x_k$ for $0 \leq k \leq p-1$ is the component-wise sum of the d-tuples i and x_k. This mapping is used to specify the neighbourhood of any cell i from Z^d relative to the neighbourhood index X. For a configuration c, let c^p : $(Z^d)^p \longrightarrow V^p$ be defined by

$$c^p(i_0, i_1, \ldots, i_{p-1}) = (c(i_0), c(i_1), \ldots, c(i_{p-1})).$$

Let C_A be the set of all configurations in A. The mapping $S_A : C_A \longrightarrow C_A$ will be defined from the local transformation f as follows : for any configuration c in A, $S_A(c) = c'$ if, and only if $c' = f(c^p(N_X(i)))$ for any i in Z^d. That is, c' is given by the following diagram:

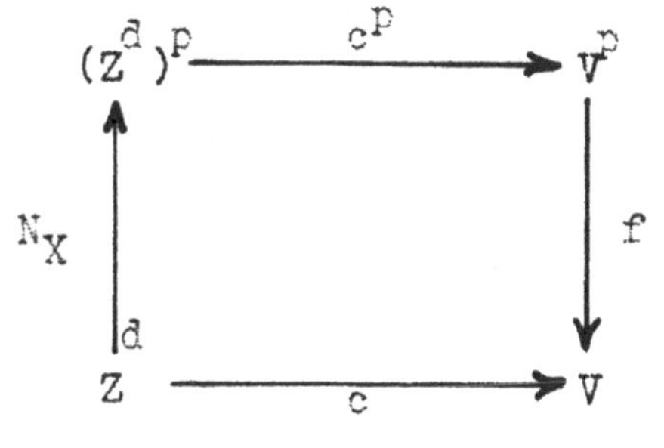

The mapping S_A will be called the parallel map for A. We shall defie the mapping S_A^n recursively as follows:

for integer $n \geq 1$, $S_A(c) = S_A(c)$; $S_A^n(c) = S_A(S_A^{n-1}(c))$,

where c is a configuration in A.

CONFIGURATIONS.

Let us define now some general properties of configurations which we are going to investigate in the sequel. The majority of the definitions is due to Yaku [8]. By C_A we shall denote the set of all configurations in a cellular automaton A, C_A^F will denote the set of all configurations with finite support in A. Clearly, $C_A^F \subseteq C_A$ for any cellular automaton A. S_A will be the parallel map for A.

A configuration $c \in C_A$ is said to be quiescent if the set sup(c) is empty. A non-quiescent configuration $c \in C_A$ is vanishing if there is a positive integer k such that $S_A^k(c)$ is quiescent, and it is suicidal if the previous condition holds for k=1. Clearly, the suicidal configurations form a subset of the set of vanishing configurations in a cellular automaton.

A configuration $c \in C_A$ is Garden-of-Eden if for any $c' \in C_A$, $S_A(c') \neq c$ holds. A configuration $c \in C_A^F$ is finitary Garden-of-Eden if $S_A(c') \neq c$ is fulfiled for any $c' \in C_A^F$.

A configuration $c \in C_A$ is stable if $S_A(c)=c$. Thus, it is easily to see that c is stable iff for any positive integer n, $S_A^n(c)=c$. A configuration $c \in C_A$ is cyclic if there exist an integer $n \geq 2$ such that $S_A^n(c)=c$. A configuration $c \in C_A$ is erasable if there is a configuration $c' \in C_A$ such that $c \neq c'$ and $S_A(c)=S_A(c')$. A configuration $c \in C_A^F$ is finitary erasable if there is a configuration $c' \in C_A^F$ such that $c \neq c'$ and $S_A(c)=S_A(c')$ holds.

Given a configuration $c \in C_A$, any configuration $c' \in C_A$ for which holds $S_A(c')=c$ is said to be the father of c. A configuration $c \in C_A$ has the Grandfather property (abbr. GF-property) if each configuration $c' \in C_A$ which is a father of c, is Garden-of-Eden. A configuration $c \in C_A^F$ has the finitary Grandfather property (abbr. FGF-property) if each configuration $c' \in C_A^F$ which is a father of c, is finitary Garden-of-Eden. Finally, a stable configuration $c \in C_A$ has the Unique Father property (abbr. UF-property) if c is the only father of itself.

RESULTS.

In this chapter we shall present some results on existence and recognizability of certain previously defined general properties of configurations. In general, we are going to investigate here two kinds of decision questions: first, the existence of a configuration which fulfils certain general property in an arbitrary d-dimensional cellular automaton; and second, if a configuration is given, whether or not we can effectively recognize certain general property of this configuration in a cellular automaton. More precisely, these decision questions can be formulated in the following way:

1. Given a general property of configurations, does a configuration with this property exist in a cellular automaton ?

2. Given a configuration in a cellular automaton, can we recognize certain (given) property of this configuration ?

In the sequel, problems of the first type will be referred to as existential, and of the second type as qualitative ones.

Let us formulate now several decision questions for some of previously defined general properties of configurations in cellular automata. In what follows, our considerations on the questions will be first restricted only for elements of C_A^F (i.e., for configurations with finite support only), and then we shall extend our results also for the set C_A of all configurations in a cellular automaton A (of course, as far as it is possible).

Def.1. The Existential Father Problem (abbr. EF-problem) for configurations in cellular automata is the following:

Given a configuration $c \in C_A^F$ ($c \in C_A$) in a cellular automaton A, does there exist a configuration $c' \in C_A^F$ ($c' \in C_A$) such that c' is the father of c ?

Let $\mathfrak{A}$ be the class of all d-dimensional cellular automata with the dimension $d \geq 2$. Then we can state the following results:

Theorem 1. The EF-problem is unsolvable for the class $\mathfrak{A}$ of cellular automata and for configurations from C_A^F (i.e., with finite support), $A \in \mathfrak{A}$.

Corollary. The EF-problem is unsolvable for the class $\mathfrak{A}$ of cellular automata and for configurations from C_A, $A \in \mathfrak{A}$.

Def.2. The Qualitative Father Problem (abbr. QF-problem) for configurations in cellular automata is the following:

Given a configuration $c \in C_A^F$ ($c \in C_A$) in a cellular automaton A, is a configuration $c' \in C_A^F$ ($c' \in C_A$) the father of c ?

This problem is for the set C_A^F of configurations with finite support in any d-dimensional cellular automaton A (for $d \geq 1$) trivially solvable. For the set C_A of all configurations in A it is an open problem which is not trivial because of possible infiniteness of both c and c′.

Let us define next decision questions which are generalizations of some problems posed by J.H.Conway for his well-known game LIFE (see e.g., [4], [7]).

Def.3. The Existential Grandfather Problem (abbr. EGF-problem) for configurations in cellular automata is the following:

Does there exist in a cellular automaton A a configuration $c \in C_A$ with the GF-property ?

The Finitary Existential Grandfather Problem (abbr. Finitary EGF-problem) for configurations in cellular automata is the following:

Does there exist in a cellular automaton A a configuration $c \in C_A^F$ (i.e., with finite support) with the FGF-property ?

The solvability of both EGF-, and Finitary EGF- problems is an open question. But we are able to give results for the following decision questions:

Def.4. The Qualitative Grandfather Problem (abbr. QGF-problem) for configurations in cellular automata is the following:

Given a configuration $c \in C_A$ in a cellular automaton A, has c the GF-property ?

The Finitary Qualitative Grandfather Problem (abbr. Finitary QGF-problem) for configurations in cellular automata is the following:

Given a configuration $c \in C_A^F$ in a cellular automaton A, has c the FGF-property ?

Theorem 2. The QGF-problem is unsolvable for the class $\mathfrak{A}$ of cellular automata and for configurations from C_A, $A \in \mathfrak{A}$.

Theorem 3. The Finitary QGF-problem is unsolvable for the class $\mathfrak{A}$ of cellular automata and for configurations from C_A^F (i.e., with finite support), $A \in \mathfrak{A}$.

Let us define two further problems which we are going to investigate. Both problems are generalizations of certain questions formulated by J.H.Conway for the game LIFE (compare [4], [7]).

Def.5. The Existential Unique Father Problem (abbr. EUF-problem) for configurations in cellular automata is the follwing:

Does there exist in a cellular automaton A a stable configuration $c \in C_A^F$ ($c \in C_A$) with the UF-property ?

The solvability of the EUF-problem is an open question for C_A^F as well as for C_A, where A is a cellular automaton. Nevertheless, we can present some answers for the following decision question:

Def.6. The Qualitative Unique Father Problem (abbr. QUF-problem) for configurations in cellular automata is the following:

Given a stable configuration $c \in C_A^F$ ($c \in C_A$) in a cellular automaton A, has c the UF-property ?

Theorem 4. The QUF-problem is unsolvable for the class $\mathfrak{K}$ of cellular automata and for configurations from C_A^F (i.e.,with finite support), $A \in \mathfrak{K}$.

Corollary. The QUF-problem is unsolvable for the class $\mathfrak{K}$ of cellular automata and for configurations from C_A, $A \in \mathfrak{K}$.

CONCLUSION.

Let us present at this place a review of results for several decision questions on configurations in cellular automata, which can be formulated as particular cases of the general questions defined at the beginning of this paper. All considered questions are arranged in the following table, where they are classified into two classes:

(i) the existential questions,

(ii) the qualitative questions,

both separatelly for the sets C_A^F, and C_A of configurations.

In the table, U means that the question is unsolvable, S means solvability, T denotes trivial cases, and the questionmark means that the answer is unknown (as far as the author knows). Sign "-" means that the question is not defined.

The dimension of cellular automata for which the result holds, is always indicated; $\mathfrak{K}$ denotes the class of all d-dimensional cellular automata with the dimension $d \geq 2$, $\mathfrak{J}$ is the class of all one-dimensional cellular automata, and finally, $\mathfrak{C}$ denotes the class of all cellular automata with an arbitrary dimension.

Question	for C_A^F		for C_A	
	existential	qualitative	existential	qualitative
Garden-of-Eden	-	-	S ($\mathfrak{J}$), ? ($\mathfrak{R}$)	U ($\mathfrak{R}$)
Finitary Garden of-Eden	S ($\mathfrak{J}$), ? ($\mathfrak{R}$)	U ($\mathfrak{R}$)	-	-
erasable conf.	-	-	S ($\mathfrak{J}$), ? ($\mathfrak{R}$)	U ($\mathfrak{R}$)
fin.erasable c.	S ($\mathfrak{J}$), ? ($\mathfrak{R}$)	U ($\mathfrak{R}$)	-	-
vanishing conf.	U ($\mathfrak{R}$)	U ($\mathfrak{R}$)	U ($\mathfrak{R}$)	U ($\mathfrak{R}$)
suicidal conf.	U ($\mathfrak{R}$)	T ($\mathfrak{R}$)	U ($\mathfrak{R}$)	?
stable conf.	?	T ($\mathfrak{C}$)	?	?
cyclic conf.	?	?	?	?
Father Problem	U ($\mathfrak{R}$)	T ($\mathfrak{C}$)	U ($\mathfrak{R}$)	?
GF-problem	-	-	?	U ($\mathfrak{R}$)
Fin.GF-problem	?	U ($\mathfrak{R}$)	-	-
UF-problem	?	U ($\mathfrak{R}$)	?	U ($\mathfrak{R}$)

ACKNOWLEDGMENT. The author is greatly indebted to Dr.I.M.Havel for his selfsacrificing help and for many suggestional remarks.

REFERENCES.

[1] AMOROSO,S.;COOPER,G. Garden-of-Eden theorem for finite configurations. Proc.Amer.Math.Soc. 26 (1970),158-164.

[2] AMOROSO,S.;PATT,Y.N. Decision procedures for surjectivity and injectivity of parallel maps for tessellation structures. Journal Comp. Sys.Sci. 6 (1972),448-464.

[3] CODD,E.F. Cellular Automata. Academic Press,New York,1968.

[4] GARDNER,M. On cellular automata,self-reproduction,the Garden-of-Eden,and the game "life". Sci.Amer. 224 (1971),112-117.

[5] HVORECKY,J. Homogénne štruktúry. Unpublished manuscript (1974).

[6] MINSKI,M.L. Computation:Finite and Infinite Machines. Prentice-Hall, 1967.

[7] WAINWRIGHT,R.T. Lifeline. A private publication on the game "life", New York, 1972.

[8] YAKU,T. The constructibility of a configuration in a cellular automaton. Journal Comp.Sys.Sci. 7 (1973),481-496.

[9] YAMADA,H.;AMOROSO,S. Tessellation automata. Inf.Control 14 (1969), 299-317.

[10] YAMADA,H.;AMOROSO,S. A completeness problem for pattern generation in tessellation automata.Journal Comp.Sys.Sci. 4 (1970),137-176.

FINITE AUTOMATA ACCEPTATION OF INFINITE SEQUENCES

K. Wagner, L. Staiger
Sektion Mathematik der Friedrich-Schiller-Universität
69 Jena - DDR

All known papers about finite automata acceptation of infinite sequences are concerned with the question which sets of infinite sequences are in principle acceptable by finite automata. There are given notions of acceptation by which all sets of sequences of this class can be accepted. For example McNAUGHTON shows in [2] that the finite nondeterministic automata using BÜCHIs notion of acceptation ([1]) accept the same class of sets of infinite sequences as the finite deterministic automata using MÜLLERs notion of acceptation ([3]). Moreover this class correspond to the class of regular sets of infinite sequences introduced by McNAUGHTON in [2] . RABIN shows in [4] that no larger classes can be accepted using other notions of acceptation. Up to now it was an open problem which subclasses of the class of regular sets of infinite sequences can be accepted by finite deterministic or nondeterministic automata using suitable notions of acceptation. Furthermore there is also a topologic question. TRACHTENBROT shows in [7] that every regular set of infinite sequences is a $F_{\sigma\delta}$ -set and a $G_{\delta\sigma}$ -set with respect to the following metric

$$\varrho(\xi, \xi') =_{df} \begin{cases} \dfrac{1}{\inf\{n, \xi(n) \neq \xi'(n)\}}, & \text{if } \xi \neq \xi' \\ 0, \text{ if } \xi = \xi' \end{cases}$$

where $\xi(n)$ is the n-th letter of the sequence ξ . Is there another way to characterize the lower topologic types? This question can be answered affirmative.

For a finite initial deterministic (nondeterministic) MEDWEDJEW-automaton $\mathfrak{A}$ let $\Phi_{\mathfrak{A}}(\xi)$ be the sequence of states (the set of possible sequences of states) of $\mathfrak{A}$ corresponding to the input of the sequence ξ .

For a infinite sequence ξ we define

$$E(\xi) =_{df} \{x;\ \text{card}\ \{n,\ \xi(n) = x\} > 0\}$$

$$U(\xi) =_{df} \{x;\ \text{card}\ \{n,\ \xi(n) = x\} = \aleph_0\}\ .$$

Let $\mathfrak{A}$ be a finite deterministic MEDWEDJEW-automaton, $\mathfrak{Z}$ a set of subsets of the set of states of $\mathfrak{A}$, $\alpha \in \{E,U\}$ and $\sigma \in \{=,\subseteq,\sqcap\}$ (where $\sqcap$ is a binary relation with $B \sqcap B' \Leftrightarrow B \cap B' \neq \emptyset$). Then we define the following notion of acceptation T^{α}_{σ}

$$T^{\alpha}_{\sigma}\ (\mathfrak{A},\mathfrak{Z}) =_{df} \{\xi;\ \exists Z'(Z' \in \mathfrak{Z} \wedge \alpha(\Phi_{\mathfrak{A}}(\xi))\ \sigma\ Z')\}\ .$$

In the case of a nondeterministic MEDWEDJEW-automaton we define

$$T^{\alpha}_{\sigma}\ (\mathfrak{A},\mathfrak{Z}) =_{df} \{\xi;\ \exists Z' \exists \eta\ (Z' \in \mathfrak{Z} \wedge \eta \in \Phi_{\mathfrak{A}}(\xi) \wedge \alpha(\eta)\ \sigma\ Z')\ .$$

For example, if $\mathfrak{A}$ is a deterministic MEDWEDJEW-automaton we have MÜLLERs notion of acceptation with

$$T^{u}_{=}\ (\mathfrak{A},\mathfrak{Z}) =_{df} \{\xi,\ \exists Z'(Z' \in \mathfrak{Z} \wedge U(\Phi_{\mathfrak{A}}(\xi)) = Z')\}$$

$$= \{\xi;\ U(\Phi_{\mathfrak{A}}(\xi)) \in \mathfrak{Z}\}\ .$$

If $\mathfrak{A}$ is a nondeterministic MEDWEDJEW-automaton, we have BÜCHIs notion of acceptation with

$$T^{u}_{\sqcap}\ (\mathfrak{A},\mathfrak{Z}) = \{\ \xi;\ \exists Z' \exists \eta\ (Z' \in \mathfrak{Z}\ \wedge\ \eta \in \Phi_{\mathfrak{A}}(\xi) \wedge U(\eta) \cap Z' \neq \emptyset\ )\}$$

$$= \{\ \xi\ ;\ \exists \eta\ \ (\eta \in \Phi_{\mathfrak{A}}(\xi) \wedge U(\eta) \cap \bigcup \mathfrak{Z} \neq \emptyset)\}$$

Now we can represent a part of our results in the following table which we have to understand in this way: if we read G_δ in the line D and in the column $T^{u}_{\sqcap}$ then F is a regular G_δ -set iff there exist a finite deterministic MEDWEDJEW-automaton $\mathfrak{A}$ and a system of sets $\mathfrak{Z}$ with $F = T^{u}_{\sqcap}\ (\mathfrak{A},\mathfrak{Z})$. The framed results are due to McNAUGHTON, RABIN and TRACHTENBROT.

	$T^{E}_{\subseteq}$	$T^{E}_{\sqcap}$	$T^{E}_{=}$	$T^{u}_{\subseteq}$	$T^{u}_{\sqcap}$	$T^{u}_{=}$
D	closed	open	$F_\sigma \cap G_\delta$	F_σ	G_δ	$F_{\sigma\delta} \cap G_{\delta\sigma}$
ND	closed	open	F_σ	F_σ	$F_{\sigma\delta} \cap G_{\delta\sigma}$	$F_{\sigma\delta} \cap G_{\delta\sigma}$

Furthermore we can give a characterization without using the notion of automaton of these topological types of sets of infinite sequences.

Let X be a finite alphabet. We denote by X^* the set of all finite sequences (words) over X and by X^ω the set of all infinite sequences over X.

For $p \in X^*$, $\xi \in X^\omega$, $W \subseteq X^*$ and $F \subseteq X^\omega$ we define

$$p \sqsubset \xi \;=_{df}\; \exists \eta (\eta \in X^{\omega} \wedge \xi = p \cdot \eta),$$
$$A(\xi) =_{df} \{p ; p \sqsubset \xi\} \subseteq X^{*},$$
$$lsW =_{df} \{\xi ; A(\xi) \subseteq W\} \subseteq X^{\omega},$$
$$W . W =_{df} \{p.q ; p,q \in W\},$$
$$W^{\omega} =_{df} W.W.W \ldots \subseteq X^{\omega}$$

and
$$W . F =_{df} \{p \cdot \xi ; p \in W \wedge \xi \in F\} \subseteq X^{\omega} .$$

We say that $W \subseteq X^{*}$ is total unorderd with respect to the initial word relation (W t.u.i.) iff there don't exist words $p,q \in W$ and $r \in X^{*}$ with $r \neq e$ (e denotes the empty word) and $p.r = q$.

Again we represent our results in a table which we explain by the following example: F is a G_{δ} -set iff there exist a natural number n, t.u.i. regular sets $W_1,\ldots,W_n$, $V_1,\ldots,V_n$ with $F = \bigcup_{i=1}^{n} W_i \cdot V_i^{\omega}$.

topologic type	representation	conditions
closed	$F = lsW$	W regular
open	$F = W . X^{\omega}$	W regular
$F_{\sigma} \wedge G_{\delta}$	$F = \bigcup_{i=1}^{n} W_i \cdot lsV_i$	W_i t.u.i., regular V_i regular
F_{σ}	$F = \bigcup_{i=1}^{n} W_i \cdot lsV_i$	W_i, V_i regular
G_{δ}	$F = \bigcup_{i=1}^{n} W_i \cdot V_i^{\omega}$	W_i, V_i t.u.i., regular
$F_{\sigma\delta} \wedge G_{\delta\sigma}$	$F = \bigcup_{i=1}^{n} W_i \cdot V_i^{\omega}$	W_i, V_i regular

The last result of this table is due to McNAUGHTON and TRACHTENBROT.

R E F E R E N C E S

[1] BÜCHI, J. R. On a decision method in restricted second order arithmetic. Proc. Intern. Congr. Logic, Method. and Philos. Sci. 1960, Stanford Univ. Press, Stanford, Calif., 1 - 11

[2] McNAUGHTON, R. Testing and generating infinite sequences by a finite automaton. Inf. and Control. 9 (1966), 521 - 530

[3] MÜLLER, D. E. Infinite sequences and finite machines. AIEE Proc. Fourth Annual Symp. Switching Circuit Theory and Logical Design, 1963, 3 - 16

[4] RABIN, M. O. Decidability of second-order theories and automata of infinite trees. Trans. Am. Math. Soc. 141 (1969), 1 - 35

[5] STAIGER, L.; WAGNER, K. Automatentheoretische und automatenfreie Charakterisierungen der topologischen Klassen regulärer Folgenmengen. EIK, to appear

[6] STAIGER, L. Analog teoremy Ginsburga- Rosa dlja posledovatjelnostnych operatorov i reguljarnych mnoschestv posledovatjelnostej. Sbornik trudov Vytsch. Zentr. Ak. Nauk SSSR, to appear

[7] TRACHTENBROT, B. A.; BARSDIN, J. M. Konjetschnyje avtomaty, isdvo. Nauka, Moskva 1970

R-FUZZY AUTOMATA WITH A TIME-VARIANT STRUCTURE

W. Wechler
Technische Universität Dresden
Sektion Mathematik
8027 Dresden, German Democratic Republic

The purpose of this note is to establish a KLEENE-MYHILL characterization of the behaviour of R-fuzzy automata with a time-variant structure. By generalizing the formalism of FLIESS-SCHÜTZENBERGER (cf. [3]) with the aid of so-called input categories the same problem was solved in [6].

State transitions of a R-fuzzy automaton over a finite alphabet X, which was introduced in [9], are described by a mapping of X into the set $(R)_n$ of all nxn matrices with coefficients from a semiring R, where n is the number of states. In [9] it is shown that deterministic, non-deterministic, stochastic, fuzzy, and linear space automata are included in this general model. For instance, if we use the BOOLEAN semiring $R_B = \{0,1\}$ with 1+1=1, then the appropriate R-fuzzy automaton is a deterministic or non-deterministic automaton.

From this point of view the transition function of a (deterministic or non-deterministic) time-variant automaton (cf. [1,5]) can be regarded as a mapping of the CARTESIAN product $T \times X$ into $(R_B)_n$ in which the time T is the set of natural numbers. Substituting an arbitrary semiring for R_B leads to the following

DEFINITION. A R-fuzzy automaton A over X with a time-variant structure is a 4-tuple $A = (S,d,\sigma_0,\sigma_1)$ with the following meanings: $S = \{s_1,s_2,\dots,s_n\}$ is the finite set of states, d is a mapping of $T \times X$ into $(R)_n$ and σ_0,σ_1 are n-dimensional row and column vectors with coefficients from R respectively.

The behaviour of usual time-variant automata are represented by metaregular events which are special mappings of the free semigroup X* of all words over X including the empty word e into R_B. Since the class of all metaregular events is not closed under product and star-operation (cf. [8]) a KLEENE-MYHILL theorem does not exist too. In order to obtain such a theorem also in this case, two new operations - splice product and splice star - for families of events are defined by BAER and SPANIER [2]. A family of events is a mapping of $T \times X^*$ into R_B.

For describing behaviour of R-fuzzy automata with a time-variant structure the transition function d must be extended to a mapping $\underline{d}$: $T \times X^* \rightarrow (R)_n$. In analogy to [1,5] the extension $\underline{d}$ is defined recursively by

$$\underline{d}(t,e) = 1 \quad \text{(unit matrix)},$$

$$\underline{d}(t,wx) = \underline{d}(t,w)\cdot d(t+|w|,x)$$

for all $t \in T$, $w \in X^*$, $x \in X$. $|w|$ denotes the length of w.

Now, to every R-fuzzy automaton A with a time-variant structure can be associated a mapping f_A: $T \times X^* \rightarrow R$ by $f_A(t,w) = \sigma_0 \cdot \underline{d}(t,w) \cdot \sigma_1$ for all $t \in T$ and $w \in X^*$. In general, a mapping f: $T \times X^* \rightarrow R$ is called a family of R-fuzzy events (cf. [9]) or, shortly, a family.

DEFINITION. A family f: $T \times X^* \rightarrow R$ is said to be acceptable if a R-fuzzy automaton A over X with a time-variant structure exists such that the equation $f = f_A$ holds.

In the following, acceptable families or, in other words, the behaviour of R-fuzzy automata with a time-variant structure shall be characterized. For this purpose suitable operations in the set F(R) of all families must be found.

DEFINITION. Let $f,f' \in F(R)$ and $r = (r_t)_{t \in T}$ be a series with $r_t \in R$ for all $t \in T$.

(1) The scalar product rf is defined by

$$(rf)(t,w) = r_t \cdot f(t,w) \quad \text{for all } t \in T,\ w \in X^*.$$

(2) The sum f + f' is defined by

$$(f + f')(t,w) = f(t,w) + f'(t,w) \quad \text{for all } t \in T,\ w \in X^*.$$

(3) The product f·f' is defined by

$$(f \cdot f')(t,w) = \sum_{\substack{w_1,w_2 \in X^* \\ w_1 w_2 = w}} f(t,w_1) \cdot f'(t+|w_1|,w_2) \quad \text{for all } t \in T, w \in X^*.$$

(4) If $f(t,e) = 0$ for any $t \in T$ then the iteration f^* is defined by $f^*(t,e) = 1$ for all $t \in T$ and

$$f^*(t,w) = \sum_{k=1}^{|w|} \sum_{\substack{w_1, w_2, \ldots, w_k \in X^* \\ w_1 w_2 \ldots w_k = w}} f(t,w_1).f(t+|w_1|,w_2)\ldots f(t+|w_{k-1}|,w_k)$$

for all $t \in T$ and $w \in X^*$ with $w \neq e$.

Let $\mathrm{supp}\, f = \{w \in X^* | f(t,w) \neq 0$ for some $t \in T\}$ be the support of a family f, then the smallest set of families containing all families with a finite support which is closed under the four operations are denoted by $F(R)_{mr}$.

DEFINITION. The elements of $F(R)_{mr}$ are called metaregular families of R-fuzzy events.

THEOREM. Any acceptable family of R-fuzzy events is metaregular.

The proof given in [7] can be deduced in analogy to [2] by means of a recursive rule. In order to reverse the Theorem we have to define derivatives of families.

DEFINITION. Let f be a family and $w \in X^*$. The derivative $D_w f$ of f with respect to w is defined by

$$(D_w f)(t,w') = \begin{cases} f(t-|w|,ww') & \text{if } t \geq |w| \\ 0 & \text{if } t < |w| \end{cases} \quad \text{for any } w \in X^*.$$

With help of the properties of derivatives (cf. [7]) the following assertion can be proved.

LEMMA. Let f be a metaregular family. Then there is a finite number of metaregular families $f_1=f, f_2, \ldots, f_n$ such that for all $w \in X^*$

$$D_w f_i = \sum_{j=1}^{n} r_{ij}(w) f_j \quad \text{for } i = 1,2,\ldots,n$$

where $r_{ij}(w)$ are series' over R for $i,j = 1,2,\ldots,n$.

From this, similarly to the usual case (cf. [4]), the following theorem can be derived.

THEOREM. Every metaregular family of R-fuzzy events is acceptable.

The characterization of the behaviour of R-fuzzy automata with a time-variant structure is now an immediate consequence of both Theorems.

REFERENCES

[1] AGASANDYAN, G.A. Automata with a variable structure. Dokl. Akad. Nauk SSSR 174(1967), 529-530.

[2] BAER, R.M., SPANIER, E.H. Referenced automata and metaregular families. J. Comput. System Sci. 3(1969), 423-446.

[3] FLIESS, M. Applications of formal series with non-commutative variables. Lecture Notes in Computer Science, this vol.

[4] INAGAKI, Y., SUGINO, K., FUKUMURA, T. Algebraic properties of quasi-regular expressions and linear space automata. Systems-Computers-Controls 1(1970), 17-26.

[5] SALOMAA, A. On finite automata with a time-variant structure. Information and Control 13(1968), 85-98.

[6] WECHLER, W. Zur Verallgemeinerung des Theorems von KLEENE-SCHÜTZENBERGER auf zeitvariable Automaten. Will appear in Elektron. Informationsverarbeit. Kybernetik.

[7] WECHLER, W. Analyse und Synthes zeitvariabler R-fuzzy Automaten. ZKI Informationen (Akad. d. Wiss. der DDR) 1(1974), Berlin 1974.

[8] WECHLER, W., AGASANDYAN, G.A. Automata with a variable structure and metaregular languages. Izv. Akad. Nauk SSSR Tehn. Kibernet. No. 1(1974), 146-148.

[9] WECHLER, W., DIMITROV, V. R-fuzzy automata. Proc. IFIP Congress 74. North-Holland Publishing Co., Amsterdam-London 1974.

FUNCTIONS COMPUTABLE IN THE LIMIT BY PROBABILISTIC MACHINES

R.V.Freivald
Computing Center
of Latvian State University
Riga, U.S.S.R.

The following question was considered in [1] : is there anything that can be done by a machine with an access to random inputs that cannot be done by deterministic machines. It was shown that much depend on the probabilities of the elementary activities of the random element. If these probabilities are not real constructive numbers (definition see [2]), then probabilistic machines can easily do something more. Thereby we follow many other authors and restrict all probabilistic machines below to differ from corresponding deterministic ones only in having the simplest random number generator which produces output values 0 or 1 equiprobably by the scheme of Bernoullian trials, i.e. outputs generated at different moments are independent.

The probabilistic space is introduced in the same way as in [1] . All the sets in the definitions and proofs below turn out to be measurable.

Several definitions of probabilistic enumerability were considered in [1]. It was shown that only recursively enumerable sets (i.e. sets enumerable by deterministic machines) can be enumerated with probability exceeding a real constructive number. These results implied an illusion that everything that can be done by a probabilistic machine with a high constructive probability can also be done by an appropriate deterministic machine.

It was shown in [4] that the reality is slightly different. There exists an immune set $A \in \Pi_1$ ([3] contains definitions of the immunity and classes of Kleene-Mostowski hierarchy) such that for every $\varepsilon > 0$ there exists a probabilistic machine enumerating some set at every realization of the computation process, and it turns out with probability exceeding $1-\varepsilon$ that the enumerated set is an infinite subset of A . Some other examples of problems solvable by probabilistic machines but unsolvable by deterministic ones were found later (see [5]). All these examples have a common feature: the result of the computation is a set of integers with a certain property, and different sets can be obtained at different realizations of the computation process.

We investigate two generalizations of the notion of the recursiveness below. We will point out that one of the generalizations have certain peculiarities making the analogues of the main results in [1] to fail. Concrete functions are proved to be weak computable in the limit (see Definition 3 below) by probabilistic machines but not by deterministic ones.

Intuitive notion of computation in the limit is clear enough. Process of programming can be considered as a typical example. Programmer usually cannot write a complicated program without errors. Thereby debugging is needed. Errors are stepwise eliminated and after some time the program works correctly for any input data. But one can never be absolutely sure that all the errors are already eliminated.

This peculiarity of the programming process is taken for basis to the intuitive notion of computation of a function in the limit. Instead of producing the final result the algorithm for computation in the limit a hypothetical result on a special " tableau ", where any natural number can be displayed. This allows the algorithm to propose a value κ_1 as the result, to remove it after some time, to propose another value κ_2 , etc.

Let the algorithm start its work at the value x of the argument. If for some n a value κ_n appears on the " tableau " at some moment and it is never removed or changed, then we call κ_n the value of function $f(x)$ computed in the limit; otherwise $f(x)$ is not defined.

This intuitive notion can be made precise. To do it we must use as the algorithm for computation in the limit a two-tape Turing machine, one tape being ordinary one (working tape) and the other one being output tape for printing the hypotheses $\kappa_1, \kappa_2, \dots$

The value of the argument is written on the working tape and the output tape is empty at the beginning of the work. The head on the output tape is writing-only and cannot move left. During the work this head prints a sequence of natural numbers $\kappa_1, \kappa_2, \dots$ (say, in binary notion) and separating symbols between them. We call the record of a number κ_i completed if at least one separating symbol is printed after κ_i and the head has moved right from it. An arbitrary number of separating symbols is allowed between neighbouring hypotheses. Hence every filling of the output tape or its fragment defines an empty, finite or infinite sequence of natural numbers records of which are completed. The numbers not followed by separating symbols are not taken into consideration.

We call a number b the limit of a sequence $\kappa_1, \kappa_2, \dots$ if: 1) the sequence $\kappa_1, \kappa_2, \dots$ is infinite, and 2) only finite number of elements of the sequence differ from b.

It can easily be seen that the following two definitions are equivalent.

DEFINITION 1. We call a function $\varphi(x)$ computable in the limit if there exists a machine $\mathfrak{M}$ such that when $\mathfrak{M}$ works at arbitrary x, it prints a finite output sequence $\kappa_1, \kappa_2, \ldots$ with last element y iff $\varphi(x) = y$.

DEFINITION 2. We call a function $\varphi(x)$ computable in the limit if there exists a machine $\mathfrak{M}$ such that when $\mathfrak{M}$ works at arbitrary x, 1) an infinite output sequence $\kappa_1, \kappa_2, \ldots$ is obtained, and 2) the limit of the sequence equals y iff $\varphi(x) = y$.

A function is computable in the limit iff its graph is in the class Σ_2 of Kleene-Mostowski hierarchy.

DEFINITION 3. We call a function $\varphi(x)$ weak computable in the limit if there exists a machine $\mathfrak{M}$ such that when $\mathfrak{M}$ works at arbitrary x, it prints an infinite output sequence with limit y iff $\varphi(x) = y$.

A function φ is weak computable in the limit iff both: 1) the domain of φ can be represented as difference of two sets from Σ_2, 2) φ can be extended to a partial function computable in the limit, i.e. to a function, the graph of which is in Σ_2.

(The class of all sets representable as difference of two sets from Σ_2 includes $\Sigma_2 \cup \Pi_2$ and is contained in $\Sigma_3 \cap \Pi_3$).

Probabilistic machine for computation in the limit (abbreviation: PMCL) differs from the machine described above only in having the simplest Bernoullian random number generator.

DEFINITION 4. We call a function $\varphi(x)$ computable in the limit with probability exceeding p if there exists a PMCL $\mathfrak{M}$ such that when $\mathfrak{M}$ works at arbitrary x : 1) $\mathfrak{M}$ prints an infinite output sequence at any realization of the computation process, 2) if $\varphi(x)$ is defined, then the probability of printing an output sequence with limit $\varphi(x)$ exceeds p , 3) for every y not equal to $\varphi(x)$ the probability of printing an output sequence with limit y does not exceed p.

DEFINITION 5. We call a function $\varphi(x)$ weak computable in the limit with probability exceeding p if there exists a PMCL $\mathfrak{M}$ such that when $\mathfrak{M}$ works at arbitrary x : 1) if $\varphi(x)$ is defined, then the probability of printing an infinite output sequence with limit $\varphi(x)$

exceeds p , 2) for every y not equal to $\varphi(x)$ the probability of printing an infinite output sequence with limit y does not exceed p.

DEFINITION 6. We call a set A recursive in the limit (weak recursive in the limit) with probability exceeding p if the characteristic function of the set A is computable in the limit (weak computable in the limit) with probability exceeding p.

DEFINITION 7. We call a set A enumerable in the limit (weak enumerable in the limit) with probability exceeding p if the partial characteristic function of the set A is computable in the limit (weak computable in the limit) with probability exceeding p.

THEOREM 1. If p is a real constructive number ($0 \leq p < 1$), then a function φ is computable in the limit with probability exceeding p iff φ is computable in the limit by deterministic machines.

PROOF. SUFFICIENCY. Immediate.
NECESSITY. Let PMCL $\mathfrak{M}$ compute the function φ in the limit with probability exceeding p . The set α^b of all realizations of the computation process of $\mathfrak{M}$ at x such that the limit of the output sequence is b , can be represented as union $\bigcup_{i=1}^{\infty} \alpha_i^b$, where the set α_i^b consists of all realizations of the computation process of $\mathfrak{M}$ at x such that all the elements of the output sequence printed not earlier than at the i -th tact is equal to b.

p is a real constructive number. Hence exists an effective process $\mathfrak{A}$ with arguments: program of the machine $\mathfrak{M}$, natural numbers x, b, i and rational q , that terminates iff the probabilistic measure of α_i^b for $\mathfrak{M}$ at x is smaller than $p+q$.

$\alpha_1^b \subseteq \alpha_2^b \subseteq \alpha_3^b \subseteq \ldots$ It follows that the probabilistic measure of α^b exceeds p iff there exists α_i^b with probabilistic measure exceeding p . Hence φ can be computed in the limit by the following deterministic machine $\mathfrak{M}'$.

Let $\tau_1, \tau_2, \tau_3, \ldots$ be an arbitrary monotone recursive sequence of positive rational numbers with the limit 0. The machine $\mathfrak{M}'$ goes through triples of natural numbers (b,i,j) in order of their Cantor's numbers. When a triple (b,i,j) is considered, $\mathfrak{M}'$ starts the process $\mathfrak{A}$ at $\mathfrak{M}, x, b, i, \tau_j$ The machine $\mathfrak{M}'$ prints an output value b at every moment until the process $\mathfrak{A}$ teminates. When $\mathfrak{A}$ terminates $\mathfrak{M}'$ prints a value $b+1$ and goes to the next triple (b', i', j') Hence the output sequence of $\mathfrak{M}'$ limits in b iff there exist such i and j that the probabilistic measure of α_i^b is at least $p+\tau_j > p$.

COROLLARY 1. If p is a real constructive number ($0 \leq p < 1$), then a set A is enumerable in the limit with probability exceeding p iff $A \in \Sigma_2$.

COROLLARY 2. If p is a real constructive number ($0 \leq p < 1$), then a set A is recursive in the limit with probability exceeding p iff $A \in \Sigma_2 \cap \Pi_2$.

STATEMENT 1. If p is a real constructive number ($0 \leq p < 1$), then a set A is weak enumerable in the limit with probability exceeding p iff $A \in \Sigma_3$.

PROOF. SUFFICIENCY. We will first regard the case $p=0$. Let R be a general recursive predicate such that $x \in A \Leftrightarrow \exists i \forall j \exists \kappa R(x,i,j,\kappa)$. We will construct a PMCL $\mathfrak{M}$ which weak enumerates the set A in the limit. At the beginning $\mathfrak{M}$ disregards x and counts how many times in succession 0 is the output value of the Bernoullian generator. The result of the count is 0 with probability 2^{-1}, 1 with probability $2^{-2}, \ldots, i$ with probability $2^{-i-1}, \ldots$ Let the result be i_0 . After that $\mathfrak{M}$ computes $R(x,i_0,0,0)$, $R(x,i_0,0,1)$, $R(x,i_0,1,2), \ldots$ until the first value " true " appears. Then $\mathfrak{M}$ prints an output value 1 and begins successive computing of $R(x,i_0,1,0)$, $R(x,i_0,1,1)$, $R(x,i_0,1,2), \ldots$ When among these values " true " is found $\mathfrak{M}$ prints another value 1 and goes to compute $R(x,i_0,2,0)$, $R(x,i_0,2,1)$, $R(x,i_0,2,2), \ldots$, etc. If $\exists i \forall j \exists \kappa R(x,i,j,\kappa)$ and i_1 is the smallest value such that $\forall j \exists \kappa R(x,i_1,j,\kappa)$, then $\mathfrak{M}$ prints an infinite sequence of ones with the probability not smaller than 2^{-i_1-1}. If $\neg \exists i \forall j \exists \kappa\, R(x,i,j,\kappa)$ then there are no realizations of the computation process by $\mathfrak{M}$ at x with an infinite output sequence.

To complete the proof we now regard the case $p>0$. p is a real constructive number. It implies the existence of a process $\mathcal{L}$ perfomable by an ordinary probabilistic Turing machine such that $\mathcal{L}$ terminates with probability p. The required PMCL $\mathfrak{M}$ executes two processes in parallel: the process $\mathcal{L}$ and the process described above (for the case $p=0$). If the process $\mathcal{L}$ terminates, then execution of the process described for the case $p=0$ is stopped too and $\mathfrak{M}$ starts printing numbers 1 every moment. Hence the probability of printing an infinite sequence of ones exceeds p iff $x \in A$. $\mathfrak{M}$ prints no other numbers but 1 .

NECESSITY. For simplicity's sake we assume that the output of the Bernoullian generator is read once in every tact. Some of these readings are fictitious and the realizations of the computation process are the same in fact. Nevertheless, when counting realizations we will regard them as different. Hence 2^t realizations of the first t tacts of the work are possible.

Our proof is based on the following important fact. A countable union of zero probability events is a zero probability event. Hence the criterium of weak computability in the limit with probability exceeding p can be described as follows: there exist a rational positive q and a natural n such that for every natural r there exists a natural t such that among all 2^t realizations of the first t tacts of work of the machine $\mathfrak{M}$ at x there are at least $(p+q)\cdot 2^t$ realizations such that at least r output values are printed during the first t tacts and all of them but the first n values are equal to 1. p is a real constructive number, hence the previous sentence describes a formula with recursive matrix and $\exists\forall\exists$ -type prefix.

COROLLARY. There exists a set A such that for every real constructive p ($0 \leq p < 1$) A is weak computable in the limit with probability exceeding p , but A is not weak computable in the limit by deterministic machines.

STATEMENT 2. If p is a real constructive number and a partial function φ is weak computable in the limit with probability exceeding p , then the graph of φ is in Σ_3 .

PROOF. Let a PMCL $\mathfrak{M}$ weak compute the function φ in the limit with probability exceeding p. We can easily transform $\mathfrak{M}$ into a machine weak computing the graph of φ in the limit with probability exceeding p. Hence the graph of φ is in Σ_3 , by Statement 1.

THEOREM 2. A function φ is weak computable in the limit with probability exceeding 0 iff its graph is in Σ_3.

PROOF. NECESSITY. By Statement 2.
SUFFICIENCY. It follows from Statement 1 that the graph of the function φ can be weak enumerated in the limit with probability exceeding 0 by a PMCL $\mathfrak{M}$, every output value of which is equal to 1. The machine $\mathfrak{M}$ can be transfofmed into a PMCL $\mathfrak{M}'$ weak computing the function φ in the limit with probability exceeding 0 as follows. At the beginning $\mathfrak{M}'$ counts how many times in succession 0 is the output value of the Bernoullian generator. Let the result be i . Then $\mathfrak{M}'$ simulates the

work of $\mathfrak{M}$ at pair $<x,i>$. Whenever $\mathfrak{M}$ must print number 1, $\mathfrak{M}'$ interrupts the simulation, prints i instead of 1 and then continues the simulation.

STATEMENT 3. If the range of a function φ consists of no more than κ elements, p is a real constructive number, $0 \leq p < \frac{1}{\kappa}$ and the graph of φ is in Σ_3, then φ is weak computable in the limit with probability exceeding p.

Statement 3 is a sufficient condition for the weak computability by PMCL's. We will improve this condition to be the criterium (see Theorem 3 below). We need a lemma now for Theorem 3. Let D_u denote a finite set with canonical index u (canonical index enables one to see an explicit listing of all the elements of the set as well as the number of elements of the set; cf. [3], § 5.6).

LEMMA. There exists a general recursive function $g(\kappa,n,x,i,j)$ such that: 1) if $\kappa=0$ or $\kappa=1$, then $g(\kappa,n,x,i,j)=0$, 2) for every $\kappa \geq 2, n, x, i, j$ $D_{g(\kappa,n,x,i,j)}$ contains no more than $\kappa-1$ elements, 3) for every $\kappa \geq 2, n, x, i, j$ $D_{g(\kappa,n,x,i,j+1)} \subseteq D_{g(\kappa,n,x,i,j)}$ and $D_{g(\kappa,n,x,i,j+1)} \subseteq D_{g(\kappa,n,x,i+1,j)}$ 4) for every $\kappa \geq 2, n, x$ if the PMCL with number n at x weak computes a result y in the limit with probability exceeding p, and $\frac{1}{\kappa} \leq p < 1$, then $y \in \lim_i \lim_j D_{g(\kappa,n,x,i,j)}$.

PROOF. We consider all the realizations of the computation process of the PMCL with number n at x during the first $i+j$ tacts to define $g(\kappa,n,x,i,j)$ There are 2^{i+j} realizations considered, by the agreement on counting the realizations in the proof of Statement 1. We divide them into classes $K_{-1}, K_0, K_1, K_2, \ldots$ We place a realization into the class K_{-1} if record of no output value is completed up to the i-th tact. We place a realization into the class $K_\tau (\tau \geq 0)$ if the last output value completed up to the i-th tact equals τ.

We are not interested in K_{-1}. Let move off from any other class K_τ all the realizations at which during the $(i+1)$-th, $(i+2)$-th, ..., $(i+j)$-th tacts an output value differring from τ was completed. The remaining realizations form the class K'_τ.

We are now able to define $g(\kappa,n,x,i,j)$. If $\kappa=0$ or $\kappa=1$, then $g(\kappa,n,x,i,j)=0$. If $\kappa \geq 2$, then $g(\kappa,n,x,i,j)$ is the canonical index of the finite set of all τ such that K'_τ contains more than $\frac{1}{\kappa} \cdot 2^{i+j}$ realizations. Assertions 1),2),3) of Lemma follow immediately. Assertions 1),2),3) guaranty the existence of the limit $\lim_j D_{g(\kappa,n,x,i,j)}$ for any

κ, n, x, i, inclusion $\lim_j D_{g(\kappa,n,x,i,j)} \subseteq \lim_j D_{g(\kappa,n,x,i+1,j)}$ for any κ,n,x,i and the existence of the limit $\lim_i \lim_j D_{g(\kappa,n,x,i,j)}$ for any κ,n,x. We will now prove the assertion 4). Let the PMCL with number n at x weak compute a result y in the limit with probability exceeding $p \geq \frac{1}{\kappa}$. If the probabilistic measure of the set α of all the realizations at which an infinite output sequence with limit y is printed, exceeds $\frac{1}{\kappa}$, then there exists i_0 such that the probabilistic measure of the set α_{i_0} of all the realizations at which the last output value completed up to the i_0-th tact is y, and no other output values are completed after the i_0-th tact, exceeds $\frac{1}{\kappa}$. It follows that such y is contained in $D_{g(\kappa,n,x,i,j)}$ for every $i \geq i_0$ and every j Hence $y \in \lim_i \lim_j D_{g(\kappa,n,x,i,j)}$.

THEOREM 3. Let p be a real constructive number and $\kappa \geq 1$ be a natural number such that $\frac{1}{\kappa+1} \leq p < \frac{1}{\kappa}$. A function φ is weak computable in the limit with probability exceeding p iff the graph of φ is in Σ_3 and there exists a general recursive function $h(x,t)$ such that: 1) for every x,t $D_{h(x,t)}$ contains not more than κ elements, 2) for every x if $\varphi(x)$ is defined, then there exists t_0 such that for every $t > t_0$ $\varphi(x) \in D_{h(x,t)}$.

PROOF. NECESSITY. It follows from Statement 2 that the graph of φ is in Σ_3 Let the function φ be weak computed in the limit with probability exceeding p by the PMCL with number n. Let g denote the function defined in Lemma. We take $g(\kappa+1,n,x,t,0)$ for $h(x,t)$ The limit $\lim_i \lim_j D_{g(\kappa+1,n,x,i,j)}$ exists for every κ,n,x. Hence exist i_0, j_0 such that for every $j > j_0$ $D_{g(\kappa+1,n,x,i_0,j_0)} = \lim_i \lim_j D_{g(\kappa+1,n,i,j)}$. Assertion 3) of Lemma shows that i_0+j_0 can be taken for t_0 in assertion 2) of Theorem 3.
SUFFICIENCY. The function h will be used to define κ auxiliary functions $h_1, h_2, \ldots, h_\kappa$. To define $h_1(x,0), h_2(x,0), \ldots, h_\kappa(x,0)$ we consider the set $D_{h(x,0)}$. Let be $D_{h(x,0)} = \{y_1, \ldots, y_s\}, s \leq \kappa$. We define $h_1(x,0) = y_1, \ldots, h_s(x,0) = y_s, h_{s+1}(x,0) = b+1, \ldots, h_\kappa(x,0) = b+\kappa-s$ where b is the maximum element in $\{y_1, \ldots, y_s\}$. Suppose for induction that $h_1(x,t-1), \ldots, h_\kappa(x,t-1)$ are defined. To define $h_1(x,t), h_2(x,t), \ldots, h_\kappa(x,t)$ we consider $D_{h(x,t)} = \{z_1, z_2, \ldots, z_m\}, m \leq \kappa$. Let be $\{z_1, z_2, \ldots, z_m\} \cap \{h_1(x,t-1), h_2(x,t-1), \ldots, h_\kappa(x,t-1)\} = \{u_1, \ldots, u_q\}$, where $u_1 = h_{i_1}(x,t-1), \ldots, u_q = h_{i_q}(x,t-1)$. We define $h_{i_1}(x,t) = u_1, \ldots, h_{i_q}(x,t) = u_q$. We give values from $\{z_1, \ldots, z_m\} \setminus \{u_1, \ldots, u_q\}$ for the other functions. If some functions are not defined yet, they get values $b+1, b+2, \ldots$ where b is the maximum element in $\{z_1, \ldots, z_m\} \cup \{h_1(x,t-1), \ldots, h_\kappa(x,t-1)\}$.

We have $p < \frac{1}{\kappa}$. It follows from Statement 1 that there exists a PMCL $\mathfrak{M}$ weak enumerating the graph of φ in the limit with probability exceeding κp, provided that every output value printed by $\mathfrak{M}$ equals 1.

Hence the following PMCL $\mathfrak{M}'$ can be used for weak computation of the function φ in the limit with probability exceeding p. At the beginning $\mathfrak{M}'$ equiprobably chooses one of the numbers $1,2,\ldots,K$. Let τ be chosen. Then $\mathfrak{M}'$ computes sequence $h_\tau(x,0), h_\tau(x,1),\ldots$ and at the same time simulates the work of $\mathfrak{M}$ at pair $<x, h_\tau(x,0)>$ until a t_1 appears such that $h_\tau(x,t_1) \neq h_\tau(x,t_1-1)$. Whenever $\mathfrak{M}$ must print the output value 1, $\mathfrak{M}'$ interrupts the simulation, prints $h_\tau(x,0)$ instead of 1 and then continues the simulation of $\mathfrak{M}$. If the value t_1 appears, then $\mathfrak{M}'$ prints a pair of two different output values, ends the simulation of $\mathfrak{M}$ at the pair $<x, h_\tau(x,0)>$ and switches over to simulation of $\mathfrak{M}$ at $<x,h_\tau(x,t_1)>$. If a $t_2>t_1$ appears for which $h_\tau(x,t_2)\neq h_\tau(x,t_2-1)$, then $\mathfrak{M}'$ prints a pair of two different output values again and switches over to the simulation of $\mathfrak{M}$ at $<x, h_\tau(x,t_2)>$, etc.

If the limit $\lim_t h_\tau(x,t)$ does not exist, then infinite number of pairs of two different values is printed, and the output sequence has no limit. Let the limit $\lim_t h_\tau(x,t)$ exist. If $\lim_t h_\tau(x,t) = \varphi(x)$, then the conditional probability (suppose the value τ is chosen) of printing an infinite sequence with limit equal to $\lim_t h_\tau(x,t)$ exceeds Kp. If $\lim_t h_\tau(x,t) \neq \varphi(x)$, then the probability does not exceed Kp. In any case $\mathfrak{M}'$ does not print infinite convergent sequences with the limit not equal to $\lim_t h_\tau(x,t)$. The desired result follows.

COROLLARY 1. Let p_1 and p_2 be real constructive numbers such that $0 \leq p_1 \leq p_2 < 1$. If a function φ is weak computable in the limit with probability exceeding p_2 then φ is weak computable in the limit with probability exceeding p_1.

COROLLARY 2. Let p_1 and p_2 be real constructive numbers. Let there exist a natural number K such that $\frac{1}{K+1} \leq p_1 \leq p_2 < \frac{1}{K}$. Then a function φ is weak computable in the limit with probability exceeding p_1 iff φ is weak computable in the limit with probability exceeding p_2.

COROLLARY 3. There exists a total function f such that for every real constructive p ($0 \leq p < \frac{1}{2}$) f is weak computable in the limit with probability exceeding p ,but φ is not weak computable in the limit by deterministic machines.

COROLLARY 4. If $\frac{1}{2} \leq p < 1$, then a total function f is weak computable in the limit with probability exceeding p iff f is computable in the limit by deterministic machines.

STATEMENT 4. It is possible to find effectively for every natural $\kappa \geqslant 2$ a number (in the principal " computable " indexing of all partial Σ_3-functions) of a total function f such that: 1) the range of f contains no more than κ different elements, 2) the graph of f is in $\Sigma_3 \cap \Pi_3$ and 3) if $p \geqslant \frac{1}{\kappa}$ then f is not weak computable in the limit with probability exceeding p.

PROOF. We define an auxiliary function $h(x,i,j)$ as the smallest number not in $D_{g(\kappa,x,x,i,j)}$ where g is the function defined in Lemma. It is easy to see that the values of h do not exceed $\kappa-1$. It follows by Lemma that for every x,i there exists the limit $\lim_j h(x,i,j)$ and for every x there exists the limit $\lim_i \lim_j h(x,i,j)$. Hence the graph of f is in $\Sigma_3 \cap \Pi_3$. From the assertion 4) of Lemma follows that f is not weak computable in the limit with probability exceeding p.

COROLLARY 1. There exists a total function f_1 such that the graph of f_1 is in $\Sigma_3 \cap \Pi_3$ and for every $p>0$ (even if p is not constructive) f_1 is not weak computable in the limit with probability exceeding p.

PROOF. Let $f_2, f_3, f_4, \ldots$ denote functions corresponding to $\kappa = 2,3,4,\ldots$ in Statement 4. Let $c(x,y), l(x), r(x)$ denote Cantor's pair functions. Then $f_1(x) = f_{2+l}(r(x))$.

COROLLARY 2. There exists a total function f such that the graph of f is in Π_3 and for every $p \in [0,1)$ f is not weak computable in the limit with probability exceeding p.

PROOF. It follows by relativization of arguments in [6], § 5 that there exists a total function $g(x)$ the graph of which is in Π_3 but not in Σ_3. We define

$$f(x) = \begin{cases} g(n), & \text{if } x = 2n \\ f_1(n), & \text{if } x = 2n+1 \end{cases}$$

where f_1 is defined in Corollary 1.

Corollaries 1,2 and Statement 4 imply

THEOREM 4. Let p_1 and p_2 be real constructive numbers and $0 \leqslant p_1 \leqslant p_2 < 1$. If there exists a natural number κ such that $p_1 < \frac{1}{\kappa} \leqslant p_2$, then the class $\mathfrak{F}_{p_2}$ of all functions weak computable in the limit with probability exceeding p_2 is properly contained in the class $\mathfrak{F}_{p_1}$ of all functions weak computable in the limit with probability exceeding p_1 Otherwise $\mathfrak{F}_{p_1} = \mathfrak{F}_{p_2}$.

REFERENCES

[1] LEEUW,K.DE ; MOORE,E.F. ; SHANNON,C.E. ; SHAPIRO,N. Computability by probabilistic machines. Automata Studies, Annals of Mathematics Studies, № 34, Princeton U. Press, Princeton, N.J., 1956.

[2] KUSHNER,B.A. Lectures in constructive mathematical analysis (Russian). Nauka, Moscow, 1973.

[3] ROGERS,H. Theory of recursive functions and effective computability. Mc Graw-Hill, New York, 1967.

[4] BARZDIN,J.M. On computability by probabilistic machines (Russian). Dokladi AN SSSR 189 (1969), № 4.

[5] ZVONKIN,A.K. ; LEVIN,L.A. Complexity of finite objects and basing of the notions of information and randomness by means of the theory of algorithms (Russian). Uspehi matematicheskih nauk 25 (1970), № 6.

[6] PODNIEKS,K.M. On reducibilities of classes of functions (Russian). Uravnenija matematicheskoi fiziki i teorija algoritmov, Latvian State University, Riga, 1972.

SOME PROPERTIES OF LIMIT RECURSIVE FUNCTIONS

B. Goetze and R. Klette
Section of Mathematics, Friedrich-Schiller-University
69 Jena, UHH, German Democratic Republic

The limit recursive functions are important in the theory of inductive inference. In this paper we will present some properties of limit recursive functions, which show, that the theory of these functions is very similar to the theory of recursive functions. Corresponding with GOLD [1] we define the limit operator L:

Definition: Let F be a (n+1)-ary function of natural variables. We define the n-ary function L(F) in the following way:

$$L(F)(x_1,\dots,x_n) = y \Longleftrightarrow_{Df} \exists t_o \forall t (t_o \leq t \rightarrow F(t,x_1,\dots,x_n) = y).$$

It is customary to use the symbol "lim":

$$L(F)(x_1,\dots,x_n) = \lim_t F(t,x_1,\dots,x_n).$$

Further we will use the following notations:

$\mathfrak{F} =_{Df}$ the set of all full defined functions of natural variables,
$Pr =_{Df}$ the set of all primitive recursive functions,
$G =_{Df}$ the set of all (general) recursive functions and
$Pa =_{Df}$ the set of all partial recursive functions.

GOLD has proved in [1] :

(A) $Pa \subset L(Pr) = L(G) \subset L(Pa)$,

(B) $G \subset L(G) \cap \mathfrak{F} = L(Pa) \cap \mathfrak{F}$ and

(C) $L(G) \cap \mathfrak{F} \nsubseteq Pa$.

Further it is ease to understand, that

(D) $L(G) \cap \mathfrak{F} \subset L(G)$ and

(E) $Pa \nsubseteq L(G) \cap \mathfrak{F}$.

Definition: a) $\mathcal{L}_f =_{Df} L(G) \cap \mathfrak{F}$,
b) $\mathcal{L}_g =_{Df} L(G)$ and

c) $\mathcal{L}_{pa} =_{Df} L(Pa)$.

The elements of $\mathcal{L}_{pa}$ are called limit recursive functions. With (A),...,(E) and $G \subset Pa$ we have the structure

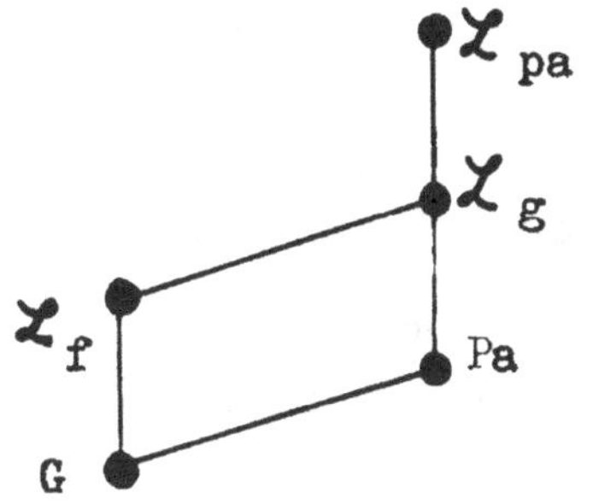

Now we pay attention to the question if the classes $\mathcal{L}_f$, $\mathcal{L}_g$ and $\mathcal{L}_{pa}$ are closed by applying of the usual operators of the theory of recursive functions:
substitution (SUB), primitive recursion (R) and the mu operator (M).
We have prooved

Theorem 1. a) $\mathcal{L}_f$, $\mathcal{L}_g$ and $\mathcal{L}_{pa}$ are closed by applying of SUB and R.
b) $\mathcal{L}_g$ and $\mathcal{L}_{pa}$ are closed by applying of M.

Not all of these results are new. Mr. R. V. Freivald from Riga told us at this symposium, that $\mathcal{L}_g$ is the class of all functions, which are computable by orakel machines with the orakel set O'. From this fact also follows, that $\mathcal{L}_g$ is closed by applying of SUB, R and M. Now we pay attention to the problem of carrying over properties of recursive functions (for instance the fixed-point theorem by Kleene and Rice's theorem) to the theory of limit recursive functions. Let φ be a Gödel numbering of Pa. With φ_z^n we denote that n-ary recursive function, which has the number z. Now we define a Gödel numbering of $\mathcal{L}_{pa}$.

$$\psi_z^n =_{Df} L(\varphi_z^{n+1})$$

This stands for

$$\psi_z^n(x_1,\dots,x_n) =_{Df} \lim_t \varphi_z^{n+1}(t,x_1,\dots,x_n).$$

The following theorems 2 and 3 justify to call ψ a Gödel numbering of $\mathcal{L}_{pa}$.

Theorem 2. (enumeration theorem). For every $n \geq 1$, there exists a function $U^{n+1} \in \mathcal{L}_{pa}$, such that for all $z, x_1,\dots,x_n$,

$$\psi_z(x_1,\dots,x_n) = U^{n+1}(z,x_1,\dots,x_n).$$

Theorem 3. (s-m-n theorem). For every m, n ≥ 1, there exists a general recursive function s_n^{m+1}, such that for all z, $x_1,\ldots,x_n$, $y_1,\ldots,y_m$,

$$\Psi_z(y_1,\ldots,y_m,x_1,\ldots,x_n) = \Psi_{s_n^{m+1}(z,y_1,\ldots,y_m)}(x_1,\ldots,x_n).$$

It is very easy to carry over the prooves of these theorems from the theory of recursive functions. Further we prooved:

Theorem 4. (fixed-point theorem).

a) For every $f^1 \in \mathcal{L}_{pa}$, there exists a natural number n_o, such that $\Psi_{n_o} = \Psi_{f(n_o)}$.

b) For every $n \geq 1$ and every $f^{n+1} \in \mathcal{L}_{pa}$, there exists a general recursive function p^n, such that for all $x_1,\ldots,x_n$,

$$\Psi_{p(x_1,\ldots,x_n)} = \Psi_{f(p(x_1,\ldots,x_n),x_1,\ldots,x_n)}.$$

Theorem 5. (Like Rice's theorem). For every $n \geq 1$ let $\mathcal{G}$ be a class with $\emptyset \subset \mathcal{G} \subset \mathcal{L}_{pa}^n$ and $M =_{Df} \{ z : \Psi_z^n \in \mathcal{G} \}$. Then the characteristic function χ_M of the set M isn't in $\mathcal{L}_{pa}$. We say, that M isn't limit recursive.

The called properties show, that the theory of limit recursive functions is similar to the theory of recursive functions.

REFERENCES

[1] GOLD, E. M. Limit-Recursion. J. Symbolic Logic, 30(1965), 28-48.

ON SOME APPROXIMATION PROBLEMS OF CONTINUOUS COMPUTATION

B. Konikowska
Computation Center
Polish Academy of Sciences
Warsaw, Poland

1. INTRODUCTION

There are two basic types of a computation: a discrete computation, performed in digital computers, and a continuous one, which is realized in analog computers. Evidently, the theoretical computer science contains many well-known models of computers performing discrete computation. However, there has been little attempt to define an abstract model of a computer performing continuous computation. Of course, such a computer is a special case of a continuous time system but the problems of system theory do not coincide with the problems of computation.

In [3] we have defined the notion of a continuous machine of memory length τ, being a general model of a computer performing continuous computation. This machine is defined as a certain kind of an operator extending functions defined in $\langle 0,\tau)$ to functions defined in $\langle 0,\infty)$. In [2] it is shown that the analog computer solving a linear differential equation with constant coefficients can be defined as a special case of a continuous machine.

The notion of a continuous machine induces in a natural way a new, machine-oriented notion of a computable function of real variable. Namely, we say that a function f is τ-computable iff it is one of the extensions generable by some continuous machine of memory length τ. The basic properties of τ-computable functions were examined in [3].

This paper is a continuation of [3] (though the knowledge of [3] is not required of the reader). Here we are concerned with two approximation problems connected with the notion of a τ-computable function. The first of them is the problem of approximating an arbitrary real function by a sequence of τ-computable functions. The second problem is implied by the fact that in practice one often approximates the functions generable by analog computers by means of digital analyzers, or some special programs realized on universal digital computers. However, this is done in an experimental way, without any general theory substantiating these methods. Hence our problem is as follows: can every τ-computable function be approximated by a sequence of functions generable in some sense by means of a discrete computation?

It turns out that both the problems have positive solutions. Of course, in a general case we can only prove the existence of a required approximation (f_n) without giving any effective formula for f_n. However, in the case of the second problem, we are able to give an effective approximation for any function generable by the analog computer solving a linear differential equation with constant coefficients.

2. CONTINUOUS MACHINES AND τ-COMPUTABLE FUNCTIONS

In this section we shall quote some basic definitions and results from [3]. The reader is referred there for the proofs of these results and more information about the discussed notions.

We begin with fixing the notation. By Df and Rf we denote the domain and the range of a function f, respectively. If $A \subset Df$, then by $f|_A$ we mean the restriction of f to A, i.e. $D(f|_A) = A$ and $(f|_A)(x) = f(x)$ for $x \in A$. For any two sets A, B, by B^A we denote the set of all total functions $f: A \to B$, and by $B^{[A]}$ the set of all partial functions $f: A \to B$. R is the set of real numbers, I - the set of integers, N - the set of natural integers, $N^0 = N \cup \{0\}$, and $\emptyset$ is the empty set.

For any $0 \leqslant a \leqslant b \leqslant \infty$, $a \neq \infty$, we denote

$$\{a,b) = \begin{cases} \langle a,b), & \text{if} \quad a < b \\ a \ , & \text{if} \quad a = b \end{cases}$$

Let X be a non-empty set, to be fixed for the sequel with exception of the cases when we explicitly assume that X = R. We denote

$$\mathfrak{F}_\infty \equiv \mathfrak{F} = X^{\langle 0,\infty)}$$

and, for any $\tau \geqslant 0$,

$$\mathfrak{F}_\tau = X^{\{0,\tau)}, \qquad \mathfrak{U}_\tau = \mathfrak{F}^{[\mathfrak{F}_\tau]}$$

Elements of $\mathfrak{U}_\tau$ will be called operators. If $A \in \mathfrak{U}_\tau$ and $f \in DA$, then we write Af instead of A(f).

We define the operation of shift $*$ as follows: if $0 \leqslant a \leqslant b \leqslant \infty$, $a \neq \infty$, and $f: \{a,b) \to X$, then $f^* \in \mathfrak{F}_{b-a}$ and $f^*(x) = f(a+x)$ for $x \in \{0,b-a)$.

For any $f\colon \langle 0,a) \to X$ $(0 \leqslant a \leqslant \infty)$ and any $\langle c,d) \subset \langle 0,a)$, we denote

$$f_{|c,d} \equiv f_{c,d} = (f|_{\langle c,d)})^*$$

Definition 1. For any $\tau \geqslant 0$, by a continuous machine of memory length τ we understand any operator $M \in \mathcal{U}_\tau$ such that:

(i) $(\forall h \in DM)((Mh)|_{\langle 0,\tau)} = h)$

(ii) $(\forall f \in RM)(\forall a \geqslant 0)(f_{a,\infty} \in RM)$

The set RM will be called the set of computations of M, and each element of this set will be called a computation of M.

Clearly, (i) means that M assigns to every function $h \in DM$ one of its extensions to $\langle 0,\infty)$. Condition (ii) means that the range of M is closed under shifting functions to the left. A "computation" of M is in fact a function generable by M.

For any $\tau \geqslant 0$, the set of all continuous machines of memory length τ is denoted by $\mathfrak{M}_\tau$.

The notion of a continuous machine induces in a natural way the following notions of a computable function of real variable:

Definition 2. For any $\tau \geqslant 0$, a function $f \in \mathfrak{F}$ is said to be τ-computable iff there exists $M \in \mathfrak{M}_\tau$ such that f is a computation of M, i.e. $f \in RM$. A function $f \in \mathfrak{F}$ is said to be absolutely computable iff it is τ-computable for every $\tau > 0$.

Theorem 1. A function $f \in \mathfrak{F}$ is τ-computable iff for any $a,b \geqslant 0$ such that $f_{a,a+\tau} = f_{b,b+\tau}$, then $f_{a,\infty} = f_{b,\infty}$.

Corollary 1. If a function $f \in \mathfrak{F}$ is τ_1-computable and $\tau_2 \geqslant \tau_1$, then f is τ_2-computable.

The above corollary implies that every 0-computable function is absolutely computable. Of course, the converse statement is false.

3. APPROXIMATION OF REAL FUNCTIONS BY τ-COMPUTABLE FUNCTIONS

In this section we consider the case of $X=R$. The corresponding set $\mathfrak{F} \equiv R^{\langle 0,\infty)}$ is denoted by $\mathfrak{F}(R)$.

From Theorem 1 it follows that some functions in $\mathfrak{F}(R)$ are not τ-computable for any $\tau \geqslant 0$. Hence it is natural to ask if every function in $\mathfrak{F}(R)$ can be approximated by a sequence of τ-computable functions for some $\tau \geqslant 0$. We shall prove that the answer is positive, even strongly so, for we can obtain uniform approximation by 0-computable functions. Of course, as the approximated function is quite arbitrary, we can only show the existence of such an approximation without giving any effective formula for it.

Theorem 2. Any function $f \in \mathfrak{F}(R)$ is the limit of a sequence (f_n) of 0-computable functions which converges uniformly in $\langle 0,\infty)$.

Proof. From Theorem 1 it follows immediately that each injective function in $\mathfrak{F}(R)$ is 0-computable. Hence it suffices to show that f is a limit of a uniformly convergent sequence of injective functions.

Denote by Q the set of rational numbers, and let $Q' = R-Q$. Consider now an arbitrary $n \in N$. As Q is dense in R, then there exists $g_n : \langle 0,\infty) \rightarrow Q$ such that

$$(\forall x \geqslant 0)(|f(x) - g_n(x)| \leqslant \tfrac{1}{2n}) \tag{1}$$

Let $\sim$ be a binary relation in the set $Q'_n = (0,\frac{1}{2n}) \cap Q'$ such that $x \sim y \Leftrightarrow x-y \in Q$. Evidently, $\sim$ is an equivalence relation, and, for any $x \in Q'_n$,

$$[x]_\sim \equiv \{y \in Q'_n : x \sim y\} = \{x+q : q \in (-x,-x+\tfrac{1}{2n}) \cap Q\}$$

Hence $[x]_\sim$ is denumerable for each $x \in Q'_n$. As $Q'_n = \bigcup_{x \in Q'_n} [x]_\sim$ and Q'_n is not denumerable, then the set $Q'_n/_\sim \equiv \{[x]_\sim : x \in Q'_n\}$ cannot be denumerable. Choosing one element from each class in $Q'_n/_\sim$, we obtain a non-denumerable set Y_n such that

$$Y_n \subset (0, \tfrac{1}{n}) \wedge (\forall y,y' \in Y_n)(y \neq y' \Rightarrow y-y' \notin Q) \tag{2}$$

As Y_n is equipotential with $\langle 0,\infty)$, then there exists an injective function $h_n : \langle 0,\infty) \rightarrow Y_n$. Let $f_n = g_n + h_n$, and suppose that $f_n(x) =$

$f_n(x')$ for some $x,x' \geqslant 0$. Then $g_n(x) + h_n(x) = g_n(x') + h_n(x')$, whence $h_n(x') - h_n(x) = g_n(x) - g_n(x') \in Q$ (for $Rg_n \subset Q$). Since $Rh_n \subset Y_n$, this implies $h_n(x) = h_n(x')$ by (2). As h_n is injective, this yields $x=x'$. Hence f_n is injective. Moreover, by (1) and (2) we have

$$(3) \qquad |f(x) - f_n(x)| \leqslant |f(x) - g_n(x)| + |h_n(x)| \leqslant \frac{1}{2n} + \frac{1}{2n} = \frac{1}{n}$$

for $x \geqslant 0$. As $n \in N$ was arbitrary, then from (3) and preceding remarks it follows that $(f_n)_{n \in N}$ is a sequence of injective functions which converges to f uniformly in $\langle 0,\infty)$, q.e.d.

From the proof of Theorem 2 it follows that $f_1,f_2,\ldots$ can be quite arbitrary injective functions. As f itself was arbitrary, this is hardly suprising. However, if f is continuous in $\langle 0,\infty)$, we would like to approximate it by continuous τ-computable functions. We shall prove that such an approximation exists, though it is slightly "weaker" than in Theorem 2 - namely, $f_n \rightarrow f$ almost uniformly in $\langle 0,\infty)$ and $f_1,f_2,\ldots$ are absolutely computable. The functions $f_1,f_2,\ldots$ will be "condensing" broken lines.

Let us denote by R^∞ the set of all infinite sequences of real numbers. For any $c \in R^\infty$ and any $k \in N^0$, the k-th element of the sequence c is denoted by $c(k)$. In other words, if $c \in R^\infty$, then $c = (c(0), c(1),\ldots)$.

Definition 3. For any $c \in R^\infty$, and any $h > 0$, by the broken line connecting the points $(c(k),kh)$ for $k \in N^0$, in symbols b_c^h, we mean the only function in $\mathfrak{F}(R)$ such that:

$$\text{(i)} \qquad (\forall\, k \in N^0)\left(b_c^h(kh) = c(k)\right)$$

$$\text{(ii)} \qquad (\forall\, k \in N^0)\left(\forall\, x \in \langle kh,(k+1)h)\right)\left(b_c^n(x) = b_c^h(kh) + \frac{x-kh}{h}\left(b_c^h((k+1)h) - b_c^h(kh)\right)\right)$$

Lemma 1. Let $f \in \mathfrak{F}(R)$, $c_n \in R^\infty$ and $h_n \in R$, $h_n > 0$ for $n \in N$. If f is continuous in $\langle 0,\infty)$, $\lim\limits_{n\to\infty} h_n = 0$ and

$$(4) \qquad (\forall\, T > 0)\left(\lim_{n\to\infty} \max_{k=0,1,\ldots,\left[\frac{T}{h_n}\right]} |f(kh_n) - c_n(k)| = 0\right)$$

then the sequence $b_{c_n}^{h_n}$ converges to f almost uniformly in $\langle 0,\infty)$.

Proof. Denote $f_n = b_{c_n}^{h_n}$ for $n \in N$. We have to show that

(5) $(\forall T>0)(\forall \varepsilon>0)(\exists n_0 \in N)(\forall n>n_0)(\forall x \in \langle 0,T\rangle)(|f(x)-f_n(x)|<\varepsilon)$

Let us fix an arbitrary $T>0$, and let $T'=T+1$. Now consider an arbitrarily fixed $\varepsilon>0$. As f is continuous in $\langle 0,T'\rangle$, then from the fact that this interval is closed and bounded it follows that f is uniformly continuous in $\langle 0,T'\rangle$. Hence there exists $\delta \in (0,1)$ such that

(6) $(\forall x',x'' \in \langle 0,T'\rangle)(|x'-x''|<\delta \Rightarrow |f(x')-f(x'')|<\frac{\varepsilon}{6})$

As $f_n(kh_n) = b_{c_n}^{h_n}(kh_n) = c_n(k)$, then by (4) we have

$$\lim_{n\to\infty} \max_{k=0,1,\dots,\left[\frac{T'}{h_n}\right]} |f(kh_n)-f_n(kh_n)| = 0$$

Hence there exists $n_1 \in N$ such that

(7) $(\forall n>n_1)(\forall k \in \{0,1,\dots,\left[\frac{T'}{h_n}\right]\})(|f(kh_n)-f_n(kh_n)|<\frac{\varepsilon}{6})$

Further, as $h_n \to 0$, then there exists $n_2 \in N$ such that $h_n<\delta$ for $n>n_2$. Let $n_0 = \max(n_1,n_2)$. We will show that for each $n>n_0$ $|f(x)-f_n(x)|<\varepsilon$ for all $x \in \langle 0,T\rangle$, which means that (5) is satisfied. Thus let $n>n_0$ and consider any $x \in \langle 0,T\rangle$. As $h_n<\delta$ (for $n>n_2$), then there exists $k \in N^0$ such that

$$x-\delta < kh_n \leq x < (k+1)h_n < x+\delta$$

Since $x+\delta \leq T+1 = T'$, then $k,k+1 \leq \left[\frac{T'}{h_n}\right]$. Considering $n>n_1$, we have by (7)

(8) $|f(ih_n)-f_n(ih_n)|<\frac{\varepsilon}{6}, \quad i=k,k+1$

As $ih_n \in \langle 0,T'\rangle$ and $|x-ih_n|<\delta$ for $i=k,k+1$, then (6) implies that

(9) $|f(x)-f(ih_n)|<\frac{\varepsilon}{6}, \quad i=k,k+1$

From (8) and (9) we obtain

(10) $\quad |f(x) - f_n(ih_n)| \leqslant |f(x) - f(ih_n)| + |f(ih_n) - f_n(ih_n)| < \frac{\varepsilon}{3}$,

$$i = k, k+1.$$

As $kh_n \leqslant x < (k+1)h_n$ and $f = b_{c_n}^{h_n}$, then by Definition 3 and (10)

$$|f(x) - f_n(x)| = \left|f(x) - f_n(kh_n) - \frac{x-kh_n}{h_n}(f_n(k+1)h_n) - f_n(kh_n))\right|$$

$$\leqslant |f(x) - f_n(kh_n)| + \frac{|x-kh_n|}{h_n}|f_n((k+1)h_n) - f_n(kh_n)|$$

$$\leqslant \frac{\varepsilon}{3} + \frac{h_n}{h_n}(|f_n((k+1)h_n) - f(x)| + |f(x) - f_n(kh_n)|) < \varepsilon, \quad \text{q.e.d.}$$

Theorem 3. Any function $f \in \mathfrak{F}(R)$ continuous in $\langle 0,\infty)$ is the limit of a sequence of absolutely computable functions continuous in $\langle 0,\infty)$ which converges almost uniformly in $\langle 0,\infty)$.

Proof. For any $n \in N$, let $c_n \in R^\infty$ be any sequence such that:

(11) $$(\forall k \in N^o)\left(\left|f(\tfrac{k}{n}) - c_n(k)\right| < \tfrac{1}{n}\right)$$

and, for any $k \in N$, $c_n(k) \neq c_n(i)$ for $i = 0,\dots,k-1$, $c_n(k) - c_n(k-1) \neq c_n(i) - c_n(i-1)$ for $i = 1,\dots,k-1$. Evidently, such a sequence c_n exists, for, taking $c_n(0) = f(0)$, we can easily prove the existence of $c_n(k)$ $(k=0,1,\dots)$ by induction on k. We define $f_n = b_{c_n}^{1/n}$ for $n \in N$. It is easy to see that f_n is continuous in $\langle 0,\infty)$ and:

(12) $$(\forall k,l \in N^o)\left(k \neq l \Rightarrow f_n(\tfrac{k}{n}) \neq f_n(\tfrac{l}{n}) \wedge f_n(\tfrac{k+1}{n}) - f_n(\tfrac{k}{n}) \neq f_n(\tfrac{l+1}{n}) - f_n(\tfrac{l}{n})\right)$$

(13) $$(\forall k \in N^o)(\forall x \in \langle \tfrac{k}{n}, \tfrac{k+1}{n}))\left(f_n(x) = f_n(\tfrac{k}{n}) + n(x - \tfrac{k}{n})\left(f_n(\tfrac{k+1}{n}) - f_n(\tfrac{k}{n})\right)\right)$$

As f is continuous in $\langle 0,\infty)$, $\frac{1}{n} \to 0$ and $\lim_{n\to\infty} \max_{k \in N^o} \left|f(\frac{k}{n}) - c_n(k)\right| = 0$ by (11), then by Lemma 1 $f_n \to f$ almost uniformly in $\langle 0,\infty)$.

Hence it suffices to show f_n is absolutely computable for any $n \in N$. Thus consider an arbitrary $\tau > 0$ and suppose that $f_{n|a,a+\tau} = f_{n|b,b+\tau}$ for some $a,b \geqslant 0$. It is easy to see that there exist $h_1,h_2 > 0$ such that $h_1 < h_2 \leqslant \tau$ and $\frac{k}{n} \notin \langle a+h_1, a+h_2)$, $\frac{k}{n} \notin \langle b+h_1, b+h_2)$ for $k \in N^o$. Hence there exist $k,l \in N^o$ such that $\langle a+h_1, a+h_2) \subset (\frac{k}{n}, \frac{k+1}{n})$

and $\langle b+h_1, b+h_2) \subset (\frac{l}{n}, \frac{l+1}{n})$. As $h_1 \leqslant h_2 \leqslant \tau$, then

$$(14) \quad f_{n|a+h_1,a+h_2} = \left(f_{n|a,a+\tau} \big| \langle h_1,h_2)\right)^* = \left(f_{n|b,b+\tau} \big| \langle h_1,h_2)\right)^*$$

$$= f_{n|b+h_1,b+h_2}$$

Since by (13) $f_n'(x) = n(f_n(\frac{i+1}{n}) - f_n(\frac{i}{n}))$ for $x \in (\frac{i}{n}, \frac{i+1}{n})$, $i = k,l$, this implies

$$f_n(\frac{k+1}{n}) - f_n(\frac{k}{n}) = f_n(\frac{l+1}{n}) - f_n(\frac{l}{n})$$

whence $k = l$ by (12). Thus $\langle a+h_1,a+h_2)$, $\langle b+h_1,b+h_2) \subset (\frac{k}{n}, \frac{k+1}{n})$. As $f_n(\frac{k}{n}) \neq f_n(\frac{k+1}{n})$, then (13) implies that f_n is strictly monotonic in $(\frac{k}{n}, \frac{k+1}{n})$. Hence from (14) it follows that $a+h_1 = b+h_1$, or $a = b$, which yields $f_{n|a,\infty} = f_{n|b,\infty}$. Thus f_n is τ-computable by Theorem 1. As τ was an arbitrary positive number, hence f_n is absolutely computable, q.e.d.

4. DISCRETE MACHINES AND n-COMPUTABLE SEQUENCES

In this section we quote (with certain minor modifications) some basic definitions and results given by Z. GRODZKI [1] which will be used in the sequel of the paper. From now on we deal only with the case of $X = R$.

Definition 4. Let $n \in N$. By an infinite discrete machine of memory length n we mean any total function $\Pi: R^n \to R$. For any $p = (x_0, \ldots, x_{n-1}) \in R^n$, by the computation of Π beginning at p, in symbols $\mathcal{C}_\Pi(p)$, we mean the unique sequence $c \in R^\infty$ such that $c(k) = x_i$ for $i = 0,\ldots,n-1$, and $c(k+n) = \Pi(c(k),\ldots,c(k+n-1))$ for $k \in N^o$.

Definition 5. For any $n \in N$, a sequence $c \in R^\infty$ is said to be n-computable, iff there exists an infinite discrete machine Π of memory length n and $p \in R^n$ such that $c = \mathcal{C}_\Pi(p)$.

Theorem 4. A sequence $c \in R^{\infty}$ is n-computable iff for any $k,l \in N^{o}$ such that $(c(k),\dots,c(k+n-1)) = (c(l),\dots,c(l+n-1))$, then $c(k+n) = c(l+n)$.

For any $n \in N$, the set of all n-computable sequences in R^{∞} is denoted by C_n.

Corollary 2. If $c \in C_n$, $k \in N^{o}$, $x \in R$ and $c(k+r) = x$ for $r = 0,1,\dots,n$, then $c(k+r) = x$ for $r \in N^{o}$.

5. APPROXIMATION OF τ-COMPUTABLE FUNCTIONS BY DISCRETELY n-GENERABLE τ-COMPUTABLE FUNCTIONS

Consider a sequence $c \in C_n$ and $h > 0$. We can assign to c a function $\bar{c}: \{kh : k \in N^{o}\} \to R$ such that $\bar{c}(kh) = c(k)$. Connecting the points of the diagram of $\bar{c}$ by a broken line, we obtain a continuous function which can be said to be generated by c. As c is an n-computable sequence, it is natural to call this function discretely n-generable. This amounts to the following definition:

Definition 6. For any $n \in N$, a function $f \in \mathcal{F}(R)$ is said to be discretely n-generable iff there exist $c \in C_n$ and $h > 0$ such that $f = b_c^h$.

We can now distinguish in the class of all continuous n-computable functions a subclass consisting of discretely n-generable τ-computable functions. Roughly speaking, we can say that a function in this subclass is obtained by first performing a discrete computation c and then connecting the points of a diagram assigned to c by means of a trivial kind of continuous computation. Now we shall try to answer the following question: Can we approximate each continuous τ-computable function by a sequence of n-generable $\bar{\tau}$-computable functions for some $n \in N$, $\bar{\tau} \geq 0$?

Note that the restriction to continuous τ-computable functions is unavoidable if we want to obtain an approximation at each point. If we approximate f by $f_n = b_{c_n}^{h_n}$, then we can only try to obtain a good approximation in the set $B = \{kh_n : k \in N^{o}\}$, for f_n is uniquely determined by $f_n|_B$. Hence if f is not continuous, we will never obtain a good approximation at the points $kh_n < x < (k+1)h_n$, because, even for very small h_n, the values of f at these points can be very distant from the values of f at $kh_n(k+1)h_n$.

Theorem 5. Any function $f\in\mathfrak{F}(R)$ continuous in $\langle 0,\infty)$ is the limit of a sequence of discretely 1-generable absolutely computable functions which converges almost uniformly in $\langle 0,\infty)$.

Proof. For any $n\in N$, let c_n be the sequence defined in the proof of Theorem 3, and let $f_n = b^{1/n}_{c_n}$. As $c_n(k) \neq c_n(l)$ for $k \neq l$, $k,l\in N^0$, then c_n is 1-computable by Theorem 4, whence f_n is discretely 1-generable for each $n\in N$. By the proof of Theorem 3, f_n is absolutely computable for each $n\in N$, and $f_n \rightarrow f$ almost uniformly in $\langle 0,\infty)$, q.e.d.

As we see, the answer is even better then we have expected, for the required approximation (f_n) exists for any continuous functions $f\in\mathfrak{F}(R)$. Since this function was arbitrary, we have proved only the existence of f_n.

In [2] it was shown that the analog computer solving a linear differential equation with constant coefficients can be defined as a special case of a continuous machine. Namely, the following definition was proved to be valid:

Definition 7. Let $a_0,\ldots,a_{n-1}$, $b\in R$. For any $\tau > 0$, by the analog computer of memory length τ solving the equation

$$y^{(n)} + a_{n-1}y^{(n-1)} + \ldots + a_0y = b$$

we mean the unique continuous machine $M\in\mathfrak{M}_\tau$ whose set of computations is the set of all functions in $\mathfrak{F}(R)$ satisfying this equation.

We shall prove now that for any computation of such an analog computer there exists an effectively defined approximation by n-generable τ-computable functions.

Lemma 2. Consider $a_0,\ldots,a_{n-1},b,\alpha_0,\ldots,\alpha_{n-1},T\in R$ and $h_k\in R$, $h_k > 0$ $(k = 1,2,\ldots)$ such that $\lim_{k\to\infty} h_k = 0$. For any $k\in N$, let $c_k = (c_k(0),\ldots, c_k([\frac{T}{h_k}]))$ be the unique sequence of real numbers such that

$$c_k(i) = \sum_{l=0}^{i} \binom{i}{l} \alpha_l \, h_k^l \,, \qquad i = 0,\dots,n-1,$$

(15) $$c_k(i+n) = h_k^n\left(b - \sum_{s=0}^{n-1}\left(\sum_{r=s}^{n} \frac{(-1)^{r+s}}{h_k^r}\binom{r}{s} a_r\right) c_k(i+s)\right),$$

$$i = 0,\dots,\left[\frac{T}{h_k}\right] - n$$

Then $\lim_{k\to\infty} \max_{i=0,\dots,\left[\frac{T}{h_k}\right]} \left| y(ih_k) - c_k(i)\right| = 0$, where y is the solution of the initial problem

(16) $$\begin{cases} y^{(n)}(x) + a_{n-1}\, y^{(n-1)}(x) + \dots + a_o y(x) = b, & 0 \leqslant x \leqslant T, \\ y(0) = \alpha_o,\ y'(0) = \alpha_1, \dots, y^{(n-1)}(0) = \alpha_{n-1} \end{cases}$$

The proof, which is based on some results of the numerical analysis, is given in [4].

Lemma 3. Let $\Pi : R^n \to R$ be a function such that

(17) $$\Pi(x_o,\dots,x_{n-1}) = v_o x_o + \dots + v_{n-1}x_{n-1} + v_n$$

for any $(x_o,\dots,x_{n-1}) \in R^n$, where $v_o,\dots,v_n \in R$. Then, for any $p \in R^n$ and any $h > 0$, $b^h_{\mathfrak{C}_\Pi(p)}$ is an nh-computable function.

Proof. Let $c = \mathfrak{C}_\Pi(p)$, $f = b^h_c$, $t_k = kh$ and $f^k = f(t_k)$ for $k \in N^o$. Then:

(18) $$(\forall k \in N^o)(f^{k+n} = \Pi(f^k,\dots,f^{k+n-1}))$$

(19) $$(\forall k \in N^o)(\forall x \in \langle t_k, t_{k+1})) \left(f(x) = f^k + \frac{x - t_k}{h}(f^{k+1} - f^k)\right)$$

Suppose that $a, b \geqslant 0$ and $f_{a,a+nh} = f_{b,b+nh}$. Then there exist $k, l \in N^o$ such that $t_k \leqslant a < t_{k+1}$, $t_l \leqslant b < t_{l+1}$.

(i) Consider first the case when $a - t_k = b - t_l$, and denote $d = t_{k+1} - a \equiv t_{l+1} - b$. Then $d \leqslant h$ and $d = h$ iff $a = t_k$, $b = t_l$. As $f(a+u) = f(b+u)$ for $0 \leqslant u < nh$, then we have

$$f^{k+r} = f(t_{k+r}) = f(t_{k+1}+(r-1)h) = f(a+d+(r-1)h)$$

$$= f(b+d+(r-1)h) = f(t_{l+1}+(r-1)h) = f(t_{l+r}) = f^{l+r}$$

for $r = \varepsilon, \varepsilon+1, \dots, \varepsilon+n-1$, where $\varepsilon \in \{0,1\}$ and $\varepsilon = 0$ iff $a = t_k$, $b = t_l$. Considering $(f^o, f^1, \dots) = c$ and Theorem 4, this implies $f^{k+\varepsilon+r} = f^{l+\varepsilon+r}$ for $r \in N^o$, whence $f_{t_{k+\varepsilon},\infty} = f_{t_{l+\varepsilon},\infty}$. As $f_{a,t_{k+\varepsilon}} = f_{a,a+\varepsilon d} = f_{b,b+\varepsilon d} = f_{b,t_{l+\varepsilon}}$, this yields $f_{a,\infty} = f_{b,\infty}$.

(ii) It remains to consider the case when $a-t_k \neq b-t_l$. Then $a \neq t_k$ or $b \neq t_l$. Without any loss of generality, we can assume that $a \neq t_k$. Thus we have $t_k < a < t_{k+1}$, $t_l \leq b < t_{l+1}$. Since $f_{a,a+nh} = f_{b,b+nh}$, then for any $\varepsilon', \varepsilon'' \geq 0$ such that $\varepsilon' \leq \varepsilon'' \leq nh$ we have $f_{a+\varepsilon',a+\varepsilon''} = f_{b+\varepsilon',b+\varepsilon''}$. Let $d = \min(a-t_k, t_{k+1}-a)$, and consider an arbitrarily fixed $r \in \{1,\dots,n\}$. Denoting $\varepsilon' = t_{k+r}-d-a$, $\varepsilon'' = t_{k+r}+d-a$, we have $\varepsilon' \leq \varepsilon''$, $\varepsilon' \geq t_{k+1} - (t_{k+1}-a) - a = 0$ and $\varepsilon'' \leq t_{k+n} + a-t_k - a = nh$. Hence

$$f_{t_{k+r}-d,t_{k+r}+d} = f_{a+\varepsilon',a+\varepsilon''} = f_{b+\varepsilon',b+\varepsilon''} = f_{b-a+(t_{k+r}-d),b-a+(t_{k+r}+d)}$$

which yields

(20) $\quad (\forall x \in \langle t_{k+r}-d, t_{k+r}+d))(f(x) = f(b-a+x))$

Now denote $d_1 = a-t_k$, $d_2 = b-t_l$. Then $d_1 \neq d_2$ and $0 < d_i < h$, $i = 1,2$, whence $0 < |d_1-d_2| < h$. As $b-a = t_l+d_2-t_k-d_1 = (l-k)h-(d_1-d_2)$, this yields $b-a \neq mh$ for $m \in I$, whence $b-a + t_{k+r} \neq t_p$ for $p \in N^o$. Since from (19) it follows that f is differentiable in $R - \{t_p : p \in N^o\}$, this implies that f is differentiable at $b-a+t_{k+r}$. Hence from (20) it follows that f is differentiable at t_{k+r}. As $r \in \{1,\dots,n\}$ was arbitrary, this is true for $r = 1,\dots,n$. Since from (19) it follows that, for any $p \in N$, f is differentiable at t_p iff $f^p - f^{p-1} = f^{p+1} - f^p$, this implies $f^{k+1} - f^k = f^{k+2} - f^{k+1} = \dots = f^{k+n+1} - f^{k+n}$. Denoting $f^{k+1} - f^k = \delta$, we obtain $f^{k+r} - f^{k+r-1} = \delta$ for $r = 1,\dots,n+1$, whence

(21) $\quad f^{k+r} = f^k + r\delta, \qquad r = 0,1,\dots,n+1$

As by (17) $f^{k+n} = \Pi(f^k,\dots,f^{k+n-1})$ and $f^{k+n+1} = \Pi(f^{k+1},\dots,f^{k+n})$, then from (17) and (21) it follows that

$$(22) \qquad f^k + n\delta = v_o f^k + v_1(f^k+\delta) + \dots + v_{n-1}(f^k+(n-1)\delta) + v_n,$$

$$(23) \qquad f^k + (n+1)\delta = v_o(f^k+\delta) + v_1(f^k+2\delta) + \dots + v_{n-1}(f^k+n\delta) + v_n$$

Subtracting (22) from (23), we obtain

$$(24) \qquad (v_o + \dots + v_{n-1})\,\delta = 0$$

Suppose first that $\delta = 0$. Then by (21) we have $f^{k+r} = f^k$ for $r = 0,\dots,n+1$, whence $f^{k+r} = f^k$ for $r \in N^o$ by Corollary 2. Considering (19), this implies $f_{t_k,\infty} \equiv f^k$. Hence $f_{a,\infty} \equiv f^k$ and $f_{b,b+nh} = f_{a,a+nh} \equiv f^k$. As $t_l \leqslant b < t_{l+1}$, this yields $f^{l+\varepsilon+r} = f^k$ for $r = 0,\dots,n-1$, where $\varepsilon \in \{0,1\}$ and $\varepsilon = 0$ iff $b = t_l$. Thus $(f^{l+\varepsilon},\dots, f^{l+\varepsilon+n-1}) = (f^k,\dots, f^{k+n-1})$. Since $(f^o, f^1,\dots) = c\ C_k$, then by Theorem 4 $f^{l+\varepsilon+n} = f^{k+n}$. Hence $f^{l+\varepsilon+r} = f^k$ for $r = 0,\dots,n$, which by Corollary 2 implies $f^{l+\varepsilon+r} = f^k$ for $r \in N^o$. Thus $f_{t_{l+\varepsilon},\infty} \equiv f^k$. Since $f_{b,t_{l+\varepsilon}} \equiv f^k$, this means that $f_{b,\infty} \equiv f^k \equiv f_{a,\infty}$.

Assume now that $\delta \neq 0$. Then (24) implies that

$$(25) \qquad v_o + \dots + v_{n-1} = 1$$

Hence from (22) it follows that

$$(26) \qquad v_1\delta + 2v_2\delta + \dots + (n-1)v_{n-1}\delta + v_n = n\delta$$

From (19) and (21) we can deduce that

$$(27) \qquad (\forall x \in \langle t_k, t_{k+n+1}))\left(f(x) = f^k + \frac{\delta}{h}(x-t_k)\right)$$

As $f_{b,b+nh} = f_{a,a+nh}$ and $\langle a,a+nh) \subset \langle t_k, t_{k+n+1})$, this implies

$$(28) \qquad (\forall u \in \langle 0,nh))\left(f(b+u) = f^k + \frac{\delta}{h}(a+u-t_k)\right)$$

Since $t_l \leqslant b < t_{l+1}$, then this yields

$$f^{l+\varepsilon+r} = f^k + \frac{\delta}{h}(a + (t_{l+\varepsilon+r}-b) - t_k) = f^k + \frac{\delta}{h}(a+t_{l+\varepsilon}+rh-b-t_k)$$

$$= f^k + \frac{\delta}{h}(a+(t_{l+\varepsilon}-b)-t_k) + r\delta = f^{l+\varepsilon} + r\delta$$

for $r = 0,\dots,n-1$, where $\varepsilon\in\{0,1\}$ and $\varepsilon = 0$ iff $b = t_l$. Let $p\in\{k,l+\varepsilon\}$, $p = k$ iff $a \leqslant b$, and let $d = \min(a,b)$. Considering (21) and the last result, we have $f^{p+r} = f^p + r\delta$ for $r = 0,\dots,n-1$. Suppose $f^{p+s} = f^p + s\delta$ for $s<r$, where $r \geqslant n$. Then by (17), (25) and (26) we have

$$f^{p+r} = \Pi(f^{p+r-n},\dots, f^{p+r-1}) = \Pi(f^p+(r-n)\delta,\dots, f^p+(r-1)\delta)$$

$$= v_0(f^p+(r-n)\delta) + v_1(f^p+(r-n+1)\delta) +\dots+ v_{n-1}(f^p+(r-1)\delta) + v_n$$

$$= (v_0+\dots+v_{n-1})(f^p+(r-n)\delta) + v_1\delta + 2v_2\delta +\dots+ (n-1)v_{n-1}\delta + v_n$$

$$= f^p + (r-n)\delta + n\delta = f^p + r\delta$$

Hence by induction $f^{p+r} = f^p + r\delta$ for $r\in N^0$. Considering (19), this yields $f(x) = f^p + \frac{\delta}{h}(x-t_p)$ for $x \geqslant t_p$. Hence $f'(x) = \frac{\delta}{h}$ for $x>t_p$. As by (27) and (28) $f(x) = \frac{\delta}{h}$ for $d<x<d+nh$ and $t_p<d+nh$, then $f(x) = \frac{\delta}{h}$ for $x>d$. Since $\delta\neq 0$ and f is continuous at d, this implies that f is strictly monotonic in $\langle d,\infty)$. Considering that $\langle a,a+nh), \langle b,b+nh)\subset\langle d,\infty)$ and $f_{a,a+nh} = f_{b,b+nh}$, this yields $a = b$. q.e.d.

Theorem 6. Let f be an arbitrary computation of the analog computer of memory length $\tau > 0$ solving the equation

$$y^{(n)} + a_{n-1}y^{(n-1)} +\dots+ a_0 y = b$$

For any $k\in N$, let $\Pi_k: R^n\to R$ be a total function defined by the formula

$$\Pi_k(x_0,\dots,x_{n-1}) = \frac{1}{k^n}\left(b - \sum_{s=0}^{n-1}\left(\sum_{r=s}^{n}(-1)^{r+s}k^r\binom{r}{s}a_r\right)x_s\right),$$

and let $c_k = \tau_{\Pi_k}(x_0^{(k)},\dots,x_{n-1}^{(k)})$, where $x_i^{(k)} = \sum_{l=0}^{i}\binom{i}{l}\frac{f^{(l)}(0)}{k^l}$.

Then, for any $\tau > 0$, $\left(b_{c_k}^{1/k}\right)_{k \geq [\frac{n}{\tau}]+1}$ is a sequence of discretely n-generable τ-computable functions which converges to f almost uniformly in $\langle 0, \infty)$.

Proof. Denote $f_k = b_{c_k}^{1/k}$ for $k \in N$. Then, by the definition of c_k and Π,

$$c_k(i) = \sum_{l=0}^{i} \binom{i}{l} \frac{f^{(l)}(0)}{k^l}, \qquad i = 0, \dots, n-1,$$

$$c_k(i+n) = \frac{1}{k^n}\left(b - \sum_{s=0}^{n-1}\left(\sum_{r=s}^{n} (-1)^{r+s} k^r \binom{r}{s} a_r\right) c_k(i+s)\right), \quad i \in N^0,$$

Hence, for any $T > 0$, the sequence $(c_k(0), \dots, c_k([Tk]))$ satisfies conditions (15) for $\alpha_i = f^{(i)}(0)$ $(i = 0, \dots, n-1)$ and $h_k = \frac{1}{k}$. As f is the solution of the corresponding initial problem (16) and $\frac{1}{k} \to 0$, then by Lemma 2

$$\lim_{k\to\infty} \max_{i=0,\dots,[kT]} \left| f\left(\frac{i}{k}\right) - c_k(i) \right| = 0$$

for any $T > 0$. Hence from Lemma 1 it follows that $f_n \to f$ almost uniformly in $\langle 0, \infty)$.

Evidently, f_k is discretely n-generable for $k \in N$, because $c_k \in C_n$. Moreover, as Π_k is of the form (17), then from Lemma 3 it follows that f_k is $\frac{n}{k}$-computable for $k \in N$. Hence if $\tau > 0$, then by Corollary 1 f_k is τ-computable for all k such that $\frac{n}{k} \leq \tau$, i.e. for any $k \geq [\frac{n}{\tau}] + 1$, q.e.d.

REFERENCES

[1] GRODZKI, Z. The k-machines. Bull. Acad. Polon. Sci., Sér.Sci. math., astronom. et phys., 18 (1970), pp. 399 - 402

[2] KONIKOWSKA, B. Formalization of the notion of an analog computer described by a linear differential equation with constant coefficients. Ibid., 20 (1972), pp. 1015 - 1020.

[3] KONIKOWSKA, B. Continuous machines. Information and Control, 22 (1973), pp. 353 - 372.

[4] KONIKOWSKA, B. Maszyny liczące o czasie ciągłym [in Polish]. PWN, Warszawa 1973.

SET-THEORETIC PROPERTIES OF PROGRAMS IN STORED PROGRAM COMPUTERS

W. Kwasowiec

Computation Centre
Polish Academy of Sciences
00-901 Warsaw, P.O.Box 22, POLAND

PAWLAK [1] has given a model of the stored program computer. He has introduced a notion of the program in this model and has formally given the meaning of a program (called the realization) in a stored program computer. These notions were investigated at the MFCS Semester in the Stefan Banach International Mathematical Centre (for example PAWLAK [2]). We shall base ourselves on Pawlak's notions (with slight modifications sometimes) and we shall give these notions which will be necessary for our investigations. We are interested in investigation of properties of programs and their realizations.

1. PROGRAMMING LANGUAGE

Let $\mathcal{A} = A \cup \{f_1, \ldots, f_k, \alpha, \mathrm{STOP}, \rightarrow, (,), ,\}$ - alphabet, where

A - the set of addresses, arbitrary elements which do not belong to the rest of the alphabet,

f_i - names of binary functions,

α - the name of an operator.

Let 1 be a distinguished element of A called the instruction counter. We adopt the following denotation: $A' = A - \{1\}$.

DEFINITION. The set of terms is the least set T such that

1° $A \subset T$

2° $\alpha(t) \in T$ for every $t \in T$

3° $f_i(t,t') \in T$ for all $t,t' \in T$, $i \leq k$.

DEFINITION. The set of instructions is the following set

$$\mathcal{R} = \{ t \longrightarrow t' : \quad t,t' \in T \} \cup \{STOP\} .$$

Let $R \subset \mathcal{R}$ be the set of instructions of our computer.

DEFINITION. By a program we mean a pair $\langle \varphi, a \rangle$ (abbr. φ^a) where φ is a partial function, $\varphi: A' \longrightarrow R$ such that the domain of the function φ (in symbols $Dom(\varphi)$) is finite and $a \in Dom(\varphi)$. The address a is called the start of the program φ^a.

Two partial functions f,g are said to be consistent if $f(x) = g(x)$ for each $x \in Dom(f) \cap Dom(g)$. Two programs φ^a, ψ^b are said to be consistent if functions φ, ψ are consistent and $a = b$.

Let f,g and φ^a, ψ^a be consistent. By the union of f,g (in symbols $f \cup g$) we mean the function whose diagram is the union of diagrams of functions f,g. By the intersection of f,g (in symbols $f \cap g$) we mean the function whose diagram is the intersection of diagrams of functions f,g. By the union of programs φ^a, ψ^a we mean the program $\langle \varphi \cup \psi, a \rangle$ (abbr. $(\varphi \cup \psi)^a$). By the intersection of programs φ^a, ψ^a we mean the program $\langle \varphi \cap \psi, a \rangle$ (abbr. $(\varphi \cap \psi)^a$).

2. MODEL OF THE STORED PROGRAM COMPUTER

DEFINITION. By a stored program computer we mean the system

$$M = \langle C, \pi \rangle$$

composed of two main components: the memory C (elements of which are called memory states) and the control π, partial function $\pi: C \longrightarrow C$.

These two components will be determined by means of the following primary objects: A, B, 1, R, $\varkappa$, λ, ρ. The objects A, 1, R were defined before.

We assume the set B to include the set A. Now we may define the memory C as a set of partial functions from A into B ($C \subseteq B^A$) such that $c(1) \in A$ for each $c \in C$.

By $\varkappa$ we mean a one-to-one function, $\varkappa: R \longrightarrow B$ (called the coding function). We may introduce an auxiliary function, called the actual instruction selector, $\gamma: C \longrightarrow R$ defined in the following way:

$$\gamma(c) = \varkappa^{-1}(c(c(1))).$$

We assume λ to be a function, called the next instruction selector, $\lambda : C \longrightarrow C$ that satisfies the following conditions:

1° $\lambda(c) \mid A' = c \mid A'$ for each $c \in C$

2° $c_1(1) = c_2(1) \implies \lambda(c_1)(1) = \lambda(c_2)(1)$ for all $c_1, c_2 \in C$.

By ρ we shall denote a function $\rho : R \times C \longrightarrow C$, called the realization, to be defined later. Therefore the control π will be also defined later.

DEFINITION. An arbitrary program φ^a is said to be stored in a state c if $c(1) = a$ and $\varkappa^{-1}(c(b)) = \varphi(b)$ for all $b \in Dom(\varphi)$.

By C^{φ^a} we shall denote the set of all states in which the program φ^a is stored.

THEOREM 1. Programs φ^a, ψ^a are consistent iff

$$C^{\varphi^a} \cap C^{\psi^a} \neq \emptyset .$$

Proof. If φ^a, ψ^a are consistent then $\varphi(x) = \psi(x)$ for all $x \in Dom(\varphi) \cap Dom(\psi)$. Therefore we may define a function c_0 in the following way:

$$c_o(x) = \begin{cases} a & \text{for } x = 1 \\ \varkappa(\varphi(x)) & \text{for } x \in Dom(\varphi) \\ \varkappa(\psi(x)) & \text{for } x \in Dom(\psi) - Dom(\varphi). \end{cases}$$

Of course, we have $c_o \in C^{\varphi^a}$, $c_o \in C^{\psi^a}$. Hence $C^{\varphi^a} \cap C^{\psi^a} \neq \emptyset$.

On the contrary, let φ^a, ψ^a be programs satisfying $C^{\varphi^a} \cap C^{\psi^a} \neq \emptyset$. So there exists a state $c \in C^{\varphi^a} \cap C^{\psi^a}$. Since $c \in C^{\varphi^a}$, we have $c(1) = a$ and $\varkappa^{-1}(c(x)) = \varphi(x)$ for all $x \in Dom(\varphi)$. Since $c \in C^{\psi^a}$, we have $c(1) = a$ and $\varkappa^{-1}(c(x)) = \psi(x)$ for all $x \in Dom(\psi)$. Therefore programs φ^a, ψ^a are consistent.

3. SEMANTICS

Let $c \in C$.

DEFINITION. The <u>valuation</u> in the state c is the function $v_c: T \longrightarrow B$ satisfying the following conditions:

1° $v_c(a) = a$ for each $a \in A$

2° $v_c(\alpha(t)) = c(v_c(t))$ for each $t \in T$

3° $v_c(f_i(t,t')) = \bar{f}_i(v_c(t), v_c(t'))$ for all $t, t' \in T$, $i \leq k$,

where $\bar{f}_i$ is a function $\bar{f}_i: B \times B \longrightarrow B$.

Now the realization $\rho: R \times C \longrightarrow C$ will be defined for a given instruction r. Thus we shall write it rather as $\rho_r: C \longrightarrow C$.

DEFINITION. The <u>realization</u> of an instruction r is the function $\rho_r: C \longrightarrow C$ which is the empty function whenever r= STOP, otherwise for an arbitrary $r = t \longrightarrow t'$ we have $\rho_r(c) = c'$ such that

$$c'(a) = \begin{cases} v_c(t) & \text{for } a = v_c(t') \\ c(a) & \text{for } a \neq v_c(t'). \end{cases}$$

Now we are able to define the control π of the stored program computer M.

DEFINITION.

$$\pi(c) = \rho_{\gamma(c)} \circ \lambda(c)$$

Therefore during the action of the control π the following two actions are executed simultaneously:

1° the next instruction selector λ changes the content of the instruction counter l and the address which contains the code of the next instruction will be the new content of l,

2° from the actual memory state the actual instruction selector γ decodes the instruction to be executed by the realization ρ.

By the <u>output function</u> of the computer M we mean the function $f_M: C \longrightarrow C$ defined as follows

$$f_M(c) = \pi^k(c) ,$$

where k is the least number, which depends on c, satisfying the following condition: $\pi^k(c) \notin \mathrm{Dom}(\pi)$.

DEFINITION. By the <u>realization of a program</u> φ^a we mean the function $\rho_{\varphi^a}: C \longrightarrow C$ defined as follows

$$\rho_{\varphi^a} = f_M \mid C^{\varphi^a} .$$

THEOREM 2. If programs φ^a, ψ^a are consistent then

$$\rho_{(\varphi \cup \psi)^a} = \rho_{\varphi^a} \cap \rho_{\psi^a} .$$

Proof. First we shall prove the inclusion $\rho_{\varphi^a} \cap \rho_{\psi^a} \subseteq \rho_{(\varphi \cup \psi)^a}$. Let ρ_{φ^a} and ρ_{ψ^a} be defined at c. They give the same result because they are some iterations of the control π and the number of iterations depends only on the state c. Since we have $c \in C^{\varphi^a}$, $c \in C^{\psi^a}$ and φ^a, ψ^a are consistent, we obtain $c \in C^{(\varphi \cup \psi)^a}$. Since the result of the function $\rho_{(\varphi \cup \psi)^a}$ is again an iteration of the control π at c, by analogy to the previous considerations we obtain

$$\rho_{(\varphi \cup \psi)^a}(c) = \rho_{\varphi^a}(c) = \rho_{\psi^a}(c).$$

On the contrary, let $c \in \mathrm{Dom}(\rho_{(\varphi \cup \psi)^a})$. Thus $c \in C^{\varphi^a}$, $c \in C^{\psi^a}$. On the basis of the previous part of this proof we obtain the equality of our functions.

THEOREM 3. If programs φ^a, ψ^a are consistent then

$$\rho_{(\varphi \cap \psi)^a} = \rho_{\varphi^a} \cup \rho_{\psi^a} .$$

Proof. First we shall prove the inclusion $\rho_{\varphi^a} \cup \rho_{\psi^a} \subseteq \rho_{(\varphi \cap \psi)^a}$.

Let $c \in C^{\varphi^a}$. Therefore $c \in C^{(\varphi \cap \psi)^a}$. On account of the proof of Theorem 2 we obtain

$$\rho_{(\varphi \cap \psi)^a}(c) = \rho_{\varphi^a}(c).$$

Since φ^a, ψ^a are consistent, we may set $c \in C^{\psi^a}$. By analogy we obtain

$$\rho_{(\varphi \cap \psi)^a}(c) = \rho_{\psi^a}(c).$$

On the contrary, let $c \in \mathrm{Dom}(\rho_{(\varphi \cap \psi)^a})$. Since programs φ^a, ψ^a are consistent, we have $c \in C^{\varphi^a}$ or $c \in C^{\psi^a}$. On the basis of the previous part of our proof in these both cases the results of corresponding realizations at c are equal.

COROLLARY 1. If a program φ^a is an extension of a program ψ^a (in the sense that the function φ is an extension of the function ψ), then ρ_{ψ^a} is an extension of ρ_{φ^a}.

Proof. This corollary results from Theorem 2 because the union of two functions is an extension of each of these functions and each realization is an extension of the intersection of realizations of two programs.

COROLLARY 2.

$$\rho_{\varphi^a} = \bigcup \{\rho_{\psi^a} : \quad \psi^a \text{ is an extension of } \varphi^a\}$$

Proof. The corollary follows from Theorem 3 because the intersection of all programs which are extensions of a given program gives us this program.

The above properties (in particular both corollaries) are essential for such program which is "open", i.e. which forms a part of another program. Therefoee, e.g. by Corollary 2, the realization of such program is continued everyway (through realizations of all programs which are extensions of the program).

REFERENCES

[1] PAWLAK, Z. A mathematical model of digital computers. Proc. of 1-st GI Conference on Formal Languages and Automata Theory, pp.16-22. Lecture Notes in Computer Science, Springer-Verlag, Berlin-Heidelberg-New York, 1973.

[2] PAWLAK, Z. Theory of computing systems. MFCS Semester, Stefan Banach International Mathematical Centre, Warsaw, 1974 (unpublished lecture notes).

CLASSIFICATION OF PROGRAMS OF A SPC

Z. Raś
Institute of Mathematics
University of Warsaw

A main problem in a mathematical theory of computing machines is to find a possibly simple mathematical model of a computer which could in a suitable way describe its action. The investigations carried on by various authors , for instance KALMAR , ELGOT , ROBINSON [1,2] based on models with too complicated structures making impossible the consideration of more sophisticated problems , or on too general models in order to formulate fundamental notions connected with a computing machine. The investigations by PAWLAK [3] achieved to a concept of a SPC being a mathematical model of a computing machine sufficiently adequate and rather simple. The notion of a program in SPC to be here introduced is a generalization of that due to VAN BA [4] . Computations in SPC will be taken as a basis for a classification of programs.

In Sec. 1 a model of SPC is presented. A manner of a decomposition of programs is discussed in Sec. 2. Sec. 3 deals with a decomposition of computations. There is also considered a connection between a decomposibility of programs and a decomposibility of computations. A method of a classification of programs is presented in Sec. 4.

1. THE DEFINITION OF SPC

By SPC we shall mean a pair $M=\langle C,\Pi\rangle$ such that $C \subseteq B^A$, where A, B are any sets and Π is an arbitrary partial function , $\Pi : C \longrightarrow C$. The set A is called the set of addresses , the set B - the alphabet , the set C - the memory and the transition function Π - the control of the computer M. We assume that the following conditions hold :

1. $A \subseteq B$

2. $c(1) \in A$ for every $c \in C$, where 1 is a distinguished element $1 \in A$, called the instruction register.

Now we shall make a language $\mathcal{R}$ which will be called the instruction language.

Let $\mathcal{A} = A \cup \{f_1, f_2, \ldots, f_k, (\, ,) \, , : \, , \alpha \, , \rightarrow\}$ be the set of symbols of the language .

By the set of terms we mean the least set T such that :

1. $A \subset T$

2. $\alpha(t) \in T$ for every $t \in T$

3. $f_i(t',t) \in T$ for each $i \leqslant k$ and $t,t' \in T$

By the instruction language we mean the set $\mathcal{R} = \{t \longrightarrow t' : t,t' \in T\}$.

We assume that a certain set $R \subset \mathcal{R}$ is connected with the computer M. We shall call it the instruction list of M.

For a given state $c \in C$ we define the valuation v_c of terms. It is the function $v_c : T \longrightarrow B$ such that :

1. $v_c(a) = a$ for every $a \in A$

2. $v_c(\alpha(t)) = c(v_c(t))$ for every $t \in T$

3. $v_c(f_i(t,t')) = f_i(v_c(t), v_c(t'))$ for each $i \leqslant k$ and $t,t' \in T$, where $f_i : B \times B \longrightarrow B$ for every $i \leqslant k$.

By the realization of the instruction $r = t \longrightarrow t'$ we mean the function $\varrho_r : C \longrightarrow C$ such that

$$[\varrho_r(c)](x) = \begin{cases} v_c(t) & \text{for } x = v_c(t') \\ c(x) & \text{for } x \neq v_c(t') \end{cases}$$

Let $\mathcal{H}$ be a one-to-one function $\mathcal{H} : R \longrightarrow B$. We call it the coding function. Let us denote $\gamma(c) = \mathcal{H}^{-1}(c(c(1)))$. In addition we assume that for the computer M a function $\lambda : C \longrightarrow C$ is defined and we assume too that the function λ satisfies:

1. $\lambda(c)/A - \{1\} = c/A - \{1\}$
2. $(\forall c,c' \in C)[c(1) = c'(1) \Rightarrow (\lambda(c))(1) = (\lambda(c'))(1)]$

The function λ can be called the function changing the instruction counter.

Now we define the control π of the computer M . For every $c \in C$

$$\pi(c) = \varrho_{\gamma(c)} \lambda(c)$$

Therefore we can write the computer M in the following way by using its main primary notions : $M = \langle C, R, \varrho, \mathcal{H}, \lambda, 1 \rangle$.

By a computation of M we understand an arbitrary sequence $p = c_1, c_2, c_3, \ldots$ such that

1. $c_1 \in D_\pi$

2. $c_{i+1} = \begin{cases} \Pi(c_i) & : c_i \in D_\Pi \\ \text{undefined} & : c_i \notin D_\Pi \end{cases}$

The set of all computations of M we denote by C_M .

2. ON SOME PROPERTIES OF PROGRAMS

Let $M = (C, R, \varrho, \mathcal{H}, \lambda, 1)$ be any SPC .

Definition 1. Every finite $U \subset A \times R$ such that U is a function is called a program.

Definition 2. Let $c \in C$ be a state of the memory of a SPC. If $U^c = \{\langle a, \mathcal{H}^{-1}(c(a))\rangle : a \in Dom(c)\} \cap (A \times R)$ is a finite set, then it will be called the program of the state c.

Thus arbitrary, finite set of label instructions with various addresses is called a program. Such a definition of a program is a natural generalization of machine programs. The acceptance of this simple definition is very convenient to further investigations. On the other hand a program in a state c is a maximal set of label instructions connected in a natural way with the state c.

We assume that SPC satisfies the following conditions :

1. $C = B^{[A]}$

2. $(\forall c \in C)[U^c = U^{\Pi(c)}]$

The adjoing of those conditions to be satisfied by SPC will turn out very convenient in Sec. 3. Now, we shall define a binary relation on $A \times R$ which is a kind of a relation of a potential successor . For any $u_1, u_2 \in A \times R$ we adopt

$$u_1 \mathcal{N} u_2 \equiv (\exists c_1, c_2 \in C)(\forall i)[\langle c_i(1), \mathcal{H}^{-1}(c_i^2(1))\rangle = u_i \ \& \ \Pi(c_1) = c_2]$$

The transitive closure of $\mathcal{N}$ in U we denote by D_U . Thus for any $u_1, u_2 \in A \times R$

$$uD_U u' \equiv (\exists \{u_i\}_{i=1}^{n} \subset U)(\forall i \leq n-1)[u_i \mathcal{N} u_{i+1} \ \& \ u_1 = u \ \& \ u_n = u']$$

Definition 3. Let U be an arbitrary program. A set $U' \subset U$ will be said to be a set of generators of U provided that :

$$(\forall u \in U)(\exists u' \in U')[u' D_U u]$$

Now, we shall introduce a notion of a computation of programs, to be denoted by "$\odot$".

Let $\{U_k\}_{k \in K}$ be the family of all programs and $\mathcal{A}_k = \{U : U \subset U_k\}$, $k \in K$. For any programs U_1 , U_2 we assume that :

$U_1 \odot U_2$ is determined iff the following conditions are satisfied:

1. $U_1 \cap U_2 = \emptyset$

2. $(\exists k \in K)[U_1 \in \mathcal{A}_k \,\&\, U_2 \in \mathcal{A}_k]$

3. if $U \subset U_1 \cup U_2$ and U is a cycle then $U \subset U_1$ or $U \subset U_2$

4. there exist a minimal set U_2^o of generators of U_2 such that $U_2^o \subset \{u : (\exists u_1 \in U_1)[u_1 \mathcal{R} u]\}$

If $U_1 \odot U_2$ is determined then $U_1 \odot U_2 \overset{df}{=} U_1 \cup U_2$

The relation $\mathcal{R}$ as considered here is a generalization of a usual relation of a successor, generated by a computation. More intuitively it is a generalization of a step of the action of a machine. The advantage of this relation is its independence of the machine computations and the fact that it is defined on the whole set $A \times R$. This simplifies fundamentally the formulation of further notions and theorems. A similar advantage characterizes also the introducing of sets of programs $\{\mathcal{A}_k\}_{k \in K}$. Moreover, these sets will play an important part by the composition of computations to be considered in Sec. 3.

Definition 4. A program U will be called decomposable if there exists programs U_1, U_2 such that $U = U_1 \odot U_2$.

In the opposite case the program U we call an atom

Theorem 1. Let U have a minimal set of generators whose pover is equal to 1. Then following conditions are equivalent:

1. U is an atom

2. D_U is an equivalence relation on U or $\mathrm{card}(U) = 1$.

Theorem 2. The pair $(\mathcal{A}_k, \odot)$, $k \in K$ is a partial algebra. The least set of generators is equal to the set of all atoms of $\mathcal{A}_k$.

Theorem 3. Every SPC determines uniqualy a class $\{(\mathcal{A}_k, \odot)\}_{k \in K}$ of partial algebras.

Theorem 4. If U is a program such that U is a finite set, then U we can decomposed into atoms.

Definition 5. A program with a minimal set of generators whose number is equel p will be called the program of the type p.

Theorem 5. Let U be an arbitrary program. Then the following conditions are equivalent:

1. The program U can be uniquely decomposed on atoms of the type 1

2. D_U is a connective relation on U

Observe that in theorem 4 the uniqueness of the decomposition is not quaranteed. Moreover atoms do not need to be of type 1.

3. ON SOME PROPERTIES OF COMPUTATIONS.

In Sec. 2 the operation of a composition of programs was introduced It turned out that every program can be decomposed on atoms. Necessary and sufficient conditions for the decomposibility of a program on atoms of type 1 were formulated. In a natural way a question arises whether it is possible to introduce in an analogous manner an operation of a composition of computations in SPC and whether it is possible to find a connection between a decomposition of a computation and a decomposition of a program assigned to this computation in a suitable way . In order to solve the question in what a way to associate a program with a computation we return to the conditions adjoined on the class SPC in Sec. 2.

Consider an arbitrary computation of SPC and two arbitrary their states c_1 , c_2 . The first condition ensures that $U^{c_1} = U^{c_2}$. Thus a program of an arbitrary state of a computation can be interpreted as a program of this computation.

Definition 6. Let $p = \langle c_i : 0 \leq i < m \rangle$ be any computation of M. We say that p is a computation over an algebra $(\mathcal{A}_k, \odot)$ if :

1. $U^{c_0} \in \mathcal{A}_k$
2. $\bigcup_{i=0}^{m-1} (\mathrm{Dom}(c_i) - \mathrm{Dom}(U^{c_0})) \cap \mathrm{Dom}(U_k) = \emptyset$

Example 1. Let M be a SPC such that A is a set of natural numbers, B is a set of integers and $\mathcal{H} : R \longrightarrow B-A$. We assume that $U_k = \{\langle i, \mathcal{H}^{-1}(-i) \rangle : i \in \{4,5,6,10\}\}$. Let us assume in the sequel that $p_1 = \langle c_i : 1 \leq i \leq 3 \rangle$ is a computation defined as follows

	1	1	2	3	4	5	6	7	8	9	10
$c_1 \equiv$	4			2	-4	-5					
$c_2 \equiv$	5			2	-4	-5			1		
$c_3 \equiv$	6			2	-4	-5		2	1		

We observe that the computation p_1 is the computation over $(\mathcal{A}_k, \odot)$.

Now Im going to introduce a notion of a composition of any two computations.

Let us take two arbitrary computations $p_1 = \langle c_i^1 : 1 \leq i \leq n \rangle$, $p_2 = \langle c_i^2 : 1 \leq i < m \rangle$, $(n < \infty , m \leq \infty)$ over an algebra $(\mathcal{A}_k, \odot)$.

We assume that :

$p_1 \odot p_2$ is determined $\stackrel{df}{\equiv}$

1. $U^{c_1^1} \cap U^{c_1^2} = \emptyset$
2. $c_n^1/(\mathrm{Dom}(c_n^1) \cap \mathrm{Dom}(c_1^2)) = c_1^2/(\mathrm{Dom}(c_n^1) \cap \mathrm{Dom}(c_1^2))$
3. $(\mathrm{Dom}(c_n^1) - \mathrm{Dom}(c_1^2)) \cap \bigcup_{i=1}^{m-1} \mathrm{Dom}(c_i^2) = \emptyset$

If $p_1 \odot p_2$ is determined then we put $p_1 \odot p_2 = \langle c_i : 1 \leq i < r \rangle$ where

1. $c_i/\mathrm{Dom}(c^j_{i-(j-1)(n-1)}) = \begin{cases} c_n^1 & : j=1 \ \& \ 1 \leq i \leq n \\ c^2_{i-n+1} & : j=2 \ \& \ i \geq n+1 \end{cases}$
2. $c_i/(\mathrm{Dom}(c_n^1) - \mathrm{Dom}(c_1^2)) = c_n^1/(\mathrm{Dom}(c_n^1) - \mathrm{Dom}(c_1^2))$ for $i \geq n+1$
3. $c_i/(\mathrm{Dom}(c_1^2) - \mathrm{Dom}(c_n^1)) = c_1^2/(\mathrm{Dom}(c_1^2) - \mathrm{Dom}(c_n^1))$ for $1 \leq i \leq n$
4. $\mathrm{Dom}(c_i) = \begin{cases} \mathrm{Dom}(c_i^1) \cup (\mathrm{Dom}(c_1^2) - \mathrm{Dom}(c_n^1)) & : i \leq n \\ \mathrm{Dom}(c^2_{i-n+1}) \cup (\mathrm{Dom}(c_n^1) - \mathrm{Dom}(c_1^2)) & : i > n \end{cases}$

Example 2. Let M be SPC and let p_1 be a computation as considered in Example 1. We assume now that $p_2 = \langle c_i : 4 \leq i \leq 6 \rangle$ is the following computation

	1	1	2	3	4	5	6	7	8	9	10
$c_4 \equiv$	6		4				-6			1	-10
$c_5 \equiv$	10		2				-6			1	-10
$c_6 \equiv$	4		2				-6			1	-10

Clearly p_2 is a computation over an algebra $(\mathcal{A}_k, \odot)$ where $U_k = \{\langle i, \mathcal{K}^{-1}(-i) \rangle : i \in \{4,5,6,10\}\}$.

We observe that $p_1 \odot p_2$ is determined. From here $p_1 \odot p_2 = \langle c_i : 7 \leq i \leq 11 \rangle$ where

	1	1	2	3	4	5	6	7	8	9	10
$c_7 \equiv$	4		4	2	-4	-5	-6			1	-10
$c_8 \equiv$	5		4	2	-4	-5	-6		1	1	-10

	1	1	2	3	4	5	6	7	8	9	10
$c_9 \equiv$	6		4	2	-4	-5	-6	2	1	1	-10
$c_{10} \equiv$	10		2	2	-4	-5	-6	2	1	1	-10
$c_{11} \equiv$	4		2	2	-4	-5	-6	2	1	1	-10

This example shows that the composition of two computations not always is a computation. The second condition adopted additionally for the class SPC in Sec. 2 ensures that the sequence of states obtained as a result of the composition of two computations is either a computation or a beginning of a computation.

Theorem 6. For any computations p_1 , p_2 , p_3 over an algebra $(\mathcal{A}_k, \odot)$

1. $p_1 \odot (p_2 \odot p_3)$ is determined iff $(p_1 \odot p_2) \odot p_3$ is determined

2. if $p_1 \odot (p_2 \odot p_3)$ is determined then $p_1 \odot (p_2 \odot p_3) = (p_1 \odot p_2) \odot p_3$.

Definition 7. A computation p is said to be decomposable if there exist computations p_1 , p_2 such that $p = p_1 \odot p_2$.

In the opposite case we say that p is an atom.

Theorem 7. If U^c is a program then the computation $p = c, c_1, \ldots$ we can decomposed into atoms.

Let $p = c, c_1, c_2, \ldots$ be any computation of SPC. Observe that the statements:

1. the decomposability of a computation p implices the decomposibility of a program U^c .

2. the decomposibility of a program U^c implices the decomposibility of a computation p .

not always are true.

The following question arises: is it possible to indicate a class of computations of a SPC satisfying 1, 2. Before answering this question we shall introduce an auxiliary notion.

For an arbitrary memory state $c \in C$ we shall define the data region of an instruction $r \in R$ at the state c and we shall denote it $D_c(r)$.

In order to this end first we define the date region of a term

$t \in T$ at the state $c \in C$ which we denote $D_c(t)$, in the following way :

1. $D_c(t) = \emptyset$ for every $t \in A$
2. $D_c(\alpha(t)) = D_c(t) \cup v_c(t)$ for every $t \in T$
3. $D_c(f_i(t,t')) = D_c(t) \cup D_c(t')$ for each $i \leq k$ and $t,t' \in T$

Let us given an arbitrary instruction $r = t \longrightarrow t' \in R$. By the data region of the instruction r at the state $c \in C$ we mean

$D_c(r) = D_c(t) \cup D_c(t')$

By the result region of the instruction r at the state $c \in C$ we mean :

$$Re_c(r) = \{v_c(t')\}$$

Now for any computation $p = \langle c_i : 1 \leq i < n \rangle$ let

$$\mathcal{L}_p = \bigcup_{i=1}^{n-1} [D_{c_i}(\mathcal{H}^{-1}(c_i^2(1))) \cup Re_{c_i}(\mathcal{H}^{-1}(c_i^2(1)))]$$

The set $\mathcal{L}_p$ is said to be the active field of the computation p.

Let $p = \langle c_i : 1 \leq i < n \rangle$ be any computation of SPC. Assume that

$p \in C_M^o \equiv (\forall i < n)[c_i = c_i / \mathcal{L}_p]$

Theorem 8. A pair $(C_M^o, \odot)$ is a subalgebra of $(C_M, \odot)$.

For any computations being elements of the set C_M^o the following theorem can be proved.

Theorem 9. Let $p = \langle c_i : 1 \leq i < n \rangle$ be any computation of the set C_M^o satisfying for every $i < n$ the condition :

$Dom(U^{c_i}) \cap D_{c_i}(\mathcal{H}^{-1}(c_i^2(1))) \subset \{c_i(1)\}$

If $U^{c_1} = U_1 \odot U_2$ then there exist states $c^1, c^2 \in C$ such that :

$U_1 = U^{c^1}$, $U_2 = U^{c^2}$ and $p = p_1 \odot p_2$ where c^i is the start state of p_i for $i=1,2$.

Thus we indicated a subclass of a class of computations of a SPC, such the elements satisfy 2. In order to solve the problem connected with 1 with every computation $p = c, c_1, \ldots$ of the machine M we associate a relation $\mathcal{R}_p \subset U^c \times U^c$.

Let $p = \langle c_i : 1 \leq i < n \rangle$ and $u_1 = \langle a_1, r_1 \rangle$, $u_2 = \langle a_2, r_2 \rangle \in$

U^{c_1} . We assume that :

$$u_1 \mathcal{N}_p u_2 \equiv (\exists i<n)\,[c_{i-1}(1) = a_1 \;\&\; c_i(1) = a_2\,] .$$

Theorem 10. Let $p = p_1 \odot p_2 \in C_M^o$ where c , c_1 , c_2 are the start states of p, p_1, p_2 respectively. Let $\mathcal{N}_p/U^c = \mathcal{N}/U^c$. Then $U^c = U^{c_1} \odot U^{c_2}$.

Now , we shall formulate a theorem which is an analogy of Theorem 2 in Sec. 2.

Theorem 11. The set of each indecomposable computations is the least set of generators of $(C_M, \odot)$.

Theorem 12. Every computation in C_M^o we can uniquely presented as a composition of atoms in C_M^o .

Given an arbitrary computation p , it can be decomposable on indecomposable parts. Every indecomposable part will be restricted to its active field. The theorem 12 shows a way of dividing the time of performing a computation into the least in a sence time sections. It shows also which part of the machine memory in these time sections is active.

4. CLASSIFICATION OF PROGRAMS.

We observe now that some computations comput the same things. So itś quite natural to introduce some strong congruence relation in $(C_M^o, \odot)$. Let´s assume that ϱ is a strong congruence relation in $(C_M^o, \odot)$.

We shall define now some set of expresions C_M^ϱ and the partial operation $\odot_\varrho$ on C_M^ϱ .

Let p_1 , p_2 ,..., p_n be arbitrary computations in C_M^o . We assume that :

$$p_1 \odot_\varrho p_2 \odot_\varrho \ldots \odot_\varrho p_n \in C_M^\varrho \equiv (\exists p_i' \in C_M^o)(\forall i \leq n)\,[\,p_i \,\varrho\, p_i' \;\&\; p_1' \odot p_2' \odot \ldots \odot p_n' \in C_M^o\,]$$

Therefore we have obtained the partial algebra $(C_M^\varrho, \odot_\varrho)$. The setof generators of this algebra is equel C_M^o .

There arises a question how to cary on the classification of the elements of the algebra $(C_M^\varrho, \odot_\varrho)$. Of course we should define some 2-argument relation in C_M^ϱ . This relation ought to take into consideration the length of computations and the structure of programs which are associated with computations. However it does not need to take into consideration the memory ocupied by computations because C_M^o is the setof generators of the partial algebra $(C_M^{\varsigma}, \odot_{\varsigma})$. The definition of such a relation is not easy and it would lead us to rather long discusions. I have chosen another way.

Let p , $p' \in C_M^{\varsigma}$. We assume that

$$p \underset{\varsigma}{\subsetneq} p' \overset{df}{\equiv} p = p_1 \odot_{\varsigma} p_2 \odot_{\varsigma} \dots \odot_{\varsigma} p_n \ \& \ (\forall i)\ [p_i \text{ - indecomposable}]$$
$$\& \ p' = p_1' \odot_{\varsigma} p_2' \odot_{\varsigma} \dots \odot_{\varsigma} p_n' \ \& \ (\forall i)\ [p_i \varsigma p_i']$$

Let us note that the relation is reflexive and transitive on C_M^{ς} . Thus $(C_M^{\varsigma}, \underset{\varsigma}{\subsetneq})$ is a quasi ordered set. We observe that this relation takes into consideration only the length of computations. Hence it does not satisfy our requirements. The construction of the set C_M^o from C_M was performed in such a way that the relation does not need to take into consideration the memory ocupied by computations. Now we shall construct the set $B_M^{\varsigma} \subset C_M^{\varsigma}$ such that " $\underset{\varsigma}{\subsetneq}$ " considered on B_M^{ς} does not need to take into consideration the structure of programs which are associated with computations. For that purpose we shall introduce the notion of a characteristics of a computation in C_M^o .

Let $p \in C_M^o$. From theorem 12 it follows that $p = p_1 \odot p_2 \odot \dots \odot p_k$ where $p_i \in C_M^o$ and p_i is an atom for each $i \in \{1,2,3,\dots,k\}$.

Let's assume that $p_i = c_i, c_i^1, c_i^2, \dots$. To every p_i we shall assign a system $(U^{c_i}, \mathcal{N}_{p_i})$ which can be interpreted as a graph. We shall denote by n_i the number of cycles in the graph $(U^{c_i}, \mathcal{N}_{p_i})$.

Consider a sequence $(h_1, h_2, \dots, h_{k+1})$ such that :

1. $h_1 = \operatorname{card}(\bigcup_{\substack{i=1 \\ n_i \neq 0}}^{k} U^{c_i})$

2. $(\forall i)(2 \leqslant i \leqslant k)(h_i \geqslant h_{i+1})$

3. $(h_2, h_3, \dots, h_{k+1})$ is a permutation of the sequence $(n_1, n_2, \dots, n_k)$

The sequence $(h_1^*, h_2^*, \dots, h_s^*)$ such that :

1. $(\forall i \leqslant s)[h_i = h_i^* \neq 0]$

2. $h_{s+1}^* = 0$

is said to be a characteristics of the computation p .

Theorem 13. Every computation $p \in C_M^o$ has exactly one characteristics .

Now let H denote the set of the characteristics of all computations in C_M^o and let " $\leqslant$ " denote the ordering relation on H which is defined as follows :

for any $h_1 = (h_1^1, h_1^2, \ldots, h_1^n)$, $h_2 = (h_2^1, h_2^2, \ldots, h_2^m) \in H$

$h_1 \leq h_2 \equiv$ one of the following conditions is satisfied :

1. $(\exists s)(2 \leq s \leq \min\{m,n\})(\forall i)(2 \leq i < s)[(h_1^i = h_2^i) \ \& \ (h_1^s < h_2^s)]$
2. $(\forall i)(2 \leq i \leq n)(h_1^i = h_2^i) \ \& \ [(n < m) \vee (n = m \ \& \ h_1^1 < h_2^1)]$

It is easy to verify that $(H, \leq)$ is lineary ordered. Now we may construct a set B_M^{ϱ} . Similarly as in the case of the construction of C_M^{ϱ} we shall start on defining a set B_M^o .

Let $p \in C_M^o$ be a computation having a characteristics h . Then

$$p \in B_M^o \overset{df}{\equiv} (\forall p' \in C_M^o)[p \varrho p' \rightarrow h \leq h']$$

where h' is a characteristics of p'.

We define the set B_M^{ϱ} on the basis of B_M^o . Similarly as the set C_M^{ϱ} was defined on the basis of C_M^o .

Theorem 14. $(B_M^{\varrho}, \odot_{\varrho})$ is a subalgebra of $(C_M^{\varrho}, \odot_{\varrho})$.

Theorem 15. For any $p_1 \odot_{\varrho} p_2 \odot_{\varrho} \ldots \odot_{\varrho} p_n \in C_M^{\varrho}$ there exist $p_1' \odot_{\varrho} p_2' \odot_{\varrho} \ldots \odot_{\varrho} p_n' \in B_M^{\varrho}$ such that $(\forall i)[p_i \varrho p_i']$.

Notice that $(B_M^{\varrho}, \subseteq_{\varrho})$ is quasi ordered. The relation $\subseteq_{\varrho}$ restricted to the set B_M^{ϱ} has to depend only on the lengths of computations. Thus it is a relation which compares expressions in a precise way.

The question arises how to compare the programs of SPC .

Let U_1 , U_2 be any programs and C_{M,U_1} , C_{M,U_2} the sets of computations in C_M^o which are associated with these programs in a natural way . We adopt

$U_1 \prec_{\varrho} U_2$ iff the following three conditions are satisfied :

1. $(\forall p_1 \in C_{M,U_1})(\exists p_2 \in C_{M,U_2})[p_1 \varrho p_2]$
2. $(\forall p_2 \in C_{M,U_2})(\exists p_1 \in C_{M,U_1})[p_2 \varrho p_1]$
3. $(\forall p_1 \in C_{M,U_1})(\forall p_2 \in C_{M,U_2})[p_1 \varrho p_2 \rightarrow p_1 \subseteq_{\varrho} p_2]$

The comparison of programs for which C_{M,U_1} , C_{M,U_2} are subsets of B_M^o is precise similarly as comparison of expressions in B_M^{ϱ} .

Literature references

1 Elgot,C.; Robinson,A. Randon-access Stored-program machines:

An Approach to Programming Languages, J. Assoc. Computing machinery , vol. 11 , no 4 , 1954 , 365-399 .

[2] KALMAR, L. _Les calculatrices automatiques comme structures algebriques_ , "previsions , Calculs et realites" , Paris 1965 , 9-22.

[3] PAWLAK, Z. _Maszyny programowane_, Algorytmy , 10 , 1969 , 5-19.

[4] VAN BA , N. _Semiprograms of address machines and their realizations_ , Bull. Acad. Polon. Sci., ser. Sci. Math. Astronom. Phys., 19 1971 , 1109-1115.

THE ALGEBRAIC APPROACH TO THE THEORY OF COMPUTING SYSTEMS

Jerzy Tiuryn
Institute of Mathematics
University of Warsaw

Warsaw, Poland

1. INTRODUCTION.

Investigations of adequate mathematical model of digital computer have lasted for a few years. But when a digital computer was well represented by some suggested model, this model had extremely complicated algebraic structure and it couldn't be studied by modern algebraic methods. On the other hand if investigated model has a simple algebraic structure (e.g. a unary algebra) then lot of notions associated with digital computers had to be excluded from such a model (e.g. programs). The starting-point of this paper is the notion of stored program computer presented by PAWLAK,Z. in [4]. The stored program computers have a very rich algebraic structure and because of difficulties mentioned above to each stored program computer a new kind of object is associated, more useful in algebraic studies; it's called a M-groupoid. Such associations were done very often in mathematics. To investigate properties of some objects we associate a new kind of objects. And we find the properties of our investigated objects from studies of objects associated with them (e.g. associating to first order predicate calculus the Tarski-Lindenbaum algebra (see [6]), to given Boolean algebra - the Stone space (see [6]), to given topological space - the fundamental group (see [7]), to given finite automaton - the input monoid (see [1])).

Such an approach often makes possible simple proofs of complex results. On the other hand it's good to be aware of differences between an associated object and the investigated one (it means how much information about the invastigated object is contained in the associated object). Theory of categories will be useful for it (it will be shown, that the assotiation between stored program computers and M-groupoids is a functor from the category of stored program computers to the category of M-groupoids). It will be shown that stored program computers and M-groupoids are closely related, namely theirs categories are equivalent.

So it's possible to associate the stored program computer with M-groupoid and inversely to associate the given M-groupoid with some stored program computer. Construction described in this paper makes possible to prove some properties of stored program computer, by proving corresponding properties of M-groupoids (thank to this, it has been proved for instance, that any group (up to isomorphism) is an automorphism group of some stored program computer).

The paper is divided into four parts.

In the first part there are introduced the definitions of stored program computer, M-groupoid and the basic notions of theory of categories. The definitions of a homomorphism of stored program computer and M-groupoid are given as well.

In the second part the equivalence of the stored program computers category and M-groupoids category is proven (Representation Theorem). It also contains the corollaries of that theorem.

The natural topology on M-groupoid is defined in the third part of this paper. It can be shown that some notions received up to now have a very simple topological interpretation (e.g. homomorphisms must be continuous in this topology).

The last part contains the notion of fixed program in M-groupoid and the notion of reduced fixed program.

It should be noticed, that M-groupoids can be associated with many different models of computers (e.g. with adress machines defined by PAWLAK, Z. in [5]). One can show that the category of adress machines and the category of M-groupoids are equivalent, too.

2. PRELIMINARY DEFINITIONS.

We begin with basic definitions in theory of categories.

Definition 2.1. A category $\mathcal{O}\!\!\mathcal{l}$ is given by :

1. Class $\mathcal{O}\!\!\mathcal{l}^{\circ}$, which elements are called the objests of the category $\mathcal{O}\!\!\mathcal{l}$.
2. For each pair of objects $(A,B)\in\mathcal{O}\!\!\mathcal{l}^{\circ}\times\mathcal{O}\!\!\mathcal{l}^{\circ}$ there is given a set $\mathrm{Hom}_{\mathcal{O}\!\mathcal{l}}(A,B)$, it is called the set of all morphisms in $\mathcal{O}\!\!\mathcal{l}$ from A to B.
3. For each triple of objects (A,B,C) there is given a function (composit function) $V^{\mathcal{O}\!\mathcal{l}}_{A,B,C}: \mathrm{Hom}_{\mathcal{O}\!\mathcal{l}}(A,B)\times\mathrm{Hom}_{\mathcal{O}\!\mathcal{l}}(B,C)\longrightarrow\mathrm{Hom}_{\mathcal{O}\!\mathcal{l}}(A,C)$.

   If $\alpha\in\mathrm{Hom}_{\mathcal{O}\!\mathcal{l}}(A,B)$, $\beta\in\mathrm{Hom}_{\mathcal{O}\!\mathcal{l}}(B,C)$ then $V^{\mathcal{O}\!\mathcal{l}}_{A,B,C}(\alpha,\beta)$ is called the composition of morphisms α and β and it will be denoted by $\beta\alpha$.

Moreover, the following axioms must be satisfied:

(i) If $(A',B')\neq(A,B)$ then $\mathrm{Hom}_{\mathcal{O}\!\mathcal{l}}(A',B')\cap\mathrm{Hom}_{\mathcal{O}\!\mathcal{l}}(A,B)=\phi$.

(ii) If $\alpha\in\mathrm{Hom}_{\mathcal{O}\!\mathcal{l}}(A,B)$, $\beta\in\mathrm{Hom}_{\mathcal{O}\!\mathcal{l}}(B,C)$, $\gamma\in\mathrm{Hom}_{\mathcal{O}\!\mathcal{l}}(C,D)$ then $\gamma(\beta\alpha)=(\gamma\beta)\alpha$.

(iii) For each object $B\in\mathcal{O}\!\!\mathcal{l}^{\circ}$ there exists a morphism $\iota_B\in\mathrm{Hom}_{\mathcal{O}\!\mathcal{l}}(B,B)$ such that:

a) for each $A \in \mathcal{A}^o$ and $\alpha \in \mathrm{Hom}_{\mathcal{A}}(A,B)$ we have $\iota_B \alpha = \alpha$

b) for each $C \in \mathcal{A}^o$ and $\beta \in \mathrm{Hom}_{\mathcal{A}}(B,C)$ we have $\beta \iota_B = \beta$.

$\alpha \in \mathrm{Hom}_{\mathcal{A}}(A,B)$ will be denoted by $A \xrightarrow{\alpha} B$ or $\alpha : A \longrightarrow B$.

Definition 2.2. Let $\mathcal{A}$, $\mathcal{B}$ be categories. By a functor F from $\mathcal{A}$ to $\mathcal{B}$ we shall understand an arbitrary function, which the morphisms of the category $\mathcal{A}$ maps into the morphisms of the category $\mathcal{B}$ and the objects of $\mathcal{A}$ maps into the objects of $\mathcal{B}$ and which satisfy the following axioms:

1. If $A \in \mathcal{A}^o$ then $F(\iota_A) = \iota_{F(A)}$.
2. If $\alpha \in \mathrm{Hom}_{\mathcal{A}}(A,B)$ then $F(\alpha) \in \mathrm{Hom}_{\mathcal{B}}(F(A),F(B))$.
3. If $\alpha_1 \in \mathrm{Hom}_{\mathcal{A}}(A,B)$, $\alpha_2 \in \mathrm{Hom}_{\mathcal{A}}(B,C)$ then $F(\alpha_2\alpha_1) = F(\alpha_2)F(\alpha_1)$.

If F is a functor from $\mathcal{A}$ to $\mathcal{B}$ then it may be written as $F: \mathcal{A} \longrightarrow \mathcal{B}$.

Definition 2.3. Let $\mathcal{A}$ be a category, then $\alpha \in \mathrm{Hom}_{\mathcal{A}}(A,B)$ is an isomorphism if there exists a morphism $\beta \in \mathrm{Hom}_{\mathcal{A}}(B,A)$ such that:

$$\alpha\beta = \iota_B \quad \text{and} \quad \beta\alpha = \iota_A .$$

Definition 2.4. Categories $\mathcal{A}$ and $\mathcal{B}$ are equivalent if there exist two functors $F: \mathcal{A} \longrightarrow \mathcal{B}$, $G: \mathcal{B} \longrightarrow \mathcal{A}$ and two families of isomorphisms $(\tau_A : A \longrightarrow G\circ F(A))_{A \in \mathcal{A}^o}$ and $(\mu_B : B \longrightarrow F\circ G(B))_{B \in \mathcal{B}^o}$ such that:

(i) for each morphism $\alpha \in \mathrm{Hom}_{\mathcal{A}}(A,A')$ the following diagram

$$\begin{array}{ccc} A & \xrightarrow{\tau_A} & G\circ F(A) \\ \downarrow{\scriptstyle \alpha} & & \downarrow{\scriptstyle G\circ F(\alpha)} \\ A' & \xrightarrow{\tau_{A'}} & G\circ F(A') \end{array}$$

is commutative

(ii) for each morphism $\beta \in \mathrm{Hom}_{\mathcal{B}}(B,B')$ the following diagram

$$\begin{array}{ccc} B & \xrightarrow{\mu_B} & F\circ G(B) \\ \downarrow{\scriptstyle \beta} & & \downarrow{\scriptstyle F\circ G(\beta)} \\ B' & \xrightarrow{\mu_{B'}} & F\circ G(B') \end{array}$$

is commutative.

The examples above notions can be found in excellent book by MAC - LANE,S. [3].

If X and Y are any sets then the set of all partial functions from X to Y will be denoted by $pf(X \longrightarrow Y)$. If $f \in pf(X \longrightarrow Y)$ then Dom(f) denotes the domain of the function f.

Now we shall define a stored program computer after PAWLAK,Z. [4] .

By a stored program computer we mean a pair $M = \langle C_M, \pi_M \rangle$ such that:

- $C_M \subseteq pf(A_M \longrightarrow B_M)$, where A_M and B_M are non-empty sets called respectively: set of adresses and alphabet. The set C_M will be called the memory of M.

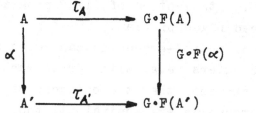

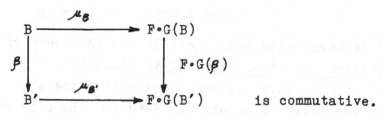

- $\pi_M \in pf(C_M \longrightarrow C_M)$ - control of computer M.
- $A_M \subseteq B_M$.
- For each $c \in C_M$, $c(1_M) \in A_M$, where $1_M \in A_M$ is distinguished element called instruction counter.

With each stored program computer M we'll associate the following notions:

- $F_M = \{f_1,\dots,f_k\}$ the set of function symbols such that $F_M \cap A_M = \emptyset$.
- Symbol $\alpha_M \notin B_M \cup F_M$.
- Now we can define the set of terms T_M as a least set satisfying the following conditions:

  T.1. $B_M \subseteq T_M$

  T.2. If $t \in T_M$ then $\alpha_M(t) \in T_M$

  T.3. If $t_1,t_2 \in T_M$ and $f \in F_M$ then $f(t_1,t_2) \in T_M$.
- By instruction we'll mean each expression of the form: $t_1 \longrightarrow t_2$ where $t_1,t_2 \in T_M$.
- Let's denote by R_M the set of instructions of computer M (this set depends on the computer M and doesn't need to contain all instructions).
- Subsequently, to each function symbol $f \in F_M$ is associated a partial function $\tilde{f}: B_M \times B_M \longrightarrow B_M$.
- Such representation determines a family of partial functions $\left\{V_c^M: T_M \longrightarrow B_M \mid c \in C_M\right\}$ defined in the following way: let $c \in C_M$, then

  V.1. $V_c^M(b) = b$ for each $b \in B_M$

  V.2. If $t \in T_M$ then

$$V_c^M(\alpha_M(t)) = \begin{cases} c(V_c^M(t)), & \text{if } V_c^M(t) \in \mathrm{Dom}(c) \\ \text{undefined, otherwise} \end{cases}$$

  V.3. If $f \in F_M$ and $t_1,t_2 \in T_M$ then

$$V_c^M(f(t_1,t_2)) = \begin{cases} \tilde{f}(V_c^M(t_1),V_c^M(t_2)), & \text{if } (V_c^M(t_1),V_c^M(t_2)) \in \mathrm{Dom}(\tilde{f}) \\ \text{undefined, otherwise} \end{cases}$$

- Each instruction $r = t_1 \longrightarrow t_2 \in R_M$ determines a partial function $\varsigma_r^M \in pf(C_M \longrightarrow C_M)$ (called a realization of instruction r) defined as follows:

$$c \in \mathrm{Dom}(\varsigma_r^M) \quad \text{iff} \quad t_1,t_2 \in \mathrm{Dom}(V_c^M)$$

and the function $\hat{c} \in pf(A_M \longrightarrow B_M)$ defined as follows:

$$\hat{c}(x) = \begin{cases} V_c^M(t_1) \ , & \text{if } x \in V_c^M(t_2) \\ c(x) \ , & \text{otherwise} \end{cases}$$

belongs to the set C_M.

Let $c \in Dom(\varsigma_r^M)$, then we define the function ς_r^M by $\varsigma_r^M(c) = \hat{c}$.

- The instruction $r = t_1 \longrightarrow t_2$ will be called:
  a) <u>jump instruction</u> if for each $c \in C_M$, $V_c^M(t_2) \neq 1_M$
  b) <u>modification instruction</u> if for each $c \in C_M$, $V_c^M(t_2) = c(1_M)$
  c) a modification instruction will be called <u>unconditional modification instruction</u> if for each $c_1, c_2 \in C_M$, $V_{c_1}^M(t_1) = V_{c_2}^M(t_1)$.
- Let's consider partial surjection $\mathcal{H}_M \in pf(B_M \longrightarrow R_M)$, so called <u>decoding function.</u>
- Such a function ($\mathcal{H}_M$) determines the following function γ_M, such that $\gamma_M \in pf(C_M \longrightarrow R_M)$. Let $c \in C_M$, then

$$\gamma_M(c) = \begin{cases} \mathcal{H}_M(c(c(1_M))), & \text{if } c(c(1_M)) \in Dom(\mathcal{H}_M) \\ \text{undefined, otherwise} \end{cases}$$

- We assume also that each computer M posses <u>a counter function</u> i.e. function $\lambda_M : C_M \longrightarrow C_M$ such that:
  λ.1. For each $c \in C_M$, $\lambda_M(c)\Big|_{A_M - \{1_M\}} = c\Big|_{A_M - \{1_M\}}$
  λ.2. For each $c_1, c_2 \in C_M$, if $c_1(1_M) = c_2(1_M)$ then $\lambda_M(c_1)(1_M) = \lambda_M(c_2)(1_M)$.
- The functions defined above determine <u>the control of the computer M</u> in the following way: let $c \in C_M$, then

$$\pi_M(c) = \begin{cases} \lambda_M \circ \varsigma^M_{\gamma_M(c)}(c), & \text{if } c \in Dom(\gamma_M) \cap Dom(\varsigma^M_{\gamma_M(c)}) \\ \text{udefined, otherwise} \end{cases} \qquad (2.1)$$

So, in sequel, thinking about the computer $M = \langle C_M, \pi_M \rangle$ we'll assume that we know all primary notions associated with M i.e. C_M, R_M, $\mathcal{H}_M$, λ_M, 1_M, $\tilde{F}_M = \{ \tilde{f} \mid f \in F_M \}$, then the control of the computer M will be given by (2.1).

Now we define the notion of a homomorphism between two computers.

<u>Definition 2.5.</u> If $M_i = \langle C_{M_i}, \pi_{M_i} \rangle$ for $i = 1,2$ are stored program computers then a partial function $h : C_{M_1} \longrightarrow C_{M_2}$ will be called a <u>homomorphism</u> M_1 into M_2 if the following conditions are satisfied:

H.1. $h \circ \lambda_{M_1} \circ \varsigma^{M_1}_{\gamma_{M_1}(c)} = \lambda_{M_2} \circ \varsigma^{M_1}_{\gamma_{M_2}(h(c))} \circ h$, for each $c \in C_{M_1}$

(here $\circ$ denotes ordinary composition of partial functions and if $c \notin Dom(\gamma_{M_1})$ then $\varsigma^{M_1}_{\gamma_{M_1}(c)}$ can be treated as the totaly undefined function).

H.2. If $c_1, c_2 \in C_{M_1}$ are two memory states such that

$$c_1(l_{M_1}) = c_2(l_{M_1}) \quad \text{and} \quad \gamma_{M_1}(c_1) \doteq \gamma_{M_1}(c_2)$$

(here equality with dot denotes the following property: if one side of an equality is defined then other is defined as well and they are equal)

then:

H.2.a. $c_1 \in \mathrm{Dom}(h)$ iff $c_2 \in \mathrm{Dom}(h)$

H.2.b. Moreover, if $c_1, c_2 \in \mathrm{Dom}(h)$ then

$$h(c_1)(l_{M_2}) = h(c_2)(l_{M_2}) \quad \text{and} \quad \gamma_{M_2}(h(c_1)) \doteq \gamma_{M_2}(h(c_2)).$$

Note that if $c \in C_M$ then $\lambda_M \circ \varrho^M_{\gamma_M(c)}$ denotes activity of the stored program computer M fixed by the state c i.e.

- putting out an instruction $\gamma_M(c)$,
- taking realization of this instruction $\varrho^M_{\gamma_M(c)}$,
- changing contents of instruction counter $\lambda_M \circ \varrho^M_{\gamma_M(c)}$.

So, after adopting the notation $r^M_c \overset{df}{=} \lambda_M \circ \varrho^M_{\gamma_M(c)}$, the condition H.1. can be presented in the form of the following commutative diagram:

$$\begin{array}{ccc} C_{M_1} & \xrightarrow{\;h\;} & C_{M_2} \\ {\scriptstyle r^{M_1}_c}\downarrow & & \downarrow{\scriptstyle r^{M_2}_{h(c)}} \\ C_{M_1} & \xrightarrow{\;h\;} & C_{M_2} \end{array} \qquad (\text{for each } c \in C_{M_1})$$

which seems to be a natural condition postulated for homomorphisms.

By <u>a labeled instruction</u> of the stored program computer M we'll mean a pair $\langle a, r \rangle$ where $a \in A_M$, $r \in R_M$. We say that state $c \in C_M$ <u>is ready to realize a labeled instruction $\langle a, r \rangle$</u> if $c(l_M) = a$ and $\gamma_M(c) = r$.

The H.2.a. condition is natural and H.2.b. condition says that homomorphisms must preserve the following property: "to be ready to realize the same labeled instruction".

It is easy to check the following result.

<u>Proposition 2.1.</u> <u>Stored program computers with homomorphisms form a category.</u>

The category of stored program computers will be denoted by $\mathcal{C}$.

If ϱ is an equivalence relation on the set X and $x \in X$ then by $[x]_\varrho$

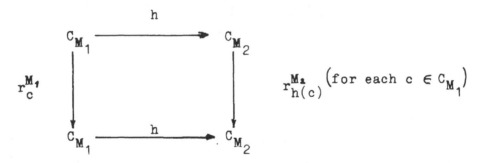

we'll mean an equivalence class of relation ϱ, which contains x (i.e. an abstract element of the quotient set X/ϱ), and by $\overline{[x]}_\varrho$ we'll mean the set of this elements of the set X which are in the relation ϱ with the element x . So we'll always distinguish $[x]_\varrho$ and $\overline{[x]}_\varrho$. Now, we can give a definition of a M-groupoid.

Definition 2.6. By a M-groupoid we mean a triple $G = \langle X, \cdot, \varrho \rangle$ where:

M.1. $\langle X, \cdot \rangle$ is a groupoid with zero i.e. X is a set, $\cdot : X \times X \longrightarrow X$ is a binary operation on X such that there exists an element $0 \in X$ such that $x \cdot 0 = 0 \cdot x = 0$ for all $x \in X$.

M.2. ϱ is an equivalence relation on X satisfying the following conditions:

M.2.a. $(\forall x,y \in X) \left[x \varrho y \Rightarrow (\forall z \in X) \left[x \cdot z = y \cdot z \right] \right]$

M.2.b. $\text{card}\,(\overline{[0]}_\varrho) = 1$.

Definition 2.7. If $G_i = \langle X_i, \cdot, \varrho_i \rangle$ for i = 1,2 are M-groupoids then a function $h : X_1 \longrightarrow X_2$ is called a homomorphism of G_1 into G_2 if:

G.1. h is a homomorphism of groupoids with zero i.e.

1. $(\forall x,y \in X_1) \left[h(x \cdot y) = h(x) \cdot h(y) \right]$
2. $h(0) = 0$

G.2. $(\forall x,y \in X_1) \left[x \varrho_1 y \Rightarrow h(x) \varrho_2 h(y) \right]$.

It is easy to see that the following satement holds.

Proposition 2.2. M-groupoids with homomorphisms form a category.

This category will be denoted by $\mathfrak{M}$.

3. THE REPRESENTATION THEOREM

At first we show, how to each stored program computer one can associate some M-groupoid.

Associate to each stored program computer $M = \langle C_M, \pi_M \rangle$ a symbol 0_M not belonging to C_M. Suppose M is a computer, determine $\mathcal{G}(M) = \langle X, \cdot, \varrho \rangle$ where:

1. $X = C_M \cup \{0_M\}$
2. Operation $\cdot$ we define in the following way, let $x,y \in X$, then:

$$x \cdot y = \begin{cases} \lambda_M(\varrho^M_{\gamma_M(x)}(y)), & \text{if } x \in \text{Dom}(\gamma_M) \text{ and } y \in \text{Dom}(\varrho^M_{\gamma_M(x)}) \\ 0_M, & \text{otherwise} \end{cases}$$

3. Let $\varrho \subseteq X \times X$ be a relation defined as follows:

$$(x,y) \in \varrho \quad \text{iff} \quad (x = 0_M = y) \text{ or } \left[x,y \in C_M,\ x(1_M) = y(1_M) \text{ and } \gamma_M(x) \doteq \gamma_M(y) \right]$$

Notice that:

- $\langle X, \cdot \rangle$ is a groupoid with zero ($0_M \in X$ plays a role of zero).
- ϱ is an equivalence relation on the set X, moreover:

  a) Suppose $(x,y) \in \varrho$, let $z \in X$.

If $x = O_M = y$ then $x \cdot z = O_M = y \cdot z$.
If $x, y \in C_M$ and $x \in Dom(\gamma_M)$ then $y \in Dom(\gamma_M)$ and $\gamma_M(x) = \gamma_M(y)$ hence $\lambda_M \circ \varsigma^M_{\gamma_M(x)} = \lambda_M \circ \varsigma^M_{\gamma_M(y)}$ which implies $x \cdot z = y \cdot z$.
If $x, y \in C_M$ and $x \notin Dom(\gamma_M)$ then $y \notin Dom(\gamma_M)$ so $x \cdot z = O_M = y \cdot z$.
In this way we have shown that ϱ satisfies M.2.a. condition of the definition 2.6.

b) Fact, that ϱ satisfies M.2.b. condition of the definition 2.6. follows immediately from the definition of ϱ.

In this manner we have shown that $\mathcal{G}(M)$ is a M-groupoid.
Suppose $M_i = \langle C_{M_i}, \Pi_{M_i} \rangle$ for $i = 1,2$ are stored program computers and $h : C_{M_1} \longrightarrow C_{M_2}$ is a homomorphism. Let $\mathcal{G}(M_i) = \langle X_i, \cdot, \varrho_i \rangle$ be M-groupoids associated with M_i for $i = 1,2$. Define a mapping $\mathcal{G}(h) : X_1 \longrightarrow X_2$ as follows:

$$\mathcal{G}(h)(x) = \begin{cases} h(x), & \text{if } x \in Dom(h) \\ O_M, & \text{otherwise} \end{cases}$$

It can be shown that $\mathcal{G}(h)$ is a homomorphism of M-groupoids and that:
Proposition 3.1. $\mathcal{G} : \mathfrak{C} \longrightarrow \mathfrak{M}$ is the functor.
It is not easy to define in the natural way the functor from the category $\mathfrak{M}$ to $\mathfrak{C}$.
Now we give such construction.
Associate to each M-groupoid $G = \langle X, \cdot, \varrho \rangle$ some function $\bar{w}_G : X/_\varrho \longrightarrow X$ such that $[\bar{w}_G([x]_\varrho)]_\varrho = [x]_\varrho$ for all $x \in X$ (the function $\bar{w}_G$ chooses from each class of the relation ϱ just one element).
Let $w_G : X \longrightarrow X$ be a function defined as follows:

$$w_G(x) = \bar{w}_G([x]_\varrho) \quad \text{for all } x \in X.$$

Note that $\ker(w_G) = \varrho$.
Moreover associate to each M-groupoid $G = \langle X, \cdot, \varrho \rangle$ the following symbols not belonging to X: $\alpha_G, f_G, a_G, 1_G$.
Let $G = \langle X, \cdot, \varrho \rangle$ be the M-groupoid. Define a stored program computer $\mathcal{M}(G) = \langle C_{\mathcal{M}(G)}, \Pi_{\mathcal{M}(G)} \rangle$ in the following way:

- $A_{\mathcal{M}(G)} = \{a_G, 1_G\}$, $B_{\mathcal{M}(G)} = (X \setminus \{0\}) \cup A_{\mathcal{M}(G)}$.
- To each $x \in X \setminus \{0\}$ associate the function $c_x : A_{\mathcal{M}(G)} \longrightarrow B_{\mathcal{M}(G)}$ described by the following conditions:

$$c_x(a_G) = x, \qquad c_x(1_G) = a_G.$$

  Let $C_{\mathcal{M}(G)} = \{ c_x \mid x \in X \setminus \{0\} \}$.
- Let $F_{\mathcal{M}(G)} = \{f_G\}$ and $\tilde{f}_G : B_{\mathcal{M}(G)} \times B_{\mathcal{M}(G)} \longrightarrow B_{\mathcal{M}(G)}$ be the partial function defined as follows:

$$\tilde{f}_G(b_1, b_2) = \begin{cases} b_1 \cdot b_2, & \text{if } b_1 \cdot b_2 \neq 0 \\ \text{undefined}, & \text{otherwise} \end{cases}$$

- $R_{\mathcal{M}(G)} = \{ f_G(w_G(y), \alpha_G(a_G)) \longrightarrow a_G \mid y \in X - \{0\} \}$.
- Let $\mathcal{H}_{\mathcal{M}(G)} : B_{\mathcal{M}(G)} \longrightarrow R_{\mathcal{M}(G)}$ be the partial function defined as follows:

$$\mathcal{H}_{\mathcal{M}(G)}(b) = \begin{cases} f_G(w_G(b), \alpha_G(a_G)) \longrightarrow a_G, & \text{if } b \in X - \{0\} \\ \text{undefined}, & \text{otherwise} \end{cases}$$

$\mathcal{H}_{\mathcal{M}(G)}$ is obviously the partial surjection.

- Let $\lambda_{\mathcal{M}(G)} = id_{C_{\mathcal{M}(G)}}$.

Then it easy to check that above conditions uniquely describe the stored program computer $\mathcal{M}(G)$.

Suppose $G_i = \langle X_i, \cdot, \rho_i \rangle$ for i = 1,2 are two M-groupoids and $h : X_1 \longrightarrow X_2$ the homomorphism of M-groupoids. We'll define a mapping $\mathcal{M}(h) : C_{\mathcal{M}(G_1)} \longrightarrow C_{\mathcal{M}(G_2)}$ as follows, let $c_x \in C_{\mathcal{M}(G_1)}$, then:

$$\mathcal{M}(h)(c_x) = \begin{cases} c_{h(x)}, & \text{if } h(x) \neq 0 \\ \text{undefined}, & \text{otherwise} \end{cases} \tag{3.1}$$

Further in this paper we'll need the following lemma:

Lemma 3.1. Suppose $G = \langle X, \cdot, \rho \rangle$ is the M-groupoid. Let $y \in X - \{0\}$ and $\mathcal{H}_{\mathcal{M}(G)}(y) = r$, then:

(i) $r = \gamma_{\mathcal{M}(G)}(c_y)$

(ii)
$$\rho_r^{\mathcal{M}(G)}(c_x) = \begin{cases} c_{y \cdot x}, & \text{if } y \cdot x \neq 0 \\ \text{undefined, otherwise} \end{cases}$$

Proof. Equality (i) is obvious because $c_y(c_y(1_G)) = y$.

(ii). Because $(y, w_G(y)) \in \rho$, then $y \cdot x = w_G(y) \cdot x$ for all $x \in X$. Let's taken $c_x \in C_{\mathcal{M}(G)}$, such that $y \cdot x \neq 0$ (then $w_G(y) \cdot x \neq 0$).

Because $r = f_G(w_G(y), \alpha_G(a_G)) \longrightarrow a_G$, then:

1. $V_{c_x}^{\mathcal{M}(G)}(a_G) = a_G$
2. $V_{c_x}^{\mathcal{M}(G)}(f_G(w_G(y), \alpha_G(a_G))) = \tilde{f}_G(w_G(y), x) = w_G(y) \cdot x = y \cdot x.$

Note that if $y \cdot x = 0$ then $V_{c_x}^{\mathcal{M}(G)}(f_G(w_G(y), \alpha_G(a_G)))$ is not defined.

So, if $y \cdot x \neq 0$ then:

$$\left(\varsigma_r^{\mathcal{M}(G)}(c_x)\right)(b) = \begin{cases} y \cdot x, & \text{if } b = a_G \\ c_x(b), & \text{if } b \neq a_G \end{cases}$$

Hence $\varsigma_r^{\mathcal{M}(G)}(c_x) = c_{y \cdot x}$. If, however $y \cdot x = 0$ then $\varsigma_r^{\mathcal{M}(G)}(c_x)$ is not defined which gives (ii). □

By the above lemma it can be proven that if $h : G_1 \longrightarrow G_2$ is a homomorphism of M-groupoids then $\mathcal{M}(h)$ defined by (3.1) is a homomorphism of computers $\mathcal{M}(G_1)$ into $\mathcal{M}(G_2)$.

Showing that $\mathcal{M}$ preserves the composition of homomorphisms and $\mathcal{M}(\iota_G) = \iota_{\mathcal{M}(G)}$ one can obtain the following result:

Proposition 3.2. $\mathcal{M} : \mathfrak{M} \longrightarrow \mathcal{C}$ is the functor.

Now we can present the main result of this paper.

Theorem 3.1. (Representation theorem)

The categories $\mathfrak{M}$ and $\mathcal{C}$ are equivalent.

Proof. In accordance with the definition 2.4 it suffice to define two families of isomorphisms $(\tau_M : M \longrightarrow \mathcal{M} \circ \mathcal{G}(M))_{M \in \mathcal{C}^o}$ and $(\mu_G : G \longrightarrow \mathcal{G} \circ \mathcal{M}(G))_{G \in \mathfrak{M}^o}$ which provides commutability of the appropriate diagrams.

(i) Let $M = \langle C_M, \Pi_M \rangle$ be a stored program computer, let $\mathcal{G}(M) = \langle X, \cdot, \varsigma \rangle$ be a M-groupoid associated with M. Let $\mathcal{M} \circ \mathcal{G}(M) = \langle C_*, \Pi_* \rangle$ be a stored program computer associated with the M-groupoid $\mathcal{G}(M)$.

Let's define a mapping $\tau_M : C_M \longrightarrow C_*$ defined as follows:

$$\tau_M(x) = c_x \quad \text{for all } x \in C_M.$$

We'll show that τ_M is an isomorphism between the computers M and $\mathcal{M} \circ \mathcal{G}(M)$.

Notice that for all $x, y \in C_M$ we have:

$$y \in \mathrm{Dom}(\varsigma^M_{\gamma_M(x)}) \quad \text{iff} \quad c_y \in \mathrm{Dom}(\varsigma^*_{\gamma_*(c_x)}) \tag{3.2}$$

Indeed, $y \in \mathrm{Dom}(\varsigma^M_{\gamma_M(x)})$ iff $x \cdot y \neq 0$ iff $c_y \in \mathrm{Dom}(\varsigma^*_{\gamma_*(c_x)})$.

Let $x \in C_M$ and $y \in \mathrm{Dom}(\varsigma^M_{\gamma_M(x)})$ then by lemma 3.1 we obtain

$$\tau_M \circ \lambda_M \circ \varsigma^M_{\gamma_M(x)}(y) = \tau_M(x \cdot y) = c_{x \cdot y} = \varsigma^*_{\gamma_*(c_x)}(c_y) =$$

$$= \lambda_* \circ \varsigma^*_{\gamma_*(\tau_M(x))} \circ \tau_M(y).$$

So from (3.2) and above equalities we have

$$\tau_M \circ \lambda_M \circ \varrho^M_{\gamma_M(x)} = \lambda_* \circ \varrho^*_{\gamma_*(\tau_M(x))} \circ \tau_M, \text{ for all } x \in C_M \qquad (3.3)$$

Because τ_M is the total function, then to show that τ_M is the homomorphism it is sufficient to show H.2.b of the definition 2.5.
To do it, we show that for each $x_1, x_2 \in C_M$ the following statement holds:

$$\left[x_1(l_M) = x_2(l_M),\ \gamma_M(x_1) \doteq \gamma_M(x_2)\right] \quad \text{iff}$$

$$\left[c_{x_1}(l_*) = c_{x_2}(l_*),\quad \gamma_*(c_{x_1}) \doteq \gamma_*(c_{x_2})\right] \qquad (3.4)$$

Because $c_{x_i}(l_*) = a_*$ and $\gamma_*(c_{x_i}) = f_*(w_*(x_i), \alpha_*(a_*)) \longrightarrow a_*$, for $i = 1,2$ so $c_{x_1}(l_*) = c_{x_2}(l_*)$ and

$\gamma_*(c_{x_1}) \doteq \gamma_*(c_{x_2})$ iff $w_*(x_1) = w_*(x_2)$ iff $(x_1,x_2) \in \varrho$ iff $x_1(l_M) = x_2(l_M)$ and $\gamma_M(x_1) \doteq \gamma_M(x_2)$.

Then, by (3.3), (3.4) and the definition of τ_M we have that τ_M is the homomorphism.
τ_M is bijection and we can reformulate (3.3) in the following form

$$\lambda_M \circ \varrho^M_{\gamma_M(\tau_M^{-1}(c_x))} \circ \tau_M^{-1} = \tau_M^{-1} \circ \lambda_* \circ \varrho^*_{\gamma_*(c_x)}, \text{ for all } c_x \in C_*$$

Moreover from (3.4) we obtain that τ_M^{-1} fulfil the condition M.2.b of the definition 2.5.
So we obtain that $\tau_M : M \longrightarrow \mathcal{M}\cdot\mathcal{G}(M)$ is the isomorphism for each $M \in \mathcal{C}^{\circ}$.

Suppose $h : M_1 \longrightarrow M_2$ is a homomorphism of computers. It is easy to see that the mapping $\mathcal{M}\cdot\mathcal{G}(h) : \mathcal{M}\cdot\mathcal{G}(M_1) \longrightarrow \mathcal{M}\cdot\mathcal{G}(M_2)$ is the homomorphism and $\mathcal{M}\cdot\mathcal{G}(h)$ is described by the following formula:

$$\mathcal{M}\cdot\mathcal{G}(h)(c_x) = \begin{cases} c_{h(x)}, & \text{if } x \in Dom(h) \\ \text{undefined, otherwise} \end{cases}$$

So the following diagram

$$\begin{array}{ccc} M_1 & \xrightarrow{\ M_1\ } & \mathcal{M}\circ\mathcal{G}(M_1) \\ {\scriptstyle h}\big\downarrow & & \big\downarrow{\scriptstyle \mathcal{M}\circ\mathcal{G}(h)} \\ M_2 & \xrightarrow{\ M_2\ } & \mathcal{M}\circ\mathcal{G}(M_2) \end{array}$$

is commutative.
(ii) Suppose $G = \langle X, \cdot, \varrho \rangle$ is a M-groupoid and $\mathcal{M}(G) = M = \langle C, \Pi \rangle$ the stored program computer associated with G. Let $\mathcal{G}\circ\mathcal{M}(G) = \langle X_*, \cdot, \varrho_* \rangle$ be the M-groupoid associated with $\mathcal{M}(G)$.
From the definitions of the functors $\mathcal{M}$ and $\mathcal{G}$ we have:

1) $X_* = C \cup \{0_M\} = \{c_x \mid x \in X \setminus \{0\}\} \cup \{0_M\}$.

2) Let's denote 0_M as c_0, then

$$c_x \cdot c_y = \begin{cases} \lambda_M \cdot \varrho^M_{\gamma_M(c_x)}(c_y) & \text{if} \quad c_y \in \mathrm{Dom}(\varrho^M_{\gamma_M(c_x)}) \\ c_0 \quad , \text{otherwise} & \end{cases}$$

From (ii) of the lemma 3.1 we have that $c_x \cdot c_y = c_{x \cdot y}$.

3) $(c_x, c_y) \in \varrho_*$ iff $\left[c_x(1_G) = c_y(1_G) \text{ and } \gamma_M(c_x) = \gamma_M(c_y)\right]$
but the last condition is equivalent to the following $(x,y) \in \varrho$ (c.f.proof of (3.4)).

Let $\mu_G : X \longrightarrow X_*$ be a function defined as follows:

$$\mu_G(x) = c_x \quad \text{for all } x \in X.$$

Then from 1), 2), 3) we have that μ_G is the isomorphism
$\mu_G : G \longrightarrow \mathcal{G} \cdot \mathcal{M}(G)$.

Moreover, if $h : G_1 \longrightarrow G_2$ is a homomorpism of M-groupoids then immediately by the definition of functors $\mathcal{M}$ and $\mathcal{G}$ we have that:

$$\mathcal{G} \cdot \mathcal{M}(h)(c_x) = c_{h(x)} \ , \quad \text{for all } c_x \in X_{1*} \ .$$

So, the following diagram is commutatuve.

$$\begin{array}{ccc} G_1 & \xrightarrow{\ \mu_{G_1}\ } & \mathcal{G} \cdot \mathcal{M}(G_1) \\ h \downarrow & & \downarrow \mathcal{G} \cdot \mathcal{M}(h) \\ G_2 & \xrightarrow[\ \mu_{G_2}\ ]{} & \mathcal{G} \cdot \mathcal{M}(G_2) \end{array}$$

□

Corollary 3.1. (Normal form theorem)
Each stored program computer M is isomorphic to some stored program comuter M_* , and M_* has the following form:

(i) card $(A_{M_*}) = 2$;

(ii) All memory states are total functions:

(iii) card $(F_{M_*}) = 1$;

(iv) R_{M_*} doesn't contain the jump instructions but it contains only modification instructions;

(v) $\lambda_M = id_{C_*}$;

In [8] has been shown the following result.

Theorem 3.2. Each group (up to isomorphism) is an automorphism group of some groupoid.

By this theorem and the representation theorem we obtain the following result.

Corollary 3.2. Each group (up to isomorphism) is an automorphism group of some stored program computer.

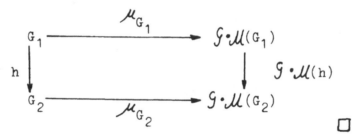

Proof. Let H be a group. By the theorem 3.2 we have that there exists a groupoid $\bar{G} = \langle X, \cdot \rangle$ such thet $Aut(\bar{G}) \cong H$. The groupoid $\bar{G}$ can be treated as the M-groupoid $G = \langle X, \cdot, \Delta_X$ where $\Delta_X = \{(x,x) \mid x \in X\}$, then $Aut(\bar{G}) = Aut(G)$.

Let $M = \mathcal{M}(G)$. Then $Aut(M) \cong Aut(G)$ because the functor $\mathcal{M}$ determines the equivalence between the categories $\mathfrak{M}$ and $\mathcal{C}$ hence (c.f. [3])

1. $f \in Aut(G)$ iff $\mathcal{M}(f) \in Aut(M)$
   (" $\Rightarrow$ " because $\mathcal{M}$ is functor, " $\Leftarrow$ " because $\mathcal{M}$ is full and faightful functor).
2. $\mathcal{M} : Hom_{\mathfrak{M}}(G,G) \longrightarrow Hom_{\mathcal{C}}(M,M)$ is bijective.
3. $\mathcal{M}(h_1 \circ h_2) = \mathcal{M}(h_1) \cdot \mathcal{M}(h_2)$ for all $h_1, h_2 \in Hom_{\mathfrak{M}}(G,G)$.

So $\mathcal{M}$ determines the isomorphism $Aut(M) \cong Aut(G)$. □

4. NATURAL TOPOLOGY ON M-GROUPOIDS.

Let $G = \langle X, \cdot, \varrho \rangle$ be a M-groupoid. Let us consider a family of sets of the form $\mathcal{B} = \{ \overline{[x]}_\varrho \mid x \in X \}$.

Because ϱ is the equivalence relation the family $\mathcal{B}$ has the following properties:

1) $(\forall U_1, U_2 \in \mathcal{B})(\forall x \in U_1 \cap U_2)(\exists U \in \mathcal{B}) \quad [x \in U \subseteq U_1 \cap U_2]$

2) $(\forall x \in X)(\exists U \in \mathcal{B}) \ [x \in U]$.

Let $\mathcal{D}_\varrho$ be the topology generated by the base $\mathcal{B}$ (c.f. [2] th. 1.2.1). The topology $\mathcal{D}_\varrho$ is said to be natural topology on the M-groupoid G. So, a subset $U \subseteq X$ is open (in $\mathcal{D}_\varrho$) iff U is a union of some equivalence classes of the relation ϱ .

The following theorems can be proven.

Theorem 4.1. Let $G = \langle X, \cdot, \varrho \rangle$ be a M-groupoid and $\mathcal{D}_\varrho$ the natural topology on G. Then the following conditions hold:

(i) $F \subseteq X$ is closed iff it is open;

(ii) Let $x \in X$, then the one element family $\mathcal{B}(x) = \{ \overline{[x]}_\varrho \}$ is a base of the space $(X, \mathcal{D}_\varrho)$ at the point x;

(iii) Suppose $A \subseteq X$, then

$$Cl(A) = \bigcup_{x \in A} \overline{[x]}_\varrho$$

where Cl(A) denotes the closure of the set A;

$$Int(A) = \{ x \in X \mid \overline{[x]}_\varrho \subseteq A \}$$

where Int(A) denotes the interior of the set A;

(iv) The space $(X, \mathcal{D}_\varrho)$ is T_0- space iff $\varrho = \Delta_X$. If $\varrho = \Delta_X$ then $(X, \mathcal{D}_\varrho)$ is the discrete space;

(v) If $G_1 = \langle X, \cdot, \varrho_1 \rangle$ is a M-groupoid, then $\varrho_1 \subseteq \varrho$ iff $\mathcal{D}_\varrho \subseteq \mathcal{D}_{\varrho_1}$

Theorem 4.2. Suppose we are given M-groupoids $G_i = \langle X_i, \cdot, \varrho_i \rangle$ for

$i = 1,2$ and a mapping $h : X_1 \longrightarrow X_2$, the following conditions are equivalent:

(i) h is a homomorphism of M-groupoids;

(ii) h is continuous (in the natural topologies) homomorphism of the groupoids $\langle X_i, \cdot \rangle$ $(i = 1,2)$ preserving zero.

Definition 4.1. Let $G = \langle X, \cdot, \varrho \rangle$ be a M-groupoid.

(i) By a right (a left) translation we mean a mapping $\mu_a : X \longrightarrow X$, $a \in X$ ($\tau_a : X \longrightarrow X$, $a \in X$) defined by $\mu_a(x) = x \cdot a$ ($\tau_a(x) = a \cdot x$) for $x \in X$.

(ii) G is to be called a rightside (a leftside) continuous M-groupoid if all right (left) translations are continuous (in the topology $\mathcal{D}_\varrho$).

(iii) G is to be called a topological M-groupoid if G is rightside as well as leftside continuous.

Proposition 4.1. Each M-groupoid is rigtside continuous.

Theorem 4.3. Let $G = \langle X, \cdot, \varrho \rangle$ be a M-groupoid. The following conditions are equivalent:

(i) G is topological ;

(ii) G is leftside continuous ;

(iii) ϱ is the congruence on the groupoid $\langle X, \cdot \rangle$;

(iv) ϱ is the left congruence on the groupoid $\langle X, \cdot \rangle$;

(v) $\cdot : X \times X \longrightarrow X$ is continuous function (on the set $X \times X$ is the Tychonoff topology).

Definition 4.2. Let $M = \langle C, \Pi \rangle$ be a stored program computer. Each partial function $f \in pf(C \longrightarrow C)$ can be extended to the function $f^* : C \cup \{0_M\} \longrightarrow C \cup \{0_M\}$ in the following way:

$$f^*(c) = \begin{cases} f(c), & \text{if } c \in Dom(f) \\ 0_M, & \text{otherwise} \end{cases}$$

We say that f is continuous if f^* is continuous function in the natural topology on $\mathcal{G}(M)$.

The following result can be proven.

Theorem 4.4. Let $M = \langle C, \Pi \rangle$ be a stored program computer. If R_M doesn't contain the jump instructions and each modification instruction contained in R_M is the unconditional modification instruction ϱ_r^M is continuous for all $r \in R_M$.

Remark: By representation theorem the jump instructions can be eliminated. Let us observe, however, that all instructions of the computer $\mathcal{M}(G)$ are modification instructions and they don't have to be the unconditional instructions.

5. FIXED PROGRAMS IN M-GROUPOIDS.

From the definition of the functor $\mathcal{S}$ it follows that if $G = \langle X, \cdot, \varrho \rangle$ is a M-groupoid then $[x]_\varrho$ one can to treat as a labeled instruction and $\overline{[x]}_\varrho$ as a set of states, which actually induce an application of the instruction $[x]_\varrho$.

The instruction $[0]_\varrho$ will play the role of the halt instruction.

By the realization of an instruction $[x]_\varrho$ we'll mean the left translation induced by x (let us observe that the realization of the instruction is well defined by M.2.a. of the definition 2.6.).

For $x \in X$, by a computation begining with x we'll mean the sequence $x_o, x_1, \ldots, x_n, \ldots$ of the elements of X such that:

1) $x_o = x$;
2) $x_{i+1} = x_i$ for $i = 0,1,2,\ldots$

The computation is said to be finite if all but finite number of elements of sequence are equal to zero.

Let $Y \subseteq X$, let's define a sequence of sets:

$$Y_o = Y, \quad Y_{n+1} = \{ y^2 \mid y \in Y_n \} \quad \text{for } n = 0,1,2,\ldots$$

Let

$$Y^* = \bigcup_{n=1}^{\infty} Y_n .$$

Now we can define the notion of a fixed program in given M-groupoid.

Definition 5.1. Let $G = \langle X, \cdot, \varrho \rangle$ be a M-groupoid. By a fixed program in G we mean the triple

$$P = \langle Y_p, \{ [x_o]_\varrho, \ldots, [x_n]_\varrho \}, [x_o]_\varrho \rangle$$

such that:

1) $x_i \in X$ for $i = 0,1,2,\ldots,n$
2) $Y_p \subseteq \overline{[x_o]}_\varrho$
3) $Y_P^* \subseteq \bigcup_{i=0}^{n} \overline{[x_i]}_\varrho \overset{df}{=} \overline{P}$.

The set Y_P is to be called the set of data of a program P. Intuitively, by data of a program P we'll mean such states x in which the program is stored and the whole information which it has to process.

The set $\{ [x_o]_\varrho, \ldots, [x_n]_\varrho \}$ will be called the set of labeled instructions of the program P, and $[x_o]_\varrho$ the begining instruction.

Let us suppose $P = \langle Y_p, \{ [x_o]_\varrho, \ldots, [x_n]_\varrho \}, [x_o]_\varrho \rangle$ is a program in the M-groupoid $G = \langle X, \cdot, \varrho \rangle$ let $y_1 \in Y_P$. We present a schema of the run of the program P with data y_1.

1. In the first step to the state y_1, the labeled instruction $[x_o]_\varrho$ is applied (notice $y_1 \in \overline{[x_o]}_\varrho$) .

2. Suppose, in the i-th step (i > 0) to the state $y_i \in \overline{P}$ the labeled instruction $[x_{j_i}]_\varrho$ $(0 \leq j_i \leq n)$ is applied and $y_i \in [x_{j_i}]_\varrho$.
As a result we obtain the state $\tau_{x_{j_i}}(y_i) = x_{j_i} \cdot y_i$ but $y_i \in \overline{[x_{j_i}]_\varrho}$ hence $x_{j_i} \cdot y_i = y_i^2$.
So, from the state y_i the M-groupoid G "goes" to the state $y_{i+1} = y_i^2$.
By 3) of the definition 5.1. $y_{i+1} \in \overline{P}$.
There are possible two following cases:
a) $y_{i+1} = 0$, then we say that the run of the program P with data y_1 is finished with result y_i.
b) $y_{i+1} \neq 0$, then to the state y_{i+1} the labeled instruction $[y_{i+1}]_\varrho$ is applied (such an istruction exists in the set of instruction of the program P because $y_{i+1} \in \overline{P}$). Obviously $y_{i+1} \in \overline{[y_{i+1}]_\varrho}$ and we return to 2.

It may occure, that program P has a minimal set of instructions in such sence that for each instruction r of the program P there exists a data $y \in Y_P$ such that the instruction r during the run of the program P is executed. Such a program will be called a reduced program.
It leads to the following definition.

Definition 5.2. Let P be a fixed program in a M-groupoid G. P is said to be a reduced program if

$$\overline{P} \subseteq Cl(Y_P^*)$$

Remark By 3) of definition 5.1. we obtain $Cl(Y_P^*) \subseteq \overline{P}$. So the fixed program P in G is reduced iff

$$\overline{P} = Cl(Y_P^*)$$

REFERENCES

[1] ARBIB, M.A. Theories of Abstract Automata, Englewood Cliffs, N.J., Prentice-Hall, 1969.

[2] ENGELKING,R. Outline of General Topology, North-Holland Publ. Comp., Amsterdam, 1968.

[3] MAC-LANE,S. Categories for the Working Mathematician, Springer-Verlag 1971.

[4] PAWLAK,Z. A Mathematical Model of Digital Computers, in Proc. Conf. on Theory of Autom. and Form. Lang., Bonn, 1973, Springer-Verlag, 16-22.

[5] PAWLAK,Z. On the Notion of a Computer, Logic, Methodology and Philosophy of Science III, Amsterdam, 1967, 255-267.

[6] RASIOWA,H.; SIKORSKI,R. The Mathematics of Methamathematics, P.A.N. Monogr. Matematyczne, P.W.N. Warszawa, 1963.

[7] SPANIER,E.H. Algebraic Topology, Mc Graw-Hill, New York,1966.

[8] TIURYN,J. Groupoids with given Automorphism Group, Bull. Acad. Polon. Sci. Ser. Sci. Math. Astronom. Phys., to appear.

CONTINUOUS SIMPLE Z-MACHINES, Z-COMPUTABLE FUNCTIONS AND SETS OF FUNCTIONS OF n REAL VARIABLES

W. Żakowski
Institute of Mathematics, Technical University,
00-661 Warsaw, Poland

1. INTRODUCTION

The main objective of the paper is a study of continuous machines introduced by B. Konikowska (the example of which are analog computers). The presented approach, however, could be also considered from the point of view of computable function of a real variable (introduced by S. Mazur) offering a new notion of computability, much closer to the existing computer praxis as the previous one. The idea of computable function by continuous machines is closely related to the theory of differential equations, however, not very much has been gained in the field, so only some remarks concerning the matter are available in the paper.

2. BASIC NOTIONS AND DEFINITIONS

Let $\mathcal{R}$ be the set of all real numbers, and $\mathcal{R}^+$ - the set of all non-negative real numbers. By $\mathcal{N}_0$ we denote the set of all non-negative integers, by $\mathcal{N}$ - the set $\mathcal{N}_0 - \{0\}$, and by $\emptyset$ - the empty set.

Let n denote an arbitrary, but fixed, positive integer. By (t,x) we denote the point $(t,x_2,\dots,x_n) \in \mathcal{R}^n$ if $n \geqslant 2$, and the point $(t) \in \mathcal{R}$ if $n=1$. We define the subset Ω_n of $\mathcal{R}^n$ as follows: $\Omega_n = \{(t,x):\ t \in \mathcal{R}^+ \wedge\ x \in \mathcal{R}^{n-1}\}$ if $n \geqslant 2$, and $\Omega_1 = \mathcal{R}^+$.

If A is an operator (i.e. a mapping), then its domain is denoted by DA, and its range by RA. For any $Q \subseteq DA$, the restriction of

A to Q is denoted by $A|Q$.

Let X denote an arbitrary, but fixed, non-empty set, and Z – an arbitrary, non-empty subset of Ω_n. By $\mathcal{F}_Z^{(n)}$ we denote the set of all mappings $f\colon Z \to X$; we put $\mathcal{F}^{(n)} = \mathcal{F}_{\Omega_n}^{(n)}$. By $\mathcal{A}_Z^{(n)}$ we denote the set of all operators A such that $\emptyset \neq DA \subseteq \mathcal{F}_Z^{(n)}$ and $RA \subseteq \mathcal{F}^{(n)}$.

If $a \in \mathcal{R}^+$, then by Z_a we denote the set of all $(t,x) \in \Omega_n$ such that $(t-a,x) \in Z$.

By the shift operator we mean the operator $P^{(n)}$ which assigns to every mapping $f\colon Z_a \to X$, where $a \in \mathcal{R}^+$, the mapping $f^*\colon Z \to X$ such that $f^*(t,x) = f(t+a,x)$ for $(t,x) \in Z$. If $f \in \mathcal{F}^{(n)}$, then we put $f_{Z_a} = (f|Z_a)^*$, and, in particular, $f_a = f_{Z_a}$ for $Z = \Omega_n$.

DEFINITION 1. An operator $M \in \mathcal{A}_Z^{(n)}$ is called a n-dimensional simple continuous Z-machine iff

$$\forall_{f \in DM} \left[(Mf)|Z = f \right] \tag{1}$$

and

$$\forall_{f \in RM} \ \forall_{a \in \mathcal{R}^+} \ (f_a \in RM) \tag{2}$$

The set of all n-dimensional simple continuous Z-machines is denoted by $\mathfrak{M}_Z^{(n)}$. If $M \in \mathfrak{M}_Z^{(n)}$, then the elements of the set DM are called initial functions of the machine M, and the elements of the set RM – the computations of this machine.

The notion of a n-dimensional simple continuous Z-machine is a generalization of the notion of a simple continuous machine with the memory length τ, introduced and examined by B. Konikowska [1-3], in case of n=1 and $Z = \langle 0;\tau)$ or $Z = \{0\}$. Consequently, some of the author's results are generalization of the corresponding results in [1-3] and are similar to the author's results in [4-6].

3. THE BASIC PROPERTIES OF n-DIMENSIONAL SIMPLE CONTINUOUS Z-MACHINES

THEOREM 1. Any n-dimensional simple continuous Z-machine is a bijection.

P r o o f . If $f_1, f_2 \in DM$ and $Mf_1 = Mf_2$, then by (1) we have $f_1 = (Mf_1)|Z = (Mf_2)|Z = f_2$.

THEOREM 2. If $M \in \mathfrak{M}_Z^{(n)}$, then $f_{Z_a} \in DM$ and $Mf_{Z_a} = f_a$ for any $f \in RM$, $a \in \mathcal{R}^+$.

P r o o f. By (2) we have $f_a \in RM$ for any $f \in RM$, $a \in \mathcal{R}^+$. From Theorem 1 follows that there exists exactly one function $g \in DM$ such that $Mg = f_a$. Hence we have

$$g = (Mg)|Z = f_a|Z = (f|Z_a)^* = f_{Z_a}$$

by (1). Consequently, $f_{Z_a} \in DM$ and $Mf_{Z_a} = f_a$ for any $f \in RM$, $a \in \mathcal{R}^+$.

THEOREM 3. If $M \in \mathfrak{M}_Z^{(n)}$, $f, h \in RM$, $a, b \in \mathcal{R}^+$ and $f_{Z_a} = h_{Z_b}$, then $f_a = h_b$.

P r o o f. By Theorem 2 we have $f_a = Mf_{Z_a} = Mh_{Z_b} = h_b$.

THEOREM 4. If $M \in \mathfrak{M}_Z^{(n)}$ and $\sup\{t : (t,x) \in Z\} = \omega < \infty$ then $f_t = (Mf_{Z_{t-\omega}})_\omega$ for any $f \in RM$, $t \geqslant \omega$.

P r o o f. Let $a = t - \omega$. By Theorem 2 we have

$$(Mf_{Z_{t-\omega}})_\omega = (f_{t-\omega})_\omega = f_t.$$

DEFINITION 2. A set $G \subseteq \Omega_n$ is said to be a streak-set iff there exists a positive real number τ such that

$$G = \{(t,x) : 0 \leqslant t < \tau \wedge x \in \mathcal{R}^{n-1}\}$$

if $n \geqslant 2$, and $G = \langle 0; \tau)$ if $n = 1$.

The number τ will be called the width of the streak-set G.

COROLLARY 1. If $M \in \mathfrak{M}_Z^{(n)}$ and Z is a streak-set with the width τ then by Theorem 4 for any $t \geqslant \tau$, and any $x \in \mathcal{R}^{n-1}$ if $n \geqslant 2$, $f(t,x)$ is uniquely determined by the values of f in the set $Z_{t-\tau}$, i.e. in the set $\{(s,x): t-\tau \leqslant s < t \wedge x \in \mathcal{R}^{n-1}\}$ if $n \geqslant 2$, and $\langle t-\tau; t)$ if $n = 1$. Consequently, in this case, the number τ will be called the memory length of M.

THEOREM 5. If

1° X is a normed space with the norm $|\cdot|$

2° Z is a streak-set with the width τ

3° $M \in \mathfrak{M}_Z^{(n)}$

4° $h \in \mathcal{F}^{(n)}$, $f = h+g \in RM$

5° $\underset{\varepsilon>0}{\forall}\ \underset{T>0}{\exists}\ \underset{(t,x)\in\Omega_n}{\forall} [t \geqslant T \Rightarrow |h(t,x)| < \varepsilon]$

6° $\underset{(t,x)\in\Omega_n}{\forall}\ \underset{k\in\mathcal{N}}{\forall} [g(t,x) = g(t+k\cdot\tau, x)]$

7° $[(\underset{m\in\mathcal{N}}{\forall} f_m \in DM) \wedge (\underset{f_0\in\mathcal{F}_Z^{(n)}}{\exists}\ \underset{(t,x)\in Z}{\forall} \lim_{m\to\infty} f_m(t,x) = f_0(t,x))] \Rightarrow f_0 \in DM$

then $(g|Z) \in DM$.

P r o o f. By 1°, 4° and 5° we have

$$\underset{m\in\mathcal{N}}{\forall}\ \underset{k_m\in\mathcal{N}}{\exists}\ \underset{(t,x)\in\Omega_n}{\forall} [t \geqslant k_m\cdot\tau \Rightarrow |f(t,x) - g(t,x)| < \tfrac{1}{m}].$$

Hence, by 2°, 3° and 6°,

$$\underset{m\in\mathcal{N}}{\forall}\ \underset{k_m\in\mathcal{N}}{\exists}\ \underset{(t,x)\in Z}{\forall} [|f_{Z_{k_m\cdot\tau}}(t,x) - g(t,x)| < \tfrac{1}{m}]$$

By Theorem 2, $f_{Z_{k_m\cdot\tau}} \in DM$ for every $m \in \mathcal{N}$. Consequently, $(g|Z) \in DM$ by 7°.

COROLLARY 2. If the assumptions $1^\circ - 6^\circ$ of Theorem 5 are satisfied, then

$$\underset{\varepsilon>0}{\forall}\ \underset{f_\varepsilon\in DM}{\exists}\ \underset{(t,x)\in Z}{\forall} [|f_\varepsilon(t,x) - g(t,x)| < \varepsilon]$$

REMARK 1. The functions f, h and g have the following phisical interpretations: non-established state, transistory state and established state, respectively.

4. SOME PROPERTIES OF Z-COMPUTABLE FUNCTIONS

DEFINITION 3. A function $f \in \mathcal{F}^{(n)}$ is said to be Z-computable iff there exists $M \in \mathfrak{M}_Z^{(n)}$ such that $f \in RM$.

THEOREM 6. In order that a function $f \in \mathcal{F}^{(n)}$ be Z-computable, a necessary and sufficient condition is:

$$\forall_{a,b \in \mathcal{R}^+} \left[f_{Z_a} = f_{Z_b} \Rightarrow f_a = f_b \right] \tag{3}$$

P r o o f. If a function $f \in \mathcal{F}^{(n)}$ is Z-computable, then, by Definition 3 and Theorem 3, f satisfies condition (3). Now let us assume that a function $f \in \mathcal{F}^{(n)}$ satisfies (3) and let M be an operator such that $DM = \{f_{Z_a}: a \in \mathcal{R}^+\}$ and $Mf_{Z_a} = f_a$. Then $M \in \mathfrak{A}_Z^{(n)}$ and M satisfies (1), because

$$(Mf_{Z_a})|Z = f_a|Z = f_{Z_a} \quad \text{for any } a \in \mathcal{R}^+.$$

Moreover, M satisfies also (2), because $RM = \{f_a: a \in \mathcal{R}^+\}$ implies $(f_a)_b = f_{a+b} \in RM$ for any $b \in \mathcal{R}^+$. Consequently, $M \in \mathfrak{M}_Z^{(n)}$ and $f = f_0 \in RM$, which ends the proof.

THEOREM 7. If $f \in \mathcal{F}^{(n)}$ is Z-computable, and $Z \subset G \subseteq \Omega_n$, then f is G-computable.

P r o o f. For any $a,b \in \mathcal{R}^+$ we have

$$f_{G_a} = f_{G_b} \Rightarrow f_{Z_a} = f_{Z_b} \Rightarrow f_a = f_b$$

by the assumption and by Theorem 6. Consequently, f satisfies the sufficient condition of G-computability.

DEFINITION 4. A function $f \in \mathcal{F}^{(n)}$ is said to be Z-injective iff

(4) $$f_{Z_a} \neq f_{Z_b} \text{ for any } a,b \in \mathcal{R}^+,\ a \neq b.$$

REMARK 2. In the case of n = 1, the notion of an Z-injective function is a generalization of the notion of an injective function ($Z = \{0\}$).

THEOREM 8. A function $f \in \mathcal{F}^{(n)}$ is Z-computable iff exactly one of the following conditions is satisfied:

1° f is Z-injective,

2° there exists $\alpha, \beta \in \mathcal{R}^+$, $\alpha \neq \beta$, such that $f_{Z_\alpha} = f_{Z_\beta}$, and, for any $a,b \in \mathcal{R}^+$ such that $a < b$, $f_{Z_a} = f_{Z_b}$ implies that f_a is periodic of period b-a with respect to the variable t.

P r o o f. A function $f \in \mathcal{F}^{(n)}$ satisfies (3) if and only if it either satisfies (4) or it does not satisfy this condition, but for any $a,b \in \mathcal{R}^+$ such that $a < b$ from $f_{Z_a} = f_{Z_b}$ it follows that $f_a = f_b$. In the first case the function f is Z-injective. In the second case we observe, that for any $a,b \in \mathcal{R}^+$ such that $a < b$ the equality $f_a = f_b$ holds iff $f_a(t,x) = f_a(t+k\cdot(b-a),x)$ for each $(t,x) \in \Omega_n$ and $k \in \mathcal{N}_0$, i.e. iff f_a is periodic of period b-a with respect to the variable t.

COROLLARY 3. Any Z-injective function is Z-computable.

COROLLARY 4. If there exists a,b $^+$, a b, such that $f_{Z_a} = f_{Z_b}$ and f_a is not periodic of period b-a with respect to the variable t, then f is not Z-computable.

Let $\mathfrak{S}_n$ be the family of all non-empty subsets of the set Ω_n.

THEOREM 9. If a predicate U(f,Z) of the variables $f \in \mathcal{F}^{(n)}$ and $Z \in \mathfrak{S}_n$ is a necessary condition for a function f to be Z-computable, then the predicate $U(f,\Omega_n)$ is true in the domain $\mathcal{F}^{(n)}$.

P r o o f. Since an n-dimensional simple continuous Ω_n-machine is an identity mapping, we have DM = RM for any $M \in \mathfrak{M}^{(n)}_{\Omega_n}$.

Consequently, each function $f \in \mathcal{F}^{(n)}$ is Ω_n-computable, because it is a computation of the Ω_n-machine M such that $DM = \{f_a : a \in \mathcal{R}^+\}$ and $Mf = f$. Since $U(f,\Omega_n)$ is a necessary condition for a function f to be Ω_n-computable, then the predicate $U(f,\Omega_n)$ is true for every $f \in \mathcal{F}^{(n)}$.

REMARK 3. The condition (3) is a predicate $U(f,Z)$ such that the assumptions of Theorem 9 are satisfied. For $Z = \Omega_n$ we have $f_{Z_a} = f_a$, $f_{Z_b} = f_b$ and (3) is obviously true for any $f \in \mathcal{F}^{(n)}$.

Let $\overline{\overline{G}}$ denote the cardinality of the set G, and let $\overline{\overline{\mathcal{R}}} = \mathfrak{c}$.

THEOREM 10. If $f \in \mathcal{F}^{(n)}$, $(t_0,x_0) \in Z$, and the cardinality of the set X-Rf is at least $\mathfrak{c}$, then there exists a Z-computable function g such that $g(t,x) = f(t,x)$ for any $(t,x) \in \Omega_n - \{(t,x_0) : t \geqslant t_0\}$.

P r o o f. Let $Y \subseteq X - Rf$ and $\overline{\overline{Y}} = \mathfrak{c}$. There exists a one-to-one mapping $h : \{(t,x_0) : t \geqslant t_0\} \to Y$. We define a function g as follows: $g(t,x) = f(t,x)$ for $(t,x) \in \Omega_n - \{(t,x_0) : t \geqslant t_0\}$, and $g(t,x_0) = h(t,x_0)$ for $t \geqslant t_0$. The function g is Z-injective, consequently, it is Z-computable by Corollary 3.

COROLLARY 5. If $f \in \mathcal{F}^{(n)}$ and the cardinality of the set X-Rf is at least $\mathfrak{c}$, then for every Z there exists a Z-computable function g whose values differ from the values of f at most in the set $\{(t,x_0) : t \geqslant t_0\}$, where (t_0,x_0) is an arbitrary point of the set Z.

THEOREM 11. If X is a metric space, $(t_0,x_0) \in Z$, $f \in \mathcal{F}^{(n)}$ is a function continuous in the subset $\{(t,x_0) : t \geqslant t_0\}$ of Ω_n, $n \geqslant 2$, and the cardinality of X-Rf is at least $\mathfrak{c}$, then there exists a Z-computable function g such that

$$f(t,x) = g(t,x) \text{ for any } (t,x) \in \Omega_n - \{(t,x_0) : t \geqslant t_0\}$$

and

$$f(t,x_0) = \lim_{(t,x) \to (t,x_0)} g(t,x) \quad \text{for any} \quad t \geqslant t_0.$$

P r o o f. Let g denote a function defined in the proof of the Theorem 10. The function g is Z-computable. Moreover, for any $t \geqslant t_0$ we have

$$f(t,x_0) = \lim_{(t,x)\to(t,x_0)} f(t,x) = \lim_{(t,x)\to(t,x_0)} g(t,x)$$

since the function f is continuous in any point of $\{(t,x_0) : t \geqslant t_0\}$, and $f(t,x) = g(t,x)$ for $(t,x) \in \Omega_n - \{(t,x_0) : t \geqslant t_0\}$.

COROLLARY 6. If the assumptions of Theorem 11 are satisfied, then there exists a machine $M \in \mathfrak{M}_Z^{(n)}$ and a computation g of this machine which after modifying to a continuous function in the set $\{(t,x_0) : t \geqslant t_0\}$ is equal to the function f.

COROLLARY 7. If X is a metric space, $f \in \mathcal{F}^{(n)}$ is a function continuous in the set Ω_n, $n \geqslant 2$, and the cardinality of X-Rf is at least $\mathfrak{c}$, then for every Z there exists a Z-computable function g such that

$$\lim_{(t,y)\to(t,x)} g(t,y) = f(t,x)$$

for any $(t,x) \in \Omega_n$.

5. ALMOST Z-COMPUTABLE FUNCTIONS

Let δ denote an arbitrary positive real number. By $\mathcal{B}_\delta^{(n)}$ we denote the family of all non-empty subsets of Ω_n such that for any $G \in \mathcal{B}_\delta^{(n)}$ there exists a point $(t_0,x_0) \in G$ such that $(t,x_0) \in G$ for any $t \in (t_0-\delta;\ t_0+\delta)$. If $P_0 = (t_0,x_0) \in \Omega_n$, $\delta > 0$, then by $\mathcal{E}_{P_0,\delta}^{(n)}$ we denote the set of all points (t,x_0) such that $t = t_0+k\cdot\delta$, where $k \in \mathcal{N}_0$.

DEFINITION 5. A function $f \in \mathcal{F}^{(n)}$ is said to be almost Z-computable iff there exists $P_0 \in \Omega_n$, $\delta > 0$ and a Z-computable function g such that $f(t,x) = g(t,x)$ for any $(t,x) \in \Omega_n - \mathcal{E}_{P_0,\delta}^{(n)}$.

COROLLARY 8. If a function $f \in \mathcal{F}^{(n)}$ is almost Z-computable, then there exists a Z-computable function g whose values differ from the values of f at most in a discrete subset of the straight line in Ω_n.

THEOREM 12. If $f \in \mathcal{F}^{(n)}$ and the set X-Rf is infinite, then the function f is almost Z-computable for any $Z \in \bigcup_{\delta>0} \mathcal{B}_\delta^{(n)}$.

P r o o f. Let (y_k) denote an infinite sequence of the points of X-Rf such that $y_r \neq y_l$ for $r \neq l$. Since $Z \in \bigcup_{\delta>0} \mathcal{B}_\delta^{(n)}$, then there exist a point $P_o = (t_o, x_o) \in Z$ and $\delta_o > 0$ such that $(t, x_o) \in Z$ for any $t \in (t_o - \delta_o; t_o + \delta_o)$. We define a function g as follows: $g(t,x) = f(t,x)$ for $(t,x) \in \Omega_n - \mathcal{E}^{(n)}_{P_o, \delta_o}$, and $g(t_k, x_o) = y_k$ for $t_k = t_o + k \cdot \delta_o$, $k \in \mathcal{N}_o$. As the function g is Z-injective, then it is Z-computable by Corollary 3. Consequently, f is almost Z-computable by Definition 5.

COROLLARY 9. If the assumptions of Theorem 12 are satisfied, then for every $Z \in \bigcup_{\delta>0} \mathcal{B}_\delta^{(n)}$ there exist a point $P_o \in \Omega_n$, $\delta_o > 0$, and a Z-computable function g whose values differ from the values of the function f at most in the set $\mathcal{E}^{(n)}_{P_o, \delta_o}$.

THEOREM 13. Let X be a metric space. Suppose there exists $\delta > 0$ and $P_o = (t_o, x_o)$ such that $(t, x_o) \in Z$ for any $t \in (t_o - \delta; t_o + \delta)$. If $f \in \mathcal{F}^{(n)}$ is continuous in each point of the set $\mathcal{E}^{(n)}_{P_o, \delta}$, and the set X-Rf is infinite, then there exists a Z-computable function g such that

$$f(t,x) = g(t,x) \quad \text{for any} \quad (t,x) \in \Omega_n - \mathcal{E}^{(n)}_{P_o, \delta} ,$$

and

$$f(t,x_o) = \lim_{(s,x_o)\to(t,x_o)} g(s,x_o) \quad \text{for any} \quad (t,x_o) \in \mathcal{E}^{(n)}_{P_o, \delta} .$$

P r o o f. We define a function g as follows: $g(t,x) = f(t,x)$ for $(t,x) \in \Omega_n - \mathcal{E}^{(n)}_{P_o, \delta}$, and $g(t_k, x_o) = y_k$ for $t_k = t_k + k \cdot \delta$, $k \in \mathcal{N}_o$, where (y_k) is an infinite sequence of the points of X-Rf such that

$y_r \neq y_1$ for $r \neq 1$. As the function g is Z-injective, then it is Z-computable. Moreover, for any $(t,x_o) \in \mathcal{E}^{(n)}_{P_o,\delta}$ we have

$$f(t,x_o) = \lim_{(s,x_o)\to(t,x_o)} f(s,x_o) = \lim_{(s,x_o)\to(t,x_o)} g(s,x_o)$$

since the function f is continuous in any point of $\mathcal{E}^{(n)}_{P_o,\delta}$, and $f(t,x) = g(t,x)$ for any $(t,x) \in \Omega_n - \mathcal{E}^{(n)}_{P_o,\delta}$.

COROLLARY 10. If the assumptions of Theorem 13 are satisfied, then there exists a machine $M \in \mathfrak{M}^{(n)}_Z$ and a computation g of this machine which after modifying to a continuous function in the set $\mathcal{E}^{(n)}_{P_o,\delta}$ is equal to the function f.

COROLLARY 11. If X is a metric space, $f \in \mathcal{F}^{(n)}$ is continuous in the set Ω_n and the set X-Rf is infinite, then for every $Z \in \bigcup_{\delta>0} \mathcal{B}^{(n)}_\delta$ there exists a Z-computable function g such that

$$\lim_{(s,x)\to(t,x)} g(s,x) = f(t,x) \quad \text{for any} \quad (t,x) \in \Omega_n.$$

6. SOME PROPERTIES OF Z-COMPUTABLE SETS

DEFINITION 6. A set $F \subseteq \mathcal{F}^{(n)}$ is said to be Z-computable iff there exists $M \in \mathfrak{M}^{(n)}_Z$ such that $F = RM$.

THEOREM 14. In order that a non-empty set $F \subseteq \mathcal{F}^{(n)}$ be a Z-computable, a necessary and sufficient condition is:

$$\forall_{f,g \in F} \left[f_Z = g_Z \Rightarrow f = g \right] \tag{5}$$

and

$$\forall_{f \in F} \; \forall_{a \in \mathcal{R}^+} \; f_a \in F \tag{6}$$

P r o o f. If a set $F \subseteq \mathcal{F}^{(n)}$ is Z-computable, then Definition 6 and Theorem 3 (a = b = 0) imply (5), and Definition 6 and condition (2) imply (6). Now let us assume that a non-empty set $F \subseteq \mathcal{F}^{(n)}$ satisfies conditions (5) and (6). Let M be an operator such that DM = $\{f_Z : f \in F\}$ and $Mf_Z = f$. We have $M \in \mathfrak{A}_Z^{(n)}$. Obviously, the operator M satisfied (1). By (6) it satisfies also condition (2). Consequently, $M \in \mathfrak{M}_Z^{(n)}$. As RM = F, this implies that the set F is Z-computable.

DEFINITION 7. A non-empty set $F \subseteq \mathcal{F}^{(n)}$ is said to be closed under the operation of shift iff $f_a \in F$ for any $f \in F$, $a \in \mathcal{R}^+$.

DEFINITION 8. A non-empty set $F \subseteq \mathcal{F}^{(n)}$ is said to be Z-injective iff $f_Z \neq g_Z$ for any $f, g \in F$, $f \neq g$.

From our definitions and Theorem 14 we have immediately:

THEOREM 15. A non-empty set $F \subseteq \mathcal{F}^{(n)}$ is Z-computable iff the following conditions are satisfied:

1° F is Z-injective,

2° F is closed under the operation of shift.

Let Φ_n be the family of all non-empty subsets of the set $\mathcal{F}^{(n)}$, and Φ_n^* - the family of all subsets of the set $\mathcal{F}^{(n)}$ which are closed under the operation of shift.

THEOREM 16. If a predicate W(F, Z) of the variables $F \in \Phi_n$ and $Z \in \mathfrak{S}_n$ is a necessary condition for a set F to be Z-computable, then the predicate $W(F, \Omega_n)$ is true in the domain Φ_n^*.

P r o o f. Any set $F \in \Phi_n^*$ is Ω_n-computable, since F = RM for $M \in \mathfrak{M}_{\Omega_n}^{(n)}$ such that DM = F and Mf = f. Since $W(F, \Omega_n)$ is a necessary condition for a set F to be a Ω_n-computable set, then the predicate $W(F, \Omega_n)$ is true for every $F \in \Phi_n^*$.

COROLLARY 12. Obviously $\mathcal{F}^{(n)} \in \Phi_n^*$. Hence if the assumptions of Theorem 16 are satisfied, then the proposition $W(\mathcal{F}^{(n)}, \Omega_n)$ is true.

REMARK 4. The conjunction of conditions (5) and (6) is a predicate $W(F,Z)$ such that the assumptions of Theorem 16 are satisfied. For $Z = \Omega_n$ we have $f_Z = f$, $g_Z = g$, and in this case the conjunction (5) and (6) is obviously true for any $F \in \Phi_n^*$.

DEFINITION 9. A non-empty set $G \subseteq \Omega_n$ is said to be a t-trail set iff $(t_0,x) \in G$ implies $(t,x) \in G$ for any $0 \leq t \leq t_0$.

By T_n we denote the family of all t-trail sets of Ω_n.

Let $\mathcal{K}_Z^{(n)}$ be the set of all Z-computable functions of $\mathcal{F}^{(n)}$.

THEOREM 17. If $Z \in T_n$ and $\overline{\overline{Z}} = \mathfrak{c}$, then $\overline{\overline{\mathcal{K}_Z^{(n)}}} = \overline{\overline{\mathcal{F}^{(n)}}}$.

P r o o f. Obviously, $\overline{\overline{\mathcal{K}_Z^{(n)}}} \leq \overline{\overline{\mathcal{F}^{(n)}}}$, since $\mathcal{K}_Z^{(n)} \subseteq \mathcal{F}^{(n)}$. We shall prove that $\overline{\overline{\mathcal{F}^{(n)}}} \leq \overline{\overline{\mathcal{K}_Z^{(n)}}}$. Let μ denote an arbitrary, but fixed, element of X. By $\mathcal{F}_{Z,\mu}^{(n)}$ we denote the set of all $f \in \mathcal{F}^{(n)}$ such that $f(t,x) = \mu$ for any $(t,x) \in \Omega_n - Z$. The set $\mathcal{F}_{Z,\mu}^{(n)}$ is Z-injective and closed under the operation of shift. Consequently, $\mathcal{F}_{Z,\mu}^{(n)}$ is Z-computable by Theorem 15. Since $\mathcal{F}_{Z,\mu}^{(n)} \subseteq \mathcal{K}_Z^{(n)}$, we have

$$\overline{\overline{\mathcal{F}_{Z,\mu}^{(n)}}} \leq \overline{\overline{\mathcal{K}_Z^{(n)}}} \tag{7}$$

On the other hand

$$\overline{\overline{\mathcal{F}_{Z,\mu}^{(n)}}} = \overline{\overline{\mathcal{F}_Z^{(n)}}} = \overline{\overline{X^Z}} = \overline{\overline{X^{\mathfrak{c}}}} = \overline{\overline{X^{\Omega_n}}} = \overline{\overline{\mathcal{F}^{(n)}}}$$

Hence, by (7) we have $\overline{\overline{\mathcal{F}^{(n)}}} \leq \overline{\overline{\mathcal{K}_Z^{(n)}}}$ which completes the proof.

REMARK 5. If $Z \in T_n$, $\overline{\overline{Z}} = \mathfrak{c}$, then $\overline{\overline{\mathcal{K}_Z^{(n)}}} = \overline{\overline{X}}^{\mathfrak{c}}$. In particular we have in this case $\overline{\overline{\mathcal{K}_Z^{(n)}}} = 1$ for $\overline{\overline{X}} = 1$ and $\overline{\overline{\mathcal{K}_Z^{(n)}}} \geq \mathfrak{c}^{\mathfrak{c}} > \mathfrak{c}$ for $\overline{\overline{X}} \geq 2$. It is interesting, because, for example, the set of all continuous real functions defined in the domain Ω_n is a set of cardinality $\mathfrak{c}$. More generally, the set of all real Baire's functions determined in the domain Ω_n is also a set of cardinality $\mathfrak{c}$. Consequently, if the assumptions of Theorem 17 are satisfied, $X \subseteq \mathcal{R}$, and $\overline{\overline{X}} \geq 2$, then there exist Z-computable functions which are not Baire's functions.

THEOREM 18. For any $M_1, M_2 \in \mathfrak{M}_Z^{(n)}$, $M_1 = M_2$ iff $RM_1 = RM_2$.

P r o o f. If $M_1 = M_2$, then obviously we have $RM_1 = RM_2$. Now let us assume that $RM_1 = RM_2$. Then

$$DM_1 = \{f_Z : f \in RM_1\} = \{f_Z : f \in RM_2\} = DM_2.$$

Let $h \in DM_1$. We define $h^{(1)} = M_1 h$ and $h^{(2)} = M_2 h$. Thus by (1) $h_Z^{(1)} = h_Z^{(2)} = h$. Since $h^{(1)}, h^{(2)} \in RM_1$ and RM_1 is a Z-computable set, this implies $h^{(1)} = h^{(2)}$ by Theorem 14. Consequently, $M_1 = M_2$.

COROLLARY 13. If $F \subseteq \mathcal{F}^{(n)}$ is a Z-computable set, then there exists exactly one $M \in \mathfrak{M}_Z^{(n)}$ such that $F = RM$.

In [3] a certain connection between the theory of τ-computable sets and the initial-value problems for ordinary linear differential equations is examined. We have also noticed a connection between the theory of Z-computable sets of functions and some initial-value problems of the theory of partial differential equations.

It is known that the equation

$$u_{xx} - c^2 u_{tt} = 0, \qquad c > 0, \tag{8}$$

possesses exactly one solution $u(t,x) \in C^2(\Omega_2)$ satisfying the initial conditions

$$u(0,x) = f(x) \in C^2(\mathcal{R}) \quad \text{and} \quad u_t(0,x) = g(x) \in C^1(\mathcal{R}).$$

Let $u^{f,g}(t,x)$ denote this solution, and let

$$\Sigma = \{u^{f,g}(t,x) : f \in C^2(\mathcal{R}) \wedge g \in C^1(\mathcal{R})\}.$$

Now assume that $X = \mathcal{R}$. We shall prove that Σ is a Z-computable set for each streak-set

$$Z = \{(t,x) : 0 \leqslant t < T \wedge x \in \mathcal{R}\}.$$

In fact, for any $u^{(1)}(t,x), u^{(2)}(t,x) \in \Sigma$, if $u_Z^{(1)} = u_Z^{(2)}$, then $u^{(1)}(0,x) = u^{(2)}(0,x)$ and $u_t^{(1)}(0,x) = u_t^{(2)}(0,x)$; consequently, $u^{(1)} = u^{(2)}$. Now, for any $u(t,x) \in \Sigma$ and any $a \in \mathcal{R}^+$, the function

$u_a(t,x) \in C^2(\Omega_2)$ satisfies equation (7), $u_a(0,x) = u(a,x) \in C^2(\mathcal{R})$ and $(u_a)_t(0,x) = u_t(a,x) \in C^1(\mathcal{R})$, i.e. $u_a(t,x) \in \sum$. Consequently, the set $\sum$ is Z-computable by Theorem 14. We observe, that, by Corollary 13, for any fixed streak-set Z there exists exactly one two-dimensional simple continuous Z-machine M such that $\sum = RM$.

REFERENCES

[1] KONIKOWSKA, B. Continuous machines, τ-computations and τ-computable sets. Bull. Acad. Polon. Sci., Ser. Sci. Math., Astronom. Phys. 19 (1971), 525-530.

[2] KONIKOWSKA, B. On some properties of continuous machines. Ibid., 531 - 538.

[3] KONIKOWSKA, B. Maszyny liczące o czasie ciągłym (Continuous machines) [in Polish]. PWN, Warszawa (1973).

[4] ŻAKOWSKI, W. On some properties of n-dimensional simple continuous machines. Bull. Acad. Polon. Sci., Sér. Sci. Math., Astronom. Phys., 1 (1974), 81 - 85.

[5] ŻAKOWSKI, W. On τ-computability of functions and sets of functions of n real variables. Bull. Acad. Polon. Sci., Sér. Sci. Math., Astronom. Phys. 9 (1974), [in print].

[6] ŻAKOWSKI, W. On τ-computability and almost τ-computability of functions of n real variables. Demonstr. Math., 4 (1974), [in print].

AN APPROACH TO CORRECTNESS PROOFS OF SEMICOROUTINES

by

Ole-Johan Dahl

Abstract. The paper discusses local correctness criteria and local correctness proofs of semicoroutines subject to certain simplifying assumptions. A nontrivial worked example is given.

1. Introduction.

An important goal in programming is to construct programs that are easy to understand. A good way to achieve understanding of a program is to prove that it is correct. Since a program easily proved correct is probably easy to understand, one looks for program structuring mechanisms which admit simple and powerful proof rules. A simple correctness proof is not necessarily easy to find, unless certain key assertions about the program variables are given. Therefore such assertions should be provided with the program text as comments, and in such quantity that the construction of a correctness proof is trivial.

In the present paper we shall discuss correctness criteria and correctness proofs of coroutines. More specifically we consider so called <u>semicoroutines</u> as defined by Wang and Dahl [1] and expressed in a slightly modified Simula 67. A class of semicoroutines is thus defined by a class declaration, say C.

```
class C; ⟨class body⟩;
```

A semicoroutine of the class C is a dynamic instance of the class body, and is named by a reference variable, say X.

```
X :- new C
```

In general any number of semicoroutines of the same class (or different ones) may coexist. We assume for simplicity that each semicoroutine is named by one and only one reference variable throughout its life.

Consider a process consisting of the execution of a master program M and a single semicoroutine X. It can be viewed as two separate processes operating in parallel, but such that only one is executing at a time, while the other is waiting.

Control is transferred from M to X at the time when X is generated, i.e. when M executes the generator "new C", and whenever M executes "call(X)". Control returns to M whenever X executes a "detach" statement, and at the time of termination of X.

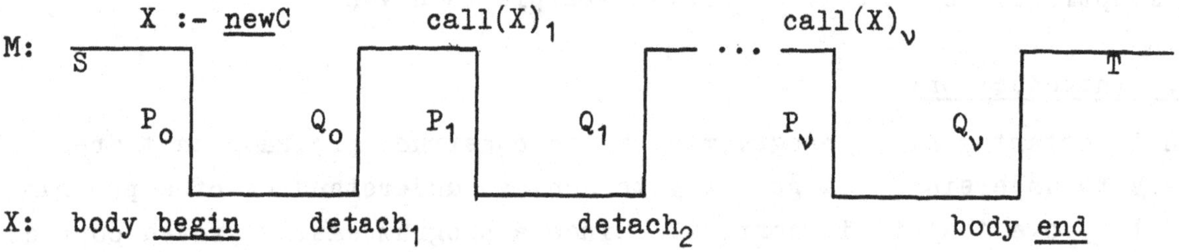

The figure gives a pictorial representation of the sequence of events in time. There is a mapping which maps each event call(X) onto some occurrence of call(X) in the program text of M, and similarly for the other events of M and X.

Understanding the processes M and X requires a prior knowledge (except in special cases) of the interface between them. The interface consists of assertions $P_0, P_1, P_2, \ldots$ and $Q_0, Q_1, Q_2, \ldots$ characterizing the state vector at the times of transition of control from M to X and from X to M respectively (see the figure). Assuming that M calls X ν times, after which X terminates, we can formulate a proof rule for the process as a whole with a formalism similar to that of Hoare.

$$\frac{P_0\{X :- \underline{\text{new}}C\}\, Q_0,\ \forall t \in [1,\nu]: P_t\{\text{call}(X)_t\}Q_t \vdash S\{M\}T,\quad \forall t \in [1,\nu]: Q_{t-1}\{\text{detach}_t\}P_t \vdash P_0\{\text{body of } C\}Q_\nu}{S\{M,C\}T}$$

The rule as it stands leaves little hope of providing a correctness proof of the semicoroutine separately from M, or any clue as to what the criterion of its correctness should be. A major difficulty is the fact that the assertions P_t and Q_t in general are predicates on the whole state vector. This reflects the fact that Simula 67 permits the entire state vector to be accessible to both the master program and the semicoroutine.

In order to simplify matters we partition the state vector s into three parts: a local to M, b local to X, and a communication area c. (In Simula 67 the locality criteria could be enforced by a compiler by outlawing references to nonlocals from within class bodies as well as remote references into class bodies; however, some additional syntax would be needed to identify the communication area. We do not wish to consider questions of syntax here).

M. Clint, in his treatment of coroutines [2], requires a similar partitioning of the state vector, and (1) is an elaboration and adaptation of his proof rule for cooperating routines. Clint adds the following proof rule for each detach statement in X,

(2) $$\frac{\vdash Q\{detach\}P}{\vdash Q \wedge \forall c(P \supset B)\{detach\}B}$$

where P and Q are predicates on c and B is an arbitrary predicate on (b,c). The rule expresses the fact that the local quantities b are unchanged across a detach statement.

A similar rule holds for each statement call(X) in M, where A is an arbitrary predicate on (a,c).

(3) $$\frac{\vdash P\{call(X)\}Q}{\vdash P \wedge \forall c(Q \supset A)\{call(X)\}A}$$

The rules (2) and (3) show that predicates on c alone bracketing call(X) or detach may be extended to predicates on the whole accessible part of the state vector. Consequently it is sufficient that the P_i and Q_i of (1) be predicates on the communication area alone. This is the simplification which arises from partitioning the state vector as above.

The problem of mapping (1) onto the program texts of M and X is solved in principle by introducing two "mythical" program variables: γ local to M whose value is the number of times that "call(X)" has been performed, and δ local to X whose value is the number of times that "detach" has been performed (in X). By definition the following relations hold (see the figure above).

Within M: $\gamma < \nu \supset \gamma + 1 = \delta$ (after the generation of X),

within X: $\delta = \gamma$,

and $\gamma = \delta = 0$ initially.

We may notice in passing that $\gamma = \nu$ implies $\delta = \nu$ in M, because the last return to M is through the termination of X, not by a detach operation. It follows that X is callable if and only if $\delta - \gamma = 1$.

Writing P(c,t) for P_t and Q(c,t) for Q_t rule (1) gets the following form.

$$\frac{P(c,0)\{X := \underline{new}C\}Q(c,0),\ 0 \leq \gamma < \nu \wedge P(c,\gamma+1)\{call(X)\}Q(c,\gamma) \vdash S\{M\}T \qquad 0 \leq \delta < \nu \wedge Q(c,\delta)\{detach\}P(c,\delta) \vdash P(c,0)\{body\ of\ C\}Q(c,\nu)}{\vdash S\{M,C\}T} \quad (1')$$

(2) and (3) may be replaced the following slightly stronger rules.

$$\frac{\vdash Q\{detach\}P}{\vdash Q \wedge \forall c(P^{\delta}_{\delta+1} \supset B^{\delta}_{\delta+1})\{detach\}B} \quad (2')$$

$$\frac{\vdash P\{call(X)\}Q}{\vdash P \wedge \forall c(Q^{\gamma}_{\gamma+1} \supset A^{\gamma}_{\gamma+1})\{call(X)\}A} \quad (3')$$

These rules, in addition to the constancy of ordinary local quantities, express the facts that detach increases δ by 1, and call(X) increases γ by 1.

Termination of X is not essential for the correct behaviour of M. For instance, if M calls X μ times, $\mu < \nu$, then from the point of view of X the $(\mu+1)$'th dynamic instance of detach does not terminate, and neither does X. On the other hand, if X terminates too early, i.e. $\nu < \mu$, then the $(\nu+1)$'th dynamic instance of call(X) will not terminate properly. Thus it is important that a semicoroutine carries on "long enough" without terminating. In fact, from the point of view of a master program a non-terminating semicoroutine is "safer" than one which terminates. This indicates that expressions of the form

P{body}Q

are not necessarily useful as correctness criteria for a semicoroutine viewed separately from its master program. The requirement that it behave according to given interface specifications may be more relevant. It is certainly true that a proof using (1'), given proper termination, permits us to infer the validity of the interface assumptions. Thus an indirect proof of a given semicoroutine may be constructed by first writing a master program reflecting its intended use, and then proving the combined program. However, we investigate below some special cases when correctness criteria are easily formulated and proved locally.

2. Producer/consumer relationships.

We impose a producer/consumer relationship on the pair M,X by defining the communication area c to be a set of read-only variables with respect to one of them (the consumer).

Assume that X is the producer and M the consumer. Let the states of the communication area c at successive executions of detach be $c_0, c_1, c_2, \ldots$. Then the interface specifications are

$$P_t : c = c_{t-1}, \quad Q_t : c = c_t.$$

If the semicoroutine X is a selfcontained process receiving no inputs, the whole sequence c_t must be completely determined by the initial state of X. We may conclude that $c_{t+1} = f(c_t, t)$. Then by a simple formal derivation (3') reduces to

$$\text{(3c)} \qquad \vdash_i A^{\gamma}_{\gamma+1}{}^{,c}_{,f(c,\gamma)} \{\text{call}(X)\}\ A,$$

where $\vdash_i$ means "deductible from the interface specifications".

(Assumption of (3'): $c = c_\gamma \{\text{call}(X)\}\ c = c_\gamma$.

Conclusion of (3') $\quad c = c_\gamma \wedge \forall c(c = c_{\gamma+1} = f(c_\gamma, \gamma) \supset A^{\gamma}_{\gamma+1})\{\text{call}(X)\}\ A,$

where the precondition reduces to that of (3c).)

(3c) states the intuitively obvious fact that the effect of call(X), as seen from M is an assignment $c := f(c,\gamma)$ to the communication variable(s) (disregarding the effect on the mythical γ). A motivation for using a semicoroutine, rather than a procedure f, to perform the computation is that the former may utilize local state information to reduce the work involved. In contrast a procedure would have to regenerate such information from the parameter values at each activation. This is true even if f does not depend on γ, as shown by the example of section 3.

The proof rule (2') for the detach statement of X reduces to

$$\vdash_i B^{\delta}_{\delta+1}\{\text{detach}\}B$$

which is simple and intuitively obvious. But it does not contribute much to proving that the semicoroutine behaves according to specifications. What must be proved is that

$$B^{c}_{f(c,\delta-1)}\{E\}B$$

for any sequence E of events occurring between two successive dynamic instances of detach. Since such event sequences are not in general mapped onto syntactic components of the program text, proof rules derived from program structure are not immediately helpful.

As an aid for proving and annotating the semicoroutine we may introduce a mythical local variable c' whose value is the state of the communication area at the time of the last execution of detach. Noting that $c' = c_{\delta-1}$ holds on either side of any detach we may derive from (2') the rule

(2p) $\vdash_i c = f(c',\delta-1) \wedge B^{\delta,c'}_{\delta+1,c}\{\text{detach}\}\ B \wedge c = c'$

which defines that a mythical assignment c' := c is an implicit side effect of the detach operation. The assertion $c = f(c',\delta-1)$ is what must be proved for every textual occurrence of detach in the semicoroutine. Technically it is a hypothesis about the interface, to be inserted in front of detach as indicated by (2p) (and also at body <u>end</u>). The hypothesis is proved valid when it has been verified, working backwords through the program text, that c = c' is true after each occurrence of detach (and also at body <u>begin</u>). The initial value of c' is defined equal to the initial state of the communication area c, before the first "output" c_0 has been produced. If that state is undefined, the value of $f(c',-1)$ should be independent of c'.

Consider next the case that X is the consumer and M is the producer, and let again $c_0, c_1, c_2, \ldots$ be the sequence of states produced and consumed. Frequently the purpose of a consuming semicoroutine is such that any functional relation between consecutive inputs is irrelevant, if indeed it exists at all. For instance, the purpose could be to perform certain statistical measurements on the sequence consumed, or to compute some function of the input, given that it is a character sequence with a given syntactic structure.

Clearly the behaviour of the semicoroutine will depend on the inputs. Let b_t be the local state at the time of the event detach_t (see the figure above), we may write

$$b_{t+1} = f(b_t, c_t, t), \quad t = 0,1,\ldots.$$

However, the examples above suggest that it may be more useful to define the current local state as a function of that part of the input sequence which has so far been consumed.

(4) $$b_{t+1} = F(\langle c_0, c_1, \ldots, c_t \rangle), \quad t = 0,1,\ldots$$

Also the interface specifications may take the form of predicates on the sequence transmitted. In our case the producer M must guarantee the validity of P_t, whereas X has no other interface obligation than leaving the communication area c unchanged.

(5) $$P_t\colon\ P(\langle c_0, c_1, \ldots, c_t \rangle) \wedge c = c_t, \quad Q_t\colon\ c = c_t.$$

Notice that the predicate P, as well as the function F of (4) are implicitly parameterized by t, since the length of the sequence parameter is by definition equal to t+1. In order to make sense the predicate P must be monotonic with respect to the sequence length.

(6) $$P(\langle c_0, c_1, \ldots, c_t \rangle) \supset P(\langle c_0, c_1, \ldots, c_s \rangle) \quad \text{for} \quad s < t;$$
$$\text{and} \quad P(\langle\ \rangle) = \underline{\text{true}}.$$

We may map (4) and (5) onto the program text by introducing a mythical variable Hc called the <u>communication</u> <u>history</u>, whose value shall be the sequence of values produced by M. Hc is extended by an element equal to the current value of c as the result of an implied side effect of the call(X) operation. We derive the following proof rules from (2') and (3').

(2c) $\vdash_i \forall c'(P(\langle Hc,c'\rangle) \supset B^{Hc,c}_{\langle Hc,c'\rangle,c'})\{detach\}\ B$

(3p) $\vdash_i P(\langle Hc,c\rangle) \wedge A^{Hc}_{\langle Hc,c\rangle}\{call(X)\}\ A$

(2c) expresses that detach has the implied side effects of assigning new values to the communication area, and appending them to the communication history. It follows that $c = last(Hc)$ everywhere in X.

The predicate B could have the form $b = F(Hc^-) \wedge P(Hc)$, where Hc^- denotes the sequence obtained from Hc by deleting its last element, i.e. that part of the communication history which has so far been "digested" by X. Then the following rule is derived from (2c) and (6).

(2c') $\vdash_i P(Hc) \supset b = F(Hc)\{detach\}\ b = F(Hc^-) \wedge P(Hc)$

The precondition of (2c') is what must be proved for every occurrence of detach (and body <u>end</u>). The proof is established by working backwards through the program text and proving that the postassertion of (2c') for each occurrence of detach implies whatever assertion has been constructed at that point. (At body <u>begin</u> $b = F(\langle\ \rangle)$ must hold).

For a terminating consumer semicoroutine a correctness criterion of the form

(7) $P_o\{body\}\ P(H_c) \supset b = F(Hc)$

is meaningful.

The concept of communication history is useful for selfcontained producer semicoroutines as well. The mythical variable Hc may be used instead of the variables γ, δ, and c' introduced above. The rule (2p) takes the following form

(2p') $\vdash_i c = f'(Hc) \wedge B^{Hc}_{\langle Hc,c\rangle}\{detach\}\ B,$

where $f'(Hc) = f(last(Hc), length(Hc)-1)$, f as in (2p).

If the semicoroutine terminates, the correctness criterion (where S is a specified sequence)

(8) $P_0\{body\}\ Hc = S$

is adequat, because it characterizes the total behaviour of the semi-coroutine as seen from an external point of view.

Frequently a producer X with respect to a communication area c may be a consumer with respect to an area d. X may be a semicoroutine with respect to c and a master program with respect to d, or vice versa. In both cases, assuming that X terminates, a relevant correctness criterion is obtained as a "combination" of (7) and (8),

(9) $P_0\{body\}\ P(Hd) \supset Hc = F(Hd)$,

where P(Hd) is the interface assumption on the consumed sequence. In some cases one would require of X that it behave in a predictable way for any arbitrary input sequence. In that case the interface assumption is void (excepting declared properties of the area d), and (9) might be replaced by a criterion of the following form

$$P_0\{\text{body of } X\}\ Hc = \underline{\text{if}}\ P(Hd)\ \underline{\text{then}}\ F(Hd)\ \underline{\text{else}}\ E(Hd),$$

where E(Hd) might contain "error messages".

3. A worked example.

As a nontrivial example we choose an adaptation of a program given by D.E. Knuth [4] for producing all permutations of the numbers 1,2,...,n according to a method developed by Trotter.

The permutation sequence is generated by successive interchanges of neighbour elements, which makes the algorithm very efficient.

In order to give a rough indication of the method we list below the complete Trotter sequences T_n of the numbers $\{1,2,\ldots,n\}$ for $n = 2,3,4$.

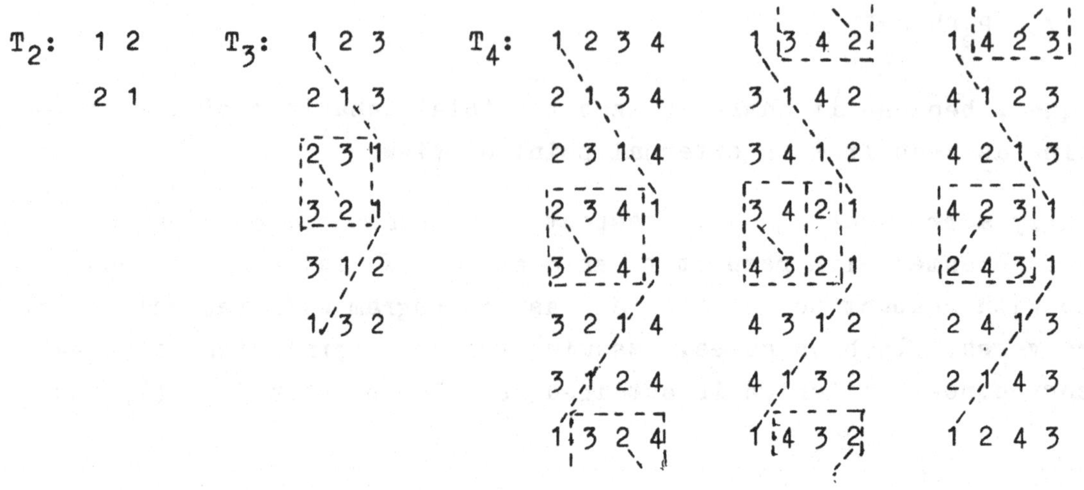

In general T_n of $\{1,2,\ldots,n\}$ is obtained from T_{n-1} of $\{2,3,\ldots,n\}$ by expanding each element X of the latter sequence into a subsequence of T_n. The subsequence is obtained from X by inserting the digit 1 in all possible positions. Then, by induction, T_n sequences through all permutations exactly once. By inserting the 1's alternately from left to right and from right to left it turns out that successive permutations are produced by always swapping neighbour elements.

The algorithm may be structured as a cooperation of n semicoroutines, each assigned to move a certain digit back and forth within a certain substring. In the program below the semicoroutines are of the class "Gdigit", and are called G[1],G[2],...,G[n]. G[k] is assigned to move the number n-k+1, k = 1,2,...,n.

The whole cooperation, including a master program "Main", is defined as a producer semicoroutine of the class "Tpermuter", which terminates after having produced the sequence T_n, where n is a parameter.

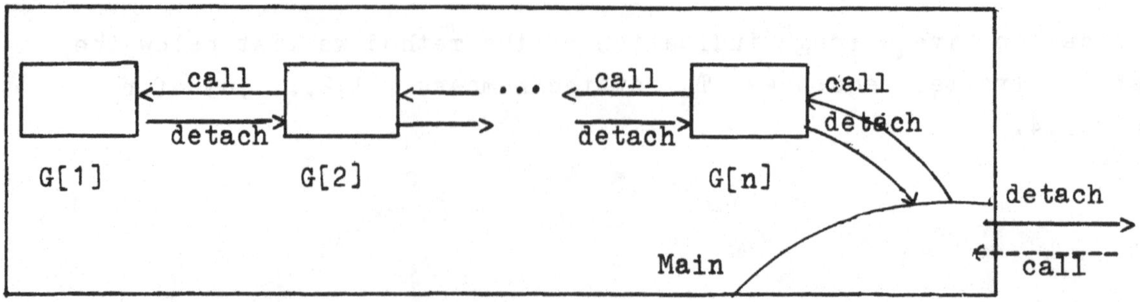

Tpermuter

The communication area of the Tpermuter consists of the quantities

Boolean more;   **integer array** p[1:n];

where p sequences through the permutations, and more is **true** until finally it is set to **false** to signal the end og the sequence. The correctness criterion with respect to p is that $Hp = T_n$ immediately before termination, provided that $n \geq 1$.

```
class Tpermuter(integer n);
begin Boolean more;  integer array p[1:n];
      integer t;  ref(Gdigit) array G[1:n];

      class Gdigit(integer k);
      begin integer i;
            i := 0; p[k] := k;
            if k = 1 then detach; more := false
            else G[k-1] :- new Gdigit(k-1);
                 loop: loop: detach;
                       while i < k-1:
                             swap(p[t+i],p[t+i+1]);
                             {0 ≤ i < k-1} i := i+1;
                       repeat; {i = k-1}
                       call(G[k-1]);
                       loop: detach;
                       while i > 0:
                             swap(p[t+i],p[t+i-1]);
                             {0 < i ≤ k-1} i := i-1;
                       repeat;  {i = 0}
                       t := t+1; call(G[k-1];
                 repeat
            fi
      end of Gdigit;
```

```
Main: more := true;  G[n]:- new Gdigit(n); {p = (1,2,...,n)}
      loop: detach; t := 1; call(G[n]); while more repeat
  {Hp = T_n}
  end of Tpermuter;
```

One syntactic construct of the program text deserves a comment. Let SL stand for statement list and BE stand for Boolean expression. Then

$$\underline{\text{loop}}\text{: } SL_1;\ \underline{\text{while}}\ BE\text{: } SL_2;\ \underline{\text{repeat}}$$

is a generalization of the while- and repeat-statements of Pascal. The while-clause represents the loop test and exit, which may occur anywhere in the loop. If the while-clause is missing, the loop is nonterminating. The following proof rule is valid for the complete construct.

$$\frac{\vdash P\{SL_1\}\ Q,\ \vdash Q \wedge BE\{SL_2\}P}{\vdash P\,\{\underline{\text{loop}}\text{: } SL_1;\ \underline{\text{while}}\ BE\text{: } SL_2;\ \underline{\text{repeat}}\}\ Q \wedge \sim BE}$$

We may simplify the correctness proof of the Tpermuter class by observing that the variable i of G[k] (k = 1,2,...,n) is equal to the inversion count of the digit n-k+1 associated to G[k].

(10) $i = inv(n-k+1)$

An inversion count inv(d) with respect to a permutation p is the number of digits greater than d which occur to the left of d in p.

(10) is obviously valid initially since p is initialized to (1,2,...,n) and all i's to zero. We now prove informally that the operations performed by an arbitrary G[k] from one detach to the next leave (10) unchanged. The proof is based on the assertions occurring in the program text above and two additional invariants for G[k].

(11) $\forall j \in [t, t+k-1]: p[j] \geq n-k+1$

(12) $p[t+i] = n-k+1$

Assume that (10) holds for G's to the right of G[k]. Since G[k] is operating each of those G's is at rest in one of its call-statements. Consequently the corresponding i's have extreme values, 0 or k'-1 for G[k'] $(k < k' \leq n)$. Furthermore t is one larger than the number of such i's equal to zero. (10) now implies that the associated digits, 1,2,...,n-k, are collected at the left and right ends of p, t-1 of them at the left end. We may conclude that the k largest numbers of p, n-k+1,...,n, are collected within the segment s = p[t:t+k-1], (11). By the bounds on i within the innermost loops of G[k], its swap operations can only move digits of the segments, thus preserving (11). Initially the digit n-k+1 is positioned at the left end of s and i = 0, which means that (12) is satisfied. It is obviously preserved by the operations on p and i in G[k].

It only remains to show that the validity of (11) and (12) is preserved by the operation call(G[k-1]). But by induction any G[k'] (k'< k) can only operate on a subsegment of s which does not contain the digit n-k+1. (12) shows that (10) is valid for G[k], since inv(n-k+1) must be equal to its relative position i in s. This completes our informal proof of (10) for all G's.

There is a one-one correspondance between n'th order permutations and their inversion tables

inv(1), inv(2),...,inv(n),

and since $0 \leq inv(k) \leq n-k$, an inversion table read backwards is a number in the base (1,2,...,n) number system. It is easily seen that the sequence of such numbers which corresponds to the Trotter permutation sequence is a base (1,2,...,n) "reflected Gray code sequence" $S_{1,n}$, where each digit position is counted up and down alternately, and only one digit is changed at each step.

$S_{1,4}$	T_4				
0000	1234	0020	1342	0110	1423
0001	2134	0021	3142	0111	4123
0002	2314	0022	3412	0112	4213
0003	2341	0023	3421	0113	4231
0013	3241	0123	4321	0103	2431
0012	3214	0122	4312	0102	2413
0011	3124	0121	4132	0101	2143
0010	1324	0120	1432	0100	1243

By (10) the "array" G.i of variables G[1].i,G[2].i,...,G[n].i contains the reversed inversion table of p. We may therefore prove the correctness of the Tpermuter by regarding G.i as its communication area and proving that its communication history Hi satisfies (13) immediately prior to termination (for $n \geq 1$).

(13) $$Hi = S_{1,n}$$

In order to carry out a (more) formal proof of (13) we need a formal definition of $S_{1,n}$.

$$S_{n+1,n} = \overline{S}_{n+1,n} = \langle \varepsilon \rangle$$

(14)
$$R_{o,k,n} = \langle\ \rangle$$
$$R_{i+1,k,n} = \langle R_{i,k,n}, i|S^{(i)}_{k+1,n} \rangle \quad (i = 0,1,\dots,k-1)$$
$$S_{k,n} = R_{k,k,n} \qquad (k = n,n-1,\dots,1)$$

$S_{k,n}$ is a base $(k,k+1,\dots,n)$ reflected Gray code sequence. $\overline{S}$ stands for the sequence S reversed, and $S^{(i)}$ for S reversed i times, i.e.

$$S^{(i)} = \underline{\text{if}}\ \text{even}(i)\ \underline{\text{then}}\ S\ \underline{\text{else}}\ \overline{S}$$

i|S is the sequence obtained from S by extending each element of S by the digit i at the left, and ε is a digit string of length zero.

By defining $R'_{i,k,n}$ such that $\langle R'_{i,k,n}, \overline{R}_{i,k,n} \rangle = \overline{S}_{k,n}$ we derive

(15)
$$R'_{k,k,n} = \langle\ \rangle$$
$$R'_{i,k,n} = \langle R'_{i+1,k,n}, i|S^{(i+1)}_{k+1,n} \rangle \quad (i = k-1, k-2,\dots,0)$$
$$\overline{S}_{k,n} = R'_{o,k,n} \quad (k = n,n-1,\dots,1).$$

In our correctness proof we may disregard all statements operating on the quantities p and t as being irrelevant. The proof techniques of section 2 may be applied if we regard each Gdigit semicoroutine G[k] as a producer-consumer with respect to its left and right neighbours (or Main). It turns out that the direction of information flow is formally determined by our choice of communication areas, and two different correctness proofs may thus be obtained.

The most intuitively natural choice is perhaps to define G[1:k-1].i to be the communication area linking G[k] to its left neighbour ($k \geq 2$). Then G[k] consumes the next element of the sequence $S_{1,k-1}$ produced by G[k-1] and produces a subsequence of $S_{1,k}$ by appending different i-values at the right end.

However, given the definition (14) a more direct correctness proof is constructed as follows. In order to clarify the terminology we call G.i the <u>external</u> communication area linking the Tpermuter as a whole to its unspecified master. Hi is the corresponding external communication history. We now define the <u>internal</u> communication area connecting G[k] to its right neighbour (or Main) to be a slice of width [k+1:n] of the mythical variable Hi, i.e. the current external communication history of the variables G[k+1].i,....,G[n].i. The slice is denoted Hi[k+1:n].

Formally G[k] "consumes" from G[k+1] (or Main) the current value of Hi[k+1:n] by a detach operation, and it "produces" the current value of Hi[k:n] by an operation call(G[k-1]) (for $k \neq 1$). Since consecutive values produced by G[k] are functionally related, we may use the techniques displayed in the first half of section 2 for a local correctness proof of G[k] ($2 \leq k \leq n$). We introduce three mythical local variables for G[k] (cf. section 2), γ, δ, and H', the last one denoting the output last produced. Let Hin_δ mean the value consumed by detach number δ, and let $Hout_\gamma$ mean the value produced by call number γ. Then we state the following interface assumptions and corresponding proof rules applicable in G[k].

(16) $Hin_\delta = \langle Hin_{\delta-1}, S^{(\delta-1)}_{k+1,n} \rangle \quad (Hin_0 = \langle\ \rangle)$,

(17) $Hout_\gamma = \langle Hout_{\gamma-1}, S^{(\gamma-1)}_{k,n} \rangle \quad (Hout_0 = \langle\ \rangle)$,

(18) $\vdash_i P^{\delta, Hin}_{\delta+1, \langle Hin, S^{(\delta)}_{k+1,n} \rangle} \{detach\}\ P$,

(19) $\vdash_i Hout = \langle H', S^{(\gamma)}_{k,n} \rangle \wedge P^{\gamma, H'}_{\gamma+1,\ Hout} \{call(G[k-1])\}\ P \wedge H' = Hout$,

where Hin means Hi[k+1:n] and Hout means Hi[k:n].

Below is given a fully annotated version of the main loop of G[k]($k \neq 1$), irrelevant operations omitted. The program text constitutes a framework for a local correctness proof of G[k]. A formal proof consists in verifying that the assertions in the text are mutually related as required by the proof rules established for the various statements and constructs.

Since the outer loop is nonterminating the formal objective is to derive

$$P_o\{\text{outer loop}\}\ \underline{\text{false}}$$

using the proof rule

$$\frac{\vdash P\ \{SL\}\ P}{\vdash P\ \{\underline{\text{loop}}\text{: SL; }\underline{\text{repeat}}\}\ \underline{\text{false}}}$$

to achieve that objective.

$\{2 \le k \le n \wedge i=\gamma=\delta=0 \wedge Hi[k:n] = H' = \langle\ \rangle\}$

<u>loop</u>: $\{i = 0 \wedge even(\gamma) \wedge even(\delta) \wedge Hi[k:n] = H'\}$

  <u>loop</u>: $\{0 \le i < k \wedge even(\gamma) \wedge even(\delta+i) \wedge Hi[k:n] = \langle H', R_{i,k,n}\rangle\}$

    detach;

    $\{0 \le i < k \wedge even(\gamma) \wedge odd(\delta+i) \wedge Hi[k:n] =$

    $\langle H', R_{i,k,n}, i|S^{(\delta-1)}_{k+1,n}\rangle = \langle H', R_{i,k,n}, i|S^{(i)}_{k+1,n}\rangle = \langle H', R_{i+1,k,n}\rangle\}$

  <u>while</u> i < k-1: i := i+1;

  <u>repeat</u>;

  $\{i=k-1 \wedge even(\gamma) \wedge odd(\delta+i) \wedge Hi[k:n] = \langle H', R_{k,k,n}\rangle = \langle H', S^{(\gamma)}_{k,n}\rangle\}$

  call(G[k-1]);

  $\{i=k-1 \wedge odd(\gamma) \wedge odd(\delta+i) \wedge Hi[k:n] = H'\}$

  <u>loop</u>: $\{0 \le i < k \wedge odd(\gamma) \wedge odd(\delta+i) \wedge Hi[k:n] = \langle H', R'_{i+1,k,n}\rangle\}$

    detach;

    $\{0 \le i < k \wedge odd(\gamma) \wedge even(\delta+i) \wedge Hi[k:n] =$

    $\langle H', R'_{i+1,k,n}, i|S^{(\delta-1)}_{k+1,n}\rangle = \langle H', R'_{i+1,k,n}, i|S^{(i-1)}_{k+1,n}\rangle = \langle H', R'_{i,k,n}\rangle\}$

  <u>while</u> i > 0: i := i-1;

  <u>repeat</u>;

  $\{i=0 \wedge odd(\gamma) \wedge even(\delta) \wedge Hi[k:n] = \langle H', R'_{o,k,n}\rangle = \langle H', S^{(\gamma)}_{k,n}\rangle\}$

  call(G[k-1]);

<u>repeat</u>;

In applying (18) to each occurrence of detach, notice that Hin of (18) is the slice of width [k+1:n] of the sequence mentioned in the precondition. The contents of the remaining slice [k:k] is defined by the local variable i.

The local correctness proof shows the validity of the output assumption (17), given the input assumption (16). In order to prove the cooperation as a whole we have to show that (16) is valid. For $k \neq n$ we have (cf. section 2, page 4) $G[k].\delta = G[k+1].\gamma$ whenever G[k] is operating. It follows immediately that (17) applied to G[k+1] implies (16) applied to G[k]. For $k = n$ (16) requires that the values consumed should increase by one element of length zero at a time ($S_{n+1,n} = \overline{S}_{n+1,n} = \langle \varepsilon \rangle$ by (14)). Since G[n] has the input communication area Hi[n+1:n] of with zero, and there is precisely one ("external") detach for every call(G[n]) in Main, the values produced by Main are those required.

The final step in the proof of the Tpermuter follows by considering G[1]. It does not enter its main loop, but perfoms its first and only detach immediately after initialization. This detach consumes through Hi[2:n] the output produced by G[2] in its first call, which according to (17) is $S_{2,n}$. Since the variable i of G[1] remains equal to zero, it follows that the complete external communication history Hi has the value $0|S_{2,n} = R_{1,1,n} = S_{1,n}$ at the moment when G[1] emerges from its detach. Since the variable "more" is now set to <u>false</u>, Main exits from its loop and terminates immediately upon regaining control.

Returning to the original Tpermuter communicating through the quantities "more" and p, we have established the following result for its total behaviour,

$$n \geq 1 \,\{\text{body}\}\, H = \langle \underline{\text{true}}|T_n, \underline{\text{false}}|\text{some } p\rangle$$

where H is the complete output history, and the last element of H is produced as the result of termination. The latter should be regarded as an "end of file" signal by the master program.

Acknowledgements.

The author wishes to thank Arne Wang for constructive criticesm and help in cleaning up formal derivations. D.E. Knuth, in addition to formulating the Tpermuter class, also provided the material on the Trotter algorithm and its connection to Gray codes at one of his lectures at the University of Oslo, [5]. Thanks are also due to IFIP WG 2.3 for reacting to a talk on "histories", which may have clarified the author's ideas on the subject more than those of the committee members.

References.

[1] A. Wang, O.-J. Dahl: Coroutine sequencing in a block structured environment. BIT 11(1971), pp. 425-449.

[2] M. Clint: Program proving: Coroutines. Acta Informatica 2 (1973), pp. 50-63.

[3] O.-J. Dahl, E.W. Dijkstra, C.A.R. Hoare: Structured programming. Academic Press, 1972.

[4] D.E. Knuth: A review of "Structured programming". STAN-Cs-73-371.

[5] D.E. Knuth: Selected topics in computer science. Lecture Note Series, Mathematical Institute, University of Oslo (1973).

TOWARDS AN UNDERSTANDING OF COMPLEX PROCESSES

P. Dembiński
Computation Centre
Polish Academy of Sciences
00 901 Warsaw, PKiN, P.O. Box 22

1. INTRODUCTION

A complex process is, roughly speaking, a process which is the result of an arrangement of other processes in order to make them cooperate in a given sense. These processes are explicitly pointed in the parallel case but also a sequential process can be considered as a very special kind of cooperation between processes implicit in it. The above approach allows to investigate problems both in parallel and sequential programming within one general theory of processes. The similar idea may be found in [7].

The central notion in this approach is that of modelling processes within a given process. It follows some ideas described in [8].

The paper consists of two parts. The first deals with sequential processes. The adopted model was introduced by Mazurkiewicz in [2] and is a particular case of the concept investigated by many authors under different names (e.g. iterative systems [1], machines [6]). In that part we give some results concerning the relationships between properties of a process and any of its parts (modelled processes). In particular we deal with determinancy and the input-output relation.

In the second part we give a short outline of how the notion of the process can be generalized to describe the possible realizations of a multiprogramming concept of the concurrent statement (e.g. [4],[5]):

$$\underline{\text{cobegin}}\ P_1;P_2;\ldots;P_n\ \underline{\text{coend}}$$

where $P_1,P_2,\ldots,P_n$ are interacting statements, i.e. sharing common variables.

2. PROCESSES (SEQUENTIAL)

Let us begin with very simple examples explaining the notion of modelling.

EXAMPLE 1. Suppose that at a given point of time we have observed only the limited part of the system (process), e.g. by experiments. Suppose than that we have observed the following cycles (Fig.1):

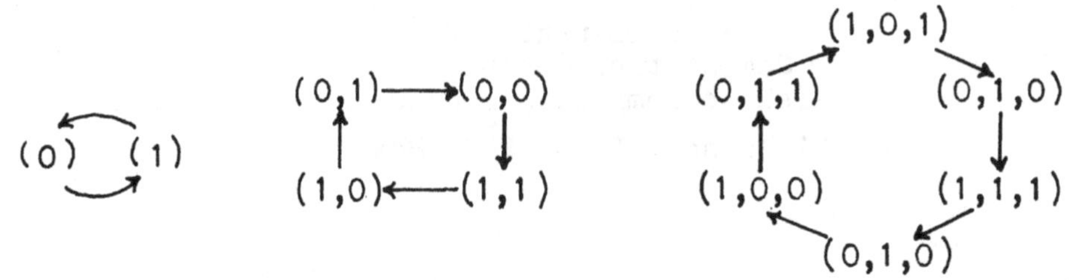

Fig. 1

We have than three processes $P_i = (S_i, F_i)$, $i = 1,2,3$, with:

$S_1 = \{(0),(1)\}$,

$S_2 = \{(0,0),(0,1),(1,0),(1,1)\}$,

$S_3 = \{(1,0,1),(0,1,1),(1,0,0),(0,1,0),(1,1,1),(0,1,0)\}$,

and transition relations (functions) described by the above diagrams.

We look now for a process which is modelling each of the three processes. The first and simplest solution is given by the process:

$P = (S_1 \times S_2 \times S_3,\ F_1 \times F_2 \times F_3)$.

Suppose that we are not satisfied and look for more "economical" solution. Then the process $P = (S,F)$ described by the diagram below (Fig. 2) is another candidate.

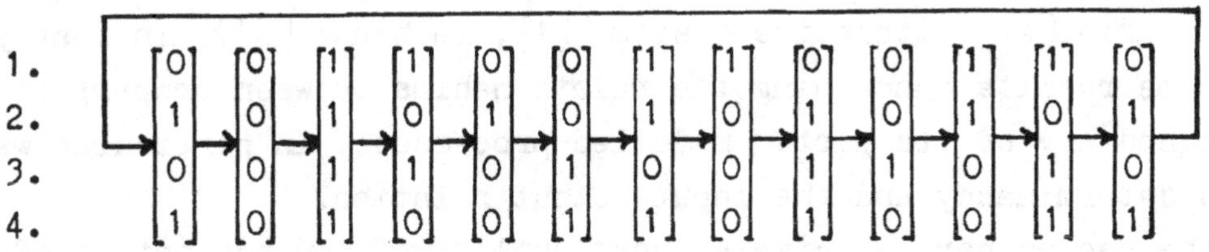

Fig. 2

Let us explain now that the process P is modelling processes P_i in the same sense as in the first solution.

Let $I = \{1,2,3,4\}$ and $J \subsetneq I$. We define an equivalence relation $=_J$ in the set S as follows:

$$s =_J s' \equiv (\forall i \in J)\ p_i(s) = p_i(s')$$

where p_i denotes i-th projection. It is easy to check that for $J = \{2\}$, $J = \{1,2\}$ or $J = \{2,3,4\}$, $=_J$ is a congruence, hence F_J: $S/=_J \longrightarrow S/=_J$ with:

$$F_J([s]_J) = [F(s)]_J$$

is well defined. If now $P_J = (S/=_J, F_J)$ then $P_{\{2\}}$, $P_{\{1,2\}}$, $P_{\{2,3,4\}}$ are isomorphic with P_1, P_2, P_3 respectively.

The situation is much more complicated when processes act, for instance, with different speed or they have to be arranged in such a way that the resulting process satisfies certain condition, e.g. computes a function. This is just the case in programming and to describe these situations a control part of a process is needed.

EXAMPLE 2. Consider an Algol-like program:

σ: r := 0
v: <u>if</u> n = 0 <u>then</u> stop;
r := r+n^2+1; n:= n-1; <u>goto</u> v;

with n $\in$ <u>in</u> (integers), r $\in$ <u>re</u> (reals). We can associate with it a process P with the set of states S = <u>in</u>×<u>re</u> described by the diagram on Fig.3.

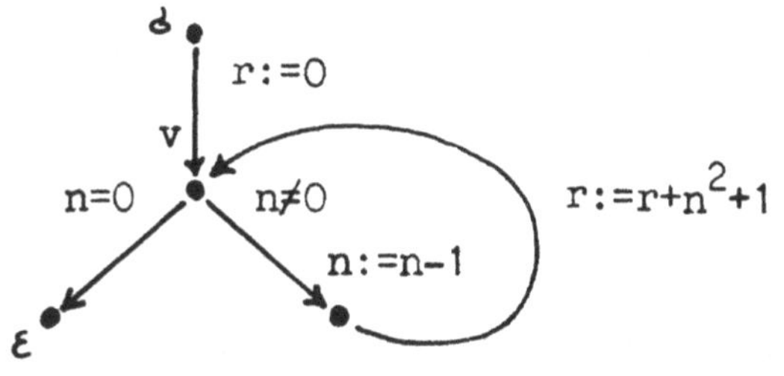

Fig. 3

From a slightly different point of view the process P can be seen as a result of arranging processes P_1, P_2 (Fig.4) in such a way that the following condition holds: for every pair (n,r) $\in$ <u>in</u>×<u>re</u> whenever P stops then as result we obtain the pair:

$$(0 , \sum_{k=1}^{n} (k^2+1)).$$

Process P is still modelling P_1, P_2 in the similar manner as in the first example (it will be shown precisely later).

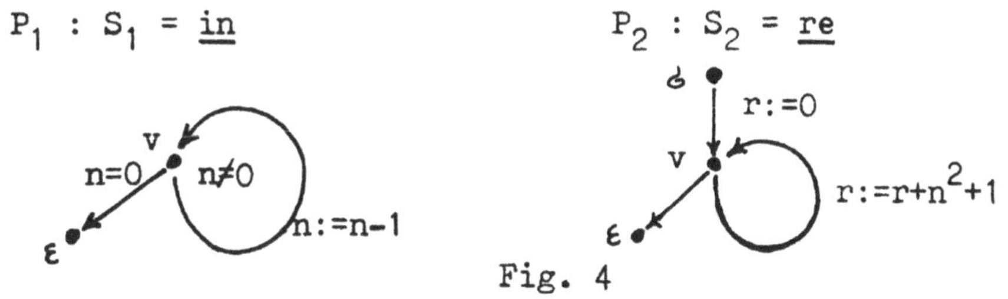

Fig. 4

Define now some basic notions.

By a <u>process</u> (MAZURKIEWICZ [2]) we mean every system P = (S,V,σ,ε,I) where:

S is a set of states of P,

V is a set of control states (or labels) of P,

$\iota, \varepsilon \in V$ are initial and terminal label of P respectively

I is a finite set of triples of the form (v,R,w) with v,w in V, $v \neq \varepsilon$, and R a binary relation in the set S - the set of instructions of P.

Elements of the set:

$$E_P = \{R : (\exists\, v,w \in V)(v,R,w) \in I\}$$

will be called elementary actions of P.

By the computation of the process P we mean any sequence:

$$(v_0,s_0),(v_1,s_1),\ldots,(v_n,s_n),\ldots$$

such that:

$$(\forall i \geqslant 0)(\exists (v_i,R_i,v_{i+1}) \in I)\ s_i R_i s_{i+1} .$$

Let $P_i = (S_i, V_i, \iota_i, \varepsilon_i, I_i)$, i = 1,2, be two processes. The pair of functions $h = (h_S, h_V)$ where:

$$h_S: S_1 \longrightarrow S_2 , \qquad h_V: V_1 \longrightarrow V_2$$

will be called a homomorphism if the following conditions are satisfied:

1. $h_V(\iota_1) = \iota_2$, $h_V(\varepsilon_1) = \varepsilon_2$;
2. for every computation $(v_0,s_0),(v_1,s_1),\ldots,(v_n,s_n),\ldots$ of P_1 there is a computation $(w_0,t_0),(w_1,t_1),\ldots,(w_m,t_m),\ldots$ of P_2 such that:
   a. $t_0 = h_S(s_0)$,
   b. $(\forall i \geqslant 0)(\exists\, k > i)(\forall i \leqslant j \leqslant k)\ t_i = h_S(s_j) \,\&\, w_i = h_V(v_j)$.

In other words this special kind of homomorphism preserves initial and terminal control states, computation (but not the length of it) , and for every instruction (v,R,w) in I_1 either there is an instruction $(h_V(v),R',h_V(w))$ in I_2 or $h_V(v) = h_V(w)$.

Let S be a set, A an equivalence in S and R any binary relation in S. Define a relation $R_A \subseteq S/A \times S/A$ as follows:

$$[s]_A R_A [t]_A \equiv (\exists\, s' \in [s]_A)(\exists\, t' \in [t]_A)\ s'Rt'$$

It is easy to verify the following properties for every two binary relations Q,R and an equivalence relation A.

1. $(Q \cup R)_A = Q_A \cup R_A$,
2. $(Q \cap R)_A \subseteq Q_A \cap R_A$,
3. $(QR)_A \subseteq Q_A R_A$,
4. $(Q^*)_A \subseteq (Q_A)^*$

($Q^* = \bigcup_{n=0}^{\infty} Q^n$, $Q^0 = Id$, $Q^{n+1} = QQ^n$, and Id denotes the identity relation)

Consider now a process $P = (S, V, \delta, \varepsilon, I)$ and an equivalence relation A in the set of states S. By the A-agrregated process of the process P we mean a process $P_A = (S/A, V, \delta, \varepsilon, I_A)$ with I_A defined as follows:

$$(v, R_A, w) \in I_A \equiv (v, R, w) \in I \quad .$$

We are now in position to express precisely what we mean saying that a process is modelling some other processes.

A process P is modelling processes $P_1, P_2, \ldots, P_n$ if there are equivalence relations $A_1, A_2, \ldots, A_n$ in the set of states of P such that for every $i = 1,2,\ldots,n$, P_i is a homomorphic image of P_{A_i} (P_{A_i} is the A_i-agrregated process of P).

In order to illustrate the above notions let us return to the second example.

EXAMPLE 2 (continued). In our formalizm we have:

$$P = (\underline{in} \times \underline{re}, \{\delta, v, w, \varepsilon\}, \delta, \varepsilon, I)$$
$$I = \{(\delta, R_1, v), (v, R_2, \varepsilon), (v, R_3, w), (w, R_4, v)\}$$

where:

$$R_1 = \{(n,r),(n,0)\}$$
$$R_2 = \{(0,r),(0,r)\} \subset Id$$
$$R_3 = \{(n,r),(n-1,r) : n \neq 0\}$$
$$R_4 = \{(n,r),(n,r+n^2+1)\}$$

Equivalences:

$$A_{in} : (n,r) A_{in} (m,s) \equiv n = m$$
$$A_{re} : (n,r) A_{re} (m,s) \equiv r = s$$

The aggregated processes $P_{A_{in}}$, $P_{A_{re}}$ are described on Fig.5.

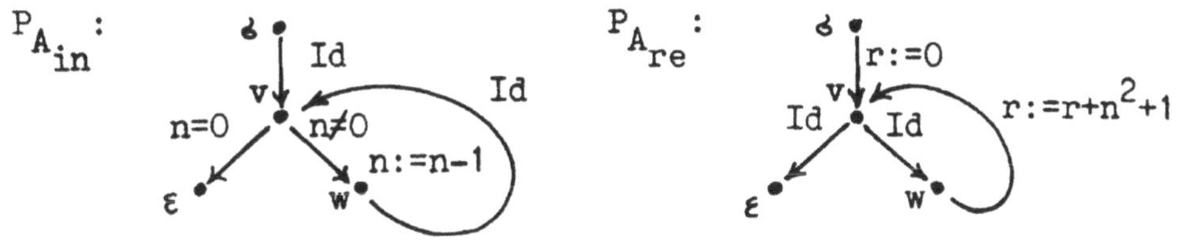

Fig. 5

The required homomorphisms are:

1. In the case of $P_{A_{in}}$ and P_1:

$h_S([n,r]) = n;$

$h_V(\alpha) = h_V(v) = h_V(w) = v \ , \ h_V(\varepsilon) = \varepsilon$.

2. In the case of $P_{A_{re}}$ and P_2:

$h_S([n,r]) = r$

$h_V(\alpha) = \alpha, \ h_V(\varepsilon) = \varepsilon \ , \ h_V(v) = h_V(w) = v$.

We can say roughly that aggregated processes of a given process represent the way in which the instructions of a modeled processes are arranged within the modelling one in order to achieve the required goal (in the above example to compute the sum of squares of the succesive n integers).

We are going now to formulate some results which connect properties of a given process with the same properties of its parts (its aggregated processes), thus, by an appropriate homomorphisms, with the properties of modelled processes.

Define first an auxiliary relation $R^A \subseteq S \times S/A$ for a given set S, an equivalence relation A, and binary relation R in the set S:

$$sR^A[t]_A \equiv (\exists t' \in [t]_A)\ sRt'$$

The following two conditions express the dependences between the choosen equivalence relation A and a relation R.

$$W(R,A) \equiv (\forall s,t \in S)\ sR^A[t]_A \Rightarrow (\forall s' \in [s]_A \cap Dom(R))\ s'R^A[t]_A$$

$$V(R,A) \equiv (\forall s \in S)\ s \in Dom(R) \Rightarrow [s]_A \subset Dom(R)$$

where $Dom(R) = \{ s \in S:\ (\exists t \in S)\ sRt \}$.

We shall deal first with functionality and determinancy of processes.

A process is <u>functional</u> if all its elementary actions are partial functions.

A process is <u>deterministic</u> if for every state s and label v there is no two instructions (v,R,u) , (v,Q,w) of the process with $u \neq w$ and $s \in Dom(R) \cap Dom(Q)$.

Let P be a process and let A be an equivalence relation in the set of its states.

PROPOSITION 1. P_A is functional if and only if for every elementary action $R \in E_P$, R^A is a partial function and $W(R,A)$ holds.

Observe that in general P does not need to be functional if P_A is for some A. The opposite situation we have with the determinancy what is the content of the next Proposition.

PROPOSITION 2. If there is an equivalence relation A such that P_A is deterministic then P is deterministic.

The determinancy of P is not sufficient to make P_A deterministic (see $P_{A_{re}}$ in Example 2).

PROPOSITION 3. If P is deterministic and for every elementary action $R \in E_P$, V(R,A) holds then P_A is deterministic.

In the theory of programs the input-output relation in the set of states (state vectors) is of the main interest. In our formalism the <u>input-output</u> <u>relation</u> (or <u>resulting</u> <u>relation</u>) Res_P of a process P is defined in the following way:

$$sRes_P t \equiv \text{there is a finite computation } (v_0,s_0),(v_1,s_1),\ldots,(v_n,s_n)$$

$$\text{with: } v_0 = \delta,\ v_n = \varepsilon,\ s_0 = s \text{ and } s_n = t.$$

Following the closure theorem in [2] and the properties of the relation R_A we have immediately:

$$(Res_P)_A \subseteq Res_{P_A}$$

On the other hand we have $(Res_P)_{A_{in}} = Res_{P_{A_{in}}}$ in our Example. It can be proved that.

THEOREM 1. $(Res_P)_A = Res_{P_A}$ if and only if for every elementary action $R \in E_P$, both W(R,A) and V(R,A) hold.

3. INTERACTING PROCESSES

The facts thus far considered have been concerned with sequential processes. In the sequel we shall try to outline how the described model, with slight modifications, can be used as a suitable tool to investigate both parallel and sequential cases.

The idea consists in describing the class of possible processes which realize (or model) the programming concept of the concurrent statement:

<u>cobegin</u> $P_1;P_2;\ldots;P_n$ <u>coend</u>

where $P_1,P_2,\ldots,P_n$ are processes which can access common variables, i.e. interacting processes.

Programming methods (e.g. critical regions,[5]) aim to assure certain instructions of the processes within the statement of an exclusive access to the shared variables or, in other words, they resolve of so called conflict situations. To some extent the meaning of a method can be represented as one of the processes realizing the above concurrent statesment.

We denote by A, B universal countable sets. All the sets of states considered in the sequel will be of the form $S = A_1^B$ (the set of all functions in A_1 with values in B) where A_1 is a subset of A.

Let $S = A_1^B$ and let R be a binary relation in S. Define for every $s_1, s_2 \in S$ such that $s_1 R s_2$ a set $Out(R,s_1,s_2) \subset A$ as follows:

$$a \in Out(R,s_1,s_2) \equiv s_1(a) \neq s_2(a) .$$

By the realization of the relation R we mean a tenary relation $\bar{R} \subseteq S \times S \times S$ given by:

$$(s_1,s_2,s_3) \in \bar{R} \equiv (\exists s' \in S)[\, s_1 R s' \,\&\, (\forall a \in Out(R,s_1,s'))\, s'(a) = s_3(a) \,\&$$
$$\&\, (\forall a \notin Out(R,s_1,s'))\, s_3(a) = s_2(a)\,].$$

By the notion of the realization of an action R we are able to express the fact that during the period of time needed to execute R the actual state of the process can be changed by another action executed simultaneously.

Assume in the sequel that V is an universal set (of control states). Any element of V^2 will be called the itermediary control state. By n-dimentional control state ($n \geq 1$) we mean a vector $[v_1, v_2, \ldots, v_n]$ with $v_i \in V \cup V^2$, and such that there is $1 \leq i \leq n$ that $v_i \in V$. We denote by $CS_n(V)$ the set of all n-dimentional control states over V. A n-dimentional control state describes a "control situation" at a given point of time while n processes are running simultaneously (any process either is in one of its own control state or is executing an action - is in an intermediary state . However not all these "control situations" are interesting. The next definition distinguish pairs of n-dimentional control states which are of particular interest.

We say that two n-dimentional control states $[v_1, v_2, \ldots, v_n]$ and $[w_1, w_2, \ldots, w_n]$ are neighbors if the following conditions are satisfied:

i. if $v_i \in V$, $w_i \in V^2$ then $w_i = v_i u$ for some u in V;

ii. if $v_i \in V^2$, $w_i \in V$ then $v_i = u w_i$ for some u in V;

iii. if $v_i, w_i \in V^2$ then $v_i = w_i$;

iv. there is exactly one $1 \leq i \leq n$ such that $w_i \in V$ and $v_i \neq w_i$.

Let us denote by $\bar{v}$ a vector $[v_1, v_2, \ldots, v_n]$.

By a n-dimentional process (over the base A, B, V) we mean any system $P^n = (S, CS_n(V), \bar{\alpha}, \bar{\varepsilon}, I)$ where:

$S = A_1^B$ ($A_1 \subseteq A$) is the set of states of P,

$\bar{\alpha} = [\alpha_1, \alpha_2, \ldots, \alpha_n]$, $\bar{\varepsilon} = [\varepsilon_1, \varepsilon_2, \ldots, \varepsilon_n]$ are n-dimentional initial and terminal control state respectively provided $\alpha_i, \varepsilon_i \in V$ for every $i = 1, 2, \ldots, n$

I is a finite set of triples of the form $(\bar{v}, R, \bar{w})$ - called the set of instructions of P^n - where: $\bar{v}, \bar{w}$ are neighbors, $\bar{v} \neq \bar{\varepsilon}$ and R is a binary relation in S.

A computation of a n-dimentional process P^n is any sequence $(\bar{v}_0, s_0)$, $(\bar{v}_1, s_1), \ldots, (\bar{v}_n, s_n), \ldots$ where $\bar{v}_k = [v_k^1, v_k^2, \ldots, v_k^n]$ and:

1. $\bar{v}_0 = \bar{\alpha}$;
2. $(\forall k \geqslant 0)(\exists (\bar{v}_k, R, \bar{w}_{k+1}) \in I)(s_{i_k}, s_k, s_{k+1}) \in \bar{R}$ & $i_k = \max_{j \leqslant k}(v_k^j \in V)$

(recall that $\bar{R}$ denotes the realizaton of R).

Clearly now, any 1-dimentional process is a process in the previously described sense, with only one technical restriction, due to the (iv) of the definition of neighbors, that no instruction of the form (v, R, v) can occur. The same (iv) gives us another unessential restriction saying that at any point of time only one instruction can complete its action.

Let $P^n = (S, CS_n(V), \bar{\alpha}, \bar{\varepsilon}, I)$ be a process. Assume that $A_1^B = S$ and let $A_2 \subseteq A_1$. An equivalence relation $=_{A_2}$ is defined as follows:

$$s_1 =_{A_2} s_2 \equiv (\forall a \in A_2)\ s_1(a) = s_2(a)$$

Let $\{i_1, i_2, \ldots, i_k\} \subset \{1, 2, \ldots, n\}$. Define a process $P^k = (A_2^B, CS_k(V), \bar{\alpha}', \bar{\varepsilon}', I')$ where:

$$\bar{\alpha}' = [\alpha_{i_1}, \alpha_{i_2}, \ldots, \alpha_{i_k}] \quad , \quad \bar{\varepsilon}' = [\varepsilon_{i_1}, \varepsilon_{i_2}, \ldots, \varepsilon_{i_k}] \quad ,$$

$$(\bar{v}', R_{A_2}, \bar{w}') \in I' \equiv (\exists (\bar{v}, R, \bar{w}) \in I)\ (\forall\ 1 \leqslant j \leqslant k)\ v_j' = v_{i_j}\ \&\ w_j' = w_{i_j}$$

and R_{A_2} is defined by:

$$(\forall s_1, s_2 \in A_2^B)\ s_1 R_{A_2} s_2 \equiv (\exists s_1' \in [s_1]_{A_2})(\exists s_2' \in [s_2]_{A_2})\ s_1' R s_2'$$

The process P^k will be called a k-projection process of P^n with respect to the set $i_1, i_2, \ldots, i_k$ and A_2 (shortly a k-projection process).

We are going now to generalize the notion of modelling introduced before.

A k-dimentional process P^k is modelled within a process P^n ($k \leq n$) if there is a k-projection process of P^n isomorphic with P^k.

Suppose now that we consider n many-dimentional processes $P_1^{i_1}, P_2^{i_2}, \ldots, P_n^{i_n}$ ($i_k \geq 1$) with the sets of states $S_k = A_k^B$. Let $i = i_1 + i_2 + \ldots + i_n$.

We say that an i-dimentional process P^i is a concurrent realization of $P_k^{i_k}$, $k = 1,2,\ldots,n$, if each process $P_k^{i_k}$ is modelled within the process P^i and two natural conditions are satisfied:

1. every two projection sets $\{k_1^j, k_2^j, \ldots, k_{i_j}^j\}$, $\{k_1^m, k_2^m, \ldots, k_{i_m}^m\}$ are disjoint ($j,m \leq n$, $k_l^j, k_l^m \in \{1,2,\ldots,i\}$);
2. $\bigcup_{j=1}^{n} \{k_1^j, k_2^j, \ldots, k_{i_j}^j\} = \{1,2,\ldots,i\}$, $S = \left(\bigcup_{j=1}^{n} A_j\right)^B$

In this sense we have the whole class of realizations of the statment

cobegin $P_1; P_2; \ldots; P_n$ coend

for arbitrary processes P_i.

Observe the following facts: each n-dimentional process is a concurrent realization of its 1-dimentional coordinate processes, and:

cobegin P_1; cobegin $P_2; P_3$ coend; coend $\subseteq$ cobegin $P_1; P_2; P_3$ coend

(i.e. every concurrent realization of the left hand side statement is a realization of the right hand side statement). We can conclude that the real subject of interest is a class of concurrent realizations of 1-dimentional (sequential) processes. The extreme cases in this class are, so called, pseudo-concurrent realizations in which for every instruction $([v_1, v_2, \ldots, v_n], R, [w_1, w_2, \ldots, w_n])$, $v_i, w_i \in V$ ($i = 1,2,\ldots n$). The content of the previous section corresponds to the above considerations restricted to the pseudo-concurrent realizations.

The above general notion of the process and the concurrent realization makes possible, at least, to express precisely what we mean by the particular multiprogramming concept. In addition to that it makes possible to understand concurrency in time independent terms, postulated e.g. in [5], without any restrictions assumed in advance. It gives, at last, the general framework within which both sequential programming and multiprogramming concepts can be studied.

REFERENCES

[1] BLIKLE,A. Iterative systems; an algebraic approach. Bull. Acad. Polon. Sci., Ser. Math. Phys. Astronom., 1(1971).

[2] BLIKLE,A.; MAZURKIEWICZ,A. An algebraic approach to the theory of programs, algorithms, languages and recursiveness. Math. Found. Comp. Sci. I (Proc. Symp. Warsaw-Jablonna), 1972 , Warsaw 1972.

[3] DEMBINSKI,P. Data aggregations in algorithms. CC PAS Reports, 147(1974).

[4] DIJKSTRA,E.,W. Cooperating sequential processes. Programming Languages, F. Genuys ed. , Academic Press, New York 1968.

[5] HANSEN,P.,B. Concurrent programming concepts. Comp. Surv. 5(1973).

[6] PAWLAK,Z. Stored program computers. Algorytmy 5(1969).

[7] WINKOWSKI,J. Concurrent programs. This issue.

[8] ZEIGLER,B.,P. Towards a formal theory of modelling and simulation: structure preserving morphisms. Jour. ACM, 19(1972).

SIMULATION

A.Skowron
Institute of Mathematics
Warsaw University
Poland

INTRODUCTION

There are two reasons which justify the need for a more precise notion of simulation.

One of them resides in the fact, that definitions of that notion which may be encountered in literature do not express one basic feature of simulation: that in the process of imitating one machine or program by another it is essential that some properties be preserved. This requirement has been taken into account in the definition of simulation suggested in the present paper. Considering that the notion of an iterative system (machine) proposed in [1] proved to be a convenient tool for describing and examining objects such as: machine, program, algorithm etc.; we introduce the notion of simulation of one iterative system by another.

The second reason seems to be need of incorporating into the mathematical foundations of Computer Science some general notion which would make it possible to compare objects of interest for computer scientists such as machines, programs, algorithms etc. It is felt that the notion of functions computable by these objects is very often not sufficient or inconvenient for their comparison. The notion of simulation suggested here seems to be a much better tool for that.

In the present paper the notion of simulation has been formulated and illustrated by various examples. Basic algebraic properties of that notion are given.

Interesting new results may be obtained applying the notion of simulation to investigations of particular classes of iterative systems such as e.g. stored program machines [3] . Using that notion it is possible to state more precisely what a translator or simulator is and investigate their properties. The notion of simulation introduced here may become a convenient tool for examining properties of programs e.g. their correctness.

1. AUXILIARY NOTIONS AND NOTATION

$\emptyset$ stands for the empty set, $\cup$ and $\cap$ denote the set-theoretical operations of join and meet. For a family of sets $\{X_i\}_{i\in I}$, we denote its cartesian product by $\times_{i\in I} X_i$. The set of all functions from a set X into a set Y is denoted by Y^X. If $x = x_0, x_1, \ldots$ is a sequence, then $|x|$ is its length i.e. the number of its elements when it is finite and $+\infty$ otherwise. If $x = x_0, x_1, \ldots$ is a sequence ranging over X and $Y \subset X$, then x_Y stands for the subsequence of x obtained by rejecting all elements which do not belong to Y. For a sequence $x = x_0, x_1, \ldots$ over X and $\varrho \in Z^X$ we denote by $\varrho(x)$ the sequence $\varrho(x_0), \varrho(x_1), \ldots$. The initial element of a sequence x is denoted by $\mathrm{beg}\, x$.

For any relation f in the product $X \times X'$ i.e. $f \subset X \times X'$, we denote by D_f (or Df) the domain of f i.e. the set

$$\{ x : \bigvee_{y\in X'} (x,y) \in f \}$$

any by R_f (or Rf) its counterdomain i.e. the set

$$\{ y : \bigvee_{x\in X} (x,y) \in f \}.$$

xfy is an abbreviation of $(x,y) \in f$. For any $A \subset X'$, $f^{-1}(A)$ is the set

$$\{ x : \bigvee_{y\in A} xfy \} ,$$

called counterimage of A. For $B \subset X$, we denote by $f(B)$ (or $f[B]$) the set

$$\{ y : \bigvee_{x\in B} xfy \} ,$$

called the image of B, and by $f|B$ the relation f reduced to B

i.e. the set

$$\{(x,y) : xfy \wedge x \in B\} .$$

For any two relations $f \subset X \times X'$ and $g \subset X' \times X''$, $g \circ f$ is a new relation, called the composition of f and g, such that

$$g \circ f = \{(x,y) : \bigvee_{z \in X'} xfz \wedge zgy\} .$$

An ordered pair of the form (X, Π) , where X is a set and $\Pi \subset X \times X$, is called an iterative system [1]. X is called the set of states and Π the control of the system (X, Π) . Iterative systems will be denoted by $M, M', \ldots$. If Π is a single-valued relation in $X \times X'$, we call it a partial function and (X, Π) is called a functional iterative system. $X^{[X]}$ stands for the set of all partial functions from X into X.

A path in a system (X, Π) is any finite sequence $x_0, \ldots, x_k$ of states in X such that for every i , $x_i \Pi x_{i+1}$, where $0 \leqslant i < k$. x_0 is called the begining and x_k the end of the path. Every finite path $x_0, \ldots, x_k$ in the system (X, Π) such that $k \geqslant 1$ and $x_k \notin D\Pi$ will be called a finite computation of that system. An infinite computation of an iterative system (X, Π) is any infinite sequence $x_0, x_1, \ldots$ of states in X such that for $i = 0, 1, \ldots$

$$x_i \Pi x_{i+1} .$$

A computation of an iterative system $M = (X, \Pi)$ is any sequence which is either a finite or infinite computation of the system M. The set of all computations of an iterative system M is denoted by C_M and the set of all subsequences of sequences belonging to C_M is denoted by $\mathcal{C}_M$.

If $M = (X, \Pi)$ and $Y \subset X$, then $\overline{Y}$ is the set

$$Y \cup \Pi(Y) \cup \Pi^2(Y) \cup \ldots ,$$

which is called the closure of Y in M or the set generated by Y in M.

A relation $f_M \subset X \times X$ such that $x f_M y$ if and only if there exists a finite computation beginning with x and ending on y will be called the state relation of the iterative system M.

A subsystem of an iterative system $M = (X, \Pi)$ is any iterative system $M' = (X', \Pi')$ such that $X' \subset X$ and for arbitrary states $x, y \in X'$, $x \Pi' y$ if and only if $x \Pi y$.

For any equivalence relation $\sim$ in X we shall denote by

$[x]_\sim$ (or $[x]$) the equivalence class of $\sim$ which contains x, while $X/\sim$ will denote the set of all equivalence classes of that relation.

An equivalence relation $\sim$ in X will be called a congruence in a functional iterative system $M = (X, \pi)$ if for any states $x,y \in X$ the condition $x \sim y$ implies that $x \in D\pi$ and $y \in D\pi$ and $\pi(x) \sim \pi(y)$ or $x \notin D_\pi$ and $y \notin D_\pi$.

If $\sim$ is a congruence in a functional iterative system $M = (X, \pi)$, then by $M/\sim$ we denote the quotient functional iterative system $(X/\sim, \pi/\sim)$ such that for $x \in X$, $[x] \in D_{\pi/\sim}$ if and only if $x \in D_\pi$ and for any $x \in D_\pi$, $(\pi/\sim)[x] = [\pi(x)]$.

The notion of a stored program machine and a program, which will be subsequently used have been described in [2].

2. THE DEFINITION OF SIMULATION

We shall begin by introducing two auxiliary definitions, describing a set of properties and a simulation basis.

Let X, X', I be sets. The set $V = \{v_i\}_{i \in I}$, where $v_i \subset X \times X'$ for all $i \in I$, is called a set of properties (in $X \times X'$), and his elements are called properties.

Let $M = (X, \pi)$, $M' = (X', \pi')$ be iterative systems. A basis of a simulation of M in M' is any ordered parir form

$$B = (v, V) ,$$

where V is a set of properties in $X_1 \times X_1'$, $v \in V$, $X_1 \supset X$ and $X_1' \supset X'$. v is called the initial property of the basis B.

DEFINITION. Let $M = (X, \pi)$, $M' = (X', \pi')$ be iterative systems and $B = (v, V)$, where $V = \{v_i\}_{i \in I}$ a basis of a simulation of M in M'. An iterative system M is B-simulated by M', which is denoted by $M <_B M'$ if and only if there exists a partial function $\varrho \in X'^{[X]}$ such that:

1° $D\varrho = (\bigcup_{i \in I} Dv_i) \cap \overline{Dv}$,

2° for any $i \in I$ and $x \in D\varrho$, if $x \in Dv_i$, then $xv_i\, \varrho(x)$,

3° for any computation $\alpha \in C_M$, if $\mathrm{beg}\,\alpha \in Dv$, then $\varrho(\alpha_{D_\varrho}) \in \mathcal{C}_{M'}$.

The relation $<_B$ is called B-simulation.

The above listed conditions state that to every computation α

of the iterative system M, which starts with a state belonging to the domain of the initial property v of the simulation basis B, there is assigned a computation α' of the iterative system M'. The connection between α and α' is illustrated by fig. 1.

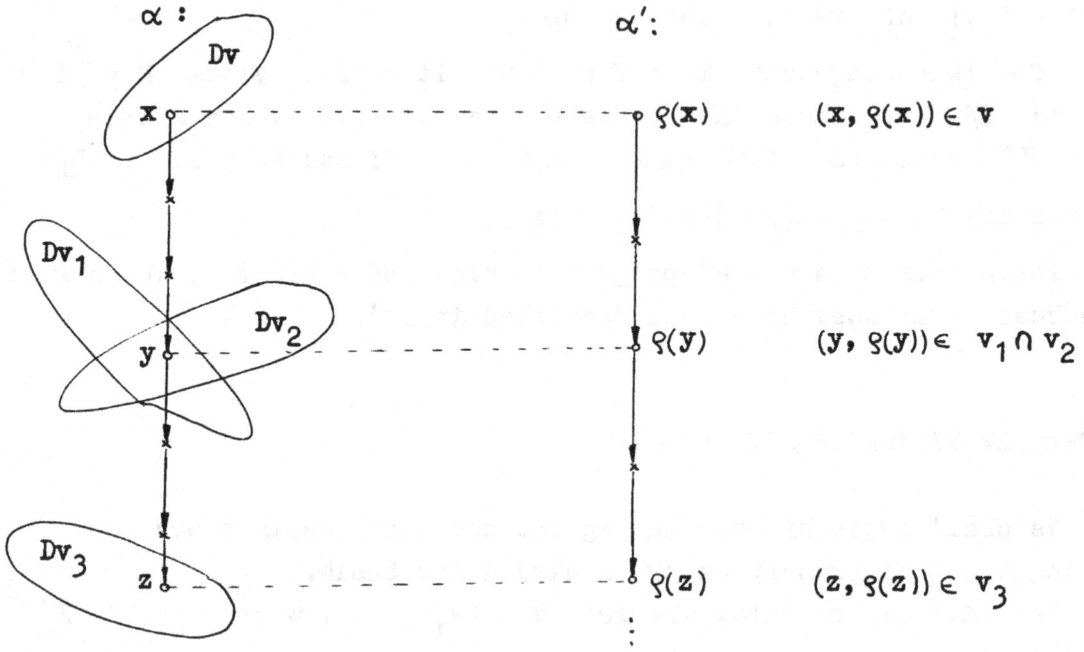

Fig. 1.

$M <_{B,\varrho} M'$ means that $M <_B M'$ and ϱ is a partial function from X into X' which satisfies conditions 1-3 from the definition of simulation.

3. EXAMPLES OF SIMULATION

Example 1. Functions computable by functional iterative systems.

Let $M = (X, \pi)$, $M' = (X', \pi')$ be functional iterative systems, Σ, Δ - finite alphabets called input and output alphabets correspondingly, i, i' - coding functions and o, o' - decoding functions such that:

$$i : \Sigma^* \longrightarrow X, \qquad i' : \Sigma^* \longrightarrow X',$$
$$o : X \longrightarrow \Delta^*, \qquad o' : X' \longrightarrow \Delta^*$$

and i, i' are one-to-one functions.

A basis of simulation of M in M' will be defined as follows:

$$B = (v, \{v, v_o\}),$$

where for any $x \in X$ and $x' \in X'$, $x v x'$ if and only if $i^{-1}(x) = i'^{-1}(x')$ and $v_o = \{(x,x') \in Rf_M \times Rf_{M'} : o(x) = o'(x')\}$.

Property 1. If $M <_B M'$ and $Dv = Ri$, then for $x \in D_{o \circ f_M \circ i}$ we have

$$(o \circ f_M \circ i)(x) = (o' \circ f_{M'} \circ i')(x).$$

Example 2. Approximation.

Let $M, M', \Sigma, \Delta, i, o, i', o', v$ be defined as in previous example. We assume that a metric d is defined in Δ^*. For a given $\varepsilon > 0$ we define a simulation basis $B_\varepsilon = (v, \{v, v_\varepsilon\})$, where

$$v_\varepsilon = \{(x,x') \in Rf_M \times Rf_{M'} : d(o(x), o'(x')) < \varepsilon\}.$$

Property 2. If $M <_{B_\varepsilon} M'$ and $Dv = Ri$, then for all $x \in D_{o \circ f_M \circ i}$

$$d((o \circ f_M \circ i)(x), (o' \circ f_{M'} \circ i')(x)) < \varepsilon .$$

Example 3. Time-regarding simulation.

Let $M = (X, \Pi)$, $M' = (X', \Pi')$ be functional iterative systems and τ, τ' functions such that $\tau : X \longrightarrow R^+$, $\tau' : X' \longrightarrow R^+$, where R^+ is the set of positive real numbers. If $x \in X$, we call $\tau(x)$ the time of M remaining in the state x; similarly, if $x' \in X'$, $\tau'(x')$ is the time of M' remaining in the state x'. Let $k \in R^+$.

We take the basis of simulation of M in M' to be the set $B_T = (v, \{v, v_o, v_T\})$, where v, v_o are defined as in example 1 and v_T is a property defined as follows: for any $x_o \in X$, $x_o' \in X'$

$x_o v_T x_o'$ if and only of $x_o v x_o'$ and $\sum_{i \leqslant |x|} \tau(x_i) = k \cdot \sum_{i \leqslant |x'|} \tau'(x_i')$,

where $x \in C_M$, $x' \in C_{M'}$, $x = x_o, \ldots, x_i, \ldots$ and $x' = x_o', \ldots, x_i', \ldots$.

$\sum_{i \leqslant |x|} \tau(x_i)$ is called the time of the computation begining with x_o.

Property 3. If $M <_{B_T} M'$ and $D_v = R_i \subset Dv_T$, then for every $x \in \Sigma^*$ the ratio of time of computation in M starting with $i(x)$ and time of computation in M' starting with $i'(x)$ is constant, equal to k and for $x \in D(o \circ f_M \circ i)$

$$(o \circ f_M \circ i)(x) = (o \circ f_{M'} \circ i')(x).$$

Example 4. Simulation of memory contents.

Let A be a set called the set of addresses, Σ - an alphabet and let $M = (X, \Pi)$, $M' = (X', \Pi')$ be functional iterative systems, where $X \subset \Sigma^A$ and $X' \subset \Sigma^A$. Let β be a one-to-one function from A into A. We shall define the property $v_\beta \subset X \times X'$ as follows:

for any $c \in X$ and $c' \in X'$, $c v_\beta c'$ if and only if $c'|R_\beta = c_\beta$, where c_β is a function from R_β into Σ such that for $x \in R_\beta$

$$c_\beta(x) = c(\beta^{-1}(x)) \quad \text{(see fig. 2).}$$

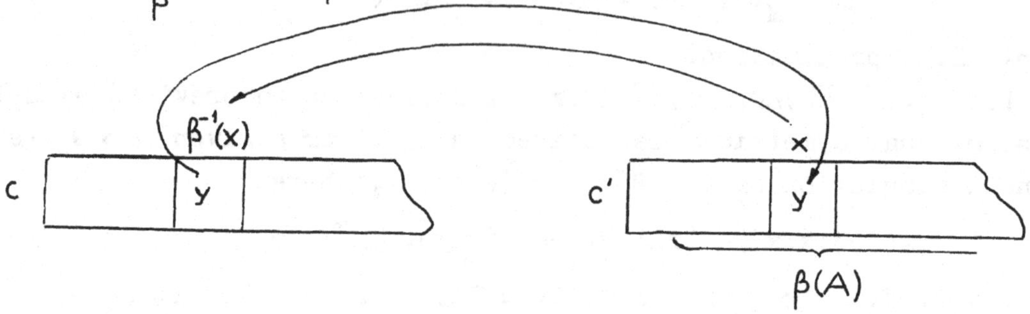

Fig. 2.

If $M <_B M'$, $B = (v, V)$ and $v_\beta \in V$, $Dv_\beta = X$, then we say that M is simulated by M' with a preservation of memory contents.

Example 5. Simulators and compilers.

We shall now give examples of notions, which will be used in [3] for investigating properties of stored program machines.

1. A simulator of an iterative system.

Let $M = (C, \Pi)$ be a stored program machine and M' a functional iterative system. If p is a program in M, we shall denote by C^p the set of all states in which p is stored and by M(p) the iterative system $(C^p, \Pi|C^p)$. Suppose $B = (v, V)$ is a basis of simulation of M' in M(p) such that $Rv \subset C^p$. We shall say that p is a B-simulator of M' in M if and only if

$$M' <_B M(p).$$

2. A simulator of a program set.

Let $M = (C, \Pi)$, $M' = (C', \Pi')$ be stored program machines, $\mathcal{P}$ - a set of programs in M', p - a program in M and $B = (v, V)$ - - a basis of simulation of M' in M. The program p is called B-simulator in M of the set of programs $\mathcal{P}$ if for every program $p' \in \mathcal{P}$,

$$M'(p') <_{B_{p'}} M(p),$$

where $B_{p'} = (v_{p'}, V')$ and $v_{p'} = v \cap (C'^{p'} \times C^p)$, $V' = V \cup \{v_{p'}\}$.

3. Compiler.

Let $M = (C, \Pi)$, $M' = (C', \Pi')$ be stored program machines, $\mathcal{P}$ - a set of programs in M, $\mathcal{P}'$ - a set of programs in M', $i : \mathcal{P} \longrightarrow C'$, $o : C' \longrightarrow \mathcal{P}'$ and let $B = (v, V)$ be a basis of simulation of M in M'. A program p_k in M' is called a B-compiler from the set $\mathcal{P}$ into the set $\mathcal{P}'$ if for every program $p \in \mathcal{P}$ we have $i(p) \in C'^{p_k}$ and $M(p) <_{B_p} M'(p')$ and $p' \in \mathcal{P}'$, where $p' = (o \circ f_{M'} \circ i)(p)$, $B_p = (v_p, V')$ and $v_p = v \cap (C^p \times C^{p'})$, $V' = V \cup \{v_p\}$.

4. ALGEBRAIC PROPERTIES OF SIMULATION

4.1. Composition and inversion of simulations.

In the sequel we shall present some properties of simulations concerning their composition and inversion i.e. we shall attempt to answer the following questions: When does it follow from an iterative system M being simulated by M' and M' by M'' that M is simulated by M'' ? When can we infer that M' is simulated by M assuming M is simulated by M' ?

If $B = (v, V)$ and $B' = (v', V')$ are simulation bases, then $B \circ B'$ denotes the composition of the basis B with B' i.e. a simulation basis of the form:

$$(v' \circ v, \{v_1' \circ v_1 : v_1 \in V \wedge v_1' \in V'\}).$$

THEOREM 1. Let M, M', M'' be iterative systems and let $B = (v, V)$ and $B' = (v', V')$ be bases of simulation of M in M' and of M' in M'', correspondingly, such that $Rv \cap Dv' \neq \emptyset$ and for arbitrary $v_1 \in V$ and $v_1' \in V'$, if $Rv_1 \cap Dv_1' \neq \emptyset$, then $Rv_1 \subset Dv_1'$. Then $M <_B M'$ and $M' <_{B'} M''$ imply

$$M <_{B \circ B'} M''.$$

THEOREM 2. Let $M = (X, \Pi)$, $M' = (X, \Pi')$, $M'' = (X, \Pi'')$ be iterative systems and let $B = (v, V)$ be a simulation basis such that properties belonging to V are equivalence relations in X. Then from $M <_B M'$ and $M' <_B M''$ follows $M <_B M''$.

THEOREM 3. Let $M = (X, \Pi)$, $M' = (X, \Pi')$ be iterative systems and $B = (v, V)$ a simulation basis with properties being equivalence relations in X. If $M <_{B,\varrho} M'$, ϱ is one-to-one mapping from X onto X and for every $x \in C_M$ $\varrho(x) \in C_{M'}$, then $M' <_B M$.

4.2. Representation theorems.

In definition of simulation we have formulated conditions which a partial function ϱ must satisfy when $M <_{B,\varrho} M'$. It turns out that topologies may be easily defined in the sets of states of M and M' such that if $M <_{B,\varrho} M'$, then ϱ is continuous function. The following theorem holds:

THEOREM 4. Let $V = \{v_i\}_{i\in I}$ be a set of properties in $X \times X'$ and $B = (v,V)$ a basis of simulation of M in M'. We define a set of properties V^* as follows:

$$V^* = \{\bigcap_{i\in T} v_i : T \subset I\} \cup \{\bigcup_{i\in T} v_i : T\subset I\} \cup \{\emptyset\}.$$

The conditions $M <_B M'$ and $M <_{B^*} M'$, where $B^* = (v,V^*)$ are equivalent.

The following conclusion may be inferred from the above theorem:

COROLLARY 1. Let $B = (v,V)$ be a basis of simulation of M in M' and let $V = \{v_i\}_{i\in I}$ be the set of properties of B such that

1. $\{\emptyset\} \in V$ and for any $V' \subset V$, $\bigcup V' \in V$ and $\bigcap V' \in V$,
2. for arbitrary states $x\in X$, $y\in X'$ and $v\in V$, if xvy then
$$\{i\in I : x\in Dv_i\} = \{i\in I : y\in Rv_i\}.$$

If $M <_{B,\varrho} M'$ then $T = (\bigcup_{v\in V} Dv \cap D\varrho, \{Dv\cap D\varrho\}_{v\in V})$ and $T' = (\bigcup_{v\in V} Rv\cap R\varrho, \{Rv\cap R\varrho\}_{v\in V})$ are topological spaces and ϱ is a continuous function in the space T ranging on the space T'.

When $M <_B M'$, a simulation basis B' may be often found such that

1. $M <_{B'} M'$,
2. the properties in the basis B' are disjoint,
3. every property v in the basis B is a join of some properties in B'.

THEOREM 5. Let $M = (X,\Pi)$, $M' = (X',\Pi')$ be functional iterative systems and let $B = (v_{i'},V)$, where $V = \{v_i\}_{i\in I}$, $i' \in I$ be a basis of simulation of M in M' such that for any property $v\in V$ and for arbitrary states $x\in X$ and $y\in X'$, if xvy then:

$$\{i\in I: x\in Dv_i\} = \{i\in I: y\in Rv_i\} \quad\text{and}\quad Dv_i \cap Dv_{i'} = \emptyset \text{ for } i \neq i',\ i\in I.$$

Then there exists a simulation basis B' such that

1. if $M <_B M'$, then $M <_{B'} M'$,

2. the properties in B' are disjoint i.e. for any non-equal properties v, v' in B', $Dv \cap Dv' = \emptyset$,
3. for every property $v \in V$ there exists a subset V'' of the set of properties of the basis B' such that

$$v = \bigcup_{v'' \in V''} v'' .$$

4.3. Products of iterative systems and simulation bases.

We shall consider families of iterative systems $\{M_i\}_{i \in I}$ and $\{M_i'\}_{i \in I}$ and a family $\{B_i\}_{i \in I}$ of simulation bases. We shall define the product of iterative systems and of simulation bases so as to obtain that the product of the family $\{M_i\}_{i \in I}$ is simulated by the product of the family $\{M_i'\}_{i \in I}$, if we take as a simulation basis the product of simulation bases and M_i is B_i-simulated by M_i' for $i \in I$. We shall examine two notions of product of iterative systems.

Let $\{M_i\}_{i \in I}$ be a family of iterative systems, where $M_i = (X_i, \Pi_i)$ for $i \in I$. An iterative system $M = (X, \Pi)$ such that

1. $X = \times_{i \in I} X_i$,

2. for all $z \in X$

$$\Pi[z] = \{z' \in X' : \bigwedge_{i \in I} (z(i) \Pi_i z'(i) \vee z'(i) = z(i)) \wedge \bigvee_{j \in I} z(j) \Pi_j z'(j)\},$$

will be called the product of the family $\{M_i\}_{i \in I}$ and will be denoted by $\times_{i \in I} M_i$.

Suppose $\{M_i\}_{i \in I}$ and $\{M_i'\}_{i \in I}$ are families of iterative systems and $B_i = (v_i, V_i)$ for $i \in I$ are bases of simulation of M_i in M_i', where $V_i = \{v_i^j\}_{j \in J_i}$. We shall define the product of the family of bases $\{B_i\}_{i \in I}$ - and we shall denote it by $\times_{i \in I} B_i$ - as a basis (v, V) of simulation of the product $\times_{i \in I} M_i$ in $\times_{i \in I} M_i'$ satisfying the following conditions:

1. for any $z \in \times_{i \in I} X_i$ and $z' \in \times_{i \in I} X_i'$, $z v z'$ if and only if $z(i)\ v_i\ z'(i)$ for $i \in I$,
2. for any $\omega \in \times_{i \in I} J_i$, $v_\omega \in V$, where v_ω is a property in the product

$$(\underset{i\in I}{\times} X_i) \times (\underset{i\in I}{\times} X_i')$$

such that for any $z \in \underset{i\in I}{\times} X_i$ and $z' \in \underset{i\in I}{\times} X_i'$, $z v_\omega z'$

if and only if for every $i \in I$

$$z(i)\ v_i^{\omega(i)} z'(i).$$

THEOREM 6. If $\{M_i\}_{i\in I}$, $\{M_i'\}_{i\in I}$ are families of iterative systems and for every $i \in I$

$$M_i <_{B_i} M_i' ,$$

then

$$\underset{i\in I}{\times} M_i <_{\underset{i\in I}{\times} B_i} \underset{i\in I}{\times} M_i' .$$

The notion of a product of iterative systems introduced above has the property that the product of a family $\{M_i\}_{i\in I}$ of functional iterative systems is not in general a functional iterative system. We shall now introduce the definition of a direct product of a family of iterative systems. This direct product of a family of functional iterative systems will be a functional iterative system.

Let $\{M_i\}_{i\in I}$ be a family of iterative systems, where $M_i = (X_i, \Pi_i)$ for $i \in I$. An iterative system $M = (X, \Pi)$ will be called the direct product of the family $\{M_i\}_{i\in I}$ and will be denoted by $\underset{i\in I}{\odot} M_i$ if $X = \underset{i\in I}{\times} X_i$ and for every $z \in X$,

$$\Pi[z] = \{z' \in X : \bigwedge_{i\in I} z(i)\, \Pi_i\, z'(i)\}.$$

No theorem analogous to theorem 6 holds for direct products. However, we shall obtain a similar assuming some additional conditions.

Let $M = (X, \Pi)$ be an iterative system and suppose $Y \subset X$. The distance of $x \in X$ from the set Y in the system M will be the length of the shortest path in M which starts with an element in Y and ends in x, if such a path exists, and will be equal to $+\infty$ otherwise.

THEOREM 7. Let $\{M_i\}_{i\in I}$, $\{M_i'\}_{i\in I}$ be families of iterative systems and let $B_i = (v_i, V_i)$ for $i \in I$ be bases of simualtion of M_i in M_i', $V_i = \{v_i^j\}_{j\in J}$. Let for all $i \in I$, $R\Pi_i' \cap Rv_i = \emptyset$. Suppose for any $z \in \underset{i\in I}{\times} X_i$, $z' \in \underset{i\in I}{\times} X_i'$ and $\omega \in \underset{i\in I}{\times} J_i$, if $z v_\omega z'$, then for all $j \in I$ the distances of $z'(j)$ from the counter-

-domain of the property v_j are equal. Then from $M_i <_{B_i} M_i'$ for $i \in I$ follows

$$\bigodot_{i \in I} M_i <_{\times_{i \in I} B_i} \bigodot_{i \in I} M_i' .$$

4.4. Congruences.

For given functional iterative systems M and M', for congruences $\sim$ and $\sim'$ in M and M' correspondingly and for a basis B of simulation of M in M' we shall define a basis $\bar{B}$, called an adjoint to B, so that the assumption of M being B-simulated by M' imply that the quotient system $M/\sim$ is $\bar{B}$-simulated by $M'/\sim'$.

Let $M = (X, \Pi)$, $M' = (X', \Pi')$ be functional iterative systems and $\sim, \sim'$ congruences in M and M' correspondingly. Let $B = (v,V)$ be a basis of simulation of M in M'. For every property $v \in V$ we define a property $\bar{v}$ in the set $X/\sim \times X'/\sim'$, called an adjoint property with respect to v, such that for any $\alpha \in X/\sim$ and $\beta \in X'/\sim'$, $\alpha \bar{v} \beta$ if and only if there exist $x \in \alpha$ and $y \in \beta$ such that xvy.

A simulation basis $\bar{B}$ such that $\bar{B} = (\bar{v}, \bar{V})$, where $\bar{v}$ is the property adjoint to v and $\bar{V}$ is the set of all properties adjoint to properties in V, will be called the simulation basis of $M/\sim$ in $M'/\sim'$ adjoint to B.

THEOREM 8. Let $\sim$ and $\sim'$ be congruences in functional iterative systems M and M' correspondingly and let $\bar{B}$ be a basis of simulation of $M/\sim$ in $M'/\sim'$ adjoint to B. Assume that for any property v in the basis B and for any $x, x' \in X$, $y, y' \in X'$, if $x \sim x'$, $y \sim' y'$ and xvy, then $x'vy'$ and if $x \sim x' \wedge xvy \wedge x'vy'$, then $y \sim' y'$. Then $M <_B M'$ implies $M/\sim <_{\bar{B}} M'/\sim'$.

4.5. Secondary properties.

Let $B = (v,V)$ and $B' = (v,V')$ be bases of simulation of M in M' and assume $V' \subset V$. If it follows from M being B'-simulated by M' that M is B-simulated by M', then we shall say that properties belonging to the set $V - V'$ are secondary properties of the basis B. We shall proceed with some examples of secondary properties.

Clearly every property $v_0 \in V$ such that $Dv_0 \cap \overline{Dv} = \emptyset$ is a secoundary property of this basis B.

THEOREM 9. Let M and M' be iterative systems and $B = (v,V)$ - a basis of simulation of M in M'. If v_0 is a property belonging to $V - \{v\}$ such that there exist non-empty properties $v_1, v_2 \in V - \{v_0\}$ for which $v_1 \cup v_2 = v_0$, then v_0 is a secondary property of the basis B.

THEOREM 10. Let $M = (X, \pi)$, $M' = (X', \pi')$ be iterative systems and $B = (v, V)$ - a simulation basis of M in M'. If $v_0 \in V$ is a property such that for some $v_1, v_2 \in V$

1. $v_0 = v_1 \cap v_2$,
2. $v_1 \neq v_0 \neq v_2$,

then v_0 is a secondary property of the simulation basis B.

Let $M = (X, \pi)$ be a functional iterative system, $Y \subset X$ and $x \in X$. We shall denote by $X_{x,Y}$ the set of all elements of sequences which are shortest paths starting in Y and ending on x. We shall write $M(x,Y)$ for a functional iterative system of the form $(X, \pi | X_{x,Y})$.

If $B = (v, V)$ is a basis of simulation of M in M', then a property $v_0 \in V - \{v\}$ such that

$$Dv_0 \cap \bigcup_{v \in V - \{v_0\}} Dv = \emptyset$$

$$\text{and} \quad Rv_0 \cap \bigcup_{v \in V - \{v_0\}} Rv = \emptyset$$

will be called an isolated property in B.

THEOREM 11. Let $M = (X, \pi)$, $M' = (X', \pi')$ be functional iterative systems and $B = (v, V)$ - a simulation basis of M in M'. Assume that $v_0 \in V$ is an isolated property in B and suppose

$$B' = (v, V - \{v_0\}).$$

Then, if $M <_{B',\varrho} M'$ and for each state $x \in X$ there exists a state $y \in X'$ such that the condition $x v_0 y$ implies

$$M(x, Dv) <_{B',\varrho'} M'(y, Rv) \quad \text{and} \quad \varrho^{-1}(X'_{y,Rv}) = \varrho'^{-1}(X'_{y,Rv}),$$

where $\varrho' = \varrho | X_{x,Dv}$, then $M <_B M'$.

THEOREM 12. Let $M = (X, \pi)$ and $M' = (X', \pi')$ be functional iterative systems and $B = (v, V)$ a basis of simulation of M in M'. Assume v_0 is an isolated property in B. Then, if there exists a property $v' \in V$ such that for any $x \in X$ and $y \in X'$ the condition $x v_0 y$ implies

$$\pi^{-1}(\{x\}) = Dv' \cap \overline{Dv} \qquad \text{and} \qquad \pi^{-1}(\{y\}) = Rv' \cap \overline{Rv},$$

then the property v_0 is a secondary property of the basis B.

4.6. Simulation and operations on iterative systems.

We shall consider the operations of join, meet, substitution and iteration depend on iterative systems. Theorems describing preservation of simulation by these operations will be stated.

THEOREM 13. Let M and M' be iterative systems and $B = (v,V)$ - a basis of simulation of M in M'. If $M <_B M'$, then for every subsystem M'' of M,

$$M'' <_B M'.$$

When $M = (X,\pi)$ is an iterative system such that:

(*) every state $x \in X$ is an element of some computation of M, then the set C_M unambiguously determines the iterative system M.

In the sequel we shall assume that all systems fulfill condition (*) .

If M and M' are iterative systems, then $M \wedge M'$ denote an iterative system called the meet of M and M', whose computation set is $C_M \cap C_{M'}$.

THEOREM 14. If $M' <_B M$ and $M'' <_B M$, then

$$M' \wedge M'' <_B M.$$

THEOREM 15. Let $B = (v,V)$ be a simulation basis. If $M <_B M'$ and $M_1 <_B M_1'$ and computations of the iterative system M' which start with states belonging to Rv are also computations of M_1', then

$$M \wedge M_1 <_B M' \wedge M_1' .$$

Let $M = (X,\pi)$, $M' = (X', \pi')$ be consistent functional iterative systems i.e. such that

$$\pi \mid D_\pi \cap D_{\pi'} = \pi' \mid D_\pi \cap D_{\pi'} \qquad \text{and}$$

$$(R_\pi - D_\pi) \cap D_{\pi'} = (R_{\pi'} - D_{\pi'}) \cap D_\pi = \emptyset \quad .$$

The set $C_M \cup C_{M'}$ is a set of computation of a functional iterative system, which will be called the join of M and M' and will be denoted by $M \vee M'$.

THEOREM 16. If $M <_B M'$ and $M_1 <_B M_1'$, M and M_1 as well as M' and M_1' are consistent iterative systems, then

$$M \vee M_1 <_B M' \vee M_1' .$$

We shall now define the operation of substitution. Suppose $M = (X,\pi)$, $M' = (X', \pi')$ and $M'' = (X'', \pi'')$ are functional iterative systems such that

1. $X'' \cap X = \emptyset$,

2. M' is a subsystem of the system M.

Let ϱ_1, ϱ_2 be functions such that

$$\varrho_1 : \{x \in X : x \in D_{\pi'} \wedge (\pi^{-1}\{x\} = \emptyset \vee \bigvee_{y \in D_\pi - D_{\pi'}} \pi(y) = x)\} \to X'',$$

$$\varrho_2 : Rf_{M''} \xrightarrow{1-1} Rf_{M'} .$$

A (ϱ_1, ϱ_2)- substitution of M'' for M' in the system M is an iterative system (X_s, π_s) denoted by

$$Sub_{M,\varrho_1,\varrho_2}(M'/M'') ,$$

such that

1. $X_s = X \cup X''$,

2. $$\pi_s(x) = \begin{cases} \pi''(\varrho_1(x)) & \text{if } x \in D_{\pi'} \wedge \pi^{-1}\{x\} = \emptyset \wedge \varrho_1(x) \in D\pi'' \\ \pi(x) & \text{if } x \in D_\pi - D_{\pi'} \wedge \pi(x) \notin D\pi' \\ \varrho_1(\pi(x)) & \text{if } x \in D_\pi - D_{\pi'} \wedge \pi(x) \in D\pi' \\ \pi''(x) & \text{if } x \in D_{\pi''} \\ \pi(\varrho_2(x)) & \text{if } x \in Rf_{M''} \wedge \varrho_2(x) \in D_\pi \\ \text{undefined in the remaining cases.} \end{cases}$$

THEOREM 17. Let M, M', M'' be functional iterative systems and ϱ_1, ϱ_2 - functions such that the (ϱ_1, ϱ_2) - substitution of M'' for M' in M is defined. Let $B = (v,V)$ be a simulation basis of transitive properties such that $M_o <_{B,\bar{\varrho}} M$ and $Rv'' \subset Dv''$ for $v'' \in V$. If

$$M' <_{B',\varrho} M'' , \quad \bar{\varrho}(Dv) \subset D_\pi - D_{\pi'} ,$$

where $B' = (v',V)$ and $Dv' \supset D\varrho_1$ and $\varrho_1 \subset \varrho$, $\varrho_2^{-1} \subset \varrho$, then

$$M_o <_B Sub_{M,\varrho_1,\varrho_2}(M'/M'') .$$

If $M = (X,\pi)$ is a functional iterative system, then a partial function

$$f \in X^{[X]}$$

such that $D_f \subset Rf_M$ will be called the iteration function for M. A functional iterative system (X,π^*) such that

$$\pi^*(x) = \begin{cases} \pi(x) & \text{if } x \in D\pi \\ f(x) & \text{if } x \in D_f \\ \text{undefined otherwise,} \end{cases}$$

will be called an f-iteration of the system M and will be denoted by $*(M,f)$.

THEOREM 18. Let $B = (v,V)$ be a basis of simulation of M in M'. If $M <_{B,\varrho} M'$ and f,f' are iteration functions for M and M' correspondingly such that $R_f \subset Dv$ and for every $x \in D_f$ $\varrho(f(x)) = f'(\varrho(x))$, then $*(M,f) <_B *(M',f')$.

References

[1] PAWLAK Z., Computers [in Polish], Algorytmy 10 (1969), 5-19.

[2] ——— A mathematical model of digital computers, Proc. Conf. on Theory of Autom. and Formal Lang., Bonn, 1973.

[3] SKOWRON A., Simulation [in Polish], CC PAS Reports [in press].

[4] ZEIGLER P., Towards a formal theory of modeling and simulation: structure preserving morphisms, Journal of ACM 19 (1972), 742-764.

CONCURRENT PROGRAMS

J. Winkowski
Computation Centre of PAS
00-901 Warsaw, PKiN, POBox 22

ABSTRACT

The paper refers to the question how programs can be executed concurrently. To answer this question the following problem will be considered.

Given some programs according to which some instructions are to be performed in a given environment. Does exist a program any performance of which runs accordantly with all the given programs simultaneously? How many programs with this property do exist? How to find them?

To make this problem precise some ideas similar to those of BURSTALL [1] and GOGUEN [2], [3] will be used to define programs and related notions in the categorical language.

PROGRAMS IN AN ENVIRONMENT

After the definition by BURSTALL and GOGUEN a <u>program</u> is a functor P from the category Pa(G) of the paths of a graph G (<u>control-flow-graph</u>) into the category Rel of sets and binary relations. Nodes represent <u>control states</u>. Paths composed of edges represent <u>control flows</u>. Sets corresponding to nodes are the sets of possible <u>states of data which are to be processed</u>. Relations corresponding to paths consist of possible <u>data state changes</u> when the control moves along the paths. Any change is determined by two states: one- before, and the second- after the change.

Since the mentioned authors consider a single program they assume implicitly that <u>the only data state changes are those due to performances of the program instructions</u>. This point of view must be rejected however if one has to do with several programs which refer to common data and are to be executed simultaneously. There are situations where some instructions of one of programs can be performed when the control of another is remaining in a node. It is necessary to know therefore <u>what data state changes are possible when the control of a</u>

program is being in a node or is moving along a path rather then to know what this program does.

As for data state changes which are possible in a given node, it is reasonable to think about them as about changes up to an equivalence. In consequence of that changes should be admitted as possible ones when the control is moving along a path if they are equivalent to a possible change with respect to the initial and final states.

Dealing with several programs which are to be executed simultaneously in an environment $\mathcal{E}$ composed of their data and themselves we shall therefore replace the category Rel by the category with objects being equivalences in subsets of the set of the environment states and with morphisms which for each pair of objects E,F are the binary relations R satisfying the conditions:

$$RE=R, \quad FR=R$$

(here RE and FR denote the usual compositions $E \circ R$ and $R \circ F$ of the considered binary relations). This category characterizes to some extent the environment $\mathcal{E}$ and will be denoted by $\tilde{\mathcal{E}}$.

Programs we are talking about could be formally defined as functors from categories of paths of their control-flow-graphs into $\tilde{\mathcal{E}}$. As a matter of fact, in order to be able to consider several programs which are to be executed simultaneously as a single program, we will have to use the following more general definition.

Definition 1 A program in an environment $\mathcal{E}$ is a functor P from a category C into the category $\tilde{\mathcal{E}}$.

A more detailed argumentation will be given later. For the time being we shall give a very simple example where categories of paths of some graphs are sufficient.

Let us consider two programs, say A and B, according to which two persons (called also A and B) act who need use from time to time a thing for a period. There is only one thing and each of the persons can not use it when his partner is just using it. The thing may be therefore in one of the states:

atA, atB, free

These are states of the environment $\mathcal{E}_{A,B}$ which consists of the considered thing and of A and B.

Both the programs run according to the following control-flow-graph:

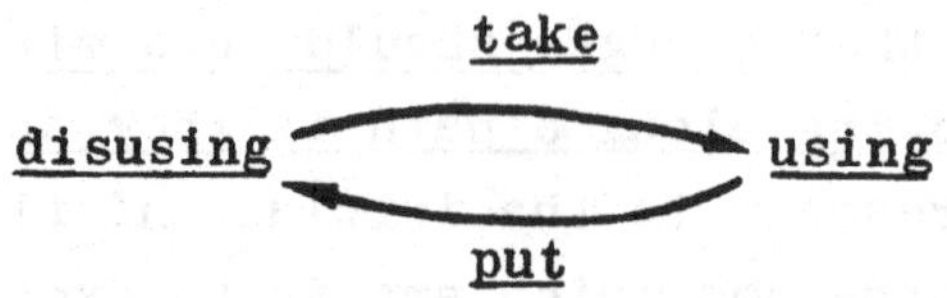

which will be denoted by G_A or G_B.

The possible environment states in the control state disusing of A are atB and free and the possible environment state changes are from atB to free and conversely. Therefore:

A(disusing) = {(atB, atB), (free, free), (atB, free), (free, atB)}

The only possible environment state in the control state using of A is atA and no changes are possible so that:

A(using) = {(atA, atA)}

The possible environment state changes when the control of A moves from disusing to using along the edge take are from atB or free to atA so that:

A(take) = {(atB, atA), (free, atA)}

The changes which are possible when the control moves from using to disusing along put are from atA to atB or free and:

A(put) = {(atA, atB), (atA, free)}

Other changes can be obtained by composing the above ones along suitable paths.

By similar argumentation:

B(disusing) = {(atA, atA), (free, free), (atA, free), (free, atA)}
B(using) = {(atB, atB)}
B(take) = {(atA, atB), (free, atB)}
B(put) = {(atB, atA), (atB, free)}

SIMULTANEOUS EXECUTION OF PROGRAMS

Simultaneous execution of programs like those A,B can be treated as an execution of a special single program Φ which may be thought as "to execute A and B simultaneously".

Possible control states of Φ are, in fact, pairs (n_A, n_B) of control states n_A, n_B of A and B respectively. Similarly, possible control flows of Φ are pairs (p_A, p_B) of control flows of A and B, i.e. pairs of paths of G_A and G_B. In other words, the control states of Φ are some objects and the control flows of Φ are some morphisms of the product $Pa(G_A) \times Pa(G_B)$ of the categories $Pa(G_A), Pa(G_B)$. Therefore, if we want to describe the resulting program Φ as a functor Φ, the functor Φ should be defined in a subcategory of $Pa(G_A) \times Pa(G_B)$. In general, such a subcategory is not of the form $Pa(G)$. It is just the main reason of admittance of arbitrary categories as domains of programs (in the place of categories of the form $Pa(G)$) in our definition.

The only possible environment state when A and B are simultaneously in the control state disusing is free. The only possible environment state when A is in disusing and simultaneously B is in using is atB. The only possible environment state when A is in using and simultaneously B is in disusing is atA. Moreover, A and B can not be simultaneously in the control state using.

The possible environment state changes are: from free to atB when A remains in the control state disusing and B moves from disusing to using along the edge take, from atB to free when A remains in disusing and B moves from using to disusing along put, from free to atA when A moves from disusing to using along take and B remains in disusing, from atA to free when A moves from using to disusing along put and B remains in disusing, and those composed of the mentioned.

Therefore, the possible control states of Φ are:

(disusing,disusing),(disusing,using),(using,disusing)

and the possible control flows are those composed of:

$$(\text{disusing},\text{disusing}) \xrightarrow{(\text{disusing},\text{take})} (\text{disusing},\text{using})$$

$$(\text{disusing},\text{using}) \xrightarrow{(\text{disusing},\text{put})} (\text{disusing},\text{disusing})$$

$$(\text{disusing},\text{disusing}) \xrightarrow{(\text{take},\text{disusing})} (\text{using},\text{disusing})$$

$$(\text{using},\text{disusing}) \xrightarrow{(\text{put},\text{disusing})} (\text{disusing},\text{disusing})$$

They form a subcategory $\mathcal{F}$ of $Pa(G_A) \times Pa(G_B)$, and the functor Φ describing our resulting program is defined for the control states and flows from $\mathcal{F}$ by the formulae:

$$\Phi(\underline{disusing}, \underline{disusing}) = \{(\underline{free}, \underline{free})\}$$
$$\Phi(\underline{disusing}, \underline{using}) = \{(\underline{atB}, \underline{atB})\}$$
$$\Phi(\underline{using}, \underline{disusing}) = \{(\underline{atA}, \underline{atA})\}$$
$$\Phi(\underline{disusing}, \underline{take}) = \{(\underline{free}, \underline{atB})\}$$
$$\Phi(\underline{disusing}, \underline{put}) = \{(\underline{atB}, \underline{free})\}$$
$$\Phi(\underline{take}, \underline{disusing}) = \{(\underline{free}, \underline{atA})\}$$
$$\Phi(\underline{put}, \underline{disusing}) = \{(\underline{atA}, \underline{free})\}$$

together with the composition rule:

$$\Phi(q_A p_A, q_B p_B) = \Phi(q_A, q_B)\,\Phi(p_A, p_B)$$

holding for paths $q_A p_A, q_B p_B$ composed of p_A, q_A and p_B, q_B respectively.

It is easy to see that any performance of Φ runs accordantly with A and B simultaneously.

We constructed the program Φ by determining which control states and flows of A and B were possible simultaneously in the given environment and what could be the corresponding environment states and state changes. It is not so easy to do that in more complicated cases. Therefore, we shall try to characterize programs we are looking for in the categorical language and to find universal methods of determining them by categorical means.

A CHARACTERIZATION OF SIMULTANEITY

To get a precise characterization and a way of determining the programs which could be thought as "to execute simultaneously some given programs in some given environment" we shall use a notion of homomorphism between programs in an environment.

GOGUEN defined a homomorphism from a program $Pa(G) \xrightarrow{P} Rel$ to another program $Pa(H) \xrightarrow{Q} Rel$ as a pair (f, λ) composed of a functor $Pa(G) \xrightarrow{f} Pa(H)$ and of a natural transformation $P \xrightarrow{\lambda} Qf$. For our program notion his definition has the following form.

Definition 2 A homomorphism from a program $C \xrightarrow{P} \tilde{\mathcal{E}}$ in an environment $\mathcal{E}$ to another program $D \xrightarrow{Q} \tilde{\mathcal{E}}$ in the same environment $\mathcal{E}$ is a pair (f,λ) composed of a functor $C \xrightarrow{f} D$ and of a natural transformation $P \xrightarrow{\lambda} Qf$.

Any two homomorphisms:

$$P \xrightarrow{(f,\lambda)} Q \text{ from } C \xrightarrow{P} \tilde{\mathcal{E}} \text{ to } D \xrightarrow{Q} \tilde{\mathcal{E}}$$

and

$$Q \xrightarrow{(g,\mu)} R \text{ from } D \xrightarrow{Q} \tilde{\mathcal{E}} \text{ to } X \xrightarrow{R} \tilde{\mathcal{E}}$$

can be composed into a homomorphism:

$$P \xrightarrow{(h,\nu)} R \text{ from } C \xrightarrow{P} \tilde{\mathcal{E}} \text{ to } X \xrightarrow{R} \tilde{\mathcal{E}}$$

according to the rules:

$$h=gf, \quad \nu(a)=\mu(f(a))\lambda(a) \text{ for any object } a \text{ of } C$$

and all the programs in the environment $\mathcal{E}$ and homomorphisms between them with such a composition form a category. This category will be denoted by Prog($\mathcal{E}$).

Now we are going to study how relationships among the above described programs A,B and Φ can be expressed in terms of homomorphisms.

First of all, the subcategory $\mathcal{F}$ of $Pa(G_A) \times Pa(G_B)$, that which is the domain of the functor Φ, can be projected into $Pa(G_A)$ and $Pa(G_B)$ by the functors:

$$\mathcal{F} \xrightarrow{f} Pa(G_A), \quad \mathcal{F} \xrightarrow{g} Pa(G_B)$$

those obtained by restricting the usual projections to $\mathcal{F}$.

Farther, the equivalence Φ(disusing,disusing) is contained in the equivalences A(disusing) and B(disusing), Φ(disusing,using) is contained in A(disusing) and B(using), Φ(using,disusing) is contained in A(using) and B(disusing), so that every equivalence $\Phi(n_A,n_B)$ assigned by the functor Φ to any control state (n_A,n_B) of the program Φ is contained in the equivalences $A(n_A),B(n_B)$ assigned by the functors A,B to the control states $n_A=f(n_A,n_B),n_B=g(n_A,n_B)$ of the programs A,B. Therefore, the relations $\lambda(n_A,n_B)$ defined by:

$$x\lambda(n_A,n_B)y \quad \text{iff} \quad x \text{ is in the domain of } \Phi(n_A,n_B) \text{ and } xA(n_A)y$$

are morphisms of $\tilde{\mathcal{E}}_{A,B}$ from $\Phi(n_A,n_B)$ to $A(f(n_A,n_B))$, and the relations $\mu(n_A,n_B)$ defined by:

$$x\,\mu(n_A,n_B)\,y \quad \text{iff} \quad \begin{array}{l} x \text{ is in the domain of } \Phi(n_A,n_B) \\ \text{and } xB(n_B)y \end{array}$$

are morphisms of $\mathcal{E}_{A,B}$ from $\Phi(n_A,n_B)$ to $B(g(n_A,n_B))$. Since they satisfy the following commutativity conditions:

$$\begin{array}{ccccc} A(f(m_A,m_B)) & \xleftarrow{\lambda(m_A,m_B)} & \Phi(m_A,m_B) & \xrightarrow{\mu(m_A,m_B)} & B(g(m_A,m_B)) \\ \Big\downarrow{\scriptstyle A(f(p_A,p_B))} & & \Big\downarrow{\scriptstyle \Phi(p_A,p_B)} & & \Big\downarrow{\scriptstyle B(g(p_A,p_B))} \\ A(f(n_A,n_B)) & \xleftarrow[\lambda(n_A,n_B)]{} & \Phi(n_A,n_B) & \xrightarrow[\mu(n_A,n_B)]{} & B(g(n_A,n_B)) \end{array}$$

for any control flow $(m_A,m_B) \xrightarrow{(p_A,p_B)} (n_A,n_B)$ of Φ, the family λ of $\lambda(n_A,n_B)$ is a natural transformation:

$$\Phi \xrightarrow{\lambda} Af$$

and the family μ of $\mu(n_A,n_B)$ is a natural transformation:

$$\Phi \xrightarrow{\mu} Bg$$

as well.

The pairs (f,λ) and (g,μ) are, in fact, homomorphisms from Φ to A and B respectively. They characterize, to some extent, the relationships occuring among A,B and Φ.

There are, of course, other programs in the category Prog($\mathcal{E}_{A,B}$) with homomorphisms to A and B so that existence of the homomorphisms:

$$\begin{array}{ccc} & \Phi & \\ {\scriptstyle (f,\lambda)} \swarrow & & \searrow {\scriptstyle (g,\mu)} \\ A & & B \end{array}$$

does not characterize Φ completly. Another property of Φ is that all what the program Φ does comes from A and B only. This property can be assured by the fact that Φ is some "subproduct" of A and B.

By subproducts of families of objects of any category we shall mean objects defined formally as follows.

Definition 3 A subproduct of objects $a_i, i \in I$ of a category C is an object a of C together with some morphisms $a \xrightarrow{\alpha_i} a_i, i \in I$ such that for any object b of C with morphisms $b \xrightarrow{\beta_i} a_i, i \in I$ there is at most one morphism $b \xrightarrow{\beta} a$ which (if any) makes all the diagrams:

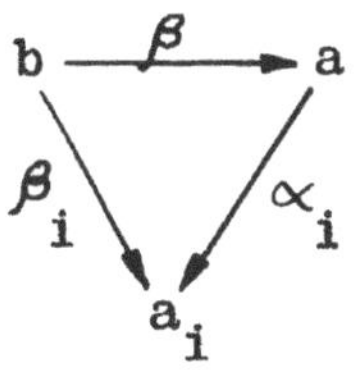

commutative. The morphisms $a \xrightarrow{\alpha_i} a_i, i \in I$ are called canonical ones.

Of course, any object which is isomorphic with a subproduct of some objects is a subproduct of these objects too.

As it will be shown later, the property of a program P from Prog($\mathcal{E}$) to be a subproduct of some programs P_i from Prog($\mathcal{E}$) enables to identify any action of P when the correspondent actions of P_i are given.

There may be a number of non-isomorphic programs which are subproducts of some given programs. In particular, some fragments of subproducts are subproducts as well. Usually, our main interest is to determine the subproducts which are "maximal".

A maximal subproduct notion can be introduced due to the following lemma.

Lemma Let objects a,b of C be subproducts of $a_i, i \in I$ with the canonical morphisms $a \xrightarrow{\alpha_i} a_i$, $b \xrightarrow{\beta_i} a_i$ respectively, and let $a \xrightarrow{\alpha} b$ be a morphism satisfying the conditions $\alpha_i = \beta_i \alpha, i \in I$. Then α is a monomorphism. If there exist also a morphism $b \xrightarrow{\beta} a$ satisfying the conditions $\beta_i = \alpha_i \beta, i \in I$ then $\beta\alpha = 1_a$, $\alpha\beta = 1_b$, so that α and β are isomorphisms.

Proof Let us take two morphisms $x \xrightarrow{\xi} a$, $x \xrightarrow{\xi'} a$ with $\alpha\xi = \alpha\xi'$

and consider $\xi_i=\alpha_i\xi$, $\xi_i'=\alpha_i\xi'$. Since $\xi_i=\beta_i\alpha\xi$ and $\xi_i'=\beta_i\alpha\xi'$, we have $\xi_i=\xi_i'$. Since a is a subproduct of a_i and α_i are its canonical morphisms, there is at most one morphism η with $\xi_i=\alpha_i\eta$ for $i\in I$, so that $\eta=\xi=\xi'$. Since $\alpha_i=\alpha_i\beta\alpha$ and $\beta_i=\beta_i\alpha\beta$ and both a,b are subproducts, we have $\beta\alpha=1_a$, $\alpha\beta=1_b$. ⁎

Definition 4 A subproduct a of objects $a_i, i\in I$ of C with the canonical morphisms $a\xrightarrow{\alpha_i}a_i$ is called maximal one iff for any subproduct b of $a_i, i\in I$ with the canonical morphisms $b\xrightarrow{\beta_i}a_i$ every morphism $a\xrightarrow{\alpha}b$ satisfying the conditions $\alpha_i=\beta_i\alpha, i\in I$ is an isomorphism.

Of course, any product is a maximal subproduct and subproducts are its subobjects. However, if any product of a_i does not exist then there may be many non-isomorphic maximal subproducts of a_i.

Maximal subproducts and subproducts of programs correspond (up to isomorphisms) to the various ways in which the given programs and their fragments can be executed simultaneously. We shall study that in the following. First of all, we shall try to explain what a structure subproducts of programs have.

SUBPRODUCTS OF PROGRAMS

In order to compute how some given programs can be executed simultaneously in a given environment we need a characterization of subproducts of programs.

The form of subproducts of programs which are to be executed in some environment $\mathcal{E}$ can be characterized as follows.

Theorem 1 Let $C\xrightarrow{P}\widetilde{\mathcal{E}}$ be a subproduct of programs $C_i\xrightarrow{P_i}\widetilde{\mathcal{E}}$, $i\in I$ and $P\xrightarrow{(f_i,\lambda_i)}P_i$ its canonical homomorphisms. Then:

(1) C is isomorphic with a subcategory C' of the product $\prod C_i$ of C_i, $i\in I$,

(2) if $\prod C_i\xrightarrow{c_i}C_i$ are the projections of $\prod C_i$ onto the corresponding C_i then there exists unique isomorphism $C\xrightarrow{\varphi}C'$ such that f composed of φ and of the inclusion of C' in $\prod C_i$ satisfies the conditions $f_i=c_if, i\in I$,

(3) for every object a of C the object P(a) is a subproduct of $P_i(f_i(a)), i\in I$ with the canonical morphisms $P(a)\xrightarrow{\lambda_i(a)}P_i(f_i(a))$.

Proof There exists unique functor $C \xrightarrow{f} \prod C_i$ which satisfies the conditions $f_i = c_i f, i \in I$.

Let us consider any category D with functors $D \xrightarrow{g_i} C_i, i \in I$. There exists unique functor $D \xrightarrow{g} \prod C_i$ satisfying the conditions $g_i = c_i g, i \in I$. Taking the constant program $D \xrightarrow{P_0} \widetilde{\mathcal{E}}$ which has the value $\emptyset$ (the empty set) and the morphisms $\emptyset \xrightarrow{\mu_i(d)} P(g_i(d))$ with $\mu_i(d) = \emptyset$ for any object d of D we get the homomorphisms $P_0 \xrightarrow{(g_i, \mu_i)} P_i, i \in I$. Therefore, there is at most one homomorphism $P_0 \xrightarrow{(h, \nu)} P$ satisfying the conditions $(g_i, \mu_i) = (f_i, \lambda_i)(h, \nu), i \in I$. But for any $D \xrightarrow{h} C$ the natural transformation $P_0 \xrightarrow{\nu_0} Ph$ defined by $\nu_0(d) = \emptyset$ for any object d of D satisfies the conditions $\mu_i(d) = \lambda_i(h(d))\nu_0(d), i \in I$, d - an object of D, so that $(g_i, \mu_i) = (f_i, \lambda_i)(h, \nu_0)$ for $i \in I$. Hence, there is at most one $D \xrightarrow{h} C$ such that $g_i = f_i h$ for $i \in I$ and C must be a subproduct of $C_i, i \in I$ with the canonical morphisms $C \xrightarrow{f_i} C_i$.

Since C is a subproduct of $C_i, i \in I$ and $C \xrightarrow{f_i} C_i$ are its canonical morphisms, the functor f must be injective. Namely, for any $D \xrightarrow{g} \prod C_i$ there is at most one $D \xrightarrow{h} C$ with $fh = g$ because such a functor should satisfy the conditions $c_i g = f_i h, i \in I$. Hence, f is mono and therefore injective.

Now, we can simply define C' as the image of C under f and φ as the unique functor $C \xrightarrow{\varphi} C'$ which, when composed with the inclusion of C' in $\prod C_i$, gives f.

To prove the third part of the theorem, let us take any object a of C and any object E of $\widetilde{\mathcal{E}}$ with some morphisms $E \xrightarrow{\mu_i} P_i(f_i(a))$, $i \in I$.

Taking the category 1 which consists of an object 0 and morphism 1_0 only, the program $1 \xrightarrow{P_E} \widetilde{\mathcal{E}}$ with $P_E(0) = E$, the functors $1 \xrightarrow{g_i} C_i$ with $g_i(0) = f_i(a)$, and the natural transformations $P_E \xrightarrow{\nu_i} P_i g_i$ with $\nu_i(0) = \mu_i$, we get the homomorphisms $P_E \xrightarrow{(g_i, \nu_i)} P_i, i \in I$. Hence, there is at most one homomorphism $P_E \xrightarrow{(g, \nu)} P$ with $(g_i, \nu_i) = (f_i, \lambda_i)(g, \nu), i \in I$ and therefore at most one morphism $E \xrightarrow{\nu} P(a)$ with $\mu_i = \lambda_i(a)\nu, i \in I$. As result, $P(a)$ is a subproduct of $P_i(f_i(a))$ and $P(a) \xrightarrow{\lambda_i(a)} P_i(f_i(a))$ are its canonical morphisms. *

This theorem informs us what a structure have programs we are looking for. It enables to reduce our problem to seeking for subproducts in the category $\widetilde{\mathcal{E}}$.

The following theorem indicates how to use subproducts in $\widetilde{\mathcal{E}}$ for constructing subproducts of programs from Prog($\mathcal{E}$).

<u>Theorem 2</u> Let $C_i \xrightarrow{P_i} \tilde{\mathcal{E}}, i \in I$ be programs from Prog($\mathcal{E}$) and C a subcategory of the product $\prod C_i$ of $C_i, i \in I$ with the restricted projections $C \xrightarrow{f_i} C_i, i \in I$.

If for every morphism $a \xrightarrow{\alpha} b$ of C there exist a subproduct P(a) of $P_i(f_i(a)), i \in I$ with the canonical morphisms $P(a) \xrightarrow{\lambda_i(a)} P_i(f_i(a))$, a subproduct P(b) of $P_i(f_i(b)), i \in I$ with the canonical morphisms $P(b) \xrightarrow{\lambda_i(b)} P_i(f_i(b))$, and a morphism $P(a) \xrightarrow{P(\alpha)} P(b)$ such that $P_i(f_i(\alpha))\lambda_i(a) = \lambda_i(b)P(\alpha)$ for $i \in I$ (there is at most one such a morphism) then the mapping defined by $a \longmapsto P(a)$, $b \longmapsto P(b), \alpha \longmapsto P(\alpha)$ is a program $C \xrightarrow{P} \tilde{\mathcal{E}}$, and it is a subproduct of $C_i \xrightarrow{P_i} \tilde{\mathcal{E}}, i \in I$ with the canonical homomorphisms $P \xrightarrow{(f_i, \lambda_i)} P_i$, where λ_i are composed of $\lambda_i(a)$ corresponding to the objects a of C.

<u>Proof</u> The only morphism u satisfying the conditions $P_i(f_i(1_a))\lambda_i(a) = \lambda_i(a)u, i \in I$ is $1_{P(a)}$ so that $P(1_a) = 1_{P(a)}$.

If a morphism $a \xrightarrow{\gamma} c$ of C is composed of morphisms $a \xrightarrow{\alpha} b$, $b \xrightarrow{\beta} c$ then $P(a) \xrightarrow{P(\gamma)} P(c)$ is the only morphism such that $P_i(f_i(\gamma))\lambda_i(a) = \lambda_i(c)P(\gamma)$ for $i \in I$. But $P_i(f_i(\alpha))\lambda_i(a) = \lambda_i(b)P(\alpha)$ and $P_i(f_i(\beta))\lambda_i(b) = \lambda_i(c)P(\beta)$ so that $P_i(f_i(\gamma))\lambda_i(a) =$ $P_i(f_i(\beta))P_i(f_i(\alpha))\lambda_i(a) = P_i(f_i(\beta))\lambda_i(b)P(\alpha) = \lambda_i(c)P(\beta)P(\alpha)$ for $i \in I$ and therefore $P(\beta)P(\alpha) = P(\gamma)$.

Hence, P is a functor i.e. a program $C \xrightarrow{P} \tilde{\mathcal{E}}$. It is also easy to see that $P \xrightarrow{(f_i, \lambda_i)} P_i$ are homomorphisms.

Let us consider any program $D \xrightarrow{Q} \tilde{\mathcal{E}}$ with homomorphisms $Q \xrightarrow{(g_i, \mu_i)} P_i, i \in I$. Since C is a subcategory of the product $\prod C_i$ there is at most one functor $D \xrightarrow{g} C$ with $g_i = f_i g$ for $i \in I$. Since each P(a) is the subproduct of $P_i(f_i(a))$ with the canonical morphisms $P(a) \xrightarrow{\lambda_i(a)} P_i(f_i(a))$ there is at most one morphism $Q(d) \xrightarrow{\nu_d} P(g(d))$ such that $\mu_i(d) = \nu_d \lambda_i(g(d))$ for $i \in I$. Hence, there is at most one homomorphism $Q \xrightarrow{(g, \nu)} P$ such that $(g_i, \mu_i) = (f_i, \lambda_i)(g, \nu)$ for $i \in I$. Therefore, P is a subproduct of P_i and (f_i, λ_i) are its canonical homomorphisms. ж

Using some isomorphic subproducts in $\tilde{\mathcal{E}}$ instead of the given ones in the above described construction of a subproduct of programs from Prog($\mathcal{E}$) we get an <u>isomorphic</u> subproduct. It results from the following theorem.

Theorem 3 Let $C \xrightarrow{P} \tilde{\mathcal{E}}$ be a subproduct of $C_i \xrightarrow{P_i} \tilde{\mathcal{E}}, i \in I$ and $P \xrightarrow{(f_i,\lambda_i)} P_i$ its canonical homomorphisms. Let for every object a of C: Q(a) be a subproduct of $P_i(f_i(a)), i \in I$ which is isomorphic with P(a), $Q(a) \xrightarrow{\mu_{ia}} P_i(f_i(a))$ its canonical morphisms, and $Q(a) \xrightarrow{\varphi_a} P(a)$ the corresponding isomorphism. Then the correspondence $a \longmapsto Q(a)$ can be extended to a program $C \xrightarrow{Q} \tilde{\mathcal{E}}$ by assuming $Q(\alpha) = \varphi_b^{-1} P(\alpha) \varphi_a$ for every morphism $a \xrightarrow{\alpha} b$ of C, this program is a subproduct of $P_i, i \in I$, it is isomorphic with P, its canonical homomorphisms are $Q \xrightarrow{(f_i,\mu_i)} P_i$ with $\mu_i(a) = \mu_{ia}$, and the homomorphism $Q \xrightarrow{(1_C,\varphi)} P$ with $\varphi(a) = \varphi_a$ is an isomorphism between Q and P.

Proof By the theorem 2 Q is a subproduct of P_i and $Q \xrightarrow{(f_i,\mu_i)} P_i$ are its canonical homomorphisms. Since every φ_a is an isomorphism in $\tilde{\mathcal{E}}$ the homomorphism $(1_C,\varphi)$ is an isomorphism in Prog($\mathcal{E}$). *

The above theorems give us a method of constructing subproducts of programs. As this method is based on finding out subproducts in the corresponding category $\tilde{\mathcal{E}}$ this last task becomes very important one. Therefore, some more detailed studies of subproducts in categories of the type $\tilde{\mathcal{E}}$ are needed.

SUBPRODUCTS IN CATEGORIES WHICH DESCRIBE ENVIRONMENTS

Now we are going to give a method for computing subproducts in categories of the type $\tilde{\mathcal{E}}$ for various environments $\mathcal{E}$. This method is based on a characterization of subproducts in such categories.

Subproducts in the category $\tilde{\mathcal{E}}$ which corresponds to some environment $\mathcal{E}$ have the following property.

Theorem 4 Given any family of objects $E_i, i \in I$ of $\tilde{\mathcal{E}}$. Every subproduct of $E_i, i \in I$ is isomorphic to a subproduct E of $E_i, i \in I$ with the canonical morphisms $E \xrightarrow{\lambda_i} E_i, i \in I$ where:

(1) the domain of E is contained in the union of the domains of E_i, $i \in I$,

(2) if x is in the domain of E then xEy iff for every $i \in I$ both x and y belong or do not belong simultaneously to the domain of E_i and xE_iy if they belong,

(3) for every $i \in I$ $x\lambda_i y$ iff x is in the domain of E and xE_iy.

Moreover, the subproduct E is the only subproduct of $E_i, i \in I$ isomorphic with the given one that has reflexive all the canonical morphisms.

<u>Proof</u> For any equivalence R and for any element x we denote by $[x]_R$ the set of all the elements which are R-equivalent with x. Of course, $[x]_R$ is non-empty iff x belongs to the domain of R.

The empty set is the only subproduct of the empty family of objects so that the theorem is trivial in this case.

Let I be non-empty and let F be a subproduct of $E_i, i \in I$ with the canonical morphisms $F \xrightarrow{\mu_i} E_i, i \in I$. Let I_x be the set of $i \in I$ with non-empty $[x]_{E_i}$, i_x the relation which holds between x and the elements of $[x]_{E_i}$, and $[x]_{E_i}\mu_i$ the inverse-image of $[x]_{E_i}$ under μ_i.

There is at most one relation R satisfying the conditions $R\{(x,x)\}=R$, $FR=R$ and $\mu_i R=i_x$ for $i \in I$. Hence, there is at most one set f which is union of some sets of the form $[y]_F$, meets all $[x]_{E_i}\mu_i$ with $i \in I_x$, and is disjoint with $[y]_{E_j}\mu_j$ if y is not E_j-equivalent with x for some $j \in I$. Being unique it must be of the form $[y]_F$ for some y. When such a set exists we denote it by f_x. It is empty iff $I_x=\emptyset$, i.e. iff x does not belong to the domain of any of $E_i, i \in I$.

If the set f_x is defined then it must be contained in $[x]_{E_i}\mu_i$ with $i \in I_x$, its elements must be F-equivalent if any, and for every y with $I_y=I_x$ which is E_i-equivalent with x for all $i \in I_y=I_x$ the set f_y is defined and $f_y=f_x$.

If $I_y \neq I_x$ then there exists i, say in I_y, which is not in I_x, so that y belongs to the domain of E_i and x does not belong. But f_y (if defined) is then disjoint with $[x]_{E_i}\mu_i$ which contains f_x (if defined) and therefore f_x, f_y can not be simultaneously defined and equal.

If $I_y=I_x$ but x is not E_i-equivalent with y for some $i \in I_x=I_y$ then f_x (if defined) is contained in $[x]_{E_i}\mu_i$ and disjoint with $[y]_{E_i}\mu_i$ which contains f_y (if f_y is defined). Finally, f_x, f_y can not be simultaneously defined and equal if $I_y \neq I_x$ or if $I_y=I_x$ and x,y are not E_i--equivalent for some $i \in I_x=I_y$.

The relation E defined by the formula:

$$xEy \text{ iff } I_x \text{ is non-empty, } f_x \text{ is defined, } I_x=I_y\text{, and } xE_iy \text{ for } i \in I_x=I_y$$

is an equivalence and satisfies (1),(2).

For every x with non-empty $[x]_E$ the set f_x is defined and non--empty. For the relation α defined by the formula:

$$x\alpha y \text{ iff } x_E \text{ is non-empty and } y \text{ is in } f_x$$

xEz implies $\alpha[x]_E = \alpha[z]_E$ because f_x, f_z are defined and equal. There are also no non-E-equivalent x,y in the domain of E with equal f_x, f_y. Moreover, every non-empty $[y]_F$ is of the form f_x for some x from the domain of E because in the other case there would be no x with non--empty I_x and $[x]_{E_i}\mu_i, i \in I_x$ containing $[y]_F$ so that there would be a non-empty relation R (for instance, that holding between some z and the elements of $[y]_F$) with empty $\mu_i R, i \in I$, and F would not be a subproduct (the conditions $\mu_i R = \emptyset, i \in I$ are satisfied by the empty relation R too). As result, α is an isomorphism between E and F.

Taking $\lambda_i = \mu_i \alpha$ we have $x \lambda_i y$ iff x is in the domain of E and there exists some z with $x \alpha z$ and $z \mu_i y$. Therefore, $x \lambda_i y$ iff x is in the domain of E and $z \in f_x \subseteq [y]_{E_i} \mu_i$. But the last condition implies $zE_i y$, so that $xE_i y$. Conversely, if x is in the domain of E and $xE_i y$ then $f_x \subseteq [y]_{E_i} \mu_i$ and there exists z in f_x with $zE_i y$, so that $x \alpha z$ and $xE_i y$.

The last part of the theorem results from the fact that α is E when for every $i \in I$ $x \mu_i y$ iff x is in the domain of F and $xE_i y$. ∗

<u>The conditions (1),(2),(3) do not guarantee, however, that E is a subproduct of $E_i, i \in I$.</u> There are equivalences and relations satisfying (1),(2),(3) which are not subproducts. For instance, taking:

$$E_1 = \{(a,a),(a,b),(b,b),(b,a),(c,c),(c,d),(d,d),(d,c)\}$$
$$E_2 = \{(a,a),(a,c),(c,c),(c,a),(b,b),(b,d),(d,d),(d,b)\}$$
$$E = \{(a,a),(b,b),(c,c),(d,d)\}$$
$$\lambda_1 = E_1$$
$$\lambda_2 = E_2$$

we have E, λ_1, λ_2 satisfying (1),(2),(3) for E_1, E_2 but there are different relations:

$$R = \{(a,b),(a,c)\}$$
$$S = \{(a,a),(a,d)\}$$

with $\lambda_1 R = \lambda_1 S$, $\lambda_2 R = \lambda_2 S$.

The above situation arises because E and λ_1, λ_2 do not have of an important property of subproducts in considered categories. This property is that <u>the canonical morphisms of any subproduct in $\mathcal{E}$ are sufficient for distinguishing essentially different subsets of the subproduct domain</u>.

Theorem 5 Let E be any subproduct of objects $E_i, i \in I$ of $\tilde{\mathcal{E}}$ and $E \xrightarrow{\lambda_i} E_i$ its canonical morphisms. Then E and $E \xrightarrow{\lambda_i} E_i$ have the following property:

(4) any subsets A,B of the domain of E which are closed with respect to E (i.e. contain together with x all y with xEy) are equal iff their images $\lambda_i A$, $\lambda_i B$ under λ_i are equal for every $i \in I$.

Proof Let us consider the relations R_A, R_B defined as follows:

xR_Ay iff $x=x_0$ and y belongs to A
xR_By iff $x=x_0$ and y belongs to B

The images $\lambda_i A, \lambda_i B$ of A and B under λ_i are equal for every $i \in I$ iff $\lambda_i R_A = \lambda_i R_B$ for every $i \in I$. But this holds iff $R_A = R_B$ i.e. A=B. ✱

Knowing the property (4) of subproducts in $\tilde{\mathcal{E}}$ we are in a position to prove the following theorem.

Theorem 6 Let $E_i, i \in I$ be arbitrary objects of $\tilde{\mathcal{E}}$, E an equivalence satisfying the conditions (1),(2), and $E \xrightarrow{\lambda_i} E_i, i \in I$ the morphisms defined by (3). Then E is a subproduct of $E_i, i \in I$ and $E \xrightarrow{\lambda_i} E_i$ are its canonical morphisms iff the condition (4) is satisfied.

Proof Let F be any object of $\tilde{\mathcal{E}}$ and $F \xrightarrow{r_i} E_i, i \in I$ some morphisms.

If there exist two morphisms $F \xrightarrow{R} E$ and $F \xrightarrow{S} E$ such that $r_i = \lambda_i R$, $r_i = \lambda_i S$ for $i \in I$ then the images Rx and Sx of any x under R and S are equal due to (4). But it means R=S, so that E is a subproduct of $E_i, i \in I$ and $E \xrightarrow{\lambda_i} E_i$ are its canonical morphisms. ✱

This theorem, together with the theorem 4, gives a method for constructing any subproducts in $\tilde{\mathcal{E}}$. Of course, equivalences like those in the theorem 6 are maximal subproducts if they are maximal of those satisfying the condition (4).

For instance, in the above considered example

$$F = \{(a,a),(d,d)\}, \quad G = \{(b,b),(c,c)\}$$

are maximal subproducts of E_1 and E_2.

COMPUTING OF SUBPRODUCTS OF PROGRAMS

Now we can describe how to compute subproducts of programs.

Having some programs $C_i \xrightarrow{P_i} \tilde{\mathcal{E}}, i \in I$ which are to be executed simultaneously in some environment $\mathcal{E}$ we try, first of all, to compute some subproducts $P((a_i)_{i\in I})$ of $P_i(a_i), i \in I$ for all the families $(a_i)_{i\in I}$ of objects a_i of the corresponding C_i and the canonical morphisms:

$$P((a_i)_{i\in I}) \xrightarrow{\lambda_i((a_i)_{i\in I})} P_i(a_i)$$

of these subproducts.

Doing that we choose subproducts with <u>reflexive</u> canonical morphisms because our interest is to find such a program that the possible environment states and state changes corresponding to its control states and flows are just some possible environment states and state changes corresponding to the suitable control states and flows of the given programs. Other choices could lead to programs <u>isomorphic</u> with those we are looking for (theorem 3).

It is far the best to choose some <u>maximal</u> subproducts because there is then a chance to construct a maximal subproduct of the given programs.

When the subproducts $P((a_i)_{i\in I})$ and their canonical morphisms:

$$P((a_i)_{i\in I}) \xrightarrow{\lambda_i((a_i)_{i\in I})} P_i(a_i)$$

are chosen we consider the families $(\alpha_i)_{i\in I}$ of morphisms $a_i \xrightarrow{\alpha_i} b_i$ of $C_i, i \in I$ and determine the unique existing morphisms:

$$P((a_i)_{i\in I}) \xrightarrow{P((\alpha_i)_{i\in I})} P((b_i)_{i\in I})$$

which satisfy the conditions:

$$P_i(\alpha_i)\lambda_i((a_i)_{i\in I}) = \lambda_i((b_i)_{i\in I})P((\alpha_i)_{i\in I})$$

for $i \in I$.

Having these we look for a maximal subcategory C of the product $\prod C_i$ of $C_i, i \in I$ with existing and non-empty $P((\alpha_i)_{i\in I})$ for all the morphisms:

$$(a_i)_{i\in I} \xrightarrow{(\alpha_i)_{i\in I}} (b_i)_{i\in I}$$

of C.

When such a subcategory C is chosen we construct a program $C \xrightarrow{P} \mathcal{E}$ as it was described in the theorem 2. Due to this theorem the constructed program is a subproduct (usually a maximal one) of the given programs.

For instance, in the case of the previously described programs A,B our procedure looks as follows.

We have:

$$A(\underline{disusing}) = \{(\underline{atB},\underline{atB}),(\underline{free},\underline{free}),(\underline{atB},\underline{free}),(\underline{free},\underline{atB})\}$$
$$A(\underline{using}) = \{(\underline{atA},\underline{atA})\}$$
$$B(\underline{disusing}) = \{(\underline{atA},\underline{atA}),(\underline{free},\underline{free}),(\underline{atA},\underline{free}),(\underline{free},\underline{atA})\}$$
$$B(\underline{using}) = \{(\underline{atB},\underline{atB})\}$$

so that the equivalence:

$$\Phi(\underline{disusing},\underline{disusing}) = \{(\underline{free},\underline{free})\}$$

is a maximal subproduct of A($\underline{disusing}$),B($\underline{disusing}$) and the morphisms:

$$\Phi(\underline{disusing},\underline{disusing}) \xrightarrow{\lambda_A(\underline{disusing},\underline{disusing})} A(\underline{disusing})$$
$$\Phi(\underline{disusing},\underline{disusing}) \xrightarrow{\lambda_B(\underline{disusing},\underline{disusing})} B(\underline{disusing})$$

with:

$$\lambda_A(\underline{disusing},\underline{disusing}) = \{(\underline{free},\underline{free}),(\underline{free},\underline{atA})\}$$
$$\lambda_B(\underline{disusing},\underline{disusing}) = \{(\underline{free},\underline{free}),(\underline{free},\underline{atB})\}$$

are its canonical morphisms.

It results from the theorem 6 and from the fact that the only subsets of the domain of $\Phi(\underline{disusing},\underline{disusing})$ are $\{\underline{free}\}$ and the empty set and they have different images under $\lambda_A(\underline{disusing},\underline{disusing})$, $\lambda_B(\underline{disusing},\underline{disusing})$ as well as from the fact that the images of $\{\underline{free}\}$ and $\{\underline{free},\underline{atA}\}$ under $\lambda_A(\underline{disusing},\underline{disusing})$,$\lambda_B(\underline{disusing},\underline{disusing})$ are the same and the images of $\{\underline{free}\}$ and $\{\underline{free},\underline{atB}\}$ are the same too.

By similar arguments:

$$\Phi(\underline{disusing},\underline{using}) = \{(\underline{atB},\underline{atB})\}$$

with

$$\Phi(\underline{disusing},\underline{using}) \xrightarrow{\lambda_A(\underline{disusing},\underline{using})} A(\underline{disusing})$$
$$\Phi(\underline{disusing},\underline{using}) \xrightarrow{\lambda_B(\underline{disusing},\underline{using})} B(\underline{using})$$

$$\lambda_A(\underline{disusing},\underline{using}) = \{(\underline{atB},\underline{atB}),(\underline{atB},\underline{free})\}$$
$$\lambda_B(\underline{disusing},\underline{using}) = \{(\underline{atB},\underline{atB})\}$$

is a maximal subproduct of A(<u>disusing</u>) and B(<u>using</u>),

$$\Phi(\underline{using},\underline{disusing}) = \{(\underline{atA},\underline{atA})\}$$

with

$$\Phi(\underline{using},\underline{disusing}) \xrightarrow{\lambda_A(\underline{using},\underline{disusing})} A(\underline{using})$$
$$\Phi(\underline{using},\underline{disusing}) \xrightarrow{\lambda_B(\underline{using},\underline{disusing})} B(\underline{disusing})$$
$$\lambda_A(\underline{using},\underline{disusing}) = \{(\underline{atA},\underline{atA})\}$$
$$\lambda_B(\underline{using},\underline{disusing}) = \{(\underline{atA},\underline{atA}),(\underline{atA},\underline{free})\}$$

is a maximal subproduct of A(<u>using</u>) and B(<u>disusing</u>), and finally

$$\Phi(\underline{using},\underline{using}) = \emptyset$$

with

$$\lambda_A(\underline{using},\underline{using}) = \lambda_B(\underline{using},\underline{using}) = \emptyset$$

is a maximal subproduct of A(<u>using</u>) and B(<u>using</u>).

The only morphism:

$$\Phi(\underline{disusing},\underline{disusing}) \xrightarrow{\Phi(\underline{disusing},\underline{take})} \Phi(\underline{disusing},\underline{using})$$

which makes commutative the diagram:

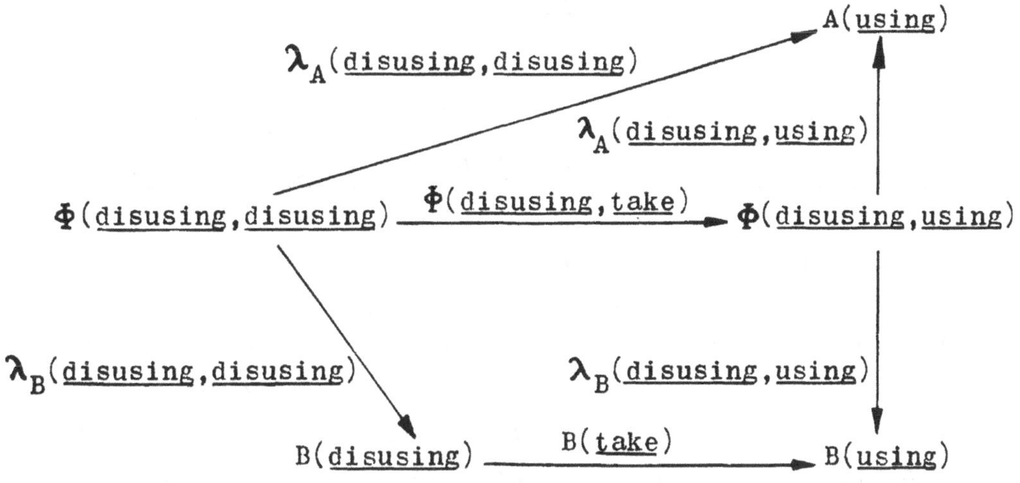

is that with

$$\Phi(\underline{\text{disusing}},\underline{\text{take}}) = \{(\underline{\text{free}},\underline{\text{atB}})\}$$

as the following picture shows

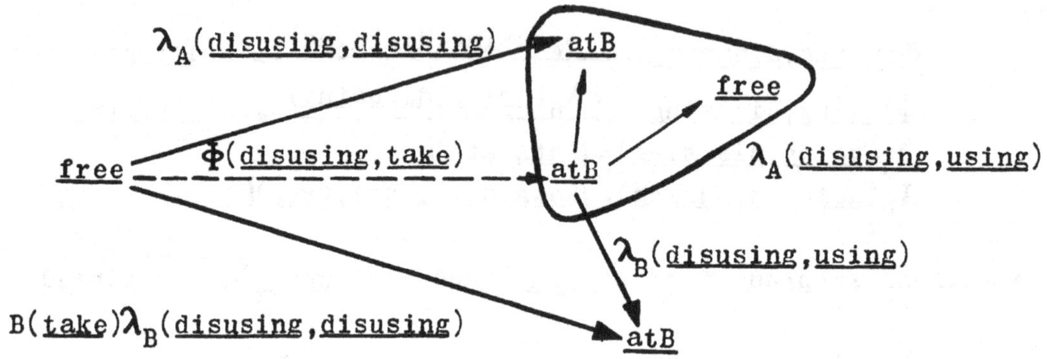

In the same way we find:

$$\Phi(\underline{\text{disusing}},\underline{\text{put}}) = \{(\underline{\text{atB}},\underline{\text{free}})\}$$
$$\Phi(\underline{\text{take}},\underline{\text{disusing}}) = \{(\underline{\text{free}},\underline{\text{atA}})\}$$
$$\Phi(\underline{\text{put}},\underline{\text{disusing}}) = \{(\underline{\text{atA}},\underline{\text{free}})\}$$

so that the subcategory C of $Pa(G_A) \times Pa(G_B)$ with existing and non--empty $\Phi(\alpha_A,\alpha_B)$ for its morphisms is that generated by the morphisms:

$$(\underline{\text{disusing}},\underline{\text{disusing}}) \xrightarrow{(\underline{\text{disusing}},\underline{\text{take}})} (\underline{\text{disusing}},\underline{\text{using}})$$
$$(\underline{\text{disusing}},\underline{\text{using}}) \xrightarrow{(\underline{\text{disusing}},\underline{\text{put}})} (\underline{\text{disusing}},\underline{\text{disusing}})$$
$$(\underline{\text{disusing}},\underline{\text{disusing}}) \xrightarrow{(\underline{\text{take}},\underline{\text{disusing}})} (\underline{\text{using}},\underline{\text{disusing}})$$
$$(\underline{\text{using}},\underline{\text{disusing}}) \xrightarrow{(\underline{\text{put}},\underline{\text{disusing}})} (\underline{\text{disusing}},\underline{\text{disusing}})$$

and Φ can be uniquely extended to the program $C \xrightarrow{\Phi} \tilde{\mathcal{E}}_{A,B}$ which was already described in the initial part of the paper.

The above illustrates how programs which consist in simultaneous execution of some given programs can be computed provided they are formally defined as subproducts of the given programs. This enables to study in a precise way such phenomena as deadlock, mutual exclusion, and others.

RECAPITULATION

Our main aim was to answer how some given programs which were to be executed in some environment containing their data and themselves could be executed simultaneously. To attain it we were looking for programs running in accordance with all the given ones simultaneously.

Programs under consideration were formally defined as functors from categories of control flows to categories of environment state changes, analogously as it was done by GOGUEN. A notion of homomorphism between programs was introduced similar to that of GOGUEN and programs we were looking for were formally characterized as some subproducts (definition 3) in a category of programs and homomorphisms between programs.

Next, we proved theorems which explained how to compute subproducts of programs using subproducts in the suitable category of environment state changes.

Finally, we characterized subproducts in categories of environment state changes getting in this way a method for computing them. As result, we got a method of computing of subproducts of programs.

REFERENCES

[1] BURSTALL,R.M. An Algebraic Description of Programs with Assertions, Verification and Simulation. Proc. of an ACM Conf. on Proving Ass. about Prog., Las Cruces, N. Mexico, 1972

[2] GOGUEN,J.A. On Homomorphisms, Simulations, Correctness, and Subroutines of Programs and Program Schemes. Proc. of 1972 IEEE Symp. on Switching and Automata Theory, 1972

[3] GOGUEN,J.A. On Homomorphisms, Correctness, Termination, Unfoldments, and Equivalence of Flow Diagram Programs. Technical Report, Computer Science Dep., School of Engin. and Appl. Sc., University of California, Los Angeles, 1973

ULTRALINEAR EXPRESSIONS

J.P. CRESTIN
Ecole Nationale Supérieure
de Techniques Avancées. Paris.

Abstract : The bracket operation, $[A, B] = \{a\,b\,\tilde{a}' : (a, a') \in A,\ b \in B\}$ is used jointly with product and union to define ultralinear languages. General properties of this operation and of the operator on families of languages associated with it are given. A decomposition of the family of ultralinear languages into a semi-lattice of principal semiAFLs is obtained by these means.

INTRODUCTION

One of the most promising means of investigation in formal languages theory seems to be the use of algebraic operators on languages and families of languages. The introduction of syntactical operators by S. Greibach [7] was a first step in this direction. Following a previous work of the author with L. Boasson and M. Nivat [2], the properties of the bracket operation are further investigated. They are applied to the study of subfamilies of the family of ultralinear linear languages, a well-known family of context-free languages. The use of bracket operation permits us to define very easily ultralinear semiAFLs , represented by "ultralinear expressions", which form a semi-lattice covering the whole family of ultralinear languages. Strict inclusion relations between these semiAFLs will follow directly from the previous general results.

After recalling the basic notions needed (§1), we give some fundamental properties of the bracket operation (§2). The third paragraph is devoted to the definition of principal semi AFLs of ultralinear languages. In the fourth paragraph we use the properties of bracket operation to prove some strict inclusion relations among these families.

1. PRELIMINARY DEFINITIONS

We introduce here the fundamental operators we shall use thereafter for the definition of families of ultralinear languages.

For any monoid M, with operation . and unit element 1, and any parts A and B of M, we shall write

$A.B = \{a.b : a \in A, b \in B\}$ (also denoted by AB)

$A \cup B$ for the set union of A and B

A^* for the submonoid of M generated by A.

Consider a free monoid $M = X^*$ generated by the alphabet X, let I be the set consisting of the single element 1. If $f = x_1 \ldots x_n \in X^*$, $x_i \in X$, we write $\tilde{f} = x_n \ldots x_1$. The operation ~, called reversal or mirror image, is an involutory anti-isomorphism of X^*.

The cartesian product $X^* \times X^*$ with operation $(a, a').(b,b') = (a.b, a'.b')$ forms a monoid.

If $A \subset X^* \times X^*$ and $B \subset X^*$, let $[A, B] = \{a\, b\, \tilde{a'} : (a, a') \in A, b \in B\}$

The family of *rational subsets* of a monoid M is the smallest family of subsets of M containing the finite sets and closed under operations $\cup$, . and * . A rational (or regular) language is any rational subset of a free monoid. Rat_2 will denote the family of rational subsets of the cartesian product of a free monoid by itself.

A *rational transduction* [8] is a rational subset of the cartesian product of two free monoids. If $\tau \subset X^* \times Y^*$ is a rational transduction, we shall write $\tau(L) = \{v : \exists u \in L \quad (u, v) \in \tau\}$. A language is any subset of a free monoid.

A *semiAFL* $\mathcal{L}$ is a nonempty family of languages closed under union and rational transductions (i.e. $\tau(L) \in \mathcal{L}$ if $L \in \mathcal{L}$)(*). $\mathcal{L}$ is said principal if there exists a language L such that, for each L' in $\mathcal{L}$, there is a rational transduction τ such that $L' = \tau(L)$. L is a generator of $\mathcal{L}$ and we write $\mathcal{L} = \mathcal{M}(L)$.

We introduce now different operators on semiAFLs :

DEFINITION 1.

For any families of languages $\mathcal{L}$, $\mathcal{L}'$, let us denote by :

$\mathcal{L} \vee \mathcal{L}'$	the smallest semiAFL including $\mathcal{L}$ and $\mathcal{L}'$
$\mathcal{L} \otimes \mathcal{L}$	the smallest semiAFL containing L.L' for any L in $\mathcal{L}$, L' in $\mathcal{L}'$
$[\mathcal{L}]$	the smallest semiAFL containing [A, L] for any A in Rat_2 and L in $\mathcal{L}$.

The following properties are proved in [2] and [7] :

PROPOSITION 1

Let $\mathcal{L}$ and $\mathcal{L}'$ be principal semi AFLs respectively generated by L and L' . Let a, b be new letters not occuring in L or L', and $S = \{(u, u) : u \in \{a,b\}^*\}$. Then the semi AFLs $\mathcal{L} \vee \mathcal{L}'$, $\mathcal{L} \otimes \mathcal{L}'$ and $[\mathcal{L}]$ are principal. More precisely, $L \cup a L'$ is a generator for $\mathcal{L} \vee \mathcal{L}'$, L a L' a generator for $\mathcal{L} \otimes \mathcal{L}'$, [S,L] a generator for $[\mathcal{L}]$.

Ultralinear languages first defined by Banerji [1] and studied by Ginsburg and Spanier [6] are the languages generated by nonterminal bounded grammars. The importance of previous operators for this family of languages comes from the following characterization :

PROPOSITION 2

The family of ultralinear languages is the smallest family of languages, UL, containing the finite languages, and the sets [A, L] for all A in Rat_2 and L in $\mathcal{L}$

(*) We consider here only full semi AFLs as defined by Greibach [7].

and closed under union and product.

As UL forms a semi AFL, we have

$$UL = UL \otimes UL = [UL] = UL \vee UL$$

So any family of languages defined from the unitary family {I} by use of operations $\vee$, $\times$, [ ] is a subfamily of UL. These families will be the main concern of this paper.

A particularly important such family is the family of *linear languages* [4] which we characterize using the following result :

PROPOSITION 3 [8]

For any linear language L, there exists an element A of Rat_2 such that $L = [A, I]$

It comes then from proposition 1:

COROLLARY

The family Lin of linear languages is a principal semi AFL equal to [{I}] and generated by

$$L = [S, I] = \{f\tilde{f} : f \in \{a, b\}^*\}$$

2. SOME PROPERTIES OF THE BRACKET OPERATOR ON FAMILIES OF LANGUAGES

We give here the fundamental properties of the bracket operator we shall use in the last paragraph for proving strict inclusions between families of ultralinear languages.

Let us first recall a result from [3]

PROPOSITION 4

If $\mathcal{L}$ is a semi AFL, $L \subset X^*$, a and b two letters not belonging to X, and if $[(a, b)^* , L]$ belongs to the rational closure of $\mathcal{L}$ (i.e. the closure of $\mathcal{L}$ by the operations $\cup$, . and $*$), then L belongs to $\mathcal{L}$.

The following result is a refinement of a result in [2] :

THEOREM 1

Let $\mathcal{L}$ be a semi AFL, L_1 and L_2 two languages over disjoint alphabets, and let $L_1.L_2$ belong to $[\mathcal{L}]$, then one of the following holds :

a) L_1 is rational and $L_2 \in [\mathcal{L}]$

b) L_2 is rational and $L_1 \in [\mathcal{L}]$

c) L_1 , L_2 and $L_1.L_2$ belong to $\mathcal{L}$.

PROOF

Let $L_1 \subset X_1^*$, $L_2 \subset X_2^*$, $X_1 \cap X_2 = \emptyset$.

Let ϕ_1 and ϕ_2 be homomorphisms from $(X_1 \cup X_2)^* = X^*$ into itself defined by

$$\phi_1 (x) = x \text{ if } x \in X_1 \text{ , } 1 \text{ if } x \in X_2$$

$$\phi_2 (x) = 1 \text{ if } x \in X_1 \text{ , } x \text{ if } x \in X_2$$

From $L_1 L_2 \in [\mathcal{L}]$ and from proposition 1 of [2], it follows that there exists a finite number p of elements A_i in Rat_2 and M_i in $\mathcal{L}$ such that

$$(\alpha) \quad L_1 L_2 = \bigcup_{i=1}^{p} [A_i , M_i]$$

The condition $[A_i , M_i] \subset X_1^*. X_2^*$ implies that for each i in [1, p], at least one of the following holds :

$$(1) \quad A_i \subset X_1^* \times X_2^* , M_i \subset X_1^* X_2^*$$

$$(2) \quad A_i \subset X_1^* X_2^* \times X_2^* , M_i \subset X_2^*$$

$$(3) \quad A_i \subset X_1^* \times X_1^* X_2^* , M_i \subset X_1^*$$

Let π_1 , π_2 be the two projections from $X^* \times X^*$ into X^* . As no confusion arises, we shall write for $A \subset X^* \times X^*$

$$\phi_j (A) = \{(\phi_j (u), \phi_j (v)) : (u, v) \in A\}$$

We can suppose that for i = 1, p_1, (1) holds, for i = p_1 + 1, p_2 (2) holds and that for i = p_2 + 1, p (3) holds.

Let then

for i = 1, p_1 $\quad A_i^1 = \pi_1 (A_i)$, $A_i^2 = \pi_2 (A_i)$, $M_i^1 = \phi_1 (M_i)$, $M_i^2 = \phi_2 (M_i)$

for i = p_1 +1, p_2 $\quad B'_i = \phi_1 (\pi_1 (A_i))$, $A'_i = \phi_2 (A_i)$

for i = p_2 +1, p $\quad A''_i = \phi_1 (A_i)$, $B''_i = \phi_2 (\pi_2 (A_i))$

Applying ϕ_1 and ϕ_2 to (α), we get then

$$L_1 = \bigcup_{i=1}^{p1} A_i^1 \; M_i^1 \bigcup_{i=p_1+1}^{p2} B'_i \bigcup_{i=p_2+1}^{p} [A''_i , M_i]$$

and $$L_2 = \bigcup_{i=1}^{p_1} M_i^2 \; A_i^2 \bigcup_{i=p_1+1}^{p_2} [A'_i , M_i] \bigcup_{i=p_2+1}^{p} B''_i$$

From these and the definitions of A_i^1 , A_i^2 , M_i^1 ... , we get :

$$[A_i , M_i] \subset A_i^1 M_i^1 M_i^2 A_i^2 \subset L_1 L_2 \text{ for } i = 1, p_1$$

$$\bigcup_{i=p_1+1}^{p_2} [A_i , M_i] \subset (\bigcup_{i=p_1+1}^{p2} B'_i) (\bigcup_{i=p_1+1}^{p2} [A'_i , M_i]) \subset L_1 L_2$$

and $\bigcup_{i=p_2+1}^{p} [A_i , M_i] \subset (\bigcup_{i=p_2+1}^{p} [A''_i , M_i]) (\bigcup_{i=p_2+1}^{p} B''_i) \subset L_1 L_2$

Let $B' = \bigcup_{i=p_1+1}^{p_2} B'_i$, $B'' = \bigcup_{i=p_2+1}^{p} B''_i$

$$L' = \bigcup_{i=p_1+1}^{p_2} [A'_i , M_i] , \quad L'' = \bigcup_{i=p_2+1}^{p} [A''_i , M_i]$$

$$H_1 = \bigcup_{i=1}^{p_1} M_i^1 A_i^1 , \quad H_2 = \bigcup_{i=1}^{p_1} M_i^2 A_i^2$$

$$H'_1 = L' - H_1 - B' , \quad H'_2 = L'' - H_2 - B''$$

We can write now

$$L_1 L_2 = \bigcup_{i=1}^{p_1} A_i^1 M_i^1 M_i^2 A_i^2 \cup B' L' \cup L'' B''$$

or (β) $L_1 L_2 = \bigcup_{i=1}^{p_1} A_i^1 M_i^1 M_i^2 A_i^2 \cup B' H_2 \cup H_1 B'' \cup B' B'' \cup B'H'_2 \cup H'_1 B''$

The A_i^j , B' and B'' are rational languages, L' and L'' belong to $[\mathcal{L}]$

From the definition of H'_2 , the elements of $L_1 H'_2$ may belong only to the term $B' H'_2$ in the expression (β). Therefore $L_1 H'_2 = B' H'_2$ and either $B' = L_1$ or $H'_2 = \emptyset$.

For the same reason, considering $H'_1 L_2$, we have either $B'' = L_2$ or $H'_1 = \emptyset$.

In the case $B' = L_1$, L_1 is rational and $L_2 \in [\mathcal{L}]$. In the case $B'' = L_2$, L_2 is rational and $L_1 \in [\mathcal{L}]$. In both cases, the theorem holds.

In the case $H'_1 = H'_2 = \emptyset$, we can write

$$L_1 L_2 = \bigcup_{i=1}^{p_1} A_i^1 M_i^1 M_i^2 A_i^2 \cup B' H_2 \cup H_1 B'' \cup B' B''$$

$$= \bigcup_{i=1}^{p_1} A_i^1 M_i A_i^2 \cup B' H_2 \cup H_1 B'' \cup B' B''$$

As A_i^1 and A_i^2 are rational, $A_i^1 M_i A_i^2$ $(i = 1, p_1)$, H_1 and H_2 are in $\mathcal{L}$. As B' and B'' are rational, $H_1 B''$, $B'H_2$, $B' B''$ are also in $\mathcal{L}$. As $\mathcal{L}$ is closed by union, $L_1 L_2$ is in $\mathcal{L}$. $L_1 = \phi_1 (L_1 L_2)$, $L_2 = \phi_2 (L_1 L_2)$ are in $\mathcal{L}$ as a homomorphisms are rational transductions.

We deduce now frome these properties two technical lemmas :

LEMMA 1

Let $\mathcal{L}$ be a semiAFL not closed under product, then $\mathcal{L}^p \underline{\not\subset} [\mathcal{L}^p]$ for any $p > 1$ (*)

PROOF

If $\mathcal{L}$ is not closed under product, we have $\mathcal{L} \underline{\not\subset} \mathcal{L}^2 \underline{\not\subset} \dots \underline{\not\subset} \mathcal{L}^p$

Let $L \in \mathcal{L}^p - \mathcal{L}$, $L \subset X^*$, a, b two letters not in X . $L' = [(a,b)^*, L]$ belongs to $[\mathcal{L}^p]$. Should L' belong to $\mathcal{L}^p$, then L' should belong to $\mathcal{L}$ from proposition 4, which is not possible.

LEMMA 2

Let $\mathcal{L}$ be a semiAFL such that $\mathcal{L} \subset [\mathcal{L}]$, then $[\mathcal{L}]$ is not closed by product with Lin.

PROOF

Let $L_1 \in [\mathcal{L}] - \mathcal{L}$, L_2 any non-rational linear language, both over disjoint alphabets. As any semiAFL contains the family of rational languages, L_1 is not rational. Should $L_1 L_2$ belong to $[\mathcal{L}]$, then from theorem 1 L_1 should belong to $\mathcal{L}$ which is a contradiction.

3. SYMMETRIC ULTRALINEAR FAMILIES

We use here the operators on families of languages defined in the previous paragraph to build ultralinear expressions representing principal subsemiAFLs of the family of ultralinear languages, the symmetric ultralinear families.

DEFINITION 2

A symmetric ultralinear expression (SUE) is any well-formed expression written with constant I and operators $\times$, $\vee$, [ ] .

It is clear that each ultralinear expression $\mathcal{E}$ represents a family $\mathcal{L}$ of languages which is a semiAFL included in the family of ultralinear languages. We shall call any such family a *symmetric ultralinear family* (SUF). When no confusion arises, we shall use the same notation for an expression and its value.

DEFINITION 3

Let ϕ be the formal substitution defined on symmetric ultralinear expressions by ϕ ([) = [S.(c,c'),

ϕ (]) =]

ϕ ($\times$) = . d

(*) $\mathcal{L}^p$ denotes here $\mathcal{L}^{p-1} \otimes \mathcal{L}$

ϕ (v) = $\cup\, d_i$ if it is the ith v in the expression

ϕ (I) = I

where a, b, c, c', d, d_i are different letters.

For any SUE $\mathcal{C}$ representing $\mathcal{L}$, ϕ ($\mathcal{C}$) is a language trivially included in $\mathcal{L}$.

Moreover, it follows by induction from proposition 1 :

THEOREM 2

For any SUE $\mathcal{C}$ representing the family $\mathcal{L}$, $\mathcal{L}$ is a principal semiAFL generated by ϕ ($\mathcal{C}$).

The language L can be constructed from the symmetric language [S, I] by insertions, unions and products, wherefrom the name of symmetric families. There are of course many ultralinear semiAFLs which are not symmetric, for instance among the linear languages, the families

$\mathcal{M}$ ({a^n b^n : n ≥ 0}), $\mathcal{M}$ ({a^n b^m : n ≥ m}), etc ... are not symmetric.

Example : The SUF $\mathcal{L}$ = $[[I]^2]$ ⊗ [I] is generated by the language

$$L = \phi\ (\mathcal{L}) = [S(c,c'),\ [S(c,c'),I].d[S(c,c'),I]].d[S(c,c'),I]$$

$$= \{f_1\ c\ f_2\ cc'\ \tilde{f}_2\ \ d\ f_3\ cc'\tilde{f}_3\ c'\tilde{f}_1\ d\ f_4c'\tilde{f}_4\ :\ f_i \in \{a,\ b\}^*\}$$

It is clear from proposition 2 that any such language belongs to some SUF, so that UL equals the union of all SUF. We shall see now the inclusion relations among those families which trivially constitute an upper semi-lattice.

DEFINITION 4.

Let $\mathcal{C}$ and $\mathcal{C}$ ' be two SUE, we shall write $\mathcal{C} \geq \mathcal{C}'$ if $\mathcal{C} = \mathcal{C}'$ or if $\mathcal{C}'$ can be obtained from $\mathcal{C}$ by deletion of symbols v , ⊗ or of pairs of matching brackets.

Let L = ϕ ($\mathcal{C}$), L' = ϕ ($\mathcal{C}'$), we can easily exhibit a rational transduction τ, erasing the pairs $\tilde{f}$, f in L corresponding to deleted brackets, such that

$$L' = \tau\ (L)$$

Therefore $\mathcal{M}$ (L') ⊂ $\mathcal{M}$(L) and

THEOREM 3

Let $\mathcal{L}$ and $\mathcal{L}'$ be two SUF respectively represented by SUE $\mathcal{C}$ and $\mathcal{C}$ ', then $\mathcal{C} \geq \mathcal{C}'$ implies $\mathcal{L} \supset \mathcal{L}'$

Remark : It can be shown that the SUF are exactly the families of languages generated by the ultralinear grammar forms of Cremers and Ginsburg [5]. Thus these families can also be very easily defined by the form of their grammars.

4. SOME STRICT INCLUSION RELATIONS

We shall restrict ourselves here to homogenous ultralinear families, which form a subset of SUF and cover the whole family of ultralinear languages. The proofs of strict inclusions are direct consequences of the second paragraph's technical lemmas The general relations of inclusion between SUF need some more material which would be too long to introduce here.

Let $\mathcal{L}_1 = \mathrm{Lin}$, $\mathcal{L}_k = (\mathrm{Lin})^k$, $\mathcal{L}_{k,1} = [L_k]$

and for any positive integers $k_1 , \ldots, k_p$

$$\mathcal{L}_{k_1 , \ldots k_p} = [\mathcal{L}_{k_1, \ldots k_{p-1}}]^{k_p}$$

We shall only consider those expression where $k_i = 1$ implies $k_{i+1} \neq 1$, as trivially holds

$$\mathcal{L}_{k_1 , \ldots k_{i-1}, 1, 1, k_{i+2} , \ldots k_p} = \mathcal{L}_{k_1, \ldots k_{i-1}, 1, k_{i+2}, \ldots k_p}$$

We shall call these expressions homogenous ultralinear expressions (HUE).

It is clear that, for any SUF $\mathcal{L}$, there exists a HUE $\mathcal{L}'$ containing $\mathcal{L}$, so that

$$\mathrm{UL} = \bigcup_{\mathcal{L} \text{ an HUE}} \mathcal{L}$$

Moreover, the partial order defined for SUE can be defined here as :

DEFINITION 5

Let $s = (k_1 , \ldots k_p)$, $s' = (k'_1 , \ldots, k'_{p'})$, then we shall write $s \geq s'$ if and only if there exists $0 < i (1) < \ldots < i (p) < p$ such that $k_{i(j)} \geq k'_j$ for all j in $[1, p]$

As a consequence from §3, we have $\mathcal{L}_s \supset \mathcal{L}_{s'}$ if $s \geq s'$. More precisely, we have :

THEOREM 4

If $s > s'$ (i.e. $s \geq s'$ and $s \neq s'$), we have $\mathcal{L}_s \underline{\not\supset} \mathcal{L}_{s'}$

PROOF

It clearly suffices to show that for all $k_1, \ldots k_p$,

$$\mathcal{L}_{k_1, \ldots, k_{p+1}} \underline{\not\supset} \mathcal{L}_{k_1 , \ldots k_p}$$

and $\mathcal{L}_{k_1 , \ldots k_p,1} \underline{\not\supset} \mathcal{L}_{k_1 , \ldots k_p}$

As Lin is not closed under product, we have $\mathcal{L}_1 \subsetneq \mathcal{L}_2 \subsetneq \dots \subsetneq \mathcal{L}_k$
Let us suppose that

$$\mathcal{L} = \mathcal{L}_{k_1, \dots k_p, 1} \subsetneq \mathcal{L}_{k_1, \dots k_{p,2}} = \mathcal{L}^2$$

That means that $\mathcal{L}$ is not closed under product, so that we have

$$\mathcal{L} \subsetneq \mathcal{L}^2 \subsetneq \mathcal{L}^3 \subsetneq \dots \subsetneq \mathcal{L}^r$$

or $\mathcal{L}_{k_1, \dots k_p, r-1} \subsetneq \mathcal{L}_{k_1, \dots k_{p,r}}$ for all r.

It follows from Lemma 1 that

$$\mathcal{L}_{k_1, \dots k_{p,r}} \subsetneq \left[\mathcal{L}_{k_1, \dots k_{p,r}}\right] = \mathcal{L}'$$

and from Lemma 2 that $\mathcal{L}'$ is not closed by product. The theorem follows by induction

As we can obviously extract from the $\mathcal{L}_s$ an infinite chain

$$\mathcal{L}_{s_1}, \mathcal{L}_{s_2} \dots$$

such that $s_i < s_{i+1}$ for all i and $\bigcup_{i=1}^{\infty} \mathcal{L}_{s_i} =$ UL, a consequence of this theorem is that the $\mathcal{L}_{s_i}$ form an infinite strictly increasing chain of semiAFLs the union of which is UL, so that we have here a new proof of the well known result that UL is not a principal semiAFL.

REFERENCES

1. R.B. BANERJI, Phrase structure language, finite machines and channel capacity, *Information and Control* 16, (1963), 153-162.

2. L. BOASSON, J.P. CRESTIN, M. NIVAT, Familles de langages translatables et fermées par crochet, *Acta Informatica* 2 (1973), 383- 393.

3. L. BOASSON, M. NIVAT, Sur diverses familles de langages fermées par transduction rationnelle, *Acta Informatica* 2 (1973), 180-188.

4. N. CHOMSKY, M.P. SCHUTZENBERGER, The algebraic theory of context-free languages, in *Computer Programming and Formal System* , Ed. P. Braffort, D. Hirschberg, North-Holland, Amsterdam (1967), 118-161.

5. A.B. CREMERS, S. GINSBURG, Context-free grammar forms, in *Automata, Languages and Programming*, Ed. J. Loeckx, Springer Verlag, Berlin (1974), 364-382.

6. S. GINSBURG, E.H. SPANIER, Finite-turn pushdown automata, *SIAM J. Control* 4 (1966), 429-453

7. S. GREIBACH, Syntactic operators on full semiAFLs, *J. Comput. System Sciences* 6 (1972), 30-76

8. M. NIVAT, Transduction des langages de Chomsky, *Annales de l'Institut Fourier* 18 (1968), 339-456.

A FAMILY OF ALGEBRAIC SYSTEMS RELATED TO THE THEORY OF EQUATIONS ON FREE MONOIDS

Max FONTET
Institut de Programmation
Université PARIS 6 - PARIS (FRANCE)

ABSTRACT :

We present some recent combinatorial results on a family of algebraic systems, called bipermutational π - systems, which allow us to determine the structure of the solutions of bipermutational equations on the free monoid X^* (each member of the equation containsexactly one occurrence of each letter of X). Thus, for each bipermutational π - system, we exhibit a class of characteristic elements called special bipermutations.

1. INTRODUCTION

1.1. Equations on free monoïds.

Given a finite non empty set X(whose elements are called letters and form an alphabet) and X^* the free monoïd of base X (whose elements are called words), a pair of words (we say a biword) $B = (f,f')$ determines an equation in the free monoid X^*. A solution of the equation is a pair (Y^*, Φ), Y^* being the free monoïd generated by the set Y and Φ a morphism of X^* on Y^* such $f\Phi = f'\Phi$.

We say that a biword is valid iff the corresponding equation admits a solution $(\mathbb{N}, \varphi)$ where $\mathbb{N}$ is the additive monoïd of the non negative integers and φ is a morphism of X^* on $\mathbb{N}$ which sends no letter on 0 . This means that the equation has a non degenerate solution. For such an equation (f, f'), the characterization of the set of pairs (Y^*,Φ) leads to the study of the "general solution" of the equation and, as a fundamental subproblem, to the determination of the maximum number of independant verbally parameters, Par(f,f'), which measures the strength of constraints exerted by the equation on the words f and f'. For more details on that general problem, the reader is refered to the works of A. LENTIN [4, 5].

1.2. π - systems

Let n be a positive integer and $[n]$ the set $\{i \ ; \ i \in \mathbb{N} : 1 \le i \le n\}$. A word f of length, $|f| = n$, on the alphabet X can be considered as a map $f : [n] \to X$. If $i \overset{f}{\mapsto} x$, we write $f^{(i)} = x$ and we say that i is the ordinal in f of this occurence of x. The letter $f^{(1)}$ is called the initial in $f^{(n)}$ the ultimate. The concatenation of the words f and f'

$$f : [n] \to X \qquad\qquad f' : [n'] \to X$$

is defined by

$$g = ff' : [n + n'] \to X$$

were $\quad i \overset{g}{\mapsto} f^{(i)} \qquad 1 \le i \le n$

$\qquad\quad i \overset{g}{\mapsto} f'^{(i)} \qquad n < i \le n'$

The number of occurences of the letter x in the word f, $|f|_x$ is called the degree in x of f.

The well known lemma of F.W. LEVI [7] plays a fundamental part in the theory of the free monoids. We can state it as follows :

If four words f_1, f_2, f_3, f_4 of X^* satisfy the condition $f_1 f_2 = f_3 f_4$, then

- either $|f_1| > |f_3|$ in which case there exist three words u,v,w, of X^* such that

$$f_1 = u\,v\ ,\ f_2 = w,\quad f_3 = u\ ,\quad f_4 = v\,w\ ;$$

- or $|f_1| < |f_3|$ then we have similarly

$$f_1 = u,\quad f_2 = v\,w\ ,\quad f_3 = u\,v \qquad f_4 = w\ ;$$

- or finally $|f_1| = |f_3|$ in which case $|f_2| = |f_4|$

and $\qquad f_1 = f_3 = u \qquad\qquad f_2 = f_4 = w.$

The methodical use of this lemma for solving the equations in free monoids leads to introduce some unary operations on the biwords. The operation of left (resp. right) initial pivot π (resp. π') sends a biword $B = (f, f')$ on a biword $B_1 = B\,\pi$ (resp. $B_2 = B\,\pi'$) where B_1 (resp. B_2) is constructed from B by replacing each occurence of the letter $f^{(1)} = x$ (resp. $f'^{(1)} = y$) by the word yx (resp. xy) and by simplifying the initial letters.

Example : (a b c a c, d d c) = π (a bac, c d d c)
(b a a c, c d d a c) = π'(a bac, c d d c)

The π - operations are defined iff $x \neq y$. But they have an equational meaning iff π (B) and π'(B) are valid biwords.

The algebraic system generated by these operations is called a π-system.

It is clear that every solution of B_1 is able to give by "retracing" a solution of B which can be described with an operator ρ. If Φ_1 is a solution of B_1 , ρ provides the solution Φ of B

$$z\,\Phi = z\,\Phi_1 \qquad\qquad z \neq x$$

$$z\,\Phi = (y\,\Phi_1)\quad(x\,\Phi_1)$$

Similarly we can define ρ' corresponding to π'. By the duality : initial-ultimate, we can again define two operations $\tilde{\pi}$ and $\tilde{\pi}'$: the pu - operations.

2. BIPERMUTATIONAL π - SYSTEMS

2.1. Definition : bipermutation

Let X ! the subset of words of degre one in all the letters of X. A bipermutation is, by definition, a biword on X !. The equation naturally associated is called a bipermutational equation.

2.2. Definition : type of a bipermutation

Let B (f,f') a bipermutation on an alphabet X of cardinality n. The surjective map $X \mapsto [n]$ defined by $f^{(i)} \mapsto i$ can be extended in a morphism of $X^* \mapsto [n]^*$. This morphism sends f' on an element of [n] ! called the type of the bipermutation B.

For example, X = {a, b, c, d, e, f} the bipermutation B = (a b c d e f, f c b e d a) has the type 632 541.

2.3. Definition : rank and place of a letter

For a bipermutation B, we call rank of x (written rk(x)) and place of x (written pl(x)) the ordinal of x in f and in f' respectively.

2.4. Definition : undecomposable bipermutation

A bipermutation B =(f, f') is undecomposable iff X cannot be divided in two sets Y and Z such that (f, f') = (g h, g' h')

$$g,\ g' \in Y\,! \quad\text{and}\quad h,\ h' \in Z\,!$$

From an equational point of view, we have only to consider undecomposable bipermuations. It is obvious that the equation associated to a decomposable bipermutation can be decomposed in two independant equations.

Later on, we will consider only undecomposable bipermutations.

2.5. Bipermutational π - system

For these π - systems, the π - operations have specific properties. Thus, if $B = (f, f')$ with

$$f = f^{(1)} \ldots\ldots\ldots\ldots f^{(n)}$$

$$f' = f'^{(1)} \ldots\ldots\ldots\ldots f'^{(n)}$$

we have for $B' = B\,\pi = (g, g')$

$$g = f$$

$$g' = f'^{(2)} \ldots\ldots f'^{(\alpha-1)}\; f'^{(1)}\; f'^{(\alpha)}\; f'^{(\alpha+1)} \ldots\ldots f'^{(n)}$$

if $f^{(1)} = f'^{(\alpha)}$.

The operation π preserves the ranks and permute circularly the letters having a place less than α . It has an inverse π^{-1} such that $B\pi^{-1} = B\,\pi^{\alpha}$.

The same results dualy hold for π'.

The π - system generated by an undecomposable bipermutation contains only undecomposable bipermutations.

It is also easy to see that

$$\text{Par}\ (f, f') = \text{Par}\ (\pi(f,f'))$$

and that this number is an invariant for the π-system.

2.6. Definition : reducible bipermutations

A bipermutation B on the alphabet X is immediately (or directly) reducible in y iff there exists a bipermutation B' on the alphabet $Y = X \setminus \{y\}$ and a letter t of Y such that B, $B\,\pi$ or $B\,\pi'$ is the image of B' by a morphism $\delta : Y^* \to X^*$ defined by $z\,\delta = z$ if $z \neq t$, $t\,\delta = yt$.

A bipermutation B on the alphabet X is mediately (or indirectly) reducible iff $B\,\tilde{\pi}$ or $B\,\tilde{\pi}'$ is immediately reducible in a letter.

2.7. The boundary permutation

Being given any bipermutation $B = (f, f')$ on the alphabet X of cardinality n, it is always possible to make the following construction :

(1) X_1 and X_2 being distinguishable copies of X, let us define the morphism $\delta : X^* \to (X_1 \cup X_2)^*$ such that $x\,\delta = x_1\, x_2$. The bipermutation (f, f') is sent on the biword $(f\,\delta, f'\delta)$.

(2) Identifying $f_1^{(1)}$ with $f_1'^{(1)}$ and $f_2^{(n)}$ with $f_2'^{(n)}$, let us form from X_1 and X_2 the quotient alphabet Z_1 and Z_2. The class $\{f_1^{(1)}, f_1'^{(1)}\}$ is the initial class i and the class $\{f_2^{(n)}, f_2'^{(n)}\}$ is the ultimate class ü. The natural morphisms from X_j to Z_j (j=1,2) send $(f\,\delta, f'\,\delta)$ on a biword on $Z_1 \cup Z_2$ $(\bar{f}, \bar{f}')$.

(3) Simplifying $\bar{f}$ and $\bar{f}'$ to the initials by ĭ and to the ultimates by ü, we obtain a biword (τ, τ') on $Z = Z_1 \times Z_2$.

Example :

$$B = (a\ b\ c\ d\ e\ f\ g\ h\ k,\ e\ g\ f\ k\ a\ d\ c\ b\ h)$$

(1) $\delta\ B = (a_1a_2b_1b_2c_1c_2d_1d_2e_1e_2f_1f_2g_1g_2h_1h_2k_1k_2,$

$e_1e_2g_1g_2f_1f_2k_1k_2a_1a_2d_1d_2c_1c_2b_1b_2h_1h_2)$

(2) $\breve{\imath} = \{a_1, e_1\}$ $\quad$ $\ddot{u} = \{k_2, h_2\}$

(3) $\tau = (a_2, b_1)\ (b_2, c_1)\ (c_2, d_1)\ (d_2, \breve{\imath})\ (e_2, f_1)\ (f_2, g_1)\ (g_2, h_1)\ (\ddot{u}, k_1)$

$\tau' = (e_2, g_1)\ (g_2, f_1)\ (f_2, k_1)\ (\ddot{u}, \breve{\imath})\ (a_2, d_1)\ (d_2, c_1)\ (c_2, b_1)\ (b_2, h_1)$

It is clear that τ and τ' define two bijections from Z_2 on Z_1.

Definition

The permutation $\sigma = \tau'\,\tau^{-1}$ of the symmetric group $\mathfrak{S}_{Z_2}$ is the boundary permutation of the bipermutation $B = (f, f')$.

In the example, we have $\sigma = (\ddot{u}\ d_2\ b_2\ g_2\ e_2\ f_2)\ (c_2\ a_2)$

It is easy to verify that $B\,\sigma = B\,\pi\,\sigma = B\,\pi'\,\sigma$.

Proposition

The boundary permutation is an invariant of the bipermutational π - system.

We can now state the theorem of A.LENTIN giving the number Par(f, f') for a bipermutation.

Theorem : [4, 6]

Given a bipermutation $B = (f, f')$ on an alphabet X, we have

$\text{Par}(f, f') = \frac{1}{2}[z(\sigma) + \text{card}(X) - 1]$ where $z(\sigma)$ designates the number of cycles of the boundary permutation of B.

The cycle of σ containing the ultimates $\ddot{u}$ will be designated by γ ; its behaviour is different from that of the other cycles for many properties.

3. THE TECHNICAL TOOLS OF THE THEORY

The study of the bipermutational π - systems needs some specific tools which are on the border of the combinatorial theory of the free monoids and of the theory of the symmetric groups. This paragraph tries to sum up all the important notions we have to use later on. For the proofs the reader is referred to previous quoted works.

3.1. Nodes and Nodal systems.

3.1.1. In a π - system, an undecomposable bipermutational for which $\ddot{u} = \check{i}$ is called a node.

Proposition : [4]

In each π - system generated by an undecomposable bipermutation, there is at least one node.

3.1.2. Nodal operations.

Given a node N, for each pair (x, y) of $X \times X$ with $x \neq y$, we associate a nodal operation x/y defined by

(1) If N is equal to

$$(af_1\, x\, f_2\, y\, f_3\, q,\; q\, g_1\, x\, g_2\, y\, g_3 a) \quad f_i, g_i \in X^*, \; i = 1,2,3$$

then $B\, x/y = (af_1\, y\, f_3\, x\, f_2\, q\,,\; q\, g_1\, y\, g_3\, x\, g_2\, a)$

(2) if not, x/y is not defined.

3.1.3. Nodal system

Given a node N, the nodal system NOD(N) is the minimal set of nodes containing N which is closed under nodal operations.

Theorem : [8, 9]

The nodal system NOD(N) generated by a node N is exactly constituted by all the nodes of the π - system $\mathbb{P}(N)$ generated by the node N.

3.1.4. Reversed π - systems

The reversed π - systems are the π - systems which are generated by the bipermutations $B = (f, \tilde{f})$ where $\tilde{f}$ is the mirror image of f.

If the alphabet X on which they are constructed is of cardinality n, their cardinality is $2^{n-1} - 1$. They are the only π - systems having a trivial nodal system. Therefore, their properties do not follow the general rule.

3.2. The fixing operator

The fixing operator is a projection operator of the symmetric group $\mathfrak{S}_A$ acting on a set A on the stabilizator of a subset E of A.

Definition [3, 4]

Let E be a finite subset of A, then the fixing operator of E in A Φ_A^E is the operator which sends $\mathfrak{S}_A$ on itself in the following way :

Let $\sigma \in \mathfrak{S}_A$ $\qquad \bar{\sigma} = \Phi_A^E(\sigma)$

(i) for x in E, $x\bar{\sigma} = x$ (every element of E is fixed, whence the name of the operator)

(ii) for a in A\E $a\bar{\sigma}^{\,n}$ where n is the least positive integer such that $a\sigma^n$ is in A\E. The finitness of E assumes the existence of n.

This operator does not respect the composition of maps in general. We have some theorems for particuliar cases :

Theorem : [3, 4]

Let $E = \{i, j\}$, the identity $\varphi\,\psi\,\theta = 1$ implies $\bar{\varphi}\,\bar{\psi}\,\bar{\theta} = 1$ iff one of the following conditions is satisfied :

(1) i and j are fixed points of one of the three permutations φ, ψ, θ.

(2) i (resp.j) is sent on j (resp. i) by two of these permutations.

3.3. $\bar{\pi}$ - systems

Given an undecomposable bipermutation B on an alphabet X of cardinality n, we define for a subset Y of X, which does not contain the initials and the ultimates of B, two unary operations $\bar{\pi}_Y$ and $\bar{\pi}'_Y$; $\pi_Y(B)$ (resp. $\bar{\pi}'_Y$ (B)) is equal to $\pi^i(B)$ (resp. $\pi'^j(B)$) where i is the least positive integer such that the initial letter of the right (resp. left) word of $\pi^i(B)$ (resp. $\pi'^j(B)$) is not in Y.

A $\bar{\pi}$ - system $\mathbb{R}(B, Y)$ is the minimal set of bipermutations containing B which is closed under the operations $\bar{\pi}_Y$ and $\bar{\pi}'_Y$.

Let φ^Y be the morphism of free monoid defined by

$x\,\varphi^Y = x$ if $x \notin Y$

$x\,\varphi^Y = e$ (empty word) if $x \in Y$

The bipermutation $\hat{B} = B\,\varphi^Y$ if it is undecomposable on $X \setminus Y$, generates a $\hat{\pi}$ - system $\hat{\mathbb{P}}$ which is isomorphic to $\mathbb{R}(B,Y)$

If σ is the boundary permutation of the π - system $\mathbb{P}$ generated by B, the boundary permutation of $\hat{\mathbb{P}}$ is

$$\hat{\sigma} = \Phi_{X_2}^{Y_2}(\tau')\ \Phi_{X_2}^{Y_2}(\tau^{-1})$$, but in general it is different from $\Phi_{X_2}^{Y_2}(\sigma)$.

For a general theory, the reader is referred to M. MORCRETTE [8, 9, 10]

3.4. Indirectly reducible π - systems

A π - system is an indirectly reducible π- system iff it is generated by an indirectly reducible permutation.

Proposition :

A π - system is indirectly reducible iff the cycle of the ultimates γ of its boundary permutation σ is a 1 - cycle.

Every node in such a π - system has a letter which is at once of rank 2 and of place 2.

Definition Being given a bipermutation B on an alphabet X and a letter x of X, we call predecessors of x in B the pair of letters (y, z) such that $y_2 = x_1\,\tau^{-1}$ and $z_2 = x_1\,\tau'^{-1}$

Let $\mathbb{P}_x$ be the set of bipermutations of an indirectly reducible π-system $\mathbb{P}$ such that the letter x admits the pair of ultimates (a,q), which are left fixed by the the π operations, as predecessors. Thus, we have a partition of $\mathbb{P}$ in card (X) - 2 classes :

$$\mathbb{P} = \bigcup_{x \in X - \{a,\, q\}} \mathbb{P}_x$$

<u>Theorem</u> : [1]

Let N_x be a node of $\mathbb{P}_x$. $\mathbb{P}_x$ is a $\bar{\pi}$ - system equal to $\mathbb{R}$ (N_x, {x})

Therefore, it is possible to embed any π - system in an indirectly reducible π - system without any constraint.

3.5. <u>Strong couples</u>

In a π-system $\mathbb{P}$ on an alphabet X of cardinality n a couple of letters (x, y) is a strong couple iff there exists a node such that rk(x)=pl(y)=n-1.

Diagonal couples can exist only in directly reducible π - systems.

<u>Theorem</u> : [4]

In a π-system different from a reverse π-system with a boundary permutation σ, every couple of letters different from the ultimates (x, y) such that $y\,\sigma = x$ is a strong couple.

3.6. <u>Permutations naturally attached to a bipermutation B ; Representable permutations</u>.

We attach to a bipermutation B = (f,f') on the alphabet X an element of the symmetric group $\mathfrak{S}_X$ defined by

$$\theta_B = \theta \binom{f'}{f}$$

This permutation induces a solution of the bipermutational equation associated to B by connecting a verbal parameter with each orbit of θ.

Moreover, θ induces in $\mathfrak{S}_{Z_1}$ and in $\mathfrak{S}_{Z_2}$ two permutations θ_1 and θ_2, linked together by the relation $\theta_2 = \tau'\theta_1\tau^{-1}$, which are the <u>permutations naturally attached to B</u>. When B is a node, Z_1 and Z_2 are identified with $Z = (X - \{f^{(n)}, f'^{(n)}\}) \cup \{\ddot{u}\}$. Then, $\theta_2 = \theta_1 = \ddot{\theta}$ and $\sigma = \theta^{-1}\,\tau\,\theta\,\tau^{-1}$; $\ddot{\theta}$ is constructed from θ by replacing the 2 - cycle ($f^{(n)}$) by the 1-cycle (ü).

We say that a permutation is <u>representable</u> in a π - system $\mathbb{P}$ iff there is a node N of $\mathbb{P}$ for which it is the permutation naturally attached to N.

3.7. Decompositions of the boundary permutation of a π - system $\mathbb{P}$.

3.7.1. Let A a set and $\mathfrak{S}_A$ the corresponding symmetric group. For $\sigma \in \mathfrak{S}_A$ a decomposition of σ in a product of two involutions

- we say a biinvodecomposition or for short a b i d - is intraorbital iff the orbits of the two involutions are included in the orbits of σ and extraorbital if not.

Proposition [3, 4]

Every permutation has intraorbital b i d. It has extraorbital ones iff it possesses at least two distinct orbits of the same cardinality.

3.7.2. Let n be a positive integer and $[0, n-1]$ the set $\{i, i \in \mathbb{N} ; 0$ $\{i, i \in \mathbb{N} ; 0 \leq i \leq n-1\}$. All the intraorbital decompositions of a cycle of length n $\Gamma = (0....n-1)$ are given by

$$\Gamma = \alpha_k \alpha_{k+1} \qquad k \in [0, n-1]$$

$$\alpha_k : [0, n-1] \to [0, n-1]$$

$$i \mapsto k - i \pmod{n}$$

All the extraorbital decompositions of two cycles of length n Γ_0 and Γ_1 are given by $\Gamma_0 \Gamma_1 = \beta_k \beta_{k+1} \qquad k \in [0, n-1]$

$$\beta_k : [0, n-1] \times [0, 1] \to [0, n-1] \times [o, 1]$$

$$(i, j) \mapsto (k - i \pmod{n}, \quad j + 1 \pmod{2})$$

3.7.3. Useful b i d

A b i d of the boudary permutation σ of a π - system $\mathbb{P}$, $\sigma = \varepsilon \varepsilon'$, is a useful b i d iff it satisfies the conditions :

i) ε and ε' are conjugate

ii) $\ddot{u}$ is a fixed point of ε

iii) There exits a 2-cycle of ε which defines a strong couple.

3.8. Fundamental theorem

Now, it is possible to state the fundamental theorem of the theory of the bipermutational π - systems, which gives all the deep algebraic properties of the π - systems.

Theorem [4, 1]

An involution is representable in a π - system $\mathbb{P}$ iff it is the first factor of a useful b i d of the boundary permutation of P.

3.9. Automorphisms of π - systems : isotypies

An automorphism of a π - system $\mathbb{P}$ is a permutation of the elements of $\mathbb{P}$ which commutes with the π - operations.

It is easy to see that the automorphisms preserve the types of the bipermutations ; so, we call them isotypies.

The boundary permutation being also preserved, the group of the isotypies can be considered as a subgroup of the stabilizator of the boundary permutation in the corresponding symmetric group.

A complete study of this group [1] has established that its structure depends on the class formula of the permutation $\sigma\gamma^{-1}$ where σ is the boundary permutation and γ the cycle of σ containing ü. The group can be characterized in terms of wreath products.

Later on, we will only use the following automorphisms :

Proposition

In a π - systems $\mathbb{P}$ with a boundary permutation σ, every pair of cycles, different from γ, defines an isotypy of P iff they form an even permutation.

4. SPECIAL BIPERMUTATIONS

4.1. The boundary permutations is not a characteristic invariant of the π - system. The two bipermutations (a b c d e f, f e d c b a) and (a d c b e f, f c d e b a) have the same boundary permutation σ = (ü d b e c) but they are not in the same π - system, the first one being the only node of its system (3.1.4)

For lack of a characteristic algebraic invariant, we try to characterize the π - systems in a combinatorial way. Among all the bipermutations of a

π - system, we try to find a characteristic family of bipermutations as small as possible. Thus, we introduice the special bipermutations.

4.2. Special bipermutations

A node S of a π - system P is a special bipermutation iff

$S = (a\, f_1 \ldots\ldots f_t\, q,\; q\, \tilde{f}_1 \ldots\ldots\ldots \tilde{f}_t\, a)$ where $\tilde{f}_i$ is the mirror image of f_i $f_i \in X^*$ $i \in [\,t\,]$ and if the involutions naturally attached to S define an intraorbital decomposition of the boundary permutation.

This condition implies that the fixed points of the boundary permutation are fixed points of the permutation naturally attached to the bipermutation S. Whe the boundary permutation has no 1 - cycle, this condition is useless.

We need a technical proposition to prove the existence of special bipermutations in every π - system.

4.3. Proposition

Given a π - system $\mathbb{P}$ on an alphabet X, different from a reverse π - system or a reducible π - system constructed with a reverse π - system, for every cycle Γ of the boundary permutation of P of length greater than 2, there exists a bipermutation B and a triplet of letters of Γ (r, s, t) such that

$$B = (a\, f\, r\, s\, t\, f'\, q,\; q\, g\, r\, t\, s\, g'\, a)$$

$$f, f', g, g' \in X^*$$

$$\Gamma = (t\, r\, s \ldots.)$$

Proof : We use a recurrence argument on the cardinality of the alphabet X. It is easy to verify directly the property when Card (X) $\leq$ 6.

Let Γ be a cycle of length greater than 2.

There exists a strong couple (s,r) in Γ such that $s \neq r$ (3.5) and a bipermutation.

$$B' = (a\, f_1\, r\, f_2\, s\, q, q\, g_1\, s\, g_2\, r\, a)$$

$$f_1, f_2, g_1, g_2 \in X^*$$

- If $f_2 = 1$ (the empty word) and $f_1 \neq 1$, we have

$$B' = (a\, f_{11}\, t\, f_{12}\, r\, s\, q,\; q\, g_1\, t\, s\, g_2\, r\, a)$$

By the nodal operation t/r, we have

$B = B'\ t/r = (a\ f_{11}\ r\ s\ t\ f_{12}\ q,\ q\ g_1\ r\ t\ s\ g_2\ a)$ which is the bipermutation we were looking for.

The case where $g_1 = 1$ can be solved in the same way. Dual arguments are valid when $g_2 = 1$.

Now we will suppose that $f_2 \neq 1$ and $g_2 \neq 1$.

●● If $g_2 = \tilde{f}_2$, by the hypotheses, we have $|f_1| \geq 1$ and $|f_2| \geq 2$.

So, there exists a letter u such that

$$B' = (a\ f_{11}\ u\ f_{12} r\ x_1 x_2 \ldots x_n\ s\ q,\ q\ g_{11}\ u\ g_{12}\ s\ x_n\ x_{n-1} \ldots x_1\ r\ a)$$

with $g_{12} \neq 1$ and $f_{12} \neq 1$

By the nodal operation u/x_n, we have

$$B'' = B'\ u/x_n = (a\ f_{11}\ x_n\ s\ u\ f_{12}\ r\ x_1 \ldots x_{n-1}\ q,\ q\ g_{11} x_n \ldots x_1 r\ u\ g_{12} s\ a)$$

The two words $s\ u\ f_{12}\ r\ x_1 \ldots x_{n-1}$ and $x_{n-1} \ldots x_1\ r\ u\ g_{12}\ s$ cannot be mirror image of each other.

Thus it is always possible to suppose that the bipermutation is such that $g_2 \neq \tilde{f}_2$.

●●● Using the π - operations, we obtain from B', with suitable powers k and k':

by π^k $(a\ f_1\ t\ f_2\ s\ q,\ s\ g_2\ t\ q\ g_1\ a)$

by $\pi'^{k'}$ $(f_2\ a\ f_1\ t\ s\ q,\ s\ g_2\ t\ q\ g_1\ a)$

Let x be the initial of f_2.

<u>1st case</u> : If x is a letter of g_1, by the operation π we obtain

$$B'' = (x\ f_{21}\ a\ f_1\ t\ s\ q,\ g_2\ t\ q\ g_{11}\ s\ x\ g_{12}\ a)$$

The $\bar{\pi}$ - system $\mathbb{R}(B'', \{s\})$ is isomorphic with the π - system generated by $B'' \varphi_{\{s\}}$ which is undecomposable (3.3)

This system contains a node (3.1.1.) and so $\mathbb{R}(B'', \{s\})$ contains a node N where $t = s\tau^{-1}$.

$N = (a\ f'_1\ r\ s\ u\ f'_2\ q,\ q\ g'_1\ r\ u\ g'_2\ a)$

By the nodal operation r/u, we obtain r/u, we obtain

$(a\ f'_{31}\ t\ f'_{32}\ \ r\ s\ q,\ q\ g'_{31}\ t\ s\ g'_{32}\ r\ a)$

and finally by t/r we have

$(a\ f'_{31}\ r\ s\ t\ f'_{32}\ q,\ q\ g'_{31}\ \ r\ t\ s\ g'_{32}\ a)$ which is the bipermutation we were looking for.

2sd case : If x is letter of g_2 and if no left factors of f_2 and g_2 are words on the same alphabet, we apply the same argument.

Otherwise $f_2 = f'_2\ f''_2 \qquad g_2 = g'_2\ g''_2$

where f'_2 and g'_2 are the shortest left factors of f_2 and g_2 which are on the same alphabet. Let u be a common letter of f'_2 and g'_2.

- If there is common letter v for f''_2 and g''_2

from $B' = (a\ f_1\ t\ f'_{21}\ u\ f'_{22}\ f''_{21}\ \ v\ f''_{22}\ s\ q,\ s\ g'_{21}\ \ u\ g'_{22}\ g''_{21}\ \ v\ g''_{22}\ ta)$

by the nodal operations u/v and t/v we have

$B'' = (a\ f_1\ u\ f'_{22}\ f''_{21}\ t\ f'_{21}\ v\ f''_{22}\ s\ q,\ q\ g_1\ s\ g'_{21}\ v\ g''_{22}\ u\ g'_{22}\ g''_{21}\ t\ a)$

It is easy to see that we are able to apply the same argument as in the first case.

- If f''_2 and g''_2 have no letter in common, B is such that, the words f_1, f'_2, f''_2 are constructed respectively on the same alphabets as g''_2, g'_2, g_1 .

If $g''_2 \neq f_1$ (resp. $f''_2 \neq g_1$), there is a letter v which is common between f_1 (resp. g_1) and g''_2 (resp. f''_2) such that by the nodal operations v/t (resp. v/s) and u/v we have a bipermutation for which we apply the same arguments as in the first case.

Finally, B' can be

$(a\ f_1\ t\ f'_2\ g_1\ s\ q,\ q\ g_1\ s\ g'_2\ f_1\ t\ a)$

but, by the hypotheses, we are sure that $g'_2 \neq \widetilde{f'_2}$. It is enough to solve the problem for the π - system generated by

$(a\ t\ f'_2\ s\ q,\ q\ s\ g'_2\ \ t\ a)$

for which we apply the recurrence argument.

4.4. Theorem [1]

An involution is representable by a special bipermutation in a π - system $\mathbb{P}$ iff it is the first factor of a useful intraorbital b i d of the boundary permutation of $\mathbb{P}$.

Proof • The necessary part of the theorems is obvious.

• • Every π - system can be embed in an indirectly reducible π - system without any constraint (3.4)

Thus, it is the same to prove that for every indirectly reducible π - system and for every involution first factor of a useful intraorbital decomposition of the boundary permutation having a distinguished fixed point, this involution is represented by a special bipermutation having the distinguished fixed point as the letter of rank 2 and place 2.

The theorem is true for the reverse π - systems which have only one special bipermutation and for which the boundary permutation has only one useful b i d.

It is also easy to prove the theorem for π - systems with an involutive boundary permutation [1,2]

For all the other cases, we use a recurrence argument on the cardinality n of the alphabet. We can verify directly the property for $n \leq 5$.

Let $\mathbb{P}$ be a π - system on an alphabet X of cardinality n. Let Γ be a cycle of the boundary permutation of length m $(m > 2)$. By the proposition 4.3., there is a bipermutation

$$B = (a\ f\ r\ s\ t\ f'\ q,\ q\ g\ r\ t\ s\ g'\ a) \quad \text{with} \quad \Gamma = (t\ r\ s \ldots.)$$

Since $s = t\,\tau^{-1}$ and $s = t\,\tau'$, we can apply to the fixing operator $\Phi^{\{s,t\}}_{Z_2}$ the theorem 3.2.

Thus $\bar{\sigma} = \bar{\tau}'\,\bar{\tau}^{-1}$

where $\bar{\sigma}$ is the boundary permutation of the π - system generated by $B\ \varphi\ \{s,t\}$.

We construct $\bar{\sigma}$ from σ by replacing the cycle Γ by the cycle $\bar{\Gamma} = (t\,\sigma^{-1}\ r\ s\ \sigma \ldots)$

Let consider an involution having r as a fixed point which is the first factor of a useful intraorbital b i d of $\bar{\sigma}$. We apply the recurrence argument taking r for the letter of rank 2 and place 2. Thus, we have the special bipermutation

$$(a\ r\ f_1 \ldots\ldots\ldots f_k\ q,\ q\ r\ \tilde{f}_1 \ldots\ldots \tilde{f}_k\ a)$$

which gives in $\mathbb{P}$ the special bipermutation

$$(a\ r\ s\ t\ f_1 \ldots f_k q,\ q\ r\ t\ s\ \tilde{f}_1 \ldots\ldots\ldots \tilde{f}_k\ a)$$

Using the isotypies of the π - system $\mathbb{P}$ (3.9.) , it is possible to put in place 2 and in rank 2 every letter of a cycle of length m of σ and for a given letter of rank 2 and place 2, it is possible to represent all the first factors of useful intraorbital decompositions of σ.

This constrcution can be done for every cycle of length m $(m > 2)$ of σ.

If σ contains some cycles of length 2, there is in $\mathbb{P}$ a special bipermutation

$$(a\ v\ f\ h_1 \ldots k_k\ g\ q,\ q\ v\ f'\ h'_1 \ldots\ldots h'_k\ g'a)$$

where $h_i = r_i\ s_i\ t_i\ u_i$ $\qquad h'_i = r_i\ u_i\ s_i,\ i \in [k]$

By a nodal operation v/r_i, it is possible to bring r_i in place 2 and in rank 2, and by an isotypy, every letter of the cycles of length 2.

For the fixed points of σ , it is also easy to verify the property.

4.5. Corollaire :

Every π - system constains at least one special bipermutation.

Proof : This property proceeds from the fact that every boundary permutation has at least one useful intraorbital decomposition (3.7)

5. CONCLUSION

Now, it is possible to look at a classification of the bipermutational equations with the special bipermutations. The problem is still open. But we are quite sure that the family of special bipermutations is a good characteristic family of bipermutations for a π - system. M. MORCRETTE has a program which has construted the list of special bipermutations for the π - system on alphabets of cardinality less or equal than 1 2 [8]. In the case of π-systems with an involutive boundary permutation, the classification is done [2]

B I B L I O G R A P H Y

[1] FONTET, M. : Etude des polyautomorphismes des π - systems bipermutationels. Thèse de 3e cycle (1973)

[2] FONTET, M. : π - systèmes involutifs. Communication to Journées de la Société Mathématique de France Montpellier (1974), to be published in Cahiers Mathématiques-Montpellier.

[3] FONTET, M. and A. LENTIN : Fixateurs et biinvodecompositions C.R. Acad. Sci. Paris, série A, 270, (1970), 848 - 850. and Séminaire M. P. Schützenberger - A. Lentin et M. Nivat, 1969/70, Exp. N°9, 14p. (Institut Henri Poincarré, Paris)

[4] LENTIN, A. : Equations dans les monoïdes libres Gauthier Villars (1972) Paris.

[5] LENTIN, A. : Equations in free monoids Proceeding of the First Colloquim in Automata, Languages and Programming (3-7 july 1972) edited by M. M. NIVAT North-Holland (1973).

[6] LENTIN, A : Problèmes posés en théorie des permutations pour la résolution des équations dans les monoïdes libres. Permutations - Actes du colloque sur les permutations Paris (10-13 juillet 1972) Gauthier-Villars Paris (1974).

[7] LEVI, F.W. : On semi-groups, Bull. Calcultta Math. Soc., (1944), 144-146.

[8] MORCRETTE, M. : Sur quelques systèmes algebriques et catégories de systèmes algébriques suscités par la théorie des équations dans le monoïde libre. Thèse de 3e cycle, Paris (1973)

[9] MORCRETTE, M. : Sur une catégorie de systèmes algébriques qui ont pour ensemble de base des ensembles de couples de permutations. Permutations - Actes du colloque sur les permutations Paris (10-13 juillet 1972) Gauthier Villars Paris (1974)

[10] MORCRETTE, M. : Catégories de systèmes algèbriques suscitées par la théorie des équations dans le monoïde libre. Communication to Journées de la Société Mathématique de France-Montpellier (1974) to be published in Cahiers Mathématiques-Montpellier.

STRETCHING BY PROBABILISTIC TREE AUTOMATA AND SANTOS GRAMMARS

Marek Karpiński

The Mathematical Institute of the
Polish Academy of Sciences, Poznań 61725, Poland.

ABSTRACT. The characterization theorems on Santos grammars [8] by means of pseudo probabilistic tree languages stretchings have been given. They are all derivable from the Equivalence Theorems on probabilistic tree languages settled in [2].

INTRODUCTION

We shall employ the standard terminology from [2], not yet repeating here all the definitions. So as to find the paper completely self-contained, the reader is referred to the introductory sections of [2] or [3] where the detailed expositions of all the notions needed are to be found.

Keeping this we shall use the abbreviations p.PCLs and p.PCFLs for the cut point and functional pseudo probabilistic climbing languages. q.PCLs and PCLs will stand for the quasi probabilistic and probabilistic languages, respectively.

1. PRELIMINARIES

ω denotes the set of natural numbers. An ordinal will be identified with the set of all its predecessors. The cardinality of a set A is denoted by $|A|$. A nonempty, finite set will be called an alphabet.

A^* will mean the free monoid over A with the empty word Λ; $A^+ = A^* \setminus \{\Lambda\}$. l denotes the length function on A^*. If $x,y \in A^*$ $(B,C \subseteq A^*)$, then xy (BC) will mean the result of concatenating x with y. If $x = a_1 \dots a_{l(x)} \in A^*$, then $x^i = a_i$, $1 \leq i \leq l(x)$, and $x^i = \Lambda$ for other i. For a function $f : B \rightarrow A^*$, f^i will mean the function defined by $f^i(b) = f(b)^i$.

On A^* we define the partial ordering $\preccurlyeq$ by $x \preccurlyeq y$ if $xv = y$ for some $v \in A^*$; supposing now that A is linearly ordered by $\leq$ we introduce the lexicographical ordering $\preccurlyeq_*$ and the onefold lexicographical ordering $\preccurlyeq_1$ by

(1) $x \preccurlyeq_* y$ if (i) $x \preccurlyeq y$ or (ii) $x = wav$ and $y = wbz$ where $a,b \in A$ and $a < b$;

and

(2) $\preccurlyeq_1$ being the extension of $\preccurlyeq$ defined by (ii) with the empty words v and z.

Now let B be an arbitrary subset of A^*. For $x \in A^*$ we denote

$$\langle x \rangle_B = \left| \{ a \mid a \in A, xa \in B \} \right| .$$

A (<u>finite</u>) <u>tree</u> T is a finite subset of ω^* such that $x \in T$ and $x' \preccurlyeq_1 x$ imply $x' \in T$. A <u>valued tree</u> over an alphabet Σ (Σ-tree) is a pair $t = (T,v)$ where T is a tree and v is a function $v : T \rightarrow \Sigma$.

The <u>frontier</u> of a tree T is the set $Ft(T) = \{ x \mid x \in T, \langle x \rangle_T = 0 \}$ and the <u>frontier sequence</u> $\overline{Ft}(T)$ is the word with the mapping $i \mapsto \overline{Ft}(T)^i$ being the natural enumeration of Ft(T) according to $\preccurlyeq_*$.

Define also the interior of T as the set $Int(T) = T \setminus Ft(T)$. For a Σ-tree $t = (T,v)$, the frontier of t is the set $ft(t) = v(Ft(T))$ and the frontier sequence is the word $\overline{ft}(t) = v(\overline{Ft}(T)^1)\dots v(\overline{Ft}(T)^n)$, $n = |Ft(T)|$. The interior of T will be the set $int(t) = v(Int(T))$.

The set of all valued (Σ-) trees will be denoted by $\mathcal{T}$ ($\mathcal{T}_\Sigma$). The set of all valued trees $t = (T,v)$ such that $T \subseteq n^*$, $n \in \omega$, is denoted by $\mathcal{T}^{(n)}$.

2. SANTOS GRAMMARS

R and R_1 denote the set of real numbers and the set of nonnegative reals, respectively. Any function from $\mathcal{T}$ into R will be referred to as a random function.

The following definitions are variations of the notions due essentially to E.G. Santos [8]. (We deal here with context free grammars only).

Definition 2.1. A pseudo probabilistic Santos grammar (p.SG) over an alphabet Σ is a quadruple $\mathcal{G} = (V,Z,P,v_0)$ where V is a finite set, the set of variables, Z is a finite subset of $(V \cup \Sigma)^+$, the generatrix set, P is a finite family $\{\varrho_i\}_{i<n}$ of functions $\varrho_i : V \times Z \to R$, the (selective) seize functions, and $v_0 \in V$ is the axiom of the grammar.

n is the index of $\mathcal{G}$. The order of $\mathcal{G}$ is the maximal length of words in Z.

A p.SG $\mathcal{G}$ will be called nonnegative (nn.) if its seize functions range over R_1.

Definition 2.2. A probabilistic Santos grammar (SG) is a nn. p.SG $\mathcal{G}$ with the seize functions ϱ_i satisfying $\sum_{z \in Z} \varrho_i(v,z) = 1$.

Definition 2.3. A weighted grammar (WG) is a p.SG of index 1. An α-normalized WG, $\alpha \in R_1$, is a nn. WG with the seize function ϱ

ranging over $[0,1]$ and such that $\sum_{z \in Z} \varrho(v,z) \leq \alpha$.

A <u>generation</u> (g.) <u>tree</u> of a p.SG $\mathcal{G}$ (of the index n) is a $(V \cup \Sigma)(n \cup \{\Lambda\})$-tree $t = (T,v)$, $Int(T) \neq \emptyset$, such that :
(1) $v^1(\Lambda) = v_0$; (2) $v^1(x0)\dots v^1(x(\langle x\rangle_T - 1)) \in Z$ for $\langle x\rangle_T \neq 0$;
(3) $v(x) \in \Sigma$ for $\langle x\rangle_T = 0$.

Denote the set of all g.trees of $\mathcal{G}$ by $D(\mathcal{G})$.

The <u>generatrix function</u> of $\mathcal{G}$ is the real function $\varphi_{\mathcal{G}}: D(\mathcal{G}) \to R$ such that $\varphi_{\mathcal{G}}((T,v)) = \prod_{x \in Int(T)} \varrho_{v^2(x)}(v^1(x), \overline{v^1(x)})$ where $\overline{v^1(x)} = v^1(x0)\dots v^1(x(\langle x\rangle_T - 1))$.

Define now, for $x \in \Sigma^+$ and a $n \cup \{\Lambda\}$ -tree $t = (T,v_1)$, $ft(t) = \{\Lambda\}$, the set

$D(\mathcal{G};x,t) = \{(T,v_2) \mid (T,v_2) \in D(\mathcal{G}),\ \overline{ft}((T,v_2)) = x,\ v_2^2 = v_1\}$.

A <u>control function</u> of $\mathcal{G}$ (c.f.) is any function from the set $\{(T,v_1) \mid v_1 = v_2^2,\ (T,v_2) \in D(\mathcal{G})\}$ into R.

Given a set of c.f.'s A.

A set $B \subseteq \Sigma^+$ will be called an <u>A-controlled pseudo probabilistic Santos language</u> (A-c. p.SL) if there is a p.SG, a function $f \in A$, and a number $\varepsilon \in R_1$ such that

$B = S_A(\mathcal{G},\varepsilon) = \{x \mid x \in \Sigma^+,\ \sup_t f(t)(\sum_{t' \in C} \varphi_{\mathcal{G}}(t')) > \varepsilon\ ,\ C = D(\mathcal{G};x,t)\}$. (1)

A set $B \subseteq \Sigma^+$ will be called <u>A-c. interacting p.SL</u> (A-c. p.ISL) if there is a p.SG $\mathcal{G}_1$, the functions $f_1, f_2 \in A$, and a nn. p.SG $\mathcal{G}_2$ such that

$$B = S_A(\mathcal{G}_1,\mathcal{G}_2) = \{x \mid x \in \Sigma^+,\ \exists\, t\,[f_1(t) \sum_{t' \in C_1} \varphi_{\mathcal{G}_1}(t') > f_2(t) \sum_{t' \in C_2} \varphi_{\mathcal{G}_2}(t'),$$
$$C_i = D(\mathcal{G}_i;x,t)]\} .$$

---

(1) The sum $\sum_{t' \in C} \varphi_{\mathcal{G}}(t')$ for the empty set C is taken to mean 0.

If the above is fulfilled for a set A comprising only the constant functions, or equivalently, when we are substituting the unit functions for the functions f in the above formulas, we obtain the (pure) p.SLs and the (pure) p.ISLs, respectively. In this case we ommit the subscript A under the languages operators.

Subsequently, when the defining grammars are the SGs, we get the probabilistic languages, abr., SLs and ISLs.

γ_A and $\mathcal{S}_A$ will stand for the families of A-c. p.SLs and A-c. SLs, whereas $\mathcal{I}\gamma_A$ and $\mathcal{I}\mathcal{S}_A$ for the families of A-c. p.ISLs and A-c. ISLs, respectively. We ommit a subscript A to denote the appropriate families of pure languages.

$\gamma^{(i)}(j)$, $\mathcal{S}^{(i)}(j)$ will mean the families of p.SLs and SLs due to the grammars of the order i and the index j.

WLs will be due to WGs, i.e. p.SGs of index 1. A WL B is called α-normalized if there is an α-normalized WG $\mathcal{G}$ such that $B = S(\mathcal{G}, \varepsilon)$ for some $\varepsilon \in R_1$.

3. CHARACTERIZATION THEOREMS

A set $B \subseteq \Sigma^+$ is said to be stretched by a set $A \subseteq \mathcal{F}$ if $B = \overline{ft}(A)$. A set $A \subseteq \mathcal{F}$ is called primitive if $\left|\bigcup_{t \in A} \mathrm{int}(t)\right| \leq 1$ (and n-primitive if $\left|\bigcup_{t \in A} \mathrm{int}(t)\right| \leq n$).

The representation theorems on probabilistic climbing languages read as follows.

Theorem 3.1 [2]. I. Any p.PCFL is a q.PCL.

II. Any p.PCL is a q.PCL.

III. If $A \subseteq \Sigma^+$ is stretched by a p.PCL, then so is by a PCL from $\mathcal{F}^{(2)}$.

Theorem 3.2 [2].I. Given a set $A \subseteq \Sigma^+$. A is a WL if and only if it is stretched by a primitive p.PCL.

II. Given a number α, $1<\alpha \in R_1$. Any WL is an α-normalized WL. The same does not hold for $\alpha = 1$.

Now p.CFs and CFs will stand for the random functions computable by the pseudo probabilistic and probabilistic climbing automata, respectively (see [2],[3]).

We shall need the following results.

Theorem 3.3. If f_1, f_2 are p.CFs (CFs), then so is $f_1 f_2$.

Theorem 3.4. If $A \subseteq \Sigma^+$ is stretched by a p.PCL, then so is by a 2-primitive p.PCL from $\gamma^{(2)}$.

Given a p.SG $\mathcal{G}$. For $x \in \Sigma^+$ and a $n \cup \{\Lambda\}$-tree t, $ft(t) = \{\Lambda\}$, define

$$\Phi_{\mathcal{G}}(x,t) = \sum_{t' \in B} \varphi_{\mathcal{G}}(t'),\ B = D(\mathcal{G};x,t).$$

Theorem 3.5. For a random function f the following two statements are equivalent

(1) There is a p.SG $\mathcal{G}$ such that $f((T,v_1)) = \Phi_{\mathcal{G}}(\overline{ft}((T,v_1)),(T,v_2))$ with $v_2|A$ isomorphic to $v_1|A$, $A = Int(T)$.

(2) f is a p.CF.

The characterization theorem is

Theorem 3.6. Given a set $A \subseteq \Sigma^+$. A is a p.SL (SL) if and only if it is stretched by a p.PCL (PCL).

Consequently Theorem 3.1 yields

Theorem 3.7. $\mathcal{S} = \Upsilon$.

Combining Theorem 3.1 with Theorems 3.2, 3.4 we get more closely

Theorem 3.8. $\mathcal{S}^{(2)}(2) = \Upsilon$. The second number 2 is the minimal one preserving the identity.

Using now the closure result from Theorem 3.3 we have

Theorem 3.9. For any set A of p.CFs, $\mathcal{S} = \mathcal{T}_A$.

Eventually, Theorems 3.3 and 3.1 entail

Theorem 3.10. The identity $\mathcal{S} = \mathcal{I}\mathcal{T}_A$ does hold for any set A of p.CFs.

Proofs of the above theorems will appear elsewhere.

REFERENCES

1. C.A.Ellis, Probabilistic tree automata, Information and Control 19 (1971), 401-416.

2. M.Karpiński, Equivalence results on probabilistic tree languages, to appear.

3. M.Karpiński, Probabilistic climbing and sinking languages, Bull. Acad. Polon. Sci. Sér. Sci. Math. Astronom. Phys. 22/10 (1974).

4. M.Magidor and G.Moran, Probabilistic tree automata and context free languages, Israel J. Math. 8 (1970), 340-348.

5. M.O.Rabin, Mathematical theory of automata, Proc. Sympos. Appl. Math., Vol. 19, Amer. Math. Soc., Providence, R.I., 1968, pp. 153-175.

6. A.Salomaa, Probabilistic and weighted grammars, Information and Control 15 (1969), 529-544.

7. E.S.Santos, Computability by probabilistic Turing machines, Trans. Amer. Math. Soc. 159 (1971), 165-184.

8. E.S.Santos, Probabilistic grammars and automata, Information and Control 21 (1972), 27-47.

9. E.S.Santos, Regular probabilistic languages, Information and Control 23 (1973), 58-70.

TOP DOWN VERSUS BOTTOM UP SYNTAX ANALYSIS REVISED

J. Král
Institute of Computation Techniques
Horská 3
128 00 Praha 2, Czechoslovakia

We shall attempt to show that the problem of syntax analysis in compiler differs a bit from the problem of syntax analysis in formal language theory. This leads to a modified problem of syntax analysis and to a new model of grammars allowing to state the modified problem of the syntax analysis in a formal way. This allows to reformulate the problem of the top-down parsing and puts some new light on the problem of left factoring and covering of a grammar.

We assume that the reader is familiar with the theory of formal languages ([5] , [1]). The problem of syntax analysis in the theory of formal languages can be formulated as a problem to insert into the parsed string x "marks" (flags) enabling to construct (collaterally or ex-post) the phrase marker for x.

Let us have (as an example) the grammar G1 with the initial symbol < cond. expression > and the set of rules (the strings enclosed in < > and capital letters are nonterminals, small letters, digits, underlined strings, and other symbols are terminals).

1. < cond. expression > → if <Bool. expression > then < expression > else < expression > fi
2. < cond. expression > → if < Bool. expression > then < expression > fi
3. < expression > → < factor > + < expression >
4. < expression > → < factor >
5. < factor > → < simple expression > * < factor >
6. < factor > → < simple expression >
7. < simple expression > → < cond. expression >
8. < simple expression > → < identifier >

9. < simple expression> → (<expression >)
10. < Bool. expression >→<identifier > ∧ < Bool. expression >
11. < Bool. expression >→<identifier > ∨ < Bool. expression >
12. < Bool. expression >→<identifier >
13. < identifier > ⟶ b
14. < identifier > ⟶ i
15. < identifier > ⟶ j

Let us have the string

$$\underline{\text{if}}\ \ b\ \ \underline{\text{then}}\ \ i + i * i\ \ \underline{\text{fi}} \tag{1}$$

The (top-down) parse of the string (1) (in an obvious notation) is as follows

$$[_1\ \underline{\text{if}}\ [_{12}[_{13}\ b\ ]_{13}]_{12}\ \underline{\text{then}}\ [_3[_6[_8[_{14}\ i\ ]_{14}]_8]_6 + [_4[_5[_8[_{14}\ i\ ]_{14}]_8 * [_6[_8[_{14}\ i\ ]_{14}]_8]_6]_5]_4]_3\ \underline{\text{fi}}\ ]_1 \tag{2}$$

$[_3\ x\ ]_3$ denotes that the substring x was generated by aplication the rule number 3. The corresponding phrase marker is (we use the obvious abbreviations CE denotes <cond. expression>).

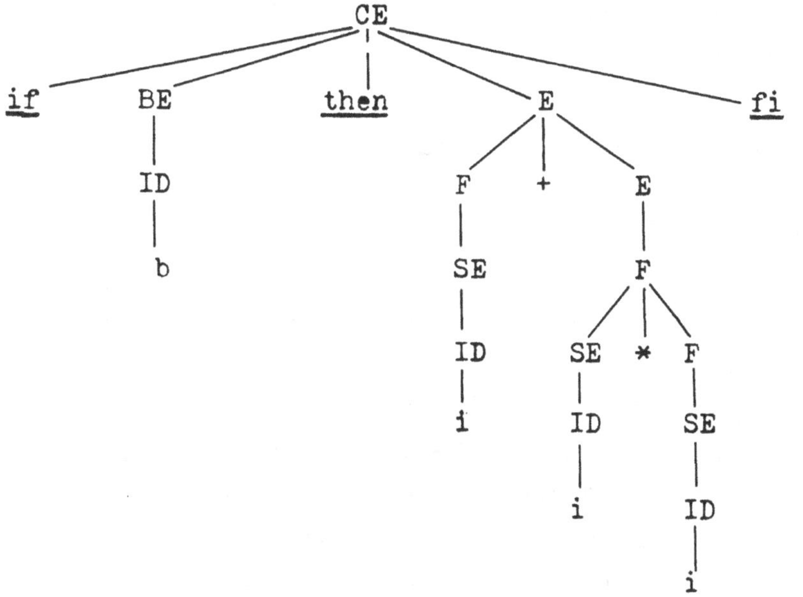

(2′)

The "parse" (2′) is in some sense less explicit (for an automaton or a compiler) than the parse (2) as the rule applied at a node must be determined from the successor nodes, the rule itself is not given explicitly in (2′).

The grammar G1 is not a top down or LL(1) grammar ([2]) so the parse (2) cannot be obtained by a simple left - to - right scan. This follows from the fact that there are strings derived from <cond. expression> by application of the rule 1 as the first one and by application of the rule 2 having common initial substrings (prefixes of arbitrary length.

Our grammar can be converted into the top-down or LL(1) one ([2] , [5] , [4]) using the wellknown method of left factoring. By the method of left factoring the first two rules of G1 are transformed into (for example)

1′. < cond. expression > → if < Bool. expression > then < expression > else <cond. end >

2′. < cond. end > → fi

2". < cond. end > → else <expression > fi

Similar transformations can be made for other rules. The parse for the string (1) in the modified grammar is (we give only the relevant information)

$$[_{1'} \ \underline{\text{if}} \ [_{2'} \ \ldots . \ ]_{2'} \ \underline{\text{then}} \ [_{3'} \ \ldots . \ ]_{3'} \ [_{2'} \ \underline{\text{fi}} \ ]_{2'} \ ] \qquad (2")$$

Now we leave the theory of formal languages and turn to the problem of compiler writing. Let us put the question when and why can we use the method of left factoring? Such a question can seem irrelevant as the method of the left factoring is commonly used. But in our example we can use the method of left factoring only under the (implicit) Assumption A that the translation (and even the sequence of calls of the semantic routines called during the translation) of the substring" x = if <Bool.expression> then

< expression > in <u>if</u> < Bool. expression > <u>then</u> < expression > <u>fi</u> is the same as translation of the substring x in <u>if</u> < Bool. expression > <u>then</u> < expression > <u>else</u> < expression > <u>fi</u>. This situation is so common in programming languages that the method of left factoring can be usually used in compilers without the explicit assumption that the translation of common prefixes is the same. In the case that it holds we can in parse (2) mark the "opening syntactic brackets" by left hand sides of rules instead of rule numbers. In our example we obtaing

$$[_{CE}\ \underline{if}\ [_{BE}\ [_{ID}\ b]_{13}]_{12}\ \underline{then}\ [_{E}\ [_{F}\ [_{SE}\ [_{ID}\ i\ ]_{14}]_{8}]_{6} + [_{E}\ [_{F}\ [_{SE}\ [_{ID}\ i]_{14}]_{8} * [_{F}\ [_{SE}\ [_{ID}\ i]_{14}]_{8}]_{6}]_{5}]_{4}]_{3}\ \underline{fi}]_{1} \qquad (2+)$$

But it can be again made only if the semantic actions bounded on the "opening of a handle" depends only on the left hand side of the corresponding rule (Assumption B), but not on the right hand side i. e. they are for all the rules having A as the left hand side the same).

Assumption B is also fulfilled for programming languages and commonly used methods of translation. Our examples show that the translation process ("calls of semantic routines") must be somewhat taken into account. We note that a compiler writer would usually treat the parse (2+) as the top-down one althought from the point of view of the formal languages theory such a parse is semi-top-down ([6]).

Now we can turn to the problem how to connect the parse with the translation (with semantic routines). We shall firstly assume, that on the "opening of a handle" no semantic action is bounded (Assumption B+). In order make the things clearer we shall firstly discuss the wellknown De Remer [9] method of parsing applied on the grammar G2 with the initial symbol S and the rules:

0.$S' \longrightarrow\ \vdash S' \dashv$		3.$A \longrightarrow aa$	
1.$S' \longrightarrow Aa$		4.$B \longrightarrow Ab$	
2.$S' \longrightarrow Bb$			

Under the Assumption B^+ we let us further assume that, for example, during the analysis after the $\vdash$ is read up (and the analysis of a S-phrase starts) some "semantic" action S_{01}, say, is performed. Let us put the symbols of such actions (semantic symbols) into the rules. We obtain the <u>Compiler grammar</u> for G2.

$$
\begin{array}{lll}
0.\ S & \longrightarrow & \vdash S_{01}\ S' S_{02} \dashv\ S_{03} \\
1.\ S' & \longrightarrow & A\ S'_{11}\ a\ S'_{12} \\
2.\ S' & \longrightarrow & B\ S'_{21}\ b\ S'_{22} \\
3.\ A & \longrightarrow & a\ A_{31}\ a\ A_{32} \\
4.\ B & \longrightarrow & A\ B_{41}\ b\ B_{42}
\end{array}
$$

N_{ij}, where N is a nonterminal, are semantic symbols. If the action denoted by N_{ij} is the "do nothing" one N_{ij} is said to be empty (or dummy) symbol.

Now we reconstruct DeRemer's automaton in order to obtain a transducer in the following way.

If in DeRemer's automaton (see [9], [3]) a transition is performed from the state containing the configuration $T \to x.a\ y$ to the state with the configuration $T \to xa.y$ then in our transducer the move is performed from the state with the configuration $T \to x.a\ N_{ij}\ y'$ (y' is the string y with inserted semantic symbols) to the state with configuration $T \to x\ a.y'$ and N_{ij} is produced on output. If two different semantic symbols are to be produced during the translation the <u>semantic conflict arise</u>. We shall assume the semantic symbols fulfils the requirements that if two semantic symbols are produced during a transition T then both symbols are the same (or denote the same action).

The transducer for the grammar G2 is given in the Table I.

State number	Configuration set in state	Transition	Semantic conditions	Output
1.	$S \rightarrow .\vdash S_{01}\ S' S_{02} \dashv S_{03}$	$\xrightarrow{\vdash} 2$		$\vdash S_{01}$
2.	$S \rightarrow \vdash . S' S_{02} \dashv S_{03}$	$\xrightarrow{S'} 3$		S_{02}
	$S' \rightarrow .A\ S'_{11}\ a\ S'_{12}$	$\xrightarrow{A} 5$	$S'_{11} = B_{41}$	S'_{11}
	$S' \rightarrow .B\ S'_{21}\ b\ S'_{22}$	$\xrightarrow{B} 8$		S'_{21}
	$A \rightarrow .a\ A_{31}\ a\ A_{32}$	$\xrightarrow{a} 10$		$a\,A_{31}$
	$B \rightarrow .A\ B_{41}\ b\ B_{42}$	$\xrightarrow{A} 5$		B_{41}
3.	$S \rightarrow \vdash S' . \dashv S_{03}$	$\xrightarrow{\dashv} 4$		$\dashv S_{03}$
4.	$S \rightarrow \vdash S' \dashv .$	$\xrightarrow{\#}$ Accept		-
5.	$S' \rightarrow A.a\ S'_{12}$	$\xrightarrow{a} 6$		$a\,S'_{12}$
	$B \rightarrow A.b\ B_{42}$	$\xrightarrow{b} 7$		$b\,B_{42}$
6.	$S' \rightarrow Aa.$	$\xrightarrow{\#} A$		-
7.	$B \rightarrow Ab.$	$\xrightarrow{\#} A$		-
8.	$S' \rightarrow B\ .\ b\ S'_{22}$	$\xrightarrow{b} 9$		bS'_{22}
9.	$S' \rightarrow Bb.$	$\xrightarrow{\#} A$		-
10.	$A \rightarrow a.a\ A_{32}$	$\xrightarrow{a} 11$		aA_{32}
11.	$A \rightarrow aa.$	$\xrightarrow{\#} A$		-
A		reduce state		
Accept		accepting state		

Table I

The work of our transducer for the string ⊢ aabb ⊣ is described in Table II (see [9])

Input string	Action	Stack (before reading)	Transition to	State	Output (compiler parse)
⊢ aabb ⊣	read		2	1	⊢ S_{01}
aabb ⊣	read	⊢	10	2	a A_{31}
abb ⊣	read	⊢ 2, a	11	10	a A_{32}
bb ⊣	-	⊢ 2, a 10, a	A	11	-
bb ⊣	reduce	⊢ 2, a 10, a	2	A	-
Abb ⊣	read	⊢	5	2	$B_{41}=S'_{11}$
bb ⊣	read	⊢ 2, A	7	5	bB_{42}
b ⊣		⊢ 2, A 7, b	A	7	-
b ⊣	reduce	⊢	2	A	-
Bb ⊣	read	⊢	8	2	S'_{21}
b ⊣	read	⊢ 2, B	9	8	bS'_{22}
⊣		⊢ 2, B 8, b	A	9	-
⊣	reduce	⊢	2	A	-
S′ ⊣	read	⊢ 2, S′	3	2	⊣ S_{02}
⊣	read	⊢ 2, S′	4	3	S_{03}
		⊢ 2, S′3 ⊣	Accept	4	-

Table II

The output of our transducer called compiler parse is

$$\vdash S'_{01} \quad a\, A_{31} \quad a\, A_{32} \quad B_{41} \quad b\, B_{42} \quad S'_{21} \quad b\, S'_{22} \quad S_{02} \dashv S_{03}$$

The phrase marker of our string is

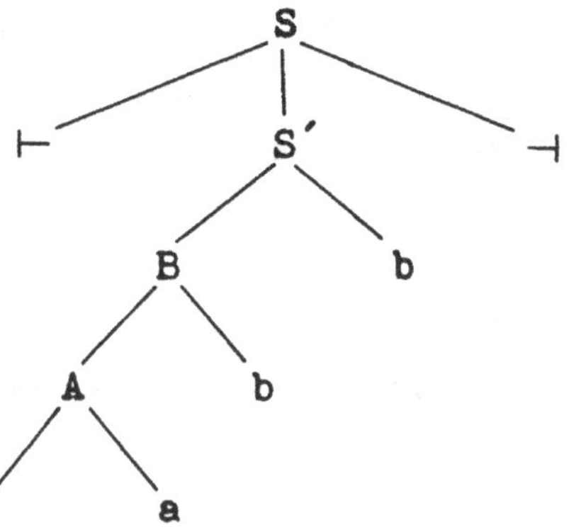

In majority of cases our "compiler parse" will be satisfactory and felt as top-down one (i. e. no extra scan is required in order to complete the parse information).

Now we attempt to weaken the Assumption B.
Let us cancel the assumption B. Then we must modify our transducer in the following way. (i) We must assume that the i-th rule with the left hand side N starts with the (opening) semantic symbol N_{io} (say). (ii) If in the state S the closure set (see [9]) is nonempty then (1) if the closure set contains the configuration $X \to .\, w'$ where $X \to .\, w'$ is i-th rule X_{io} is produced and contatenated from right with the sequence of symbols T produced on each transition to S in the original version of our transducer; (2) if $X \to .\, w'$, $Y \to .z$ and $X \overset{*}{\Longrightarrow} Yy$ where $X \to w$ and $Y \to z$ are i-th and j-th rule then TX_{io} and the string TX_{io} is produced on output. Generally on output the set TQ of strings of semantic symbols is associated with a transition. The set Q contains all strings of the form $N_{io}\ R_{jo}\ W_{ko}$ ... having the property that if the R_{jo} is after N_{io} then r_i : $N \to w_i$ contributes to the closure set and $w_i \overset{*}{\Longrightarrow} Rx$; x is a string.

If Q has more than one element, then a semantic conflict arises. It follows.

If A is an left recursive symbol, the rule r_L : $A \longrightarrow .w$ contributes to the closure set of a state, and $w \stackrel{*}{\Longrightarrow} A\ z$ then A_{LO} must be empty.

In our example the only state with nonempty closure set is the state 2, achievable from the state 1 only. So the output in the first row of the table I is $S_{01}\ S'_{10}\ A_{30}$ or $S_{01}\ S'_{20}\ B_{40}\ A_{30}$. It must be therefore $S_{10}\ A_{30} = S'_{20}\ B_{40}\ A_{30}$ so B_{40} must be empty and $S'_{20} = S'_{10}$. The transducer modified in the just described way will be called T - transducer.

<u>Theorem 1.</u> If each state of DeRemer contains at most one configuration then there can be no conflict between the semantic symbols in the corresponding T - transducer

<u>Proof:</u> Obvious

The Theorem 1 has a very important consequence. We shall state them in an informal way. It is known from [7] that if a grammar is the top-down one the DeRemer automaton for it has at most one configuration in the basic set [9] in each state. It follows from the Theorem 1 that T transducer cannot have semantic conflict between not opening semantic symbols. (So from the point of wiew of a compiler it behaves almost like a <u>top-down</u> method). The methods having such a property will be called latently top-down.

The DeRemer method is therefore latently top-down.

The methods which are not latently top-down are the precedence. methods. The substantial property of precedence parsing is the fact, that until the whole handle is separated there is no information allowing to detect in what handle is of what rules the analysis is just being proceded.

It is question whether the precedence parse can be modified in order to obtain the potentialy top-down parsing method based on precedence relations. It seems that such a method is not easy to find.

On the other hand bounded context parsing methods can be easily modified to obtain potentially top-down variant of them. We shall give the main ideas of construction on the following example of the top-down grammar G3

1. $C \longrightarrow$ if B then E fi
2. $B \longrightarrow I \vee B_1$
3. $B_1 \longrightarrow$
4. $B_1 \longrightarrow E$
5. $E \longrightarrow I$
6. $I \longrightarrow i$

The compiler grammar for G3 is obvious. The rule 3 has in the compiler grammar the form $B_1 \longrightarrow B_{30}\ \ B_{31}$. The bounded context parse of if $i \vee i$ then i fi is (the lines over symbols denotes matched symbols on stack and on input, the not changed items are often omitted)

input	stack	Action	Output
$\overline{\text{if}}$ $i \vee i$ then i fi		read	C_{00}if
$\bar{i} \vee i$ then i fi	$C_{00}\overline{\text{if}}$	new	C_{11}
	$C_{00}\text{if}\ \overline{C}_{11}$	new	B_{20}
	$C_{00}\text{if}\ C_{11}\overline{B}_{20}$	new	E_{50}
	$C_{00}\text{if}\ C_{11}B_{20}I_{60}$	new, read	$I_{60}i$
$\bar{\vee}\, i$ then i fi	$C_{00}\text{if}\ C_{11}B_{20}\overline{I_{60}\ i}$	reduce	I_{61}
	$C_{00}\text{if}\ C_{11}B_{20}\ I$	new read	$B_{21}\vee$
$\bar{i}$ then i fi	$C_{00}\text{if}\ C_{11}B_{20}\ I\ \overline{B_{21}\vee}$	new	B_{22}
	$C_{00}\text{if}\ C_{11}B_{20}\ I\ B_{21}\vee\overline{B_{22}}$	new,new	B_{40}
	$\ldots\ldots\ldots\ B_{21}\vee\overline{B_{22}B_{40}}$	new	E_{50}
$\bar{i}$ then i fi	$\ldots\ldots\ldots\ IB_{21}\vee\overline{B_{22}B_{40}E_{50}}$	new	I_{60}
	$\ldots\ldots\ldots\ \vee B_{22}B_{40}E_{50}E_{60}$	read	i
$\overline{\text{then}}$ i fi	$\ldots\ldots\ldots\ E_{50}\overline{I_{60}\ i}$	reduce	I_{61}
	$\ldots\ldots\ldots\ \overline{E_{50}\ I}$	new, reduce	E_{50}
	$\ldots\ldots\ldots\ \overline{I\ B_{21}\vee B_{22}B_{1}}$	new, reduce	B_{23}

C_{00} **if** C_{01} B read **then**

... etc ...

The bounded context parsing can be therefore modified in order to work in the top down manner. This reflects the fact, that, intuitively speaking, if a bounded context parsing is used the "top-down parts" of a grammar can be parsed in the top-down manner, a fact well-known to compiler writers.

We note, however, the semantic symbols must be used to control the work of the parser. They need not be used for DeRemer´s parser. It follows that, intuitively speaking, bounded context parsing has weaker top down features.

It seems, that the latently top-down methods are better suited to compiler writing. Moreover the LR(k) methods seem to have in some sense both "stronger top-down properties" that the bounded context parsing (BRC) methods (see the examples) and both LR(k) and BRC methods have more strong top-down features that the precedence methods. This is, perhaps, one reason why so much of study is devoted to the LR(k) parsing in the last years.

It follows further, that there is no strong difference between the top-down and bottom up parsing as it can seem. A slight modification of some bottom-up methods can made them to work in a (compiler) top-down fashion as long as possible. There is, of course, the open problem if the power of such methods for error recovery is also comparable with the power of classical top-down methods.

Now we turn to the LR(k) methods. There is the question: "Have some LR(k) methods more strong top-down features than some other ones?" The answer is yes. For example the modification MR of DeRemer parser discussed in the first part in [3] has the property, that the closure set in each state MR is not greater that the closure set of some state of a DeRemer automaton R if such an automaton R can be constructed for the given grammar (i. e. to each state S in MR there is a state S´of the automaton R containing all the configurations of the state S). It follows that the restrictions on semantic symbols in MR cannot be stronger that the restrictions in the DeRemer parser. We can easily verify that the only restriction on semantic symbols for the grammar G2 (see [3] page 6) in MR is $S'_{10} = S'_{20}$ (i. e. for opening symbols). It follows that the method discussed in the first part of [3] has stronger the top-down features than the DeRemer method.

The compiler grammars differ from the usual compiler writing systems in the way that the semantic symbols can be inserted "inside the handles", an i. e. they are not bounded on reductions only. The situation that a semantic action is bounded on the reduction only can be in compiler grammars descrited by the requirements that all the semantic symbols except the symbols at the ends of handles are empty (see [1]). The above given examples show, that it is very often not necessary to postpone all the semantic decision in such a way. Moreover if such a postponing cannot be made we must artifically replace one rule by a set of rules. This, however, causes that the grammar of the parser differs from the grammar defining the source language more than it is necessary and that is unpleasant as this makes the changes in the parser (needed for example for error recovery) which must at present state of the art be made "by hands" more difficult and it also causes not necessary structuring of the analysed text introduced via auxiliary nonterminals.

The compiler grammars allow to make clearer the definition of covering (see [11]). A compiler grammar G′covers the compiler grammar G with respect to a parsing method M if (i) the compiler grammar G defines for each $x \in L(G)$ and only for $x \in L(G)$ a compiler parse equivalent to that one defined by the compiler grammar G. (Two compiler parses are equivalent if they are equal after deleting all occurences of empty symbols).

(ii) each right-hand side of a rule in G is a right-hand side of a rule in G - and

(iii) each nonterminal in G is a nonterminal in G . G′ weakly covers G if the condition (i) only is fulfilled.

For any compiler grammar G corresponding to the grammar G1 the semantic symbols F_{60}, F_{61} and SE_{80}, SE_{81} are very likely to be empty. If this is the case any compiler grammar corresponding to the grammar replacing each derivation of the form ⟨factor⟩ => ⟨ identifier⟩ can cover G and the phrase marker (2′) then can have the form

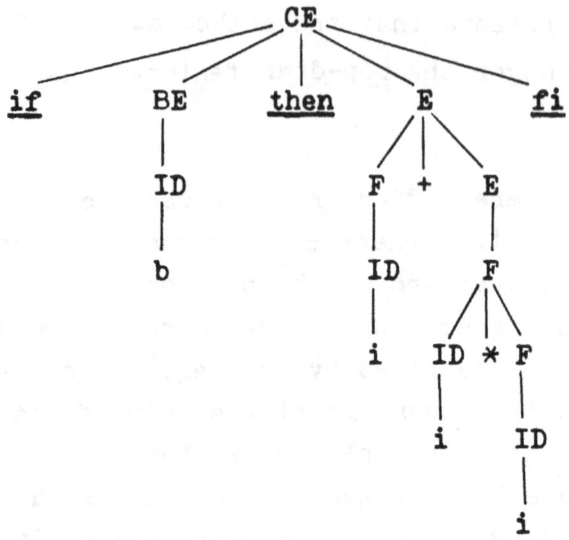

(2 *)

Now we turn to the top-down methods. We assume that the Assumption A holds. Let us describe the grammar G1 in a concise grafic form (see [6]) i. e. in the form of "diagrams"

<cond. expression >

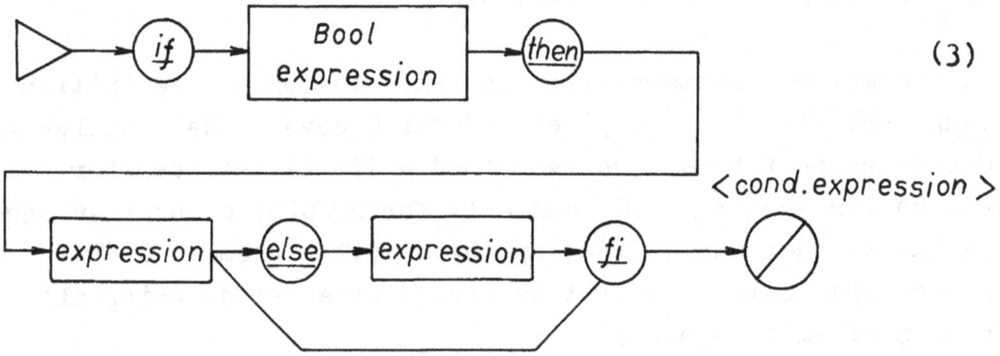

(3)

The notation is selfexplanatory, we note only that the terminals are surrounded by circles, the nonterminals by oblongs.

<expression >

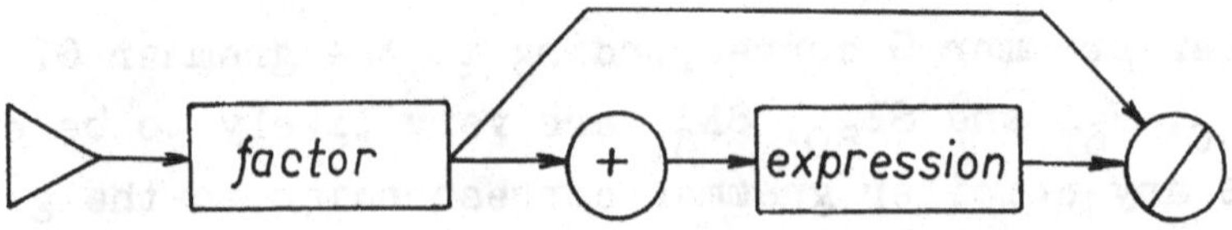

(3')

< factor >

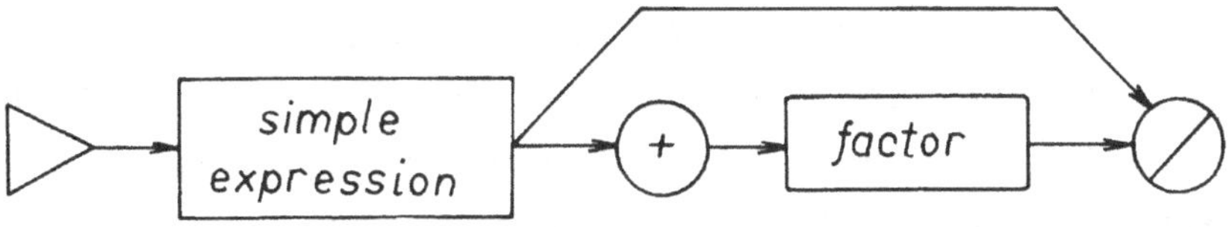

(3")

<simple expression >

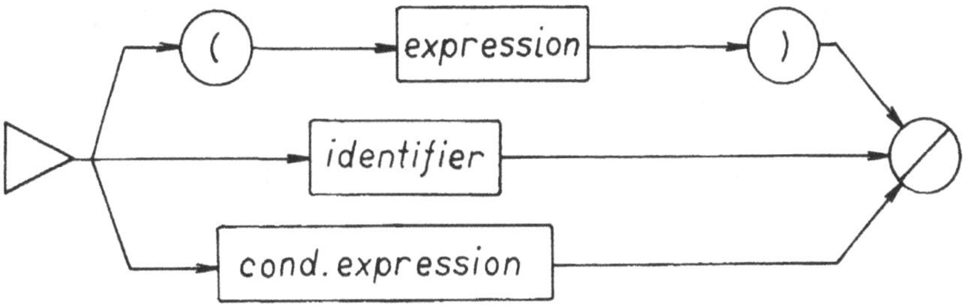

(3‴)

< Bool expression >

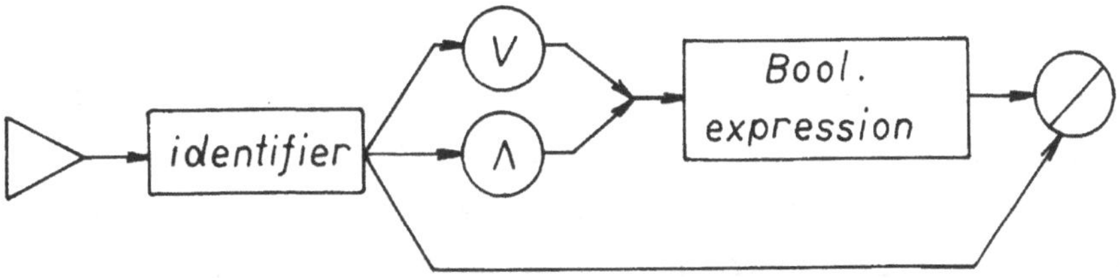

(3 *)

As the grammar G1 is left factorisable (see [3]) part two) the diagrams (3) through (3*) can be under Assumption A treated as a form of flow charts of a program where oblongs denotes (recursive) calls of routines. For example (3) can be converted into a program (fi matches if)

```
if readsymbol = "if" then  read else  error fi;
call Bool expression;
if read symbol = "then" then read else error fi;
call expression;
ℓ : if read symbol = "fi" then exit fi;
if read symbol = "else" then read else error fi
call expression; goto ℓ;
```

This is, of course, the method of recursive procedures, one of the oldest methods of parsing. This method is latently top-down as it can be easily seen. We note however that it has stronger top-down features than the LR(k) methods as for LL(k) grammar there can be no conflicts between opening semantic symbols. Note that no left factoring is necessary. The method of recursive procedures has some great advantages. First: The method allows a concise very acceptable notation (see [3]). For example the parser for Algol 68 can be writen on 12 pages.

Second: It allows to elaborate easily the construction like

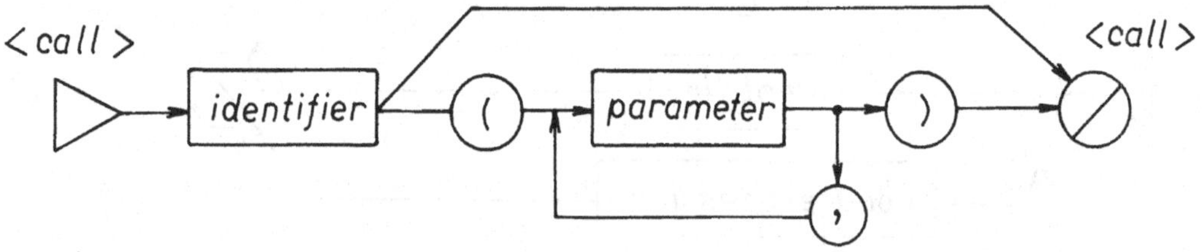

without introducing any auxiliary nonterminals. We are working, in fact, with "grammars" with the rules of the form (nonterminal, regular event). This concept can be easily formalized (see [3])

Third: The whole parse is near to the human understanding of a text and the changes in the parser can be easily performed. The tendency to form subroutines is in the direction of new programming technology (structured programming). The main disadvantage is due to the impossibility to parse some types of constructions in top down manner (see [2]). We note, that the power of the method of diagrams can be substantially strengthened by the methods described in [3] A practical application, of the ideas from [3] can be found in [12] . Like in the compiler grammars we can insert the semantic symbols with the transition (edges) in the diagram. For example if (3) is a part of an Algol 68 - like parser the semantic symbols are distinguished by card - like shapes; semantic actions "then", "else" causes the action "range begin", "if" causes " range end".

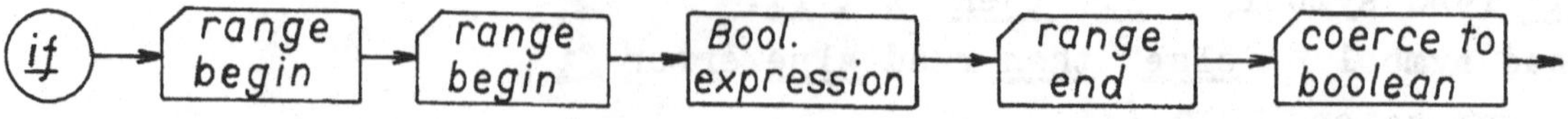

see next page

continued from the previous page

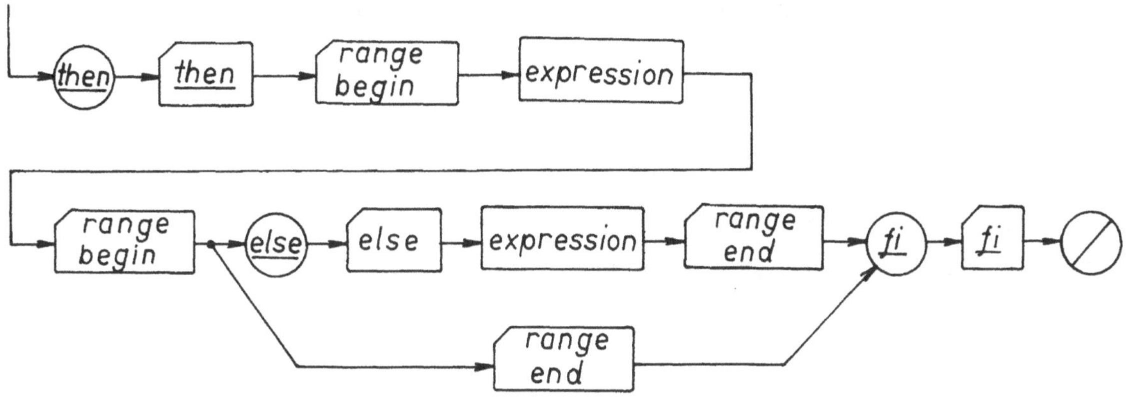

If the methods form [3] are to be used certain restrictions must be impossed on semantic symbols if the grammar under the discussion is not a top-down one, but we do not discuss detais here, the reader is referred to [8] . We state here the main result from [8] . If the translation has the property that the semantic symbol to be produced in a given place of the input text depends only on the limited right context and (possibly whole) left context of the given place in the input text then the modified method of recursive procedures can realize translation for each LR(k) grammar.

Conclusions:

We attempted to show that by introducing some means allowing to produce compiler parse can help us to make a bit clearer some things in parsing. It can also make the whole problem of compiler writing easier. It allows to define a semi-top-down parsing and to compare "degrees of top-down-ness" in methods which are treated in literature as the bottom-up ones.

The separation of the problem of syntax analysis from the problems of semantics was a great step forward in compiler writing. Now, it seems, the time comes, when it is necessary to reinvolve a certain formalized aspects of semantics back into the syntact analysis. The reasons for it are not only those given above. For example in FORTRAN the construction A(I,J,K) can be either a procedure call or an indexed variable. This "ambiguity" can be resolved by introducing a new nonterminal "call or indexed variable". In the transition diagram notation the translation can be the following

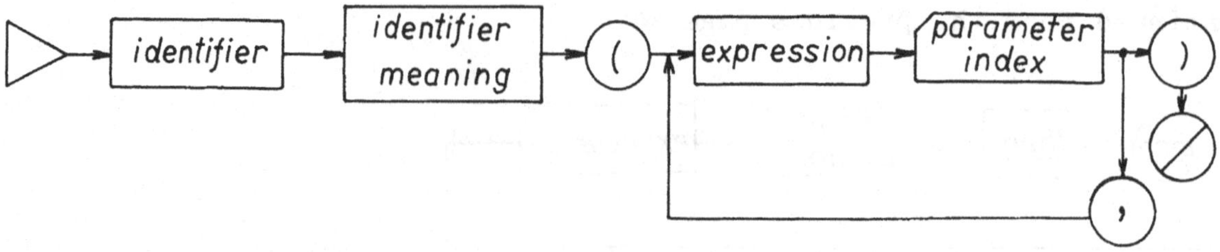

which seems to be near to the process in which a human being analyzes the text. "Parameter/index" uses the information formed in "identifier meaning".

We have defined the potentially top-down methods and we have shown that a lot of wellknown parsing methods are potentially top-down ones. For the compiler writer a method has the top down property if the compiler parse can be produced during one scan. This can be formulated as follows.

F o r t h e c o m p i l e r w r i t e r t h e m e t h o d i s t h e t o p - d o w n o n e i f i n e a c h p l a c e o f a p r o g r a m t h e s e m a n t i c r o u t i n e s t o b e c a l l e d a r e u n i q u e l y d e t e r m i n a b l e u n d e r t h e a s s u m p t i o n t h a t t h e w h o l e l e f t c o n t e x t a n d o n l y a l i m i t e d r i g h t c o n t e x t i n t h e i n p u t s t r i n g i s k n o w n (without knowing the rest of the phrase under elaboration).

We have also shown, that there are diferences between top-down methods in the respect that some methods works in (compiler) top-down fashion with less requirements impossed on semantic symbols. The class of potentially top-down methods has therefore some subclasses of methods differing in the "top-down-ness", i.e. subclasses of the methods differing in their ability to parse in a "compiler-top-down" manner. To each such a subclass there is a certaing class of compiler grammars (i. e. grammars with semantic symbols) "compiler-top-down" parsable.

References

[1] GRIES,D., Compiler Construction for Digital Computers, John Wiley, New York, 1971.

[2] ROZENKRANTZ, D.J.; STEARNS, R.E. Properties of Deterministic Top-Down Grammars, Inf. and Control 17 (Oct.1970).

[3] KRÁL, J.; DEMNER, J. Semi-Top-Down Syntactic Analysis, Report of the Institute of Computation Techniques, Prague 1973.

[4] WOOD, D. The Theory of Left Factored Languages II, The Comp. Journal 13 (1970), 12 - 20.

[5] AHO, A.V.; ULLMANN, J.D. The Theory of Parsing, Translation and Compiling, Prentice Hall International, London, 1972.

[6] KRÁL, J. A Concise Graphic Form of Description of Algol 68 Syntax, to appear in Information Processing Machines No 19.

[7] KRÁL, J.; DEMNER, J. A Note on the Number of states of the DeRemer's Recognizer, Inf. Proc. Letters 2 (1973), 22 - 23.

[8] KRÁL, J. Semi-Top-Down Transition Diagrams Driven. Syntax Analysis, Preliminary Report ÚVT 5-6/74, Institute of Computation Techniques, May 1974

[9] DeREMER, F.L. Simple LR(k) Grammars, Comm. of ACM 14 (1971), 453-460.

[10] FELDMAN, J.; GRIES, D. Translator Writing Systems, Comm. ACM 11 (1968), 77 - 103.

[11] GRAY, J. Precedence Parsers for Programming Languages, Ph.D. Thesis, Univ. of California, Berkeley

[12] KRÁL, J.; MOUDRÝ, J.; NADRCHAL, J. Construction of a Syntax Parser for an Algol 68 Compiler, to appear in Information Processing Machines No 19.

[13] HAVEL, I. M. Strict Deterministic Languages. Ph.D. Thesis Univ. of California, Berkeley 1971.

SUBSTRING LANGUAGES

J. Małuszyński
Computation Centre
Polish Academy of Sciences
P.O.Box 22 00-901 Warsaw PKiN

INTRODUCTION

The syntax of programming languages is usually described by context-free grammars. However, the parsers consist very often of two devices: a scanner that reduces substrings of a given string and a syntax analyzer that deals with partially reduced strings. Such an approach is as a rule based on the experience of the compiler designer. This paper gives him a tool for the examination of languages to distinguish sets of substrings that could be reduced regardless of their contexts. The tool is a notion of a substring language of a given language. Any substring language is a set of substrings of strings of a given language. It is determined by a given language and an ordered pair of arbitrary other languages over the same alphabet.

We are particularly interested in the substring languages of context-free languages. The objects of our considerations are those of them which are determined by pairs of regular languages; we call them CFR-substring languages. We prove that any CFR-substring language is a context -free language and we give a method for constructing grammars that generate such languages. We show a connection between CFR-substring languages and grammars of the original languages. It turns out that any CFR-substring language S of a given language L is a substitution of context-free languages into a regular language Q_S over the alphabet of a grammar that generates L. This fact enables us to construct two -pass parsers for any context-free language. In the paper we discuss additional conditions, necessary for good efficiency of such parsers.

DEFINITIONS

In this section we give a method for distinguishing substrings of strings of a given language. The idea of this method is expressed by the definition of a substring language.

Let T be an alphabet and L - a language over T. A string ω_0 is a substring of a string ω over T iff there exist strings π and Θ such that $\omega = \pi\omega_0\Theta$. A prefix of a string ω is any such string π that $\omega = \pi\gamma$ for some string γ . The prefix language of L is the set of all prefixes of all strings belonging to L. A postfix of a given string ω is any such string γ that $\omega = \pi\gamma$ for some string π. The postfix language of L is the set of all postfixes of all strings belonging to L. If we wish to distinguish a substring of a given string, we should specify an ordered pair of strings over T: the prefix and the postfix of a given string. Such a pair (π, Θ) can be used as well to determine a set $S(\pi, \Theta)$ of substrings of strings of a given language:

$$S(\pi,\Theta) = \{\gamma \mid \pi\gamma\Theta \in L\}$$

Any ordered pair (π, Θ) of strings over T we call a context and any string in $S(\pi, \Theta)$ - a detached substring of the context (π, Θ) We will specify sets of contexts as Cartesian products of languages and we will consider the corresponding sets of detached substrings.

Definition 1

Let T be an alphabet and L, C_1, C_2 - languages over T. By a substring language of L generated by the Cartesian product $C_1 \times C_2$ we mean the following set:

$$S_L(C_1,C_2) = \{\gamma \mid \exists \pi \in C_1 \exists \Theta \in C_2 \ \ \pi\gamma\Theta \in L\}$$

Example 1

Denoting by Sb(L) the set of all substrings of all strings of L by Pr(L) the prefix language of L and by Ps(L) the postfix language of L we can see that for any language L over T the following holds:

$$S_L(\{\varepsilon\},\{\varepsilon\}) = L \quad \text{/where } \varepsilon \text{ is the empty string/}$$
$$S_L(T^*, T^*) = Sb(L)$$
$$S_L(\{\varepsilon\}, T^*) = Pr(L)$$
$$S_L(T^*, \{\varepsilon\}) = Ps(L)$$

It follows from the definition of a substring language that:

1. If $L_1 \subset L_3$ and $L_2 \subset L_4$ then $S_L(L_1,L_2) \subseteq S_L(L_3,L_4)$.
2. For any L_1,L_2,L_3 over T
$$S_L(L_1 \cup L_2,L_3) = S_L(L_1,L_3) \cup S_L(L_2,L_3)$$
$$S_L(L_1,L_2 \cup L_3) = S_L(L_1,L_2) \cup S_L(L_1,L_3).$$
3. For any L_1,L_2,L_3 over T
$$S_L(L_1 \cap L_2,L_3) \subseteq S_L(L_1,L_3) \cap S_L(L_2,L_3)$$
$$S_L(L_1,L_2 \cap L_3) \subseteq S_L(L_1,L_2) \cap S_L(L_1,L_3).$$

CFR-SUBSTRING LANGUAGES

In this section we consider the substring languages of Context -Free languages determined by Cartesian products of Regular languages. We call them CFR-substring languages.We prove that each CFR-substring language is a context-free language and we give a method for constructing grammars of such languages./By a grammar of the language we mean any grammar generating it/.

Let L be a context-free language over an alphabet T and R_1,R_2 regular languages over T. Assume $G = (V,T,P,\sigma)$ to be a grammar of L in the Chomsky normal form. Such a grammar exists if the empty string does not belong to L. In the opposite case we can consider the language $L - \{\varepsilon\}$. We proceed as follows:

1. We construct context-free grammars G_{Pr} and G_{Ps} and we prove that G_{Pr} is a grammar of the prefix language of L and G_{Ps} is a grammar of the postfix language of L. Hence Pr(L) and Ps(L) are context-free.
2. We prove that for any regular set R over T a subset of Pr(L) defined as follows $Pr(L,R) = \{\theta \mid \exists \zeta \in Ps(L) \cap R \ \ \theta\zeta \in L\}$ is a context-free language. Pr(L,R) consists of all detached substrings of all such contexts (ε, ζ) that $\zeta \in Ps(L) \cap R$.
3. Similarly one can prove that for any regular set R over T the follo-

wing subset of Ps(L): $Ps(L,R) = \{\zeta \mid \exists \theta \in Pr(L)\cap R \;\; \theta\zeta \in L\}$ is a context -free language. Ps(L,R) consists of all detached substrings of all such contexts (θ, ε) that $\theta \in Pr(L)\cap R$.

4. From the definition of a substring language we obtain at once that

$$S_L(R_1,R_2) = Ps(Pr(L,R_2),R_1) = Pr(Ps(L,R_1),R_2)$$

As a conclusion we obtain the following theorem:

__Theorem 1__

Let T be an alphabet, L a context-free language over T and R_1,R_2 regular languages over T. The substring language $S_L(R_1,R_2)$ is a context -free language.

We describe now an algorithm that for any context-free grammar $G = (V,T,P,\sigma)$ in the Chomsky normal form gives a grammar G_{Ps}. To define that grammar we choose the elements of the quadruple $(V_{Ps},T_{Ps},P_{Ps},\sigma_{Ps})$ as follows:

1. Let $V = \{v_1,v_2,\dots,v_n,t_1,t_2,\dots,t_m\}$ where v_i are nonterminal symbols and t_j - terminal ones , for $i = 1,2,..n$, $j = 1,2,...m$. Then $V_{Ps} \overset{df}{=} \{v_1,v_2,\dots,v_n,v_1',v_2',\dots,v_n',v_1'',v_2'',\dots,v_n'',t_1,\dots,t_m\}$ where all v_i's and all v_i''s are new symbols, not belonging to V.

2. $T_{Ps} \overset{df}{=} T$

3. The set P_{Ps} consists of all productions belonging to P and the following additional ones:

(i) $\sigma' \to \sigma$

(ii) For each production $v_k \to v_pv_q$ in P we have in P_{Ps} the following ones: $v_k' \to v_p'v_q$, $v_k'' \to v_p''v_q'$, $v_k'' \to v_p''v_q''$.

(iii) For each production $v_k \to t_l$ in P we have in P_{Ps} the following ones: $v_k' \to \varepsilon$, $v_k'' \to \varepsilon$.

4. $\sigma_{Ps} \overset{df}{=} \sigma$

Denoting $\mathcal{L}(G_{Ps})$ the language generated by the grammar G_{Ps} we can express the result of the above construction in the following lemma.

__Lemma 1__

$\mathcal{L}(G_{Ps}) = Ps(L)$

Proof. We show that $Ps(L) \subseteq \mathcal{L}(G_{Ps})$ and then the inverse inclusion.

Assume $\omega \in Ps(L)$. By the definition there exists such string ζ that $\zeta\omega \in L$. Then there exists at least one leftmost derivation of $\zeta\omega$ according to G :

$$\sigma \Rightarrow z_{11}\ldots z_{1m_1} \Rightarrow z_{21}z_{22}\ldots z_{2m_2} \Rightarrow \ldots \Rightarrow z_{k1}\ldots z_{km_k} \Rightarrow \zeta\omega \; ; \; k \geqslant 1 \; , \; m_i \geqslant 1$$

$z_{ij} \in V$ for $i = 1,2,\ldots,k$ $j = 1,\ldots,m_i$.

For each $i = 1,2,\ldots,k$ there exists such p_i that

1. For each $j < p_i$ z_{ij} derives a substring of ζ ,
2. For each $j > p_i$ z_{ij} derives a substring of ω ,
3. z_{ip_i} derives a nonempty substring of ζ and a substring of ω /possibly empty/.

Consider the following sequence of strings:

$$\sigma', \tilde{z}_{11}\ldots\tilde{z}_{1m_1}, \tilde{z}_{21}\ldots\tilde{z}_{2m_2}, \ldots, \tilde{z}_{k1}\ldots\tilde{z}_{km_k} \quad \text{where}$$

$$\tilde{z}_{ij} = \begin{cases} \varepsilon & \text{iff } z_{ij} \in T \text{ and } j \leqslant p_i \\ z_{ij} & \text{iff } z_{ij} \in V \text{ and } j > p_i \\ z'_{ij} & \text{iff } z_{ij} \in V-T \text{ and } j < p_i \\ z''_{ij} & \text{iff } z_{ij} \in V-T \text{ and } j = p_i \end{cases}$$

This sequence is a leftmost derivation of ω according to G_{Ps}. Hence $\omega \in \mathcal{L}(G_{Ps})$ and $Ps(L) \subseteq \mathcal{L}(G_{Ps})$.

We show now the inverse inclusion. Assume $\omega \in \mathcal{L}(G_{Ps})$. Then there exists a leftmost derivation of ω according to G_{Ps}.

$$\sigma' \Rightarrow u_{11}\ldots u_{1n_1} \Rightarrow u_{21}u_{22}\ldots u_{2n_2} \Rightarrow \ldots \Rightarrow u_{q1}u_{q2}\ldots u_{qn_q} \Rightarrow \omega; \quad q \geqslant 1 \text{ and}$$

for $i = 1,2,\ldots q$ and $j = 1,2,\ldots,n_i$ $u_{ij} \in V_{Ps}$.

We define the following homomorphism $\delta : V_{Ps} \to V$:

For each $u \in V_{Ps}$

$$\delta(u) = \begin{cases} u & \text{if } u \in V \\ \text{such } v \text{ that } v' = u \text{ or } v'' = u & \text{if } u \in (V_{Pr} - V) \end{cases}$$

Consider the sequence of strings:

$$\sigma, \gamma_1 \delta(u_{11}\ldots u_{1n_1}), \gamma_2 \delta(u_{21}\ldots u_{2n_2}), \ldots \gamma_q \delta(u_{q1}\ldots u_{qn_q})$$

where γ_i are defined as follows:

1. $\gamma_1 = \varepsilon$
2. For each $1 \leqslant i < q$

$$\gamma_{i+1} = \begin{cases} \gamma_i t & \text{if } u_{i+1\,1}\ldots u_{i+1\,n_{i+1}} = u_{i2}\ldots u_{in_i} \\ \gamma_i & \text{in the opposite case} \end{cases}$$

where t is such a terminal symbol that the production $\delta(u_{i1}) \to t$ belongs to P. By the definition of P_{Ps} there exists at least one t with the above property. Observe that $\delta(\omega) = \omega$ and for each i=2,...q $\gamma_{i-1}\,\delta(u_{i-1\,1}\ldots u_{i-1\,n_{i-1}}) \overset{*}{\underset{G}{\Rightarrow}} \gamma_i\,\delta(u_{i1}\ldots u_{in_i})$. Hence $\gamma_q\,\delta(u_{q1}\ldots u_{qn_q})$ $= \gamma_q\omega$ and $\gamma_q\omega \in L$. Thus $\omega \in Ps(L)$ q.e.d.

We construct now a grammar $G_{Pr} = (V_{Pr}, T_{Pr}, P_{Pr}, \sigma_{Pr})$:

1. $V_{Pr} \overset{df}{=} V_{Ps}$
2. $T_{Pr} \overset{df}{=} T_{Ps} = T$
3. The set P_{Pr} consists of all productions of P and the following additional ones:

(i) $\sigma' - \sigma$

(ii) For each production $v_k \to v_p v_q$ in P we have in P_{Pr} the following ones: $v'_k \to v_p v'_q$, $v'_k \to v'_p v''_q$, $v''_k \to v''_p v''_q$.

(iii) For each production $v_k \to t_1$ in P we have in P_{Pr} the following ones: $v'_k \to \varepsilon$, $v''_k \to \varepsilon$.

4. $\sigma_{Pr} \overset{df}{=} \sigma'$

The following lemma holds:

<u>Lemma 2</u>

$(G_{Pr}) = Pr(L)$

We omit the proof of this lemma because it is very similar to the proof of the lemma 1.

We restrict now the set of considered prefixes to those strings of Pr(L) that belong to a given regular set R and we examine the set of corresponding postfixes.

<u>Lemma 3</u>

For any context-free languge L and any regular set R the set **Pr**(L,R) /defined at the beginning of this section/ is a context-free language.

Proof. We can assume without loss of generality that $\varepsilon \notin L$ and $\varepsilon \notin R$. If $\varepsilon \in R$ then $Pr(L,R) = Pr(L - \{\varepsilon\}, R - \{\varepsilon\})$ L and Pr(L,R) is context-free iff the language $Pr(L - \{\varepsilon\}, R - \{\varepsilon\})$ is context-free. Let $G = (V,T,P,\sigma)$ be a grammar of L in the Chomsky normal form and $A = (T,S,s_0,S_1,f)$ a finite deterministic automaton - an acceptor of the language R /as defined in SALOMAA, A. [3], p.27/. S_1 is a finite set of final states. Let $S_1 = \{s_1,\ldots,s_n\}$ and denote

$A_i = (T,S,s_0,\{s_i\},f)$, $i = 1,\ldots,n$ R_i - the language accepted by A_i.

Clearly, $R = R_1 \cup R_2 \cup \ldots \cup R_n$ and $Pr(L,R) = Pr(L,R_1) \cup \ldots \cup Pr(L,R_n)$. We construct now a context-free grammar $\hat{G}_i$ of the language $Pr(L,R_i)$. Let $\hat{G}_i = (\hat{V}_i, \hat{T}_i, \hat{P}_i, \hat{\sigma}_i)$ where:

1. $\hat{V}_i = V \cup (V_{Pr} - V) \times S \times S$

The alphabet $\hat{V}_i$ consists of two disjoint sets: the set V and a set of triples. The first element of any triple is an "additional" symbol of the alphabet of the grammar G_{Pr}, the next two ones are states of the acceptor A.

2. $\hat{T}_i = T$

3. $\hat{P}_i$ consists of P and all productions having one of the following forms:

(i) $(v',s_j,s_k) \rightarrow (w',s_j,s_p)(z'',s_p,s_k)$ where $s_j,s_k,s_p \in S$ and $v \rightarrow wz$ is a production in P ;

(ii) $(v',s_j,s_k) \rightarrow w(z',s_j,s_k)$ where $s_j,s_k \in S$ and $v \rightarrow wz$ is a production in P ;

(iii) $(v'',s_j,s_k) \rightarrow (w'',s_j,s_p)(z'',s_p,s_k)$ where $s_j,s_k,s_p \in S$ and $v \rightarrow wz$ is a production in P ;

(iv) $(v',s_j,s_k) \rightarrow (a,s_j,s_k)$ where $s_j,s_k \in S$ and $v \rightarrow a$ is a production in P ;

(v) $(v'',s_j,s_k) \rightarrow (a,s_j,s_k)$ where $s_j,s_k \in S$ and $v \rightarrow a$ is a production in P ;

(vi) $(a,s_j,s_k) \rightarrow \varepsilon$ where $a \in T$ and $f(s_j,a) = s_k$.

4. $\hat{\sigma}_i = (\sigma',s_0,s_i)$

First components of triples in the productions of the form (i)÷(iii) preserve the derivation according to the grammar G_{Pr}. First components of triples in the productions of the form (iv) and (v) derive postfixes to be cut off. Productions of the form (vi) cut off postfixes under the condition that they are accepted by the acceptor A_i. By the definition a string ω belongs to $Pr(L,R_i)$ iff there exists such θ that $\omega\theta \in L$ and θ is accepted by A_i. Hence $Pr(L,R_i) = \mathcal{L}(\hat{G}_i)$ q.e.d.

In a similar way one can prove the following lemma:

<u>Lemma 4</u>

For any context-free language L and any regular set R the set

Ps(L,R) is a context-free language.

Lemma 4 completes the proof of the theorem 1. We described an algorithm that enables us to construct a grammar of any CFR-substring language. The input data for the algorithm is a context-free grammar in the Chomsky normal form and FS-acceptors of the regular languages that specify a substring language. On the output we get a context-free grammar of the substring language. A restricted version of this algorithm has been implemented on ODRA 1204 computer/MAŁUSZYŃSKI, J.[2] /

In the next section we show a connection between CFR-substring languages and grammars of original languages. We give now certain auxiliary results concerning the languages Pr(L,R) and Ps(L,R) to be used in the next section. We show, that for any grammar G in the Chomsky normal form the language $Pr(\mathcal{L}(G),R)$ can be obtained from a regular set Z_R over the alphabet of G by a context-free substitution. A similar result can be proved for Ps(L,R).

Lemma 5

Let $G = (V,T,P,\sigma)$ be a context-free grammar in the Chomsky normal form and R a regular language over T. There exists such a regular set Z_R over V that $Pr(\mathcal{L}(G),R) = \{\omega \in T^* \mid \exists \alpha \in Z_R \quad \alpha \overset{*}{\underset{G}{\Rightarrow}} \omega\}$

Proof. It was shown above that for any G $Pr(\mathcal{L}(G),R) = Pr(\mathcal{L}(G),R_1)$ ... $Pr(\mathcal{L}(G),R_n)$, where R_i are disjoint components of R and n equals the number of final states of the acceptor of R. It suffices then to prove the lemma for a component R_i of R. In the proof of the lemma 3 we described an algorithm, that for given G and R_i produces a grammar $\hat{G}_i = (\hat{V}_i,\hat{T}_i,\hat{P}_i,\hat{\sigma}_i)$ that generates $Pr(\mathcal{L}(G),R_i)$. By the definition $\hat{V}_i = V \cup U_i \cup W_i$ where U_i is a set of triples of the form (v', s_j,s_k) and W_i is a set of triples of the form (v'',s_j,s_k) /s_j,s_k are states of the acceptor of R_i and v',v'' are auxiliary symbols - see proof of the lemma 3/. Observe that each non-triple of $\hat{V}_i$ cannot derive accordingly to G_i any string in which triples occur. Consider then the grammar $\check{G}_i = (\check{V}_i,\check{T}_i,\check{P}_i,\check{\sigma}_i)$ defined as follows:

$\check{V}_i = \hat{V}_i$

$\check{T}_i = V$

$\check{P}_i = \hat{P}_i \cap ((\check{V}_i - V) \times \check{V}_i^*) = \hat{P}_i - P$

$\check{\sigma}_i = \hat{\sigma}_i = (\sigma', s_0,s_i)$.

Clearly $\mathcal{L}(G_i) \subset V^*$. It can be shown that $Pr(\mathcal{L}(G),R)$ is the set of terminal strings that can be derived from the strings of $\mathcal{L}(G_i)$ accordingly to the grammar G i.e. $Pr(\mathcal{L}(G),R_i) = \{\omega \in T^* | \exists \alpha \in \mathcal{L}(\check{G}_i) \quad \alpha \overset{*}{\underset{G}{\Rightarrow}} \omega\}$

To complete the proof it suffices to show that $\mathcal{L}(\check{G}_i)$ is a regular language. Observe, that each nonterminal of the form (v'',s_j,s_k) derives accordingly to $\check{G}_i$ either no terminal string at all or at most the empty string. One can construct an equivalent grammar without these nonterminals. Consider the grammar $\bar{G}_i = (\bar{V}_i,\bar{T}_i,\bar{P}_i, \bar{\sigma}_i)$ defined as follows:

1. $\bar{V}_i$ is the subset of $\check{V}_i$ obtained by removing all nonterminals of the form (v'',s_j,s_k) i.e. $\bar{V}_i = \check{V}_i - W_i$
2. $\bar{T}_i = \check{T}_i = V$
3. $\bar{P}_i = P_{0i} \cup \check{P}_i \cap (\bar{V}_i \times \bar{V}_i^*)$

where $P_{0i} = \{a \to b \mid \exists c \in W_i \quad c \overset{*}{\underset{\check{G}_i}{\Rightarrow}} \varepsilon \ , \ (a \to bc) \in \check{P}_i\}$

4. $\bar{\sigma}_i = \check{\sigma}_i = \hat{\sigma}_i = (\sigma',s_0,s_1)$

$\bar{G}_i$ is a right-linear grammar equivalent to $\check{G}_i$. Therefore $\mathcal{L}(\check{G}_i)$ is a regular language with the needed properties q.e.d.

It can be seen that for each $v \in \hat{V}_i$ there exists such a regular set Z_v over V that

$$\{\omega \in T^* | v \overset{*}{\underset{\hat{G}_i}{\Rightarrow}} \omega\} = \{\omega \in T^* | \exists \xi \in Z_v \quad \xi \overset{*}{\underset{G}{\Rightarrow}} \omega\}$$

We will use this fact in the sequel.

In a similar way one can prove the following lemma:

<u>Lemma 6</u>

Let $G = (V,T,P,\sigma)$ be a context-free grammar in the Chomsky normal form and R a regular language over T. There exists such a regular set Y_R over V that $Ps(\mathcal{L}(G),R) = \{\omega \in T^* | \exists \alpha \in Y_R \quad \alpha \overset{*}{\underset{G}{\Rightarrow}} \omega\}$

CFR-SUBSTRING LANGUAGES AND TWO-PASS PARSING

In this section we show that any CFR-substring language S of a given language L enables us to design two-pass parser for those strings of L in which occur substrings belonging to S. Assume $G = (V,T,P,\sigma)$ is a context-free grammar in the Chomsky normal form and $L = \mathcal{L}(G)$.

<u>Theorem 2</u>

For any CFR-substring language S of L there exists such a regular language Q_S over V that $S = \{\omega \in T^* | \exists \Theta \in Q_S \ \Theta \overset{*}{\underset{G}{\Rightarrow}} \omega\}$

Proof. Assume S is determined by the pair (A,B) where A and B are regular languages over T. By the definition S = Ps(Pr(L,B),A). Hence by the lemma 3 there exists a context-free grammar that generates Pr(L,B). We can assume without loss of generality that the acceptor of B has only one final state s_1. Using the construction described in the proof of the lemma 3 we obtain the grammar $\hat{G}_1$ with an alphabet $\hat{V}_1$. One can easily construct an equivalent grammar in the Chomsky normal form with the same alphabet $\hat{V}_1$. By the lemma 5 there exists a regular language Y_A over V_1 such that $S = \{\omega \in T^* | \exists \alpha \in Y_A \ \alpha \overset{*}{\underset{\hat{G}_1}{\Rightarrow}} \omega\}$. On the other hand for each $v \in \hat{V}_1$ there exists such a regular language Z_V that the set of strings that can be derived from v accordingly to $\hat{G}_1$ is the same as the set of strings over T that can be derived accordingly to G from all strings of Z_v. Hence we can obtain Q_S from Y_A by the substitution of the languages Z_v q.e.d.

The theorem 2 enables us to construct two-pass parsers. If a terminal string ω belongs to L and ω is of the form $\omega_1\omega_0\omega_2$ where ω_0 belongs to S then there exists $\Theta \in Q_S$ such that $\Theta \overset{*}{\underset{G}{\Rightarrow}} \omega_0$ and $\omega_1 \Theta \omega_2$ is a sentential form. In the first pass we can distinguish and reduce all non-overlapping ω_0s of ω and in the second one - to parse the partially reduced string. Such an approach have sense provided that:

1. For each ω_0 belonging to S there exists only one such Θ in Q_S that Θ derives ω_0.
2. Each string of L has a substring belonging to S.

If the condition 1 is not satisfied then we have such ω_0s that can be reduced in different ways and we do not know which of these ways is the proper one. It may cause backtracking and the loss of efficiency If the condition 2 is not satisfied then there exist such strings belonging to L that cannot be reduced by the scanner. For these strings the first pass is useless and causes the loss of parsing efficiency. How one can find such CFR-substring languages of L that satisfy the conditions? This question remains open.

CONCLUSIONS

The paper gives a method for distinguishing sets of substrings of strings of a given language L over an alphabet T. These sets are called substring languages of L. We defined a special class of substring languages, so called CFR-substring languages. Each CFR-substring language is a context-free language. We gave an algorithm that produces grammars for CFR-substring languages. This algorithm enables us to construct two-pass parsers for L. However, it is only an auxiliary tool; we can see whether a chosen CFR-substring language induces an efficient two-pass parser or not, but we do not know how find such one that induces an efficient parser. The algorithm for constructing grammars of CFR-substring languages can be used for error recovery. Let ω_1 and ω_2 be strings in T^*. Find a string ω belonging to L with the prefix ω_1 and the postfix ω_2. The set of all solutions of this problem is the language $\omega_1 S_L(\{\omega_1\},\{\omega_2\})\omega_2$. By the theorem 1 the language $S_L(\{\omega_1\},\{\omega_2\})$ is a context-free language and using our algorithm we can construct a grammar that produces this language. The set of all non-empty substring languages of L is a semilattice with respect to the set-theoretical inclusion. The greatest element of this semilattice is the set Sb(L) of all substrings of all strings of L and the minimal ones are all substring languages $S_L(\{\alpha\},\{\beta\})$ where $\alpha,\beta \in T^*$. Using the described method one has a limited possibility of distinguishing subsets of Sb(L). To increase the selectivness one should find a way of distinguishing subsets of the minimal substring languages.

REFERENCES

[1] MAŁUSZYNSKI,J.: Subproblems of recognitions problems. Lecture Notes in Computer Science 2(1973), 294-300, (Proc. of 1GI Conf. on Formal Languages and Automata Theory). Springer-Verlag, Berlin-Heidelberg-New York 1973.

[2] MAŁUSZYNSKI,J.: Regular structures in programming languages. Theory of Programming Languages Semantics and Compiling,(Proc. Conf., Frankfurt/Oder, 1974) - to appear in EIK

[3] SALOMAA,A.: Formal languages. Academic Press, New York 1973.

DEFINING LANGUAGES BY MAZURKIEWICZ ALGORITHMS

W.A.Owsianiecka
Mathematical Institute, Polish Academy of Sciences
Sniadeckich 8, 00-950 Warsaw, Poland

1.INTRODUCTION

The Mazurkiewicz algorithms have been orginally introduced (in [1] and [2]) as models of computer programs. In this paper they are shown to be good mathematical means in defining formal languages. In fact after a minor modification one can consider them both as acceptors and generators. New classes of languages are defined and investigated. In particular, the theorems proved concern their closure properties and position within the Chomsky hierarchy.

2.BASIC NOTIONS

The reader is assumed to be familiar with basic notions of the theory of formal languages.

Let X be a set. Any subset $Q \subseteq X \times X$ is called a binary relation in X. We write xQy instead of $(x,y) \in Q$. By I_X (or simply, I if X is fixed) we denote the identity relation in X.

Let $Q,T \subseteq X \times X$. By QT we denote the composition of Q and T defined as follows:

$$xQTy \Longleftrightarrow [(\exists z)\ xQz \ \&\ zTy]$$

The n-th power of Q and the iteration of Q are binary relations in X defined as follows:

of strings of a given language L over an alphabet T. These sets are called substring languages of L. We defined a special class of substring languages, so called CFR-substring languages. Each CFR-substring language is a context-free language. We gave an algorithm that produces grammars for CFR-substring languages. This algorithm enables us to construct two-pass parsers for L. However, it is only an auxiliary tool; we can see whether a chosen CFR-substring language induces an efficient two-pass parser or not, but we do not know how find such one that induces an efficient parser. The algorithm for constructing grammars of CFR-substring languages can be used for error recovery. Let ω_1 and ω_2 be strings in T^*. Find a string ω belonging to L with the prefix ω_1 and the postfix ω_2. The set of all solutions of this problem is the language $\omega_1 S_L(\{\omega_1\},\{\omega_2\})\omega_2$. By the theorem 1 the language $S_L(\{\omega_1\},\{\omega_2\})$ is a context-free language and using our algorithm we can construct a grammar that produces this language. The set of all non-empty substring languages of L is a semilattice with respect to the set-theoretical inclusion. The greatest element of this semilattice is the set Sb(L) of all substrings of all strings of L and the minimal ones are all substring languages $S_L(\{\alpha\},\{\beta\})$ where $\alpha,\beta \in T^*$. Using the described method one has a limited possibility of distinguishing subsets of Sb(L). To increase the selectivness one should find a way of distinguishing subsets of the minimal substring languages.

REFERENCES

[1] MAŁUSZYNSKI,J.: Subproblems of recognitions problems. Lecture Notes in Computer Science 2(1973), 294-300, (Proc. of 1GI Conf. on Formal Languages and Automata Theory). Springer-Verlag, Berlin-Heidelberg-New York 1973.

[2] MAŁUSZYNSKI,J.: Regular structures in programming languages. Theory of Programming Languages Semantics and Compiling,(Proc. Conf., Frankfurt/Oder, 1974) - to appear in EIK

[3] SALOMAA,A.: Formal languages. Academic Press, New York 1973.

Q-algorithm), if for each instruction $[Q;R] \in \mathbb{P}$ there exist α in V, u_1, u_2 in V^* such that $Q = \{(\alpha w, u_1 w u_2) \mid w \in V^*\}$. PD-algorithms can be regarded as a particular case of Q-algorithms.

An algorithm $A = (\Omega, V, \sigma, \mathbb{P})$ is called a <u>complex</u> algorithm (abbr. C-algorithm), if for each instruction $[Q;R] \in \mathbb{P}$ there exist u_1 in V^+, u_2, u_3 in V^* such that $Q = \{(u_1 w, u_2 w u_3) \mid w \in V^*\}$. Similarly as above Q-algorithms constitute a particular case of C-algorithms.

A binary relation R in Ω is said to be <u>FC-computable</u> (<u>PD,Q, C-computable</u>) over a set $\mathfrak{A}$ of binary relations in Ω, if there exists a FC-algorithm (PD,Q,C-algorithm respectively) A with $Res_A = R$ and $E_A \subseteq \mathfrak{A} \cup \{I\}$. The set of all relations FC-computable (PD,Q,C-computable) over $\mathfrak{A}$ is denoted by $FC(\mathfrak{A})$ ($PD(\mathfrak{A}), Q(\mathfrak{A}), C(\mathfrak{A})$ respectively).

The following two theorems are proved in [1]:

<u>Theorem 2.1.</u> For any set $\mathfrak{A}$ of binary relations in Ω, $FC(\mathfrak{A})$ and $PD(\mathfrak{A})$ are closed under the operation of union, composition and iteration.

<u>Theorem 2.2.</u> For any set $\mathfrak{A}$ of binary relations in Ω

$$FC(FC(\mathfrak{A})) = FC(\mathfrak{A}) \ , \ PD(PD(\mathfrak{A})) = PD(\mathfrak{A}) \ .$$

The following theorems are proved in [3]:

<u>Theorem 2.3.</u> For any set $\mathfrak{A}$ of binary relations in Ω, $Q(\mathfrak{A})$ and $C(\mathfrak{A})$ are closed under the operation of union.

<u>Theorem 2.4.</u> For any set $\mathfrak{A}$ of binary relations in Ω

$$Q(PD(\mathfrak{A})) = Q(\mathfrak{A}) \ , \ C(PD(\mathfrak{A})) = C(\mathfrak{A}) \ .$$

3.ACCEPTORS AND LANGUAGES

Let Σ be an arbitrary (finite) alphabet to be fixed for the sequel. By $\mathfrak{A}_1$ we denote a family of binary relations in Σ^* defined as follows:

$$\mathfrak{A}_1 = \{R \mid (\exists a,b \in \Sigma \cup \{\varepsilon\})\ R = \{(axb,x) \mid x \in \Sigma^*\}\} .$$

The elements of $\mathfrak{A}_1$ are called <u>erasing relations</u>.

Let $\mathfrak{A}_2$ be a subfamily of $\mathfrak{A}_1$ such that

$$\mathfrak{A}_2 = \{R \mid (\exists a \in \Sigma \cup \{\varepsilon\})\ R = \{(ax,x) \mid x \in \Sigma^*\}\} .$$

The elements of $\mathfrak{A}_2$ are called <u>left-side erasing relations</u>.

By an <u>acceptor</u> we mean any algorithm $A = (\Omega, V, \sigma, \mathbb{P})$ such that $\Omega = \Sigma^*$ and $E_A \subseteq \mathfrak{A}_1$ (i.e. each elementary action of the algorithm A is an erasing relation).

An acceptor $A = (\Sigma^*, V, \sigma, \mathbb{P})$ is said to be a <u>left-side acceptor</u> if $E_A \subseteq \mathfrak{A}_2$ (i.e. if it has only left-side erasing relations as its elementary actions).

By a <u>language</u> acceptable by an acceptor $A = (\Sigma^*, V, \sigma, \mathbb{P})$ we mean the set $LA(A) = \{x \mid x \in \Sigma^* \ \&\ x\mathrm{Res}_A\, \varepsilon\}$.

A language L over an alphabet Σ is said to be <u>FC-acceptable</u> (<u>PD,Q,C-acceptable</u>), if there exists a FC-acceptor (PD,Q,C-acceptor respectively) $A = (\Sigma^*, V, \sigma, \mathbb{P})$ with $LA(A) = L$. The class of all FC-acceptable (PD,Q,C-acceptable) languages over Σ is denoted by $\mathcal{L}_{FC}$ ($\mathcal{L}_{PD}, \mathcal{L}_Q, \mathcal{L}_C$ - respectively).

A language L over Σ is called <u>left-side FC-acceptable</u> (<u>left-side PD,Q,C-acceptable</u>), if there exists a left-side FC-acceptor (left-side PD,Q,C-acceptor resp.) $A = (\Sigma^*, V, \sigma, \mathbb{P})$ with $LA(A) = L$. The class of all left-side FC-acceptable (left-side PD,Q,C-acceptable) languages is denoted by $\mathcal{L}_{LFC}$ ($\mathcal{L}_{LPD}, \mathcal{L}_{LQ}, \mathcal{L}_{LC}$ - resp.).

Let $\mathcal{L}_R, \mathcal{L}_{CF}$ and $\mathcal{L}_{CS}$ denote the classes of all regular, context-free and context-sensitive languages over an alphabet Σ respectively.

The following theorems about hierarchy of the classes of languages defined above can be proved.

Theorem 3.1. (MAZURKIEWICZ [2])

$$\mathcal{L}_{LFC} = \mathcal{L}_{R} \, , \; \mathcal{L}_{LPD} = \mathcal{L}_{CF} \, .$$

Theorem 3.2.

$$\mathcal{L}_{LFC} \subsetneq \mathcal{L}_{FC} \, .$$

The latter is proved by showing that the well known context-free language $L = \{x\hat{x} \mid x \in \{a,b,c\}^*\}$ belongs to $\mathcal{L}_{FC}$.

Theorem 3.3.

$$\mathcal{L}_{FC} \subseteq \mathcal{L}_{LPD} \, .$$

Theorem 3.4.

$$\mathcal{L}_{LPD} \subsetneq \mathcal{L}_{PD} \, , \; \mathcal{L}_{LPD} \subsetneq \mathcal{L}_{LQ} \, .$$

The latter is proved by showing that the context-sensitive language $L = \{a^n b^n a^n \mid n=1,2,\dots \;\&\; a,b \in \Sigma\}$ is both in $\mathcal{L}_{PD}$ and in $\mathcal{L}_{LQ}$.

Corollary 3.1.

$$\mathcal{L}_{FC} \subsetneq \mathcal{L}_{PD} \, .$$

Theorem 3.5. (MAZURKIEWICZ [3])

$$\mathcal{L}_{LQ} \subsetneq \mathcal{L}_{LC} \, .$$

Corollary 4.1. and the well known fact that $\mathcal{L}_{CS}$ is not closed under an arbitrary homomorphism imply immediately what follows:

Corollary 3.2.

$$\mathcal{L}_{LQ} \neq \mathcal{L}_{CS} \, .$$

Let $\longrightarrow$ and $\Longrightarrow$ denote the inclusions $\subseteq$ and $\subsetneq$ respectively. Now we can summarise the above theorems by the following diagram:

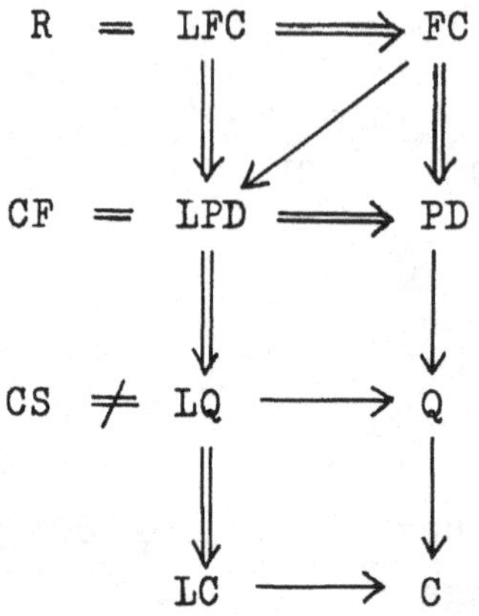

4.CLOSURE PROPERTIES OF CLASSES OF LANGUAGES

Theorems 2.1. and 2.3. imply what follows:

Theorem 4.1. $\mathcal{L}_{FC}$, $\mathcal{L}_{PD}$, $\mathcal{L}_{LQ}$, $\mathcal{L}_{Q}$, $\mathcal{L}_{LC}$ and $\mathcal{L}_{C}$ are closed under the operation of union.

Theorem 4.2. $\mathcal{L}_{FC}$, $\mathcal{L}_{PD}$, $\mathcal{L}_{Q}$ and $\mathcal{L}_{C}$ are closed under the operation of mirror reflection.

Let $\mathcal{L}$ be a class of languages over Σ . By a substitution of languages in $\mathcal{L}$ we mean any operation S defined recursively on the class of all languages over Σ in the following way:

1. $S(\{\varepsilon\}) = \{\varepsilon\}$,
2. $S(\{a\}) \in \mathcal{L}$ for each a in Σ ,
3. $S(\{aw\}) = S(\{a\}) \cdot S(\{w\})$ for any a in Σ and w in Σ^*,
4. $S(L) = \bigcup_{w \in L} S(\{w\})$ for any language L over Σ .

Theorem 4.3. $\mathcal{L}_{FC}$ is closed under any operation of substitution of regular languages.

The proof of the above theorem bases on Theorem 2.2..

Basing on Theorems 2.2. and 2.4. the following theorem can be proved:

Theorem 4.4. $\mathcal{L}_{PD}$, $\mathcal{L}_{LQ}$, $\mathcal{L}_{Q}$, $\mathcal{L}_{LC}$, $\mathcal{L}_{C}$ are closed under any operation of substitution of context-free languages.

Theorems 4.3. and 4.4. imply immediately what follows:

Corollary 4.1. $\mathcal{L}_{FC}$, $\mathcal{L}_{PD}$, $\mathcal{L}_{LQ}$, $\mathcal{L}_{Q}$, $\mathcal{L}_{LC}$, $\mathcal{L}_{C}$ are closed under any homomorphism.

REFERENCES

[1] BLIKLE,A.J.; MAZURKIEWICZ,A. An algebraic approach to the theory of programs, algorithms, languages and recursiveness. Mathematical Foundation of Computer Sciences (Int. Symp. and Sum. Sch., Warsaw, Jablonna, 1972).

[2] MAZURKIEWICZ,A. Algorithms and grammars.(to appear).

[3] OWSIANIECKA,W.A. Mazurkiewicz algorithms as a tool for defining formal languages.(in polish), unpublished doctoral dissertation.

COMPLEXITY AND NORMAL FORMS OF CONTEXT-FREE LANGUAGES.

A. Piricka
Mathematical Institute
Slovak Academy of Science

Obrancov mieru 41, 886 25 BRATISLAVA
Czechoslovakia

INTRODUCTION.

Descriptional complexity of languages is one of the interesting parts of language theory at the present time. The grammatical complexity of languages deals with those measures of complexity which are based on characteristic features of the underlying grammars.

In this paper we shall consider context-free grammars and languages only. Given a measure for grammars, its extension to the measure of languages depends on the class of grammars taken into consideration. We shall investigate the case that the measure depends on some of the classes of grammars in well-known normal forms. In this way we obtain so called bounded complexity measures. We shall study the relationships between bounded and unbounded complexity measures, where unbounded measures are defined with respect to the complete class of context-free grammars.

PRELIMINARIES.

1. DEFINITIONS. The basic definitions and notations of the theory of context-free grammars (cfg) and languages (cfl) are due to GINSBURG [2] .

We shall discuss here the following grammatical measures: *Var, Prod, Symb, Ind, Dep, Lev, NLev, Hei*. All of them are functions from the set of all cfg's to the set of integers. For a cfg $G = \langle V,\Sigma,P,\sigma\rangle$ we denote by $Var(G)$ the number of variables in G and by $Prod(G)$ the number of productions in G. $Symb(G)$ is the length of a cfg G, i.e. $Symb(G) = 2\ Prod(G) + \sum_{(A\to\alpha)\in P} |\alpha|$; $|\psi|$ denotes the length of the word ψ.

The measure *Ind* is defined as follows: Index of a derivation τ: $w_1, w_2, \ldots, w_s$ (abbreviated as $Ind(\tau)$) is the smallest integer j such that none of the words w_t, $1 \le t \le s$, has more than j occurrences of nonterminals. For $x \in L(G)$; $Ind(x) = \min \{ Ind(\tau)$: τ is a derivation of x from σ in G $\}$ and index of a grammar G is defined by $Ind(G) = \max \{Ind(x) : x \in L(G) \}$.

Further measures are based on the notion of the grammatical level. If $G = \langle V,\Sigma,P,\sigma\rangle$ is a cfg and A,B are variables we put $A \rhd B$ iff there are strings x,y such that $(A \to xBy) \in P$. Relation $\overset{*}{\rhd}$ is a reflexive and transitive closure of the relation $\rhd$. A subset $Q \subseteq P$ is said to be a grammatical level of G iff $(A \to \alpha) \in Q$ implies that $[\ (B \to \beta) \in Q$ is equivalent to $A \overset{*}{\rhd} B$ and $B \overset{*}{\rhd} A\ ]$. The number of variables on the left sides of the rules in a grammatical level Q is said to be depth of Q and is denoted by $Dep(Q)$. A grammatical level Q is termed nontrivial if $Dep(Q) > 1$. Let Q_1, Q_2 be levels of G. Then $Q_1 \ge Q_2$ iff there are $(A \to \alpha) \in Q_1$ and $(B \to \beta) \in Q_2$ such that $A \overset{*}{\rhd} B$.
$Dep(G) = \max \{Dep\ Q : Q$ is a grammatical level of $G\}$. $Lev(G)$ is the number of the grammatical levels in G , $NLev(G)$ is the number of nontrivial grammatical levels in G. Let G be a cfg and $Q_1, Q_2, \ldots, Q_r$ be levels of G such that $\sigma \in Q_1$. Then $Hei(Q_1)=1$, $Hei(Q_s)=h$ for $s>1$ iff there is

a Q_t such that $Hei(Q_t)=h-1$ and $Q_t \geq Q_s$. The height of a grammar G is defined by $Hei(G)=\max\{Hei(Q_t): t=1,2,\ldots,r\}$.

There are many ways how to associate a measure of complexity of languages with a given measure of grammars. A natural extension is for a given measure K and a particular language L to put $K(L)=\min\{K(G) : L(G)=L\}$. For ψ being a class of grammars $K_\psi(L)$ denotes the measure K bounded to ψ and is defined as follows $K_\psi(L)= \min\{K(G): G \in \psi, L(G)=L\}$.

In this paper some classes of normal form grammars are considered. Grammars of a class ψ are said to be in a normal form if for every cfl L, $\varepsilon \notin L$ there is a cfg $G \in \psi$ such that $L(G)=L$.

The following classes are considered:

$\mathcal{E}$ - ε-free grammars. (The productions of type $A \to \varepsilon$ are not admissible),

$\mathcal{R}$- ε-free grammars without productions of the type $A \to B$.

$\mathcal{P}$- class of perfectly reduced grammars. (A grammar $G= \langle V,\Sigma,P,\sigma \rangle$ is said to be perfectly reduced -see GRUSKA [3] - iff

i/ G is ε-free,

ii/ G is reduced (i.e. for each $A \in V-\Sigma$ there are $x,y,z \in \Sigma^*$ such that $\sigma \overset{*}{\Rightarrow} xAy \overset{*}{\Rightarrow} xzy$),

iii/ there are no productions of the form $A \to B$, $B \in V-\Sigma$ in P,

iv/ $A \rhd A$ for $A \in V-(\Sigma \cup \{\sigma\}$).)

$\mathcal{Ch}$- class of grammars in Chomsky normal form. (The only productions which are admissible are of types $A \to BC$ and $A \to a$; $A,B,C \in V-\Sigma$, $a \in \Sigma$).

2. FORMULATION OF THE PROBLEM. If ψ is any subset of the set of all cfg's then trivialy $K_\psi(L) \geq K(L)$ for $L=L(G)$, $G \in \psi$. The aim of this paper is to answer for the class $\psi \in \{\mathcal{E}, \mathcal{R}, \mathcal{P}, \mathcal{Ch}\}$ of grammars in normal form the following questions: How big can the difference $K_\psi(L)-K(L)$ be for $L \in \{L=L(G): G \in \psi\}$? Does there exist a recursive function ν

such that $K_\psi(L) \leq \nu(K(L))$?

CLASSIFICATIONS BOUNDED TO $\mathcal{E}$ AND $\mathcal{R}$.

These problems have been first discussed by GRUSKA [5] for $\psi = \mathcal{E}$. Results for the class $\psi = \mathcal{R}$ have been mentioned in [4]. If $K_\psi(L) = K(L)$ for all $L = L(G)$, $G \in \psi$ then the class ψ is said to be K-dense.

THEOREM 1. i/ Class $\mathcal{E}$ is K-dense for $K \in \{Var, Ind, Dep, Lev, NLev, Hei\}$.

ii/ For every integer n there is a language L_n such that $Prod(L_n) = 2$ and $Prod_\varepsilon(L) \geq n$.

iii/ $Symb_\varepsilon(L) \leq 10\ Symb(L)$ for any language $L \not\ni \varepsilon$.

THEOREM 2. i/ Class $\mathcal{R}$ is K-dense for $K \in \{Var, Ind, Dep, Lev, NLev, Hei\}$.

ii/ $K_{\mathcal{R}}(L) \leq \frac{1}{2} K^2(L)$ for K being $Prod$ or $Symb$, and this estimation cannot be improved more then by a constant.

CLASSIFICATIONS BOUNDED TO $\mathcal{P}$ AND $\mathcal{Cl}$.

For the class of perfectly reduced grammars there is a simple algorithm how to transform a given cfg into an equivalent perfectly reduced grammar.(See [3].).Using that algorithm and a fact that there is exactly one perfectly reduced grammar generating a given finite language one can obtain

THEOREM 3. i/ $\mathcal{P}$ is K-dense for $K \in \{Var, Dep, Lev, NLev, Hei\}$.

ii/ For every integer n there is a finite language L_n such that $Prod(L_n) = 3$ and $Prod\ (L_n) \geq n$.

iii/ For every integer n there is a regular language L_n such that $Ind(L_n) = 2$ and $Ind_{\wp}(L_n) = n$.

iv/ For every integer n there is a finite language L_n such that $Symb_{\wp}(L_n) > n\ Symb(L_n)$.

It can be shown that the following languages satisfy the theorem 3: The language $L_n = (a \cup b)^n$ for the measures *Prod* and *Symb* and the language $L_n = \{a^{i_1} b c^{i_1} \dots a^{i_n} b c^{i_n} : i_t \in N, 1 \le t \le n\}$ for the measure *Symb*.

Because of the restriction on the length of rules of the grammars in Chomsky normal form relationships between $K_{\mathcal{Ch}}(L)$ and $K(L)$ have quite different character. The class $\mathcal{Ch}$ is not K-dense for any above defined measure of complexity.

THEOREM 4. For any $K \in \{Var, Prod, Lev, NLev, Dep, Hei\}$ and any integer n there is a language L_n with property $K(L_n) = 1$ and $K_{\mathcal{Ch}}(L_n) = n$.

The following languages satisfy the theorem 4:

i/ if $K \in \{Var, Prod, Lev, Hei\}$ then the finite language $L_n = \{a^{2^{n-1}}\}$.

ii/ if $K = Dep$ then the linear language generated by grammar

$$A \to a^{2i} b B a^{2i-1} b$$

$$B \to a^{2i} b B a^{2i-1} b \mid \varepsilon ; \quad 1 \le i \le n-1 .$$

iii/ if $K = NLev$ then the linear language $L_n = L(G_n) - \varepsilon$, where G_n is given by rules

$$A \to a^{2i} b A\, a^{2i-1} b \mid A \qquad 1 \le i \le n-1$$

$$A \to a^{2n} b A\, a^{2n-1} b \mid \varepsilon$$

Quite different situation is in the case of measures *Ind* and *Symb*. The following theorem indicates that the restriction to the class $\mathcal{Ch}$ cannot change the measure *Ind* very much.

THEOREM 5. i/ $Ind(L) \le Ind_{\mathcal{Ch}}(L) \le 1 + Ind(L)$ for all languages L, $\varepsilon \notin L$.

ii/ There is a finite language over one-element alphabet such that $Ind_{\mathcal{Ch}}(L) = 1 + Ind(L)$ and a linear language such that $Ind(L) = Ind_{\mathcal{Ch}}(L)$.

In the case of the measure $Symb_{\mathcal{CR}}$ we have two results. The first one is for the case that the alphabet is fixed and the second result is for general case. Here by $\mathcal{L}_{CF(n)}$ we denote the class of cfl´s over n-symbol alphabet and by $\mathcal{L}_{\varepsilon F}$ the complete class of ε-free cfl´s.

THEOREM 6. i/ Let $L \in \mathcal{L}_{CF}$. Then $Symb_{\mathcal{CR}}(L) < 7\ Symb_{\mathcal{R}}(L)$.

ii/ Let $L \in \mathcal{L}_{CF(n)}$. Then $Symb_{\mathcal{CR}}(L) < 4\ Symb_{\mathcal{R}}(L) + 3n$.

The constants 7 and 4 in these estimations are the smallest possible.

REFERENCES.

[1] Brauer,W. On grammatical complexity of context-free languages. Proceedings of MFCS´73,(1973) High Tatras, 191-196.

[2] Ginsburg,S. The mathematical theory of context-free languages. McGraw-Hill,New York 1966.

[3] Gruska,J. Some classifications of context-free languages. Information and Control 14(1969), 152-179.

[4] Gruska,J. Descriptional complexity of context-free languages. Proceedings of MFCS´73,(1973) High Tatras, 71-83.

[5] Gruska,J. A note on ε-rules in context-free grammars.(In print)

THE AXIOMATIZATION PROBLEM OF A THEORY OF LINEAR LANGUAGES

G. Wechsung

Sektion Mathematik der Friedrich-Schiller-Universität Jena

69 Jena, DDR, Schillerstraße

INTRODUCTION

An important problem of formal language theory is the algebraic characterization of suitable classes of languages. The first example has been given by S. C. KLEENE ([2]) in 1956 who proved the class of regular languages over X to be the closure of the set of all finite subsets of X^* with respect to the operations $\cup$, $\cdot$, * (union, concatenation and iteration). Ten years later A. SALOMAA found a finite axiom system for the KLEENEan algebra ([3]). In 1971 J. P. McWHIRTER ([4]), J. GRUSKA ([1]) and M. K. YNTEMA ([5]) found independently algebraic characterizations of the class of contextfree languages. These algebras, however, have the property that the number of necessary operations grows with growing cardinality of the underlying alphabet.

In this paper we are concerned only with linear languages. If we introduce one additional symbol $*$ which is, roughly speaking, a marker of the middle of the words it is possible to regard the class of linear languages over X as an algebra with three operations $\cup$, $\circ$, $^{\circledast}$ independently from the cardinality of X. $\circ$ is not far from the new operations introduced by GRUSKA, McWHIRTER and YNTEMA.

Two different theories describing the equivalence of linear terms will be regarded. Both are not effective enumerable and hence fail to be axiomatizable.

COMPOSITION OF LINEAR LANGUAGES

This section of the paper gives a motivation of our subsequent definition of the multiplication operation for linear languages. Let A,B be linear languages generated by grammars G_A, G_B and let $A_{i_1} \longrightarrow u_{i_1}, \ldots , A_{i_s} \longrightarrow u_{i_s}$ be the terminal rules of G_A. We fixe arbitrary factorizations

$$(F) \qquad \begin{array}{c} u_{i_1} = u_{i_1 1} u_{i_1 2} \\ \vdots \\ u_{i_s} = u_{i_s 1} u_{i_s 2} \end{array}$$

and form the new rules

$$A_{i_1} \longrightarrow u_{i_1 1} S u_{i_1 2}$$
$$\vdots$$
$$A_{i_s} \longrightarrow u_{i_s 1} S u_{i_s 2}$$

where S is the start symbol of G_B. These rules, the nonterminal rules of G_A and all the rules of G_B constitute a new grammar G_F which describes a certain superposition of the languages A and B. A special case of this superposition is the concatenation of regular sets. However, in the case of linear languages we have many different operations: We have to insert strings from B into certain positions of those parts of strings from A which arise by terminal substitution. These positions cannot be found without using an auxiliary symbol # not belonging to X. For this reason we turn from A to a language $A_F^{\#}$ substituting the terminal rules $A_{i_j} \longrightarrow u_{i_j}$ by the new rules $A_{i_j} \longrightarrow u_{i_j 1} \# u_{i_j 2}$. The index F shows that $A_F^{\#}$ depends on the factorization (F). If the homomorphism h from $(X \cup \{\#\})^*$ onto X^* is defined by $h(\#) = e$, $h(x_i) = x_i$ for $x_i \in X$ we have $h(A_F^{\#}) = A$. Two different factorizations give rise to different languages $A_F^{\#} \neq A_{F'}^{\#}$. But because on $h(A_F^{\#}) = h(A_{F'}^{\#})$ the only difference between them consists in a different preparation for a composition with a third language B.

THE ALGEBRA $\mathfrak{L}$

The last remarks justify the following definitions.

__Def.__: $W =_{df} X^* \cdot \{\#\} \cdot X^*$, $W_r =_{df} X^* \cdot \{\#\}$, $W_l =_{df} \{\#\} \cdot X^*$,

$$\mathfrak{P}(W) =_{df} \{U : U \subseteq W\} ,$$

$$E =_{df} \{U : U \subseteq W \wedge U \text{ finite}\} ,$$

$$E_r =_{df} \{U : U \subseteq W_r \wedge U \text{ finite}\} ,$$

$$E_l =_{df} \{U : U \subseteq W_l \wedge U \text{ finite}\} .$$

__Def.__: For $A, B \subseteq W$ we define

$$A \circ B =_{df} \{a_1 b a_2 : a_1 \# a_2 \in A \wedge b \in B\}$$

$$A^{\circledast} =_{df} \bigcup_{i=0}^{\infty} K_i \ , \ K_0 =_{df} \{\#\} \ , \ K_{i+1} =_{df} K_i \circ A.$$

__Corollary__: $\mathfrak{W} =_{df} [\mathfrak{P}(W), \cup, \circ, ^{\circledast}]$ is an algebra.

Corollary 2: In $\mathcal{W}$ the following identities are valid (A,B,C are arbitrary elements from $\mathcal{R}(W)$):

(I)	$A \cup (B \cup C) = (A \cup B) \cup C$	(II)	$A \cup A = A$
(III)	$(A \cup B) = (B \cup A)$	(IV)	$A \cup \emptyset = A$
(V)	$A \circ (B \circ C) = (A \circ B) \circ C$	(VI)	$\emptyset \circ A = \emptyset$
(VII)	$A \circ (B \cup C) = (A \circ B) \cup (A \circ C)$	(VIII)	$(A \circ B) \cup C = (A \circ C) \cup (B \circ C)$
(IX)	$\emptyset^{\circledast} \circ A = A$	(X)	$A^{\circledast} = \emptyset^{\circledast} \cup (A^{\circledast} \circ A)$
(XI)	$A^{\circledast} = (\emptyset^{\circledast} \cup A)^{\circledast}$.		

The proofs are straightforward.

Let Γ be the closure operator of $\mathcal{W}$ and let us define $L =_{df} \Gamma(E)$, $L_r =_{df} \Gamma(E_r)$, $L_l =_{df} \Gamma(E_l)$. Then the following statements are obvious.

Corollary 3: (1) The algebras $\mathcal{L}_r =_{df} [L_r, \cup, \circ, ^{\circledast}]$ and $\mathcal{L}_l =_{df} [L_l, \cup, \circ, ^{\circledast}]$ are subalgebras of the algebra $\mathcal{L} =_{df} [L, \cup, \circ, ^{\circledast}]$.

(2) $\mathcal{L}_r$ is isomorphic to the algebra $\mathcal{R} =_{df} [R, \cup, \cdot, ^{*}]$ of the algebra of the regular sets over X.

(3) $\mathcal{L}_l$ is anti-isomorphic with respect to $\circ$ to $\mathcal{R}$.

By the same arguments as in the case of the regular sets we can prove the following statements.

Lemma 1: Let $A, C \subseteq W$, $\# \notin A$. Then the equation (1)

(1) $$Z = (A \circ Z) \cup C$$

has the only solution

$$Z = A^{\circledast} \circ C.$$

Theorem 1: $A \in L$ if and only if there are a finite number of sets $A_1 = A, A_2, \ldots, A_n \subseteq W$ and finite sets $U_{ij}, V_i \subseteq W$ with the property $\# \notin U_{ij}$ and which satisfy the system

(2) $$A_i = \bigcup_{j=1}^{n} U_{ij} \circ A_j \cup V_i, \quad i = 1, \ldots, n.$$

Taking into account the well known close relationship between equations of the form (2) and corresponding (linear) grammars we can state the last result in the following form

Theorem 2: If $A \in L$ then $h(A)$ linear over X.

If B linear over X then every A with $h(A) = B$ belongs to L.

Remark: Theorem 2 shows that $\mathcal{L}$ can be regarded as algebra of the linear languages over X although the elements of $\mathcal{L}$ differ from linear languages in that their words contain exactly one more additional symbol # (the substitution marker). Thus we succeeded in giving an inner algebraic description of the class of the linear languages without using the notions "grammar" or "automaton".

THE LINEAR THEORIES

In order to set up a logical theory of the linear languages we use as <u>individual constants</u> the elements of

$$I =_{df} \{0\} \cup \{\xi_i : 1 \le i \le n\} \cup \{\eta_i : 1 \le i \le n\} ,$$

furthermore the unary <u>function constant</u> $\langle\ \rangle$ and the binary function constants + and $\cdot$ and the binary <u>predicate constants</u> $\approx$, $\sim$.

Definition of <u>linear terms</u>:

Linear terms are exactly the elements of the free algebra with the operations $+$, $\cdot$, $\langle\ \rangle$ and the generating system I. We design the set of these terms by Θ while Θ_r, Θ_l design the subsets of Θ which are generated by the sets $\{0, \xi_1, \dots, \xi_n\}$ resp. $\{0, \eta_1, \dots, \eta_n\}$.

Definition of <u>formulas</u>:

If α and β are linear terms $\alpha \approx \beta$ and $\alpha \sim \beta$ are called formulas. Other formulas don't exist.

Definition of the <u>standard interpretation</u> φ :

φ is the homomorphism from the free algebra $[\Theta, +, \cdot, \langle\rangle]$ onto the algebra $\mathcal{L}$ ($+$, $\cdot$, $\langle\ \rangle$ correspond to $\cup$, $\circ$, $\circledast$ respectivly) defined by

$$\varphi(0) = \emptyset , \qquad \varphi(\xi_i) = \{X_i \#\} , \qquad \varphi(\eta_i) = \{\# X_i\} .$$

Definition of <u>validity</u>:

$$\alpha \approx \beta \text{ is valid } \Leftrightarrow_{df} \varphi(\alpha) = \varphi(\beta)$$
$$\alpha \sim \beta \text{ is valid } \Leftrightarrow_{df} h(\varphi(\alpha)) = h(\varphi(\beta))$$

$\mathcal{T}_1 =_{df} \{ \alpha \sim \beta : \alpha \sim \beta \text{ is valid} \}$ is called the weak theory of the linear languages. $\mathcal{T}_2 = \{ \alpha \approx \beta : \alpha \approx \beta \text{ is valid} \}$ is called the strong theory of the linear languages. (If in the definition of $\mathcal{T}_1$ resp. $\mathcal{T}_2$ the range of α , β is restricted to Θ_r (or Θ_l) then we get theories of the right-linear (or left-linear) languages which coincide with SALOMAA's theory ([3]) and hence are axiomatizable.)

SUMMARY OF RESULTS

<u>Theorem 3</u>: $\mathcal{T}_1$ is not decidable, if card X $\ge$ 2.

<u>Theorem 4</u>: $\bar{\mathcal{T}}_1 =_{df} \{ \alpha \sim \beta : \alpha \sim \beta \text{ is not valid} \}$ is enumerable.

As a corollary we conclude that $\mathcal{T}_1$ is not enumerable and hence not axiomatizable.

<u>Theorem 5</u>: $\mathcal{T}_2$ is not decidable.

Theorem 6: $\mathcal{T}_2$ is not axiomatizable.

REFERENCES

(1) GRUSKA, J. A characterization of context-free languages. Journal Comput. Syst. Sci. 5 (1971), 353 - 364.

(2) KLEENE, S. C. Representation of events in nerve-nets and finite automata. Automata Studies, Princeton, 1956, 3 - 41.

(3) SALOMAA, A. Two complete axiom systems for the algebra of regular events. JACM 13, Nr. 1 (January 1966), 158 - 169.

(4) McWHIRTER, J. P. Substitution expressions. Journal Comput. Syst. Sci. 5 (1971), 629 - 673.

(5) YNTEMA, M. K. Cap expressions for context-free languages. Information and Control 18 (1971), 311 - 318.

A LATTICE-THEORETICAL APPROACH TO PROBLEM-SOLVING

Jozef Kelemen
Department of Theoretical Cybernetics
Komensky University, 816 31 Bratislava
Czechoslovakia

ABSTRACT

The starting point of this paper is Sandewall's conception of using multiple-input and multiple-output operators in problem-solving (see [3]). A formal definition of the general transformation problem is given. The conventional search-tree (or graph) is generalized into a new structure (lattice-structure with a special relation).

INTRODUCTION

The problem environments for problem-solving methods always include a (nonempty) set P of <u>abstract objects</u> and a (nonempty) finite set Q of <u>operators</u> (see [3]).

We consider that the states of a problem are (in the most general case) described by finite nonempty subsets of the set P.

We shall consider an <u>operator</u> as a mapping

$$q_i : D_i \longrightarrow 2^P \quad ,$$

where $D_i \subseteq 2^P$, $D_i \neq \emptyset$ is a domain of the operator, given usually implicitly by "conditions of applicability" of the operator. We shall denote the image of the mapping q_i by $q_i(D_i)$.

We introduce the following condition:

$$\text{if } P' \in D_i \text{ , then } q_i(P') \neq P' \quad .$$

(If $q_i(P') = P'$, then application of the operator is "nonproductive".)

Example: In the case of state description by the first-order predicate calculus methods (well-known system STRIPS;see[1]) each state is described by finite number of axioms.The set P may be understood as a set of (some) well-formed first-order formulas.Let q be an operator (for example operator in the system STRIPS).Elements of q(P') are axioms of the theory,resulting from the theory with axioms P' after application of the operator q.

A problem is given by a finite nonempty subset R (the initial set) of the set P,whose elements describe the initial state of problem,and by a finite nonempty set $M \subseteq P$ (the target set),each element of which describes one target state of the problem.We denote a problem given in such a way by (R,M).

GENERAL TRANSFORMATION PROBLEM

Let (R,M) be a problem.Let $Q_s = (q_1,\dots,q_n)$ be a finite sequence of operators (not necessary different).Let $P_s = (P_1,\dots,P_n)$ be a finite sequence of subsets of P.
Define inductively:

$$K_1 = R$$
$$K_{i+1} = q_i(P_i') \cup K_i - \bigcup_{j=1}^{i} P_j' \quad , \quad 1 \le i \le n-1 \ .$$

The general transformation problem consists in the determination of sequences Q_s and P_s with the properties:

(1) $$P_i' \in D_i \cap 2^{K_i} \ , \quad 1 \le i \le n-1$$

(2) $$K_n \cap M \neq \emptyset \ .$$

The sequence Q_s (if it exists) is called a solution of the problem (R,M).If $M \cap R \neq \emptyset$,then we put Q_s to be empty and the problem (R,M) is trivial.That means,there is no need for application of an operator for its solution.In the case of nonempty Q_s we use exactly operators from Q_s to solve the problem.

SOLUTION-STRUCTURE AND EXISTENCE OF SOLUTION

Let $(S, \sqcup, \sqcap)$ be the free lattice generated by the set P.Let x and y are elements of S.We define a relation $x \sqsubseteq y$ to mean $x = x \sqcap y$ (or $y = x \sqcup y$).

We define on $(S, \sqcup, \sqcap)$ operators corresponding to the operators from Q as follows:

Let $q_i \in Q$.The operator on $(S, \sqcup, \sqcap)$,corresponding to the operator $q_i \in Q$,is a mapping

$$\bar{q}_i : D_i \longrightarrow S \quad ,$$

where

$$\bar{D}_i =_{df} \{ s \in S \mid s = s_1 \sqcup \dots \sqcup s_m \ \& \ \{s_1, \dots, s_m\} \in D_i \}$$

and

$$\bar{q}_i(\bar{D}_i) =_{df} \{ z \in S \mid z = z_1 \sqcap \dots \sqcap z_k \ \& \ \{ z_1, \dots, z_k\} \in q_i(D_i)\}.$$

The mapping $\bar{q}_i$ is defined in figure 1.If $A = \{a_1, \dots, a_h\} \subset S$ then we write $\bigsqcup A$ for $a_1 \sqcup \dots \sqcup a_h$, and similarly $\bigsqcap A$.

Fig.1:

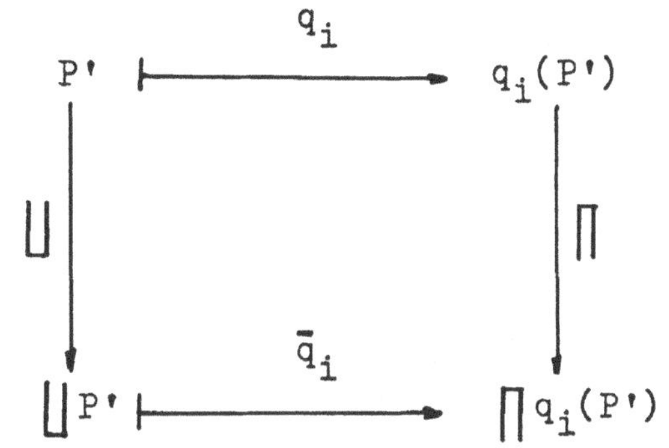

where $q_i \in Q$, $P' \in D_i$, $\bigsqcup P' \in \bar{D}_i$, $q_i(P') \in q_i(D_i)$ and $\bigsqcap q_i(P') \in \bar{q}_i\ (\bar{D}_i)$.

Let $\bar{Q}$ be the set of all operators corresponding to the operators from Q.The following axiom defines a transitive relation < on S:

$$(\forall \bar{q}_i \in \bar{Q})\ (\forall s \in S)\quad \bar{q}_i(s) < s\ ,$$

when $\bar{q}_i(s)$ is defined.

By means of partial ordering relation $\sqsubset$ and transitive relation < we define a relation $\underline{r}$:

Let $x, y \in S$.

$$x\ \underline{r}\ y \quad \Leftrightarrow_{df} (\ x \sqsubset y\ ) \vee (\ x < y\ )\ .$$

Relation $\underline{r}$ is transitive.

We shall call the pair $[(S, \sqcup, \sqcap);\ \underline{r}\ ]$ a solution-structure.

Now we shall give a necessary and sufficient condition of existence of a solution Q_s to a problem (R,M).

Theorem:

Problem (R,M) is solvable (Q_s exist) iff $\bigsqcap M\ \underline{r}\ \bigsqcup R$.

Proof: In [2] .

That condition is an analogy to the condition of existence of a path in the graph corresponding to the problem environment in conventional problem-solving theory.

The general method to solve the given problem (R,M) is to inspect nodes in the set S until one has identified a finite set $S' \subseteq S$ which forms a "bridge" between $\bigsqcap M$ and $\bigsqcup R$.Succesive nodes on this "bridge" are to satisfy the relation $\underline{r}$,and the desired result $\bigsqcap M\ \underline{r}\ \bigsqcup R$ then follows by the transitivity of $\underline{r}$.

REFERENCES

[1] FIKES,R.E.;NILSSON,N.J. STRIPS:A New Approach to the Application of Theorem Proving to Problem Solving , Artificial Intelligence 2 (1971) , 189

[2] KELEMEN,J. A generalized approach to problem-solving , (in Slovak) , Master Thesis , 1974

[3] SANDEWALL,E.J. Concepts and methods for heuristic search , Proc.Intern.Joint Conf.Artificial Intelligence,Washington,D.C., 1969

ON THE EQUIVALENCE OF PLANAR GRAMMARS AND PARALLEL PICTURE PROCESSING ALGORITHMS

Zenon Kulpa
Institute of Organization,
Management and Control Sciences
00-818 Warsaw, POLAND

1. INTRODUCTION

The purpose of this note is to sketch a way to a formal proof of the processing equivalence of planar grammars (originated by KIRSCH [3] for picture description) and simple, fully nondeterministic picture processing algorithms (in the sense of BLIKLE, MAZURKIEWICZ [2]) consisting of position-invariant (parallel) local picture processing operations (NARASIMHAN [7], ROSENFELD [8], KULPA [4]).

The equivalence we are to prove has been intuitively recognized by picture processing men [10] but no formal proof has appeared up to now. Only for string grammars there have been presented some related equivalence results (ROSENFELD [9]).

On the way to prove the main theorem we also state two theorems (on the equivalence properties of planar grammars) which are interesting results by themselves.

The style of introducing planar grammars will be similar to BIELIK's [1], and of the algorithms - that of BLIKLE, MAZURKIEWICZ [2]. For the lack of space, the proofs will not be given, but only sketched; the details can be found in KULPA [5].

2. PRELIMINARIES

Let us recall briefly a notation for algebra of relations (after BLIKLE, MAZURKIEWICZ [2]). Let X,Y,Z,W be sets, then $R \subseteq X \times Y, Q \subseteq Y \times Z$ are (binary) <u>relations</u>; $R \circ Q$ (shortly: RG) denotes a <u>composition of relations</u>; xRy means $(x,y) \in R$; WR denotes an <u>image</u> of W under R and RW is a <u>coimage</u> of W. Thus, RY is a <u>domain</u> and XR a <u>range</u> of R. The same notation will also be used for functions. R^* denotes a (reflexive and transitive) <u>closure</u> of R; for any set X, I_X denotes an <u>identity</u> (or diagonal) relation in X (i.e. aI_Xb iff $a=b$ and $a,b \in X$). Thus, I_WR is a <u>left restriction</u> and RI_W a <u>right restriction</u> of R to W.

We will denote by J the set of integers, call the set $U = J \times J$ a raster and any $(i,j) \in U$ a point. Two points (a,b), (i,j) are adjacent iff $|a-i| + |b-j| = 1$. A subset S of U is connected if any two its points can be connected by a chain of consecutively adjacent points lying entirely in S. A function $d_{ij}: U \to U$ such that $d_{ij}((x,y)) = (x+i, y+j)$ is called a displacement.

We denote by A a finite set called the alphabet and by T some subset of A called the terminal alphabet. Let $\# \notin A$ denotes a blank symbol and let $A_\# = A \cup \{\#\}$.

Definition 1. An abstract picture (or planar word) over the alphabet A is any function $p: U \to A_\#$ such that pA is a bounded (i.e. finite in this case) set of points. The set of all abstract pictures over A we will denote by $\Pi(A)$, (or Π, if A is known).

A picture p is called connected if pA is connected. A subpicture is a function $I_N p$, where N is any bounded subset of U, and p - a picture. The set of all subpictures will be denoted by $\pi(A)$, (briefly : π). By $\pi_N(A)$ we will denote the set of all subpictures with domain N.

3. PLANAR GRAMMARS

Definition 2. A generalized plannar grammar is a system $G = (A_\#, T, R)$, where A,T: alphabets (as defined above), and $R \subseteq \pi(A) \times \pi(A)$ a finite set of rules, such that for every $(u,v) \in R$, $uA_\# = vA_\#$ and $Uu \neq \{\#\}$ (i.e. the rule never creates anything on the completely empty place).

Definition 3. For some $x,y \in \Pi$ we say that x immediately produces y (written $x \underset{G}{\Longrightarrow} y$ or simply xGy) in G iff there exists a rule $r = (u,v) \in R$ and a displacement d_{ij} such that:

(i) $I_Q x = d_{ij} u$ and $I_Q y = d_{ij} v$,

(ii) $I_{U \setminus Q} x = I_{U \setminus Q} y$, where $Q = d_{ij} uA_\# = d_{ij} vA_\#$.

That is, xGy if y can be obtained from x by replacement of some subpicture of x which is identical to (appropriately displaced) left side of the rule r, by the (appropriately displaced) right side of r, leaving the rest of x unchanged.

Definition 4. The resulting relation of the grammar G is a relation $Res_G = G^* I_{\Pi(T)} \subseteq \Pi(A) \times \Pi(T)$; i.e x Res_G y if xG^*y and y is a picture over the terminal alphabet T.

Definition 5. Two grammars G and H are called W-equivalent, where W - some alphabet, iff $I_{\Pi(W)} Res_G = I_{\Pi(W)}$ Res H.

Definition 6. A planar language defined by G is a set $L_G =$

$= \sum Res_G$, where $\sum = \{\sigma \in \prod(\{s\}) \mid s \in A \setminus T \wedge card(\sigma \circ \{s\}) = 1\}$ is a set of so-called starting pictures,i.e. pictures having only one non--blank starting symbol s of the grammar.

The above formulations are, in a sense, noneffective. Namely, there is no effective way to check if some rule is in fact applicable to some arbitrary picture (because of infiniteness of the raster). It can be overcome if one requires the pictures to be connected or provides some endmarkers on the raster. Let us consider the first possibility.

Let us introduce a new, 'visible-blank' symbol $\sqcup$, let $\sqcup \in A$ and denote by $T_\sqcup$ the new terminal alphabet $T_\sqcup = T \cup \{\sqcup\}$. Introduce the 'erasing function' $h: \prod(T_\sqcup) \rightarrow \prod(T)$, such that h(x) is a picture obtained from x by replacing all occurrences of $\sqcup$ in x by $\#$, leaving other symbols unchanged.

Theorem 1. For every planar grammar $G = (A_\#, T, R)$ there exists a grammar $G' = (A_\#, T_\sqcup, R')$ such that:

(i) $Res_G = Res_{G'} \, h$ and

(ii) $(\forall (u,v) \in R')$ ($uA_\# = vA_\#$ is connected) and

(iii) if $x \in \prod$ is connected, so is every y such that $xG'^* y$.

I.e. G' is equivalent to G with respect to erasing of visible-blank symbol (i) and has rules connected (ii) and all pictures produced in the course of derivation in G' are connected, provided the starting one was (iii).

Proof. For every rule $(u,v) \in R$ change $\#$'s occuring in v to $\sqcup$'s. Then replace it by a set of rules by changing some (or all or none) of $\#$'s occuring in u to $\sqcup$'s in all possible combinations. Then make rules connected replacing every one by a set of rules resulting by connecting its (possibility) disconnected parts by connected chains with all possible assignments of symbols from $A_\# \cup T_\sqcup$ in the left and $A \cup T_\sqcup$ in the right side respectively. The set R' results. ▩

So we will restrict ourselves from now on only to connected pictures and rules, without loss of (at least practical) generality. Although not explicitly stated, the theorem has also been assumed by MILGRAM, ROSENFELD [6].

4. PARALLEL PICTURE PROCESSING ALGORITHMS

A picture processing operation (p.p.o.) is a function $\varphi: \prod \rightarrow \prod$. A p.p.o. $s_{ij} = \{(S, d_{ij}S) \mid S \in \prod\} \subseteq \prod \times \prod$, where d_{ij} - displacement is called a shifting operation.

Definition 7. A position-invariant operation is a p.p.o. ψ such that for every shifting operation s_{ij} holds $\psi s_{ij} = s_{ij}\psi$.

Definition 8. A (parallel) local operation is a p.p.o. λ such that there exists a bounded subset $N \subseteq U$ and the function f_λ : $\pi_N(A_\#) \longrightarrow A_\#$ such that for every $S \subseteq \Pi$:

$$\lambda(S) = \{((i,j),\ f_\lambda(I_N d_{ij} S)) \mid (i,j) \in U\}.$$

The set of all parallel local operations will be denoted by $\Lambda(\Pi)$.

It is easy to see that every local operation λ is fully characterized by the function f_λ. Also every local operation is position-invariant (but not the converse). Without loss of generality we may also assume N to be connected and including the point (0,0). Such an operation can be performed in parallel, i.e. one can perform the computation prescribed by f_λ for every point simultaneously.

Definition 9. A simple, fully nondeterministic parallel picture processing algorithm is a finite-control MAZURKIEWICZ's algorithm $= (\Pi(A), \{a\}, a, L)$ (BLIKLE, MAZURKIEWICZ [2]) such that

$$L = \{(\{(a,a)\}, \lambda_i) \mid \lambda_i \in \lambda_{\mathfrak{A}} \subseteq \Lambda(\Pi)\} \cup \{(\{(a,\varepsilon)\},\ I_{\Pi(T)})\}.$$

Thus, instructions of the algorithm have the same initial and terminal label a and action consisting of some parallel local operation λ_i, except for one (terminating) instruction assuring the algorithm to stop 'by end' if it produces some terminal picture. Therefore, the resulting relation is:

$$Res_{\mathfrak{A}} = \Lambda^*_{\mathfrak{A}} I_{\Pi(T)}, \text{ where } \Lambda_{\mathfrak{A}} = \bigcup \lambda_{\mathfrak{A}}$$

5. EQUIVALENCE PROOF

As it is clearly seen from the above, the only important differences between the rules of a planar grammar (Sec. 3) and λ-actions of parallel picture processing algorithms (Sec. 4) lie in the points:

(i) The rule can change several symbols at the point of its applicability, while the f_λ-function - only one.

(ii) The rule applies at a given moment at one place (although may be applicable at several places); λ changes simultaneously all points that are to be changed (i.e. acts in parallel).

Therefore, the first step in our way to prove the equivalence will be:

Theorem 2. For every planar grammar $G = (A_\#, T, R)$ there exists an A-equivalent grammar $G' = (A'_\#, T, R')$ such that, for every rule $q = (u,v) \in R'$:

(i) $(\exists!\ (m,n)\in Q)\ u(m,n) \neq v(m,n)$, i.e. a rule changes only one symbol;

(ii) if $x \underset{q}{\Rightarrow} y$ then $(\exists!\ d_{ij}) I_Q x = d_{ij}u$, i.e. a rule can be applied at at most one place, where $Q = d_{ij}uA'_{\#}$.

Proof. For (i) use the technique developed in proving the 'two-point-rules' theorem by BIELIK [1, Th. 1.4.3]. The ROSENFELD's [9, p. 289] technique for asserting analogical fact for string grammars is not applicable to two dimensions (cf. KULPA [5]). For (ii), add as symbols the 'primed' original symbols, modify rules to have exactly one primed symbol at the left and at most one at the right hand side. Introduce new rules only 'moving' a prime over the picture. Start with exactly one primed symbol in the picture (there is somewhat fine point with the equivalence as defined by Definition 5, but it can be overcome. No difficulty will arise if the equality of defined planar languages is considered instead). This method is equivalent to ROSENFELD's [9, Th. 5]. ▩

Theorem 3 (the equivalence). For any planar grammar $G = (A_{\#}, T, R)$ there exists a simple, fully nondeterministic parallel picture algorithm $\mathfrak{A} = (\Pi(A'), \{a\}, a, L)$ such that it is A-equivalent to G, and conversely - for any such an algorithm there exists an A'-equivalent planar grammar G.

Proof. The first part almost directly follows from the Theorem 2. The proof of the second part is less immediate. It requires one to construct a planar grammar which in effect applies the f_λ-functions of $\mathfrak{A}$ 'in parallel' (ROSENFELD 9), by modelling with appropriate rules, for every λ_i of $\mathfrak{A}$, a 'square' spiral extending scan of the current picture, marking the places where f_{λ_i} changes a symbol, and after recognizing that the whole picture was scanned (the use of Theorem 1 is indispensable) - scanning backwards, changing symbols at marked points and ending at the begining of the scan with a condition allowing to start a scan for another λ_i. An enormous number of new symbols and rules is required. For details see KULPA [5]. ▩

6. CONCLUSIONS

The above result can encourage some adherents of linguistic methods of picture recognition ('all the processing can be made grammatical!'), but it also is an argument for their opponents ('the algorithms do it better than your intricate and unnatural grammars!') - see [10]. The author, although promotes the linguistic (or structural) trend in pattern recognition, in this case inclines to the second opinion. If grammars can be of any use to describing or processing pictures on the raster level, another apparatus, e.g. that by SIROMONEY et al. [11] looks better suited here than above-described KIRSCH's planar grammars are.

REFERENCES

[1] BIELIK, A. Sterowana generacja słów języków planarnych (in Polish). M.Sc. Thesis, supervised by Z. Kulpa, Warsaw 1973.

[2] BLIKLE, A.; MAZURKIEWICZ, A. An algebraic approach to the theory of programs, algorithms, languages and recursiveness, Proc. MFCS 72, Warsaw 1972.

[3] KIRSCH, R.A. Computer interpretation of English text and picture patterns, IEEE Trans. on El. Comp. EC-13 (1964).

[4] KULPA, Z. A picture processing system PICTURE ALGOL 1204, Proc. VII Yugoslav Intern. Symp. FCIP 72, Bled 1972.

[5] KULPA, Z., Automatyczne przetwarzanie i analiza informacji graficznej o złożonej strukturze (in Polish), Ph.D. Thesis, Warsaw 1974 (in preparation).

[6] MILGRAM, D.L.; ROSENFELD, A. Array automata and array grammars, Information Processing 71 (Proc. IFIP 71 Congr.), North-Holland, Amsterdam 1972.

[7] NARASIMHAN, R. Labeling schemata and syntactic description of pictures, Information and Control 7 (1964).

[8] ROSENFELD, A. Picture processing by computer. Academic Press, New York 1969.

[9] ROSENFELD, A. Isotonic grammars, parallel grammars, and picture grammars, Machine Intellig. 6, Edinb. Univ. Press, Edinburgh 1971.

[10] Panel discussion on 'Are Picture Grammars of Any Use in Scene Analysis?', in: Graphic languages, North-Holland, Amsterdam 1972.

[11] SIROMONEY, G.; SIROMONEY, R.; KRITHIVASAN, K. Picture languages with array rewriting rules, Information and Control 22 (1973).

COMBINATORIAL ASPECTS OF INFORMATION STORAGE AND RETRIEVAL

Witold Lipski, Jr
Institute of the Foundations of Electronics
Technical University of Warsaw

1. INTRODUCTION

In the paper we present a combinatorial theory motivated by problems arising in organizing the memory of a computer while storing there a system of information storage and retrieval.

To describe these problems let us recall some basic definitions concerning information storage and retrieval (i.s.r.) systems from MAREK and PAWLAK [8,9]. An i.s.r. system is a quadruple consisting of the set of objects (records) X, the set of descriptors A, an equivalence R_I on the set of descriptors, the equivalence classes of which are indexed by the set of attributes I, and a function U which associates a subset of X to each descriptor. The function U can be extended in a natural way to the set of terms $\mathcal{T}$ - expressions constructed of descriptors and the operators $+, \cdot, \sim$ (interpreted as union, intersection and complementation). Thus each term t is given its value $\|t\| \subseteq X$ (in other words $\|t\|$ is the set of records relevant to a query t).

Usually there is a class of distinguished terms $\mathcal{H} \subseteq \mathcal{T}$ which are for some reasons important (e.g. there is a simple method for obtaining from their values the value of each other term). We are then interested in a file organization, i.e. an arranging of the objects in storage locations, satisfying the following two conditions:

(i) There is no redundant storage of objects, each object is stored exactly once.

(ii) The value of each distinguished term is a set consisting of objects stored in adjacent storage locations.

Such an organization enables us to retrieve the values of distinguished terms especially easily.

To each family of terms $\mathcal{H}$ there corresponds a family of subsets of X $\mathcal{M} = \{\|t\| : t \in \mathcal{H}\}$. It will be convenient to deal with families of sets instead of families of terms. Since each object is stored exactly once, it may be identified with its storage location.

To describe the adjacency of objects an additional structure on X is needed. We take as this structure a partial function $S: X \longrightarrow X$ (<u>successor function</u>) interpreted as follows: $S(x)$ is the object inspected immediately after x. Thus S corresponds to a method of retrieval which is, in turn, usually determined by the physical structure of storage media. We say that the objects of a set $B \subseteq X$ are adjacent if they form a <u>segment</u>, i.e. if there is an $x \in X$ such that $B = \{x, S(x), \ldots, S^{|B|-1}(x)\}$, where $S^0(x) = x$, $S^{n+1}(x) = S(S^n(x))$.

Our main problem is to find conditions under which a given family of sets $\mathcal{M}$ admits such a successor function that each $M \in \mathcal{M}$ is a segment, and to construct such a function. Problems of this type were considered - for a special "linear" form of S - by FULKERSON and GROSS [2], GHOSH [3] and - in the general case - by LIPSKI and MAREK [6,7] and LIPSKI [5].

Throughout the text the standard mathematical notation is used. In particular $\mathcal{P}(X)$ denotes the power set (i.e. the set of all subsets) of X, $|B|$ is the cardinality of a set B, $\mathcal{D}S$ and $\mathcal{R}S$ are the domain and the range of a function S. All the sets under consideration are assumed to be finite.

2. ADMISSIBLE FAMILIES OF SETS

Let X be a set and let $S \subseteq X \times X$ be a partial function such that $S(x) \neq x$ for each $x \in \mathcal{D}S$. It will be convenient to treat $\langle X,S \rangle$ as a directed graph with the set of vertices X and the set of edges S. $\langle X,S \rangle$ will be referred to as an <u>f-graph</u> on X (S - a <u>successor function</u>, $S(x)$ - the <u>successor</u> of x). A set $B \subseteq X$ is a <u>segment</u> in $\langle X,S \rangle$ if either $B = \emptyset$ or $B = \{x, S(x), \ldots, S^{|B|-1}(x)\}$ for a certain $x \in X$. Such an x is a <u>head</u> of B and $S^{|B|-1}(x)$ is the <u>end</u> corresponding to this head. If in addition $S^{|B|}(x) = x$ then B is a <u>cycle</u>. A segment B is <u>proper</u> if it contains no cycles, <u>final</u> if $B \setminus \mathcal{D}S \neq \emptyset$ or $B = \emptyset$, and <u>initial</u> if $B \setminus \mathcal{R}S \neq \emptyset$ or $B = \emptyset$. If a non-empty segment B is not a cycle then its unique head and end are denoted by $h(B)$ and $e(B)$ respectively.

An f-graph $\langle X,S \rangle$ is <u>linear</u> if X is a final segment in it, <u>cyclic</u> if X is a cycle in it (or $|X| \leqslant 1$), <u>acyclic</u> if there is no cycle in it. These three types of f-graphs correspond to different types of storage, e.g. magnetic tape (linear f-graphs), drums, disks (cyclic f-graphs), random-access memory organized by using chaining techniques (all the types of f-graphs including the generic one). We denote by $\mathcal{F}(X)$ the class of all f-graphs on X and by $\mathcal{LF}(X)$, $\mathcal{CF}(X)$, $\mathcal{AF}(X)$ the subclasses of linear, cyclic and acyclic f-graphs.

We say that a family $\mathcal{M} \subseteq \mathcal{P}(X)$ is <u>segmental</u> (<u>*-segmental</u>) over $\langle X,S\rangle$ if each $M \in \mathcal{M}$ is a segment (final segment) in $\langle X,S\rangle$. Our basic problem is to find out, for a given $\mathcal{M} \subseteq \mathcal{P}(X)$, whether there exists an f-graph $\langle X,S\rangle$ such that $\mathcal{M}$ is segmental over it. If $\mathcal{M}$ admits such an f-graph then it is called <u>admissible</u>.

<u>Example 2.1</u>. Let $X = \{1,2,3,4\}$, $\mathcal{M} = \{\{1,2\},\{2,3\},\{3,1\},\{2,4\},\{3,4\}\}$. It is easy to see that $\mathcal{M}$ is not admissible and that each its proper subfamily, e.g. $\mathcal{M} \setminus \{\{1,2\}\}$, is admissible (see Fig. 1.).

Now we shall define the <u>classes of admissibility</u>. To this end let $\mathcal{E} \subseteq \mathcal{F}(X)$ be a class of f-graphs (e.g. $\mathcal{F}(X)$, $\mathcal{LF}(X)$, $\mathcal{CF}(X)$, $\mathcal{AF}(X)$) and let $\mathcal{R} \subseteq \mathcal{P}(X) \times \mathcal{F}(X)$ be a relation, e.g. $\mathcal{S}$ or $\mathcal{S}^*$ defined as follows:

$\langle M,G\rangle \in \mathcal{S} \longleftrightarrow$ M is a segment in G,

$\langle M,G\rangle \in \mathcal{S}^* \longleftrightarrow$ M is a final segment in G.

We define a class $c(\mathcal{E},\mathcal{R})$ of families of subsets of X as follows:

<u>Definition 2.2</u>.

$$\mathcal{M} \in c(\mathcal{E},\mathcal{R}) \longleftrightarrow (\exists G \in \mathcal{E})(\forall M \in \mathcal{M}) \ \langle M,G\rangle \in \mathcal{R}$$

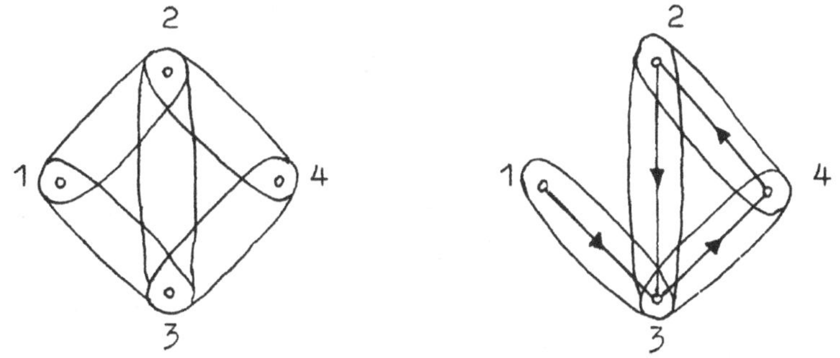

Fig. 1. An example of a non-admissible family and its admissible subfamily

The following classes of admissibility will play an important role in further considerations:

$Adm(X) = c(\mathcal{F}(X),\mathcal{S})$ - the class of <u>admissible</u> families

$\mathcal{L}(X) = c(\mathcal{LF}(X),\mathcal{S})$ - the class of <u>linear</u> families

$\mathcal{L}^*(X) = c(\mathcal{LF}(X),\mathcal{S}^*)$ - the class of <u>*-linear</u> families

$\mathcal{C}(X) = c(\mathcal{CF}(X),\mathcal{S})$ - the class of <u>cyclic</u> families

$\mathcal{A}(X) = c(\mathcal{AF}(X),\mathcal{S})$ - the class of <u>acyclic</u> families

$\mathcal{A}^*(X) = c(\mathcal{AF}(X),\mathcal{S})$ - the class of <u>*-acyclic</u> families

We say that $\langle X,S\rangle$ realizes the admissibility (linearity, etc.)

of $\mathfrak{M}$ if $\langle X,S\rangle$ is an f-graph (linear f-graph, etc.) such that $\mathfrak{M}$ is segmental over it.

<u>Definition 2.3</u>. (a) Let $\mathfrak{M}\subseteq\mathcal{P}(X)$ and let $C\subseteq X$. The <u>trace</u> of $\mathfrak{M}$ on C (in symbols $\mathfrak{M}|_C$) is a family of subsets of C defined as follows:

$$\mathfrak{M}|_C = \{M\cap C\colon M\in\mathfrak{M}\}.$$

(b) Let $\langle X,S\rangle$ be an f-graph and let $C\subseteq X$. The <u>contraction</u> of $\langle X,S\rangle$ to C (in symbols $\langle X,S\rangle|_C$) is an f-graph on C defined as follows:

$$\langle X,S\rangle|_C = \langle C,S_C\rangle,$$
$$\mathfrak{D}S_C = \{y\in C\colon\ (\exists k>0)\quad S^k(y)\in C \ \&\ S^k(y)\neq y\},$$
$$S_C(x) = S^{k_x}(x) \qquad \text{for each } x\in\mathfrak{D}S_C, \text{ where}$$
$$k_x = \min\{k\colon k>0 \ \&\ S^k(x)\in C\}.$$

Contraction and trace are used to describe the deletion of objects in an i.s.r. system.

<u>Theorem 2.4</u>. (a) The contraction preserves the type (linear, cyclic, acyclic) of an f-graph.
(b) If $\mathfrak{M}$ is segmental (*-segmental) over $\langle X,S\rangle$ then $\mathfrak{M}|_C$ is segmental (*-segmental) over $\langle X,S\rangle|_C$. ∎

<u>Corollary 2.5</u>. Let $\mathfrak{M}\subseteq\mathcal{P}(X)$ and let $C\subseteq X$. If $\mathfrak{M}\in\mathcal{K}(X)$ then $\mathfrak{M}|_C\in\mathcal{K}(C)$, where $\mathcal{K}(X)$ is one of the following classes of admissibility: $\mathrm{Adm}(X)$, $\mathcal{L}(X)$, $\mathcal{C}(X)$, $\mathcal{A}(X)$, $\mathcal{L}^*(X)$, $\mathcal{A}^*(X)$. ∎

There are some relations between different classes of admissibility. It is easy to see that $\mathrm{Adm}(X)$ is the greatest of them and that $\mathcal{L}^*(X)$ contains exactly these families which are linearly ordered by $\subseteq$. The following "local characterization" of $\mathcal{A}^*(X)$ can also be proved: $\mathfrak{M}\in\mathcal{A}^*(X)$ iff for each $M\in\mathfrak{M}$ $\mathfrak{M}|_M\in\mathcal{L}^*(M)$ (for $\mathcal{A}(X)$ and $\mathcal{L}(X)$ the analogous statement is false). $\mathcal{L}(X)\subseteq\mathcal{C}(X)\cap\mathcal{A}(X)$ but the equality does not hold since we have the following

<u>Example 2.6</u>. (WĄSOWSKA [10]) Let $X=\{1,2,\ldots,5\}$ and let $\mathfrak{M} = \{\{1,2,3\},\{1,3,4,5\},\{1,5\},\{3,4\}\}$. $\mathfrak{M}$ is cyclic and acyclic (see Fig. 2.) but it can be easily checked that it is not linear.

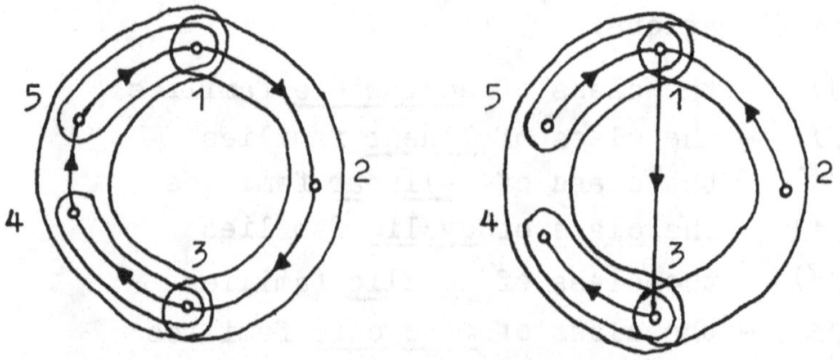

Fig. 2. An example of a family $\mathfrak{M}\in(\mathcal{C}(X)\cap\mathcal{A}(X))\setminus\mathcal{L}(X)$.

Definition 2.7. Let $\mathfrak{M} = \{M_1, M_2, \ldots, M_n\} \subseteq \mathcal{P}(X)$ and let $\varepsilon_1, \varepsilon_2, \ldots, \varepsilon_n \in \{0,1\}$. Sets of the form

$$S_{\mathfrak{M}}(\varepsilon_1, \varepsilon_2, \ldots, \varepsilon_n) = M_1^{\varepsilon_1} \cap M_2^{\varepsilon_2} \cap \ldots \cap M_n^{\varepsilon_n} \qquad (M_i^0 = X \setminus M_i,\ M_i^1 = M_i)$$

are called components (cf. KURATOWSKI and MOSTOWSKI [4]). We denote the set of all non-empty components of $\mathfrak{M}$ by $\mathcal{S}(\mathfrak{M})$.

It can be proved (cf. [5,6]) that for $\mathcal{K}(X) = \mathrm{Adm}(X), \mathcal{L}(X), \mathcal{C}(X), \mathcal{A}(X)$ $\mathfrak{M} \in \mathcal{K}(X)$ iff $\mathfrak{M} \cup \mathcal{S}(\mathfrak{M}) \in \mathcal{K}(X)$, moreover the admissibility (of class $\mathcal{K}(X)$) depends only on the fact which components are non-empty: if two families $\mathfrak{M} \subseteq \mathcal{P}(X)$, $\mathfrak{N} \subseteq \mathcal{P}(Y)$ can be indexed so that $S_{\mathfrak{M}}(\varepsilon_1, \varepsilon_2, \ldots, \varepsilon_n) = \emptyset$ iff $S_{\mathfrak{N}}(\varepsilon_1, \varepsilon_2, \ldots, \varepsilon_n) = \emptyset$ ($\mathfrak{M}$ and $\mathfrak{N}$ are similar) then $\mathfrak{M} \in \mathcal{K}(X)$ iff $\mathfrak{N} \in \mathcal{K}(Y)$.

3. DEPENDENT SETS AND EQUIVALENT FAMILIES

Let a family $\mathfrak{M}$ be segmental over $\langle X,S\rangle$. Then some sets belonging to $\mathcal{B}(\mathfrak{M})$, the Boolean algebra generated by $\mathfrak{M}$, are "forced to be segments", e.g. if $\langle X,S\rangle$ is linear and M,N are segments then $M \cap N$ is a segment in $\langle X,S\rangle$. This will be studied in a systematic way in the present section.

Let us fix a class $\mathcal{E}(X)$ of f-graphs on X and a relation of segmentality $\mathcal{R} \subseteq \mathcal{P}(X) \times \mathcal{F}(X)$ – $\langle M,G\rangle \in \mathcal{R}$ means: M is a segment (of a specified type) in the f-graph G. Define for any $\mathfrak{M} \subseteq \mathcal{P}(X)$, $\mathcal{G} \subseteq \mathcal{F}(X)$

$$\mathfrak{M}^* = \{G \in \mathcal{E}(X) : \quad (\forall M \in \mathfrak{M}) \quad \langle M,G\rangle \in \mathcal{R}\}$$

$$\mathcal{G}^* = \{M \in \mathcal{P}(X) : \quad (\forall G \in \mathcal{G}) \quad \langle M,G\rangle \in \mathcal{R}\}$$

$\mathfrak{M}^*$ is the set of all f-graphs "good" for $\mathfrak{M}$ and $\mathcal{G}^*$ is the greatest family such that each $G \in \mathcal{G}$ is "good" for it. The mappings $\mathfrak{M} \longmapsto \mathfrak{M}^*$ and $\mathcal{G} \longmapsto \mathcal{G}^*$ have the following properties:

(i) $\mathfrak{M} \subseteq \mathfrak{N} \rightarrow \mathfrak{M}^* \supseteq \mathfrak{N}^*$ $\qquad$ $\mathcal{G} \subseteq \mathcal{H} \rightarrow \mathcal{G}^* \supseteq \mathcal{H}^*$

(ii) $\mathfrak{M} \subseteq \mathfrak{M}^{**}$ $\qquad$ $\mathcal{G} \subseteq \mathcal{G}^{**}$

(iii) $\mathfrak{M}^{***} = \mathfrak{M}^*$ $\qquad$ $\mathcal{G}^{***} = \mathcal{G}^*$

being an example of a Galois connection (see COHN [1]). Let $\mathcal{K}(X) = c(\mathcal{E}(X), \mathcal{R})$ be the class of admissibility determined by $\mathcal{E}(X)$ and $\mathcal{R}$ (see Def. 2.2.).

Definition 3.1. (a) We define an operator $\mathbb{D}_{\mathcal{K}} : \mathcal{P}(\mathcal{P}(X)) \rightarrow \mathcal{P}(\mathcal{P}(X))$ as follows:

$$\mathbb{D}_{\mathcal{K}}(\mathfrak{M}) = \mathfrak{M}^{**} \quad \text{for each } \mathfrak{M} \subseteq \mathcal{P}(X).$$

(b) M is $\mathcal{K}$-dependent on $\mathfrak{M}$ if $M \in \mathbb{D}_{\mathcal{K}}(\mathfrak{M})$.

(c) $\mathcal{M}$ and $\mathcal{N}$ are <u>$\mathcal{K}$-equivalent</u> (in symbols $\mathcal{M} \underset{\mathcal{K}}{\sim} \mathcal{N}$) if $\mathcal{M}^* = \mathcal{N}^*$.

We shall show the interpretation of the above notions taking $\mathcal{K}(X) = \mathrm{Adm}(X)$ (in this case we omit "Adm" in the notation). $\mathbb{D}(\mathcal{M})$ contains exactly these subsets of X which are "forced" to be segments in each f-graph realizing the admissibility of $\mathcal{M}$. M is dependent on $\mathcal{M}$ if M is a segment in each f-graph realizing the admissibility of $\mathcal{M}$. $\mathcal{M} \sim \mathcal{N}$ if the same f-graphs realize the admissibility of $\mathcal{M}$ and $\mathcal{N}$.

The following simple lemma follows from general properties of Galois connections (see COHN [1]).

<u>Lemma 3.2</u>. $\mathbb{D}_{\mathcal{K}}$ is a closure operator, i.e. for each $\mathcal{M}, \mathcal{N} \subseteq \mathcal{P}(X)$

(a) $\mathcal{M} \subseteq \mathcal{N} \rightarrow \mathbb{D}_{\mathcal{K}}(\mathcal{M}) \subseteq \mathbb{D}_{\mathcal{K}}(\mathcal{N})$,

(b) $\mathcal{M} \subseteq \mathbb{D}_{\mathcal{K}}(\mathcal{M})$,

(c) $\mathbb{D}_{\mathcal{K}}(\mathbb{D}_{\mathcal{K}}(\mathcal{M})) = \mathbb{D}_{\mathcal{K}}(\mathcal{M})$. ∎

Notice that in general $\mathbb{D}_{\mathcal{K}}(\emptyset) \neq \emptyset$ and $\mathbb{D}_{\mathcal{K}}(\mathcal{M} \cup \mathcal{N}) \neq \mathbb{D}_{\mathcal{K}}(\mathcal{M}) \cup \mathbb{D}_{\mathcal{K}}(\mathcal{N})$.

<u>Lemma 3.3</u>. The following conditions are equivalent:

(a) $\mathcal{M} \underset{\mathcal{K}}{\sim} \mathcal{N}$

(b) $\mathbb{D}_{\mathcal{K}}(\mathcal{M}) = \mathbb{D}_{\mathcal{K}}(\mathcal{N})$

(c) Each $M \in \mathcal{M}$ is $\mathcal{K}$-dependent on $\mathcal{N}$ and each $N \in \mathcal{N}$ is $\mathcal{K}$-dependent on $\mathcal{M}$. ∎

It is easy to see that $\mathcal{M} \underset{\mathcal{K}}{\sim} \mathbb{D}_{\mathcal{K}}(\mathcal{M})$ and that $\mathcal{M} \notin \mathcal{K}(X)$ implies $\mathbb{D}_{\mathcal{K}}(\mathcal{M}) = \mathcal{P}(X)$. If we want to prove that $\mathcal{M} \in \mathcal{K}(X)$ it is sufficient to show that $\mathcal{N} \in \mathcal{K}(X)$ for a certain $\mathcal{N}$ such that $\mathbb{D}_{\mathcal{K}}(\mathcal{N}) \supseteq \mathcal{M}$ (e.g. $\mathcal{N} \underset{\mathcal{K}}{\sim} \mathcal{M}$). In order to prove that $\mathcal{M} \notin \mathcal{K}(X)$ we can take instead of $\mathcal{M}$ any family $\mathcal{N}$ with $\mathcal{N} \subseteq \mathbb{D}_{\mathcal{K}}(\mathcal{M})$ (e.g. $\mathcal{N} = \mathbb{D}_{\mathcal{K}}(\mathcal{M})$).

<u>Definition 3.4</u>. Two sets M, N <u>overlap</u> (in symbols $M \between N$) if $M \cap N \neq \emptyset \;\&\; M \setminus N \neq \emptyset \;\&\; N \setminus M \neq \emptyset$.

The following simple lemma enables us to find some (in general not all) sets dependent on a family:

<u>Lemma 3.5</u>. Let $M, N \subseteq X$ and let $x \in X$. Then

(a) $\emptyset$ and $\{x\}$ are dependent on each $\mathcal{M} \subseteq \mathcal{P}(X)$.

(b) $\emptyset, \{x\}$ and X are $\mathcal{L}$-dependent on each $\mathcal{M} \subseteq \mathcal{P}(X)$.
$M \cap N$ is $\mathcal{L}$-dependent on $\{M, N\}$.
If $M \cap N \neq \emptyset$ then $M \cup N$ is $\mathcal{L}$-dependent on $\{M, N\}$.
If $M \between N$ then $M \cap N$, $M \cup N$, $M \setminus N$, $N \setminus M$ are $\mathcal{L}$-dependent on $\{M, N\}$.

(c) $\emptyset, \{x\}, X$ and $X \setminus \{x\}$ are $\mathcal{C}$-dependent on each $\mathcal{M} \subseteq \mathcal{P}(X)$.
$X \setminus M$ is $\mathcal{C}$-dependent on $\{M\}$.
If $M \cap N \neq \emptyset$ then $M \cup N$ is $\mathcal{C}$-dependent on $\{M, N\}$.

If $M \cup N \neq X$ then $M \cap N$ is $\mathcal{C}$-dependent on $\{M,N\}$.
If $M \oplus N$ then $M \cup N$, $M \setminus N$, $N \setminus M$ are $\mathcal{C}$-dependent on $\{M,N\}$.

(d) $\emptyset$ and $\{x\}$ are $\mathcal{A}$-dependent on each $\mathcal{M} \subseteq \mathcal{P}(X)$.
$M \cap N$ is $\mathcal{A}$-dependent on $\{M,N\}$. ∎

Though the above lemma does not provide a complete description of the operators $\mathbb{D}_{\mathfrak{X}}$, nevertheless from the analysis of the algorithm given in Section 5 we can deduce the following "completeness theorem":

Theorem 3.6. Let $\mathcal{M} \in \mathcal{L}(X)$. Then $\mathbb{D}_{\mathcal{L}}(\mathcal{M})$ is the least family $\mathcal{N} \subseteq \mathcal{P}(X)$ satisfying the following conditions:

(i) $\mathcal{M} \subseteq \mathcal{N}$, $\emptyset, X \in \mathcal{N}$, $\{x\} \in \mathcal{N}$ for each $x \in X$,

(ii) if $M,N \in \mathcal{N}$ and $M \oplus N$ then $M \cup N$, $M \cap N$, $M \setminus N$, $N \setminus M \in \mathcal{N}$. ∎

Using this theorem we can construct $\mathbb{D}_{\mathcal{L}}(\mathcal{M})$ for each linear family $\mathcal{M}$ without knowing any f-graph realizing its lineatity.

By Lemma 3.5. we can construct, for a given family $\mathcal{M}$, a certain family $\mathcal{M}' \underset{\mathfrak{X}}{\sim} \mathcal{M}$ which has a more convenient structure, i.e. such a structure which enables us to find easily an f-graph "good" for it. As an example we shall consider the following important

Theorem 3.7. For every cyclic family $\mathcal{M} \subseteq \mathcal{P}(X)$ there exists a $\mathcal{C}$-equivalent linear family $\mathcal{M}'$. We can take as $\mathcal{M}'$ any family of the following form:

$$\mathcal{M}' = \{M^{\varepsilon(M)} : M \in \mathcal{M}\}$$

where $\varepsilon(M) = 1$ if $x_0 \notin M$ or 0 otherwise, and x_0 is a fixed element of X (recall that $M^1 = M$, $M^0 = X \setminus M$).

Proof: Each $M \in \mathcal{M}'$ is $\mathcal{C}$-dependent on $\mathcal{M}$ since $M \in \mathcal{M}$ or $X \setminus M \in \mathcal{M}$. Similarly each $N \in \mathcal{M}$ is $\mathcal{C}$-dependent on $\mathcal{M}'$. By Lemma 3.3. $\mathcal{M} \underset{\mathcal{C}}{\sim} \mathcal{M}'$. $\mathcal{M}'$ is linear since $x_0 \notin \bigcup \mathcal{M}'$ and the edge $\langle x_0, S(x_0)\rangle$ may be deleted from each f-graph $\langle X,S\rangle$ realizing the cyclicity of $\mathcal{M}'$. ∎

The above theorem gives a simple method of reducing the problem of finding an f-graph realizing the cyclicity of a family to the analogous problem for the linear case.

Example 3.8. Let $X = \{1,2,\dots,9\}$ and let $\mathcal{M} = \{\{1,4,5,8\}, \{2,3,5,6,9\}, \{2,4,7\}, \{2,4,6,7,8\}\}$. We take $x_0 = 8$ and we obtain $\mathcal{M}' = \{\{2,3,6,7,9\}, \{2,3,5,6,9\}, \{2,4,7\}, \{1,3,5,9\}\}$. Then we construct an f-graph $\langle X,S\rangle$ realizing the linearity of $\mathcal{M}'$ (see the algorithm in Section 5) and we add the edge $\langle e(X), h(X)\rangle$ (see Fig. 3.). The resulting f-graph realizes the cyclicity of $\mathcal{M}'$, and consequently of $\mathcal{M}$.

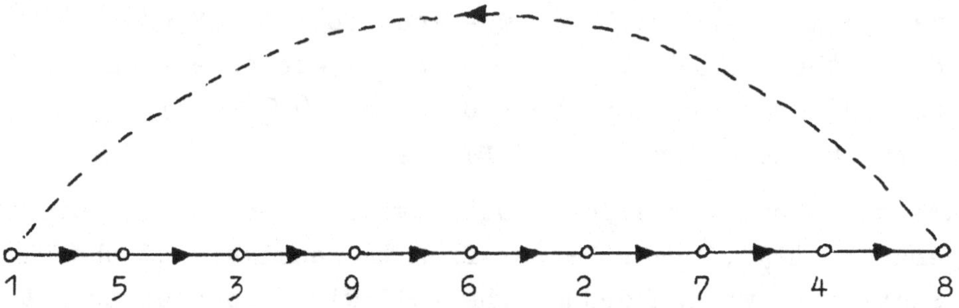

Fig. 3. Constructing an f-graph for a cyclic family of sets.

In a similar way we can construct for a given family $\mathcal{M}$ a $\mathcal{C}$-equivalent family $\mathcal{M}''$ such that $\bigcap \mathcal{M}'' \neq \emptyset$. To this end we take $\mathcal{M}'' = \{X \setminus M : M \in \mathcal{M}'\}$.

4. DECOMPOSITION THEOREM

This section is based on an idea of FULKERSON and GROSS [2]. It will be shown that the investigation of the linearity (cyclicity, etc.) of a family of sets can be reduced to similar problems for certain subfamilies of this family.

Definition 4.1. Let $\mathcal{M} \subseteq \mathcal{P}(X)$.

(a) The overlap graph $\mathcal{O}(\mathcal{M})$ is a nondirected graph with $\mathcal{M}$ as the set of vertices, two vertices M, N joined by an edge iff $M \between N$.

(b) A family $\mathcal{B} \subseteq \mathcal{M}$ is a block of $\mathcal{M}$ if $\mathcal{B}$ is the set of vertices of a component of $\mathcal{O}(\mathcal{M})$.

(c) We define a partial ordering $\leqslant$ on the set of blocks of $\mathcal{M}$ as follows:

$$\mathcal{B}_1 \leqslant \mathcal{B}_2 \longleftrightarrow (\exists M_1 \in \mathcal{B}_1)(\exists M_2 \in \mathcal{B}_2) \quad M_1 \subseteq M_2 .$$

(d) A block $\mathcal{B}$ of $\mathcal{M}$ is maximal if it is a maximal element in the ordering $\leqslant$, i.e. if there is no block $\mathcal{B}' > \mathcal{B}$.

Theorem 4.2. (a) A family $\mathcal{M}$ is linear iff all its blocks are linear.

(b) A family $\mathcal{M} \subseteq \mathcal{P}(X)$ such that $X \notin \mathcal{M}$ is cyclic in exactly two cases:

(i) All the blocks of $\mathcal{M}$ are linear (and consequently $\mathcal{M}$ is linear).

(ii) There is exactly one maximal block of $\mathcal{M}$ and this block is cyclic. All the other blocks are linear.

(c) A family $\mathcal{M}$ is acyclic iff all maximal blocks are acyclic and all the other blocks are linear.

Proof: In order to prove the necessity of the above conditions let us notice that the blocks of $\mathfrak{M}$, being subfamilies of $\mathfrak{M}$, are in the class of admissibility of $\mathfrak{M}$. Moreover, the union of each non-maximal block is contained in a certain set of $\mathfrak{M}$. This set is a segment in each f-graph realizing the linearity (cyclicity, etc.) of $\mathfrak{M}$ (it is not a cycle since we excluded the case $X \in \mathfrak{M}$ in (b)), consequently each non-maximal block must be linear. Two cases in (b) are caused by the fact that, unlike for the other classes, the union of two cyclic families $\mathfrak{M}_1$, $\mathfrak{M}_2$ such that $\bigcup \mathfrak{M}_1 \cap \bigcup \mathfrak{M}_2 = \emptyset$ need not be cyclic.

The sufficiency follows from the fact that the ordering (by a successor function) of the elements of any component is immaterial. In particular we may take such an ordering of each component of each maximal block that all the blocks of "depth" two are segmental, then, if necessary, we modify the ordering of each component of each block of "depth" two in such a way that all the blocks of "depth" three are segmental, and so on. ∎

The construction in the proof of sufficiency in the above theorem can serve as an effective algorithm for the decomposition of the problem of finding an f-graph realizing the linearity (cyclicity, etc.) of a family of sets.

5. AN ALGORITHM FOR CONSTRUCTING AN F-GRAPH REALIZING THE LINEARITY OF A FAMILY OF SETS

In virtue of Theorem 4.2. we may restrict ourselves to the case when $\mathfrak{M} \subseteq \mathcal{P}(X)$ consists of one block. Without loss of generality we may also assume that $\bigcup \mathfrak{M} = X$. Our algorithm constructs a family $\mathfrak{N} \in \mathcal{L}^*(X)$ such that each f-graph realizing the $*$-linearity of $\mathfrak{N}$ realizes the linearity of $\mathfrak{M}$ (for more details see [5]).

<u>Step 1</u>. We find a minimal "connected covering" $\mathfrak{M}_0 \subseteq \mathfrak{M}$, i.e. a minimal (with respect to $\subseteq$) family $\mathfrak{M}' \subseteq \mathfrak{M}$ such that

(i) $\bigcup \mathfrak{M}' = X$,

(ii) $\mathcal{O}(\mathfrak{M}')$ (see Def. 4.1.a) is connected.

To this end we check for each $M \in \mathfrak{M}$ whether $\mathfrak{M} \setminus \{M\}$ satisfies (i) and (ii) and, if so, delete M from $\mathfrak{M}$. The resulting family $\mathfrak{M}_0$ is a minimal "connected covering" and $\mathcal{O}(\mathfrak{M}_0)$ has the form of an elementary path (if $\mathfrak{M} \in \mathcal{L}(X)$). Let $M_0 \in \mathfrak{M}_0$ be one of its endpoints. It is easy to see that M_0 is a final or initial segment in each f-graph realizing the linearity of $\mathcal{M}$.

Step 2. Having the set M_0 we can produce another final segments (we can restrict ourselves to the case when they are final since $\langle X,S\rangle$ can be replaced, if necessary, by $\langle X,S^{-1}\rangle$). To this end we construct a family $\mathcal{N}$ - the least family $\mathcal{N}' \subseteq \mathcal{P}(X)$ such that

(i) $M_0 \in \mathcal{N}'$

(ii) If $M \in \mathcal{N}' \,\&\, N \in \mathcal{M} \,\&\, M \cap N \neq \emptyset \,\&\, N \setminus M \neq \emptyset$ then $M \cup N,\ M \setminus N \in \mathcal{N}'$.

It is easy to see that $\mathcal{N} \in \mathcal{L}^*(X)$ (if $\mathcal{M} \in \mathcal{L}(X)$) and that for each $M \in \mathcal{M}$ there are two sets $N_1, N_2 \in \mathcal{N}$ such that $M = N_2 \setminus N_1$ (recall that $\mathcal{M}$ is a block) . Now it is evident that each f-graph realizing the $*$-linearity of $\mathcal{N}$ realizes the linearity of $\mathcal{M}$ (and conversely).

Step 3. We construct an f-graph realizing the $*$-linearity of $\mathcal{N}$.

Example 5.1. Let $X = \{1,2,\dots,10\}$, $\mathcal{M} = \{\{1,2,4\},\{1,2,3,4,7,9\},\{2,5,9,10\},\{9,10\},\{1,7\},\{3,6,8\},\{1,3,4,6,7,8\}\}$. The execution of Step 1 gives $\mathcal{M}_0 = \{\{1,2,3,4,7,9\},\{2,5,9,10\},\{3,6,8\}\}$. We take $M_0 = \{2,5,9,10\}$. The whole construction is shown in Fig. 4.

The described algorithm was implemented in PL/1 on IBM 360/50. For $|X| = 50$, $|\mathcal{M}| = 100$ the execution time was 67 s.

An another algorithm (in terms of matrices of 0's and 1's) can be found in FULKERSON and GROSS [2].

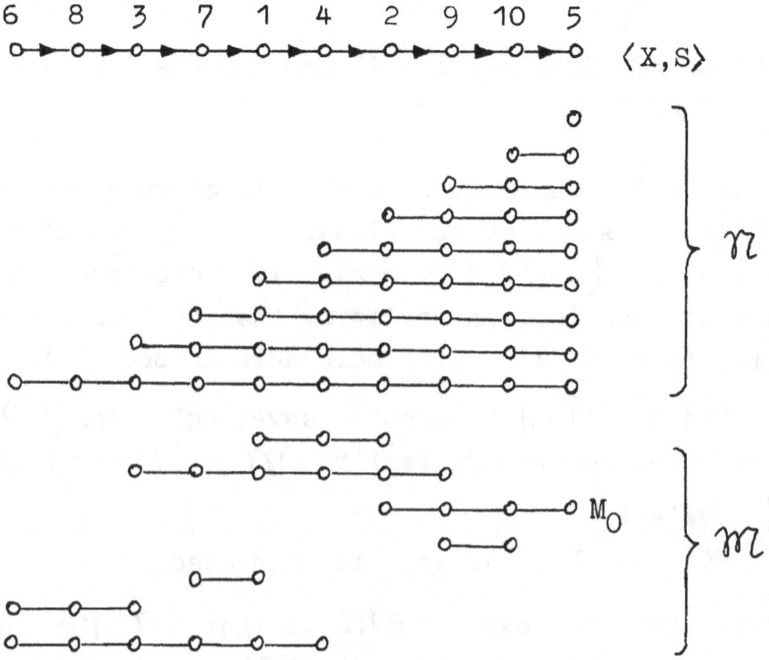

Fig. 4. Constructing an f-graph for a linear family of sets.

At the end of this section let us notice thet if we define $\mathfrak{M}' = \mathfrak{N} \cup \{X \setminus N: N \in \mathfrak{N}\}$ then $\mathfrak{M}' \underset{\mathcal{L}}{\sim} \mathfrak{M}$ and $N \in \mathfrak{M}'$ iff $X \setminus N \in \mathfrak{M}'$. By analysing the algorithm one can also prove that each component of $\mathfrak{M}$ is a segment in each f-graph realizing the linearity of $\mathfrak{M}$, i.e. $\mathcal{S}(\mathfrak{M}) \subseteq \mathbb{D}_{\mathcal{L}}(\mathfrak{M})$. These two remarks are valid only when $\mathfrak{M}$ consists of one block.

6. AUGMENTATION OF A FAMILY

The considerations of this section are motivated by problems arising in updating i.s.r. systems. There are two kinds of updating: one can change either the set of distinguished terms (queries) or the set of objects (records). This leads to the following question: How should the appropriate f-graph be modified to be good for a modified family of sets ?

All the theorems of this section are constructive, i.e. they provide an algorithm of such a modification of an f-graph. The situation is simple when a set of our family is deleted (we need not change the f-graph), or when an object $x \in X$ is deleted (we take the contraction $\langle X,S\rangle|_{X \setminus \{x\}}$, which is good for $\mathfrak{M}|_{X \setminus \{x\}}$, see Theorem 2.4.b). Now we shall study the possibility of the addition of a new set to a family.

By Theorem 4.2.a if we add to a linear family $\mathfrak{M} \subseteq \mathcal{P}(X)$ a set $M \subseteq X$ which does not overlap any set of $\mathfrak{M}$ then $\mathfrak{M} \cup \{M\}$ remains linear. Indeed, M is then a block, evidently linear. In particular M may be contained in a component of $\mathfrak{M}$ or $M \supseteq \bigcup \mathfrak{M}$. It is also easy to prove that a set M can be added to an admissible (acyclic) family $\mathfrak{M}$ without destroying the admissibility (acyclicity) provided that M meets at most one component of $\mathfrak{M}$.

Theorem 6.1. Let $\mathfrak{M} \in \mathcal{A}^*(X)$ and let $M \subseteq X$ be a set such that $\mathfrak{M}|_M \in \mathcal{L}^*(M)$. Then $\mathfrak{M} \cup \{M\} \in \mathcal{A}(X)$.

Proof: Let $\mathfrak{M}$ be $*$-segmental over an acyclic f-graph $\langle X,S\rangle$ and let $\mathfrak{M}|M$ be $*$-segmental over a linear f-graph $\langle M,S_1\rangle$. Let the f-graph $\langle X,S\rangle|_{X \setminus M}$ have k components. For each i, $1 \leqslant i \leqslant k$, there is a unique vertex of the i-th component x_i such that $x_i \notin \mathcal{D}\, S_{X \setminus M}$. Let x_0 be the end of M in $\langle M,S_1^{-1}\rangle$. Then the f-graph $\langle X,\bar{S}\rangle$, where

$$\bar{S} = S_{X \setminus M} \cup S_1^{-1} \cup \{\langle x_i,x_0\rangle : 1 \leqslant i \leqslant k\} \quad (S_1^{-1} = \{\langle x,y\rangle : \langle y,x\rangle \in S_1\})$$

realizes the acyclicity of $\mathfrak{M} \cup \{M\}$. ∎

Notice that the condition $\mathfrak{M}|_M \in \mathcal{L}^*(M)$ in the above theorem can be replaced by

$$(\exists N \in \mathfrak{M})\ M \cap \bigcup \mathfrak{M} \subseteq N$$

and that M is a final segment in $\langle X, \bar{S} \rangle$.

Example 6.2. Let $\langle X,S \rangle$ be the f-graph depicted in Fig. 5., let $\mathfrak{M}$ be a family of final segments in $\langle X,S \rangle$ (e.g. the family of all final segments in $\langle X,S \rangle$) and let $M = \{1,2,9,13\}$. The construction of $\langle X,\bar{S} \rangle$ is shown in Fig. 5.

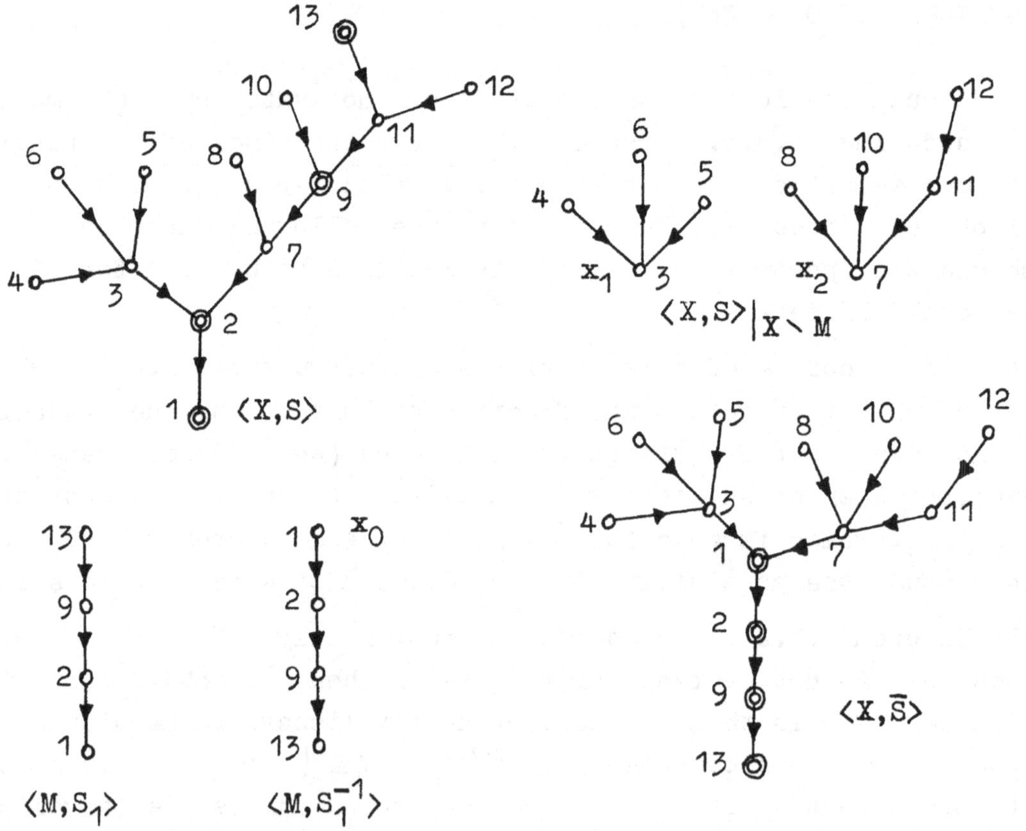

Fig. 5. Constructing the f-graph $\langle X,\bar{S} \rangle$ (see Example 6.2.).

If the f-graph $\langle X,S \rangle$ is linear then $\langle X,S \rangle$ is also linear. Hence we obtain

Theorem 6.3. (GHOSH [3]) If $\mathfrak{M} \in \mathcal{L}^*(X)$ and $M \subseteq X$ then $\mathfrak{M} \cup \{M\} \in \mathcal{L}(X)$.

Proof: If $\mathfrak{M} \in \mathcal{L}^*(X)$ then $\mathfrak{M}|_M \in \mathcal{L}^*(M)$ for each $M \subseteq X$. ∎

Theorem 6.4. Let $\mathfrak{M}_1, \mathfrak{M}_2 \in \mathcal{L}^*(X)$, $\bigcup \mathfrak{M}_1 \cap \bigcup \mathfrak{M}_2 = \emptyset$ and let $M \subseteq X$. Then $\mathfrak{M}_1 \cup \mathfrak{M}_2 \cup \{M\} \in \mathcal{L}(X)$.

Proof: Let us denote $\bigcup \mathfrak{M}_1 = A$, $\bigcup \mathfrak{M}_2 = B$. We construct linear f-graphs $\langle A,S_1 \rangle$ and $\langle B,S_2 \rangle$ realizing the linearity of $\mathfrak{M}_1 \cup \{M \cap A\}$ and $\mathfrak{M}_2 \cup \{M \cap B\}$ respectively. Then we construct arbitrary linear f-graphs $\langle M \setminus (A \cup B),S_3 \rangle$ and $\langle X \setminus (A \cup B \cup M),S_4 \rangle$. Now we "glue together"

$\langle X \setminus (A \cup B \cup M), S_4\rangle$, $\langle A, S_1\rangle$, $\langle M \setminus (A \cup B), S_3\rangle$ and $\langle B, S_2^{-1}\rangle$ by adding appropriate edges. ∎

Theorem 6.5. Let $\mathfrak{M} = \mathfrak{M}_1 \cup \mathfrak{M}_2$, where $\mathfrak{M}_1 \cup \{X \setminus N \colon N \in \mathfrak{M}_2\} \in \mathcal{L}^*(X)$, and let $M \subseteq X$. Then $\mathfrak{M} \cup \{M\} \in \mathcal{C}(X)$.

Proof: Let $\mathfrak{N} = \mathfrak{M}_1 \cup \{X \setminus N \colon N \in \mathfrak{M}_2\}$ be $*$-segmental over a linear f-graph $\langle X, S\rangle$. By Theorem 6.3. we construct an f-graph $\langle X, S_1\rangle$ realizing the linearity of $\mathfrak{N} \cup \{M\}$. Then we add the edge $\langle e(X), h(X)\rangle$ and the resulting f-graph realizes the cyclicity of $\mathfrak{M} \cup \{M\}$. ∎

Now we shall study the possibility of adding a new element to the set X, i.e. for a given $\mathfrak{M} \subseteq \mathcal{P}(X)$ we shall consider families $\overline{\mathfrak{M}} \subseteq \mathcal{P}(X \cup \{x\})$ such that $\overline{\mathfrak{M}}|_X = \mathfrak{M}$. We shall call $\overline{\mathfrak{M}}$ an extension of $\mathfrak{M}$. To each $M \in \mathfrak{M}$ there corresponds a set $\overline{M} \in \overline{\mathfrak{M}}$ equal to M or $M \cup \{x\}$. It is easy to see that $\mathfrak{M}$ and $\overline{\mathfrak{M}}$ are in the same class of admissibility if the addition of x does not create any new non-empty component, i.e. if there exists $y \in X$ such that $y \in M$ iff $x \in \overline{M}$, for each $M \in \mathfrak{M}$. In this case the necessary modification consists of adding the edge $\langle y, x\rangle$ and, if $y \in \mathcal{D}S$, replacing $\langle y, S(y)\rangle$ by $\langle x, S(y)\rangle$. One can also prove easily that the addition of x preserves the admissibility (acyclicity) provided there is at most ane $M \in \mathfrak{M}$ containing x.

Theorem 6.6. Each extension of an $*$-acyclic ($*$-linear) family is acyclic (linear).

Proof: We modify the appropriate f-graph $\langle X, S\rangle$ by adding the edges $\langle y, x\rangle$ for all $y \notin \mathcal{D}S$. ∎

Theorem 6.7. Let $|X| \geqslant 2$ and let $\overline{\mathfrak{M}} \subseteq \mathcal{P}(X \cup \{x\})$ be an extension of $\mathfrak{M} \subseteq \mathcal{P}(X)$.

(a) $\overline{\mathfrak{M}}$ is cyclic iff there exist two elements $y, z \in X$ and an f-graph $\langle X, S\rangle$ realizing the cyclicity of $\mathfrak{M}$ such that $S(y) = z$ and

(*) $\{M \in \mathfrak{M}_0 \colon y \in M \,\&\, z \in M\} \subseteq \{M \in \mathfrak{M}_0 \colon x \in \overline{M}\} \subseteq \{M \in \mathfrak{M}_0 \colon y \in M \vee z \in M\}$

where $\mathfrak{M}_0 = \{M \in \mathfrak{M} \colon M \neq \emptyset\}$.

(b) $\overline{\mathfrak{M}}$ is linear iff there exist two elements $y, z \in X$ and an f-graph $\langle X, S\rangle$ realizing the linearity of $\mathfrak{M}$ such that either $S(y) = z$ and (*) holds, or $z \notin \mathcal{D}S$ and

$$\{M \in \mathfrak{M}_0 \colon x \in \overline{M}\} \subseteq \{M \in \mathfrak{M}_0 \colon z \in M\}.$$

Proof: To prove the "if" part of the theorem we replace in $\langle X, S\rangle$ the edge $\langle y, z\rangle$ by the edges $\langle y, x\rangle$, $\langle x, z\rangle$ or (the second case in (b)) we add the edge $\langle z, x\rangle$. To prove the "only if" part we take the contraction to X of an f-graph realizing the cyclicity (linearity) of $\mathfrak{M}$. ∎

ACKNOWLEDGMENT

The author would like to thank Dr. W. Marek for many valuable discussions and suggestions.

REFERENCES

[1] COHN, P.M. Universal Algebra. Harper and Row, New York 1965.

[2] FULKERSON, D.R.; GROSS, O.A. Incidence matrices and interval graphs. Pacif. J. Math. 15(1965), 835-855.

[3] GHOSH, S.P. File organization: the consecutive retrieval property. Comm. ACM 15(1972), 802-808.

[4] KURATOWSKI, K.; MOSTOWSKI, A. Set theory. North-Holland Publishing Co., Amsterdam 1967.

[5] LIPSKI, W. Information storage and retrieval systems - mathematical foundations II. CC PAS Reports, No. 153, Warsaw 1974.

[6] LIPSKI, W.; MAREK, W. An application of graph theory to information storage and retrieval. Bull. Acad. Polon. Sci., Sér. Sci. Math. Astronom. Phys. 22(1974) (to appear in No. 7).

[7] LIPSKI, W.; MAREK, W. File organization, an application of graph theory. Automata, Languages and Programming (Proc. Collq., Saarbrücken, 1974), pp. 270-279. Springer-Verlag, Berlin - Heidelberg - New York 1974.

[8] MAREK, W.; PAWLAK, Z. On the foundations of information retrieval. Bull. Acad. Polon. Sci., Sér. Sci. Math. Astronom. Phys. 22(1974), 447-452.

[9] MAREK, W.; PAWLAK, Z. Information storage and retrieval systems - mathematical fuundations I. CC PAS Reports, No. 149, Warsaw 1974.

[10] WĄSOWSKA, M. Personal communication.

MODULAR APPROACH TO THE LOGICAL THEORY OF PROGRAMS

L.Banachowski
Institute of Mathematical Machines
Warsaw University

The aim of this paper is to present some results of investigations concerning modular properties of programs without procedures.
The modular method of writing,testing and debugging of programs is widely applied in every day practice. It is very interesting question about the significance of the modular approach to the program structure from the point of view of the logical theory of programs.
One answer is as follows: the examining of the correctness of a program has the same degree of complexity in the following two cases:
1/when we have got only two classical formulas describing an integral, input-output task of a program
2/when we have got a whole net of classical formulas describing required properties for all particular modules.
That is, supplying such a documentation of all modules is not essential with respect to the examination of the correctness property.
As a side effect of this investigations it will be shown that the theories of FLOYD[4], MANNA[5] and HOARE[6] can be formulated and completed in a uniform way by means of the extended algorithmic logic.

1.FORMAL LANGUAGE

The notions of a formal,algorithmic language and of its realization in a non-empty set J of objects and two-element Boolean algebra B_0 are based on those defined in [1],[2],[3],[7] and [8].
Substitutions/assignment statements/ are the simplest programs.
We admit the following program constructions:
<u>begin</u> K ; M <u>end</u> , <u>if</u> α <u>then</u> K <u>else</u> M and <u>while</u> α <u>do</u> K .
The algorithmic logic examines properties of programs by means of a formal language of algorithmic formulas.
The usual constructions of the first order logic are available.
Moreover we admit the following constructions:

$K\alpha$ the value of this formula is true iff the program K halts for a given valuation and the final results satisfy a formula α.

$\bigcup K\alpha$ the value of this formula is true iff for a given valuation one of the formulas $K^i\alpha$ for i being a natural number is true where K^i is the abbreviation of $\underbrace{KK\ldots K}_{\text{i-th times}}$.

$\bigcap K\alpha$ the value of this formula is true iff for a given valuation all the formulas $K^i\alpha$ for i being a natural number are true.

The algorithmic logic has the completeness property/see [2],[3], [7] and [8] /. That is, the concept of truth is identifiable with the concept of being provable for formal algorithmic theories.

Every formula can be transformed to its prenex normal form $Q_1Q_2\ldots Q_n\alpha$ where α is an open formula and for each i=1,...,n Q_i is either a classical quantifier binding an individual variable or is of the form $s\bigcup K$ or $s\bigcap K$ where s is a substitution and K is a loop-free program. Thus we can classify properties of programs by means of a configuration $Q_1Q_2\ldots Q_n$ appearing in the prenex normal form of a formula expressing given property.

2.PROPERTIES OF PROGRAMS

We shall consider the following properties of programs:

/1/partial correctness of a program K with respect to an input formula α and an output formula β - it is expressible by the formula $(K\ \underline{true} \wedge \alpha \Rightarrow K\beta)$

/2/correctness of a program K with respect to an input formula α and an output formula β -it is expressible by the formula $(\alpha \Rightarrow K\beta)$

/3/halting property of a program K - it is expressible by the formula $K\ \underline{true}$

/4/strongest verifiable consequent/introduced by FLOYD [4]/of a formula α with respect to a program K - it is expressible by the formula $\alpha K: \exists \vec{y}(\alpha(\vec{y}) \wedge K(\vec{y})(\vec{x}=\vec{y}))$ where $\vec{x}$ and $\vec{y}$ are disjoint vectors of variables

/5/adequacy of a program K with respect to an input formula α and an output formula β - it is expressible by the formula $((\alpha \Leftrightarrow K\beta) \wedge (\alpha K \Leftrightarrow \beta))$

The characterization of partial correctness of programs by means of strongest verifiable consequent is very useful.

Namely a relational system $\mathfrak{A}$ is a model of the formula $(K\ \underline{true} \wedge \alpha \Rightarrow K\beta)$ iff $\mathfrak{A}$ is a model of the formula $(\alpha K \Rightarrow \beta)$ [7] .

3. MODULAR STRUCTURE OF PROGRAMS

Let K be a fixed program.

By a module of K we mean any subexpression of K being a program.
The set of all modules of K will be denoted by Mod(K) .
A pair $H=(I,\hat{K})$ is said to be a tree of the program K if $I\subset\{1,2\}^*$, $\hat{K}:I \xrightarrow{onto} Mod(K)$ and the following conditions are fulfilled:

/1/ the empty sequence e belongs to I and $\hat{K}_e$:K

/2/ if i is in I and $\hat{K}_i$:<u>begin</u> K_1; K_2 <u>end</u> or $\hat{K}_i$:<u>if</u> α <u>then</u> K_1 <u>else</u> K_2 then i1 and i2 are in I and $\hat{K}_{i1}:K_1$, $\hat{K}_{i2}:K_2$

/3/ if i is in I and $\hat{K}_i$: <u>while</u> α <u>do</u> K_1 then i1 is in I and $\hat{K}_{i1}:K_1$

/4/ every element i in I can be obtained from the vertice e by means of the rules /2/ and /3/.

The function $\hat{K}$ is said to be a modular structure of the program K and is denoted by $\hat{K}=\{K_i\}_{i\in I}$.

For example the program M: <u>if</u> x>0 <u>then</u> <u>while</u> x≠y <u>do</u> y:=y+1 <u>else</u> x:=y has the following tree $H=(I,\hat{M})$ where $I=\{e,1,2,11\}$ and $\hat{M}_e$:M, $\hat{M}_1$:<u>while</u> x≠y <u>do</u> y:=y+1 , $\hat{M}_2$: x:=y and $\hat{M}_{11}$: y:=y+1 .

By a description of the program K we shall understand any mapping $A:I\longrightarrow F\times F$. We shall denote it by $A=\{(a_i,b_i)\}_{i\in I}$.

The formulas a_i and b_i are called an input formula and an output formula of the module $\hat{K}_i$, respectively.

The integral task is defined by the pair $A(e)=(a_e,b_e)$.

By a verification condition of a vertice i in I with respect to a description $A=\{(a_i,b_i)\}_{i\in I}$ we shall mean the formula VC_i defined as follows:

/1/ if $\hat{K}_i$:s is a substitution then $VC_i:(a_i\Rightarrow \overline{sb_i})$ where $\overline{sb_i}$ is the formula obtained from b_i by the application of the substitution s

/2/ if $\hat{K}_i$:<u>begin</u> K_1; K_2 <u>end</u> then $VC_i:((a_i\Rightarrow a_{i1})\wedge(b_{i1}\Rightarrow a_{i2})\wedge(b_{i2}\Rightarrow b_i))$

/3/ if $\hat{K}_i$:<u>if</u> α <u>then</u> K_1 <u>else</u> K_2 then $VC_i:((a_i\wedge\alpha\Rightarrow a_{i1})\wedge(a_i\wedge\neg\alpha\Rightarrow a_{i2})\wedge(b_{i1}\vee b_{i2}\Rightarrow b_i))$

/4/ if $\hat{K}_i$: <u>while</u> α <u>do</u> K_1 then $VC_i:(((a_i\vee b_{i1})\wedge\alpha\Rightarrow a_{i1})\wedge((a_i\vee b_{i1})\wedge\neg\alpha\Rightarrow b_i))$

The description A is called compatible with the program K in a class $\mathfrak{R}$ of similar relational systems if $\models_{\mathfrak{R}} \bigwedge_{i\in I} VC_i$.

Let $A=\{(a_i,b_i)\}_{i\in I}$ be a description of K and let $\mathfrak{R}$ be a class of similar relational systems.

The modular structure $\hat{K}$ is said to be partially correct with respect to A in $\mathfrak{R}$ if A is compatible with K in $\mathfrak{R}$ and for each i in I $\models_{\mathfrak{R}}(a_i\hat{K}_i\Rightarrow b_i)$.

The modular structure $\hat{K}$ is said to be correct with respect to A in $\mathfrak{R}$ if A is compatible with K in $\mathfrak{R}$ and for each i in I $\models_{\mathfrak{R}}(a_i\Rightarrow \hat{K}_i b_i)$.

THEOREM 1

The modular structure $\hat{K}$ is partially correct with respect to any compatible description A .

In practice we meet usually descriptions consisting solely of formulas of the first order predicate calculus.Such descriptions will be called classical.The following theorem establishes the complexity degrees of properties of a modular structure with respect to classical descriptions.

THEOREM 2

In every class of similar relational systems:

/1/the properties of partial correctness of a modular structure with respect to classical descriptions and of validity of formulas of the first order predicate calculus are recursively reducible to each other.

/2/the properties of correctness of a modular structure with respect to classical descriptions and of correctness of a program with respect to formulas of the first order predicate calculus are recursively reducible to each other.

4.HEREDITARY PROPERTIES OF PROGRAMS

Now we shall be concerned with the following problem:
Let χ be a property of programs with respect to input and output formulas. Is it possible to extend an association of input and output formulas to a program K , to a compatible description D such that if K has the property χ with respect to input and output formulas then each module of K has the property χ with respect to formulas assign to it by the description D ? Such a property we shall call hereditary.

THEOREM 3

In every class of similar relational systems the properties of partial correctness , correctness and adequacy are hereditary.
On the contrary the halting property is not hereditary.

As a consequence of this theorem it follows the completeness of the following system of proving partial correctness formally.
Let $\mathfrak{R}$ be a class of similar relational systems.Let E be the empty substitution x:=x .
We assume the following formulas as axioms:

$(\alpha\, E \Rightarrow \beta)$ if $\models_{\mathfrak{R}} (\alpha \Rightarrow \beta)$

$(\,\overline{s\beta}\ s \Rightarrow \beta)$

for all formulas α,β and substitutions s .
We admit also the following rules of inference:

$$\frac{\alpha E \Rightarrow \beta\ ,\ \beta K \Rightarrow \delta}{\alpha K \Rightarrow \delta} \qquad \frac{\alpha K \Rightarrow \beta\ ,\ \beta E \Rightarrow \delta}{\alpha K \Rightarrow \delta}$$

$$\frac{\alpha K_1 \Rightarrow \beta\ ,\ \beta K_2 \Rightarrow \delta}{\alpha\ \underline{\text{begin}}\ K_1 ; K_2\ \underline{\text{end}} \Rightarrow \delta} \qquad \frac{(\alpha \wedge \gamma) K_1 \Rightarrow \beta\ ,\ (\alpha \wedge \neg\gamma) K_2 \Rightarrow \beta}{\alpha\ \underline{\text{if}}\ \gamma\ \underline{\text{then}}\ K_1\ \underline{\text{else}}\ K_2 \Rightarrow \beta}$$

$$\frac{\alpha_1 K \Rightarrow \beta_1\ ,\ ((\alpha \vee \beta_1) \wedge \gamma) E \Rightarrow \alpha_1\ ,\ ((\alpha \vee \beta_1) \wedge \neg\gamma) E \Rightarrow \beta}{\alpha\ \underline{\text{while}}\ \gamma\ \underline{\text{do}}\ K \Rightarrow \beta}$$

for all programs K, K_1, K_2 , open formulas γ and arbitrary formulas $\alpha, \beta, \alpha_1, \beta_1, \delta$.

This formal system resembles the system of HOARE[5] who uses the notation $\alpha\{K\}\beta$ for the formula $(\alpha\ K \Rightarrow \beta)$.

Theorem 3 implies that:

THEOREM 4

Program K is partially correct with respect to formulas α, β in $\mathcal{R}$ iff the formula $(\alpha\ K \Rightarrow \beta)$ is provable in the formal system defined above.

5.PROPERTIES OF PROGRAMS AND SECOND ORDER LOGIC

Theorems 1 and 3 allow to deduce consequences similar to the results of MANNA[6].

We say that a formula α is F_{II}-existential / F_{II}-universal/ provided there exists a formula γ of the first order predicate calculus and a sequence of predicates $\vec{u}$ such that $\models (\alpha \Leftrightarrow \exists \vec{u}\, \gamma)$ $(\ \models (\alpha \Leftrightarrow \forall \vec{u}\, \gamma))$.

THEOREM 5

Let α, β be formulas of the first order predicate calculus and let K and M be programs.

The formulas of the form $(K\ \underline{\text{true}} \wedge \alpha \Rightarrow K\beta)$ and $(\alpha\ K \Rightarrow \beta)$ are F_{II}-existential. The formulas of the form $(\alpha \Rightarrow K\beta)$, K $\underline{\text{true}}$, $\underline{\text{true}}$ K and $(K\ \underline{\text{true}} \wedge M\ \underline{\text{true}} \wedge (K\alpha \Leftrightarrow M\beta))$ are F_{II}-universal.

On account of the deduction theorem and of the completeness theorem for extended algorithmic logic theorem 5 implies the following important fact:

THEOREM 6

Let A be a finite set of formulas of the first order predicate calculus and let $\mathcal{T}$ be the algorithmic theory based on the set A of axioms.

Let α be a F_{II}-universal formula.

Then α is a theorem of the theory $\mathcal{T}$ iff a certain formula of the first order predicate calculus is unsatisfiable.

This theorem reduces an examination of an appropriate property of programs to an automatic theorem proving based on the Herbrand theorem. However since the theorem on compactness fails to hold in algorithmic logic [8] this method of proving correctness of programs can not be used in the most important cases in which the theories of first order predicate calculus have an infinite number of axioms.

REFERENCES

[1] RASIOWA,H; SIKORSKI,R. Mathematics of metamathematics. Polish Scientific Publishers. Warsaw,1968.

[2] SALWICKI,A. Formalized algorithmic languages. Bull.Acad.Polon. Sci.,Ser.Sci.Math.Astronom.Phys. 18(1970), 227-232.

[3] KRECZMAR,A. Effectivity problems of algorithmic logic. 2-nd Colloquium on Automata,Languages and Programming. Lecture notes on Computer Science,No.14,Springer Verlag,1974.

[4] FLOYD,R.W. Assigning meanings to programs. Proc.Sym.in Applied Math.19(1967).in Mathematical aspects of Computer Science, American Mathematical Society.

[5] HOARE,C.A.R. An axiomatic basis of computer programming. Comm.ACM 12(1969),576-583.

[6] MANNA,Z. The correctness of programs. J.Comp.Syst.Sci. 3 (1969),119-127.

[7] BANACHOWSKI,L. Extended algorithmic logic and its properties. to appear in Bull.Acad.Polon.Sci.,Ser.Sci.Math.Astronom.Phys.

[8] MIRKOWSKA,M. Algorithmic logic and its applications in the theory of programs. Doct.Diss. Warsaw 1972 /in Polish/.

PROVING PROGRAMS BY SETS OF COMPUTATIONS

A.Blikle
Computation Center, Polish Academy of Sciences
PKiN P.O.Box 22, 00-901 Warsaw, Poland

ABSTRACT

By a computation of a program we mean any finite or infinite sequence of consecutive data-vector states generated by the program during a run. The set of all such computations can be considered as the program meaning. Analysing programs by sets of computations permits one to deal not only with input-output properties like correctness or termination, but also with properties of runs independently are they finite or not. In particular one can analyse system-like programs, where no output at all is expected. Given a program to be analysed we split it into a finite number of modules each of them simple enough for the set of all its computations to be obvioust. Sets of computations associated to modules are combined then into a global set in a way that is described by operational semantics. This semantics - being of litle use for program analysis - is supplemented then by a fixed point semantics that is proved equivalent to the former. Two examples of program analysis are considered: the McCarthy´s 91-procedure and a consumer-producer system-like program.

Key words and phrases: recursive procedure, set of computations, algebra of computations, operational semantics, fixed point semantics, least fixed point, greatest fixed point, deadlock.

Category numbers: CR 5.24 , AMS(MOS) 68A05, 06A23

1. INTRODUCTION

By a <u>computation</u> of a program we shall mean any finite or infinite sequence of consecutive data-vector states generated by the program during a run. E.g. if we consider a procedure FACTORIAL as below

```
procedure FACTORIAL
          integer n,s;
          begin
α1:       if  n=0  then  s:=1
          else begin
                    n:=n-1;
                    FACTORIAL;
α2:                 n:=n+1;
                    s:=s × n;
               end
          end
```

then we get the following computations, where in each pair (v_1,v_2), v_1 is the current value of n and v_2 is the current value of s:

Finite computations (for any integer i):
1) (0,i),(0,1)
2) (1,i),(0,i),(0,1),(1,1),(1,1)
3) (2,i),(1,i),(0,i),(0,1),(1,1),(1,1),(2,1),(2,2)
etc.

Infinite computations (for any integer i):
1) (-1,i),(-2,i),(-3,i),...
2) (-2,i),(-3,i),(-4,i),...
etc.

The set of all the computations of a program can be obviously regarded as its semantic description. In fact, such description is much more detailed (complete) than a usual description by means of input-output functions or relations. Analysing programs by means of computations permits one to deal not only with input-output properties, like correctness or termination, but also with properties of runs, independently are they finite or not. E.g. for the above FACTORIAL we can prove that in any finite run the current value of n never exceeds its initial value, and that in any infinite run (for negative inputs in n) an overload in n must appear. Dealing with computations one can also analyze system-like programs, where no output at all is expected (Example 2 in Sec.8).

Mathematical realization of our approach is as follows. Given a program to be analyzed we split it into a finite number of modules, e.g. assignment statements or tests, each of them simple enough for its set of computations to be obvioust. We use then a special algebra to combine these local sets of computations into a global one corresponding to the entire program. The way (succession) we combine these sets is described by operational semantics. This semantics - being of litle use for program analysis - is supplemented then by a fixed point semantics that is proved equivalent to the former. Least fixed points are used to describe the finitistic- and greatest fixed points to describe the entire (finitistic + infinitistic) behaviour of programs. The class of programs under investigations are recursive procedures without parameters.

First attempt to this approach, stimulated by REDZIEJOWSKI [10], was given in BLIKLE [3] for the case of iterative (flowchart-like) programs. The present paper extends the approach to the case of recursive procedures and specifies a calculus to be used in analyzing concrete programs. Since [3] is ruther hardly available, some main ideas are recalled here. For the sake of clarity all the proofs has been shifted to the last section. It is to be mentioned at the end that the present approach constitutes a particular case of a general lattice-oriented approach described in BLIKLE [4] and covering analysis of programs by languages, relations and sets of computations.

2. AN ALGEBRA OF ABSTRACT COMPUTATIONS

Let D be an arbitrary set to be fixed for the sequel and to be regarded as the set of data-vector states. Finite and infinite sequences over D will be called <u>abstract computations</u> and will be written as $(d_1,\dots,d_n)$, $n<\infty$ or $(d_1,d_2,\dots)$ or $(d_1,\dots,d_n)$, $n\leqq\infty$ the latter to denote a sequence that may be finite or infinite. The empty sequence is denoted by ε . We denote also:

$seq^*(D)$ - the set of all finite computations over D

$seq^{\infty}(D)$ - the set of all infinite computations over D

$seq(D) = seq^{*}(D) \cup seq^{\infty}(D)$.

Given two computations $x = (a_1,\ldots,a_n)$ and $y = (b_1,\ldots,b_m)$ with $n,m \leqq \infty$ we set

$$x \sqsubseteq y \quad \text{iff} \quad n \leqq m \text{ and } a_i = b_i \text{ for } i = 1,\ldots,n$$

In the set seq(D) we define a total binary operation called <u>composition</u>: for any $0 \leqq n < \infty$ and $0 \leqq m \leqq \infty$

$$(a_1,\ldots,a_n)\circ(b_1,\ldots,b_m) = \underline{\text{if}}\ a_n=b_1\ \underline{\text{then}}\ (a_1,\ldots,a_n,b_2,\ldots,b_m)\ \underline{\text{else}}\ \varepsilon.$$

$$(a_1,a_2,\ldots)\circ(b_1,\ldots,b_m) = (a_1,a_2,\ldots)$$

In particular we get therefrom

$\varepsilon \circ x = \varepsilon$ for all x in seq(D)
$x \circ \varepsilon = \varepsilon$ for all x in $seq^{*}(D)$
$(a,b)\circ(b) = (a)\circ(a,b) = (a,b)$
$(a,b)\circ(b,c) = (a,b,c)$ ... etc.

We can also prove that the composition is associative.

<u>Interpretation</u>: Given two programs (modules of programs) P_1 and P_2, if x is a computation in P_1 and y is a computation in P_2, then $x \circ y$ is a computation in the compound program in Fig.1 □

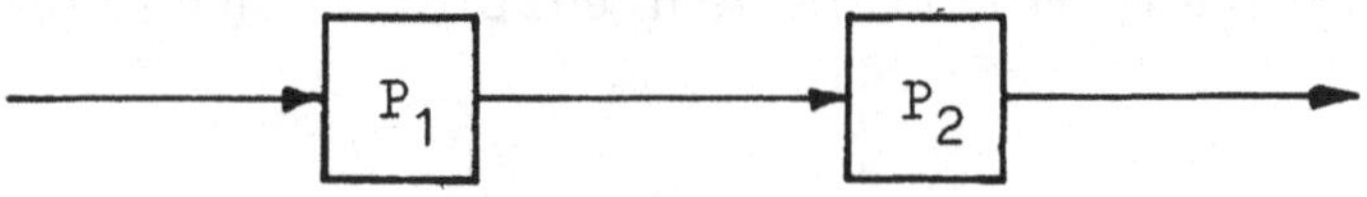

Fig.1

On the base of the binary composition " ∘ " we introduce an infinitary composition C. If $x_1,x_2,\ldots$ is an infinite sequence of computations, then $C[x_1,x_2,\ldots]$ is defined as follows:

<u>if</u> $(\exists n)(x_1\circ\ldots\circ x_n = \varepsilon)$ <u>then</u> $C[x_1,x_2,\ldots] = \varepsilon$ <u>else</u> $C[x_1,x_2,\ldots]$ is the shortest (in the obvioust sense of the word) computation in seq(D) with the property that

$(\forall n)(x_1 \circ \ldots \circ x_n \sqsubseteq C[x_1, x_2, \ldots])$.

Notice that $C[x_1,x_2,\ldots]$ as well as x_i's may be empty, finite or infinite. E.g.

$$C[(a,b),(b,c),(b,c),\ldots] = \varepsilon \quad \text{for} \quad b \neq c$$
$$C[(a,b),(b,c),(c),(c),\ldots] = (a,b,c)$$
$$C[(a,a),(a,a),\ldots] = (a,a,\ldots)$$
$$C[(a,b),(b,b,\ldots),(c,d),\varepsilon,(d),\ldots] = (a,b,b,\ldots) \quad \text{etc.}$$

3. AN ALGEBRA OF SETS OF COMPUTATIONS

By a <u>bundle of computations</u> over D we shall mean any subset of $seq(D)$ that contains the empty computation ε. Consequently

$$Bun(D) = \{B \mid B \subseteq seq(D) \ \& \ \varepsilon \in B\}$$

denotes the set of all bundles over D. The assumption that ε belongs to any bundle has a technical character and will be explained later. The set $Bun(D)$ ordered by set-theoretic inclusion is a complete set-theoretic lattice with the top element $seq(D)$ and bottom element $\{\varepsilon\}$. We shall denote

$$\underline{0} = \{\varepsilon\}$$

and we shall call it the <u>empty bundle</u>.

A bundle B will be said to be <u>finitistic</u> provided all its computations are finite, and will be said to be <u>inherently infinitistic</u> provided it is not empty and all its nonempty computations are infinite.

In the set $Bun(D)$ we define a binary operation "$\circ$" of <u>composition</u>. For any $B_1, B_2 \in Bun(D)$ we set

$$B_1 \circ B_2 = \{x \circ y \mid x \in B_1 \ \& \ y \in B_2\}.$$

As is easy to prove, this operation is associative and the bundle

$$E = \{(d) \mid d \in D\} \cup \{\varepsilon\}$$

is a neutral element of it. In what follows $(\mathrm{Bun}(D), \circ, E)$ is a monoid. One can prove also that the composition is distributive over arbitrary union, i.e. for any family $\{B_t \mid t \in T\}$ of bundles and for any bundle B we have

$$B \circ \bigcup\{B_t \mid t \in T\} = \bigcup\{B \circ B_t \mid t \in T\}$$
$$\bigcup\{B_t \mid t \in T\} \circ B = \bigcup\{B_t \circ B \mid t \in T\}$$

Moreover, for any bundle B we get

$$\underline{0} \circ B = \underline{0} \tag{1}$$
$$B \circ \underline{0} = (B \cap \mathrm{seq}^{\infty}(D)) \cup \underline{0} \tag{2}$$

Interpretation: Bundles are to be interpreted as sets of computations associated to programs and their modules. In fact we do not distinguish between programs and program modules considering them as objects of the same nature. Given two modules P_1 and P_2 with bundles B_1 and B_2 respectively, the bundle $B_1 \circ B_2$ corresponds to the compound module in Fig.1. If now $B_1 = \underline{0}$, i.e. there are neither finite nor infinite runs in P_1, then there are clearly neither finite nor infinite runs in the compound program; equation (1). If however $B_2 = \underline{0}$, then the infinite runs of P_1 are all and only runs of the compound program. This fact is expressed by (2). Formally (2) is a consequence of the assumption that ε is in any bundle, and in fact this assumption has been made in order that (2) be satisfied. □

By a generalized composition of bundles we shall mean an operation defined for all finite and infinite sequences of bundles:

1) $\mathbf{C}[\varepsilon] = E$, where ε denotes the empty sequence of bundles
   $\mathbf{C}[B_1,\ldots,B_n] = \mathbf{C}[B_1,\ldots,B_{n-1}] \circ B_n$ for $1 \leq n < \infty$
2) $\mathbf{C}[B_1,B_2,\ldots] = \{C[x_1,x_2,\ldots] \mid (\forall i \geq 1)(x_i \in B_i)\}$

This operation plays an important part in defining operational semantics of programs (Sec.6). Intuitively, finite and infinite sequences of bundles correspond to sequences of modules consecutive in program runs.

We define now three unary operations in the set $\mathrm{Bun}(D)$. For any B in $\mathrm{Bun}(D)$ we set:

<u>n-th power</u> : $B^0 = E$

$B^{n+1} = B^n \circ B \quad \text{for} \quad 0 \leqq n < \infty$

<u>finite iteration</u> : $B^* = \bigcup_{n=0}^{\infty} B^n$

<u>infinite iteration</u> : $B^\infty = \mathbf{C}[B,B,\dots]$

<u>Interpretation</u>: Given a flowchart as in Fig.2 where A and B

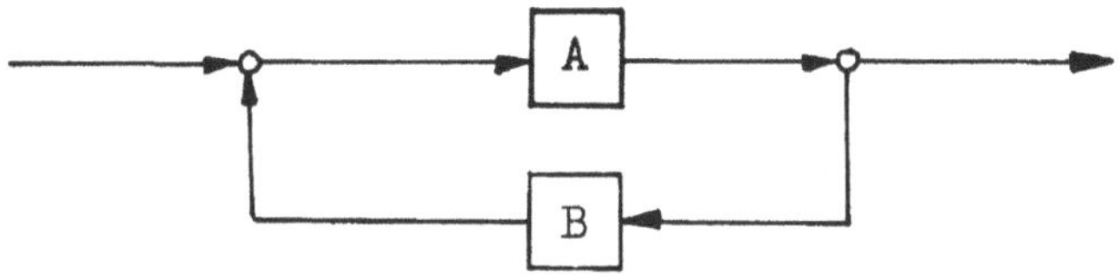

Fig.2

are appropriate bundles of computations we get

$A\circ(B\circ A)^*$ - the set of computations generated by all the finite runs of the flowchart,

$(A\circ B)^\infty$ - the set of computations generated by all the infinite runs of the flowchart,

$A\circ(B\circ A)^* \cup (A\circ B)^\infty$ - the set of computations generated by all the runs of the flowchart. □

<u>Convention</u>: We shall omit the symbol " $\circ$ " of composition and write AB instead of $A\circ B$. We shall also assume the composition to be prioritive with respect to the union, i.e. $AB \cup C$ will be written instead of $(A\circ B) \cup C$. □

The algebra of bundles as developed here is a particular case of an abstract algebra called <u>quasinet</u> which is a system $(U, \leqslant, \circ, e)$, where $(U, \leqslant)$ is a complete lattice, $(U, \circ, e)$ is a monoid, the operation " $\circ$ " is continuous in $(U, \leqslant)$ in the sense of SCOTT [11] and analogon of equation (1) is satisfied. Beside bundles, examples of other quasinets applicable to the theory of programs are generalized languages (languages with possibly infinite words) and so called δ-relations. All these examples together with a general theory of an abstract case are investigated in [4]. The case of δ-relations is described also in [5].

4. EQUATIONS

A mathematical tool to be used in our approach are <u>polynomial sets of equations</u>

$$
\begin{aligned}
X_1 &= \bigcup_{i=1}^{s_1} \varphi_{1i}(X_1,\dots,X_n) \\
&\dots \\
X_n &= \bigcup_{i=1}^{s_n} \varphi_{ni}(X_1,\dots,X_n)
\end{aligned}
\tag{3}
$$

where X_i range over Bun(D) and $\varphi_{ji} : (\mathrm{Bun}(D))^n \longrightarrow \mathrm{Bun}(D)$ are mononomials in Bun(D). By <u>mononomials</u> we mean functions that are either constant or of the form $BX_i\psi(X_1,\dots,X_n)$, where ψ is a mononomial again and $B \in \mathrm{Bun}(D)$. As is clear, each set as above can be written as one equation

$$\underline{X} = \Phi(\underline{X}) \tag{4}$$

where $\underline{X}$ ranges over n-dimentional vectors of bundles in $(\mathrm{Bun}(D))^n$. It is easy to observe now that the set $(\mathrm{Bun}(D))^n$ constitutes a complete lattice with componentwise ordering by inclusion, and that each Φ as in (4) is monotone and continuous in this lattice [11]. In what follows the set of solutions of (3) is always nonempty and moreover the least and the greatest solution always exist (see TARSKI [12]). For more details about sets of polynomial equations see [2], [4] and [6].

5. ALGORITHMS

Mathematical models of recursive procedures without parameters to be used in this approach are Mazurkiewicz pushdown algorithms. This notion was introduced in [8] and [6] over an algebra (quasinet) of binary relations. Here we modify it for the case of bundles

By a <u>Mazurkiewicz pushdown algorithm</u> (abbr. <u>PD-algorithm</u>) over Bun(D) we mean any system $A = (V, \alpha_1, \mathcal{E}, \mathbb{P})$ where

$V = \{\alpha_1,\dots,\alpha_n\}$ is a finite set of characters called <u>labels</u> or <u>procedure names</u>,

α_1 is a distinguished label called the <u>initial label</u> (it corresponds to begin in the program),

$\mathcal{E}$ is the empty string of labels (it corresponds to end)

$\mathfrak{P}$ is a finite set of triples of the form (α_i, B, z), where $\alpha_i \in V$, $B \in \mathrm{Bun}(D)$ and $z \in V^*$, such that for each α_i in V there exists $B \in \mathrm{Bun}(D)$ and $z \in V^*$ with $(\alpha_i, B, z) \in \mathfrak{P}$.

Each triple (α_i, B, z) is called an instruction and can be interpreted as a procedure declaretion, where α_i is the procedure name, B corresponds to a "segment" of procedure body free of other procedure calls - we call it action of the instruction - and z is a string of procedure names to be called (activated) in succession as they appear in z. If $z = \mathcal{E}$, then z is interpreted as the end symbol.

Considering the procedure FACTORIAL defined in Sec.1 we get the following PD-algorithm as its model:

$$\mathfrak{P} : \begin{array}{l} (\alpha_1, B_1, \mathcal{E}) \\ (\alpha_1, B_2, \alpha_1\alpha_2) \\ (\alpha_2, B_3, \mathcal{E}) \end{array} \qquad V = \{\alpha_1, \alpha_2\}$$

where

$$B_1 = \{((0,s),(0,1)) \mid s \in \mathrm{Int}\} \cup \{\mathcal{E}\}$$

$$B_2 = \{((n,s),(n-1,s)) \mid n \neq 0,\ n,s \in \mathrm{Int}\} \cup \{\mathcal{E}\}$$

$$B_3 = \{((n,s),(n+1,s \times (n+1))) \mid n,s \in \mathrm{Int}\} \cup \{\mathcal{E}\}$$

and where Int is the set of all integers.

It is to be emphasised that the choice of actions in this algorithm is arbitrary - to an extent - and depends on what we want to prove about the program. E.g. instead of B_3 we could set

$$B_3' = \{((n,s),(n+1,s),(n+1,s \times (n+1))) \mid n,s \in \mathrm{Int}\} \cup \{\mathcal{E}\}$$

A PD-algorithm where each instruction is either of the form (α_i, B, α_j) or of the form $(\alpha_i, B, \mathcal{E})$ will be said to be a finite-control algorithm (abbr. FC-algorithm). Instructions in such algorithms have natural ALGOL-like interpretation:

(α_i, B, α_j) - α_i : do B ; goto α_j

$(\alpha_i, B, \mathcal{E})$ - α_i : do B ; end

In what follows FC-algorithms are models of programs without recursive procedures (flowchart programs).

6. OPERATIONAL SEMANTICS

Every PD-algorithm over Bun(D) is assumed to generate a bundle that can be interpreted as the set of all its computations. How this bundle is defined depends clearly on the way we assume our algorithms to be executed. This way is described below.

Let $A = (V, \alpha_1, \mathcal{E}, \mathbb{P})$ be an arbitrary PD-algorithm with $V = \{\alpha_1, \dots, \alpha_n\}$. Strings in V^* will be called <u>control states</u> of the algorithm. For any instruction (α_i, B, z) the pair (α_i, z) is intended now to describe a binary relation in V^* denoted by $(\alpha_i \longrightarrow z)$ and called <u>control relation</u> of the instruction. This relation (in fact function) is defined as follows: for any y_1, y_2 in V^*:

$$y_1 \ (\alpha_i \longrightarrow z) \ y_2 \Longleftrightarrow (\exists w \in V^*)[\ y_1 = \alpha_i w \ \ \& \ \ y_2 = zw\ ]$$

In this way each instruction can modify the actual control state of the algorithm, provided it is applicable to it. Consider now a finite or infinite sequence of instructions

$$(\alpha_{i_1}, B_1, z_1), \dots, (\alpha_{i_m}, B_m, z_m) \quad ; \quad m \leqq \infty$$

such that there exists a sequence of control states $y_1, \dots, y_{m+1}$ with three following properties:

1) $y_1 = \alpha_{i_1}$
2) $(\forall j \leqq m)[\ y_j \ (\alpha_{i_j} \longrightarrow z_j) \ y_{j+1}\ ]$
3) If $m < \infty$, then $y_{m+1} = \mathcal{E}$.

Each such a sequence of instructions will be called an α_{i_1}-<u>run</u>. The corresponding sequence of actions $(B_1, \dots, B_m)$ will be called an α_{i_1}-<u>trace</u>. For each α_i in V the set of all α_i-traces is denoted by $Tr(\alpha_i)$. By $FinTr(\alpha_i)$ and $InfTr(\alpha_i)$ we denote respectively the set of all finite and infinite α_i-traces.

Observe now that any trace $(B_1, \dots, B_m)$ is a sequence of actions that can be considered as consecutive in the algorithm. The set of computations that is generated by this sequence is therefore

$$\mathbf{C}[B_1,\ldots,B_m].$$

With each α_i in V we can associate now three following bundles corresponding respectively to all, to all finite and to all infinite α_i-runs of the algorithm:

$$\mathrm{Run}(\alpha_i) = \bigcup\{\mathbf{C}(t) \mid t \in \mathrm{Tr}(\alpha_i)\}$$
$$\mathrm{Tail}(\alpha_i) = \bigcup\{\mathbf{C}(t) \mid t \in \mathrm{FinTr}(\alpha_i)\}$$
$$\mathrm{Perp}(\alpha_i) = \bigcup\{\mathbf{C}(t) \mid t \in \mathrm{InfTr}(\alpha_i)\} \qquad \text{"perpetual"}$$

where we have of course for $i \leqq n$

$$\mathrm{Run}(\alpha_i) = \mathrm{Tail}(\alpha_i) \cup \mathrm{Perp}(\alpha_i) \tag{5}$$

In what follows with every algorithm we associate tree vectors of bundles to be called respectively the Run- , Tail- and Perp-vector.

It is clear that the most relevant for proving properties of programs are in general the bundles $\mathrm{Run}(\alpha_1)$, $\mathrm{Tail}(\alpha_1)$ and $\mathrm{Perp}(\alpha_1)$ since α_1 has been assumed, by the definition, to be initial label of any algorithm. For instance, in the case of the algorithm described in Sec.5 we can prove the following:

$$\mathrm{Tail}(\alpha_1) = \bigcup_{n=0}^{\infty} B_2^n B_1 B_3^n = \{((n,s),(n-1,s),\ldots$$
$$\ldots,(0,s),(0,1),(1,1),\ldots,(n-1,(n-1)!),(n,n!)) \mid n \geqq 0,\ n,s \in \mathrm{Int}\} \cup \{\varepsilon\}$$

$$\mathrm{Perp}(\alpha_1) = B_2^{\infty} = \{((n,s),(n-1,s),\ldots) \mid n < 0,\ \ n,s \in \mathrm{Int}\} \cup \{\varepsilon\}$$

7. FIXED POINT SEMANTICS

The definition of the Run- , Tail- and Perp-vector, as given in the former section, are formulated in a way that referes to our intuitive understanding of program semantics. Here we characterize these vectors in an abstract algebraic way, that is less intuitive but in return more usefull in mathematical analysis of programs.

Let $A = (V, \alpha_1, \mathcal{E}, \mathfrak{R})$ be an arbitrary PD-algorithm with $V = \{\alpha_1, \ldots, \alpha_n\}$. Without loss of generality (i.e. without changing the Run-, Tail- and Perp-vector) we can assume that for each α_i in V and any z in V^* there is at most one B with $(\alpha_i, B, z) \in \mathfrak{R}$. Indeed, any two instructions (α_i, B_1, z) and (α_i, B_2, z) can be replaced by $(\alpha_i, B_1 \cup B_2, z)$. For each α_i and z appearing in an instruction, the only corresponding action will be denoted by B_{iz}. For any $i \leqq n$ we shall denote $V_i = \{ z \mid (\exists B)[(\alpha_i, B, z) \in \mathfrak{R}]$.

With any z in V we shall associate now a total function $\varphi_z : (\mathrm{Bun}(D))^n \longrightarrow \mathrm{Bun}(D)$, where n is the number of elements in V, defined as follows:

1) $\varphi_{\mathcal{E}}(X_1, \ldots, X_n) = E$ (see Sec.3)

2) If $z = \alpha_{i_1}, \ldots, \alpha_{i_m}$, then $\varphi_z(X_1, \ldots, X_n) = X_{i_1} \circ \ldots \circ X_{i_m}$.

E.g. if $z = \alpha_1\alpha_2\alpha_1$, then $\varphi_z(X_1, \ldots, X_n) = X_1X_2X_1$ provided $n \geqq 2$.

By the <u>canonical set of equations</u> (abbr. <u>CSE</u>) of the algorithm A we shall mean the set

$$X_1 = \bigcup_{z \in V_1} B_{1z}\varphi_z(X_1, \ldots, X_n)$$

$$\ldots$$

$$X_n = \bigcup_{z \in V_n} B_{nz}\varphi_z(X_1, \ldots, X_n)$$

E.g. for the algorithm in Sec.5 the CSE is as follows:

$$X_1 = B_2X_1X_2 \cup B_1$$

$$X_2 = B_3$$

A PD-algorithm is said to be <u>finitistic</u> provided all its actions B_{iz} are finitistic (see Sec.3).

THEOREM 1. For any PD-algorithm that is either finitistic or has the property that $\mathrm{FinTr}(\alpha_i) \neq \emptyset$ for all $i \leqq n$, the vector $(\mathrm{Tail}(\alpha_1), \ldots, \mathrm{Tail}(\alpha_n))$ is the least solution of CSE.

A PD-algorithm is said to be <u>proper</u> if for any infinite trace t of this algorithm, $\mathbf{C}(t)$ is either empty or inherently infinitistic.

Observe that in any case a PD-algorithm is supposed to be a model of a concrete program all its actions are bundles with computations of length at least 2 and in such a case the algorithm is proper.

THEOREM 2. For any proper PD-algorithm the vector $(\mathrm{Run}(\alpha_1),\ldots,\mathrm{Run}(\alpha_n))$ is the greatest solution of CSE.

It is to be emphasised that if the algorithm is not proper, then the Run-vector needs not to be a solution of CSE at all.

Let now $(Q_1,\ldots,Q_n)$ be an arbitrary solution of CSE. By Theorem 1 there exists exactly one vector $(S_1,\ldots,S_n)$ such that for any $i \leqq n$

$$Q_i = \mathrm{Tail}(\alpha_i) \cup S_i$$

with $\mathrm{Tail}(\alpha_i) \cap S_i = \underline{0}$. By Theorem 2 and equation (5) we get now

$$S_i \subseteq \mathrm{Perp}(\alpha_i) \tag{6}$$

for $i \leqq n$. This gives a nice characterization of a set of all solutions of CSE.

Observe now that for finitistic algorithms all $\mathrm{Tail}(\alpha_i)$ are of course finitistic as well. On the other hand, if an algorithm is proper, then $\mathrm{Perp}(\alpha_i)$'s are either empty or inherently infinitistic. The inclusion (6) implies now what follows:

THEOREM 3. For any proper and finitistic PD-algorithm the vector $(\mathrm{Tail}(\alpha_1),\ldots,\mathrm{Tail}(\alpha_n))$ is the only finitistic solution of CSE.

In consequence, whenever we are given a proper and finitistic PD-algorithm and a finitistic vector $\underline{T} = (T_1,\ldots,T_n)$ that is supposed to be its Tail-vector, we need not prove $\underline{T}$ to be the least solution, but just to be a solution of CSE.

In the general case of PD-algorithms there is no satisfactory fixed point characterization of $(\mathrm{Perp}(\alpha_1),\ldots,\mathrm{Perp}(\alpha_n))$. We get one, however, if we restrict our attention to FC-algorithms.

Let $A = (V, \alpha_1, \mathcal{E}, \mathcal{R})$ with $V = \{\alpha_1,\ldots,\alpha_n\}$ be an FC-algorithm.

For simplicity of notation we shall write in the sequel B_{ij} instead of $B_{i\alpha_j}$ and B_{in+1} instead of $B_{i\varepsilon}$. We shall also set $B_{ij} = \underline{0}$ whenever there is no B with $(\alpha_i, B, \alpha_j) \in \mathfrak{R}$. In this way all B_{ij} for $i \leqq n$ and $j \leqq n+1$ are defined, however not all of them are actions in **A**. The CSE for **A** can be written now in the following form:

$$\begin{aligned} X_1 &= B_{11}X_1 \cup \ldots \cup B_{1n}X_n \cup B_{1n+1} \\ &\ldots \\ X_n &= B_{n1}X_1 \cup \ldots \cup B_{nn}X_n \cup B_{nn+1} \end{aligned} \tag{7}$$

THEOREM 4. For any proper and finitistic FC-algorithm the vector $(\mathrm{Perp}(\alpha_1), \ldots, \mathrm{Perp}(\alpha_n))$ is the greatest solution of the following set:

$$\begin{aligned} X_1 &= B_{11}X_1 \cup \ldots \cup B_{1n}X_n \\ &\ldots \\ X_n &= B_{n1}X_1 \cup \ldots \cup B_{nn}X_n \end{aligned} \tag{8}$$

It should be stressed here that the first application of greatest fixed points in an analysis of infinite runs has been developed by MAZURKIEWICZ [9] in an input-output analysis of iterative processes.

Sets of equations like (7) - which are called right linear - have a nice algebraic property. There exist namely two heuristic algorithms which permit to solve (7) in such a way, that in the first case we get the least solution expressed by B_{ij}'s and the operations $\cup$, $\circ$, $*$ and in the second case we get the greatest solution expressed by B_{ij}'s and the operations $\cup$, $\circ$, $*$, ∞. Both these algorithms consists in variable elimination. For instance, if we eliminate X_1, then to obtain the least solution we replace first equation in (7) by

$$X_1 = B_{11}^{*}(B_{12}X_2 \cup \ldots \cup B_{1n}X_n \cup B_{1n+1})$$

and to obtain the greatest solution we replace it by

$$X_1 = B_{11}^{*}(B_{12}X_2 \cup \ldots \cup B_{1n}X_n \cup B_{1n+1}) \cup B_{11}^{\infty}.$$

Of course both above algorithms can be also used to solve (8). For a mathematical justification of the algorithms see [2],[4],[6] - for the first one and [3], [4] - for the second one. It is also to be stressed that first of the algorithms has been known to many authors and has been applied in algebras of languages and binary relations.

8. A NOTATION FOR PROVING PROGRAMS

To deal with concrete programs we introduce here some specific notation for bundles. This is a modification of the Mazurkiewicz notation for partial functions [6].

Let $f : D \rightarrow D$ and $p : D \rightarrow \{tt , ff\}$ be a partial function and a partial predicate in D respectively. We denote

$$[p(x) \mid x \leftarrow f(x)] = \{(d,f(d)) \mid p(d) = tt\} \cup \{\varepsilon\}$$

$$[p(x)] = \{(d) \mid p(d) = tt\} \cup \{\varepsilon\}$$

We shall also write $[d]$ instead of $[x=d]$.

Let p and q be arbitrary predicates in D and let $c = (d_1,\ldots,d_m)$ with $1 \leqq m \leqq \infty$ be an arbitrary (finite or infinite but nonempty) computation. We say c to <u>satisfy p at the entrance</u> provided $p(d_1) = tt$ and we say c to <u>satisfy q at the exit</u> provided either $m = \infty$ or $m < \infty$ & $q(d_m) = tt$. A bundle B is said to satisfy p at the entrance (exit) if all computations in B satisfy p at the entrance (exit). Notice that inherently infinitistic bundles satisfy any predicate at the exit.

Bundles of the form $[p(x)]$ are subsets of the unit E in the monoid of bundles. In consequence, for any bundle B and any predicate p we get the following subsets of B:

$[p(x)]B$ - the bundle of all computations in B that satisfy p at the entrance,

$B[p(x)]$ - the bundle of all computations in B that satisfy p at the exit.

The following facts about bundles, which appear frequently in proofs of programs, can be now easily formulated:

1) $B = [p(x)]B[q(x)]$ - B satisfies p at the entrance and q at the exit

2) $[p(x)]B = \underline{0}$ - no computation in B satisfies p at the entrance

3) $B[p(x)] = 0$ - no computation in B satisfies p at the exit

4) $[p(x)]B \subseteq B[q(x)]$ - each computation in B that satisfies p at the entrance satisfies q at the exit (partial correctness in the case $B = \mathrm{Tail}(\alpha_1)$)

Observe that 4) is equivalent to

$$[p(x)]B = [p(x)]B[q(x)]$$

and therefore 1) implies 4). In fact 1) asserts, beside the partial correctness, that any computation in B satisfies p at the entrance.

9. TWO EXAMPLES OF PROVING PROPERTIES OF PROGRAMS

Two concrete programs are analyzed here. The former is a numerical procedure. In this case the approach by bundles permits to extend the usual input-output analysis to an analysis of computations. Properties proved in this case are strong enough to imply partial and total correctness in the sense of [7]. In the latter example we investigate a system-like program that has no output at all (all runs are infinite) and we prove properties concerning deadlock and overload in this program.

EXAMPLE 1. Consider a well known procedure for the McCarthy´s 91-function

```
procedure NINETYONE
          integer x;
          begin
               if  x > 100  then  x:=x-10
               else
                   x:=x+11;
                   NINETYONE;
```

NINETYONE;

end

end

Let Int denote the set of all integers. We assume D = Int and we set the following algorithm:

$(\alpha_1, Q, \varepsilon)$ where $Q = [x>100 \mid x \leftarrow x-10]$

$(\alpha_1, F, \alpha_1\alpha_1)$ where $F = [x \leqq 100 \mid x \leftarrow x+11]$

The CSE is now as follows:

$$X = FXX \cup Q.$$

Denote (cf. Sec.8)

$$C_0 = [100]FQQ, \quad C_1 = [99]FQC_0, \quad \ldots \quad, C_9 = [91]FQC_8$$
$$C = C_0 \cup C_1 \cup \ldots \cup C_9$$

We shall prove the following:

$$\mathrm{Tail}(\alpha_1) = \bigcup_{i=1}^{\infty} F^i QCC_9^{i-1} \cup \bigcup_{i=1}^{\infty} F^i Q^2 C_9^{i-1} \cup Q \qquad (9)$$

This equation shows explicitly how the finite computations of our procedure look like. To prove it we denote

$$B_1 = \bigcup_{i=1}^{\infty} F^i QCC_9^{i-1} \qquad B_2 = \bigcup_{i=1}^{\infty} F^i Q^2 C_9^{i-1} \qquad T = B_1 \cup B_2 \cup Q$$

We can easily show now the following auxiliary properties:

1) $C = [91 \leqq x \leqq 100]C[91]$

2) $C_9 = [91]C_9[91]$

3) $B_1 = B_1[91]$

4) $B_2 = B_2[91]$

5) $[91]B_2 = \underline{0}$

6) $[91]B_1 = [91]FQC = [91]FQ[92]C = [91]FQC_8 = C_9$

7) $B_1Q = B_1[91]Q = \underline{0}$

8) $B_2Q = B_2[91]Q = \underline{0}$

9) $[100]B_1 = \underline{Q}$

10) $FQ = FQ[91 \leqq x \leqq 100]$

11) for all $1 \leqq s \leqq 9$

$$[90+s]B_1 = [90+s]FQ[91+s]C = [90+s]FQC_{10-(s+1)} = C_{10-s}$$

12) $[91 \leqq s \leqq 99]B_2 = \underline{0}$

On the strength of Theorem 3 proving (9) is equivalent to proving that T satisfies our CSE. This can be easily accomplished using 1) - - 12). The computations are left to the reader. Equation (9) shows now any finite computation of our algorithm to be an element of either B_1 or B_2 or Q. We can specify these cases in the following way:

1) for any $d > 100$

$$[d]\mathrm{Tail}(\alpha_1) = [d]Q = \{(d,d-10)\ ,\ \varepsilon\}$$

2) for any $n = 0,1,\ldots$

$$[100-11\times n]\mathrm{Tail}(\alpha_1) = [100-11\times n]B_2 = $$
$$= [100-11\times n]F^{n+1}[111]Q^2[91]C_9^n[91]$$

3) for any $n = 0,1,\ldots$ and $t = 1,\ldots,10$

$$[100-11\times n-t]\mathrm{Tail}(\alpha_1) = [100-11\times n-t]B_1 =$$
$$= [100-11\times n-t]F^{n+1}[111-t]Q[101-t]C$$
$$[91]C_9^n[91]$$

This is a total and explicite description of the set of all finite computations of our algorithm. In particular we get total correctness therefrom, since the algorithm is deterministic [4] and the set of all initial elements (entries) of computations in $\mathrm{Tail}(\alpha_1)$ equals Int.

EXAMPLE 2. Consider a sequential CONSUMER-PRODUCER program as given by flowchart in Fig.3. We shall assume s_1, s_2, q_1, q_2 to be arbitrary positive integers and x, y to be integer variables. The program contains two operational modules Q_1 and Q_2. The former can be regarded as a routine consuming x and producing y, the latter - - as a routine consuming y and producing x. The entire program is clearly supposed to run permanently and in consequence no output is expected. The program properties we shall analyze here concern occurences of deadlock and overload. <u>Deadlock</u> means that the program executes

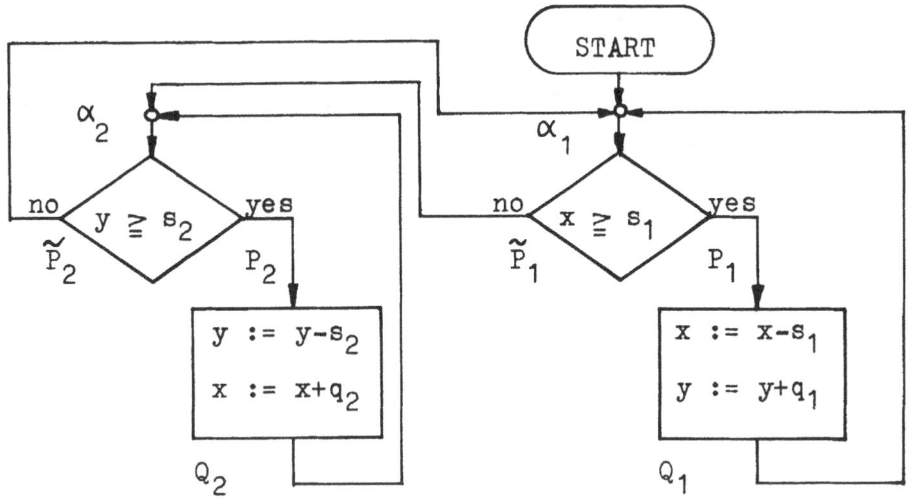

Fig.3

infinitly (permanently) the loop $(\tilde{P}_1\tilde{P}_2)^{\infty}$, and <u>overload</u> that for one or both variables x and y the sequence of corresponding successive values contains an infinite increasing subsequence of integers.

Let Nat denote the set of all natural numbers. We assume D = = Nat × Nat and we set the following algorithm:

$(\alpha_1, P_1Q_1, \alpha_1)$	where	$P_1 = [x \geqq s_1 \mid (x,y) \leftarrow (x,y)]$
$(\alpha_1, \tilde{P}_1, \alpha_2)$		$\tilde{P}_1 = [x < s_1 \mid (x,y) \leftarrow (x,y)]$
$(\alpha_2, P_2Q_2, \alpha_2)$		$Q_1 = [(x,y) \leftarrow (x-s_1, y+q_1)]$
$(\alpha_2, \tilde{P}_2, \alpha_1)$		$P_2 = [y \geqq s_2 \mid (x,y) \leftarrow (x,y)]$
		$\tilde{P}_2 = [y < s_2 \mid (x,y) \leftarrow (x,y)]$
		$Q_2 = [(x,y) \leftarrow (x+q_2, y-s_2)]$

The CSE is now as follows:

$$X_1 = P_1Q_1X_1 \cup \tilde{P}_1X_2$$
$$X_2 = P_2Q_2X_2 \cup \tilde{P}_2X_1$$

To get Run(α_1) from this set we solve it in the way as described in Sec.7 and using the equations $(P_1Q_1)^{\infty} = (P_2Q_2)^{\infty} = \underline{0}$ we get

$$\mathrm{Run}(\alpha_1) = ((P_1Q_1)^{*}\tilde{P}_1(P_2Q_2)^{*}\tilde{P}_2)^{\infty}$$

This formula is now a start point to deadlock-overload analysis. The entire analysis can be splitted into three main complementary cases that have to be splitted into subcases again. We show here only some of the subcases leaving the rest for the reader. Calculations can be found in [4].

Let n and m represent current values of x and y respectively. Denote

$$R = (P_1Q_1)^*\tilde{P}_1(P_2Q_2)^*\tilde{P}_2.$$

Case 1. $(q_1-s_2)+(q_2-s_2) > 0$: overproduction

subcase 1.1. $q_1-s_1 > 0$, $q_2-s_2 > 0$, $n \geqq s_1$, $m \geqq s_2$. In this subcase we can prove the following:

(i) for every $k \geqq 0$, $[(n,m)]R^k(\tilde{P}_1\tilde{P}_2)^\infty = \underline{0}$, i.e. deadlock never occurs

(ii) overload does occure for both x and y.

Case 2. $(q_1-s_1)+(q_2-s_2) < 0$: overdemand

In this case for any $n,m \geqq 0$ there exists $k \geqq 0$ such that

$[(n,m)]\mathrm{Run}(\alpha_1) = [(n,m)R^k(\tilde{P}_1\tilde{P}_2)^\infty$.

In words: deadlock after some finite number of steps and of course no overload as a consequence.

Case 3. $(q_1-s_1)+(q_2-s_2) = 0$: balance

subcase 3.1. $q_1-s_1 = 0$, $q_2-s_2 = 0$, $n \geqq s_1$, $m \geqq s_2$. In this subcase we can prove the following:

(i) for any $k \geqq 0$, $[(n,m)]R^k(\tilde{P}_1\tilde{P}_2)^\infty = 0$, i.e. deadlock never occurs

(ii) for any $k \geqq 0$, if $[(n,m)]T^k = [(n,m)]T^k[(n_1,m_1)]$, then $n+m = n_1+m_1$ which means that $x+y$ is an invariant of the program. In consequence the overload will not occure

10. PROOFS OF THE THEOREMS

We start with introducing some auxiliary mathematical tools. Let W be an arbitrary set. Given t_1,t_2 in seq(W) (see Sec.2) we define the concatenation $t_1 \frown t_2$ as follows:

$$t_1 \frown t_2 = \begin{cases} \text{usual concatenation} & \text{for } t_1 \text{ -finite} \\ t_1 & \text{for } t_1 \text{ -infinite} \end{cases}$$

Given two sets of strings (generalized languages, cf. [10] and [4]) $S_1, S_2 \subseteq seq(W)$, their concatenation is defined in an obvioust way:

$$S_1 \frown S_2 = \{ t_1 \frown t_2 \mid t_1 \in S_1 \ \& \ t_2 \in S_2 \}.$$

On the base of the generalized composition $\mathbf{C} : seq(Bun(D)) \longrightarrow Bun(D)$ we define now a new operation $\mathbb{C} : 2^{seq(Bun(D))} \longrightarrow Bun(D)$ whose domain is the family of sets of sequences of bundles. For any such set $S \subseteq seq(Bun(D))$:

$$\mathbb{C}(S) = \bigcup \{ \mathbf{C}(t) \mid t \in S \}$$

As it follows therefore, for any $i \leq n$

$$\begin{aligned} Run(\alpha_i) &= \mathbb{C}(Tr(\alpha_i)) \\ Tail(\alpha_i) &= \mathbb{C}(FinTr(\alpha_i)) \qquad (10) \\ Perp(\alpha_i) &= \mathbb{C}(InfTr(\alpha_i)) \end{aligned}$$

A sequence $t \in seq(Bun(D))$ is said to be <u>proper</u> if it is either finite or infinite with $\mathbf{C}(t) \subseteq seq^{\infty}(D) \cup \underline{0}$. A set $S \subseteq seq(Bun(D))$ is said to be proper, if all its elements are proper. By the definition in Sec.7 an algorithm is proper iff all its $Tr(\alpha_i)$ are proper.

LEMMA 1. For any family $\{S_p \mid p \in P\}$ with $S_p \subseteq seq(Bun(D))$ for $p \in P$ we have

$$\mathbb{C}(\bigcup_{p \in P} S_p) = \bigcup_{p \in P} \mathbb{C}(S_p)$$

LEMMA 2. For any two sets $S_1, S_2 \subseteq seq(Bun(D))$ if S_1 is proper, then

$$\mathbb{C}(S_1 \frown S_2) = \mathbb{C}(S_1)\mathbb{C}(S_2).$$

Proofs by obvioust calculations. Consider now an arbitrary PD-algorithm $A = (V, \alpha_1, \varepsilon, \mathfrak{P})$. By analogy to α_i-traces we can define <u>x-traces</u> for arbitrary x in V^*. Let $Tr(x)$ and $FinTr(x)$ denote the set of all- and all finite x-traces respectively.

LEMMA 3. For any x in $V^* - \{\varepsilon\}$, if $x = \alpha_{i_1} \ldots \alpha_{i_k}$ then

1) $Tr(x) = Tr(\alpha_{i_1})^\frown \ldots {}^\frown Tr(\alpha_{i_k})$

2) $FinTr(x) = FinTr(\alpha_{i_1})^\frown \ldots {}^\frown FinTr(\alpha_{i_k})$

The proofs of 1) and 2) are of course analogous. To prove 1) we shall show

$$Tr(x) = Tr(\alpha)^\frown Tr(x')$$

for any $x = \alpha^\frown x'$ with $\alpha \in V$ and $x' \in V^*$. Consider arbitrary t in $Tr(x)$ and let $y_1, \ldots, y_m$ with $m \leqq \infty$ be a corresponding sequence of control states (Sec.6). If there exists $k \leqq m$ with $y_k = x'$, then some initial segment of t is in $Tr(\alpha)$ and the remainder must be in $Tr(x')$. If there is no k with this property, then t is an infinite trace in $Tr(\alpha)$ and therefore $t \in Tr(\alpha)^\frown Tr(x')$. In what follows $Tr(x) \subseteq Tr(\alpha)^\frown Tr(x')$.

Let $t \in Tr(\alpha)^\frown Tr(x')$ with $t = t_1{}^\frown t_2$, $t_1 \in Tr(\alpha)$, $t_2 \in Tr(x')$. If t_1 is infinite, then of course $t = t_1 \in Tr(x)$. If t_1 is finite, then let $y_1, \ldots, y_k$ and $z_1, \ldots, z_m$ be sequences of control states corresponding to t_1 and t_2 respectively. It is easy to show that $t_1{}^\frown t_2$ is an x-trace with the sequence of control states $y_1{}^\frown z_1, \ldots$ $\ldots, y_n{}^\frown z_1, z_2, \ldots, z_m$. $\square$

LEMMA 4. For any $i \leqq n$

1) $Tr(\alpha_i) = \bigcup_{z \in V^*} \{(B_{iz})\}^\frown Tr(z)$

2) $FinTr(\alpha_i) = \bigcup_{z \in V^*} \{(B_{iz})\}^\frown FinTr(z)$

Proof is obvioust by the definitions of $Tr(\alpha_i)$ and $Tr(x)$.

PROOF OF THEOREM 1. Using (10) and all the above lemmas we show first the vector $(Tail(\alpha_1), \ldots, Tail(\alpha_n))$ to be a solution of CSE. We must prove it now to be the least one. Let then $(D_1, \ldots, D_n)$ be an arbitrary solution of CSE and let for any x in V^* and any $m \geqq 1$, $Tr^m(x)$ denote the set of all x-traces of length not greater than m. Clearly

$$\mathrm{FinTr}(x) = \bigcup_{m=1}^{\infty} Tr^m(x)$$

for any x in V^*. Let $T_i^m = \mathbb{C}(Tr^m(\alpha_i))$. By Lemma 1 we get therefrom

$$\mathrm{Tail}(\alpha_i) = \bigcup_{m=1}^{\infty} T_i^m$$

for $i = 1,\ldots,n$. We shall show that for $i \leqq n$ and $m \geqq 1$, $T_i^m \subseteq D_i$. Proof by induction on m.

Initial step: $T_i^1 = B_{i\varepsilon} \subseteq \bigcup_{z\in V^+} B_{iz}\,\varphi_z(D_1,\ldots,D_n) \cup B_{i\varepsilon} = D_i$.

Induction step: Let $T_i^k \subseteq D_i$ for $k \leqq m$ and $i = 1,\ldots,n$. Of course for any $i \leqq n$

$$T_i^{m+1} = \mathbb{C}(Tr^{m+1}(\alpha_i)) = \mathbb{C}\Big(\bigcup_{z\in V^*}\{(B_{iz})\} \frown Tr^m(z)\Big) = \bigcup_{z\in V^*} B_{iz}\,\mathbb{C}(Tr^m(z)).$$

It is also clear that for any $z = \alpha_{i(1,z)}\ldots\alpha_{i(l(z),z)}$ in V^*, where $l(z)$ is the length of z

$$Tr^m(z) \subseteq Tr^m(\alpha_{i(1,z)}) \frown \ldots \frown Tr^m(\alpha_{i(l(z),z)}).$$

Therefrom, by monotonicity of composition and by the inductive assumption we get

$$\begin{aligned} T_i^{m+1} &= \bigcup_{z\in V^*} B_{iz}\,\mathbb{C}(Tr^m(z)) \subseteq \bigcup_{z\in V^*} B_{iz}\,\mathbb{C}(Tr^m(\alpha_{i(1,z)}) \frown \ldots \\ &\ldots \frown Tr^m(\alpha_{i(l(z),z)}) \subseteq \bigcup_{z\in V^*} B_{iz}\,\varphi_z(T_1^m,\ldots,T_n^m) \subseteq \\ &\subseteq \bigcup_{z\in V^*} B_{iz}\,\varphi_z(D_1,\ldots,D_n) = D_i \end{aligned}$$ □

PROOF OF THEOREM 2. Consider an arbitrary proper PD-algorithm $A = (V, \alpha_1, \varepsilon, \mathfrak{P})$. Using (10) and lemmas from 1 to 4 we prove easily $(\mathrm{Run}(\alpha_1),\ldots,\mathrm{Run}(\alpha_n))$ to be a solution of CSE. Let now $(D_1,\ldots,D_n)$ be an arbitrary solution of CSE, i.e.

$$D_i = \bigcup_{z\in V^*} B_{iz}\,\varphi_z(D_1,\ldots,D_n) \quad \text{for } i = 1,\ldots,n \tag{11}$$

We shall prove $D_i \subseteq \mathrm{Run}(\alpha_i)$ for $i = 1,\dots,n$. We start with proving the following auxiliary assertion:

(*) For any nonempty control state $\alpha_j w$ and any computation $x \in \varphi_{\alpha_j w}(D_1,\dots,D_n)$ there exists an instruction (α_j, B_{jz}, z) such that

$$x \in B_{jz}\varphi_{zw}(D_1,\dots,D_n).$$

Indeed, let $x \in \varphi_{\alpha_j w}(D_1,\dots,D_n) = D_j\,\varphi_w(D_1,\dots,D_n)$. By (11) we get

$$x \in \bigcup_{z\in V^*} B_{jz}\,\varphi_z(D_1,\dots,D_n)\,\varphi_w(D_1,\dots,D_n).$$

Hence there exists z in V^* such that

$$x \in B_{jz}\varphi_{zw}(D_1,\dots,D_n)$$

and (α_j, B_{jz}, z) is of course an instruction in $\mathfrak{P}$ by the definition of CSE. □

By this assertion, given $i \leqq n$ and $x \in D_i = \varphi_{\alpha_i}(D_1,\dots,D_n)$ we get three sequences:

of instructions : $(\alpha_{j_1}, B_{j_1 z_1}, z_1),\dots,(\alpha_{j_s}, B_{j_s z_s}, z_s)$

of control states : $w_0,\dots,w_s$

of computations : $y_1,\dots,y_s, x_1$

with the following properties:

(i) $w_0 = \alpha_{j_1} = \alpha_i$

(ii) $w_{k-1}\ (\alpha_{j_k} \longrightarrow z_k)\ w_k$ for $k \leqq s$

(iii) $y_k \in B_{j_k z_k}$ for $k \leqq s$

(iv) $x_1 \in \varphi_{w_s}(D_1,\dots,D_n)$ whenever $s < \infty$

(v) $x = y_1 \circ \dots \circ y_s \circ x_1$

Notice that according to (*) the above sequences can be extended whenever $w_s \neq \varepsilon$, and the extended sequences satisfy (i)-(v) again. We can assume therefore our sequences to be either finite with $w_s = \varepsilon$ or infinite with $w_k \neq \varepsilon$ for all $k < \infty$. In both these cases the sequence of instructions is an α_i-run. In the former case we get $\varphi_{w_s}(D_1,\dots,D_n) = E$ (see Sec.3) and therefore

$$x = y_1 \circ \dots \circ y_s \in \mathbf{C}[B_{j_1 z_1},\dots,B_{j_s z_s}] \subseteq \mathrm{Run}(\alpha_i)$$

and in the latter case

$$C[y_1,y_2,\dots] \in \mathbf{C}[B_{j_1 z_1},B_{j_2 z_2},\dots] \subseteq \mathrm{Run}(\alpha_i)$$

with (see Sec.2)

$$y_1 \circ \dots \circ y_k \sqsubseteq x \quad \text{for} \quad k = 1,2,\dots \tag{12}$$

Observe that (12) does not imply $x = C[y_1,y_2,\dots]$ in the general case. But in our case we have assumed our algorithm to be proper, hence the trace $(B_{j_1 z_1},B_{j_2 z_2},\dots)$ is proper and $C[y_1,y_2,\dots] \in \mathrm{seq}^{\infty}(D)$. In these circumstances (12) does imply $x = C[y_1,y_2,\dots]$, hence $x \in \mathrm{Run}(\alpha_i)$. □

PROOF OF THEOREM 4. Consider a proper and finitistic FC-algorithm A_1 with the set of instructions $\mathfrak{P} = \{(\alpha_i,B_{ij},\alpha_j) \mid i \leqq n,\ j \leqq n+1\}$ and another algorithm A_2 that has been got from A_1 by setting $B_{in+1} = \underline{O}$ for $i = 1,\dots,n$. Since A_1 has been assumed finitistic, the Tail-vector of A_2 must be empty and therefore the Run-vector of A_2 equals the Perp-vector of A_1. On the other hand (7) is the CSE of A_2, hence by Theorem 2 the proof. □

REFERENCES

[1] BLIKLE, A. Nets, complete lattices with a composition. Bull. Acad. Polon. Sci., Ser. Sci. Mathemat. Astronom. Phys. 19(1971), 1123-1127

[2] BLIKLE, A. Equations in nets - computer oriented lattices. CC PAS Reports 99(1973)

[3] BLIKLE, A. An algebraic approach to programs and their computations. Math. Found. Comp. Sci. II (Proc. Symp. High Tatras, 1973) pp.17-26. High Tatras 1973

[4] BLIKLE, A. An extended approach to mathematical analysis of programs.(Roughly revised notices to lectures delivered during MFCS-74 Semester in the Intern. Mathem. S.Banach Center in Warsaw, 1974) CC

PAS Reports 169(1974)

[5] BLIKLE, A. Proving programs by δ-relations. Formalization of Semantics of Programming Languages and Writing of Compilers, (Proc. Symp. Frankfurt/Oder, 1974), Elektronische Informationesverarbeitung und Kybernetik (to appear)

[6] BLIKLE, A.; MAZURKIEWICZ, A. An algebraic approach to the theory of programs, algorithms, languages and recursiveness. Math. Found. Comp. Sci. I (Proc. Symp. Warsaw-Jablonna, 1972), Warsaw 1972

[7] MANNA, Z.; PNUELI, A. Axiomatic approach to total correctness of programs. Stanford Art. Intel. Lab., Memo AIM-210, Stanford 1973; also Acta Informatica ?(1974)

[8] MAZURKIEWICZ, A. Iteratively computable relations. Bull. Acad. Polon. Sci., Sér. Sci. Math. Astronom. Phys. 20(1972), 793-798

[9] MAZURKIEWICZ, A. Proving properties of processes. CC PAS Reports 134(1973)

[10] REDZIEJOWSKI, R.R. The theory of general events and its application to parallel programming. IBM Nordic Laboratory Sweden TP. 18.220 (1972)

[11] SCOTT, D. Outline of a mathematical theory of computations. Techn. Mon. PRG-2, Oxford 1970

[12] TARSKI, A. A lattice-theoretic fixpoint theorem and its applications. Pacific Jour. Math. 5(1955), 285-309

BASES OF PATHS IN CORRECTNESS PROOFS

V.K. Evtimov
Theoretical Cybernetics Department
Kiev State University , USSR

Using the Floyd's method of program analysis, we must cover the control-flow graph G by a set B of paths, such that the correctness of all the sequences of statements, corresponding to these paths, implies (by induction) the correctness of the whole program. Denote M(S,F) (where S and F are the sets of entry and exit nodes respectively) the set of all execution paths μ, such that start node (denoted by $b(\mu)$) belongs to S and end node (denoted by $e(\mu)$) belongs to F. Obviously, the above proof of correctness is possible, when each path $\mu \in M(S,F)$ can be represented as a concatenation of some paths from B (we say "B generates M(S,F)"). If, in addition, no proper subset of B generates M(S,F), B is called basis of the set M(S,F).

It is easy to see that each set of paths in a graph G has a finite basis whose power is not greater than the number of arcs in G. So we are interested in the minimal bases of the given set M(S,F), because using paths of a minimal basis we can prove the program for a minimal number of steps.

The control-flow graph G of each correct program satisfies the following assumption:

ASSUMPTION 1. All the nodes of G belong to the paths in M(S,F).

There exists a simple procedure reducing any given graph to a form, for which Assumption 1 holds. This allows to generalize our approach on arbitrary graphs.

Define the set $\Sigma(S\cup F)$ of linear segments as consisting of all paths σ, such that a node v is intermediate (i.e. $v\in\sigma$ and $b(\sigma)\neq v\neq e(\sigma)$) iff $v\notin S\cup F$ and only one arc comes in v and only one arc goes out of v. Let $I(v)$ and $O(v)$ denote the sets of linear segments σ for which $e(\sigma)=v$ and $b(\sigma)=v$ respectively. Consider a node $v\notin S\cup F$ which is not intermediate for any incident linear segment and does not lie on any linear segment $\sigma\in I(v)\cap O(v)$. Splitting of v is a transformation of the graph G in a graph H, constructed as follows:

1. Construct a graph G', isomorphic to the part of G, obtained after deletion of v and all its incident linear segments;

2. For each pair $(\sigma,\sigma')_i\in I(v)\times O(v)$ in G add to G'a linear segment σ_i for which $b(\sigma_i)=b(\sigma)$ and $e(\sigma_i)=e(\sigma')$. The graph thus obtained is H.

We call homomorphical extension of G a) graph $G_0=G$; b) graph G_{i+1} obtained by splitting of a node $v\notin S_i\cup F_i$ in the homomorphical extension G_i of G. The sets S_{i+1} and F_{i+1} are trivially derived from S_i and F_i, belonging to G_i' - the part of G_i, not affected by splitting.

LEMMA. If G_n is a homomorphical extension of a graph G, satisfying Assumption 1, then the set $\Sigma(S_n\cup F_n)$ of linear segments in G_n is isomorphic to some basis B_n of the set $M(S,F)$.

The above isomorphism may be easily set by matching of the graph G and inserting a rule for matches in the node splitting definition.

A very simple condition is obtained, under which the node splitting decreases the number of linear segments: each node to be splitted must have only one incoming or outgoing arc. A homomorphical extension G_m which does not contain such nodes is called restricted.

THEOREM. If G_m is a restricted homomorphical extension of a graph G, satisfying Assumption 1, then the set $\Sigma(S_m\cup F_m)$ of linear segments in G_m is isomorphic to a minimal basis B_m of the set $M(S,F)$.

This theorem points a straightforward way to the construction of minimal bases of given set $M(S,F)$.

ALGEBRAIC MODELS I

Hans-Jürgen Hoehnke
Zentralinstitut für Mathematik und Mechanik
der Akademie der Wissenschaften der DDR,
108 Berlin, Mohrenstr. 39

0. In categorical terms a general concept of a theory and of its models is described which covers the algebraic theories of LAWVERE [7] , [8] . As a special case also models of first order theories of predicate logics appear (LAWVERE [9] , [10] , VOLGER [15] , DAIGNEAULT [2] , POSEGGA [13]). GOGUEN, E. WAGNER, TATCHER, WRIGHT respectively KAPHENGST, REICHEL [6]and others have used algebraic theories on one hand and operative theories on the other in order to form programming languages. The use of algebraic model theories admitts the construction of programs (as syntactic objects) which in addition contain some or all of the logical operations of first order logics or other operations among predicates.
The use of algebraic model theories seesms also be appropriate for a categorical treatment of the GALOIS correspondence between classes of functions, closed with respect to superposition, and their invariant relations (cf. PÖSCHEL [12] , HOEHNKE [5]). In its most general case this treatment only involves the logical signs $\exists$, $\wedge$, =, and their laws.

1. Let H = $\langle H, \otimes, I\rangle$ be the free monoid, freely generated by a set J, with multiplication $\otimes : H \times H \longrightarrow H$ and identity element I.

Let

(1) $\langle \mathcal{T}, \otimes, I, c, d, t, o\rangle$

be a sequence, where $\langle \mathcal{T}, \otimes, I, c, d, t\rangle$ is a dt-symmetric category in the sense of HOEHNKE [4] with ob$\mathcal{T}$ = H, i.e., a category with finite products which are definable by $\otimes$, a terminal object I, three families of morphisms (A, B $\in$ H):

$$(1a)\quad \begin{cases} c = c_{AB}\colon A \otimes B \longrightarrow B \otimes A & \text{(symmetry)} \\ d = d_A\colon A \longrightarrow A \otimes A & \text{(diagonal)} \\ t = t_A\colon A \longrightarrow I & \text{(terminal morphism),} \end{cases}$$

and a Σ-sequence $o = \langle o_\sigma \rangle_{\sigma \in \Sigma}$ (for an index set Σ) of operations o_σ , among the Hom sets $(A, B)_{\mathcal{T}}$ of the category $\mathcal{T}$ of the form

(1b) $o_\sigma \; : (A_{\sigma 1}, B_{\sigma 1})_{\mathcal{T}} \times \cdots \times (A_{\sigma l(\sigma)}, B_{\sigma l(\sigma)})_{\mathcal{T}} \longrightarrow (A_\sigma, B_\sigma)_{\mathcal{T}}$,
having the symbol

$$\langle \sigma, \; (A_{\sigma 1}, B_{\sigma 1}), \ldots, (A_{\sigma l(\sigma)}, B_{\sigma l(\sigma)}); (A_\sigma, B_\sigma) \rangle_{\sigma \in \Sigma}$$

as the type of o. We remark, that $\langle \mathcal{T}, \otimes, I \rangle$ is a strict monoidal category in the sense of MAC LANE [11] .

If one considers $1_I\colon I \longrightarrow I$ (the identity morphism of the object I) $\in (I,I)_{\mathcal{T}}$, $c_{AB} \in (A \otimes B, B \otimes A)_{\mathcal{T}}$, $d_A \in (A, A \otimes A)_{\mathcal{T}}$, $t_A \in (A, I)_{\mathcal{T}}$ $(A, B \in H)$ as constant operations, the composition ($\cdot$) of morphisms in $\mathcal{T}$ as a sequence of operations

$$(\cdot)_{ABC}\colon (A,B)_{\mathcal{T}} \times (B,C)_{\mathcal{T}} \longrightarrow (A,C)_{\mathcal{T}} \qquad (A,B,C \in H)$$

and the product $\otimes$ in $\mathcal{T}$ as a sequence of operations

$$(\otimes)_{ABCD}\colon (A,C)_{\mathcal{T}} \times (B,D)_{\mathcal{T}} \longrightarrow (A \otimes B, C \otimes D)_{\mathcal{T}} \; (A,B,C,D \in H),$$

then the sequence (1) (for short also denoted by $\mathcal{T}$) appears as a special case of a (multi-based) algebra with a scheme of operators in the sense of HIGGINS [3] . An algebra with several carriers is also called a heterogeneous algebra in the sense of BIRKHOFF - LIPSON [1] . The carrier sets in the case of (1) are the Hom sets

(2) $\qquad (A,B)_{\mathcal{T}} \qquad (A, B \in H);$

the operations are

(3) $(\cdot)_{ABC}, \; (\otimes)_{ABCD}, \; 1_I, \; c_{AB}, \; d_A, \; t_A, \; o_\sigma \quad (A,B,C,D \in H, \sigma \in \Sigma)$.

A homomorphism $\phi : \mathcal{T} \longrightarrow \mathcal{T}'$ between heterogeneous algebras $\mathcal{T}, \mathcal{T}'$ of the form (1) is a sequence $\phi = \langle \phi_{AB} \rangle_{A,B \in H}$ of mappings

$$\phi_{AB}\colon \; (A,B)_{\mathcal{T}} \longrightarrow (A,B)_{\mathcal{T}'}$$

between the corresponding carrier sets (2) of $\mathcal{T}$ and $\mathcal{T}'$, which preserve the corresponding operations (3) of $\mathcal{T}$ and $\mathcal{T}'$.

The class of all heterogeneous algebras (1) which satisfy both the equations for dt-symmetric categories and a given system Γ of equantions (or also identical implications), in which the operations o_σ may also occur, forms a variety (resp. quasivariety). The (heterogeneous) algebras of this class are called algebraic

(o, Γ)-model theories (or for short theories) and form, together with all homomorphisms (the theory morphisms), between them a category Th.

We assume that the category $\mathcal{S}$ = Set of all sets is provided with the structure of a dt-symmetric category $\langle \mathcal{S}, \otimes, I, c, d, t \rangle$ such that to within isomorphisms $A \otimes B$ is the cartesian product of the sets A and B (but strictly-associative, cf. HOEHNKE [4]), I is a terminal object, t_A is the only terminal map, c_{AB} is the usual interchange, and d is the diagonal.

Consider the following situation in $\mathcal{S}$. Let $\Psi : J \longrightarrow \mathrm{ob}\, \mathcal{S}$ be any assignment; for short we write $\Psi(A) = \Psi_A$. Let $\mathcal{S}(\Psi) = \langle \mathcal{S}(\Psi), \otimes, I, c, d, t \rangle$ be the following category:

$\mathrm{ob}\, \mathcal{S}(\Psi) = H$,

$(A,B)_{\mathcal{S}(\Psi)} = (\Psi_{A_1} \otimes \dots \otimes \Psi_{A_n}, \Psi_{B_1} \otimes \dots \otimes \Psi_{B_m})_{\mathcal{S}}$

where

$A = A_1 \otimes \dots \otimes A_n, \quad A_i \in J$, if $A \neq I$,

$B = B_1 \otimes \dots \otimes B_m, \quad B_j \in J$, if $B \neq I$;

the composition of morphisms, the operation $\otimes$ and I, c, d, t are defined as an $\mathcal{S}$. Moreover we assume, that for every $\sigma \in \Sigma$ there is defined an $l(\sigma)$-placed operation o_σ^Ψ in $\mathcal{S}(\Psi)$,

$$o_\sigma^\Psi : (A_{\sigma 1}, B_{\sigma 1})_{\mathcal{S}(\Psi)} \times \dots \times (A_{\sigma l(\sigma)}, B_{\sigma l(\sigma)})_{\mathcal{S}(\Psi)} \longrightarrow (A_\sigma, B_\sigma)_{\mathcal{S}(\Psi)}$$

such that in $\mathcal{S}(\Psi)$ the identities and identical implications of Γ hold, i.e. $\mathcal{S}(\Psi) \in \mathrm{ob}\, \mathrm{Th}$, for all $\Psi : J \longrightarrow \mathrm{ob}\, \mathcal{S}$.

With respect to this correspondence between operations in (1) and in $\mathcal{S}(\Psi)$ an algebraic model of (1) (a $\mathcal{T}$-model, a model) in $\mathcal{S}$ is a functor $\Phi : \mathcal{T} \longrightarrow \mathcal{S}$ which (considered as a functor $\Phi : \mathcal{T} \longrightarrow \mathcal{S}(\Phi|_H)$) preserves all the dt-symmetric operations and carries o_σ into $o_\sigma^{\Phi|H}$.

A homomorphism $s: \Phi \longrightarrow \Phi' : \mathcal{T} \longrightarrow \mathcal{S}$ between models Φ, Φ' is a natural transformation s; it is already uniquely determined by the sequence $\langle s_A \rangle_{A \in J}$ $(s_A : \Phi A \longrightarrow \Phi' A)$.

The class of all $\mathcal{T}$-models in $\mathcal{S}$ together with their homomophisms form a category

$$\mathcal{S}^{(\mathcal{T})} = \mathrm{Mod}\,(\mathcal{T}, \mathcal{S}).$$

Each theory morphism X: $\mathcal{T} \longrightarrow \mathcal{T}' \in$ Th induces a functor

$$\mathcal{S}^{(X)} = \mathrm{Mod}\,(X, \mathcal{S}) \colon \mathcal{S}^{(\mathcal{T}')} \longrightarrow \mathcal{S}^{(\mathcal{T})}$$

$$\phi \colon \mathcal{T}' \to \mathcal{S} \longmapsto X\phi \colon \mathcal{T} \to \mathcal{S},$$

$$s \colon \phi \longrightarrow \phi' \colon \mathcal{T}' \to \mathcal{S} \longmapsto X * s \colon X\phi \longrightarrow X\phi' \colon \mathcal{T} \to \mathcal{S}$$

with $(X * s)_A = s_{XA} = s_A \colon \phi A \longrightarrow \phi' A \in \mathcal{S}, \quad A \in H.$

Let (Cat, $\mathcal{S}^J$) denote the comma category; its objects are the functors $\mathcal{C} \longrightarrow \mathcal{S}^J$, where $\mathcal{C} \in$ ob Cat is a category, and its morphisms are the functors $\mathcal{C} \longrightarrow \mathcal{C}'$, making the diagram

$$\begin{array}{ccc} \mathcal{C} & \longrightarrow & \mathcal{C} \\ & \searrow \quad \swarrow & \\ & \mathcal{S}^J & \end{array}$$

commutative; $\mathcal{S}^J$ is the category with Hom sets

$$(L,M)_{\mathcal{S}^J} = \langle (L,M)_{\mathcal{S}} \rangle_{A \in J} \qquad (L,\ M \in \text{ob}\ \mathcal{S}).$$

Obviously for X: $\mathcal{T} \longrightarrow \mathcal{T}' \in$ Th we have the commutative diagram

$$\begin{array}{ccc} \mathcal{S}^{(\mathcal{T}')} & \xrightarrow{\ \mathcal{S}^{(X)}\ } & \mathcal{S}^{(\mathcal{T})} \\ & {\scriptstyle U_{\mathcal{T}'}} \searrow \quad \swarrow {\scriptstyle U_{\mathcal{T}}} & \\ & \mathcal{S}^J & \end{array}$$

where $U_{\mathcal{T}}$ is the forgetful functor

$$U_{\mathcal{T}} \colon \mathcal{S}^{(\mathcal{T})} \longrightarrow \mathcal{S}^J,$$

$$\phi \longmapsto \langle \phi(A) \rangle_{A \in J},$$

$$s \colon \phi \longrightarrow \phi' \colon \mathcal{T} \to \mathcal{S} \longmapsto \langle s_A \rangle_{A \in J}.$$

Therefore

$$\mathrm{Sem} \colon \mathrm{Th}^{\mathrm{opp}} \longrightarrow (\mathrm{Cat},\ \mathcal{S}^J),$$

$$\mathcal{T} \longrightarrow U_{\mathcal{T}} \colon \mathrm{Mod}\,(\mathcal{T}, \mathcal{S}) \longrightarrow \mathcal{S}^J,$$

$$X \colon \mathcal{T} \longrightarrow \mathcal{T}' \longrightarrow \mathrm{Mod}\,(X, \mathcal{S}) \colon \mathrm{Mod}\,(\mathcal{T}', \mathcal{S}) \longrightarrow \mathrm{Mod}\,(\mathcal{T}, \mathcal{S})$$

defines a functor, called "semantics".

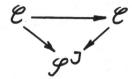

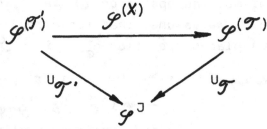

The question arises, wether there is a certain subcategory $K \subsetneq$ (Cat, $\mathcal{S}^J$) with Sem $(\mathrm{Th}^{\mathrm{opp}}) \subsetneq K$, such that Sem, regarded as a functor Sem: $\mathrm{Th}^{\mathrm{opp}} \to K$, has an adjoint Str: $K \to \mathrm{Th}^{\mathrm{opp}}$.

2. A sequence $\langle X_A \rangle_{A \in J}$ of functors $X_A: \mathcal{C} \to \mathcal{S}$ is called admissible, if the class $(A,B)_{\mathcal{R}}$ of natural transformations

(1) $r: D_n(X_{A_1} \otimes \dots \otimes X_{A_n}) \to D_m(X_{B_1} \otimes \dots \otimes X_{B_m}): \mathcal{C} \to \mathcal{S}$,

where

(2) $A = A_1 \otimes \dots \otimes A_n,\ A_i \in J$, if $A \neq I$,

$B = B_1 \otimes \dots \otimes B_m,\ B_j \in J$, if $B \neq I$,

(3) $D_n: \mathcal{C} \to \mathcal{C}^n$

$C \longmapsto \langle C, \dots, C \rangle$ (n times),

$x : C_1 \to C_2 \longmapsto \langle x, \dots, x \rangle$ (n times)

forms a set, whatever $A, B \in H$.

In this case we have a category $\mathcal{R}$ with ob $\mathcal{R} = H$ and with the sets $(A,B)_{\mathcal{R}}$ $(A, B \in H)$ as Hom sets. Then the natural transformation (1) appears as a morphism $r: A \to B \in (A,B)_{\mathcal{R}}$ of the category $\mathcal{R}$; the identity morphism $1_A: A \to A \in (A,A)_{\mathcal{R}}$ is given by the identical natural transformation

$D_n(X_{A_1} \otimes \dots \otimes X_{A_n}) \to D_n(X_{A_1} \otimes \dots \otimes X_{A_n}): \mathcal{C} \to \mathcal{S}$

and the composition of morphisms $r: A \to B$ and $s: B \to C \in \mathcal{R}$, denoted by $rs: A \to C$, is defined by composing the corresponding natural transformations (1) and

(8) $s: D_m(X_{B_1} \otimes \dots \otimes X_{B_m}) \to D_k(X_{C_1} \otimes \dots \otimes X_{C_k}): \mathcal{C} \to \mathcal{S}$,

where

$C = C_1 \otimes \dots \otimes C_k,\ C_h \in J$, if $C \neq I$,

in accordance with

$rs: D_n(X_{A_1} \otimes \dots \otimes X_{A_n}) \to D_k(X_{C_1} \otimes \dots \otimes X_{C_k}): \mathcal{C} \to \mathcal{S}$.

In $\mathcal{R}$ we define an operation $\otimes : \mathcal{R} \times \mathcal{R} \to \mathcal{R}$ as follows. For $r: A \to C$ and $s: B \to D$,

$$r \otimes s: A \otimes B \to C \otimes D$$

is defined by

$D_2(r \otimes s): D_{n+m}(X_{A_1} \otimes \dots \otimes X_{A_n} \otimes X_{B_1} \otimes \dots \otimes X_{B_m})$
$D_{k+l}(X_{C_1} \otimes \dots \otimes X_{C_k} \otimes X_{D_1} \otimes \dots \otimes X_{D_l}): \mathcal{C} \to \mathcal{S}$.

Moreover we define morphisms

$$c_{AB}: A \otimes B \longrightarrow B \otimes A \qquad (A, B \in H)$$

in $\mathcal{R}$ in accordance with

$$D_{n+m}(X_{A_1} \otimes \dots \otimes X_{A_n} \otimes X_{B_1} \otimes \dots \otimes X_{B_n})$$

$$\longrightarrow D_{m+n}(X_{B_1} \otimes \dots \otimes X_{B_m} \otimes X_{A_1} \otimes \dots \otimes X_{A_n}),$$

using the symmetry morphisms in $\mathcal{S}$,

$$c_{X_{A_1}(C) \otimes \dots \otimes X_{A_n}(C),\, X_{B_1}(C) \otimes \dots \otimes X_{B_m}(C)}$$

morphisms

$$d_A: A \longrightarrow A \otimes A \qquad (A \in H)$$

in $\mathcal{R}$ in accordance with

$$D_n(X_{A_1} \otimes \dots \otimes X_{A_n}) \longrightarrow D_{2n}(X_{A_1} \otimes \dots \otimes X_{A_n} \otimes X_{A_1} \otimes \dots \otimes X_{A_n})$$

using the diagonal morphism in $\mathcal{S}$,

$$d_{X_{A_1}(C) \otimes \dots \otimes X_{A_n}(C)}$$

and morphisms

$$t_A: A \longrightarrow I \qquad (A \in H)$$

in $\mathcal{R}$ by

$$D_n(X_{A_1} \otimes \dots \otimes X_{A_n}) \longrightarrow X_I$$

(where $X_I = D_n(X_I \otimes \dots \otimes X_I): \mathcal{C} \longrightarrow \mathcal{S}$ denotes the constant functor given by $C \longmapsto \{\emptyset\}$ and by $x: C_1 \longrightarrow C_2 \longmapsto id_{\{\emptyset\}}: \{\emptyset\} \longrightarrow \{\emptyset\}$ using the terminal morphism in $\mathcal{S}$

$$t_{X_{A_1}(C) \otimes \dots \otimes X_{A_n}(C)}: X_{A_1}(C) \otimes \dots \otimes X_{A_n}(C) \longrightarrow X_I(C).$$

Finally for every $\sigma \in \Sigma$ define a possibly partial operation

$$o_\sigma : (A_{\sigma 1}, B_{\sigma 1})_{\mathcal{R}} \times \dots \times (A_{\sigma l(\sigma)}, B_{\sigma l(\sigma)})_{\mathcal{R}} \overset{?}{\longrightarrow} (A_\sigma, B_\sigma)_{\mathcal{R}} \quad ,$$

in $\mathcal{R}$, using the corresponding operation in $\mathcal{S}(\Psi)$ (with $\Psi = \Psi_C: J \longrightarrow \mathrm{ob}\,\mathcal{S}$ given by $(\Psi_C)_A = X_A(C)$)

$$(o_\sigma(r_1: A_{\sigma 1} \longrightarrow B_{\sigma 1}, \dots, r_{l(\sigma)}: A_{\sigma l(\sigma)} \longrightarrow B_{\sigma l(\sigma)})_C$$

$$= o_\sigma^\Psi \quad ((r_1)_C, \dots, (r_{l(\sigma)})_C).$$

This operation is partial (indicated by $\overset{?}{\longrightarrow}$), since its application to natural transformations need not yield a natural transformation.

The subalgebras of $\langle \mathcal{R}, x, I, c, d, t \rangle$ that are also closed with respect to the operations o, that is, the subalgebras of $\langle \mathcal{R}, \otimes, I, c, d, t, o \rangle$, are called the theories, implicitly defined by the admissible sequence $\langle X_A \rangle_{A \in J}$ of functors X_A: $\mathcal{C} \to \mathcal{S}$. Indeed, since the equations and identical implications of Γ, which by definition hold in $\mathcal{S}(\Psi)$, also hold in these latter subalgebras, they are theories belonging to ob Th. (They could also be defined as those subalgebras of the (hyper-) product $\Pi_{C \in \mathcal{C}} \mathcal{S}(\Psi)$ consisting only of natural transformations.)

2.1. Let $\langle X_A \rangle_{A \in J}$ be an admissible sequence of functors $X_A : \mathcal{C} \to \mathcal{S}$.
(a) Given a theory $\mathcal{T} \in$ ob Th and a functor F: $\mathcal{C} \longrightarrow$ Mod $(\mathcal{T}, \mathcal{S})$ such that

$$F(C)\ (A) = X_A(C) \text{ for all } C \in \mathcal{C},\ A \in J,$$

$$F(u)_A\ (=F(u)(A)) = X_A(u) \text{ for all } u: C_1 \longrightarrow C_2 \in \mathcal{C},\ A \in J,$$

then the category $\mathcal{Q}$ with

$$(A,B)_{\mathcal{Q}} = \{\langle F(C)(a) \mid C \in \mathcal{C} \rangle \mid a \in (A,B)_{\mathcal{T}}\}$$

is a theory $\in$ ob Th, implicitely defined by $\langle X_A \rangle_{A \in J}$.
(b) Let $\mathcal{Q}$ ($\subseteq \mathcal{R}$) be a theory $\in$ ob Th, implicitely defined by $\langle X_A \rangle_{A \in J}$.
Then we get a functor $F' : \mathcal{C} \longrightarrow$ Mod $(\mathcal{Q}, \mathcal{S})$ (having the properties which are established in (a) (with F' instead of F)) as follows:

$$C \longmapsto F'(C), \text{ where}$$
$$F'(C)(A) = X_{A_1}(C) \otimes \dots \otimes X_{A_n}(C),$$
$$F'(C)(r) = r_C \text{ for } r \in (A,B)_{\mathcal{Q}}\ ;$$
$$u: C_1 \longrightarrow C_2 \longmapsto F'(u): F'(C_1) \longrightarrow F'(C_2), \text{ where}$$
$$F'(u)_A = X_{A_1}(u) \otimes \dots \otimes X_{A_n}(u),$$

with $A = A_1 \otimes \dots \otimes A_n$ and $A_i \in J$, if $A \neq I$.

Proof. (a) To see that $\langle F(C)(a) \mid C \in \mathcal{C} \rangle$: $D_n(X_{A_1} \otimes \dots \otimes X_{A_n}) \longrightarrow D_m(X_{B_1} \otimes \dots \otimes X_{B_m})$ (with $B = B_1 \otimes \dots \otimes B_m$ and $B_j \in J$, if $B \neq I$) is a natural transformation, we need only check commuativ ity of the diagram ($u: C_1 \to C_2 \in \mathcal{C}$):

$$\begin{array}{ccc} & X_{A_1}(u) \otimes \dots \otimes X_{A_n}(u) & \\ X_{A_1}(C_1) \otimes \dots \otimes X_{A_n}(C_1) & \longrightarrow & X_{A_1}(C_2) \otimes \dots \otimes X_{A_n}(C_2) \\ F(C_1)\,(a) \downarrow & & \downarrow F(C_2)\,(a) \\ X_{B_1}(C_1) \otimes \dots \otimes X_{B_m}(C_1) & \longrightarrow & X_{B_1}(C_2) \otimes \dots \otimes X_{B_m}(C_2) \\ & X_{B_1}(u) \otimes \dots \otimes X_{B_m}(u) & \end{array}$$

Indeed, since $F(C):\mathcal{T} \longrightarrow \mathcal{S}$ preserves the operation $\otimes$, we have

$(X_{A_1}(u) \otimes \dots \otimes X_{A_n}(u))F(C_2)(a)$

$= (F(u)_{A_1} \otimes \dots \otimes F(u)_{A_n})F(C_2)(a)$

$= F(u)_{A_1 \otimes \dots \otimes A_n} F(C_2)\,(a) = F(u)_A\, F(C_2)(a)$

$= F(C_1)(a)\; F(u)_B = F(C_1)(a)\; F(u)_{B_1 \otimes \dots \otimes B_m}$

$= F(C_1)(a)\; (F(u)_{B_1} \otimes \dots \otimes F(u)_{B_m})$

$= f(C_1)(a)(X_{B_1}(u) \otimes \dots \otimes X_{B_m}(u)).$

As $F(C)(a)\; F(C)(b) = F(C)(ab)$ and $F(C)(1_A) = id_{F(C)(A)}$ show $\mathcal{Q}$ is closed under composition of morphisms and contains identity morphisms. Since $F(C)(a) \otimes F(C)(b) = F(C)(a \otimes b)$, $\mathcal{Q}$ is closed under $\otimes$. Since $F(C)$ preserves $o_{\mathcal{C}}$, $\mathcal{Q}$ is closed with respect to $o_{\mathcal{C}}$. Moreover $F(C)$ preserves c_{AB}, d_A, t_A, therefore $\mathcal{Q}$ also contains c_{AB}, d_A, t_A. Thus $\mathcal{Q}$ is a subalgebra of $\langle \mathcal{R}, \otimes, I, c, d, t, o\rangle$ and consequently $\mathcal{Q} \in$ ob Th.

(b) Since $\mathcal{Q}$ is a subalgebra of $\mathcal{R}$, $F'(C): \mathcal{Q} \longrightarrow \mathcal{S}$ is a model of $\mathcal{Q}$.

3. Let $\langle X_A \rangle_{A \in J}$ be an admissible sequence of functors $X_A: \mathcal{C} \longrightarrow \mathcal{S}$ and D_J be the functor

$$D_J: \mathcal{C} \longrightarrow \mathcal{C}^J,$$
$$C \longmapsto \langle C \rangle_{A \in J},$$
$$j: C_1 \longrightarrow C_2 \longmapsto \langle u \rangle_{A \in J}.$$

Form the functor

$$\Pi_{A \in J} X_A : \mathcal{C}^J \longrightarrow \mathcal{C}^J,$$

$$\langle C \rangle_{A \in J} \qquad \langle X_A(C) \rangle_{A \in J},$$

$$\langle u_A : C_1 \longrightarrow C_2 \rangle_{A \in J} \longmapsto \langle X_A(u_A) \rangle_{A \in J} : \langle X_A(C_1) \rangle_{A \in J}$$

$$\longrightarrow \langle X_A(C_2) \rangle_{A \in J}.$$

The sequence $\langle X_A \rangle_{A \in J}$ uniquely determines a functor

(1) $\qquad X = D_j \, \Pi_{A \in J} X_A : \mathcal{C} \longrightarrow \mathcal{S}^J.$

The admissible sequence $\langle X_A \rangle_{A \in J}$ is called algebraic admissible, if there is at least one theory $\in$ ob Th implicitely defined by $\langle X_A \rangle_{A \in J}$. Let K be the full subcategory of $(\mathrm{Cat}, \mathcal{S}^J)$ consisting of all functors X that arise via (1) from algebraic admissible sequences $\langle X_A \rangle_{A \in J}$. If Sem $(\mathcal{T}) \in$ ob K, we may regard the functor Sem as taking values in K:

$$\mathrm{Sem} : \mathrm{Th}^{\mathrm{opp}} \longrightarrow K.$$

3.1. If Im Sem $\subseteqq$ K, then the functor

$$(X, \mathrm{Sem}(\;-\;))_K : \mathrm{Th}^{\mathrm{opp}} \longrightarrow \mathcal{S}$$

is a proper functor (in the sense of SCHUBERT (1970, I, p. 81/82)) with dominating set M of all theories $\in$ ob Th implicitly defined by $\langle X_A \rangle_{A \in J}$.

Proof. Let $\mathcal{T} \in$ ob Th and $F \in (X, \mathrm{Sem}(\mathcal{T}))_K$, i.e.,

$$\begin{array}{ccc} \mathrm{Mod}(\mathcal{T}, \mathcal{S}) & \xleftarrow{\;F\;} & \mathcal{C} \\ {\scriptstyle \mathrm{Sem}\,\mathcal{T} = U_{\mathcal{T}}} \searrow & & \swarrow {\scriptstyle X} \\ & \mathcal{S}^J & \end{array}$$

is a commutative diagram. We have to show: there are $\mathcal{Q} \in M$, $F' \in (X, \mathrm{Sem}\,\mathcal{Q})_K$ and $G^{\mathrm{opp}} : \mathcal{Q} \longrightarrow \mathcal{T} \in \mathrm{Th}^{\mathrm{opp}}$, such that the following diagram is commutative:

$$\begin{array}{ccc} \mathrm{Mod}(\mathcal{T}, \mathcal{S}) & \xleftarrow{\;F\;} & \mathcal{C} \\ {\scriptstyle \mathrm{Mod}(G, \mathcal{S})} \uparrow & \swarrow {\scriptstyle F'} & \downarrow {\scriptstyle X} \\ \mathrm{Mod}(\mathcal{Q}, \mathcal{S}) & \xrightarrow{\;U\;} & \mathcal{S}^J \end{array}$$

Choose $\mathcal{Q}$ as in 2.1.(a). Then $\mathcal{Q} \in M$. Define the functor

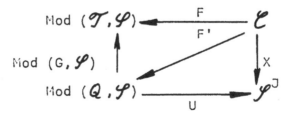

$$G: \mathcal{T} \longrightarrow \mathcal{Q},$$
$$A \longmapsto A \quad (A \in H),$$
$$a \longmapsto \langle F(C)(a) \mid C \in \mathcal{C} \rangle$$

Then $G \in$ ob Th.

Define $F': \mathcal{C} \longrightarrow \mathrm{Mod}\,(\mathcal{Q}, \mathcal{S})$ as in 2.1.(b).
Then $F' \in (X, \mathrm{Sem}\,\mathcal{Q})_K$, and

$$GF'(C) = F(C),$$
$$F'(u)_{GA}: GF'(C_1) \longrightarrow GF'(C_2)$$
$$= F'(u)_A = F(u)_A \qquad (A \in H),$$

i.e., $F'\mathrm{Mod}\,(G, \mathcal{S}) = F$.

If Sem: $\mathrm{Th}^{\mathrm{opp}} \longrightarrow K$ preserves limits, 3.1 and an adjoint functor theorem (for instance by Satz 16.4.7 of SCHUBERT (1970, II, p. 9)) delivers:

3.2. If Im Sem $\subsetneq K$ and Sem preserves limits, then the functor Sem: $\mathrm{Th}^{\mathrm{opp}} \longrightarrow K$ has an adjoint "structure"

$$\mathrm{Str}: K \longrightarrow \mathrm{Th}^{\mathrm{opp}}.$$

REFERENCES

[1] BIRKHOFF, G.B.; LIPSON, J.D.: Heterogeneous algebras. J. Combinatorial Theory 8(1970),115-133.

[2] DAIGNEAULT, A.: Lawvere's elementary theories and polyadic and cylindric algebras. Fund. Math. 66(1970),307-328.

[3] HIGGINS, P.J.: Algebras with a scheme of operators. Math. Nachr. 27(1963),115-132.

[4] HOEHNKE, H.-J.: Struktursätze der Algebra und Kompliziertheit logischer Schemata, I, II, III. Math. Nachr. (1974), im Druck.

[5] ———, Logische Kategorien und Galoissche Theorie. Manuskript 1974.

[6] KAPHENGST, H.; REICHEL, H.: Operative Theorien und Kategorien von operativen Systemen. Studien zur Algebra und ihre Anwendungen, pp. 41-56, Berlin 1972.

[7] LAWVERE, F.W.: Functorial semantics of algebraic theories. Proc. Nat.Acad.Sci. 50 (1963),869-872.

[8] ———, Some algebraic problems in context of functorial semantics of algebraic theories. Reports of the Midwest Category Seminar.II, Lecture Notes in Mathematics 61, Berlin, 1968.

[9] ———, Functorial semantics of elementary theories. J. Symbolic Logic 31(1966),294.

[10] ———, Theories as categories and the completeness theorem. J.Symbolic Logic 32(1967),562.

[11] MACLANE, S.: Kategorien. Berlin 1972.

[12] PÖSCHEL, R.: Postsche Algebren von Funktionen über einer Familie endlicher Mengen. Z. math. Logik Grundlagen Math. 19 (1973),37-74.

[13] POSEGGA, M.: Funktorielle Untersuchungen der Semantik in Modellkategorien elementarer Theorien. Manuskript 1973.

[14] SCHUBERT, H.: Kategorien, I, II. Berlin 1970.

[15] VOLGER, H.: Logical categories. Manuscript 1971.

STRUCTURED PROGRAMMABILITY OF ITERATIVE ALGORITHMS

Jacek Irlik
Institute of Mathematical Machines
Silesian Division, Katowice

The notion of FC-algorithm $A = (X, V, \sigma, \varepsilon, P)$ as introduced by Mazurkiewicz [1] has appeared to be a sensitive tool in considering various properties of iterative programs. It has been proved (MAZURKIEWICZ [1]) that

THEOREM 1A. Any FC-algorithm A such that $E_A \subseteq F \subseteq 2^{X \times X}$ has its resulting relation - Res_A - in Cl(F), i.e. in the Kleene closure of the family F.

THEOREM 2A. For any relation R in Cl(F) there exists an FC-algorithm A such that $Res_A = R$ and $E_A \subseteq F \cup \{I\}$.

On base of THEOREM 2A we may conclude informally that in order to get an algorithm for any relation R in Cl(F) the TOP-DOWN process of synthesis of the algorithm may be used. Thus we get an algorithm which is a model for a structured program.

When we restrict, however, our considerations to the case when F is a family of partial functions it appears that the process of synthesis of an algorithm for a partial function f in Cl(F) leads in general to an algorithm being nondeterministic one. This paper presents some results on the question of synthesis of deterministic algorithms.

In the sequel we shall use the same notation as it was used in [1]. In particular by RP we denote composition of relations R and P; by UR we denote an image of a set U with respect to a relation R and by $R\overline{U}$ we dentoe a coimage of a set U with respect to a relation R where $U \subseteq X$ and $R \subseteq X \times X$. Finally we shall use [U] to denote partial identity relation restricted to the set U, i.e. $U = \{(x,x) | x \in U\}$.

DEFINITION 1. We call an algorithm $A = (X, V, \sigma, \varepsilon, P)$ a DC-algorithm (deterministic & correct) iff:

(i) $f \in E_A \wedge xfy \wedge xfz \quad \Rightarrow \quad y = z$,

(ii) $(a,f,b),(a,g,c) \in P \wedge f = g \quad \Rightarrow \quad b = c$,

(iii) $(a,f,b),(a,g,c) \in P \wedge f \neq g \quad \Rightarrow \quad fX \cap gX = \emptyset$,

(iv) $x \in fX \wedge (a,f,b) \in P \quad \Rightarrow \quad (\exists z)(a,x)Tr_A^{*}(\varepsilon,z)$.

We introduce notions of some partial operations.

DEFINITION 2. A correct composition of two functions f and g, denoted f;g, is defined iff $Xf \subseteq gX$ and then

$$f;g = fg.$$

DEFINITION 3. A correct union of two functions f and g, denoted $f \Psi g$, is defined iff $fX \cap gX = \emptyset$ and then

$$f \Psi g = f \cup g.$$

DEFINITION 4. A correct iteration of a function f to a function g, denoted $f \# g$, is defined iff:

(i) $fX \cap gX = \emptyset$,

(ii) $Xf \subseteq fX \cup gX$,

(iii) $(\forall x \in fX)(\exists n \geq 0)(xf^n \in gX)$ and then

$$f \# g = f^{*}g.$$

DEFINITION 5. The structured closure of a family F of partial functions (denoted Cls(F)) is the least set U of functions such that

(i) $F \cup \{\emptyset, I\} \subseteq U$,

(ii) $f, g \in U$ and the correct operations are defined $\Rightarrow$ $f;g$, $f \Psi g$, $f \# g \in U$,

(iii) $f, [Y] \in U \quad \Rightarrow \quad [fY] \in U$,

(iv) $W \subseteq U \quad \Rightarrow \quad [\bigcup_{[Y] \in W} Y] \in U$.

Thus there is a family of partial identities included in Cls(F) and we denote the family id(F). So

$$id(F) = \{[Y] \mid [Y] \in Cls(F)\}.$$

The following two theorems may be proved.

THEOREM 1B. Any DC-algorithm A such that $E_A \subseteq F$ has its resulting relation Res_A in Cls(F).

THEOREM 2B. For any function $f \in Cls(F)$ there exists a DC-algorithm A such that $Res_A = f$ and $E_A \subseteq F \cup id(F)$.

In order to prove the theorems we can proceed analogously as to prove THEOREM 1A and THEOREM 2A. In particular, in order to prove THEOREM 1B we can make use of some special transformations of an algorithm instead of the label elimination procass used by Mazurkiewicz. The transformations are presented in the graphic form as follows.

I.A correct elimination of a label. It is possible when there is only one instruction in P starting with the label (Fig.1).

Fig.1.

II.Making a label correctly eliminable. Fig.2a and Fig.2b illustrate two possible variants of such transformation.

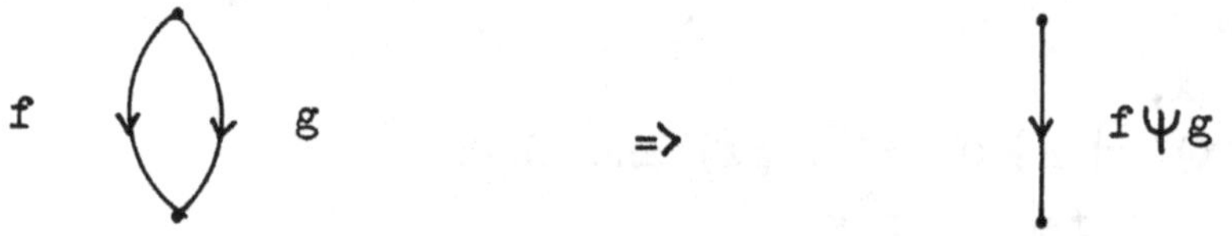

Fig.2a.

Fig.2b.

III.A structured elimination of a label. Such elimination is always possible and is illustrated by Fig.3.

The case when we cannot eliminate all labels from a given algorithm using only the transformations described in pp. I and II corresponds to the situation in which auxiliary variables are suggested to be introduced in order to translate a "goto" program into a "while" program [2]. It comes out from THEOREM 1B and THEOREM 2B that for a given algorithm which is a DC-one we can obtain, by means of the

TOP-DOWN synthesis process, an equivalent DC-algorithm in which there are some partial identities as elementary operations and which is a model of a structured program. Thus we can do the above mentioned translation by means of proper formulation of the expressions for tests in a flowchart. The transformations described in I - III followed by the TOP-DOWN process may be considered as a method of such a translation.

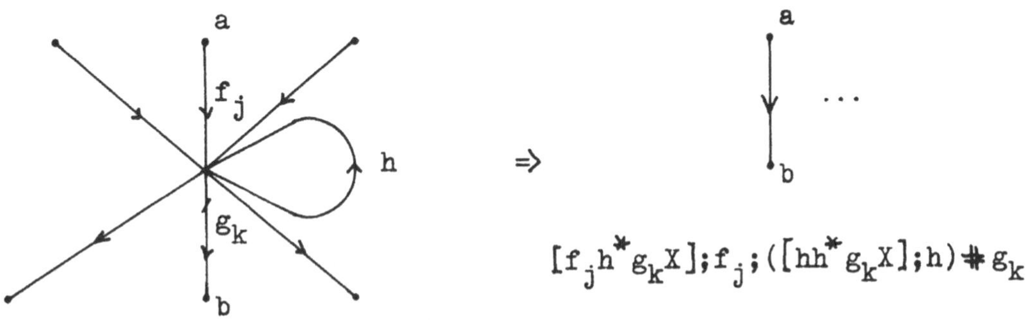

Fig.3.

EXAMPLE. Below we present, in a graphic form, a sequence of equivalent algorithms obtained by means of the above described transformations.

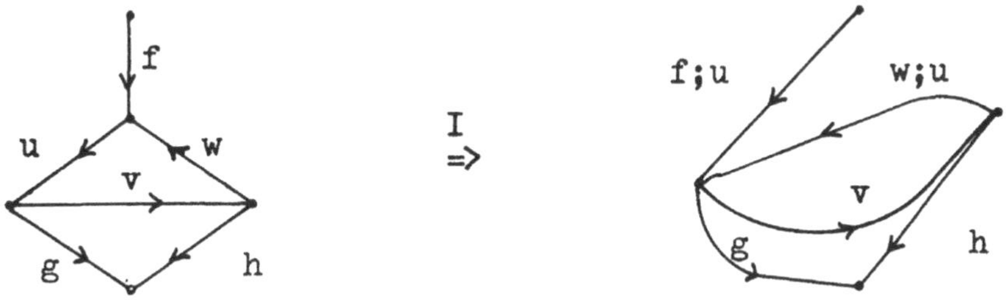

We have used here the transformation described in p.I - the correct elimination of a label. Now it is impossible to make anything but a structured elimination of a label. We get the followin graph=.

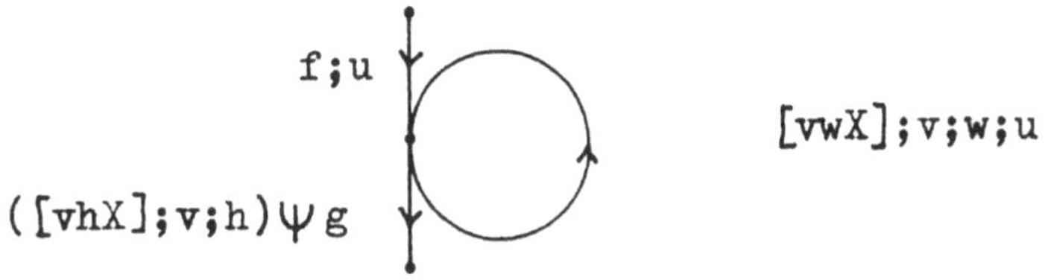

Finally we get the following expression for the resulting relation of any algorithm of the sequence

$$Res = f;u;([vwX];v;w;u)\#(g\,\psi[vhX];v;h).$$

We may easily read out a structured program from such expression. In this case we could write the following intuitively obvious text for such a program:

f;u; WHILE $x \in$ vwX DO (v;w;u); IF $x \in$ vhX THEN (v;h) ELSE g.

REFERENCES.

[1]. MAZURKIEWICZ, A. Theory of Programs and Algorithms. Lecture Notes. MFCS Semester. Stefan Banach Mathematical Center, Warsaw 1974.

[2]. ASHCROFT, E.; MANNA, Z. The Translation of 'goto' Programs into 'while' Programs. Proc. IFIP Conf. 1971.

ON EQUIVALENCE OF PROGRAMS

J.Leszczyłowski
Computation Center, Polish Academy of Sciences
PKiN P.O.Box 22, 00-901 Warsaw, Poland

1. INTRODUCTION

Problem of programs equivalence is one of the most important in the theory of programming. Pawlak's processes are used in this paper as program models. Usually two processes are called equivalent if corresponding computed functions, defined on the entire vector of program variables, are equal. This approach is not adequate in our situation where we want to distinguish a particular set of variables and describe program behaviour truncated to this set. In this paper two processes are considered equivalent provided their computed fuctions are similar in some defined mathematical sense. Main result of this paper is a theorem which permits to reduce the problem of such equivalence of programs to a local problem of similarity, in defined sense, of sets of instructions.

2. BASIC NOTIONS

Let U be an arbitrary set. By a binary relation in U we mean any subset R of $U \times U$. Let $R, Q \subseteq U \times U$, $A \subseteq U$, $a, b \in U$. We define:

identity relation: $I_U = \{(a,a) \mid a \in U\}$

composition of relations: $a\, RQ\, b$ iff $(\exists z \in U)\ (aRz \,\&\, zQb)$

composition of a set and a relation: $RA = \{b \mid (\exists a \in A)\ (bRa)\}$

n-th power of a relation: for all $n \geqslant 0$, $R^0 = I_U$, $R^n = RR^{n-1}$

$*$ and $+$ iteration of relations: $R^* = \bigcup_{n=0}^{\infty} R^n$, $R^+ = \bigcup_{n=1}^{\infty} R^n$.

3. ON EQUIVALENCE OF PROCESSES

By a process we shall mean a system:

$$P = (S , B , F , T)$$

where S is a set /of states of P /, $B \subseteq S$ is a set of initial states, $F \subseteq S$ is a set of final states and $T \subseteq (S-F) \times S$ is a binary relation called transition relation of P . We associate so called resulting relation with every process. This relation, corresponds in our model, to an input-output relation of a program. It is a binary relation with domain B and range F defined as follows:

$$Res_P = I_B T^* I_F .$$

States in our processes should be understood as full McCarthy state-vector i.e. pairs (q,v) where q is a control state /e.g. label/ and v is a current valuation of variables. Now $a \, Res_P \, b$ means that there exists $n \geq 0$ with $a \, I_B T^n I_F \, b$, i.e. starting with a in B we get b in F after a finite number of n steps.

Usually two processes are called equivalent whenever their resulting relations are equal. As has been mentioned in the introduction, this notion is sometimes to strong. We introduce therefore an alternative notion of "being a copy of" to replace the concept of equivalence in the above sense. The idea of our approach is that given two programs we want to compare them outside of the sets of their auxiliary variables.

If R_1 and R_2 are binary relations and $c: R_1 \longrightarrow R_2$ is a total function ranging over the whole R_2 , then R_2 is said to be a c-copy of R_1, in symbols $R_1 \; copy(c) \; R_2$.

Now we formulate an auxiliary notion. Let $P_i = (S_i, B_i, F_i, T_i)$ for $i=1,2$ be processes and let $C: S_1 \longrightarrow S_2$ be a total fuction. P_2 is said to be a C-COPY of P_1, in symbols $P_1 \; COPY(C) \; P_2$, if the following conditions are satisfied:

1. $(\forall s_1, s_2 \in S_1)\ [s_1 T_1 s_2 \longrightarrow C(s_1)\ (T_2 \cup I)\ C(s_2)]$

2. $(\forall s_1, s_2 \in S_2)\ [s_1 T_2 s_2 \longrightarrow (\forall s_1' \in C^{-1}(s_1))\ (\exists s_2' \in C^{-1}(s_2))\ (s_1' T_1^+ s_2')]$

3. $C(B_1) = B_2$

4. $T_2 S_2 \subseteq C(S_1)$

5. $C(F_1) = F_2$

6. $C^{-1}(F_2) \subseteq F_1$.

THEOREM. Let $P_i = (S_i, B_i, F_i, T_i)$ for $i=1,2$ be processes and let $C: S_1 \longrightarrow S_2$ be a total function.

If P_1 COPY(C) P_2, then Res_{P_1} copy(C') Res_{P_2}, where $C': B_1 \times F_1 \longrightarrow B_2 \times F_2$ and $C'(b,f) = (C(b), C(f))$.

Proof. First we have to prove two formulas:

(i) $(\forall k \geq 0)\ (\forall s_1 \in B_1)\ (\forall s_2 \in S_1)\ [s_1 T_1^k s_2 \longrightarrow C(s_1)\ T_2^* C(s_2)]$

(ii) $(\forall k \geq 0)\ (\forall s_1 \in B_2)\ (\forall s_2 \in S_2)\ [s_1 T_2^k s_2 \longrightarrow (\forall s_1' \in C^{-1}(s_1))\ (\exists s_2' \in C^{-1}(s_2))(s_1' T_1^+ s_2')]$

Since the proofs are similar, we shall show only the second one. The proof is by induction on k :

1. for $k=0$ the formula is true because of 4 in the definition above
2. let (ii) be true for some $n > 0$, let $s_1 \in B_2$, $s_2 \in S_2$ and let $s_1 T_2^{n+1} s_2$.

The latter means $(\exists z)\ (s_1 T_2^n z \ \&\ z T_2 s_2)$. By induction assumption:

$$(\forall s_1' \in C^{-1}(s_1))\ (\exists z' \in C^{-1}(z))\ (s_1' \ T_1^+ \ z') .$$

By condition 4 from definition above, we have $z \in C(S_1)$, and basing on 2 from the same definition, $(\forall z' \in C^{-1}(z))\ (\exists s_2' \in C^{-1}(s_2))\ (z' T^+ \ s_2')$.
The latter completes the proof of (ii) .

Observe now that the claim of the theorem is equivalent to conjunction of the following formulas:

(iii) $(\forall (x,y) \in Res_{P_1})\ [C(x)\ Res_{P_2}\ C(y)]$

(iv) $(\forall (x,y) \in Res_{P_2})\ (\exists (x',y') \in Res_{P_1})\ [C(x') = x \ \&\ C(y') = y]$.

Both these formulas are true. Indeed (iii) follows from (i) and 3, 5 in the definition above. Formula (iv) follows from (ii) and 3, 6 from the same definition.

Intuitively, the theorem shows the way in which proving relationships between resulting relations of two processes can be reduced to proving relationships between their sets of instructions.

This theorem has been applied in proving relationships between computability by diffrent classes of programs see [1] .

REFERENCES

[1] LESZCZYŁOWSKI, J. Mathematical models of programs with dynamic allocation of variables. Math. Found. Comp. Sci. III (Proc. Symp. Warsaw Jadwisin 1974) Springer-Verlag, Lectures Notes inComputer Science (this volume), Heidelberg

[2] MAZURKIEWICZ, A. Proving properties of processes. CC PAS Reports 134 (1974)

MATHEMATICAL MODEL OF PROGRAMS WITH DYNAMIC ALLOCATION OF VARIABLES

J.Leszczyłowski
Computation Center, Polish Academy of Sciences
PKiN P.O.Box 22, 00-901 Warsaw, Poland

1. INTRODUCTION

Our model is an extention of a model, introduced by A.Mazurkiewicz (see [1], [5]), to describe programs with fixed set of variables. In particular we can consider programs with the set of variables depending on the input, e.g. programs computing product of two vectors of arbitrary length, or programs where the set of variables changes dynamically in course of a run, e.g. recursive procedures with calls by values. Our model is intended to help in proving properties of programs with dynamic allocation of variables and to investigate the problem of definability (computability) by classes of programs with different mechanisms of variable allocation. In this paper we deal with the latter problem only. Due to the lack of space there are no proofs in the paper.

2. NOTATIONS AND BASIC IDEAS

Let N denote the set of all natural numbers. Let Z be an arbitrary set. We shall denote:

$Rel(Z)=\{R \mid R \subseteq Z \times Z\}$ - the set of all binary relations in Z

$Z^0 = \{\varepsilon\}$, where ε denotes the empty string

$Z^n = Z \times Z^{n-1}$

$$Z^* = \bigcup_{n=0}^{\infty} Z^n$$

$$Z^+ = \bigcup_{n=1}^{\infty} Z^n$$

$$[Z] = \{(z,z) \mid z \in Z\} .$$

Let x be a string in Z :

x_i - denotes the i-th component of x

$l(x)$ - denotes the length of x .

If $R_1, R_2 \in Rel(Z)$ and $c: R_1 \longrightarrow R_2$ is a total function ranging over the whole R_2 , then R_2 is said to be a c-copy of R_1 , in symbols R_1 copy(c) R_2 .

We introduce now slightly modified Mazurkiewicz algorithms to be used in our approach as models of programs. Semantics of these algorithms will be described by appropriate binary relation to be called resulting relation of an algorithm.

An algorithm is an arbitrary system of the form:

$$A = (Z , V , \sigma , P)$$

where Z is an arbitrary set, V is a finite set of symbols /labels/, $\sigma \in V$ is an initial label, P is a finite subset of $Rel(V^*) \times Rel(Z)$ called set of instructions. Intuitively Z corresponds to a set of data and for each (R,R') P , R is to represent a control part of program instruction and R' - the operational part /assignment statement, condition, etc./.

With any algorithm $A = (Z,V,\sigma,P)$ we associate now a relation $Res_A \in Rel(Z)$ to be called resulting relation of A :

$x \; Res_A \; y$ iff there exist $(v_1,x_1),\ldots,(v_n,x_n) \in V^* \times Z$ and $(R_1,R_1'), \ldots, (R_{n-1},R_{n-1}') \in P$ such that $v_1=\sigma$, $x_1=x$, $v_n=\varepsilon$, $x_n=y$ and for every $i=1,\ldots,n-1$ $(v_i,v_{i+1}) \in R_i$ and $(x_i,x_{i+1}) \in R_i'$.

Now we introduce algorithmic systems to be used in considering definability by algorithms in the above sense.

An <u>algorithmic system</u> is a triple of the form:

$$S = (D , W , F)$$

where D is a set, W is an arbitrary family of subsets of D and $F \subseteq Rel(D)$.

We shall say an algorithm $A = (Z,V,\epsilon,P)$ to be an <u>algorithm over the algorithmic system</u> $S = (D,W,F)$ if $Z = D$ and $P \subseteq Rel(V^*) \times F$.

A relation R is said to be <u>definable by algorithm</u> A iff there exists a set $Q \subseteq Z$ with $R = [Q]Res_A$. The above relation R is said to be <u>definable over algorithmic system</u> $S = (D,W,F)$ iff A is an algorithm over S and $Q \in W$.

3. PROGRAMS WITH EXTENDABLE SETS OF VARIABLES

In majority of existing mathematical models of programs, programs are assumed to operate on a fixed set of variables. This means in our terms, that $D = U^n$ where U is a range of variables and n is a fixed natural number / number of variables /. In our approach we shall assume $D = U^+$ to consider programs where the set of variables may change. In this way we are able to investigate programs of two types. Either, the set of variables is fixed for each particular input but depends on it, e.g. a program to compute product of square matrices of arbitrary demension, or the set of variables is modificated during a run, e.g. a program that calls and rejects variables dynamically. To deal with both these types of programs we introduce a notation corresponding to indexed-variable mechanism. This is a natural extention of notation introduced by Mazurkiewicz in [1] and [5].

Let U be an arbitrary set and let $n \in N$. Let $f: U^n \longrightarrow U$ be a partial fuction, $r \subseteq U^n$, and $z_1,\dots,z_n$ be partial fuctions from U^+ into N. We shall consider relations $[r(v_{z_1},\dots,v_{z_n})]$ and functions $[v_{z_1} := f(v_{z_2},\dots,v_{z_n})]$ in $Rel(U^+)$ defined as follows:

$$x\ [r(v_{z_1},\dots,v_{z_n})]\ y \quad \text{iff} \quad \begin{cases} 1. & x = y \\ 2. & (x_{z_1(x)},\dots x_{z_n(x)}) \in r \end{cases}$$

$$x\left[v_{z_1} := f\left(v_{z_2},\dots,v_{z_n}\right)\right] y \quad \text{iff} \quad \begin{array}{l} 1.\ \ l(x) = l(y) \\ 2.\ \ \text{for each } 1 \leq i \leq l(x) \\ \quad y_i = \begin{cases} f\left(x_{z_2(x)},\dots,x_{z_n(x)}\right) & \text{if } i=z_1(x) \\ x_i & \text{if } i \neq z_1(x) \end{cases} \end{array}$$

By a system basis over U we call a triple $G = \left(G_f, G_r, G_i\right)$, where:

$$\begin{array}{ll} 1. & G_f \subseteq \left\{ g \mid (\exists n \in N)\ \left(g\colon U^n \xrightarrow[\text{part.}]{} U\right)\right\} \\ 2. & G_r \subseteq \left\{ g \mid (\exists n \in N)\ \left(g \subseteq U^n\right)\right\} \\ 3. & G_i \subseteq \left\{ g \mid g\colon U^+ \xrightarrow[\text{part.}]{} N\right\} . \end{array} \qquad /1/$$

Let $G = \left(G_f, G_r, G_i\right)$ be a system basis. We shall denote:

$$\langle G\rangle = \bigcup_{n=1}^{\infty}\left(\left\{\left[v_{z_1} := f\left(v_{z_2},\dots,v_{z_n}\right)\right] \mid f \in G_f \,\&\, z_i \in G_i\right\} \cup \left\{\left[r\left(v_{z_1},\dots,v_{z_n}\right)\right] \mid r \in G_r \,\&\, z_i \in G_i\right\}\right)$$

We shall introduce now more specified algorithmic systems to distinguish between the two cases mentioned in the comentary to this section. Let G be a system basis over U . By a simple algorithmic system with basis G we mean every algorithmic system S of the form:

$$S = \left(U^+ , W , \langle G\rangle\right) .$$

Observe that elements in G_f and G_r are intended to represent primitive operations and conditions in a programing language. In what follows algorithms over simple algorithmic systems are models for programs with a fixed sets of variables.

Now we shall extend our systems to deal with algorithms that are models of programs with a modificable vector of variables.

By B we shall denote a relation in $Rel\left(U^+\right)$, defined as follows: for any $x,y \in U^+$, $x\,B\,y$ iff $y = xx_{l(x)}$. This relation is intended to describe the operation of calling new variables in a program.

By E we denote a relation in $Rel\left(U^*\right)$, defined as follows: for any $x,y \in U^*$, $x\,E\,y$ iff $y = x_1 \dots x_{l(x)-1}$ and $l(x)>1$. This relation is intended to describe the operation of rejecting existing variables.

Let $S=\left(U^+ , W , \langle G\rangle\right)$ be a simple algorithmic system. By a dynamic algorithmic system over S we mean an algorithmic system of the form:

$$SD = \left(U^+ , W , \langle G\rangle \cup \{B,E\}\right). \qquad /\ 2\ /$$

Notice that any algorithm over S is also an algorithm over SD . In what follows any relation definable over S is definable over SD as well. As turns out, the converse implication needs not to be true and depends on the basis G .

4. RESULTS

The notion of an algorithmic system as defined in Sec. 3 is intended to be general frame in describing classes of programs possibly with dynamic allocation of variables. In this section we investigate some particular subcases of this notion corresponding to some particular classes of programs. We shall investigate definabilities of relations by these particular classes.

Let $W = \{U^n \mid n = 1,2,\dots\}$ be the family of subsets in / 2 /. In this case we deal with programs where data vector has arbitrary but fixed length.

Let us consider now a correspondence between variables in real programs and components of vectors performed by algorithms in our model. To this effect we shall specify the set G_i in / 1 /. Let Da be the set of all constant functions from U^+ into N . Thus, if we want to deal with simple variables we set G_i=Da . Let t be a total function from U into N and let $Ia(t) = \{f \mid (\exists n \in N)(\forall x \in U^+)(f(x) = t(x_n))\} \cup Da$. In the case $G_i = Ia(t)$, we deal with programs with simple and indexed variables.

In some cases we want to compare programs in a way that neglects particular variables to be considered as auxiliary ones. To deal with such cases we shall define another notion of definability. A fuction $c: U^+ \times U^+ \longrightarrow U^+ \times U^+$ is said to be a projection iff there exist three natural numbers n_1, n_2, n_3 such that for all $x,y \in U^+$, if $c(x,y) = (x',y')$ then $x' = x_{n_1} \dots x_{l(x)}$ and $y' = y_{n_2} \dots y_{n_3}$.

Relation R is said to be projection definable / abbr. p-definable/ over algorithmic system S iff there exists such relation R′ definable over S and such projection c that R′ copy(c) R .

This definition of definability permits to compare in a nontrivial way definability by algorithms having a fixed set of variables with definability by algorithms where the set of variables changes dynamically. In particular - and this is motivation for p-definability - we can ask now if a relation p-definable by dynamic allocating algorithm is p-definable by an algorithm without dynamic allocation. Observe that using ordinary definability we should get in general a trivial negative answer. In fact, there exist relations with fixed length of inputs and unlimited length of outputs that are definable by dynamic allocating algorithms and are not definable by algorithms without such mechanism. Some technical results helpfull in proving p-definability of relations are given in [2], [3] .

The following results concerning definability by algorithms over different algorithmic systems are proved in [2].

THEOREM 1. There exist sets G_f, G_r , a function t and a relation R p-definable over a dynamic system with basis $(G_f, G_r, Ia(t))$ such that R is not p-definable over any dynamic system with basis (G_f, G_r, Da).

THEOREM 2. There exists a simple algorithmic system S and a relation R p-definable over SD such that R is not p-definable over S.

THEOREM 3. There exists an algorithmic system S and a relation R p-definable over S by algorithms with recursion (see [1]) that is not p-definable without recursion over S .

It is to be mentioned at the end that problem of a mathematical model for programs with dynamic allocation of variables has been also investigated by other authors (see [4], [6]) but in different way.

REFERENCES

[1] BLIKLE, A.; MAZURKIEWICZ, A. An algebraic approach to the theory of programs, algorithms, languages and recursiveness. Math. Found. Comp. Sci. I (Proc. Symp. Warsaw-Jabłonna 1972), Warsaw 1972

[2] LESZCZYŁOWSKI, J. Mathematical theory of programs with dynamic allocation of variables. Ph.D. Thesis , in preparation

[3] LESZCZYŁOWSKI, J. On equivalence of programs. Math. Found. Comp. Sci. III (Proc. Symp. Warsaw-Jadwisin 1974), Lecture Notes in Computer Science, Springer-Verlag, Heidelberg, (this volume)

[4] MAZURKIEWICZ, A. Polyadic program schemes. ibid

[5] MAZURKIEWICZ, A. Recursive algorithms and formal languages.

Bull. Acad. Polon. Sci., Ser. Sci. Math. Phys. 20 (1972), 799-803

[6] SCOTT, D.; STRACHEY, Ch. Toward a Mathematical Semantics for Computer Languages. Technical Monograph PRG-6, August 1971, Oxford University Computing Laboratory.

MATHEMATICAL FOUNDATIONS OF MOTIVATION LANGUAGES AND SYNTHESIS MAPS.

Pierangelo Miglioli

Istituto di Fisica dell'Università di Milano - Gruppo di Elettronica e di Cibernetica.

INTRODUCTION

How can we carry out the construction of a program which is adequate with respect to some previously stated goals (motivation)? Which general conditions make this task possible?

We call the above problems the problems of the synthesis of programs. Despite of its great relevance in Computer Science, very little is known on this subject from a theoretical point of view: the literature is widespread and even the most basic concepts have not an homogeneous and clear definition. In our paper we try to set up such concepts and to investigate, on the basis of the proposed definitions, the possibilities and the bounds of the synthesis approach. The treatment is made on a theoretical ground and special attention is devoted to questions involving the completeness of the considered procedures or the recursive enumerability of some classes of formulas.

More specifically, the paper considers synthesis procedures as embedded in a first order number theory. It extends the treatment of Degli Antoni - Miglioli - Ornaghi [3] and is an attempt to put it on a more general ground: so, the emphasis is on intuitionistic number theory and on the intuitionistically-well-constructed formulas (see Chapter 3) which are the core of the theory exposed in [3]; but also the classical theories and their relations to the intuitionistics ones are considered; moreover, a new class of formulas which allow the synthesis in a classical frame is defined.

Apart from general references to results about intuitionism, the paper should be self-contained in its main lines; on the other hand we cannot expose the most proofs and send the reader to a larger report [5]. Of course, the purposes of our paper make the treatment indipendent from computational aspects and from implementation on some machines: so a concrete exposition of the synthesis procedures involved is not given; for a detailed exposition of such procedures which are a development of the synthesis rules presented in [3], we send to Degli Antoni - Miglioli - Ornaghi [4].

1. - BASIC DEFINITIONS

By "synthesis procedure" we informally mean any set of rules which allow us to construct procedural definitions of functions starting from non procedural ones.

The general concept of "procedural definition" or, equivalently, of "program", is considered known: a program will be any set of statements, in some language, which allow us to compute the values of a function for some set of arguments; this function, whose domain is restricted to exactly those arguments for which the computation is defined, will be said the "input-output function of the program".

We will consider programs whose input-output functions are integer valued functions, i.e. partial functions defined, for some n, on a subset of N^n and having values in N, N being the set of the natural numbers. We assume, without further details, our programs belong to some well chosen programming language $\mathcal{L}\rho$, by which we are able to compute all partial recursive functions (p.r.f.'s).

Definition 1. Fun will be the class of all the functions $f(x_1,..,x_n)$ such that:

1) the domain D_f of $f(x_1,..,x_n)$ is a subset of N^n, for some n.

2) if $\langle \bar{x}_1,..,\bar{x}_n \rangle \in D_f$, then $f(\bar{x}_1,..,\bar{x}_n) \in N$ (we will represent a function putting into evidence its arguments by means of the variables x_1, $.,x_n$; symbols auch as $\bar{x}_1,..,\bar{x}_n$ will denote natural numbers). □

The following definition will specify the concept of "non procedural definition" of a function: a non procedural definition, which we call a "synthesis motivation", or, simply, a "motivation", will be any expression of a "motivation language".

Definition 2. We say that the couple $\langle \mathcal{L}_m, \mathcal{I} \rangle$ is a motivation language iff the following conditions are satisfied:

1) $\mathcal{L}_m$ is a language, i.e. a set of expressions on some finite alphabet which can be generated by a Turing machine or, equivalently, by a type-0 grammar.
2) $\mathcal{I}$, which we call the interpretation map of $\mathcal{L}_m$, is a map whose domain contains $\mathcal{L}_m$ and which is such that $\mathcal{I}(\mathcal{E}) \in$ Fun for every $\mathcal{E} \in \mathcal{L}_m$. □

Any synthesis procedure must define a partial map between a motivation language and a programming language; since it is a "procedure", this map must be a computable map, where "computable" is assumed equivalent to "computable by means of a Turing machine", according to Turing's and Church's thesis.

Definition 3. Let $\langle \mathcal{L}_m, \mathcal{I} \rangle$ be a motivation language and let S be a map with domain D_S; we say that S is a synthesis map defined on $\langle \mathcal{L}_m, \mathcal{I} \rangle$ if and only if the following conditions are satisfied:

1) $D_S \subseteq \mathcal{L}_m$.
2) If $\mathcal{E} \in D_S$, then $S(\mathcal{E}) \in \mathcal{L}_p$.
3) If $\mathcal{E} \in D_S$ and $f(x_1,..,x_n)$ is the input-output function of $S(\mathcal{E})$, then $\mathcal{I}(\mathcal{E}) = f(x_1,..,x_n)$.
4) S is a computable map. □

Generally a synthesis map is a partial map: in fact, in the most interesting motivation languages, if $\mathcal{E} \in \mathcal{L}_m$, then not necessarily $\mathcal{I}(\mathcal{E})$ is a computable function (a p.r.f.); so, we do not know whether a given synthesis motivation is a "good motivation" or not and we may only try to find the associated program, which may not exist. If $\mathcal{I}(\mathcal{E})$

is not a p.r.f., then the procedure must not stop: in this sense a motivation language should differ from an "high level programming language" and a synthesis procedure should differ from a "compiler".

Condition 3 of Definition 3 is an obvious soundness requisite we must impose to a map in order to have a synthesis map. It is to be remarked, however (as we shall see in an interesting case), that Condition 4 prevents some maps which satisfie Condition 3 from being synthesis maps: in fact there are cases where the class of all the motivations which can agree with Condition 3 (the class of all the "good motivations") is not a recursively enumerable set.

Definition 4. Let $\langle \mathcal{L}_{\mathcal{M}}, \mathcal{J} \rangle$ be a motivation language and let S be a synthesis map defined on $\langle \mathcal{L}_{\mathcal{M}}, \mathcal{J} \rangle$ with domain D_S; we say that S is motivationally complete with respect to $\langle \mathcal{L}_{\mathcal{M}}, \mathcal{J} \rangle$ iff the following condition is satisfied:

1) For every $\xi \in \mathcal{L}_{\mathcal{M}}$, if $\mathcal{J}(\xi)$ is a p.r.f., then $\xi \in D_S$. □

Definition 5. Let $\langle \mathcal{L}_{\mathcal{M}}, \mathcal{J} \rangle$ be a motivation language and let S be a synthesis map defined on $\langle \mathcal{L}_{\mathcal{M}}, \mathcal{J} \rangle$ with domain D_S; we say that S is weakly complete with respect to $\langle \mathcal{L}_{\mathcal{M}}, \mathcal{J} \rangle$ iff the following condition is satisfied:

1) If $f(x_1,..,x_n) \in$ Fun and $f(x_1,..,x_n)$ is a p.r.f., then there is an $\xi \in \mathcal{L}_{\mathcal{M}}$ such that:
   a_1) $\mathcal{J}(\xi) = f(x_1,..,x_n)$ and
   b_1) $\xi \in D_S$. □

Definition 6. Let $\langle \mathcal{L}_{\mathcal{M}}, \mathcal{J} \rangle$ be a motivation language and let S be a synthesis map defined on $\langle \mathcal{L}_{\mathcal{M}}, \mathcal{J} \rangle$; we say that S is complete with respect to $\langle \mathcal{L}_{\mathcal{M}}, \mathcal{J} \rangle$ iff the following conditions are satisfied:

1) S is motivationally complete with respect to $\langle \mathcal{L}_{\mathcal{M}}, \mathcal{J} \rangle$.
2) S is weakly complete with respect to $\langle \mathcal{L}_{\mathcal{M}}, \mathcal{J} \rangle$. □

As we shall see, we can define a synthesis map on an interesting motivation language which is motivationally complete but not weakly complete (even in a strenghtened sense which considers, in the definition of weak completeness, only the class of the general recursive functions): such a motivation language is not "enough powerful". On the other hand, we will be mainly interested in a motivation language on which we can define weakly complete synthesis maps; on this language, on the contrary, motivationally complete synthesis maps cannot be defined: it is "too powerful". At last, we can give a motivation language on which a complete synthesis map is definable; however, despite of this nice property, there are good reasons to consider such a motivation language unadequate from a pragmatical point of view, as we shall see.

Finally, we give the following definition, which will be useful later.

Definition 7. Let $\langle \mathcal{L}_{\mathfrak{M}1}, \mathcal{I}_1 \rangle$ and $\langle \mathcal{L}_{\mathfrak{M}2}, \mathcal{I}_2 \rangle$ be two motivation languages; let S_1 be a synthesis map defined on $\langle \mathcal{L}_{\mathfrak{M}1}, \mathcal{I}_1 \rangle$ with domain D_{S1} and let S_2 be a synthesis map defined on $\langle \mathcal{L}_{\mathfrak{M}2}, \mathcal{I}_2 \rangle$ with domain D_{S2}; we say that the map Om is an homomorphic extension of S_1 into S_2 iff the following conditions are satisfied:

1) Om is a computable map;
2) The domain of Om is D_{S1} and its range is contained in D_{S2};
3) If $\xi \in D_{S1}$, then $\mathcal{I}_1(\xi) = \mathcal{I}_2(Om(\xi))$.

We say that S_2 Homomorphically extends S_1 if there is an homomorphic extension of S_1 into S_2. □

Of course, an homomorphic extension of a sinthesis map preserves the weak completeness.

2. MOTIVATION LANGUAGES IN THE FRAME OF A FIRST ORDER NUMBER THEORY

Now, we want to describe some motivation languages. We restrict ourselves to motivation languages which are subsets of the language of a first order number theory: namely, we will consider subsets of $L_{\mathfrak{N}}$, which is the language of both Kleene's classical number theory T_{NC} and Kleene's intuitionistic number theory T_{NI} (as it is well known, these theories have the same language, i.e. the same set of well formed formulas; for reference, see [1]).

If $\mathcal{F}$ is a formula of $L_{\mathfrak{N}}$, we will represent by "$T_{NC} \vdash \mathcal{F}$" ("$T_{NI} \vdash \mathcal{F}$") the fact that $\mathcal{F}$ is provable in T_{NC} (the fact that $\mathcal{F}$

is provable in T_{NI}); moreover, we will denote by "$\mathfrak{N} \models \mathcal{F}$" the fact that $\mathcal{F}$ is valid (true) over the structure $\mathfrak{N} = \langle N, =, ', +, \cdot \rangle$ of the natural numbers.

As it is well known, if $T_{NI} \vdash \mathcal{F}$, then $T_{NC} \vdash \mathcal{F}$; the converse proposition does not hold in general.

Finally, we accept the following result, which, as a consequence of Gödel's incompleteness theorem, is a non elementary result: both T_{NC} and T_{NI} admit the structure $\mathfrak{N}$ as a model, i.e., if $T_{NC} \vdash \mathcal{F}$ ($T_{NI} \vdash \mathcal{F}$), then $\mathfrak{N} \models \mathcal{F}$.

A natural framework in which we want to define our motivation language is the class Den (which we may read as "Denoting") interpreted by the map $\mathcal{J}_{Den}$: Den and $\mathcal{J}_{Den}$ are defined below.

Definition 8. For every $\mathcal{F} \in L_{\mathfrak{N}}$, $\mathcal{F} \in$ Den iff the following conditions are satisfied:

1) $\mathcal{F} \equiv \forall x_1 \dots x_n \, (\varphi(x_1,..,x_n) \longrightarrow \exists ! \, z \, \psi(x_1,..,x_n,z))$, where "$\equiv$" denotes the identity relation between formulas.
2) $\mathfrak{N} \models \mathcal{F}$.

The formulas $\varphi(x_1,..,x_n)$ and $\psi(x_1,..,x_n,z)$ will be said the input formula of $\mathcal{F}$ and the input-output formula of $\mathcal{F}$ respectively. □

Definition 9. For every $\mathcal{F} \in$ Den, $\mathcal{J}_{Den}(\mathcal{F})$ is the function $f(x_1,..,x_n) \in$ Fun with domain D_f, which satisfies the following conditions:

1) Let $\varphi(x_1,..,x_n)$ be the input formula of $\mathcal{F}$; then $D_f = \{\langle \bar{x}_1,..,\bar{x}_n \rangle \mid \mathfrak{N} \models \varphi(\tilde{x}_1,..,\tilde{x}_n)\}$, where $\bar{x}_1,..,\bar{x}_n$ represent numbers and $\tilde{x}_1,..,\tilde{x}_n$ are the corresponding constants of $L_{\mathfrak{N}}$.
2) Let $\psi(x_1,..,x_n,z)$ be the input-output formula of $\mathcal{F}$ and let it be $\langle \bar{x}_1,..,\bar{x}_n \rangle \in D_f$; then $f(\bar{x}_1,..,\bar{x}_n)$ is the only $\bar{z}$ such that $\mathfrak{N} \models \psi(\tilde{x}_1,..,\tilde{x}_n,\tilde{z})$. □

Unfortunately, $\langle$Den, $\mathcal{J}_{Den}\rangle$ cannot be a motivation language, since Den cannot be a language, being not a recursively enumerable set.

We must therefore restrict the class Den in order to obtain motivation languages: we give the following "reasonable definitions".

Definition 10. For every $\mathcal{F} \in$ Den, $\mathcal{F} \in \mathcal{L}^C_{\mathcal{M}}$ iff $T_{NC} \vdash \mathcal{F}$; for every $\mathcal{F} \in$ Den, $\mathcal{F} \in \mathcal{L}^I_{\mathcal{M}}$ iff $T_{NI} \vdash \mathcal{F}$. □

One easily sees that $\langle \mathcal{L}^C_{\mathcal{M}}, \mathcal{J}_{Den} \rangle$ and $\langle \mathcal{L}^I_{\mathcal{M}}, \mathcal{J}_{Den} \rangle$ are motivation languages.

Definition 11. $\mathcal{F} \in \mathcal{R}^C$ iff $\mathcal{F} \in \mathcal{L}^C_{\mathcal{M}}$ and $\mathcal{J}_{Den}(\mathcal{F})$ is a p.r.f.; $\mathcal{F} \in \mathcal{R}^I$ iff $\mathcal{F} \in \mathcal{L}^I_{\mathcal{M}}$ and $\mathcal{J}_{Den}(\mathcal{F})$ is a p.r.f.. □

$\mathcal{R}^C$ and $\mathcal{R}^I$ are the classes of all the "good motivations" of $\langle \mathcal{L}^C_{\mathcal{M}}, \mathcal{J}_{Den} \rangle$ and of $\langle \mathcal{L}^I_{\mathcal{M}}, \mathcal{J}_{Den} \rangle$ respectively. Now we must show that $\mathcal{R}^I$ is properly contained in $\mathcal{R}^C$: the following proposition states much more.

Proposition 1. $\mathcal{R}^C - \mathcal{R}^I$ is not a recursively enumerable set.

Proof.

We prove in outline that the set $\mathcal{Q}$ of all the formulas $\alpha(x) \in L_{\mathcal{N}}$ such that $T_{NI} \vdash \alpha(x) \vee \neg \alpha(x)$ is recursively enumerable, but not recursive: in order to do so, we must show that $L_{\mathcal{N}} - \mathcal{Q}$ is not recursively enumerable.

Consider the class Γ of all the formulas $\gamma(x) \in L_{\mathcal{N}}$ such that $T_{NI} \nvdash \neg \forall y(\neg \gamma(y))$ and $T_{NI} \nvdash \forall y(\neg \gamma(y))$: from the proof of Proposition 8 we shall see that this class is not recursively enumerable. If $\gamma(x) \in \Gamma$, then $T_{NI} \nvdash (\forall y(\neg \gamma(y)) \wedge x=x) \vee \neg(\forall y(\neg \gamma(y)) \wedge x=x)$ and conversely; so, if we could recursively enumerate $L_{\mathcal{N}} - \mathcal{Q}$, then we could recursively enumerate Γ, a contradiction.

On the other hand, let it be

1) $T_{NI} \nvdash \overline{\beta}(x) \vee \neg \overline{\beta}(x)$

and let $\overline{\mathcal{F}}$ be so defined:

2) $\overline{\mathcal{F}} \equiv \forall x(\neg \forall z \neg ((\overline{\beta}(x) \vee \neg \overline{\beta}(x)) \wedge z=x) \longrightarrow \exists ! z((\overline{\beta}(x) \vee \neg \overline{\beta}(x)) \wedge z=x))$;

since we have

3) $T_{NI} \vdash \neg \forall z \neg ((\overline{\beta}(x) \vee \neg \overline{\beta}(x)) \wedge z=x)$,

we can prove

4) $T_{NI} \nvdash \overline{\mathcal{F}}$.

In fact, otherwise, we could prove, by 3), $T_{NI} \vdash \overline{\beta}(x) \vee \neg \overline{\beta}(x)$, which contradicts 1).

But

5) $T_{NC} \vdash \overline{\mathcal{F}}$

and $\mathcal{J}_{Den}(\overline{\mathcal{F}})$ is a p.r.f., since it is the identity function. □

The following propositions complete the picture of the "good motivations" of both $\mathcal{L}_{\mathfrak{M}}^{C}$ and $\mathcal{L}_{\mathfrak{M}}^{I}$; the proofs are not very impressive and are omitted.

Proposition 2. $\mathcal{R}^{C}$ and $\mathcal{R}^{I}$ are not recursively enumerable sets. $\square$

Proposition 3. Let $\langle \overline{\mathcal{L}}_{\mathfrak{M}}, \overline{\mathcal{J}} \rangle$ be a motivation language such that $\mathcal{L}_{\mathfrak{M}}^{I} \subseteq \overline{\mathcal{L}}_{\mathfrak{M}}$ and $\mathcal{J}_{Den} \subseteq \overline{\mathcal{J}}$; let $\overline{\mathcal{R}}$ be the class of all $\xi \in \overline{\mathcal{L}}_{\mathfrak{M}}$ such that $\overline{\mathcal{J}}(\xi)$ is a p.r.f.: then $\overline{\mathcal{R}}$ is not recursively enumerable. $\square$

Now we look at the "bad motivations" of $\mathcal{L}_{\mathfrak{M}}^{C}$ and $\mathcal{L}_{\mathfrak{M}}^{I}$, which are characterized in the following propositions; the method of the proofs looks like the one of proposition 3.

Proposition 4. $(\mathcal{L}_{\mathfrak{M}}^{C} - \mathcal{R}^{C}) - (\mathcal{L}_{\mathfrak{M}}^{I} - \mathcal{R}^{I})$ is not a recursively enumerable set. $\square$

Proposition 5. $\mathcal{L}_{\mathfrak{M}}^{C} - \mathcal{R}^{C}$ is not a recursively enumerable set. $\square$

Proposition 6. $\mathcal{L}_{\mathfrak{M}}^{I} - \mathcal{R}^{I}$ is not a recursively enumerable set. $\square$

Proposition 1 and Proposition 4 tell us that $\langle \mathcal{L}_{\mathfrak{M}}^{C}, \mathcal{J}_{Den} \rangle$ and $\langle \mathcal{L}_{\mathfrak{M}}^{I}, \mathcal{J}_{Den} \rangle$ are essentially different motivation languages and that, as a motivation language, $\langle \mathcal{L}_{\mathfrak{M}}^{C}, \mathcal{J}_{Den} \rangle$ is "better" and "worse" than $\langle \mathcal{L}_{\mathfrak{M}}^{I}, \mathcal{J}_{Den} \rangle$ at the same time.

3. SYNTHESIS MAPS DEFINED ON $\langle \mathcal{L}_{\mathfrak{M}}^{I}, \mathcal{J}_{Den} \rangle$.

Now we take into account synthesis maps having a proper subset of $\mathcal{L}_{\mathfrak{M}}^{I}$ as a domain. As a consequence of Nelson's and Kleene's realizability theory (see for references [1], starting from page 501), an intuitionistic frame is particularly suitable to the synthesis of programs: this question was pointed out by Constable [2] and systematically investigated in [3].

So, we will consider henceforth only motivation languages embedded in the intuitionistic number theory T_{NI}: in this chapter we will discuss synthesis maps defined on $\langle \mathcal{L}_{\mathfrak{M}}^{I}, \mathcal{J}_{Den} \rangle$; in the following chapters other motivation languages will be analyzed.

We start from the following theorem, which is an immediate consequence of Proposition 3.

Theorem 1. Let $\langle \overline{\mathcal{L}}_{\mathfrak{M}}, \overline{\mathcal{I}} \rangle$ be any motivation language such that

1) $\mathcal{L}^{I}_{\mathfrak{M}} \subseteq \overline{\mathcal{L}}_{\mathfrak{M}}$

and

2) $\mathcal{I}_{Den} \subseteq \overline{\mathcal{I}}$;

then any synthesis procedure defined on $\langle \overline{\mathcal{L}}_{\mathfrak{M}}, \overline{\mathcal{I}} \rangle$ is not motivationally complete. □

We have not yet shown, however, that "reasonable" synthesis maps can be defined on $\langle \mathcal{L}^{I}_{\mathfrak{M}}, \mathcal{I}_{Den} \rangle$. In order to exibit such reasonable maps, we refer to [3]: in fact we are taking from [3] some definitions and results; these results, however, will be given in a different form, according to the purpose of this paper.

Definition 12. A formula $\varphi(x_1,..,x_n)$ of $L_{\mathfrak{M}}$ is intuitionistically well constructed (i.w.c.) iff it satisfies one of the following conditions:

1) $T_{NI} \vdash \varphi(x_1,..,x_n) \vee \neg \varphi(x_1,..,x_n)$.
2) $\varphi(x_1,..,x_n) \equiv \exists y\ \varphi_1(x_1,..,x_n,y)$ and $\varphi_1(x_1,..,x_n,y)$ is i.w.c..
3) There is a formula $\overline{\varphi}(x_1,..,x_n)$ of $L_{\mathfrak{M}}$ such that
   - a_3) $\overline{\varphi}(x_1,..,x_n)$ is i.w.c.; and
   - b_3) $T_{NI} \vdash \varphi(x_1,..,x_n) \rightarrow \underline{\varphi}(x_1,..,x_n)$; and
   - c_3) $T_{NC} \vdash \varphi(x_1,..,x_n) \rightarrow \varphi(x_1,..,x_n)$.

The class of all the i.w.c. formulas will be denoted by $F_{i.w.c.}$. □

Let us explicitely remark that condition c_3) of the previous definition refers to the classical theory T_{NC}. The following definition is not, by itself, a very impressive one and in [3] it is omitted; on the other hand, it is important in order to show how the above condition c_3) extends, jointly with condition b_3), the set of the i.w.c. formulas.

Definition 13. A formula $\varphi(x_1,..,x_n)$ of $L_{\mathfrak{M}}$ is almost strongly i.w.c. iff if satisfies one of the following conditions:

1) $T_{NI} \vdash \varphi(x_1,..,x_n) \vee \neg \varphi(x_1,..,x_n)$.
2) $\varphi(x_1,..,x_n) \equiv \exists y\, \varphi_1(x_1,..,x_n,y)$ and $\varphi_1(x_1,..,x_n,y)$ is almost strongly i.w.c..

3) There is a formula $\overline{\varphi}(x_1,..,x_n)$ of $L_{\mathfrak{n}}$ such that

a'3) $\overline{\varphi}(x_1,..,x_n)$ is almost strongly i.w.c.

and

b'3) $T_{NI} \vdash \overline{\varphi}(x_1,..,x_n) \longleftrightarrow \varphi(x_1,..,x_n)$.

The set of all the almost strongly i.w.c. formulas will be denoted by $F_{a.s.i.w.c.}$. □

Definition 14. A formula $\varphi(x_1,...,x_n)$ of $L_{\mathfrak{n}}$ is strongly i.w.c. iff it satisfies one of the following conditions:

1) $T_{NI} \vdash \varphi(x_1,..,x_n) \vee \neg \varphi(x_1,..,x_n)$.

2) $\varphi(x_1,..,x_n) \equiv \exists y \ \varphi_1(x_1,..,x_n,y)$ and $\varphi_1(x_1,..,x_n,y)$ is strongly i.w.c.

The set of all the strongly i.w.c. formulas will be denoted by $F_{s.i.w.c.}$.□

Now we look at the relation existing among the three above defined sets of formulas. Before doing so we state, however, the following proposition.

Proposition 7. $F_{i.w.c.}$, $F_{a.s.i.w.c.}$ and $F_{s.i.w.c.}$ are non recursive recursively enumerable sets. □

Proposition 8. $F_{i.w.c.} - F_{a.s.i.w.c.}$ is not a recursively enumerable set.

Proof.

Let $T^1(y,x,w)$ be the universal primitive recursive predicate such that, for every $\langle \overline{y},\overline{x},\overline{w} \rangle \in N^3$, "$T^1(\overline{y},\overline{x},\overline{w})$ is true" iff "$\overline{y}$ is the Godel number of a Turing machine and $\overline{w}$ is the Godel number of a computation of this Turing machine with the input $\overline{x}$"; let $\mathcal{T}^1(y,x,w)$ be a formula of $L_{\mathfrak{n}}$ which numeralwise expresses the predicate $T^1(y,x,w)$, i.e., if "$T^1(\overline{y},\overline{x},\overline{w})$ is true" then "$T_{NI} \vdash \mathcal{T}^1(\tilde{y},\tilde{x},\tilde{w})$" and if "$T^1(\overline{y},\overline{x},\overline{w})$ is false" then "$T_{NI} \vdash \neg \mathcal{T}^1(\tilde{y},\tilde{x},\tilde{w})$": we can assume that $T_{NI} \vdash \mathcal{T}^1(y,x,w) \vee \neg \mathcal{T}^1(y,x,w)$; of course, we can prove that such a $\mathcal{T}^1(y,x,w)$ do exist. We have, under our hypotheses, that, for any couple $\langle \overline{m},\overline{n} \rangle$ of natural numbers,

$$T_{NI} \vdash \mathcal{T}^1(\tilde{m},\tilde{n},x) \vee \neg \mathcal{T}^1(\tilde{m},\tilde{n},x).$$

Now, let $\overline{m^*}$ be the Godel number of a Turing machine which computes a p.r.f. having a non recursive domain; we define the set $\mathcal{S}$ of formulas $\alpha_n(x)$ in the following way:

for every n, $\alpha_n(x) \in \mathcal{S}$ iff $\alpha_n(x) \equiv \neg \mathcal{T}^1(\widetilde{m^*},\tilde{n},x)$.

Let Γ be so defined:

for every n, $\alpha_n(x) \in \Gamma$ iff $\alpha_n(x) \in \mathcal{S}$ and $T_{NI} \nvdash \forall w(\alpha_n(w)) \vee \neg \forall w(\alpha_n(w))$; **we prove that Γ is not recursively enumerable.**

First of all, if $\alpha_n(x) \in \Gamma$, then $\mathcal{N} \models \alpha_n(\tilde{x})$ for every natural number $\bar{x}$: in fact, if $\mathcal{N} \models \neg\alpha_n(\tilde{x})$ for some $\bar{x}$, then $T_{NI} \vdash \neg \forall w(\alpha_n(w))$, a contradiction.

Now, let Γ_1 be so defined:

for every n, $\alpha_n(x) \in \Gamma_1$ iff $\alpha_n(x) \in \mathcal{S}$ and $T_{NI} \vdash \forall w\ (\alpha_n(w))$;
since Γ_1 is recursively enumerable, if Γ is recursively enumerable, then $\Gamma \cup \Gamma_1$ is recursively enumerable too.

We have that, for every formula $\alpha_n(x) \in \mathcal{S}$, $\alpha_n(x) \in \Gamma \cup \Gamma_1$ iff $\mathcal{N} \models \alpha_n(\tilde{x})$ for every natural $\bar{x}$; so, looking **at** the definition of the set $\mathcal{S}$ and under the assumption that Γ is recursively enumerable, we could recursively enumerate the set $\{\bar{n} \mid \mathcal{N} \models \forall w\ (\neg\ \mathcal{T}^1(\widetilde{m^*}, \tilde{n}, w))\}$, i.e. the set

$N - \{\bar{n} \mid \mathcal{N} \models \exists w(\ \mathcal{T}^1\ (\widetilde{m^*}, \tilde{n}, w))\}$:

since $\overline{m^*}$ is the Godel number of a Turing machine which computes a p.r.f. having a non recursive domain, we have a contradiction.

Now let it be $\alpha_n(x) \in \Gamma$; we prove that, for every strongly i.w.c. formula $\varphi(x)$ such that

1) $T_{NI} \vdash \varphi(x) \longrightarrow \neg\forall y(\alpha_n(y)) \wedge x = x$

the following fact holds:

2) $T_{NI} \nvdash \neg\forall y(\alpha_n(y)) \wedge x = x \longrightarrow \varphi(x)$.

In fact, $\varphi(x) \equiv \exists w_1 \ldots w_m\ \psi(x, w_1, \ldots, w_m)$, where $T_{NI} \vdash \psi(x, w_1, \ldots, w_m) \vee \neg\psi(x, w_1, \ldots, w_m)$; **so, from the negation of 1), we could derive**
$T_{NI} \vdash \neg\forall y(\alpha_n(y)) \longrightarrow \exists w_1 \ldots \exists w_m\ \psi(0, w_1, \ldots, w_m)$.

Now, by a well known result about intuitionistic number theories, we can derive from the above:

3) $T_{NI} \vdash \neg\forall y(\alpha_n(y)) \longrightarrow \psi(0, \tilde{w}_1, \ldots, \tilde{w}_m)$, for suitable natural numbers $\bar{w}_1, \ldots, \bar{w}_m$.

But either $T_{NI} \vdash \psi(0, \tilde{w}_1, \ldots, \tilde{w}_m)$ or $T_{NI} \vdash \neg\psi(0, \tilde{w}_1, \ldots, \tilde{w}_m)$: in the first case we have, by 1), $T_{NI} \vdash \neg\forall y\ (\alpha_n(y))$, a contradiction; in the second case we derive by contraposition in 3) that $T_{NI} \vdash \neg\neg\forall y(\alpha_n(y))$:from this, being $T_{NI} \vdash \alpha_n(y) \vee \neg\alpha_n(y)$, we obtain $T_{NI} \vdash \forall y\ (\alpha_n(y))$, again a contradiction.

4) $T_{NI} \vdash \exists y(\tau^1(\widetilde{m^*},\widetilde{n},y)) \wedge x=x \longrightarrow \neg\forall y\ (\alpha_n(y)) \wedge x=x$

and

5) $T_{NC} \vdash \neg\forall y(\alpha_n(y)) \wedge x=x \longrightarrow \exists y(\tau^1(\widetilde{m^*},\widetilde{n},y)) \wedge x=x.$

Since we immediately state that $\exists y(\tau^1(\widetilde{m^*},\widetilde{n},y)) \wedge x=x$ is i.w.c., from 4) and 5) we have that $\neg\forall y(\alpha_n(y)) \wedge x=x$ is i.w.c.; but by 1) and 2) $\neg\forall y(\alpha_n(y)) \wedge x=x$ is not strongly i.w.c. and by 2) we see that it cannot be almost strongly i.w.c..

Let $\alpha_n(x) \in \mathcal{G}-\Gamma$ and let $\psi(x) \equiv \neg\forall y(\alpha_n(y)) \wedge x=x$; since either $T_{NI} \vdash \forall y(\alpha_n(y))$ or $T_{NI} \vdash \neg\forall y(\alpha_n(y))$, we easily prove that $T_{NI} \vdash \psi(x) \vee \neg\psi(x)$ and hence that $\psi(x)$ is strongly i.w.c. and a fortiori almost strongly i.w.c..

We have just proved that a formula $\psi(x)$ such as $\neg\forall y\ (\alpha_n(y)) \wedge x=x$ is i.w.c. and not almost strongly i.w.c. iff $\alpha_n(x) \in \Gamma$; so, if $F_{i.w.c.} - F_{a.s.i.w.c.}$ were recursively enumerable, then we could recursively enumerate the set Γ too, a contradiction. □

The proof of the following proposition is rather cumbersome; it can be obtained from a counterexample given in [3] (Cex 3) and is therefore omitted.

Proposition 9. $F_{a.s.i.w.c.} - F_{s.i.w.c.}$ and $F_{i.w.c.} - F_{s.i.w.c.}$ are not recursively enumerable sets. □

The following theorem can be easily proved by induction.

Theorem 2. There is a computable map Conj such that:

1) The domain of Conj is the set $F_{i.w.c.}$.

2) If $\varphi(x_1,..,x_n) \in F_{i.w.c.}$, then

a2) $\mathrm{Conj}(\varphi(x_1,..,x_n)) \in F_{s.i.w.c.}$,

and

b2) $T_{NI} \vdash \mathrm{Conj}\ (\varphi(x_1,..,x_n)) \longrightarrow \varphi(x_1,..,x_n)$

and

c2) $T_{NC} \vdash \varphi(x_1,..,x_n) \longrightarrow \mathrm{Conj}(\varphi(x_1,..,x_n))$.

For any i.w.c. formula $\varphi(x_1,..,x_n)$, the formula $\mathrm{Conj}\ (\varphi(x_1,..,x_n))$ will be said "the conjugated by Conj" of $\varphi(x_1,..,x_n)$. □

Definition 15. Let $\varphi(x_1,..,x_n)$ be any formula of L_η; we say that $\varphi(x_1,..,x_n)$ is T_{NI}-Den- complete iff the following property is satisfied:

1) $\{\langle\bar{x}_1,..,\bar{x}_n\rangle \mid T_{NI}\vdash\varphi(\tilde{x}_1,..,\tilde{x}_n)\} = \{\langle\bar{x}_1,..,\bar{x}_n\rangle \mid \mathfrak{N}\models\varphi(\tilde{x}_1,..,\tilde{x}_n)\}$.

The formula $\varphi(x_1,..,x_n)$ is said to be T_{NC}-Den-complete iff

1') $\{\langle\bar{x}_1,..,\bar{x}_n\rangle \mid T_{NC}\vdash\varphi(\tilde{x}_1,..,\tilde{x}_n)\} = \{\langle\bar{x}_1,..,\bar{x}_n\rangle \mid \mathfrak{N}\models\varphi(x_1,..,x_n)\}$.

We will denote the class of all the T_{NI}-Den- complete formulas and of all the T_{NC}-Den-complete formulas by COM (T_{NI}) and by COM(T_{NC}) respectively. □

The following theorem, proved in [3] , states the main property of the i.w.c. formulas.

Theorem 3. $F_{i.w.c.}\subseteq$ COM(T_{NI}). □

The problem now arises of extablishing whether the T_{NI}-Den-completeness of a formula implies the i.w.c.-ness of the formula itself: we can prove the following proposition.

Proposition 10. COM(T_{NI}) and COM(T_{NC}) are not recursively enumerable sets.

Proof.

Every general recursive predicate P $(x_1,..,x_n)$ is numeralwise expressed in T_{NI} by a formula $\varphi_P(x_1,..,x_n)$ of $L_{\mathfrak{N}}$, i.e., for every $\langle\bar{x}_1,..,\bar{x}_n\rangle\in N^n$, if "$P(\bar{x}_1,..,\bar{x}_n)$ is true" then "$T_{NI}\vdash\varphi_P(\tilde{x}_1,..,\tilde{x}_n)$" and if "$P(\bar{x}_1,..,\bar{x}_n)$ is false" then "$T_{NI}\vdash\neg\varphi_P(\tilde{x}_1,..,\tilde{x}_n)$": so, every general recursive predicate is numeralwise expressed by a formula which is T_{NI}-Den-complete together to its negation. On the other hand, if a formula is T_{NI}-Den-complete together to its negation, then it numeralwise expresses a general recursive predicate.

Now let's suppose that COM(T_{NI}) is recursively enumerable: without entering into details, we see that in this case we can define a procedure which scans every not yet enumerated $\varphi(x_1,..,x_n)\in$ COM(T_{NI}) and tries to find $\neg\varphi(x_1,..,x_n)\in$ COM(T_{NI}); if $\neg\varphi(x_1,..,x_n)$ is reached, then $\varphi(x_1,..,x_n)$ is enumerated.

In this way we could recursively enumerate the set of all the general recursive predicates, a contradiction.

The proof for COM(T_{NC}) is quite similar. □

Corollary 1. COM(T_{NI}) - $F_{i.w.c.}$, COM(T_{NI})- $F_{a.s.i.w.c.}$ and COM(T_{NI}) - $F_{s.i.w.c.}$ are not recursively enumerable sets. □

Of course the T_{NC}-Den-completeness of a formula is a very strong property too. Every T_{NC}-Den-complete formula $\varphi(x_1,..,x_n)$ is such that $\{\langle \bar{x}_1,..,\bar{x}_n\rangle | \mathfrak{M} \models \varphi(\tilde{x}_1,..,\tilde{x}_n)\}$ is recursively enumerable; but the class of all all the formulas which are input formulas of some $\mathfrak{F} \in \mathfrak{R}^I$ contains much more, as we see in the following proposition.

Proposition 11. Let En be the class of all the formulas $\varphi(x_1,..,x_n)$ such that $\{\langle \bar{x}_1,..,\bar{x}_n\rangle | \mathfrak{M} \models \varphi(\tilde{x}_1,..,\tilde{x}_n)\}$ is recursively enumerable; then En - COM(T_{NC}) is not a recursively enumerable set. □

Our interest in the i.w.c. formulas is justified by the fact that the i.w.c. formulas allow us to define on $\langle \mathcal{L}^I_{\mathfrak{M}}, \mathfrak{I}_{Den}\rangle$ weakly complete synthesis maps, as it is stated in the following theorem given in [3](see [3] , Theorems 5 and 6).

Theorem 4. Let $DS_{i.w.c.}$, $DS_{a.s.i.w.c.}$ and $DS_{s.i.w.c.}$ be the sets of all the $\mathfrak{F} \in \mathcal{L}^I_{\mathfrak{M}}$ such that the input formula of $\mathfrak{F}$ is i.w.c., the input formula of $\mathfrak{F}$ is almost strongly i.w.c. and the input formula of $\mathfrak{F}$ is strongly i.w.c. respectively; we can define on $\langle \mathcal{L}^I_{\mathfrak{M}}, \mathfrak{I}_{Den}\rangle$ three synthesis maps $S_{i.w.c.}$, $S_{a.s.i.w.c.}$ and $S_{s.i.w.c.}$ which satisfie the following properties:

1) The domain of $S_{i.w.c.}$ is $DS_{i.w.c.}$.
2) The fomain of $S_{a.s.i.w.c.}$ is $DS_{a.s.i.w.c.}$.
3) The domain of $S_{s.i.w.c.}$ is $DS_{s.i.w.c.}$.
4) The synthesis maps $S_{i.w.c.}$, $S_{a.s.i.w.c.}$ and $S_{s.i.w.c.}$ are weakly complete with respect to $\langle \mathcal{L}^I_{\mathfrak{M}}, \mathfrak{I}_{Den}\rangle$. □

Of course, among the three above defined synthesis maps, the most interesting is the largest one, i.e. $S_{i.w.c.}$. We can see, however, that even $S_{s.i.w.c.}$ is weakly complete, i.e. the set $F_{s.i.w.c.}$ is sufficient to express every recursively enumerable predicate.

We have already seen how the set of the i.w.c. formulas is a sufficient formalization in T_{NI} of the concept of recursively enumerable set: in fact, every recursively enumerable set (or, equivalently, predicate) can be expressed by an i.w.c. formula and, conversely, every i.w.c. formula expresses a recursively enumerable predicate.

But even the class of the strongly i.w.c. formulas is adequate in this sense and, on the other hand, we can reach by no means, by Proposition 10, the best formalization in T_{NI} of the notion of recursively enumerable set. Now, we list some propositions which show some nice properties one should require to a "good formalization" in T_{NI} of recursively enumerable sets. It turns out that also $F_{a.s.i.w.c.}$ has these properties, while $F_{s.i.w.c.}$ has not.

I) If $\varphi_1(x_1,..,x_n)$ and $\varphi_2(x_1,..,x_m)$ are i.w.c. (a.s.i.w.c.), then :

   1) $\varphi_1(x_1,..,x_n) \wedge \varphi_2(x_1,..,x_m)$ is i.w.c. (a.s.i.w.c.)

   2) $\varphi_1(x_1,..,x_n) \vee \varphi_2(x_1,..,x_m)$ is i.w.c. (a.s.i.w.c.) .

II) There are strongly i.w.c. formulas $\varphi_1(x_1,..,x_n)$ and $\varphi_2(x_1,..,x_n)$ such that:

   1) $\varphi_1(x_1,..,x_n) \wedge \varphi_2(x_1,..,x_n)$ is not strongly i.w.c.;

   2) $\varphi_1(x_1,..,x_n) \vee \varphi_2(x_1,..,x_n)$ is not strongly i.w.c..

III) If $\varphi(x_1,..,x_n)$ is i.w.c. (a.s.i.w.c.) and $t\,(w_1,..,w_m)$ is any term of $L_{\mathcal{M}}$ whose variables are different from $x_1,\dots,x_{n-1}$, then

$$\forall\; y(y \leq t(w_1,..,w_m) \rightarrow \varphi(x_1,..,x_{n-1},t(w_1,..,w_m)))$$ is i.w.c. (a.s.w.c.).

IV) There is a strongly i.w.c. formula $\varphi(x_1,..,x_n)$ such that

$$\forall y(y \leq x_n \longrightarrow \varphi(x_1,..,x_{n-1},y))$$ is not strongly i.w.c..

4. A NON WEAKLY COMPLETE MOTIVATIONALLY COMPLETE SYNTHESIS MAP AND A COMPLETE SYNTHESIS MAP.

In $\langle \mathcal{L}^{\mathcal{I}}_{\mathcal{M}}, \mathcal{J}_{Den} \rangle$ we are far away from defining complete synthesis maps, since this motivation language is very powerful; on the other hand, the power of this language allows us to define "reasonable" weakly complete synthesis maps.

In this chapter we will see a remarkable motivation language on which a motivationally complete synthesis map is definable; this language may be seen as a restriction of $\langle \mathcal{L}^{\mathcal{I}}_{\mathcal{M}}, \mathcal{J}_{Den} \rangle$ suitable to represent total functions: in the restriction we will lose, however, the weak completeness, in any "reasonable" sense.

Finally, we will show a motivation language having an interpretation map of a kind different from $\mathcal{J}_{Den}$; on this language we will be able to define a complete synthesis map; but we will see that such a motivation language is a very unnatural one.

We start from the following definition.

Definition 16. $\mathcal{L}^{tot}_{\mathfrak{M}}$ is the set of all the formulas $\mathcal{F}\in L_{\mathfrak{M}}$ which satisfie the following conditions:

1) $\mathcal{F}\equiv\forall x_1 \ldots x_n \exists ! z\, \psi(x_1,..,x_n,z)$ for some $\psi(x_1,..,x_n,z)\in L_{\mathfrak{M}}$.

2) $T_{NI}\vdash\mathcal{F}$. □

To every $\mathcal{F}\in\mathcal{L}^{tot}_{\mathfrak{M}}$ we associate a total function of Fun by means of the interpretation map $\mathcal{J}^{tot}$ defined below.

Definition 17. For every $\mathcal{F}\in\mathcal{L}^{tot}_{\mathfrak{M}}$, $\mathcal{J}^{tot}(\mathcal{F})$ is the total function $f(x_1,..,x_n)\in$ Fun which satisfies the following condition:

1) For every $<\bar{x}_1,..,\bar{x}_n>\in N^n$, $f(\bar{x}_1,..,\bar{x}_n)$ is the only $\bar{z}$ such that $\mathfrak{N}\models\psi(\tilde{x}_1,..,\tilde{x}_n,\tilde{z})$, where $\mathcal{F}\equiv\forall x_1 \ldots x_n \exists ! z\, \psi(x_1,..,x_n,z)$ (being $T_{NI}\vdash\mathcal{F}$ this condition is equivalent to $T_{NI}\vdash \psi(\tilde{x}_1,..,\tilde{x}_n,\tilde{z})$). □

Of course $<\mathcal{L}^{tot}_{\mathfrak{M}}, \mathcal{J}^{tot}>$ is a motivation language.

As a consequence of Nelson's and Kleene's realizability theory, we can state the following theorem, which, in a different form, was proved by Nelson and Kleene (for reference, see [1] starting form page 501; see also [3]).

Theorem 5 . On $<\mathcal{L}^{tot}_{\mathfrak{M}}, \mathcal{J}^{tot}>$ we can define a synthesis map S^{tot} whose domain coincides with $\mathcal{L}^{tot}_{\mathfrak{M}}$. □

Of course, S^{tot} is motivationally complete; on the other hand, since for every $\mathcal{F}\in\mathcal{L}^{tot}_{\mathfrak{M}}$ we have that $\mathcal{J}^{tot}(\mathcal{F})$ is a total function, S^{tot} cannot be motivationally complete. But we can see that the weak incompleteness of S^{tot} has a much deeper nature, as it is stated in the following theorem (see [1], page 510, Example 2; see also [3]) .

Theorem 6 . There are general recursive functions (i.e. total p.r.f.'s) $f(x_1,..,x_n)$ such that, for no $\mathcal{F}\in\mathcal{L}^{tot}_{\mathfrak{M}}$, $\mathcal{J}^{tot}(\mathcal{F}) = f(x_1,..,x_n)$. □

Now we describe the motivation language on which we are able to define a complete synthesis map; this language will be obtained by defining an interpretation map for $\mathcal{L}^{I}_{\mathfrak{M}}$ different form $\mathcal{J}_{Den}$.

Definition 19 . For every $\mathcal{F}\in\mathcal{L}^{I}_{\mathfrak{M}}$, $\mathcal{J}_{Prov}(\mathcal{F})$ is the function $f(x_1,..,x_n)\in$ $\in$ Fun whith domain D_f, which satisfies the following conditions:

1) Let $\varphi(x_1,..,x_n)$ be the input formula of $\mathcal{F}$; then $D_f=\{\langle\bar{x}_1,..,\bar{x}_n\rangle \mid T_{NI}\vdash \varphi(\tilde{x}_1,..,\tilde{x}_n)\}$.

2) Let $\psi(x_1,..,x_n,z)$ be the input-output formula of $\mathcal{F}$ and let it be $\langle\bar{x}_1,..,\bar{x}_n\rangle\in D_f$; then $f(\bar{x}_1,..,\bar{x}_n)$ is the only $\bar{z}$ such that $T_{NI}\vdash \psi(\tilde{x}_1,..,\tilde{x}_n,\tilde{z})$. $\square$

Theorem 7 . On $\langle\mathcal{L}^I_{\mathcal{M}},\mathcal{I}_{Prov}\rangle$ we can define a syntheis map S_{Prov} whose domain coincides with $\mathcal{L}^I_{\mathcal{M}}$. $\square$

By Theorem 3 one sees that S_{Prov} extends $S_{i.w.c.}$ (i.e., the identity map defined onto $DS_{i.w.c.}$ omomorphically extends $S_{i.w.c.}$ into S_{Prov}) and that S_{Prov} is complete with respect to $\langle\mathcal{L}^I_{\mathcal{M}},\mathcal{I}_{Prov}\rangle$.

$\langle\mathcal{L}^I_{\mathcal{M}},\mathcal{I}_{Prov}\rangle$ is a very unnatural motivation language from a pragmatical point of view: in fact, if $\mathcal{F}\in\mathcal{L}^I_{\mathcal{M}}$ and $\varphi(x_1,..,x_n)$ is the input formula of $\mathcal{F}$, then, presumably, the domain that one would have for a function denoted by $\mathcal{F}$ is "the semantical domain" $\{\langle\bar{x}_1,..,\bar{x}_n\rangle \mid \mathcal{M}\models\varphi(\tilde{x}_1,..,\tilde{x}_n)\}$ and not "the intuitionistic domain" $\{\langle\bar{x}_1,..,\bar{x}_n\rangle \mid T_{NI}\vdash \varphi(\tilde{x}_1,..,\tilde{x}_n)\}$: moreover, we have a "classical domain" too, i.e. the set $\{\langle\bar{x}_1,..,\bar{x}_n\rangle \mid T_{NC}\vdash \varphi(\tilde{x}_1,..,\tilde{x}_n)\}$, which is contained in the semantical domain and contains the intuitionistic domain. So, in general, the domain of $\mathcal{I}_{Prov}(\mathcal{F})$ is a "very mysterious" domain which is not defined on a proper semantical ground. Of course, for every $\mathcal{F}\in\mathcal{L}^I_{\mathcal{M}}$, we can find a formula $\mathcal{F}'$ of $DS_{i.w.c.}$ such that $\mathcal{I}_{Den}(\mathcal{F}')=\mathcal{I}_{Prov}(\mathcal{F})$; but also $\mathcal{F}'$ is a "very mysterious" formula when compared to $\mathcal{F}$, if we assume that $\mathcal{F}$ is the "original motivation " of a problem.

To end this chapter, we remark that restricting the synthesis map S_{Prov} to the class of all the formulas of $\mathcal{L}^I_{\mathcal{M}}$ having a T_{NI}-Den-complete input formula, we obtain a map which satisfies the clauses 1), 2) and 3) of Definition 3 in order to be a synthesis map defined on $\langle\mathcal{L}^I_{\mathcal{M}},\mathcal{I}_{Den}\rangle$; unfortunately, by Proposition 10, this map cannot be a synthesis map, since it is not computable. We state this fact in the following theorem.

Theorem 8 . Let In $(COM(T_{NI}))$ be the set of all the formulas $\mathcal{F}\in\mathcal{L}^I_{\mathcal{M}}$ such that the input formula of $\mathcal{F}$ is T_{NI}-Den-Complete and let $S_{Prov}/In(COM(T_{NI}))$ be the restrinction of S_{Prov} whose domain is $In(COM(T_{NI}))$; then :

1) $In(COM(T_{NI}))\subseteq\mathcal{L}^I_{\mathcal{M}}$;

2) If $\mathcal{F} \in In(COM(T_{NI}))$, then $S_{Prov} | In(COM(T_{NI}))$ $(\mathcal{F}) \in \mathcal{L}_{\wp}$;
3) If $\mathcal{F} \in In (COM(T_{NI}))$ and $f(x_1,..,x_n)$ is the input-output function of $S_{Prov} | IN(COM(T_{NI}))$ $(\mathcal{F})$, then $\mathcal{J}_{Den}(\mathcal{F}) = f(x_1,..,x_n)$;
4) $S_{Prov} | In(COM(T_{NI}))$ is not a synthesis map defined on $\langle \mathcal{L}^{I}_{\mathcal{M}}, \mathcal{J}_{Den} \rangle$.□

From Theorem 8 we obtain the following corollary.

Corollary 2 . Let $\overline{S}$ be any synthesis map defined on $\langle \mathcal{L}^{I}_{\mathcal{M}}, \mathcal{J}_{Den} \rangle$ whose domain $D_{\overline{S}}$ is contained in In $(COM(T_{NI}))$; then there is a synthesis map $\overline{S'}$ with domain $D_{\overline{S'}}$ such that :
1) $D_{\overline{S}} \subseteq D_{\overline{S'}}$ and $D_{\overline{S}} \neq D_{\overline{S'}}$;
2) $D_{S'} \subseteq In(COM(T_{NI}))$. □

Corollary 2 asserts that, in an intuitionistic attitude we cannot obtain the "best synthesis map".

5. RECURSIVE MOTIVATION LANGUAGES AND SYNTHESIS MAPS DEFINED ON THEM.

The motivation languages we have considered in the previous chapters were not recursive motivation languages, in the sense we will define below; on the other hand, it is very desirable to define enough powerful synthesis maps on recursive languages.

In this chapter we will define a recursive motivation language on which we will be able to define two remarkable synthesis maps: the first one omomorphically extends $S_{i.w.c.}$; the second is a synthesis map of a new kind whose domain is not contained in $COM(T_{NI})$.

Definition 20. Let $\langle \mathcal{L}_{\mathcal{M}}, \mathcal{J} \rangle$ be any motivation language; we say that $\langle \mathcal{L}_{\mathcal{M}}, \mathcal{J} \rangle$ is recursive iff $\mathcal{L}_{\mathcal{M}}$ is recursive. □

Theorem 9. $\langle \mathcal{L}^{C}_{\mathcal{M}}, \mathcal{J}_{Den} \rangle$, $\langle \mathcal{L}^{I}_{\mathcal{M}}, \mathcal{J}_{Den} \rangle$, $\langle \mathcal{L}^{I}_{\mathcal{M}}, \mathcal{J}_{Prov} \rangle$ and $\langle \mathcal{L}^{tot}_{\mathcal{M}}, \mathcal{J}^{tot} \rangle$ are not recursive motivation languages. □

Now we define the recursive set $\mathcal{L}^{Part}_{\mathcal{M}}$.

Definition 21. $\mathcal{F}^{*} \in \mathcal{L}^{Part}_{\mathcal{M}}$ iff
$\mathcal{F}^{*} \equiv \exists y_1 \ldots \exists y_m \exists z^{*} \psi(x_1,..,x_n,y_1,..,y_m,z)$ for some $m \geq 0$ and $\exists y_1 \ldots$
$\ldots \exists y_m \exists z \; \psi(x_1,\ldots,x_n,y_1,..,y_m,z) \in L_{\mathcal{N}}$. □

The following definition gives the interpretation map $\mathcal{J}^{Part}$ for $\mathcal{L}^{Part}_{\mathcal{M}}$.

Definition 22. Let it be $\mathcal{F}^{*} \equiv \exists y_1 \ldots \exists y_m \exists z^{*} \psi(x_1,..,x_n,y_1,..,y_m,z)$; then

$\mathcal{J}^{Part}(\mathcal{J}^*)$ is the function $f(x_1,..,x_n)$ with domain D_f which satisfies the following conditions:

1) $D_f = \{\langle \bar{x}_1,..,\bar{x}_n\rangle \mid \mathfrak{M} \models \exists y_1 ... \exists y_m \exists z\ \psi(\tilde{x}_1,..,\tilde{x}_n,y_1,..,y_m,z)\}$;

2) If $\langle \bar{x}_1,..,\bar{x}_n\rangle \in D_f$, then there is a m+1 -tuple $\langle \bar{y}_1,..,\bar{y}_m,\bar{z}\rangle$ such that

a2) $\mathfrak{M} \models \psi(\tilde{x}_1,..,\tilde{x}_n,\tilde{y}_1,..,\tilde{y}_m,\tilde{z})$

and

b2) If $\mathfrak{M} \models \psi(\tilde{x}_1,..,\tilde{x}_n,\tilde{y}'_1,..,\tilde{y}'_m,\tilde{z}')$, then $\bar{y}_1+..+\bar{y}_m+\bar{z} \leq \bar{y}'_1+...+\bar{y}'_m+\bar{z}'$;

let Tup $(\tilde{x}_1,..,\tilde{x}_n)$ be the set of all the m+1 -tuples which satisfie a2) and b2); then $f(\bar{x}_1,..,\bar{x}_n)$ is the least $\bar{z}$ in the set Tup $(\tilde{x}_1,..,\tilde{x}_n)$. □

Remark that $\langle \mathcal{L}^{Part}_{\mathfrak{M}}, \mathcal{J}^{Part}\rangle$ is a recursive motivation language.

The following theorem (see[3]) can be proved.

Theorem 10 . Let $DS^*_{i.w.c.}$ be the set of all the formulas $\exists y_1 ... \exists y_m \exists z^* \psi(x_1,..,x_n,y_1,..,y_m,z) \in \mathcal{L}^{Part}_{\mathfrak{M}}$ such that $\exists y_1 ... \exists y_m \exists z\ \psi(x_1,...,x_n,y_1,..,y_m,z)$ is i.w.c.; then we can define on $\langle \mathcal{L}^{Part}_{\mathfrak{M}}, \mathcal{J}^{Part}\rangle$ the synthesis map $S^*_{i.w.c.}$ whose domain is $DS^*_{i.w.c.}$. □

Now we can prove that $S^*_{i.w.c.}$ omomorphically extends $S_{i.w.c.}$; but we can prove much more, i.e. that a submap of $S^*_{i.w.c.}$ defined on a remarkable subset of the strongly i.w.c. formulas of $\mathcal{L}^{Part}_{\mathfrak{M}}$ omomorphically extends $S_{i.w.c.}$. Before stating this, we give the following definitions.

Definition 23. Let $DS^{**}_{s.i.w.c.}$ be the set of all the formulas $\exists y_1 ... \exists y_m \exists z^* \psi(x_1,..,x_n, y_1,..,y_m,z) \in \mathcal{L}^{Part}_{\mathfrak{M}}$ such that $T_{NI} \vdash \exists z\ \psi(x_1,..,x_n,y_1,..,z) \vee \neg\exists z\ \psi(x_1,..,x_n,y_1,..,y_m,z)$; then $S^{**}_{s.i.w.c.}$ is the submap of $S^*_{i.w.c.}$ whose domain is $DS^{**}_{s.i.w.c.}$. □

Definition 24. $\overline{Om}^{**}$ is the computable map defined on $DS_{i.w.c.}$ which satisfies the following condition:

1) Let $\mathcal{Y} \equiv \forall x_1 ... x_n(\varphi(x_1,..,x_n) \rightarrow \exists! z\ \psi(x_1,..,x_n,z))$ be any formula of $DS_{i.w.c.}$ and let it be $Conj(\varphi(x_1,..,x_n)) \equiv \exists y_1 .... \exists y_m\ \overline{\varphi}(x_1,..,x_n,y_1,..,y_m)$, where

$T_{NI} \vdash \overline{\varphi}(x_1,..,x_n,y_1,..,y_1,..,y_m) \vee \neg\overline{\varphi}(x_1,..,x_n,y_1,..,y_m)$;

then

$Om^{**}(\mathcal{Y}) \equiv \exists y_1 ... \exists y_m \exists z^* (\overline{\varphi}(x_1,..,x_n,y_1,..,y_m) \wedge \psi(x_1,..,x_n,z))$. □

The following theorem is proved in [3] in a different form.

Theorem 11 . The computable map $\overline{Om}^{**}$ is an omomorphic extension of $S_{i.w.c.}$ into $S^{**}_{s.i.w.c.}$. □

Finally we look at a recursively enumerable set of T_{NC}-Den-complete formulas by which we will be able to define on $\langle \mathcal{L}^{\varphi \mathrm{Part}}_{\mathfrak{m}}, \mathcal{J}^{\mathrm{Part}} \rangle$ a synthesis map larger than the previous ones.

Definition 23. A formula $\varphi(x_1,..,x_n)$ of $L_{\mathfrak{n}}$ is almost constructively meaningful (a.c.m.) iff it satisfies one of the following conditions:

1) There is an i.w.c. formula $\overline{\varphi}(x_1,..,x_n)$ such that

$$T_{NC} \vdash \overline{\varphi}(x_1,..,x_n) \longleftrightarrow \varphi(x_1,..,x_n) ..$$

2) $\varphi(x_1,..,x_n) \equiv \exists y\ \varphi_1(x_1,..,x_n,y)$ and $\varphi_1(x_1,..,x_n, y)$ is a.c.m.. □

Definition 24. An a.c. m. formula $\varphi(x_1,..,x_n)$ is constructively meaningful (c.m.) if either $\varphi(x_1,..,x_n)$ is i.w.c. and $\varphi(x_1,..,x_n) \equiv \exists y \varphi_1(x_1,..,x_n,y)$ for some $\varphi_1(x_1,...., x_n,y)$ or $\varphi(x_1,..,x_n) \equiv \exists y\ \varphi_1(x_1,..,x_n,y)$ and $\varphi_1(x_1,..,x_n,y)$ is a.c.m.. □

We will denote by $F_{a.c.m.}$ the class of all the almost constructively meaningfuls formulas. The following Theorems are extablished without proof (see for reference [5]).

Theorem 11. $F_{a.c.m.} \subseteq COM(T_{NC})$.

Theorem 12. Let $DS_{c.m.}$ the class of all the formulas $\mathcal{F} \equiv \exists y_1 ... \exists y_m \exists z^* \psi(x_1,..,x_n,y_1,..,y_m,z)$ such that $\exists z \exists y_1 .... \exists y_m \psi(x_1,...,x_n, y_1,..,y_m,z)$ is c.m.; then we can define on $\langle \mathcal{L}^{\varphi \mathrm{Part}}_{\mathfrak{m}}, \mathcal{J}^{\mathrm{Part}} \rangle$ the synthesis map $S_{c.m.}$ whose domain is $DS_{c.m.}$. □

The map $S_{c.m.}$ is out from an intuitionistic attitude. In fact on an intuitive ground there are c.m. formulas (the non i.w.c. ones) which express the possibility of constructively finding objects z which are in a non constructive relation with the objects $x_1,..,x_n$, whereas in an intuitionistic attitude all the relations must be constructive. This is an example which shows how difficult is to characterize the constructive attitude needed in the approach to the synthesis of programs.

REFERENCES

[1] KLEENE, S.C.: Introduction to Metamathematics North Holland, Amsterdam (firth reprint, 1967).

[2] CONSTABLE, R.L.:Constructive Mathematics and automatic program writers IFIP Congress 1971, North Holland, Amsterdam.

[3] DEGLI ANTONI; MIGLIOLI; ORNAGHI: The Synthesis of Programs in an intuitionistic frame extended version of Top-down approach to the Synthesis of programs Colloque sur la programmation, Paris (Ap. 1974).

[4] DEGLI ANTONI; MIGLIOLI, ORNAGHI : The Synthesis of Programs as an approach to the construction of reliable Programs - Submitted to International Conference on Reliable Software 1974, Los Angeles.

[5] MIGLIOLI, P.A. : Notes on Motivation Languages and Synthesis Maps Internal report of the Gruppo Elettronica e Cibernetica, v.Viotti 5 - MIlano.

Research sponsered by CNR (Progetto per la Informatica) and by Honeywell Information System Italy (Project AST).

THE SEMANTICS OF SEMANTIC EQUATIONS

P.D.Mosses
Oxford University Computing Laboratory
Programming Research Group
45 Banbury Road, Oxford, England OX2 6PE

INTRODUCTION

The notation of so-called semantic equations can be used to give a compact description of the mathematical or denotational semantics of a programming language. It was introduced by SCOTT and STRACHEY in [4,6,7], where they gave a detailed account of the *method* of mathematical semantics. However no formal definition of the *notation* was ever formulated, and as a result the meaning and syntax of extensions to the basic notation (such as those used in the semantic equations of PAL [1], SNOBOL [9] and ALGOL 60 [2]) could not be defined formally. This has meant that there has been an element of informal description in a method which purports to give rigorous definitions of programming languages. We believe that the level of formality in semantic equations is not quite high enough to ensure completely precise and unambiguous definitions, and in this paper we attempt to remedy the situation.

After a brief summary of the method of mathematical semantics, and of the general appearance of semantic equations, we shall give an unambiguous grammar for a language called MSL (Mathematical Semantics Language), which looks quite similar to the notation of semantic equations. A semantic description of a programming language will at least be *unambiguous* if it is written in MSL, or in a simple extension of MSL (specified formally by amending the grammar). To make it also *precise*, we must give a precise definition of the semantics of MSL, and we shall indicate how this can be done. Finally we shall give a semantic description of MSL written in MSL, and point out how this circular description can be used.

As a side-effect of this formalization, semantic descriptions written in MSL are suitable for computer processing - in fact they can be used to "run" test-programs written in the described language. This enables a semantic description to be tested empirically, and also makes it possible to use a mathematical semantics of a programming language as a reference standard for compilers of that language.

MATHEMATICAL SEMANTICS

As stated in the literature [4,6,7,8], a mathematical semantics is a correspondence between the constructs or phrases of a programming language and certain abstract mathematical entities. For reasons not discussed here, these entities are always elements of complete lattices - we refer to these lattices as domains, and to their elements as values. The partial ordering of a domain usually corresponds to a notion of approximation or "defined-ness". The semantic values of basic phrases of a programming language, such as numerals and strings, are considered to be "perfectly defined", hence they form a domain with a "flat" structure (distinct proper elements are incomparable). However, the semantic values of commands and expressions are naturally considered as partial functions (e.g. the state-transformation corresponding to a while-loop), and this gives a more complex structure to the domains.

A description of the domains involved forms a useful part of a semantic description, as it allows the type of a semantic function to be expressed. The following notation is used in describing compound domains:

$D_1 \times D_2 \times \ldots \times D_n$ denotes the product of the domains $D_1, D_2, \ldots, D_n$; i.e. the domain of n-tuples $\langle d_1, d_2, \ldots, d_n \rangle$ with $d_i \in D_i$.

$D_1 \rightarrow D_2$ denotes the domain of continuous functions from D_1 to D_2. These are all total functions - those corresponding to non-terminating computations give as result the minimal (bottom) element of D_2.

$D_1 + D_2 + \ldots + D_n$ denotes (roughly speaking) the disjoint union of $D_1, D_2, \ldots, D_n$.

D^n denotes the domain of n-tuples of elements of D.

D* denotes the domain of all tuples of elements of D, i.e.

$$D^* = D^0 + D^1 + \ldots + D^n + \ldots$$

Domains may also be described by a recursive set of equations, giving each domain as a compound domain formed from other domains using the above operators. The solution of such a set of equations (up to isomorphism) always exists because only continuous functions are included in $D_1 \rightarrow D_2$. It is usually quite easy to find a domain of values for any given construct of a programming language.

A mathematical semantics is usually written as a set of semantic equations, which together define the semantic function (usually denoted by a script letter such as $\mathfrak{C}$, $\mathfrak{E}$ or $\mathfrak{F}$). Each left-hand side denotes the application of a semantic function to a compound phrase, specifying both the form of the phrase and naming its component sub-phrases. The form is specified with reference to an abbreviated BNF grammar which describes all the possible phrases of the language, and the names of the syntactic categories (subscripted if necessary) are used as "meta-variables" denoting sub-phrases. (To keep syntax and semantics separate, it is assumed that phrases are really "annotated deduction trees", i.e. parse-trees, conforming to the BNF grammar.) On the right-hand side an extension of λ-notation is used to denote a value formed from the semantic values of the sub-phrases (denoted by applications of the semantic functions to the meta-variables). The brackets ⟦ ⟧ enclose the parts of equations which denote phrases, avoiding confusion with the λ-notation.

For example, suppose the grammar includes

(1) $\quad Com ::= \ldots \mid Com\ ;\ Com \mid \ldots$

so that a command *Com* may be a sequence of two other commands. If $\mathfrak{F}$ denotes the semantic function for commands, then $\mathfrak{F}[\![Com]\!]$ denotes the semantic value of the phrase denoted by *Com*. Considering a command to specify a transformation on a state σ belonging to a domain S, we might want

(2) $\quad \mathfrak{F}[\![Com]\!] \in [S \rightarrow S]\ ;$

and then, ignoring the possibility of gotos, errors and non-termination within commands, the natural meaning of $Com_1\ ;\ Com_2$ would be the composition of $\mathfrak{F}[\![Com_1]\!]$ and $\mathfrak{F}[\![Com_2]\!]$. The semantic equation for this is

(3) $\quad \mathfrak{F}[\![Com_1\ ;\ Com_2]\!] = \lambda\sigma.\ \mathfrak{F}[\![Com_2]\!](\ \mathfrak{F}[\![Com_1]\!](\sigma))$

where our λ-notation has allowed the omission of some parentheses.

Of course semantic equations are usually much more complex than (3). For example the meaning of a command would usually depend on the previous declared meanings of the identifiers occurring in it. Using ρ to denote a function from identifiers to their meanings (an "environment") we would then write

$$(4)\qquad \mathcal{F}[\![Com_1 \ ; \ Com_2]\!](\rho) = \lambda\sigma \ . \ \mathcal{F}[\![Com_2]\!](\rho)(\mathcal{F}[\![Com_1]\!](\rho)(\sigma)).$$

Further parameters are often introduced to express various other kinds of context-dependence. To improve the readability of semantic equations, the basic notation includes several operators which abbreviate commonly-occurring expressions in λ-notation. An example is $\circ$, where $f \circ g$ abbreviates $x.f(g(x))$ - this enables (4) to be written as

$$(4)\qquad \mathcal{F}[\![Com_1 \ ; \ Com_2]\!]\rho = \mathcal{F}[\![Com_2]\!]\rho \circ \mathcal{F}[\![Com_1]\!]\rho$$

(assuming that $\circ$ has less "binding power" than application).

THE SYNTAX OF MSL

Table 1 gives an unambiguous grammar for MSL. The notation used in the grammar is basically BNF, with the addition of the Brooker convention that $\{...\}^{*?}$ allows zero or more occurrences of {...}. Syntactic categories are denoted by such names as *Seg*, *ExpA*, etc. The names *IDE*, *NUM* and *STR* denote unspecified categories of identifiers, numerals and strings respectively. We do not specify the lexical grammar of MSL, except to point out that identifiers may be subscripted, strings are delimited by " and ", and ! introduces an end-of-line comment.

Let us compare MSL to the original semantic equations notation. Table 2 provides an example of (part of) a semantic description written in both notations. A set of equations defining a semantic function (such as $\mathfrak{C}$ or $\mathfrak{E}$ in Table 2) corresponds to a *Def* of the form *IDE ParL* = *Exp* in MSL. Here the first parameter in *ParL* is $[\![t]\!]$ and *Exp* is of the form **clauses** *t* § *CaseL* $. In fact *t* denotes a node of a parse-tree, and its label (assumed to be a *STR*ing) is used to select a **case** *STR Bvs*: *Exp* from the *CaseL*. Inside the *Case*, the *Bvs* denote the branches from the node *t*, performing the same function as the meta-variables in the corresponding semantic equation. The *Exp* of the *Case* looks very similar to the right-hand side of an equation. As regards the wider structure, the *Def*s of the semantic functions are connected recursively by a *DefL*, and the final **result** *Exp* specifies the main semantic function for complete programs.

Thus the main points of difference of MSL from the basic notation of semantic equations are (i) the more explicit definition of semantic functions, and (ii) the "less sophisticated" way of denoting the form of a phrase and its components. The motivation for creating difference (ii) is perhaps not apparent from the simple example of Table 2, it comes from the desire to denote the components of a phrase such as $\langle Exp\{,Exp\}^{*?}\rangle$ without using the "..." convention - in semantic equations this phrase would be denoted by $\langle Exp_1,\ldots,Exp_n\rangle$ (where n is also a variable).

TABLE 1: MSL GRAMMAR

```
Seg   ::=  λ Bvs. Seg  |  def DefL Seg  |  result Exp

DefL  ::=  Def {and Def}*?

Def   ::=  IDE ParL = Exp  |  Bvs = Exp

Exp   ::=  let Def in Exp  |  λ Bvs. Exp  |  fix Bvs. Exp
        |  ExpA → Exp, Exp  |  clauses ExpA § CaseL $
        |  Exp OpA ExpA  |  ExpA

ExpA  ::=  ExpB OpB ExpB  |  OpC ExpB  |  OpD ExpD ExpD  |  ExpB

ExpB  ::=  ExpB OpE ExpC  |  ExpC

ExpC  ::=  ExpC ExpD  |  ExpD

ExpD  ::=  ExpD [ Exp / Exp ]  |  ⟨Exp {,Exp}*? ⟩  |  ⟨⟩  |  ( Exp )
        |  ⟦ Exp ⟧  |  IDE  |  NUM  |  STR  |  true  |  false  |  err

Bvs   ::=  ⟨ Bvs {,Bvs}*? ⟩  |  ⟨⟩  |  IDE  |  ⟦ IDE ⟧  |  ( Bvs )

ParL  ::=  Bvs ParL  |  Bvs

CaseL ::=  Case CaseL  |  Case

Case  ::=  case STR Bvs: Exp  |  default: Exp

OpA   ::=  ∘  |  *

OpB   ::=  +  |  -  |  ×  |  =  |  ≤  |  ∨  |  ∧  |  cat

OpC   ::=  ~  |  dim  |  mapn  |  mapt  |  label  |  spread

OpD   ::=  node

OpE   ::=  ↓
```

IDE, NUM, STR denote unspecified categories of identifiers, numerals and strings, respectively.

TABLE 2: EXAMPLE SEMANTIC DESCRIPTION

Syntax:

$$C ::= \quad C \; ; \; C \quad | \quad \text{dummy} \quad | \quad \text{if } E \text{ then } C \text{ else } C \quad | \quad \text{while } E \text{ do } C$$
$$E ::= \quad \text{true} \quad | \quad \sim E$$

Domains:

    S is a primitive domain of states

    T is the primitive domain of truth-values

Semantic Equations:

$$\mathcal{C} \in [C \to [S \to S]]$$

$$\mathcal{C}[\![C_1 \; ; \; C_2]\!] \qquad\qquad = \quad \mathcal{C}[\![C_2]\!] \circ \mathcal{C}[\![C_1]\!]$$
$$\mathcal{C}[\![\text{dummy}]\!] \qquad\qquad = \quad I$$
$$\mathcal{C}[\![\text{if } E \text{ then } C_1 \text{ else } C_2]\!] = \quad Cond(\mathcal{C}[\![C_1]\!], \mathcal{C}[\![C_2]\!]) \star \mathcal{E}[\![E]\!]$$
$$\mathcal{C}[\![\text{while } E \text{ do } C]\!] \qquad = \quad Y(\lambda\theta.\ Cond(\theta \circ \mathcal{C}[\![C]\!], I) \star \mathcal{E}[\![E]\!])$$

$$\mathcal{E} \in [E \to [S \to [T \times S]]]$$

$$\mathcal{E}[\![\text{true}]\!] = \quad Pair(true)$$
$$\mathcal{E}[\![\sim E]\!] = \quad (\lambda\beta.\ Pair(\sim\beta)) \star \mathcal{E}[\![E]\!]$$

MSL Version:

```
def 𝒞[t] = clauses t                 !   𝒞 ∈ [C → [S → S]]
§ case "C ; C" ⟨c₁,c₂⟩:                  𝒞[c₂] ∘ 𝒞[c₁]
  case "dummy" ⟨⟩:                       I
  case "if E then C else C" ⟨e,c₁,c₂⟩:  Cond(𝒞[c₁], 𝒞[c₂]) ⋆ 𝓔[e]
  case "while E do C" ⟨e,c⟩:            fix θ. Cond(θ∘𝒞[c],I) ⋆ 𝓔[e]
§

and 𝓔[t] = clauses t                 !   𝓔 ∈ [E → [S → [T × S]]]
§ case "true" ⟨⟩:  Pair(true)
  case "~ E" ⟨e⟩:  (λβ. Pair(~β)) ⋆ 𝓔[e]
§

and I(σ) = σ
and Cond(θ₁, θ₂)(β) = β → θ₁, θ₂
and Pair(β)(σ) = ⟨β, σ⟩

result 𝒞
```

THE SEMANTICS OF MSL

As we remarked above, we consider a semantic function to be a mapping from parse-trees of programs to their mathematical values. We intend a description in MSL to specify such a function, in the same way that a set of semantic equations does; but we have two extra requirements. The first is that we must be able to describe the correspondence between MSL descriptions and semantic functions (i.e. the semantics of our meta-language MSL) in a completely rigorous way - this will enable a semantic description in MSL to be considered really precise as well as unambiguous. The second is that MSL must be general enough, as we want to be able to describe a semantic function for *any* programming language.

We start by embedding semantic functions in a mathematical domain, so that we may think of them as ordinary mathematical values. If we regard distinct parse-trees as incomparable, then they could simply be considered as elements of a primitive domain with a "flat" structure. However, we shall need to select the branches and label of a node of a parse-tree, so it is more convenient to identify a node with a tuple. Specifically, we identify the leaves (terminal nodes) of a parse-tree with integers; and if the branches of a node are identified with values $t_1,\ldots,t_n$, we identify the node itself with the tuple $\langle t_1,\ldots,t_n,l\rangle$, where l is a string identified with the label of the node. It can be shown that distinct tuples formed in this way are indeed incomparable, so they form a flat domain, say **Tree**. We are interested in the values of a particular semantic function only on a subset of the proper elements of **Tree**, but it is convenient to extend it to all of **Tree** - this can easily be done so that the extended function is continuous. As regards the values of semantic functions, these are already mathematical; however Scott has shown that all the domains we use in mathematical semantics can be continuously embedded in one "universal" domain U, so we may consider our semantic functions to give these embedded values. Hence the mathematical value we associate with a semantic function is an element of the domain **Tree** → U.

The grammar of MSL in Table 1 enables us to form parse-trees of written MSL descriptions, which we can now imbed in **Tree**. It only remains to specify an element of **Tree** → [**Tree** → U], which will map the (tuples corresponding to) parse-trees of MSL descriptions, into the intended (embedded) semantic functions. How to do this, precisely and unambiguously? The basic notation of semantic equations might be considered rigorous enough for this one description, but we would need to give a more detailed explanation of the notation than we did above. On the other hand, to rely on a description written in MSL itself would require a proof that there is a unique minimal semantic function for MSL which is consistent with the circular description (and which gives the usual semantics to λ-abstraction etc.). The best solution seems to be to use Scott's language LAMBDA [5], which has such a simple syntax and semantics that we need not worry about the slight informality in *its* definition. We can simply write down a LAMBDA-expression ε denoting our meta-semantic function (or rather, its embedding in the domain of interpretation of LAMBDA), although lack of space prevents us from doing this here. This LAMBDA-expression then gives a precise meaning to any description in MSL, so our first requirement above is satisfied.

As regards our second requirement, Scott has shown that all "computable" values are LAMBDA-definable, where computability is defined in terms of recursive enumerability. It is reasonable to assume that the definition of the term "programming language" implies that a semantic function is computable in this sense, and as it can be shown that a value is LAMBDA-definable iff MSL-definable, we can be satisfied that MSL is general enough.

MSL can be used to abbreviate a LAMBDA-expression; in particular there is an MSL-expression ϕ which abbreviates ε above. If τ is a LAMBDA-expression denoting the parse-tree (in **Tree**) of ϕ according to the grammar of MSL, then we can formulate a check for the correctness (consistency) of ε : we must have $\varepsilon(\tau)$ equivalent to ε, in the sense that they have the same "effect" when applied to parse-trees of arbitrary semantic descriptions in MSL. This can be shown using conversion rules in LAMBDA.

We now give ϕ, the abbreviation of the formal semantics of MSL. It is hoped that the reader will be able to use it in two ways to improve his understanding of MSL. The first way is to imagine that it is written in the usual notation of semantic equations and, with the aid of the comments, to formulate an equivalence between MSL and λ-notation. The second way is to check the consistency of this equivalence with the uses of MSL-notation below.

As usual in semantic descriptions we wish to ignore the precedence information given in the unambiguous grammar of Table 1. To do this we postulate that when a parse-tree of an MSL-description is formed, the strings which label the nodes omit the last letters from *ExpA*, *ExpB*, ..., *OpA*,...; and that nodes with the label "*Exp*" are excised from the tree. We shall refer to the domains of parse-trees of MSL phrases by the names of the corresponding syntactic categories used in Table 1; with the addition of

$$Exp = ExpA + ExpB + ExpC + ExpD$$
$$Op1 = OpC$$
$$Op2 = OpA + OpB + OpD + OpE$$

The semantic domains are

$$\mathrm{I} = \{identifiers\}$$
$$\mathrm{N} = \{integers\}$$
$$\mathrm{S} = \{strings\}$$
$$\mathrm{T} = \{true, false\}$$
$$\mathrm{E} = \mathrm{N} + \mathrm{S} + \mathrm{T} + \mathrm{E}^* + [\mathrm{E} \to \mathrm{E}] + \{\mathrm{err}\}$$
$$\mathrm{Env} = \mathrm{I} \to \mathrm{E}$$

(Technical point: the projections and injections between sum domains and their summands have been omitted, as is usually done informally in semantic equations. This can be justified formally for MSL.)

The semantic functions for MSL are described as follows.

$\lambda\langle IdeVal, NumVal, StringVal\rangle$.
   ! $IdeVal \in [IDE \to \mathrm{I}]$, $NumVal \in [NUM \to \mathrm{N}]$, $StringVal \in [STR \to \mathrm{S}]$
   ! all depend on the lexical grammar (not specified here).

def $\mathcal{S}[\![t]\!]\rho$ = ! $\mathcal{S} \in [Seg \to [\mathrm{Env} \to \mathrm{E}]]$
clauses t
§ case "λ *Bvs*. *Seg*" $\langle b,s\rangle$: $\lambda\beta.\ \mathcal{S}[\![s]\!](Lay\langle\rho,\beta,b\rangle)$
   ! b can be compound $\langle b_1,\ldots,b_n\rangle$
  case "def *DefL Seg*" $\langle dl,s\rangle$: let β_1 = fix $\beta.\mathcal{D}[\![dl]\!](Lay\langle\rho,\beta,\mathcal{B}[\![dl]\!]\rangle)$
   in $\mathcal{S}[\![s]\!](Lay\langle\rho,\beta_1,\mathcal{B}[\![dl]\!]\rangle)$
   ! β_1 is a tuple of the recursive values declared in dl.
  case "result *Exp*" $\langle e\rangle$: $\mathcal{E}[\![e]\!]\rho$
§ ! A result must always end a segment.

```
and 𝔈⟦t⟧ρ =                               !     𝔈 ∈ [Exp → [Env → E]]
clauses t
§ case "let Def in Exp" ⟨d,e⟩ :           𝔈⟦e⟧(Lay⟨ρ, 𝔇⟦d⟧ρ, 𝔅⟦d⟧⟩)
    !    𝔅 extracts Bvs , 𝔇 their denotations.
  case "λ Bvs. Exp" ⟨b,e⟩ :               λβ. 𝔈⟦e⟧(Lay⟨ρ,β,b⟩)
    !    b can be compound ⟨b_1,...,b_n⟩
  case "fix Bvs. Exp" ⟨b,e⟩ :             fix β. 𝔈⟦e⟧(Lay⟨ρ,β,b⟩)
    !    ≡ Y(λ Bvs. Exp), where Y(f) = (λx.f(x(x)))(λx.f(x(x))).
  case "Exp → Exp, Exp" ⟨e_1,e_2,e_3⟩ :   𝔈⟦e_1⟧ρ → 𝔈⟦e_2⟧ρ, 𝔈⟦e_3⟧ρ
    !    ≡ e_2 or e_3, depending on e_1 being true or false.
  case "clauses Exp § CaseL ∮" ⟨e,cl⟩ :   ℭ⟦cl⟧(ρ)(𝔈⟦e⟧ρ)(err)
    !    chooses a case depending on e; valued as err if no match.
  case "Exp Op Exp" ⟨e_1,op,e_2⟩ :        𝔒_2⟦op⟧⟨𝔈⟦e_1⟧ρ, 𝔈⟦e_2⟧ρ⟩
  case "Op Exp" ⟨op,e⟩ :                  𝔒_1⟦op⟧(𝔈⟦e⟧ρ)
  case "Op Exp Exp" ⟨op,e_1,e_2⟩ :        𝔒_2⟦op⟧⟨𝔈⟦e_1⟧ρ, 𝔈⟦e_2⟧ρ⟩
  case "Exp Exp" ⟨e_1,e_2⟩ :              (𝔈⟦e_1⟧ρ)(𝔈⟦e_2⟧ρ)
    !    Function application is denoted by juxtaposition.
  case "Exp [ Exp / Exp ]" ⟨e_1,e_2,e_3⟩ : λβ.β=𝔈⟦e_3⟧ρ → 𝔈⟦e_2⟧ρ, 𝔈⟦e_1⟧ρβ
    !    used to add a layer to an environment.
  case "⟨ Exp {,Exp}*? ⟩" (es):           mapt ⟨λe. 𝔈⟦e⟧ρ, t⟩
    !    i.e. the tuple of the values of its elements.
  case "⟨⟩" ⟨⟩ :                          ⟨⟩
  case "( Exp )" ⟨e⟩ :                    𝔈⟦e⟧ρ
  case "⟦ Exp ⟧" ⟨e⟩ :                    𝔈⟦e⟧ρ
  case "IDE" ⟨i⟩ :                        ρ(IdeVal⟦i⟧)
  case "NUM" ⟨n⟩ :                        NumVal⟦n⟧
  case "STR" ⟨s⟩ :                        StringVal⟦s⟧
  case "true" ⟨⟩ :                        true
  case "false" ⟨⟩ :                       false
  case "err" ⟨⟩ :                         err
∮
```

```
and 𝓑⟦t⟧ =                              !    𝓑 ∊ [[DefL + Def] → Bvs]
clauses t
§ case "Def {and Def}*?" (ds):          node "⟨Bvs {,Bvs}*? ⟩" (mapt⟨𝓑,t⟩)
    !    In effect 𝓑 and 𝓓 reduce a DefL to  Bvs = Exp.

  case "IDE ParL = Exp" ⟨i,pl,e⟩ :      node "IDE" ⟨i⟩
    !    defines IDE to be a function.

  case "Bvs= Exp" ⟨b,e⟩ :                b
$   !    already in the "standard" form.

and 𝓓⟦t⟧ρ =                              !    𝓓 ∊ [[DefL + Def] → [Env → E]]
clauses t
§ case "Def {and Def}*?" (ds):          mapt ⟨λd.𝓓⟦d⟧ρ, t ⟩
    !    Compare 𝓔 , case "⟨Exp {,Exp}*?⟩ "

  case "IDE ParL = Exp" ⟨i,pl,e⟩ :      𝓟⟦pl⟧⟦e⟧ρ
    !       creates an abstraction for each parameter.

  case "Bvs = Exp" ⟨b,e⟩ :              𝓔⟦e⟧ρ
$

and 𝓟⟦t₁⟧⟦t₂⟧ρ =                          !    𝓟 ∊ [ParL → [Exp → [Env → E]]]
clauses t₁
§ case "Bvs ParL" ⟨b,pl⟩ :              λβ.𝓟⟦pl⟧⟦t₂⟧(Lay⟨ρ,β,b⟩)
    !    Parameters are abstracted one-by-one.

  case "Bvs" ⟨b⟩ :                      λβ.𝓔⟦t₂⟧(Lay⟨ρ,β,b⟩)
$

and 𝓒⟦t⟧ρε₁ε₂ =               !    𝓒 ∊   [[CaseL + Case] → [Env → [E → [E→E]]]]
clauses t
§ case "Case CaseL" ⟨c,cl⟩ :            𝓒⟦c⟧ρε₁(𝓒⟦cl⟧ρε₁ε₂)
    !    𝓒 tests cases sequentially.

  case "Case" ⟨c⟩ :                     𝓒⟦c⟧ρε₁ε₂
    !    ε₂ will be err for this, the last case.

  case "case STR Bvs: Exp" ⟨s,b,e⟩ :      (label ε₁)=StringVal⟦s⟧ →
                                              𝓔⟦e⟧(Lay⟨ρ,ε₁,b⟩),  ε₂

    !    so that the Bvs denote the branches of the node ε₁
  case "default: Exp" ⟨e⟩ :             𝓔⟦e⟧ρ
    !    The omission of a default case is equivalent to the insertion
    !    of default: err  after the last case.
$
```

```
and 𝒪₁⟦t⟧ε =                               !   𝒪₁ ∊ [Op₁→ [E → E]]
clauses t
§ case "~" ⟨⟩:        ~ ε                  !  [T→ T]       logical negation
  case "dim" ⟨⟩:      dim ε                !  [E* → N]     dimension of a tuple
  case "mapn" ⟨⟩:     MapN(ε)              !  see MapN
  case "mapt" ⟨⟩:     MapT(ε)              !  see MapT
  case "label" ⟨⟩:    ε↓(dim ε)            !  [E* → S]   see "node"
  case "spread" ⟨⟩:   (dim ε) - 1          !  [E* → N]   see "node"
§

and 𝒪₂⟦t⟧⟨ε,φ⟩ =                            !   𝒪₂ ∊ [Op₂→ [E² → E]]
clauses t
§ case "∘" ⟨⟩:       λβ. ε(φ(β))           !  [[E → E]² → [E → E]]
  case "*" ⟨⟩:       λβ. (λ⟨ψ,δ⟩. ε(ψ)(δ)) (φ(β))
                                           !  [[[E→E²] x [E→[E→E]]] → [E→E]]
  case "+" ⟨⟩:       ε + φ                 !  [N² → N]
  case "-" ⟨⟩:       ε - φ                 !  [N² → N]
  case "x" ⟨⟩:       ε x φ                 !  [N² → N]
  case "=" ⟨⟩:       ε = φ                 !  [D² → T]  any "flat"  D.
  case "≤" ⟨⟩:       ε ≤ φ                 !  [N² → T]
  case "v" ⟨⟩:       ε v φ                 !  [T² → T]
  case "∧" ⟨⟩:       ε ∧ φ                 !  [T² → T]
  case "cat" ⟨⟩:     ε cat φ               !  [[E* x E*] → E*]   concatenation
  case "node" ⟨⟩:    φ cat ⟨ε⟩             !  [[S x E*] → E*]
  case "↓" ⟨⟩:       ε ↓ φ                 !  [[E* x N] → E]     selection
§                                          !  note that ⟨a,b⟩↓1 = a.

and Lay⟨ρ,ε,t⟩ =                            !  Lay  ∊ [[Env x E x Bvs] → Env]
clauses t
§ case "⟨ Bvs{,Bvs}*? ⟩" (bs):  MapN ⟨ (λ⟨ρ₁,ν⟩. Lay⟨ρ₁, ε↓ν, t↓ν⟩ ),
                                          ρ, 1, spread t ⟩
     !    dim ε may be greater than   spread t,  without error.
  case "⟨⟩ " ⟨⟩:                  ρ
  case "IDE" ⟨i⟩:                 ρ[ε/IdeVal⟦i⟧]
  case "⟦ IDE ⟧" ⟨i⟩:             ρ[ε/IdeVal⟦i⟧]
  case "( Bvs )" ⟨b⟩:             Lay⟨ρ,ε,b⟩
§
```

and $MapN\langle \phi,\varepsilon,\nu,\mu\rangle$ = ! $MapN \in [[[[E\times N]\rightarrow E] \times E \times N \times N] \rightarrow E]$

$\nu \leq \mu \rightarrow MapN\ \langle \phi,\ \phi\langle \varepsilon,\nu\rangle,\ \nu+1,\ \mu\ \rangle,\ \ \varepsilon$

! applies function ϕ to partial result ε with integers:

! $\nu,\nu+1,\ldots,\mu$ (in succession) to give the final result.

and $MapT\ \langle \phi,t\rangle$ = ! $MapT \in [[[E\rightarrow E] \times E^*] \rightarrow E^*]$

$MapN\ \langle (\lambda\langle \varepsilon,\nu\rangle .\ \varepsilon$ **cat** $\langle \phi[\![t\downarrow\nu]\!]\rangle),\ \langle\rangle ,1,$ **spread** $t\ \rangle$

! applies semantic function ϕ to each branch of node t ,

! forming a tuple from the results.

result $\lambda t.\,\mathcal{S}[\![t]\!](\lambda\iota.$ **err**) ! free variables produce errors.

! End of description of MSL.

It should be noted that the above description is based on a mixture of (extended) λ-notation and LAMBDA: the notation for tuples and certain operators comes from the λ-notation used in semantic equations, whereas λ-abstractions are type-free, as in LAMBDA. This need not worry the user of the description, for he may simply forget about the absence of types and manipulate expressions just as in λ-notation. However to be more formal one should reduce all notation to LAMBDA - this can be done by valuing a tuple of MSL as a function (abstraction), and by valuing **true**, **false**, *STR*, etc. as integers, although care must be taken if we want MSL to be a clean language with expressions such as: **true + false** valued as **err**.

In conclusion we remark that MSL is not claimed to be the ultimate in notation for mathematical semantics - only that it could form a firm basis for one, and that it should enable future notation to be described more precisely, eliminating the possibility of ambiguity in the definition of the mathematical semantics of a programming language.

ACKNOWLEDGMENTS

The author is grateful for many discussions with members of the Programming Research Group, and for useful feed-back from the participants of MFCS-74.

This work was done while the author was being supported by an SRC Research Scholarship.

REFERENCES

[1] MILNE,R.E. The Formal Semantics of Computer Languages and their implementations. Ph.D. Thesis, Cambridge University, 1974; Technical Monograph PRG-13, Oxford University Computing Laboratory, Programming Research Group.

[2] MOSSES,P.D. The Mathematical Semantics of ALGOL 60. Technical Monograph PRG-12, Oxford University Computing Laboratory, Programming Research Group.

[3] MOSSES,P.D. Mathematical Semantics and Compiler Generation. Doctoral Dissertation, in preparation.

[4] SCOTT,D. Outline of a Mathematical Theory of Computation. Proc. of the Fourth Annual Princeton Conference on Information Sciences and Systems, pp. 169-176; Technical Monograph PRG-2, Oxford University Computing Laboratory, Programming Research Group.

[5] SCOTT,D. Data Types as Lattices. In preparation.

[6] SCOTT,D.; STRACHEY,C. Toward a Mathematical Semantics for Computer Languages. Proc. Symp. on Computers and Automata, Polytechnic Institute of Brooklyn, 1971; Technical Monograph PRG-6, Oxford University Computing Laboratory, Programming Research Group.

[7] STRACHEY,C. Towards a Formal Semantics. Formal Language Description Languages (Ed. T.B.Steel), pp.198 -216, North-Holland, 1966.

[8] TENNENT,R.D. Mathematical Semantics and the Design of Programming Languages, Ph.D. Thesis, University of Toronto, 1973.

[9] TENNENT,R.D. Mathematical Semantics of SNOBOL 4. Technical Report No. 73-16, Dept. of Computing and Info. Sciences, Queen's University, Kingston, Ontario.

ω^+ -VALUED ALGORITHMIC LOGIC AS A TOOL TO INVESTIGATE PROCEDURES

H.Rasiowa
Institute of Mathematics
University of Warsaw

PKiN,00-110 Warsaw,Poland

Essential progress has recently been made in a logical approach to programming theory. A logical programming theory was initiated in University of Warsaw in papers [19] - [21] and developed in [5], [7]-[17], [22] and others. Those investigations yielded what we now call algorithmic logic.

In algorithmic logic programs are treated as certain expressions of formalized languages. Procedure free programs are constructed of expressions, which are called substitutions, by means of composition, branching and iteration program operations. Realizations of these languages determine semantics of programs. Formulas in languages of algorithmic logic describe properties of programs. For instance the stop property, equivalences of programs, correctness of programs are expressible in algorithmic languages and can be examined using metamathematical methods.

A HILBERT-style formalization and GENTZEN's type formalization of algorithmic logic was established in [7], [8]. Effectivity problems connected with algorithmic logic and its applications to programming theory have been examined in [5] . Connections between programmability and recursiveness have been recently studied in [22]. Many-valued algorithmic logics were investigated in [9]-[17] . The crucial case is that of extended ω^+ -valued algorithmic logic, which is a formalized theory of programs with recursive procedures. This approach links procedures to pushdown algorithms /see [1] / and uses ω^+-valued logic to describe the action and the control functions of algorithms. Other approach to recursive procedures on the background of algorithmic logic is based on a special kind of implicit definitions.

The purpose of this paper is to present extended ω^+-valued algorithmic logic in a modified version especially suitable to investigate procedures. In this version ω^+-valued logic is used only to describe control functions of pushdown algorithms whereas the action is described by means of the two-valued logic.

1. FORMALIZED LANGUAGES OF PROCEDURES AND THEIR REALIZATIONS

Let $\mathcal{L}_o=(A_o,T,F_o)$ be an enumerable language of a first order predicate calculus without quantifiers, A_o, T and F_o being the alphabet, the set of terms and the set of formulas of $\mathcal{L}_o$, respectively. We assume that A_o is the union of the following disjoint sets: an enumerable set V of free individual variables, an enumerable set V_o of propositional variables, two-element set $\{E_o,E_\omega\}$ of propositional constants / E_o corresponding to any false statement and E_ω corresponding to any true statement/, a set Φ of functors , a non-empty set Π of predicates, a four-element set $\{\vee,\wedge,\rightarrow,\sim\}$ of propositional connectives and two-element set $\{(,)\}$ of brackets.

The following terminology and notation we shall use in the sequel. Let N and N_o denote the set of positive integers and the set of non-negative integers, respectively. By a realization of $\mathcal{L}_o$ in a non-empty set U we mean any mapping R assigning to each n-argument $/n\in N_o/$ functor φ in Φ, a function $\varphi_R:U^n\rightarrow U$, and to each predicate q in Π of n argument $/n\in N/$, a function $q_R:U^n\rightarrow\{e_o,e_\omega\}$,where e_o and e_ω are the zero element and the unit element of the two-element Boolean algebra $B_o=(\{e_o,e_\omega\},\cup,\cap,\Rightarrow,\neg)$,respectively. Valuations /to be also called state vectors/ in U are mappings $v:V\cup V_o\rightarrow U\cup\{e_o,e_\omega\}$ such that $v(x)\in U$ for each $x\in V$ and $v(p)\in\{e_o,e_\omega\}$ for each $p\in V_o$ .The set of all valuations in U will be denoted by W_U. Every realization R of $\mathcal{L}_o$ in any set $U\neq 0$ assigns to each term τ in T a function $\tau_R:W_U\rightarrow U$ /i.e. a realization of τ / and to each formula α in F_o a function $\alpha_R:W_U\rightarrow\{e_o,e_\omega\}$/i.e. a realization of α /, the propositional connectives being realized as corresponding Boolean operations in B_o. In particular, $E_{oR}(v)=e_o$ and $E_{\omega R}(v)=e_\omega$ for each v in W_U.

The alphabet A_o of $\mathcal{L}_o$ is now extended to an alphabet A_{oL} by adjoing : a set $V_L=(a_n)_{n\in N}$ of label variables, a set $E=(E_n)_{n\in N}$ of label constants, a set $(J_k)_{k\in N_o}$ of unary label connectives, a set $\{o,\veebar, o^*\}$ of program operations signs /to be called the composition sign, the branching sign and the procedure operation sign, respectively, and the set $\{[,],/\}$ of auxiliary signs.

In order to extend any realization of $\mathcal{L}_o$ in a way making possible to realize label variables, label constants and label connectives, we shall use an algebra $\mathcal{P}^o_\omega$ to be defined as follows.

Let $P_\omega=(e_i)_{o\leq i\leq\omega}$ be a chain $e_o\leq e_1\leq\ldots\leq e_\omega$ /of different elements/ of the type ω^+ ,i.e. isomorphic to the chain of ordinals not greater than ω/. Assume that e_o and e_ω coincide with the zero element and the unit element of the Boolean algebra B_o. Define on P_ω one-argument operations $j_k: P_\omega \to \{e_o, e_\omega\}$, for $k \in N_o$, thus:

(1) $\quad j_k(e_i) = e_\omega$ for $i=k$, $\qquad j_k(e_i) = e_o$ for $i \neq k$, $0 \leq i \leq \omega$.

Now we set

(2) $\quad \mathcal{P}^o_\omega = (P_\omega, (j_k)_{k \in N_o})$.

Let $L = P_\omega - \{e_o, e_\omega\}$ and let L^* be the set of all words under L /i.e. of all finite strings of elements in L/, the empty word -to be denoted by ε - included. The elements in L will be treated as labels and e_o as ε .

Given a realization R of $\mathcal{L}_o$ in $U \neq 0$, we set $E_{iR} = e_i$, $i \in N$ and $J_{kR} = j_k$, $k \in N_o$.

By label valuations or label vectors we shall understand any mapping $v_L: V_L \to L \cup \{e_o\}$, satisfying the following conditions

(v_L1) $\quad v_L(a_n) = e_o$ for some $n \in N$,

(v_L2) $\quad$ for each $n \in N$: if $v_L(a_n) = e_o$, then $v_L(a_{n+1}) = e_o$.

The set of all label vectors will be denoted by W_L. We shall identify any $v_L \in W_L$ with the sequence $(v_L(a_1), v_L(a_2), \ldots)$. It follows from (v_L1) and (v_L2) that for every label vector v_L, either v_L is $(e_o, \ldots)$ or v_L is $(e_{k_1}, e_{k_2}, \ldots, e_{k_n}, e_o, \ldots)$, where $k_i \neq 0$ for $i=1,\ldots,n$. In the first case it can be treated as the empty word ε in L^* and in the second case as the word $e_{k_1} \ldots e_{k_n} \in L^*$. Thus W_L may be identified with the set L^* of all words under L.

By a generalized valuation in $U \neq 0$ / or a state in U / we shall understand any pair $v^* = (v_L, v)$, where $v_L \in W_L$ and $v \in W_U$. The set of all states in U will be denoted by $W^*_U = W_L \times W_U$. For every term τ in T and every formula α in F_o we may treat τ_R and α_R as mappings from $W_L \times W_U$ into U and $\{e_o, e_\omega\}$, respectively. Then we set

(3) $\quad \tau_R(v_L, v) = \tau_R(v)$ and $\alpha_R(v_L, v) = \alpha_R(v)$, for each $(v_L, v) \in W_L \times W_U$.

Now we are going to define progressively a set F_LS of programs and their realizations as partial functions from the set W^*_U of states in U into W^*_U, by an established realization R of $\mathcal{L}_o$ in a set $U \neq 0$. Programs will be certain expressions constructed of elements from A_{oL}.

Atomic programs in F_LS are substituions, label substitutions and label supervisors.

The set S of substitutions consists of the following expressions

(s1) $\quad [x_1/\tau_1 \ldots x_n/\tau_n \; p_1/\alpha_1 \ldots p_m/\alpha_m]$, for n,m in N_o, where $x_1,\dots,x_n \in V$ are different individual variables, $\tau_1,\dots,\tau_n$ are any terms in T, $p_1,\dots,p_m \in V_o$ are different propositional variables and $\alpha_1,\dots,\alpha_m$ are any formulas in F_o.

The following expression is an example of a substitution

(4) $[x/x+1 \ y/y.z \ \ p_1/(x<y \wedge z=t) \rightarrow (p_1 \vee p_2)]$.

Substitutions may be translated into an Algol-like language as follows. Any substitution s in a form (sl) should be read:

$x_1:=\tau_1$ <u>and</u> ...<u>and</u> $x_n:=\tau_n$ <u>and</u> $p_1:=\alpha_1$...<u>and</u> $p_m:=\alpha_m$.

Clearly, terms play the role of arithmetic expressions while formulas play the role of Boolean expressions.

Realization R is now extended on the set S of substitutions as follows. For any $s \in S$, where s is in the form (sl), the realization s_R of s is a mapping $s_R: W_L \times W_U \rightarrow W_L \times W_U$ which is defined thus:

(sr) $s_R(v_L,v)=(v_L,v')$,where

(5) $v'(x_i)=\tau_{iR}(v)$ for $i=1,\dots,n$, $\quad v'(p_i)=\alpha_{iR}(v)$ for $i=1,\dots,m$,

(6) $v'(x) = v(x)$ for $x \in V$ and $x \neq x_i$, $i=1,\dots,n$,

(7) $v'(p) = v(p)$ for $p \in V$ and $p \neq p_i$, $i=1,\dots,m$.

In particular $[\ ]_R(v_L,v)=(v_L,v)$. Since s_R does not depend on v_L and does not change v_L it may be treated as a mapping from W_U into W_U. Therefore we shall also write $s_R(v)=v'$ and $s_R(v_L,v)=(v_L,s_R(v))$.

The set S_L^o of label substitutions consists of the expressions in the following forms:

(s_L1) $[a_1/E_{k_1}]$, $k_1 \in N$,

(s_L2) $[a_1/E_{k_1} \ a_2/a_1]$, $k_1 \in N$,

(s_L3) $[a_1/E_{k_1} \dots a_n/E_{k_n} \ a_{n+1}/a_2]$, $n>1$, $n \in N$, $k_i \in N$ for $i=1,\dots,n$,

(s_L4) $[a_1/a_2]$,

(s_L5) $[a_1/E_o]$,

(s_L6) $[\ ]$.

By S_L will be denoted the set of all label substitutions except (s_L5). The set FCS_L of finite control substitutions in S_L consists of the substitutions in the forms (s_L1), (s_L4) and (s_L6).

Realization R is now extended on S_L^o in the following way. For any $s^* \in S_L^o$, s_R^* is a mapping $s_R^*: W_L \times W_U \rightarrow W_L \times W_U$ defined thus:

(s_Lr1) $[a_1/E_{k_1}]_R(v_L,v)=(v'_L,v)$, where $v'_L(a_1)=e_{k_1}$ and $v'_L(a_n)=v(a_n)$ for $n>1$, $n \in N$.

In this case $(v_L(a_1), v_L(a_2), \ldots)$ is transformed on $(e_{k_1}, v_L(a_2), \ldots)$.

(s_Lr2) $[a_1/E_{k_1}\ a_2/a_1]_R(v_L,v) = (v'_L,v)$, where $v'_L(a_1) = e_{k_1}$ and $v'_L(a_n) = v_L(a_{n-1})$ for $n > 1$, $n \in N$.

In this case $(v_L(a_1), v_L(a_2), \ldots)$ is transformed on $(e_{k_1}, v_L(a_1), \ldots)$.

(s_Lr3) $[a_1/E_{k_1} \ldots a_n/E_{k_n}\, a_{n+1}/a_2]_R(v_L,v) = (v'_L,v)$, where $v'_L(a_i) = e_{k_i}$ for $i=1,\ldots,n$ and $v'_L(a_{n+i}) = v_L(a_{i+1})$ for $i \in N$.

In this case $(v_L(a_1), v_L(a_2), \ldots)$ is transformed on $(e_{k_1}, \ldots, e_{k_n}, v_L(a_2), \ldots)$.

(s_Lr4) $[a_1/a_2]_R(v_L,v) = (v'_L,v)$, where $v'_L(a_i) = v_L(a_{i+1})$ for $i \in N$.

In this case $(v_L(a_1), v_L(a_2), \ldots)$ is transformed on $(v_L(a_2), v_L(a_3), \ldots)$.

(s_Lr5) $[a_1/E_o]_R(v_L,v) = (v'_L,v)$, where $v'_L(a_i) = e_o$ for $i \in N$.

In this case $(v_L(a_1), v_L(a_2), \ldots)$ is transformed on $(e_o, e_o, \ldots)$.

(s_Lr6) $[\ ]_R(v_L,v) = (v_L,v)$.

Since, for any s^* in S_L^o, s_R^* does not depend on $v \in W_U$ and does not change $v \in W_U$, it may be treated as a mapping $s_R^*: W_L \to W_L$. Therefore we shall also write $s_R^*(v_L) = v'_L$ and $s_R^*(v_L,v) = (s_R^*(v_L), v)$.

The set Sp of label supervisors consists of the following expressions:

(j) $[J_k(a_n)]$, $k \in N_o$, $n \in N$.

They are realized as partial mappings from $W_L \times W_U$ into $W_L \times W_U$, namely we set

$$(jr)\quad [J_k(a_n)]_R(v_L,v) = \begin{cases} (v_L,v) & \text{if } j_k(v_L(a_n)) = e_\omega\text{, i.e. if } v_L(a_n) = e_k \\ \text{otherwise is undefined.} \end{cases}$$

Thus the realization of $[J_k(a_n)]$ checks whether $v_L(a_n) = e_k$, i.e. whether the n-th label in a label vector $(v_L(a_1), v_L(a_2), \ldots)$ is equal e_k. In other words, it is the identity mapping on the set of states (v_L,v) for which $v_L(a_n) = e_k$ and is undefined on other states.

The set I_1 of instructions of order 1 consists of the following expressions:

(il1) $o[o[[J_k(a_1)s^*]\ s]$, where $k \in N$, $s^* \in S_L$, $s \in S$,

(il2) $o[[J_k(a_1)] \vee [\alpha\, o[s_1^*\ s_1]\ o[s_2^*\ s_2]]]$, where $k \in N$, $\alpha \in F_o$, $s_1^*, s_2^* \in S_L$, $s_1, s_2 \in S$.

For brevity these expressions will be written respectively thus:

(8) $o[[J_k(a_1)]\ s^* s]$,

(9) $o[[J_k(a_1)] \veebar [\alpha\ s_1^*\ s_1\ s_2^*\ s_2]]$.

Realization R is now extended on I_1 as follows. If H in I_1 is in a form (il1), then we set

(irl1) $H_R(v_L,v) = s_R(s_R^*([J_k(a_1)]_R(v_L,v)))$, if this is defined, otherwise $H_R(v_L,v)$ is undefined.

It follows from this definition and (sr), (s_Lr1), (s_Lr2), (s_Lr3), (s_Lr4), (s_Lr6), (jr), that $H_R(v_L,v)$ is defined iff $v_L(a_1)=e_k$, and then we have

(10) $H_R(v_L,v)=s_R(s_R^*(v_L,v)) = (s_R^*(v_L), s_R(v))$.

If H in I_1 is in a form (il2), then we set

(irl2) $H_R(v_L,v) = \begin{cases} s_{1R}(s_{1R}^*([J_k(a_1)]_R(v_L,v))) & \text{if this is defined and } \alpha_R(v)=e_\omega \\ s_{2R}(s_{2R}^*([J_k(a_1)]_R(v_L,v))) & \text{if this is defined and } \alpha_R(v)=e_o \\ \text{is undefined otherwise.} & \end{cases}$

It follows from this definition and (sr), (s_Lr1), (s_Lr2), (s_Lr3), (s_Lr4), (s_Lr6), (jr), that $H_R(v_L,v)$ is defined iff $v_L(a_1)=e_k$. If it is defined, then we have

(11) $H_R(v_L,v)=(s_{1R}^*(v_L), s_{1R}(v))$ if $\alpha_R(v)=e_\omega$,

(12) $H_R(v_L,v)=(s_{2R}^*(v_L), s_{2R}(v))$ if $\alpha_R(v)=e_o$.

The realizations of instructions in I_1 suggest to call e_k the label of instructions in a form (il1) and (il2).

Example 1.

Let $H=o[[J_1(a_1)]\veebar[x=0\,[a_1/a_2][y/1][a_1/E_1\ a_2/E_2\ a_3/a_2][y/x-1]]$. Let R be the usual realization in the set of integers, $v_L=(e_1,e_o,\ldots)$, $v(x)=2$, $v(y)=3$. Then $H_R(v_L,v)=((e_1,e_2,e_o,\ldots),v')$, where $v'(x)=2$, $v'(y)=1$ and $v'(z)=v(z)$ for any individual variable z different from x and from y.

Instructions in I_1 such that all label substituions which occur in these instructions belong to FCS_L are said to be finite-control instructions in H. The set of all finite-control instructions in I_1 will be denoted by FCI_1.

The set P_1 of procedures of order 1 consists of the following expressions

(p1) $o^*[H_{k_1} t\ H_{k_1} \ldots H_{k_n}\ H_t]$, $n\in N$, where

1° $H_{k_1},\ldots,H_{k_n}$ are instructions of order 1 with different labels $e_{k_1},\ldots,e_{k_n}$, and e_{k_1} is said to be the label of (p1).

2° E_t, $t\in N$, does not occur in H_{k_i} for $i=1,\dots,n$ and is called a terminal label,

3° $H_{k_1 t} = o\big[[J_{k_1}(a_1)]\ [a_1/E_{k_1}\ a_2/E_t\ a_3/a_2][\ ]\big]$ is called a preparatory instruction,

4° $H_t = o\big[[J_t(a_1)][a_1/a_2][\ ]\big]$ is called a terminal instruction.

If $H\in P_1$ and all H_{k_i}, $i=1,\dots,n$, which occur in H belong to FCI_1, then H is said to be a finite-control procedure in P_1. The set of all finite-control procedures in P_1 will be denoted by FCP_1. Observe that $H\in P_1 - FCP_1$ if at least one of H_{k_i}, $i=1,\dots,n$, belongs to $I_1 - FCI_1$. This holds if at least one of H_{k_i} contains a label substitution in $S_L - FCS_L$, i.e. in a form (s_L2) or (s_L3).

It follows from 3°, (irl1), (10), (s_Lr3), that $H_{k_1 tR}(v_L,v)$ is defined iff $v_L(a_1)=e_{k_1}$. If it is defined, then

(13) $H_{k_1 tR}(v_L,v) = ((e_{k_1}, e_t, v_L(a_2), v_L(a_3),\dots), v)$.

Thus, if the realization $H_{k_1 tR}$ is defined for a state (v_L,v), then it maps v_L on $(e_{k_1}, e_t, v_L(a_2),\dots)$, i.e. it separates e_{k_1}, being the first label of v_L from $v_L(a_2)$ by means of the terminal label e_t.

In order to define the realization H_R of any H in P_1 we first introduce the notion of a computation.

Let $H\in P_1$ be in a form (p1). By a computation of H by realization R for a state (v_L,v) we shall understand any finite sequence of states

(c) $H_R^o(v_L,v)=(v_L^o,v^o),\dots,H_R^{\bar m+1}(v_L,v)=(v_L^{\bar m+1},v^{\bar m+1})$

such that the following conditions are satisfied:

(c1) $H_R^o(v_L,v)=(v_L^o,v^o)=H_{k_1 tR}(v_L,v)$,

(c2) for each $i=0,\dots,\bar m-1$, $H_R^{i+1}(v_L,v)=(v_L^{i+1},v^{i+1})=H_{k_j R}(v_L^i,v^i)$ for some $j=1,\dots,n$,

(c3) $H_R^{\bar m+1}(v_L,v)=(v_L^{\bar m+1},v^{\bar m+1})=H_{tR}(v_L^{\bar m},v^{\bar m})$,

(c4) all states in (c) are defined.

The number $\bar m$ is said to be the length of a computation (c) .

1.1. For every $H\in P_1$, realization R and any state $(v_L,v)\in W_L\times W_U$, there exists at most one computation of H by R for (v_L,v) and is effectively defined. Moreover, if (c) is this computation, then

(14) $v_L^{\bar m+1}=(v_L(a_2),v_L(a_3),\dots)$.

To prove the first part of 1.1 notice that $k_1,\dots,k_n$ are different and each k_i, $i=1,\dots,n$, is different from t. If $v_L(a_1)\neq e_{k_1}$, then a computation does not exist. If $v_L(a_1)=e_{k_1}$, then /by (c1), (c2), (13), (irl1), (irl2)/ (v_L^o,v^o) and (v_L^1,v^1) are defined. Suppose that for $i\geqslant 1$, (v_L^i,v^i) is defined. If $v_L^i(a_1)$ is different from e_{k_j}, $j=1,\ldots,n$, and is different from e_t, then (v_L^{i+1},v^{i+1}) is not defined and a computation does not exist. If $v_L^i(a_1)$ is equal e_{k_j}, for some $j=1,\ldots,n$, then by (c2), (v_L^{i+1},v^{i+1}) is uniquely defined. If $v_L^i(a_1)=e_t$, then (v_L^{i+1},v^{i+1}) is uniquely defined and is the last state in a computation of H by R for (v_L,v).

To prove the second part of 1.1 suppose that (c) is a computation of H by R for (v_L,v). Then, by (13), $v_L^o=(e_{k_1},e_t,v_L(a_2),\ldots)$. We shall call (e_{k_1},e_t) the active part of v_L^o, and $(v_L(a_2),\ldots)$ the passive part of v_L^o. By (irl1), (irl2), $(s_Lr1)-(s_Lr4)$, (s_Lr6), (c2) and 2°, v_L^1 is in a form

(15) $(e_{m_1},\ldots,e_{m_p},e_t,v_L(a_2),\ldots)$, where $p\in N_o$ and $m_1,\ldots,m_p$ are different from t.

In (15), $(e_{m_1},\ldots,e_{m_p},e_t)$ is said to be the active part and $(v_L(a_1),\ldots)$ the passive part. Suppose that for some i, $1\leqslant i<\bar{m}$, v_L^i has a form (15). It follows from (irl1), (irl2), $(s_Lr1)-(s_Lr4)$, (s_Lr6) (c2), 2°, that v_L^{i+1} has also a form (15). Thus every label vector $v_L^1,\ldots,v_L^{\bar{m}}$, has a form (15) with a constant passive part $(v_L(a_2),\ldots)$. Since (c) is a computation, it follows by (c3), that $v_L^{\bar{m}}=(e_t,v_L(a_2),\ldots)$. By (c3), 4° and (irl1), (s_Lr4), we have $v_L^{\bar{m}+1}=(v_L(a_2),\ldots)$.

1.2. For any H in P_1, any two states (v_L,v) and (w_L,w) in $W_L\times W_U$ such that $v_L(a_1)=w_L(a_1)$ and $v=w$, either both computations of H by realization R for (v_L,v) and for (w_L,w) exist or both do not exist. Moreover, if $(v_L^o,v^o),\ldots,(v_L^{\bar{m}+1},v^{\bar{m}+1})$, and $(w_L^o,w^o),\ldots,(w_L^{p+1},w^{p+1})$ are computations of H by R for (v_L,v) and for (w_L,w), respectively, then $\bar{m}=p$, and for each i, $1\leqslant i\leqslant\bar{m}$, $v^i=w^i$, and the label vectors v_L^i, w_L^i have the same active parts.

The proof of 1.2, based on the proof of 1.1, is left to the reader.

Theorem 1.1 enables us to extend realization R on P_1. For any H in P_1 we set

(pr1) $H_R(v_L,v)=H_R^{\bar{m}+1}(v_L,v)$ if (c) is a computation of H by R for (v_L,v), and $H_R(v_L,v)$ is not defined if a computation of H by R for (v_L,v) does not exist.

Suppose that for each $n\leqslant m$ the sets I_n of instructions of order n and the sets P_n of procedures of order n have been defined.

Then we define I_{m+1} and P_{m+1} as follows.

The set I_{m+1} of instructions of order m+1 consists of the following expressions:

(i1) $o[o[[J_k(a_1)]\ s^*]\ H_q]$, where $k \in N, H_q \in P_m$, e_q is the label of H_q, $q \in N$, $s^* \in S_L$ and is in one of the following forms

($s_L q1$) $[a_1/E_q]$,

($s_L q2$) $[a_1/E_q\ a_2/a_1]$,

($s_L q3$) $[a_1/E_q\ a_2/E_{k_2} \ldots a_n/E_{q_n}\ a_{n+1}/a_2]$, $n > 1$, $k_2, \ldots, k_n \in N$.

(i2) $o[[J_k(a_1)] \veebar [\alpha\ o[s_1^*\ H_{q_1}] o[s_2^*\ H_{q_2}]]]$, where $k \in N$, $\alpha \in F_o$, H_{q_1} and H_{q_2} are procedures of orders not greater than m, one at least of them being of order m, e_{q_1}, e_{q_2} are the labels of H_{q_1} and H_{q_2}, respectively, $q_1, q_2 \in N$, s_1^*, s_2^* are in S_L and each of them has one of the forms ($s_L q1$), ($s_L q2$), $s_L q3$).

(i3) $o[[J_k(a_1)] \veebar [\alpha\ o[s^* H_q] o[\ s_1^*\ s_1]]]$, where $k \in N$, $\alpha \in F_o$, H_q and s^* satisfy the conditions in (i1), $s_1^* \in S_L$, $s_1 \in S$.

(i4) $o[[J_k(a_1)] \veebar [\alpha\ o[s_1^* s_1]\ o[s^* H_q]]]$, where $k \in N$, $\alpha \in F_o$, $s_1^* \in S_L$, $s_1 \in S$, and H_q, s^* satisfy the conditions in (i1).

For brevity we shall write expressions (i1) - (i4) in the forms analogous to (8) and (9). For the instructions in forms (i1) - (i4), e_k is said to be their label.

The set FCI_{m+1} consists of these instructions in I_{m+1} in which do not occur label substitutions ($s_L q3$) with $n > 2$ and substitutions s_1^* in (i3), (i4) are in FCS_L.

The set P_{m+1} of procedures of order m+1 consists of the expressions

(p) $o^*[\ H_{k_1} t\ H_{k_1} \ldots H_{k_n}\ H_t]$, $n \in N$, where

(p^o) $H_{k_1}, \ldots, H_{k_n}$ are instructions of orders not greater than m and at least one of them is of order m, the labels $e_{k_1}, \ldots, e_{k_n}$ of $H_{k_1}, \ldots, H_{k_n}$, respectively, are different, and e_{k_1} is said to be the label of (p),

(p^1) the conditions 2°, 3°, 4° in (p1) are satisfied.

If $H \in P_{m+1}$ and all H_{k_i}, $i=1,\ldots,n$, which occur in H belong to $FCI_1 \cup \ldots \cup FCI_m$, then H is said to be a finite-control procedure of order m+1. The set of all finite-control procedures of order m+1 will be denoted by FCP_{m+1} .

Suppose that realization R is extended on the sets I_i and P_i for $1 \le i \le m$, the notion of computation of any $H \in P_i$ being the same as for procedures of order 1.

In order to extend R on I_{m+1} we adopt for any instruction H of order m+1, which is in a form (i1), (i2), (i3), (i4) the following definition, respectively:

(ir1) $H_R(v_L,v) = H_{qR}(s_R^*([J_k(a_n)]_R(v_L,v)))$ if the right side is defined, otherwise $H_R(v_L,v)$ is not defined,

(ir2) $H_R(v_L,v) = \begin{cases} H_{q_1R}(s_{1R}^*([J_k(a_1)]_R(v_L,v))) & \text{if this is defined and } \alpha_R(v)=e_\omega \\ H_{q_2R}(s_{2R}^*([J_k(a_1)]_R(v_L,v))) & \text{if this is defined and } \alpha_R(v)=e_o \\ \text{is undefined otherwise ,} \end{cases}$

(ir3) $H_R(v_L,v) = \begin{cases} H_{qR}(s_R^*([J_k(a_1)]_R(v_L,v))) & \text{if this is defined and } \alpha_R(v)=e_\omega \\ s_{1R}^*(s_{1R}([J_k(a_1)]_R(v_L,v))) & \text{if this is defined and } \alpha_R(v)=e_o \\ \text{is undefined otherwise,} \end{cases}$

(ir4) $H_R(v_L,v) = \begin{cases} s_{1R}^*(s_R([J_k(a_1)]_R(v_L,v))) & \text{if this is defined and } \alpha_R(v)=e_\omega \\ H_{qR}(s_R^*([J_k(a_1)]_R(v_L,v))) & \text{if this is defined and } \alpha_R(v)=e_o \\ \text{is undefined otherwise} \end{cases}$

In order to extend R on P_{m+1} we adopt for $H \in P_{m+1}$ the definition of computation of H by R for any state $(v_L,v) \in W_L \times W_U$ the same as for procedures of order 1.

1.3. If theorem 1.1 holds for all procedures of orders i, $1 \le i \le m$, then this theorem holds for the procedures of order m+1.

The proof of 1.3 is analogous to that of 1.1 and is left to the reader.

Theorems 1.1 and 1.3 make possible to extend R on P_{m+1}. For any H in P_{m+1} we set

(pr) $H_R(v_L,v) = H_R^{\bar{m}+1}(v_L,v)$ if (c) is a computation of H by R for (v_L,v), and $H_R(v_L,v)$ is undefined if a computation of H by R for (v_L,v) does not exist.

Thus the sets I_m, P_m and realization R for any H in I_m and any H in P_m are defined for each $m \in N$. Moreover the following theorems hold.

.. 1.4. For any H in P_m, $m \in N$, realization R and any state (v_L, v) in $W_L \times W_U$, there exists at most one computation of H by R for (v_L, v) and is effectively defined. Moreover, if (c) is this computation, then

(16) $v_L^{\bar{m}+1} = (v_L(a_2),\ v_L(a_3), \ldots)$.

1.5. For any H in P_m, $m \in N$, realization R and any two states $(v_L, v), (w_L, w)$ in $W_L \times W_U$ such that $v_L(a_1) = w_L(a_1)$ and $v = w$, either both computations of H by R for (v_L, v) and for (w_L, w) exist or both do not exist. Moreover, if $(v_L^o, v^o), \ldots, (v_L^{\bar{m}+1}, v^{\bar{m}+1})$ and $(w_L^o, w^o), \ldots, (w_L^{p+1}, w^{p+1})$ are computations of H by R for (v_L, v) and (w_L, w), respectively, then $\bar{m} = p$ and for each i, $1 \le i \le \bar{m}$, $v^i = w^i$, and the label vectors v_L^i and w_L^i have the same active parts.

The proof by induction with respect to $m \in N$ is left to the reader.

1.6. For any instruction H in I_m, $m \in N$, realization R and any state $(v_L, v) \in W_L \times W_U$, if $H_R(v_L, v)$ is defined and $H_R(v_L, v) = (\bar{v}_L, \bar{v})$, then $\bar{v}_L$ has one of the following forms: v_L, $(e_{k_1},\ v_L(a_1),\ v_L(a_2), \ldots)$, $(e_{k_1}, \ldots, e_{k_n},\ v_L(a_2), \ldots)$, $n \in N$, $(v_L(a_2), v_L(a_3), \ldots)$.

If H is in I_1, then the theorem holds by (irl1), (irl2), (jr), (s_Lr1)-(s_Lr4), (s_Lr6). Suppose that $H \in I_m$, $m > 1$, e_k is the label of H and $H_R(v_L, v)$ is defined. Then $v_L(a_1) = e_k$. If H is in a form (i1), then by (irl) and (jr) we have $H_R(v_L, v) = H_{qR}(s_R^*(v_L, v))$. Since s^* has one of the forms (s_Lq1)- (s_Lq3), $s_R^*(v_L, v)$ has one of the forms $(e_q, v_L(a_2), \ldots)$, $(e_q, v_L(a_1), \ldots)$, $(e_q,\ e_{k_2}, \ldots, e_{k_n},\ v_L(a_2), \ldots)$. Hence, by 1.4, $\bar{v}_L$ can be equal $(v_L(a_2),\ v_L(a_3), \ldots)$ or v_L, or $(e_{k_2}, \ldots, e_{k_n}, v_L(a_2), \ldots)$. In the last case, if $n=3$ and $k_3 = k$, we obtain a label vector in a form $(e_{k_2},\ v_L(a_1),\ v_L(a_2), \ldots)$. The proof for H in forms (i2), (i3), (i4) is analogous.

The set F_LS of programs / F_LS-expressions / is the least set of finite sequences of elements in A_{oL} satisfying the following conditions:

(f_Ls1) $S \cup S_L^o \cup Sp \cup \bigcup_{m=1}^{\infty} P_m \subset F_LS$,

(f_Ls2) if $H_1, H_2 \in F_LS$, then $o[H_1H_2] \in F_LS$,

(f_Ls3) if $H_1, H_2 \in F_LS$, then $\varkappa[\varkappa\ H_1H_2] \in F_LS$ for each $\varkappa \in F_o$.

For any $H \in S \cup S_L^o \cup Sp \cup \bigcup_{m=1}^{\infty} P_m$, H will be said to be an indecomposable program. It follows from (f_Ls1)-(f_Ls3), that $\bigcup_{m=1} I_m \subset F_LS$.

Example 2.

The following procedure $H \in P_1$-FCP_1 is an implementation of a recursive program P: $F(x) \Leftarrow$ <u>if</u> $x=0$ <u>then</u> 1 <u>else</u> $x.F(x-1)$, over N_o.

$H = o^*[H_{13}\ H_1\ H_2\ H_3]$, where

$H_{13} = o[[J_1(a_1)][\ a_1/E_1\ a_2/E_3\ a_3/a_2][\ ]]$,

$H_1 = o[[\ J_1(a_1)]_{\vee}[x=0\ [a_1/a_2][y/1][a_1/E_1\ a_2/E_2\ a_3/a_2][x/x-1]]]$,

$H_2 = o[[\ J_2(a_1)][\ a_1/a_2][x/x+1\ y/(x+1)\ .\ y]]$,

$H_3 = o[[\ J_3(a_1)][\ a_1/a_2][\ ]]$.

H_{13} is a preparatory instruction and H_3 is a terminal instruction. We adopt as R the standard realization in N_o. The following sequence of states is an example of a computation of H by R for $(v_L,v) \in W_L \times W_{N_o}$, where $v_L = (e_1, e_o, \dots)$ and $v(x)=4$, $v(y) \in N_o$, $v(z) \in N_o$ for $z \in V$. In writting state vectors in this computation we shall only give the values of the variables which occur in H.

$v_L^o = (e_1,e_3,e_o,\dots)$	$v^o(x)=4$	$v^o(y)=v(y)$
$v_L^1 = (e_1,e_2,e_3,e_o,\dots)$	$v^1(x)=3$	$v^1(y)=v(y)$
$v_L^2 = (e_1,e_2,e_2,e_3,e_o,\dots)$	$v^2(x)=2$	$v^2(y)=v(y)$
$v_L^3 = (e_1,e_2,e_2,e_2,e_3,e_o,\dots)$	$v^3(x)=1$	$v^3(y)=v(y)$
$v_L^4 = (e_1,e_2,e_2,e_2,e_2,e_3,e_o,\dots)$	$v^4(x)=0$	$v^4(y)=v(y)$
$v_L^5 = (e_2,e_2,e_2,e_2,e_3,e_o,\dots)$	$v^5(x)=0$	$v^5(y)=1$
$v_L^6 = (e_2,e_2,e_2,e_3,e_o,\dots)$	$v^6(x)=1$	$v^6(y)=1$
$v_L^7 = (e_2,e_2,e_3,e_o,\dots)$	$v^7(x)=2$	$v^7(y)=2$
$v_L^8 = (e_2,e_3,e_o,\dots)$	$v^8(x)=3$	$v^8(y)=6$
$v_L^9 = (e_3,e_o,\dots)$	$v^9(x)=4$	$v^9(y)=24$
$v_L^{10} = (e_o,\dots)$	$v^{10}(x)=4$	$v^{10}(y)=24$.

It can be proved that $H_R(v_L,v)$ is defined for each state (v_L,v) in $W_L \times W_{N_o}$ such that $v_L(a_1) = e_1$. Moreover, if $H_R(v_L,v) = (\tilde{v}_L,\tilde{v})$, then $\tilde{v}(y) = (v(x))!$.

Example 3.

The following procedure $H \in P_1\text{-}FCP_1$ is an implementation of a recursive program P: $F(x,y) \Leftarrow$ <u>if</u> x=y <u>then</u> y+1 <u>else</u> F(x ,F(x-1,y+1)), over the set C of integers.

$H = o^*[H_{13}\ H_1\ H_2\ H_3]$, where H_{13} and H_3 are the same as in Example 2 and H_1, H_2 have the following forms:

$H_1 = o[[J_1(a_1)]_{\vee}[\ x=y\ [\ a_1/a_2][z/x+1][\ a_1/E_1\ a_2/E_2\ a_3/a_2][\ x/x-1\ y/y+1]]]$,

$H_2 = o[[J_2(a_1)]\ [a_1/a_2][\ x/x+1\ y/z\ z/y+2]]$.

We adopt as R the standard realization in C. The following sequence of states is an example of a computation of H by realization R for $(v_L,v)\in W_L\times W_C$, where $v_L=(e_1,e_2,e_0,\dots)$, $v(x)=7$, $v(y)=3$, $v(z)\in C$, and $v(u)\in C$ for each $u\in V$.

$v_L^0=(e_1,e_3,e_2,e_0,\dots)$	$v^0(x)=7$	$v^0(y)=3$	$v^0(z)=v(z)$
$v_L^1=(e_1,e_2,e_3,e_2,e_0,\dots)$	$v^1(x)=6$	$v^1(y)=4$	$v^1(z)=v(z)$
$v_L^2=(e_1,e_2,e_2,e_3,e_2,e_0,\dots)$	$v^2(x)=5$	$v^2(y)=5$	$v^2(z)=v(z)$
$v_L^3=(e_2,e_2,e_3,e_2,e_0,\dots)$	$v^3(x)=5$	$v^3(y)=5$	$v^3(z)=6$
$v_L^4=(e_2,e_3,e_2,e_0,\dots)$	$v^4(x)=6$	$v^4(y)=6$	$v^4(z)=7$
$v_L^5=(e_3,e_2,e_0,\dots)$	$v^5(x)=7$	$v^5(y)=7$	$v^5(z)=8$
$v_L^6=(e_2,e_0,\dots)$	$v^6(x)=7$	$v^6(y)=7$	$v^6(z)=8$

It can be proved that $H_R(v_L,v)$ is defined for any $(v_L,v)\in W_L\times W_C$ such that $v_L(a_1)=e_1$ and $v(x)\geq v(y)$, $v(x)-v(y)$ is even. Other wise is undefined. If the conditions mentioned above are satisfied and $H_R(v_L,v)=(\bar{v}_L,\bar{v})$, then $\bar{v}(z)=v(x)+1$. The partial function

$$f(x,y)=\begin{cases} x+1 & \text{if } x\geq y \text{ and } x-y \text{ is even}\\ \text{undefined otherwise} \end{cases}$$

is the least fixpoint of the recursive program P.

Example 4.

Let G_1 be the procedure considered in Example 2 and let G_2 be the procedure considered in Example 3. The following expression

$$\underline{\vee}[(x\geq y \wedge x-y=2z)o[[a_1/E_1]\ G_2]o[o[[a_1/E_1]\ G_1][z/y]]]$$

is a F_LS-expression.

In order to extend realization R on F_LS we adopt the following additional definitions:

(f_Lsr2) $o[H_1H_2]_R(v_L,v)=H_{2R}(H_{1R}(v_L,v))$ if the right side is defined, otherwise is undefined,

(f_Lsr3) if $H=\underline{\vee}[\alpha H_1H_2]$, then

$$H_R(v_L,v)=\begin{cases} H_{1R}(v_L,v) & \text{if this is defined and } \alpha_R(v)=e_\omega\\ H_{2R}(v_L,v) & \text{if this is defined and } \alpha_R(v)=e_0\\ \text{is undefined otherwise} \end{cases}$$

These definitions are conformable to (irl1), (irl2), (irl), (ir2), (ir3), (ir4).

2. FS-EXPRESSIONS

Let $\mathcal{L}_0=(A_0,T,F_0)$ be a first order predicate language without quantfiers, as considered in Sec.1, and let A_1 be an extension of A_0 obtained by adjoining the sets $\{o, \veebar, *\}$, $\{[\ ,\ ]\ ,\ /\}$ of program operations signs and of auxiliary signs, respectively.

The set FS of FS-expressions, as introduced by SALWICKI [19], is the least set of finite sequences of elements in A_1 such that

(fs1) if $s \in S$, then $s \in FS$,

(fs2) if $K, M \in FS$, then $o[KM]$, $\veebar[\alpha KM]$, $*[\alpha K] \in FS$ for each α in F_0.

Let R be a realization of $\mathcal{L}_0$ in $U \neq 0$. Then any FS-expression K is realized as a partial function K_R from the set W_U of state vectors into W_U. More exactly, for any substitutions $s \in S$, $s_R(v)=v'$, where v' is defined in Sec.1 by (5)-(7). Moreover,

(1) $o[KM]_R(v) = M_R(K_R(v))$ if the right side is defined, and is undefined in the opposite case,

$$(2)\ \veebar[\alpha KM]_R(v) = \begin{cases} K_R(v) \text{ if this is defined and } \alpha_R(v)=e_\omega, \\ M_R(v) \text{ if this is defined and } \alpha_R(v)=e_0, \\ \text{is undefined otherwise,} \end{cases}$$

$$(3)\ *[\alpha K]_R(v) = \begin{cases} K_R^i(v), \text{ if } i \text{ is the least } j \in N_0 \text{ such that } \alpha_R(K_R^j(v))=e_\omega, \\ \qquad \text{where } K_R^0(v)=v, K_R^{j+1}(v)=K_R(K_R^j(v)) \text{ for } j \in N_0, \\ \text{is undefined if such } i \in N_0 \text{ does not exist.} \end{cases}$$

Clearly, we assume that $K_R^i(v)$ in (3) is defined.

FS-expressions $o[KM]$, $\veebar[\alpha KM]$, $*[\alpha K]$ can be tranlated into an Algol-like language as follows: if K and M are translated into programs P_K, P_M, respectively, then $o[KM]$, $\veebar[\alpha KM]$, $*[\alpha K]$ are translated into programs

<u>begin</u> P_k; P_m <u>end</u> , <u>if</u> α <u>then</u> P_K <u>else</u> P_M , <u>while</u> $\sim\alpha$ <u>do</u> P_K,

respectively.

A procedure $H \in \bigcup_{m=1}^{\infty} P_m$, $H=o^*[H_{k_1} t\ H_{k_1} \dots H_{k_n}\ H_t]$ is said to be equivalent to a FS-expression M provided for every realization R of $\mathcal{L}_o$ in any set $U \neq O$ and for every $(v_L, v) \in W_L \times W_U$ such that $v_L(a_1) = e_{k_1}$, i.e. such that the label of H is the first label in v_L,

(4) $H_R(v_L, v)$ is defined iff $M_R(v)$ is defined,

(5) if $H_R(v_L, v) = (\bar{v}_L, \bar{v})$, then $\bar{v} = M_R(v)$.

2.1. For each $M_o \in$ FS there is $H^o \in FCP_1$ such that H^o is equivalent to M_o.

If $M_o \in S$, then as H^o we can take $o^*[H_{kt}\ H_k\ H_t]$, where H_k is $o[[J_k(a_1)][a_1/a_2]\ M]$. Suppose that

$$H = o^*[H_{k_1 t_1} H_{k_1} \dots H_{k_n}\ H_{t_1}], \quad G = o^*[G_{m_1 t_2}\ G_{m_1} \dots G_{m_p}\ G_{t_2}],$$

are procedures in FCP_1 equivalent to FS-expressions K,M,respectively, and that all $k_1, \dots, k_n, t_1, m_1, \dots, m_p, t_2$, are different, which is no restriction. Suppose that $M_o = o[KM]$. For each $i=1,\dots,n$, let H'_{k_i} be the instruction obtained from H_{k_i} by the replacement of each occurrence of $[a_1/a_2]$ by $[a_1/E_{m_1}]$. Then the following H^o in FCP_1

$$H^o = o^*[H_{k_1 t_1}\ H'_{k_1} \dots H'_{k_n}\ G_{m_1} \dots G_{m_p}\ H_{t_1}]$$

is equivalent to M_o. Suppose now that $M_o = \veebar[\alpha\ KM]$. Let $k,t \in N$, $k \neq t$, and k,t be different from $k_1, \dots, k_n, t_1, m_1, \dots, m_p, t_2$. We may assume that e_k, e_t occur neither in H nor in G. Then the following H^o in FCP_1 is equivalent to M_o

$$H^o = o^*[H_{kt}\ H_k\ H_{k_1} \dots H_{k_n}\ G_{m_1} \dots G_{m_p}\ H_t], \text{ where}$$
$$H_k = o[[J_k(a_1)] \veebar [\alpha\ [a_1/E_{k_1}][\ ][a_1/E_{m_1}][\ ]]].$$

Suppose that $M_o = *[\alpha K]$. For each $i=1,\dots,n$, let H'_i be the instruction obtained of H_i by the replacement of each occurrence of $[a_1/a_2]$ by $[a_1/E_k]$. Moreover, let $k,t \in N$, $k \neq t$, k,t different from $k_1, \dots, k_n$, t_1 and let e_k, e_t do not occur in H. Then the following H^o in FCP_1 is equivalent to M_o

$$H^o = o^*[H_{kt}\ H_k\ H'_{k_1} \dots H'_{k_n}\ H_t], \text{ where}$$
$$H_k = o[[J_k(a_1)] \veebar [\alpha\ [a_1/a_2][\ ][a_1/E_{k_1}][\ ]]].$$

The following theorem is an analogue of **MAZURKIEWICZ**'s [1] theorem on the label elimination in FC-algorithms and of SALWICKI's theorem on the equivalence of FS-expressions and programs /see[20]/.

2.2. For each $H \in FCP_1$ there is a FS-expression K such that H is equivalent to K.

3. TREE FORM AND NORMAL FORM OF F_LS-EXPRESSIONS

F_LS-expressions H_1 and H_2 are said to be equivalent if for each realization R in any set $U\neq 0$ and for each state $(v_L,v)\in W_L\times W_U$

(1) $H_{1R}(v_L,v)$ is defined iff $H_{2R}(v_L,v)$ is defined, and
if $H_{1R}(v_L,v)$ is defined, then $H_{1R}(v_L,v)=H_{2R}(v_L,v)$.

If H_1,H_2 are equivalent we shall write $H_1 \approx H_2$.

3.1. The relation $\approx$ is an equivalence relation on F_LS. Moreover,

(i) if $H_1\approx H_2$, then $o[HH_1]\approx o[HH_2]$ and $o[H_1H]\approx o[H_2H]$,

(ii) if $H_1\approx H_2$ and $H_3\approx H_4$, then $\veebar[\alpha H_1H_3]\approx \veebar[\alpha\ H_2H_4]$.

3.2. For any $H_1,H_2,H_3\in F_LS$ and $\alpha\in F_o$:

(2) $o[o[H_1H_2]\ H_3]\approx o[H_1o[H_2H_3]]$,

(3) $o[\veebar[\alpha\ H_1H_2]H_3]\approx\veebar[\alpha\ o[H_1H_3]o[H_2H_3]]$.

Theorem 3.2 (2) enables us to write $o[H_1H_2H_3]$ instead of

$$o[o[H_1H_2]H_3] \quad \text{and} \quad o[H_1o[H_2H_3]].$$

More generally, we shall use the notation $o[H_1\ldots H_n]$ for all possible compositions formed of $H_1,\ldots,H_n$, $n>2$. This explains the simplified notation (8),(9) in Sec.1.

A F_LS-expression H is said to be in a semi-tree form if one of the following conditions is satisified:

(st1) H is indecomposable,

(st2) $H=o[H_1\ldots H_n]$, $n>1$, where $H_1,\ldots,H_n$ are indecomposable,

(st2) $H=o[H_1\ldots H_n\veebar[\alpha H_{n+1}H_{n+2}]]$, $n\in N_o$, where $H_1,\ldots,H_n$ are indecomposable.

A F_LS-expression H is said to be in a tree form provided that each F_LS-expression which occurs in H is in a semi-tree form. Let TF_LS be the set of all F_LS-expressions in a tree form. Then the following statement holds.

3.3. TF_LS is the least set containing indecomposable F_LS-expressions and such that

(tfs1) if $H_1,H_2\in TF_LS$ and $\alpha\in F_o$, then $\veebar[\alpha H_1H_2]\in TF_LS$,

(tfs2) if H_1 is indecomposable and $H_2\in TF_LS$, then $o[H_1H_2]\in TF_LS$.

Notice also the following simple statement.

3.4. There is a mapping $t: F_L S \to F_L S$, effectively defined which assigns to each $H \in F_L S$ a $F_L S$-expression $t(H)$ in a semi-tree form, such that $H \approx t(H)$. In particular, $t(H) = H$ for $H \in TF_L S$.

Let us set

(t1) $t(H) = H$ for indecomposable $H \in F_L S$,

(t2) $t(\veebar[\alpha H_1 H_2]) = \veebar[\alpha H_1 H_2]$,

(t3) $t(o[H_1 H_2]) = o[H_1\ t(H_2)]$ for indecomposable $H_1 \in F_L S$,

(t4) $t(o[\veebar[\alpha H_1 H_2] H_3]) = \veebar[\alpha\, o[H_1 H_3]\, o[H_2 H_3]]$.

The proof that t satisfies the required conditions refers to 3.1 and 3.2.

3.5. For each $F_L S$-expressions H there is a $F_L S$-expression H^*, effectively defined, such that $H^* \in TF_L S$ and $H \approx H^*$.

Let $t^*: F_L S \to F_L S$ be a mapping defined thus

(t^*1) $t^*(H) = t(H) = H$ for indecomposable $H \in F_L S$,

(t^*2) $t^*(\veebar[\alpha H_1 H_2]) = \veebar[\alpha\, t(H_1)\, t(H_2)]$,

(t^*3) $t^*(o[H_1 H_2]) = o[H_1\, t(H_2)]$ for indecomposable $H_1 \in F_L S$,

(t^*4) $t^*(o[\veebar[\alpha H_1 H_2]\ H_3] = \veebar[\alpha\, t(o[H_1 H_3])\, t(o[H_2 H_3])]$.

The following properties of t^* can be proved:

(4) $t^*(H) = H$ for $H \in TF_L S$,

(5) for each $H \in F_L S$, $t^*(H) \approx H$ and $t^*(H)$ is in a semi-tree form,

(6) for each $H \in F_L S$ there is $n \in N$, such that $\underbrace{t^*(\ldots(t^*}_{n \text{ times}}(H)\ldots)$ is in $TF_L S$, i.e. $t^{*n}(H) \in TF_L S$.

It follows from (4) -(6), that $H^* = t^{*m}(H)$, where m is the least n in N such that $t^{*n}(H) \in TF_L S$ satisfies the conditions required in 3.5.

3.6. Let $s_1^*, \ldots, s_n^* \in S_L^o$, $n \in N$, and let $H = o[s_1^* \ldots s_n^*]$. Then for each realization R in any set $U \neq 0$ and each state $(v_L, v) \in W_L \times W_U$, $H_R(v_L, v) = (\bar{v}_L, v)$, where $\bar{v}_L$ is effectively defined and has one of the following forms

(i) $(e_o, e_o, \ldots)$,

(ii) $(e_{k_1}, \ldots, e_{k_i}, e_o, \ldots)$, $i \in N$, independently of v_L,

(iii) $(v_L(a_m), v_L(a_{m+1}), \ldots)$, $m \in N$,

(iv) $(e_{k_1}, \ldots, e_{k_i}, v_L(a_m), v_L(a_{m+1}), \ldots)$, $i \in N$, $m \in N$.

The easy proof refers to $(s_L r1)-(s_L r6)$ and $(f_L sr2)$, $(f_L sr3)$ in Sec.1.

3.7. There is a mapping f, effectively defined, assigning to each F_LS-expression H in one of the following forms: $o[s_1^* \dots s_n^*]$, $n\in N$, $o[s_1^* \dots s_n^* [J_k(a_m)]]$, $n\in N_o$, $k\in N_o$, $m\in N$, a F_LS-expression $f(H)\in TF_LS$ such that for each realization R in a set $U\neq 0$ and each $(v_L,v)\in W_L\times W_U$ the following conditions are satisfied

(7) $H_R(v_L,v)$ is defined iff $f(H)_R(v_L,v)$ is defined,

(8) if $H_R(v_L,v)$ is defined, then $f(H)_R(v_L,v)=(v_L,v)$.

Observe, that for each (v_L,v),

(9) $H_o=o[[a_1/E_1][J_o(a_1)]]$ is undefined.

We set $f(o[s_1^* \dots s_n^*])=[\ ]$ and $f([J_k(a_m)])=[J_k(a_m)]$. Suppose that

(10) $H=o[s_1^* \dots s_n^* [J_k(a_m)]]$, $n\in N$, $k\in N_o$, $m\in N$.

It follows from 3.6 that for each $(v_L,v)\in W_L\times W_U$, $o[s_1^* \dots s_n^*]_R(v_L,v)=(\bar{v}_L,v)$ where $\bar{v}_L$ is in one of forms (i) - (iv). If $\bar{v}_L$ is $(e_o,e_o,\dots)$, independently of v_L, then we set $f(H)=[\ ]$ for k=0 and $f(H)=H_o$ for k>0. If $\bar{v}_L=(e_{k_1} \dots e_{k_1},e_o,\dots)$, independently of v_L, then we set $f(H)=[\ ]$ for k=0, m>i and for k>0, $m\leq i$, $k_m=k$, and $f(H)=H_o$ in the remaining cases. If $\bar{v}_L=(v_L(a_i),v_L(a_{i+1}),\dots)$, then we set $f(H)=[J_k(a_{i+m-1})]$. If $\bar{v}_L=(e_{k_1},\dots,e_{k_i},v_L(a_j),v_L(a_{j+1}),\dots)$, then consider two cases:

$$i < m \quad \text{and} \quad i \geqslant m .$$

If $i<m$, $m=i+p$, then we set $f(H)=[J_k(a_{j+p-1})]$. If $i\geqslant m$, then we set $f(H)=[\ ]$ for $k=k_m$ and $f(H)=H_o$ for $k\neq k_m$.

Now we shall define for the F_LS-expressions in TF_LS their diagrams, being mappings assigning to some finite sequences of elements in $\{0,1\}\cup F_o$, certain expressions in TF_LS which occur in them. Such sequences will be denoted by ι, ξ. If ι is a sequence under consideration, then $(\iota,0)$, $(\iota,1)$, (ι,α) will denote sequences obtained of ι by adjoing 0, 1, α, respectively, as the next element. We set $\iota\leq\xi$ if ι is an initial part of ξ. For any $H\in TF_LS$ the diagram of H will be denoted by Γ_H. A sequence ι in the domain of Γ_H / in symbols $\iota\in \text{Dom}\,\Gamma_H$ / will be called an end sequence if for each ξ, such that $\iota\leq\xi$, $\iota\neq\xi$, ξ doe not belong to Dom Γ_H.

The definition of Γ_H is as follows.

(γ1) If H is indecomposable, then $\Gamma_H(0)=H$ and (0) is the end sequence,

(γ2) if $H=o[H_1\dots H_n]$, where $H_1,\dots,H_n$ are indecomposable, then

$\Gamma_H(0)=H_1$, ... $,\Gamma_H(0,\dots,0_n)=H_n$, $(0,\dots,0_n)$ is the end sequence, where $(0,\dots,0_n)$ is written instead of $\underbrace{(0,\dots,0)}_{n\ \text{times}}$.

(γ3) if $H=o[H_1 \dots H_n \curlyvee[\alpha H_{n+1}H_{n+2}]]$, $n\in N_o$, $H_1,\dots,H_n$ are indecomposable, then $\Gamma_H(0)=H_1,\dots, \Gamma_H(0,\dots,0_n)=H_n$, $\Gamma_H(0,\dots,0_n,\alpha]=\curlyvee[\alpha H_{n+1}H_{n+2}]$, Suppose that $\Gamma_H(\iota,\beta)=\curlyvee[\beta H' H'']$ is defined and $\curlyvee[\beta H' H'']$ occurs in H. Then

(γ4) if H' is indecomposable, then $\Gamma_H(\iota,\beta,0)=H'$ and $(\iota,\beta,0)$ is an end sequence; if H'' is indecomposable, then $\Gamma_H(\iota,\beta,1)=H''$ and $(\iota,\beta,1)$ is and end sequence ; if $H'=o[H_1' \dots H_m']$, $H_1',\dots,H_m'$ are indecomposable, then $\Gamma_H(\iota,\beta,0)=H_1',\dots, \Gamma_H(\iota,\beta,0,\dots,0_m)=H_m'$ and $(\iota,\beta,0,\dots,0_m)$ is an end sequence; if $H''=o[H_1'' \dots H_k'']$, $H_1'',\dots,H_k''$ are indecomposable, then $\Gamma_H(\iota,\beta,1)=H_1'',\dots,\Gamma_H(\iota,\beta,1,\dots,1_k)=H_k''$ and $(\iota,\beta,1,\dots,1_k)$ is an end sequence; if $H'=o[H_1' \dots H_m' \curlyvee[\gamma H_{m+1}'H_{m+2}']]$, $m\in N_o$, then $\Gamma_H(\iota,\beta,0)=H_1'$, $\dots,\Gamma_H(\iota,\beta,0,\dots,0_m)=H_m$, $\Gamma_H(\iota,\beta,0,\dots,0_m,\gamma)=o[\gamma H_{m+1}'H_{m+2}']$; if $H''=o[H_1'' \dots H_k'' \curlyvee[\delta H_{k+1}''H_{k+2}'']]$, $k\in N_o$, then $\Gamma_H(\iota,\beta,1)=H_1'',\dots,\Gamma_H(\iota,$ $\beta,1,\dots,1_k)=H_k''$, $\Gamma_H(\iota,\beta,1,\dots,1_k,\delta)=\curlyvee[\delta H_{k+1}'',H_{k+2}'']$.

The domain of Γ_H consists of these sequences ξ, for which there is an end sequence ι, such that $\xi\leq\iota$. Observe, that for each occurrence of an indecomposable F_LS-exprssion G in H there is exactly one sequence $\iota\in \mathrm{Dom}\,\Gamma_H$ such that $\Gamma_H(\iota)=G$.

Let $\varkappa$, μ, ν be mappings from the set of all indecomposable F_LS-expressions into TF_LS which are defined as follows:

(11) $\varkappa(s)=[\ ]$, $\mu(s)=[\ ]$, $\nu(s)=s$ for each $s\in S$,

(12) $\varkappa(s^*)=[\ ]$, $\mu(s^*)=s^*$, $\nu(s^*)=[\ ]$, for each $s^*\in S_L^o$,

(13) $\varkappa([J_k(a_m)])=[J_k(a_m)]$, $\mu([J_k(a_m)]=[\ ]$, $\nu([J_k(a_m)])=[\ ]$, $k\in N_o$, $m\in N$,

(14) if $H=o^*[H_{k_1}t\ H_{k_1}\dots H_{k_n}\ H_t]$, then we set

$\varkappa(H)=[J_{k_1}(a_1)]$, $\mu(H)=[a_1/a_2]$, $\nu(H)=o[[a_1/E_{k_1}\ a_2/a_1]\,H]$.

3.8. For any indecomposable $H\in F_LS$ the following conditions are satisfied:

(15) if $H_R(v_L,v)$ is defined, then $\varkappa(H)_R(v_L,v)$ is defined and $\varkappa(H)_R(v_L,v)=(v_L,v)$,

(16) if $H_R(v_L,v)$ is defined, then $\nu(H)_R(v_L,v)$ is definded and

if $H_R(v_L,v)=(\bar{v}_L,\bar{v})$, then $\nu(H)_R(v_L,v)=(v_L,\bar{v})$,

(17) if $H_R(v_L,v)$ is defined and $H_R(v_L,v)=(\bar{v}_L,\bar{v})$, then $\mu(H)_R(v_L,v)=(\bar{v}_L,v)$,

(18) $H_R(v_L,v)$ is defined iff $\mathcal{H}(H)_R(v_L,v)$ and $\nu(H)_R(v_L,v)$ are defined

(19) $H_R(v_L,v)$ is defined iff $o[\mathcal{H}(H)\nu(H)]$ is defined, and if $H_R(v_L,v)=(\bar{v}_L,\bar{v})$, then $o[\mathcal{H}(H)\nu(H)]_R(v_L,v)=(v_L,\bar{v})$.

The notion of a diagram of $H\in TS_LF$ and theorems 3.7 and 3.8 will be applied in a construction of a normal form of any $H\in TS_LF$ and play the basic role in the proof of the main theorem of this section, which concerns normal forms and will be formulated later.

Let $H\in TS_LF$ and let Γ_H be the diagram of H. For any $\iota\in \mathrm{Dom}\,\Gamma_H$, such that $\Gamma_H(\iota)=G$ is an indecomposable F_LS-expression, by a trace of ι we shall mean the sequence $\iota_1,\dots,\iota_m$, where $\iota_i\in \mathrm{Dom}\,\Gamma_H$, $\iota_1\le\dots\le\iota_m\le\iota$, and which is composed of all $(\xi,0)$ and $(\xi,1)$ different from ι and such that $(\xi,0)\le\iota$, $(\xi,1)\le\iota$. For instance, if $\iota=(0,0,\alpha,1,1,\beta,0,0)$, then $(0),(0,0),(0,0,\alpha,1),(0,0,\alpha,1,1),(0,0,\alpha,1,1,\beta,0)$, is the trace of ι.

For each indecomposable F_LS-expression which occurs in $H\in TS_LF$ we shall consider all its occurrences. With any occurrence of an indecomposable G in H there is uniquely associated a sequence ι in $\mathrm{Dom}\,\Gamma_H$ such that $\Gamma_H(\iota)=G$. Let $\iota_1,\dots,\iota_m$ be the trace of ι. Then we set

(20) $\mu_H(\Gamma_H(\iota))=o[\mu(\Gamma_H(\iota_1))\dots\mu(\Gamma_H(\iota_m))]$.

If $\Gamma_H(\iota)=G$, G is indecomposable, and the trace of ι is empty, then

(21) $\mu_H(\Gamma_H(\iota))=[\ ]$.

Let $H\in TS_LF$ and let Γ_H be the diagram of H. By the normal form of H we shall understand a F_LS-expression nor(H) which is constructed of H by the replacement of each indecomposable $\Gamma_H(\iota)$, $\iota\in \mathrm{Dom}\,\Gamma_H$ by $o[\,f(o[\mu_H(\Gamma_H(\iota))\mathcal{H}(\Gamma_H(\iota))])\,\nu(\Gamma_H(\iota))]$.

Example 5.

$H=o[\underline{\vee}[\alpha\ o[[J_k(a_1)]\ s^*s]\,o[[J_m(a_1)]\underline{\vee}[\beta\ s_1^*s_1s_2^*s_2]]]\ o[[J_n(a_1)]\underline{\vee}[\gamma\ s_3^*s_3s_4^*s_4]]]$.

Tree form of H is H^*, where

$H^*=\underline{\vee}[\alpha\ o[[J_k(a_1)]s^*s\,[J_n(a_1)]\underline{\vee}[\gamma\,s_3^*s_3s_4^*s_4]]\ o[[J_m(a_1)]\underline{\vee}[\beta\ o[s_1^*s_1[J_n(a_1)]$
$\quad\underline{\vee}[\gamma\ s_3^*s_3s_4^*s_4]]\ o[\ s_2^*s_2[\ J_n(a_1)]\ \underline{\vee}[\gamma\ s_3^*s_3s_4^*s_4]]]]]$.

Normal form of H^* is nor(H^*) in the following form:

$\mathrm{nor}(H^*)=\underline{\vee}[\alpha\ o[[\ J_k(a_1)]\ s\ f(s^*[J_n(a_1)])\ \underline{\vee}[\gamma\,[\,]s_3[\ ]\ s_4]]\ G]$, where

$G = o[[J_m(a_1)] \veebar [\beta o[s_1 \ f(s_1^*[J_n(a_1)]) \veebar [\gamma[\ ]s_3[\ ]s_4]] \ o[s_2 \ f(s_2^*[J_n(a_1)]) \veebar [\gamma[\ ]s_3[\ ]s_4]]]]$.

The main theorem in this section explains the role of the normal form of any $H \in TF_LS$.

3.9. For any $H \in TF_LS$, every realization R in any set $U \neq 0$ and every state $(v_L, v) \in W_L \times W_U$ the following conditions are satisfied:

(i) $H_R(v_L, v)$ is defined iff $nor(H)_R(v_L, v)$ is defined,

(ii) if $H_R(v_L, v)$ is defined and $H_R(v_L, v) = (\bar{v}_L, \bar{v})$, then $nor(H)_R(v_L, v) = (v_L, \bar{v})$.

The proof of 3.9 will be omitted. The following corollary results from 3.5 and 3.9.

3.10. For any $H \in F_LS$, every realization R in any set $U \neq 0$ and every state $(v_L, v) \in W_L \times W_U$ the following conditions hold:

(i) $H_R(v_L, v)$ is defined iff $nor(H^*)_R(v_L, v)$ is defined,

(ii) if $H_R(v_L, v)$ is defined and $H_R(v_L, v) = (\bar{v}_L, \bar{v})$, then $nor(H^*)_R(v_L, v) = (v_L, \bar{v})$.

4. GENERALIZED TERMS

In this section we introduce new expressions under A_{oL} /see Sec.1/ to be called generalized terms.

The set F_LST of generalized terms is the least set of finite sequences of elements in A_{oL} which satisfies the following conditions

(gt1) if $\tau \in T$, then $\tau \in F_LST$,

(gt2) if $H \in F_LS$ and $\tau \in F_LST$, then $H\tau \in F_LST$,

(gt3) if φ is a n-argument functor in Φ and $\tau_1, \ldots, \tau_n \in F_LST$, then $\varphi(\tau_1 \ldots \tau_n) \in F_LST$.

Any realization R of $\mathcal{L}_o$ in a set $U \neq 0$ is now extended on F_LST thus. For each $\tau \in F_LST$, τ_R is a partial function from $W_L \times W_U$ into U, which is defined as follows

(gtr1) $\tau_R(v_L, v) = \tau_R(v)$ for every $\tau \in T$,

(gtr2) $H\tau_R(v_L, v) = \tau_R(H_R(v_L, v))$ if the right side is defined, and is undefined otherwise, (gtr3) $\varphi(\tau_1\ldots\tau_n)_R(v_L,v)=\varphi_R(\tau_{1R}(v_L,v),\ldots,\tau_{nR}(v_L,v))$, if $\tau_{iR}(v_L,v)$ are defined for each $i=1,\ldots,n$, and is undefined otherwise.

Example 6.

Let H be the procedure as formulated in Example 2, Sec.1, and let $\tau=Hy$ .Then

$$\tau_R(v_L,v)=Hy_R(v_L,v)=y_R(H_R(v_L,v)) .$$

In particular, if R is a standard realization in N_o, $v_L=(e_1,e_o,\ldots)$, $v(x)=4$, then $Hy_R(v_L,v)=24$.

It is easy to show on applying (gtr2) and ($f_L$sr2) in Sec.1,that the following statement holds for each realization R in any set $U\neq 0$.

4.1. For any $\tau\in F_LST$ and any $H_1,H_2\in F_LS$,

$$H_1(H_2\tau)_R(v_L,v)=o[H_1H_2]\tau_R(v_L,v) \quad \text{for each } (v_L,v) \text{ in } W_U^*.$$

It follows from 1.5 that

4.2. If $H\in\bigcup_{m=1}^{\infty}P_m$ and e_k is the label of H, then for each τ in F_LST and any v_L,w_L such that $v_L(a_1)=w_L(a_1)=e_k$

$$H\tau_R(v_L,v)=H\tau_R(v_L,v).$$

This means that either both sides are defined or both sides are undefined and if they are defined, then they are equal.

On applying generalized terms we can define a notion of the programmability of partial functions by means of recursive procedures. Let R be a realization of $\mathcal{L}_o$ in a set $U\neq 0$ and let f be a n-argument partial function from U into U. We say that f is programmable by means of a recursive procedure if there exists $H\in P_m$, $m\in N$, with a label e_k such that $x_1,\ldots,x_n$ are all its free variables /i.e. such that H_R depends on $v(x_i)$ for $i=1,\ldots,n$ / and x_{n+1} occurring in H is not free, moreover the following condition is satisfied: for each $(v_L,v)\in W_L\times W_U$, if $v_L(a_1)=e_k$, then

(1) $f(v(x_1),\ldots,v(x_n))$ is defined iff $Hx_{n+1\,R}(v_L,v)$ is defined

(2) if $Hx_{n+1\,R}(v_L,v)$ is defined, then $f(v(x_1),\ldots,v(x_n))=Hx_{n+1\,R}(v_L,v)$.

In particular, we can speak on P_1-programmable partial functions, FCP_1-programmable partial functions, P_1-FCP_1-programmable partial functions etc.

On applying 3.10 and the method similar to that used in the proof of the theorem 1.1 in [14] we can prove the following theorem, which concerns generalized terms.

4.3. Let $\varphi(H_1\tau_1 \ldots H_n\tau_n) \in F_LST$, where $H_1,\ldots,H_n \in F_LS$ and $\tau_1,\ldots,\tau_n \in T$. Then there are $H \in F_LS$ and $\tau'_1,\ldots,\tau'_n \in T$, effectively defined, such that for every realization R in any set $U \neq 0$ and for any (v_L, v) in $W_L \times W_U$,

$$\varphi(H_1\tau_1 \ldots H_n\tau_n)_R(v_L,v) = H\varphi(\tau'_1 \ldots \tau'_n)_R(v_L,v).$$

This equation means, that either both sides are defined or both are undefined, and if they are defined, then they are equal.

5. EXTENDED ALGORITHMIC LOGIC

Let $A = A_{oL} \cup \{\bigvee, \bigwedge\} \cup \{D_k\}_{k\in N}$, where $\bigvee$ and $\bigwedge$ are connectives of infinite disjunction and of infinite conjunction, respectively, and D_k, $k \in N$, are unary connectives.

We shall define a set F of generalized formulas under A. The set F is the least set satisfying the following conditions:

(f1) if $q \in \Pi$ is a n-argument predicate and $\tau_1,\ldots,\tau_n \in F_LST$, then $q(\tau_1 \ldots \tau_n) \in F$,

(f2) if $p \in V_o$, then $p \in F$,

(f3) $E_i \in F$ for each i, $0 \leq i \leq \omega$, and $a_i \in F$ for $i \in N$,

(f4) if $\alpha, \beta \in F$, then $(\alpha \vee \beta), (\alpha \wedge \beta), (\alpha \to \beta), \sim\alpha$, $D_i\alpha$ for $i \in N$, are in F,

(f5) if $\alpha \in F$ and $H \in F_LS$, then $H\alpha \in F$,

(f6) if $\alpha_1, \alpha_2, \ldots$ is a sequence of formulas in F and the set of all individual and propositional variables which occur in these formulas is finite, then $\bigvee(\alpha_1\alpha_2\ldots)$ and $\bigwedge(\alpha_1\alpha_2\ldots)$ are in F.

The condition in (f6) concerning propositional variables refers to propositional variables in V_o. Generalized formulas satisfying (f1), (f2), (f3) are said to be atomic. The set of atomic generalized formulas will be denoted by F_{at}. The system

$$\mathcal{L} = (A, T, F_o, F_LS, F_LST, F)$$

will be called a formalized language of extended algorithmic logic, or briefly, a formalized language of EAL. We adopt the following definitions

(f7) $J_o(\alpha) = \sim D_1\alpha$ and $J_k(\alpha) = \sim D_{k+1}\alpha \wedge D_k\alpha$.

Thus $J_k, k\in N_o$, can be eliminated in $[J_k(a_n)]$ by means of equations (f7).

In order to extend any realization R of $\mathcal{L}_o$ in $U\neq 0$ on $\mathcal{L}$ we adopt as a semantic basis a Post algebra of order ω^+ to be denoted by $\mathcal{P}_\omega$ and defined thus.

(1) $\mathcal{P}_\omega=(P_\omega, \cup, \cap, \Rightarrow, \rceil, (d_k)_{k\in N}, (e_i)_{0\leq i\leq\omega})$, where

(2) P_ω is defined in Sec.1 and coincides with the set of elements of $\mathcal{P}^o_\omega$,

(3) $e_i\cup e_k=e_{max(i,k)}$, $e_i\cap e_k=e_{min(i,k)}$, $e_i\Rightarrow e_k=\begin{cases} e_\omega & \text{if } i\leq k \\ e_o & \text{if } i>k\end{cases}$

(4) $\rceil e_i=e_i\Rightarrow e_o=\begin{cases} e_\omega & \text{if } i=0 \\ e_o & \text{if } i\neq 0\end{cases}$ $\quad d_k(e_i)=\begin{cases} e_\omega & \text{if } k\leq i \\ e_o & \text{if } k>i\end{cases}$

In (3) we assume that $0\leq i\leq\omega$, $0\leq k\leq\omega$, and in (4) that $0\leq i\leq\omega$, $k\in N$. Observe that the operations $\cup$, $\cap$, $\Rightarrow$, $\rceil$ restricted to $\{e_o, e_\omega\}$ coincide with the Boolean operations in the two-element Boolean algebra $B_o=(\{e_o, e_\omega\}, \cup, \cap, \Rightarrow, \rceil)$ and that $d_k(e_o)=e_o$, $d_k(e_\omega)=e_\omega$ for each $k\in N$.

Let us set

(5) $j_o(e_i)=\rceil d_1(e_i)$, $j_k(e_i)=\rceil d_{k+1}(e_i)\cap d_k(e_i)$, $k\in N$, $0\leq i\leq\omega$.

It is easy to verify, that the operations j_k, $k\in N_o$, satisfy the equations (1) in Sec.1, i.e. that they coincide, respectively, with the operations j_k, $k\in N_o$, in $\mathcal{P}^o_\omega$.

Notice, that $(P_\omega, \cup, \cap)$ is a distributive lattice with a least element e_o and a greatest element e_ω, and that this lattice is complete. This means that for each set $(e_i)_{i\in I}$ of its elements there exists the least upper bound, to be denoted by $\bigcup_{i\in I} e_i$, and the greatest lower bound, to be denoted by $\bigcap_{i\in I} e_i$.

Let R be a realization of $\mathcal{L}_o$ in a set $U\neq 0$. Generalized formulas in F will be realized as mappings from $W_L\times W_U$ into P_ω. The inductive definition is as follows.

(fr1) $\varrho(\tau_1\ldots\tau_n)_R(v_L,v)=\varrho_R(\tau_{1R}(v_L,v),\ldots,\tau_{nR}(v_L,v))$ if $\tau_{iR}(v_L,v)$ are defined for every $i=1,\ldots,n$, otherwise $\varrho(\tau_1\ldots\tau_n)_R(v_L,v)=e_o$,

(fr2) $p_R(v_L,v)=v(p)$ for each $p\in V_o$,

(fr3) $E_{iR}(v_L,v)=e_i$, $0\leq i\leq e_\omega$, $a_{iR}(v_L,v)=v_L(a_i)$, $i\in N$,

(fr4) $(\alpha\vee\beta)_R(v_L,v)=\alpha_R(v_L,v)\cup\beta_R(v_L,v)$, $(\alpha\wedge\beta)_R(v_L,v)=\alpha_R(v_L,v)\cap\beta_R(v_L,v)$, $(\alpha\rightarrow\beta)_R(v_L,v)=\alpha_R(v_L,v)\Rightarrow\beta_R(v_L,v)$, $\sim\alpha_R(v_L,v)=$

$= \neg\alpha_R(v_L,v)$, $D_k\alpha_R(v_L,v) = d_k\alpha_R(v_L,v)$, $k\in N$.

(fr5) $H\alpha_R(v_L,v) = \alpha_R(H_R(v_L,v))$ if $H_R(v_L,v)$ is defined , and
$H\alpha_R(v_L,v) = e_o$ if $H_R(v_L,v)$ is not defined,

(fr6) $\bigvee(\alpha_1\alpha_2\ldots)_R(v_L,v) = \bigcup_{i\in N}\alpha_{iR}(v_L,v)$,
$\bigwedge(\alpha_1\alpha_2\ldots)_R(v_L,v) = \bigcap_{i\in N}\alpha_{iR}(v_L,v)$.

In the equations occurring in (fr4) - (fr6), $\cup$, $\cap$, $\Rightarrow$, $\neg$, d_k, $\bigcup$ $\bigcap$ are operations in $\mathcal{P}_\omega$.

A generalized formula α in F is said to be valid in R provided that $\alpha_R(v_L,v)=e_\omega$ for each (v_L,v) in $W_L\times W_U$. If α is valid in each realization R , then it is said to be a tautology of EAL.

For every $\mathcal{A}\subset$ F and $\alpha\in$ F , α is a semantic consequence of $\mathcal{A}$, in symbols $\mathcal{A}\models\alpha$, if for every realization R in which all generalized formulas belonging to $\mathcal{A}$ are valid, α is valid in R ,too.

We set $C(\mathcal{A}) = \{\alpha\in F: \mathcal{A}\models\alpha\}$, for each $\mathcal{A}\subset F$. The system $\mathcal{S}=(\mathcal{L},C)$ is said to be a sytem of EAL. A formal consequence operation can also be introduced and a completeness theorem holds.

Various properties of procedures can be expressed by means of generalized formulas in F. For instance, let $H\in P_m$, $m\in N$. Consider $HE_\omega\in F$. It follows from (fr5), that

$HE_{\omega R}(v_L,v) = E_{\omega R}(H_R(v_L,v)) = e_\omega$ iff $H_R(v_L,v)$ is defined,

i.e. iff there exists a computation of H by realization R for the state(v_L,v) . Thus HE_ω describes the stop property for H. Suppose that e_k is the label of H, and let $\alpha,\beta\in F_o$. Consider

$(J_k(a_1)\wedge(\alpha\rightarrow H\beta))_R(v_L,v)$.

This is equal e_ω iff $v_L(a_1)=e_k$ and the condition $\alpha_R(v)=e_\omega$ implies that $\beta_R(H_R(v_L,v))=e_\omega$. Thus the generalized formula under consideration describes a correctness of H. Let $H\in P_m$, $G\in P_n$, where $m,n\in N$, and let e_k, be the label of both H and G. Then for some $\tau_1,\tau_2\in T$,

$J_k(a_1)\wedge(HE_\omega\rightarrow GE_\omega\wedge(H\tau_1=G\tau_2))\wedge(GE_\omega\rightarrow HE_\omega\wedge(H\tau_1=H\tau_2))_R(v_L,v)$

is equal e_ω iff $v_L(a_1)=e_k$, the computation of H by R for(v_L,v) exists iff the computation of G by R for (v_L,v) exists, and if both computations exist, then $\tau_{1R}(H_R(v_L,v)) = \tau_{2R}(G_R(v_L,v))$. Thus the generalized formula under consideration describes an **equivalence** of **procedures H** and G.

Let $\alpha\in F_o$ and $H=o^*[H_{k_1t}\,H_{k_1}\ldots H_{k_n}\,H_t]\in P_1$. For any $\beta,\gamma\in F$

we shall write $\beta \leftrightarrow \gamma$ instead of $(\alpha \rightarrow \beta) \wedge (\beta \rightarrow \gamma)$ .The following generalized formula in F

$$H\alpha \leftrightarrow \bigvee(o[H_{k_1}t\ H_{k_1}\ H_t]\alpha \quad o[H_{k_1}t\ H_{k_1} H_{k_1} H_t]\alpha \quad o[H_{k_1}t\ H_{k_1} H_{k_2}\ H_t]\alpha \ldots \ )$$

is a tautology of EAL. The exact definition of the sequence of gen- neralized formulas which occur on the right-hand side of $\leftrightarrow$ is easy to formulate.

On applying generalized formulas in F we can define a notion of relations programmable by means of recursive procedures.Let R be a realization in a set $U \neq 0$ of $\mathcal{L}_0$, and let $r \subset U^n$. We say that r is programmable in R by means of a recursive procedure if there exists $H \in P_m, m \in N$, with a label e_k, and a formula $\alpha \in F_0$,whose all individual variables are $x_1, \ldots, x_n$, such that the following holds:

$$(v(x_1), \ldots, v(x_n)) \in r \quad \text{iff} \quad H\alpha_R(v_L, v) = e_\omega$$

for each $(v_L, v) \in W_L \times W_U$ such that $v_L(a_1) = e_k$.

This definition is correct with respect to 1.5. In particular we can speak on P_1 -programmable relations, FCP_1-programmable relations, P_1-FCP_1-programmable relations, etc. We can also introduce a notion of a strong programmability of relations by means of recursive procedures. A relation is strongly programmable by means of a recursive procedure if it is programmable by $H\alpha$ and its complement is programmable by $H \sim \alpha$.

Investigations concerning partial functions and relations programmable by means of recursive procedures are carried out by research workers in University of Warsaw.

REFERENCES

[1] BLIKLE,A.; MAZURKIEWICZ,A. An algebraic approach to the theory of programs,algorithms,languages and recursiveness.Proc.Intern. Symp.and Summer School on Math.Found.of Comp.Sci.,Warsaw,Jabłonna, August 21-27,1972, CCPAS Reports,1972

[2] CADIOU,J.M. Recursive definitions of partial functions and their computations. Ph.D.Thesis,Computer Science Dept.,Stanford Univ.

[3] ENGELER,E. Algorithmic properties of structures,Math.Syst. Theory 1 /1967/, 183-195

[4] KARP,C.R. Languages with expressions of infinite length. North-Holland Publishing Co.,Amsterdam 1964

[5] KRECZMAR,A. Effectivity problems in algorithmic logic.

Ph.D.Thesis,Faculty of Mathematics and Mechanics,University of Warsaw, 1973

[6] MANNA,Z.; VUILLEMIN.J.Fixpoint approach to the theory of computation.Stanford Artificial Intelligence Project,Computer Science Department,School of Humanities and Sciences,Stanford University, Unpublished memo,1972

[7] MIRKOWSKA,G. On formalized systems of algorithmic logic, Bull.Ac.Pol.Sci.,Ser.Sci.Math.Astron.Phys.,19 /1971/,421-428

[8] MIRKOWSKA-SALWICKA,G.Algorithmic logic and its applications in the programming theory. Ph.D.Thesis,Faculty of Mathematics and Mechanics,University of Warsaw,1972

[9] PERKOWSKA,E. On algorithmic m-valued logics.Bull.Ac.Pol. Sci.,Ser.Sci.Math.Astron.Phys.,20 /1972/,717-719

[10] RASIOWA,H. On logical structure of programs,ibid.20 /1972/, 319-324

[11] RASIOWA,H. On a logical structure of programs,Proc.Intern. Symp.and Summer School on Math.Found.of Comp.Sci.,Warsaw,Jabłonna, August 21-27,1972,CCPAS Reports,1972

[12] RASIOWA,H. On generalized Post algebras of order ω^+ and ω^+-valued predicate calculi.Bull.Ac.Pol.Sci.,Ser.Sci.Math.Astron.Phys., 21 /1973/,209-219

[13] RASIOWA,H. On logical structure of mix-valued programs and ω^+-valued algorithmic logic.ibid. 21 /1973/,451-458

[14] RASIOWA,H. Formalized ω^+-valued algorithmic systems.ibid. 21 /1973/,559-565

[15] RASIOWA,H. On ω^+-valued algorithmic logic and related problems. CCPAS Reports,1974

[16] RASIOWA,H. A simplified formalization of ω^+-valued algorithmic logic.Bull.Ac.Pol.Sci.,Ser.Sci.Math.Astron.Phys.,22 /1974/,595-603

[17] RASIOWA,H. Extended ω^+ -valued algorithmic logic.ibid. 22 /1974/,605-610

[18] Scott,D. An outline of a Mathematical Theory of Computation. Oxford University computing Laboratory,Programming Research Group, Technical Monograph PRG 2 /November 1970/

[19] SALWICKI,A. Formalized algorithmic languages. Bull.Ac.Pol. Sci.,Ser.Sci.Math.Astron.Phys.,18 /1970/,227-232

[20] SALWICKI,A. On the equivalence of FS-expressions and programs. ibid.18 /1970/,275-278

[21] SALWICKI,A. On the predicate calculi with the iteration quantifiers.ibid. 18 /1970/,279-285

[22] SALWICKI,A. Programmability and Recursiveness /an application of algorithmic logic to procedures/. To appear in Dissertationes Mathematicae

CALL-BY-VALUE VERSUS CALL-BY-NAME: A PROOF-THEORETIC COMPARISON *)

W.P. DE ROEVER

ABSTRACT. Minimal fixed point operators were introduced by Scott and De Bakker in order to describe the input-output behaviour of recursive procedures. As they considered recursive procedures acting upon a monolithic state only, i.e., procedures acting upon one variable, the problem remained open how to describe this input-output behaviour in the presence of an arbitrary number of components which as a parameter may be either called-by-value or called-by-name. More precisely, do we need different formalisms in order to describe the input-output behaviour of these procedures for different parameter mechanisms, or do we need different minimal fixed point operators within the same formalism, or do different parameter mechanisms give rise to different transformations, each subject to the same minimal fixed point operator? Using basepoint preserving relations over cartesian products of sets with unique basepoints, we provide a single formalism in which the different combinations of call-by-value and call-by-name are represented by different products of relations, and in which only one minimal fixed point operator is needed. Moreover this mathematical description is axiomatized, thus yielding a relational calculus for recursive procedures with a variety of possible parameter mechanisms.

0. STRUCTURE OF THE PAPER

The reader is referred to section 1.2 for a leisurely written motivation of the contents of this paper.

Chapter 1. Section 1.1 deals with the relational description of various programming concepts, and introduces as a separate concept the parameter list each parameter of which may be either called-by-value or called-by-name. In section 1.2 Manna and Vuillemin's indictment of call-by-value as rule of computation is analyzed and refuted by demonstrating that call-by-value is as amenable to proving properties of programs as call-by-name.

Chapter 2. Using basepoint preserving relations over cartesian products of sets with unique basepoints, we demonstrate in section 2.1 how a variety of possible parameter mechanisms can be described by using different products of relations. In section 2.2 these relations are axiomatized.

---

*) This publication is registered as report IW 23/74 of the Mathematisch Centrum.

1. PARAMETER MECHANISMS, PROJECTION FUNCTIONS, AND PRODUCTS OF RELATIONS

1.1. *The relational description of programs and their properties*

The present paper presents an axiomatization of the input-output behaviour of recursive procedures, which manipulate as values neither labels nor procedures, and the parameters of which may be either called-by-value or called-by-name. It will be argued that, in case all parameters are called-by-name, we may confine ourselves, without restricting the generality of our results, to procedures with procedure bodies in which at least one parameter is invoked, describing calls of the remaining ones by suitably chosen constant terms.

The main vehicle for this axiomatization is a language for binary relations, which is rich enough to express the input-output behaviour of programming concepts such as the composition of statements, the conditional, the assignment, systems of procedures which are subject to the restriction stated above and which call each other recursively, and lists of parameters each of which may be either called-by-value or called-by-name.

EXAMPLE 1.1. Let D be a domain of initial states, intermediate values and final states. The *undefined* statement L: goto L is expressed by the *empty* relation Ω over D. The *dummy* statement is expressed by the *identity* relation E over D.

Define the *composition* $R_1;R_2$ of relations R_1 and R_2 by $R_1;R_2 = \{\langle x,y\rangle \mid \exists z[\langle x,z\rangle \in R_1 \text{ and } \langle z,y\rangle \in R_2]\}$. Obviously this operation expresses the composition of statements.

In order to describe the *conditional* if p then S_1 else S_2, one first has to transliterate p: Let D_1 be p^{-1}(true) and D_2 be p^{-1}(false), then the predicate p is uniquely determined by the pair $\langle p,p'\rangle$ of disjoint subsets of the identity relation defined by: $\langle x,x\rangle \in p$ iff $x \in D_1$, snd $\langle x,x\rangle \in p'$ iff $x \in D_2$, cf. Karp [6]. If R_i is the input-output behaviour of S_i, i=1,2, the relation described by the conditional above is $p;R_1 \cup p';R_2$.

Let $\pi_i: D^n \to D$ be the projection function of D^n on its i-th component, i=1,...,n, let the *converse* $\breve{R}$ of a relation R be defined by $\breve{R} = \{\langle x,y\rangle \mid \langle y,x\rangle \in R\}$, and let $R_1,\ldots,R_n$ be arbitrary relations over D. Consider $R_1;\breve{\pi}_1 \cap \ldots \cap R_n;\breve{\pi}_n$. This relation consists exactly of those pairs $\langle x,\langle y_1,\ldots,y_n\rangle\rangle$ such that $\langle x,y_i\rangle \in R_i$ for i=1,...,n. *Thus this expression terminates in* x *iff all its components* R_i *terminate in* x. Observe the analogy with the following: The evaluation of a list of parameters called-by-value terminates iff the evaluation of all its parameters terminates.

In case of a state vector of n components, an *assignment* to the i-th component of the state, $x_i := f(x_1,\ldots,x_n)$, is expressed by $\pi_1;\breve{\pi}_1 \cap \ldots \cap \pi_{i-1};\breve{\pi}_{i-1} \cap R;\breve{\pi}_i \cap \pi_{i+1};\breve{\pi}_{i+1} \cap \ldots \cap \pi_n;\breve{\pi}_n$, where the input-output behaviour of f is expressed by R. This description satisfies Hoare's axiom for the assignment (cf. section 2.2.3 of De Roever [3]). □

Note that the input-output behaviour of systems of recursive procedures has not been expressed above; this will be taken care of by extending our language for binary relations with minimal fixed point operators, introduced by Scott and De Bakker [9].

Our use of the parameter list as a separate programming concept merits some comment. In ALGOL 60 the evaluation of the parameter list $(f_1(\xi),\ldots,f_n(\xi))$ is part of the execution of the procedure call $f(f_1(\xi),\ldots,f_n(\xi))$, with ξ denoting the state vector. In case all parameters are called-by-value one might introduce $[f_1(\xi),\ldots,f_n(\xi)]$ as a separate programming concept with the following semantics: execution of $[f_1(\xi),\ldots,f_n(\xi)]$ amounts to the independent evaluation of the values of $f_1(\xi),\ldots,f_n(\xi)$, and results in the n-tuple consisting of these values. Provided all state components which are accessed in the original procedure body of f are also contained in its parameter list, the procedure call $f(f_1(\xi),\ldots,f_n(\xi))$ can then be replaced by an expression of the form $[f_1(\xi),\ldots,f_n(\xi)];P$, where P has no parameters and operates upon a state the components of which are accessed by the projection functions $\pi_1,\ldots,\pi_n$.

The generalization of this parameter list construct to the case where paremeters may also be called-by-name dictates our restriction, that, in case all parameters are called-by-name, we must confine ourselves to procedures with procedure bodies in which at least one parameter is invoked. This will be explained next.

Given a terminating call of a procedure some parameters of which are called-by-value, the remaining ones being called-by-name, the very fact of termination of this call guarantees termination of the evaluation of the parameter expressions which are called-by-value; however, the termination of this call guarantees the termination of the evaluation of a parameter expression which is called-by-name only in case its value is actually needed inside the procedure body. Thus the evaluation of some parameter expressions need not terminate at all. If one then separates the parameter list from the actual procedure call as above, one is faced with the problem that in the output of the generalized parameter list one has to handle the undefined components. In order to complete an operationally partially defined n-tuple to an output which is a formally well-defined n-tuple, we introduce a formal element, the so-called *basepoint*, whose function is merely to represent the operationally undefined components. Thus, a basepoint represents a nonterminating computation *whose value is simply not asked for*, and hence may not be transformed into any operationally well-defined value, for otherwise the relevance of our theory to actual programming gets lost. On the other hand, in case of a terminating procedure call of which *none* of its parameters terminate, e.g., the call f("L:goto L","L:goto L") of the integer procedure f(x,y);f := 1, the separation of the parameter list from the call results in an expression of the form ["L:goto L","L:goto L"];P with P always producing an *operationally completely defined* output, even if its formalized input consists of a pair of two basepoints, signalling an *operationally completely undefined* value as input; i.e., P transforms an operationally undefined value into an operationally well-defined value, in violation of the above condition. We resolve this conflict by describing calls of those procedures, which produce an operationally well-defined output by not looking at any component of their input state, by suitably chosen constant terms. E.g., any call $f(f_1(x),f_2(x))$ of f declared above, is described by $U^{2,1};p_1$, with $p_1 = \{<1,1>\}$ and $U^{2,1} = (I\times I)\times I$, where I denotes the set of integers. Hence we may assume that, in case all parameters are called-by-name, a procedure asks for the value of at least one component of its input, and that consequently, in case of a terminating call, the evaluation of the corresponding parameter expression terminates.

Next we demonstrate how certain concepts, which we need in formulating correctness properties of programs, can be expressed within the relational framework.

EXAMPLE 1.2. Let the input-output behaviour of programs S, S_1 and S_2 be described by R, R_1 and R_2, and let the (partial) predicates p and q be represented by the pairs $<p,p'>$ and $<q,q'>$ of disjoint subsets of the identity relation, cf. example 1.1. With D as above, let the *universal* relation U be defined by $U = D\times D$. $R_1 \subseteq R_2$ and $R_2 \subseteq R_1$ together express *equality* of R_1 and R_2, and will be abbreviated by $R_1 = R_2$. S_1 and S_2 are called *equivalent* iff $R_1 = R_2$. $p \subseteq R;\breve{R}$ and $p \subseteq R;U$ both express *termination* of S provided p is satisfied. $\breve{R};R \subseteq E$ expresses *functionality* of R, i.e., R describes the graph of a function.

Correctness in the sense of Hoare [5], {p}S{q}, amounts to: *if* x *satisfies predicate* p *and program* S *terminates for input* x *with output* y, *then* y *satisfies predicate* q, and is expressed by $p;R \subseteq R;q$.

The "$\circ$" operator is defined by $R\circ p = R;p;\breve{R} \cap E$. This operator has been investigated in De Bakker and De Roever [1] in order to prove (and express) various properties of <u>while</u> statements, and has been independently described in Dijkstra [4] using the term "predicate-transformer". It satisfies $R;p;\breve{R} \cap E = \{<x,y> \mid <x,y> \in E$ and $<x,y> \in R;p;\breve{R}\} = \{<x,y> \mid x=y$ and $\exists z[<x,z> \in R, <z,z> \in p$, and $<z,y> \in \breve{R}]\} =$ $= \{<x,x> \mid \exists z[<x,z> \in R$ and $<z,z> \in p]\}$. Thus, if R expresses the input-output behaviour of procedure f, and $<p,p'>$ expresses the boolean procedure p, $p(f(x)) =$ $=$ <u>true</u> iff $<x,x> \in R\circ p$. If we take for p the identically <u>true</u> predicate, represented by $<E,\Omega>$, $<x,x> \in R\circ E$ iff R is defined in x, i.e., $R\circ E$ expresses the *domain of convergence* of R. Note that $R;p;\breve{R} \cap E = R;p;U \cap E$. □

1.2. *Parameter mechanisms and products of relations*

Although in this section mostly partial functions are used, it is stressed that the formalism to-be-developed concerns a calculus of relations.

Given a set D and functions $f\colon D \to D$, $g\colon D\times D \to D$, and $h\colon D\times D\times D \to D$

(*) $\qquad <x,y,z> \longmapsto <f(y),g(x,y),h(x,z,x)>$

certainly describes a function of $D\times D\times D$ into itself. For a relational description this element-wise description is not appropriate. Therefore, when dealing with functions between or with binary relations over finite cartesian products of sets, one introduces projection functions (cf. example 1.1) in order to cope with the notion of coordinates in a purely functional (relational) way, thus suppressing any explicit mention of variables. E.g., (*) describes the function $(\pi_2;f,(\pi_1,\pi_2);g,(\pi_1,\pi_3,\pi_1);h)$. Again, this function has been described component-wise, its third component being $(\pi_1,\pi_3,\pi_1);h$. This does not necessarily imply that

(**) $$(\pi_2;f,(\pi_1,\pi_2);g,(\pi_1,\pi_3,\pi_1);h);\pi_3 = (\pi_1,\pi_3,\pi_1);h$$

holds! E.g., consider the following: f, g and h are *partial* functions, and, for some $\langle a,b,c\rangle \in D\times D\times D$, f(b) is undefined, but g(a,b) and h(a,c,a) are well-defined. Therefore $\langle f(b),g(a,b),h(a,c,a)\rangle$ is undefined as one of its components is undefined.

The problem whether or not (**) is valid turns out to depend on the particular product of relations one wishes to describe, or, in case of the input-output behaviour of procedures, on the particular parameter mechanism used.

In order to understand this, consider the values of fv(1,0) and fn(1,0), with integer procedures fv and fn declared by

<u>integer</u> <u>procedure</u> fv(x,y); <u>value</u> x,y; <u>integer</u> x,y; fv := <u>if</u> x=0 <u>then</u> 0 <u>else</u> fv(x-1,fv(x,y))

and

<u>integer</u> <u>procedure</u> fn(x,y); <u>integer</u> x,y; fn := <u>if</u> x=0 <u>then</u> 0 <u>else</u> fn(x-1,fn(x,y)).

Application of the computation rules of the ALGOL 60 report leads to the conclusion that the value of fv(1,0) is *un*defined and the value of fn(1,0) is *well*-defined and equal to 0.

In order to describe this difference in terms of different products of relations and projection functions, we first discuss two possible products of relations: the *call-by-value* product, which resembles the call-by-value concept from the viewpoint of convergence, and the *call-by-name* product, which incorporates certain properties of the call-by-name concept.

Call-by-value product: Let f_1 and f_2 be partial functions from D to D, then the call-by-value product of f_1 and f_2 is defined by $[f_1,f_2] = f_1;\breve{\pi}_1 \cap f_2;\breve{\pi}_2$, cf. example 1.1. This product satisfies the following properties:

(1) $[f_1,f_2](x) = \langle y_1,y_2\rangle$ iff $f_1(x)$ and $f_2(x)$ are both defined in x, and $f_1(x) = y_1$, $f_2(x) = y_2$.

(2) $[f_1,f_2];\pi_1 \subseteq f_1$, as $f_2(x)$, whence $\langle f_1(x),f_2(x)\rangle$, and therefore $\pi_1([f_1,f_2](x))$, may be undefined in x, although $f_1(x)$ is well-defined.

(3) In order to transform $[f_1,f_2];\pi_1$ we therefore need an expression for the domain of convergence of f_2. Using the "$\circ$" operator introduced in example 1.2, this expression is supplied for by $f_2\circ E$, as $f_2\circ E = \{\langle x,x\rangle \mid \exists y[y=f_2(x)]\}$, as follows from example 1.2. Thus we obtain $[f_1,f_2];\pi_1 = f_2\circ E\,;f_1$. □

Call-by-name product: Let f_1 and f_2 be given as above. For the call-by-name product $[f_1 \times f_2]$ of f_1 and f_2 we stipulate $[f_1 \times f_2];\pi_i = f_i$, i=1,2. Hence $\pi_i([f_1 \times f_2](x)) = f_i(x)$, even if $f_{3-i}(x)$ is undefined, i=1,2. The justification of this property originates from the ALGOL 60 call-by-name parameter mechanism for which the requirement of replacing the formal parameters by the corresponding actual parameters within the text of the procedure body prior to its execution leads to a situation in which evaluation of a particular actual parameter takes place *independent* of the convergence of the other actual parameters. Models for this product are given in the next chapter. □

Before expressing the difference between f_1 and f_2 in the more technical terms of our relational formalism, we discuss the opinion of Manna and Vuillemin [7] concerning call-by-value and call-by-name. We quote: "In discussing recursive programs, the key problem is: *What is the partial function* f *defined by a recursive program* P? There are two viewpoints:

(a) *Fixpoint approach*: Let it be the unique least fixpoint f_P.

(b) *Computational approach*: Let it be the computed function f_C for some given computation rule C (such as call-by-name or call-by-value).

We now come to an interesting point: all the theory for proving properties of recursive programs is actually based on the assumption that the function defined by a recursive program is exactly the least fixpoint f_P. That is, the fixpoint approach is adopted. *Unfortunately, almost all programming languages are using an implementation of recursion (such as call-by-value) which does not necessarily lead to the least fixpoint*. Hence they conclude: "... existing computer systems should be modified, and language designers and implementors should look for computation rules which always lead to the least fixpoint. Call-by-name, for example, is such a computation rule...".

At this point the reader is forced to conclude, that, according to Manna and Vuillemin, call-by-value should be *discarded* (as a computation rule).

Before arguing, that, *quite to the contrary, call-by-value is as suitable for proofs as call-by-name is*, (the latter being accepted by Manna c.s.), we present their argumentation for indictment of the former rule of computation.

Consider again the recursive procedure f defined by

(***) $\quad f(x,y) \Leftarrow \underline{\text{if}}\ x=0\ \underline{\text{then}}\ 0\ \underline{\text{else}}\ f(x-1,f(x,y)).$

They observe that evaluation of f(x,y), (1) using call-by-name, results in computation of $\lambda x,y.\ \underline{\text{if}}\ x\geq 0\ \underline{\text{then}}\ 0\ \underline{\text{else}}\ \bot$, (2) using call-by-value, results in computation of $\lambda x,y.\ \underline{\text{if}}\ x=0\ \underline{\text{then}}\ 0\ \underline{\text{else}}\ \bot$, provided y is defined (where $\bot$ is a formal element expressing operational undefinedness). Then they argue that the minimal fixed point of the transformation

$$T = \lambda X \cdot \lambda x,y \cdot \underline{\text{if}}\ x=0\ \underline{\text{then}}\ 0\ \underline{\text{else}}\ X(x-1,X(x,y))$$

according to the rules of the λ-calculus, where, e.g. $(\lambda u,v\cdot u)\langle x,y\rangle = x$ *holds, in-*

dependent of the value of y *being defined or not*, can be computed, for k a positive natural number, by a sequence of approximations of the form

$$T^k(\Omega) = \lambda x,y.\ \underline{\text{if}}\ x=0\ \underline{\text{then}}\ 0\ \underline{\text{else}}\ \ldots\ \underline{\text{if}}\ x=k-1\ \underline{\text{then}}\ 0\ \underline{\text{else}}\ \bot.$$

Hence the minimal fixed point $\bigcup_{i=1}^{\infty} T^i(\Omega)$ of T equals $\lambda x,y.$ $\underline{\text{if}}$ $x\geq 0$ $\underline{\text{then}}$ 0 $\underline{\text{else}}$ $\bot$. The observation that this minimal fixed point coincides with the computation of (***) using call-by-name, but is clearly different from the computation of (***) using call-by-value, then leads them to denounce call-by-value as a computation rule.

We shall demonstrate that computation of the minimal fixed point of the transformation implied by (***) *gives the call-by-value solution, when adopting the call-by-value product, while computation of the minimal fixed point of this transformation using the call-by-name product results in the call-by-name solution.* Hence we come to the conclusion that *the minimal fixed point of a transformation depends on the particular relational product used, i.e., on the axioms and rules of the formal system one applies in order to compute this minimal fixed point.*

We are now in a position to comment upon Manna and Vuillemin's point of view: as it happens they work with a formal system in which minimal fixed points coincide with recursive solutions computed with call-by-name as rule of computation. Quite correctly they observe that within such a system call-by-value does not necessarily lead to computation of the minimal fixed point. Only this observation is too narrow a basis for discarding call-by-value as rule of computation in general, keeping the wide variety of formal systems in mind.

The transformation implied by (***), using call-by-value as parameter mechanism, is expressed within our formalism by

$$\tau_v(X) = [\pi_1;p_0,\pi_2];\pi_1 \cup [\pi_1;\check{S},X];X$$

where (i) p_0 is only defined for 0 with $p_0(0) = 0$, (ii) $\check{S}$ is the converse of the successor function S, whence $\check{S}(n) = n-1$, $n \in \mathbb{N}$, $n \geq 1$.

It will be demonstrated that the minimal fixed point $\bigcup_{i=1}^{\infty} \tau_v^i(\Omega)$ of this transformation is equivalent with $\pi_1;p_0$, which is in our formalism the expression for the call-by-value solution of (***).

(1) $\tau_v^1(\Omega) = [\pi_1;p_0,\pi_2];\pi_1$ and $[\pi_1;p_0,\pi_2];\pi_1 = \pi_2\circ E\ ;\pi_1;p_0$, by a property of the call-by-value product; as totality of π_2 implies $\pi_2\circ E = E$, we obtain $\tau_v^1(\Omega) = \pi_1;p_0$.

(2) $\tau_v^2(\Omega) = \pi_1;p_0 \cup [\pi_1;\check{S},\pi_1;p_0];\pi_1;p_0$. For $[\pi_1;\check{S},\pi_1;p_0]\langle x,y\rangle$ to be defined, both $(\pi_1;\check{S})\langle x,y\rangle$ and $(\pi_1;p_0)\langle x,y\rangle$ must be defined, i.e., both $x \geq 1$ and $x = 0$ have to hold. As these requirements are contradictory, $[\pi_1;\check{S},\pi_1;p_0];\pi_1;p_0 = \Omega$, and therefore $\tau_v^2(\Omega) = \pi_1;p_0$.

(3) Assuming $\tau_v^k(\Omega) = \pi_1;p_0$, one argues similarly that $\tau_v^{k+1}(\Omega) = \pi_1;p_0$.

(4) Hence $\bigcup_{i=1}^{\infty} \tau_v^i(\Omega) = \pi_1;p_0$, which corresponds with $\lambda x,y.$ $\underline{\text{if}}$ $x=0$ $\underline{\text{then}}$ 0 $\underline{\text{else}}$ $\bot$. □

The transformation implied by (***), using call-by-name as parameter mechanism, is expressed by

$$\tau_n(X) = [\pi_1;p_0\times\pi_2];\pi_1 \cup [\pi_1;\breve{S}\times X];X.$$

We demonstrate that the minimal fixed point $\bigcup_{i=1}^{\infty} \tau_n^i(\Omega)$ of this transformation corresponds with $\lambda x,y$. if $x\geq 0$ then 0 else $\bot$, Manna and Vuillemin's call-by-name solution of (***):

(1) $\tau_n^1(\Omega) = [\pi_1;p_0\times\pi_2];\pi_1$ and $[\pi_1;p_0\times\pi_2];\pi_1 = \pi_1;p_0$, by definition of the call-by-name product; clearly $\pi_1;p_0$ corresponds with $\lambda x,y$. if $x=0$ then 0 else $\bot$.

(2) $\tau_n^2(\Omega) = \pi_1;p_0 \cup [\pi_1;\breve{S}\times\pi_1;p_0];\pi_1;p_0$, by (1); as $[\pi_1;\breve{S}\times\pi_1;p_0];\pi_1 = \pi_1;\breve{S}$, we have $\tau_n^2(\Omega) = \pi_1;p_0 \cup \pi_1;\breve{S};p_0$, corresponding with $\lambda x,y$. if $x=0$ then 0 else if $x=1$ then 0 else $\bot$.

(3) Assume $\tau_n^k(\Omega) = \pi_1;p_0 \cup \pi_1;\breve{S};p_0 \cup \ldots \cup \pi_1;\underbrace{\breve{S};\ldots\breve{S}}_{(k-1)\text{times}};p_0$. As $\tau_n^{k+1}(\Omega) = \pi_1;p_0 \cup \cup [\pi_1;\breve{S}\times\tau_n^k(\Omega)];\tau_n^k(\Omega)$, it follows from the assumption that $\tau_n^{k+1}(\Omega) = \pi_1;p_0 \cup \cup \pi_1;\breve{S};p_0 \cup \ldots \cup \pi_1;\underbrace{\breve{S};\ldots\breve{S}}_{k\text{ times}};p_0$, which corresponds with $\lambda x,y$. if $x=0$ then 0 else ... if $x=k$ then 0 else $\bot$.

(4) Hence $\bigcup_{i=1}^{\infty} \tau_n^i(\Omega) = \bigcup_{i=1}^{\infty} \pi_1;\underbrace{\breve{S};\ldots\breve{S}}_{(i-1)\text{times}};p_0$, corresponding with $\lambda x,y$. if $x\geq 0$ then 0 else $\bot$. □

2. A CALCULUS FOR RECURSIVE PROCEDURES WITH VARIOUS PARAMETER MECHANISMS

2.1. *The interpretation of products of relations*

In chapter 1 we demonstrated how the call-by-value and call-by-name parameter mechanisms could be described (from the viewpoint of convergence) within the relational framework by introduction of a call-by-value product of relations, which has been axiomatized in De Roever [2,3], and a call-by-name product of relations, which will be discussed in the present section. In particular, we introduce a product of relations describing a parameter list some components of which are called-by-value, the remaining ones being called-by-name. Section 2.2.2 contains an axiomatization of *all* these products. By replacing in the axiom system of section 5 of De Roever [2] or chapter 2 of De Roever [3] axioms C_1 and C_2 (the axioms for projection functions upon which our axiomatization of the call-by-value product was based) by the new axioms of section 2.2.2, we obtain a calculus for recursive procedures with various parameter mechanisms.

It has been argued in section 1.1 that the interpretation of the call-by-name product requires the introduction of a special element to each domain, the so-called basepoint, the function of which is merely to complete an operationally partially defined n-tuple to a formally well-defined n-tuple by representing the operationally undefined components, in case these might simply not be invoked within a procedure body (and hence are potentially redundant).

Now the very fact, that the introduction of a basepoint is so closely connected with a relation being undefined in some point, suggests using Scott's undefined value $\perp$, cf. Scott [8] as basepoint; an originally partial function then becomes a total function, which assigns the formal value $\perp$ to those elements for which the original function was undefined, and the same applies to relations: formally they become total. However, when considering *converses* of such relations-made-total, we are stuck for the following reason: *an operationally undefined value should never be transformed by any relation into an operationally well-defined value*, since otherwise the relevance to programming of a theory of such relations gets lost, for once a computer initiates an unending computation it will not produce any definite value (if left to itself). Thus we refrain from the transition of basepoints to undefined values in general.

Prior to interpreting the call-by-name product, we first define the cartesian product of domains with basepoints: The product of domains $D_1,\dots,D_n$ with basepoints $\underline{pt}_1,\dots,\underline{pt}_n$, which are contained in $D_1,\dots,D_n$, respectively, is the cartesian product of $D_1,\dots,D_n$ with basepoint $<\underline{pt}_1,\dots,\underline{pt}_n>$. □

Next we define our admissable relations. The requirement that a basepoint should not be transformed into an operationally defined value, implies conversely that, due to the presence of the conversion operator, an operationally well-defined value should never be transformed into a basepoint. Hence we must observe the following two restrictions when interpreting relations over domains with basepoints:

(1) *A basepoint should be transformed into a basepoint.* ... (2.1.1)

(2) *Only a non-basepoint can be transformed into a non-basepoint.* ... (2.1.2)

EXAMPLE 2.1. Let $D_1,\dots,D_n$ be domains with basepoints, $\underline{pt}_1,\dots,\underline{pt}_n$, respectively, then the projection function π_i: $D_1 \times\dots\times D_n \to D_i$ is defined as follows:

$$\pi_i(<x_1,\dots,x_n>) = \begin{cases} x_i, \text{provided } x_i \neq \underline{pt}_i, \\ \underline{pt}_i, \text{ in case } x_j = \underline{pt}_j,\ j=1,\dots,n, \\ \text{undefined, otherwise,} \end{cases} \quad \dots \ (2.1.3)$$

for $i=1,\dots,n$. □

At last we are in a position to discuss the interpretation of the call-by-name product:

Let $D,D_1,\dots,D_n$ be domains with basepoints $\underline{pt},\underline{pt}_1,\dots,\underline{pt}_n$, and $R_1,\dots,R_n$ be binary relations such that $R_i \subseteq D\times D_i$, for $i=1,\dots,n$, which satisfy (2.1.1) and (2.1.2). Then $[R_1\times\dots\times R_n]$ is interpreted as follows:

$$[R_1\times\dots\times R_n] = \bigcup_{\substack{I\subseteq\{1,\dots,n\} \\ \text{and } I\neq\emptyset}} \{<x,<y_1,\dots,y_n>> \mid xR_jy_j \text{ for } j\in I, \text{ and } y_j=\underline{pt}_j \text{ for } j\in\{1,\dots,n\}-I\}. \ \square$$

For example, $[R_1 \times R_2] = \{<x,<y_1,\underline{pt}_2>> \mid xR_1y_1\} \cup \{<x,<\underline{pt}_1,y_2>> \mid xR_2y_2\} \cup$ $\cup \{<x,<y_1,y_2>> \mid xR_iy_i,\ i=1,2\}$. In particular, $[E \times \Omega] = \{<x,<x,\underline{pt}>> \mid x \in D\}$.
The reader should verify himself, using the interpretation of π_i in example 2.1, that $[R_1 \times \ldots \times R_n];\pi_i = R_i$, $i=1,\ldots,n$. Notice also that
$[R_1 \times \ldots \times R_n];(\pi_{j_1};\breve{\pi}_1 \cap \ldots \cap \pi_{j_k};\breve{\pi}_k) = (R_{j_1};\breve{\pi}_1 \cap \ldots \cap R_{j_k};\breve{\pi}_k)$, for $1 \le j_1 < \ldots < j_k \le n$, i.e., a list of n parameters called-by-name, of which only the j_1-st,...,j_k-th components are invoked, is equivalent with the list of k invoked parameters which are called-by-value.

Nevertheless, for a relational calculus this element-wise description is not appropriate. Therefore we introduce the following constants:
Let $D, D_1, \ldots, D_n$ be as above, then the relation constants $*_1, \ldots, *_n$ are defined by

$$<<x_1,\ldots,x_n>,x> \in *_i \text{ iff } \begin{cases} x = \underline{pt}, \text{ in case } x_j = \underline{pt}_j,\ j=1,\ldots,n, \\ x \in D-\{\underline{pt}\}, \text{ provided } x_i = \underline{pt}_i, \text{ and} \\ \qquad x_j \neq pt_j \text{ for at least one } j,\ j \neq i, \\ \text{undefined, otherwise,} \end{cases} \qquad \ldots \quad (2.1.4)$$

for $i=1,\ldots,n$. □

The introduction of these constant is motivated by the following property: $\breve{*}_i$ transforms any non-basepoint into any n-tuple, the i-th component of which is $\underline{pt}_i$, provided this n-tuple is not composed out of basepoints altogether. Hence we have

$$[R_1 \times \ldots \times R_n] = \bigcap_{i=1}^{n} (R_i;\breve{\pi}_i \cup \breve{*}_i).$$

In general, the ALGOL 60 parameter mechanism allows within the same parameter list for a combination of parameters called-by-value and called-by-name. This combination of parameter mechanisms results in a product of relations, which reflects this mixed structure.
Let procedure f have for simplicity a parameter list of n components, the first k components of which are called-by-value, and the last n-k components of which are called-by-name. Let ξ denote a statevector. As in our formal model of description the parameter list is separated from the procedure call, cf. section 1.1, the separation of $(f_1(\xi),\ldots,f_n(\xi))$ from the call $f(f_1(\xi),\ldots,f_n(\xi))$ results in an expression of the form $[f_1(\xi) \times \ldots \times f_n(\xi)]^{\underline{value}\{1,\ldots,k\}};P$, where the value of $[f_1(\xi) \times \ldots \times f_n(\xi)]^{\underline{value}\{1,\ldots,k\}}$ is only defined in case the evaluation of the first k parameters, the call-by-value parameters $f_1(\xi),\ldots,f_k(\xi)$, terminates. Therefore a relational description of this parameter list is obtained by introducing a product of relations $[R_1 \times \ldots \times R_n]^{\underline{value}\{1,\ldots,k\}}$, which satisfies

$$[R_1 \times \ldots \times R_n]^{\underline{value}\{1,\ldots,k\}};\pi_i = R_1 \circ E ;\ldots; R_k \circ E ;R_i,$$

for $i=1,\ldots,n$.

In general, such products are interpreted as follows:
Let $D,D_1,\ldots,D_n$ be given as above. Let $J \subseteq \{1,\ldots,n\}$ and let $I = \{1,\ldots,n\}-J$. Then $[R_1 \times \ldots \times R_n]^{\underline{\text{value}}\ J}$ is defined by:

$$(\bigcap_{j\in J} R_j;\breve{\pi}_j) \cap (\bigcap_{i\in I}(R_i;\breve{\pi}_i \cup \breve{\star}_i)). \quad \square \qquad \ldots \quad (2.1.5)$$

Observe finally that both the call-by-value and the call-by-name product can be obtained as special case of the product defined above by taking $J = \{1,\ldots,n\}$ and $J = \emptyset$, respectively.

2.2. *A calculus for recursive procedures with various parameter mechanisms*

2.2.1. *Language*

The language MU^* for basepoint preserving relations over cartesian products of domains with unique basepoints, which has minimal fixed point operators, is a simple extension of the language MU, defined in De Roever [2,3].

The syntax of MU^* is obtained from the syntax of MU by adding for $n\geq 2$ the logical relation constants $\star_i^{\eta_1\times\ldots\times\eta_n,\eta}$, for $i=1,\ldots,n$, and all $\eta_1,\ldots,\eta_n$ and η, to the elementary terms of MU.

The semantics of MU^* is determined by considering binary relations over domains with unique basepoints only, observing restrictions (2.1.1) and (2.1.2), and interpreting $\pi_i^{\eta_1\times\ldots\times\eta_n,\eta_i}$ and $\star_i^{\eta_1\times\ldots\times\eta_n,\eta}$ as in (2.1.3) and (2.1.4), for $i=1,\ldots,n$, and all $\eta_1,\ldots,\eta_n$, and η. Hence

(1) $m(\Omega^{\eta,\theta}) = \{\langle \underline{pt}_\eta,\underline{pt}_\theta\rangle \mid \underline{pt}_\eta \in D_\eta,\ \underline{pt}_\theta \in D_\theta\}$, $m(E^{\eta,\eta}) = \{\langle x,x\rangle \mid x \in D_\eta\}$,
$m(U^{\eta,\theta}) = \{\langle x,y\rangle \mid x \in D_\eta - \{\underline{pt}_\eta\},\ y \in D_\theta - \{\underline{pt}_\eta\}\} \cup \{\langle \underline{pt}_\eta,\underline{pt}_\theta\rangle\}$,

(2) interpretations of elementary relation constants $A^{\eta,\theta}$ satisfy
$m(\Omega^{\eta,\theta}) \subseteq m(A^{\eta,\theta}) \subseteq m(U^{\eta,\theta})$,

(3) interpretations of pairs $\langle p^{\eta,\eta},p'^{\eta,\eta}\rangle$ of boolean constants satisfy
$m(\Omega^{\eta,\eta}) \subseteq m(p^{\eta,\eta}) \subseteq m(E^{\eta,\eta})$, $m(\Omega^{\eta,\eta}) \subseteq m(p'^{\eta,\eta}) \subseteq m(E^{\eta,\eta})$, and
$m(p^{\eta,\eta}) \cap m(p'^{\eta,\eta}) = m(\Omega^{\eta,\eta})$,

(4) interpretations of relation variables $X^{\eta,\theta}$ satisfy $m(\Omega^{\eta,\theta}) \subseteq m(X^{\eta,\theta}) \subseteq m(U^{\eta,\theta})$,

(5) the operators "$\cup$", "$\cap$", ";", "$\smile$" are interpreted as usual, and the "$-$" operator is interpreted by $m(\overline{X^{\eta,\theta}}) = (m(U^{\eta,\theta}) - m(X^{\eta,\theta})) \cup m(\Omega^{\eta,\theta})$,

(6) $\mu_i X_1\ldots X_n[\sigma_1,\ldots,\sigma_n]$ is interpreted as the i-th component of the (unique) minimal fixed point of the transformation $\langle m(\sigma_1),\ldots,m(\sigma_n)\rangle$ acting on n-tuples of relations satisfying (2.1.1) and (2.1.2), $i=1,\ldots,n$. Observe that it follows from the definitions that any fixed point of $\langle m(\sigma_1),\ldots,m(\sigma_n)\rangle$ acting on these relations satisfies (2.1.1) and (2.1.2); hence the minimal fixed point of this transformation, being the intersection of all these fixed points, satisfies (2.1.1) and (2.1.2) also.

2.2.2. *Axiomatization*

MU^* is axiomatized by replacing in the axiom system for MU, as contained in chapter 2 of De Roever [3] or section 5 of De Roever [2], axioms C_1 and C_2 by BP_1, BP_2, BP_3, BP_4 and BP_5 below: For $n \geq 2$,

BP_1 : $\vdash \star_1;\breve{\star}_1 \cap \ldots \cap \star_n;\breve{\star}_n = \Omega^{\eta_1\times\ldots\times\eta_n,\eta_1\times\ldots\times\eta_n}$

BP_2 : $\vdash \star_i^{\eta_1\times\ldots\times\eta_n,\xi} = \star_i^{\eta_1\times\ldots\times\eta_n,\theta};U^{\theta,\xi}$, $i=1,\ldots,n$,

BP_3 : $\vdash \pi_i;\breve{\pi}_i \cap \star_i;\breve{\star}_i = \Omega^{\eta_1\times\ldots\times\eta_n,\eta_1\times\ldots\times\eta_n}$, $i=1,\ldots,n$,

BP_4 : $\vdash (\pi_1;\breve{\pi}_1 \cup \star_1;\breve{\star}_1) \cap \ldots \cap (\pi_n;\breve{\pi}_n \cup \star_n;\breve{\star}_n) = E^{\eta_1\times\ldots\times\eta_n,\eta_1\times\ldots\times\eta_n}$

BP_5 : *For all* $I \subsetneq \{1,\ldots,n\}$ s.t. $I \neq \emptyset$:

$$\vdash \bigcap_{i\in I} X_i;Y_i = \{(\bigcap_{i\in I} X_i;\breve{\pi}_i) \cap (\bigcap_{i\in\{1,\ldots,n\}-I} \breve{\star}_i^{\eta_1\times\ldots\times\eta_n,\theta})\};$$
$$\{(\bigcap_{i\in I} \pi_i;Y_i) \cap (\bigcap_{i\in\{1,\ldots,n\}-I} \star_i^{\eta_1\times\ldots\times\eta_n,\xi})\},$$

and for $I = \{1,\ldots,n\}$:

$$\vdash \bigcap_{i\in I} X_i;Y_i = (\bigcap_{i\in I} X_i;\breve{\pi}_i);(\bigcap_{i\in I} \pi_i;Y_i),$$

with π_i of type $(\eta_1\times\ldots\times\eta_n,\eta_i)$, and X_i and Y_i of types (θ,η_i) and (η_i,ξ), respectively, $i=1,\ldots,n$.

The following lemma is proved in De Roever [3]:

LEMMA. *Let* $n\geq 2$, $i=1,\ldots,n$, *and* $j=1,\ldots,n$, *and* $\star_i$ *of type* $(\eta_1\times\ldots\times\eta_n,\eta_i)$, *then*

a. $\vdash \breve{\star}_i;\pi_j = U$, $i\neq j$, *and* $\vdash \breve{\star}_i;\pi_i = \Omega$.

b. *For* $n=2$: $\vdash \breve{\star}_i;\star_j = \Omega$, $i\neq j$, *and* $\vdash \breve{\star}_i;\star_i = U$.
   For $n\geq 3$: $\vdash \breve{\star}_i;\star_j = U$.

c. $\vdash \breve{\pi}_i;\pi_j = U$, $i\neq j$, *and* $\vdash \breve{\pi}_i;\pi_i = E$.

Let $[X_1 \times\ldots\times X_n]^{\underline{\text{value}}\ J}$ be defined as in (2.1.5). Then corollaries 2.1 and 2.2 follow from the above lemma and the definitions.

COROLLARY 2.1. $\vdash [X_1 \times\ldots\times X_n]^{\underline{\text{value}}\{j_1,\ldots,j_k\}};\pi_i = X_{j_1} \circ E\ ;\ldots;\ X_{j_k} \circ E\ ;X_i$, $i=1,\ldots,n$.

COROLLARY 2.2. $\vdash [X_1 \times\ldots\times X_n]^{\underline{\text{value}}\{j_1,\ldots,j_m\}};(\pi_{k_1};\breve{\pi}_1 \cap\ldots\cap \pi_{k_p};\breve{\pi}_p) =$
$= X_{j_1} \circ E\ ;\ldots;\ X_{j_m} \circ E\ ;(X_{k_1};\breve{\pi}_1 \cap\ldots\cap X_{k_p};\breve{\pi}_p)$.

REFERENCES

[1] De Bakker, J.W., and W.P. de Roever, *A calculus for recursive program schemes*, in Proc. IRIA Symposium on Automata, Formal Languages and Programming, M. Nivat (ed.), North-Holland, Amsterdam, 1972.

[2] De Roever, W.P., *Operational and mathematical semantics for recursive polyadic program schemata (extended abstract)*, in Proceedings of Symposium and Summer School "Mathematical Foundations of Computer Science", 3-8 September 1973, High Tatras, Czechoslovakia, pp. 293-298.

[3] De Roever, W.P., *Recursion and parameter mechanisms: an axiomatic approach*, in Automata, Languages and Programming, 2nd Colloquium, University of Saarbrücken, July 29 - August 2,1974, Edited by Jacques Loeckx, Lecture Notes in Computer Science no. 14, Springer-Verlag, Berlin etc., 1974.

[4] Dijkstra, E.W., *A simple axiomatic basis for programming languages constructs*, Indagationes Mathematicae, 36 (1974) 1-15.

[5] Hoare, C.A.R., *An axiomatic basis for computer programming*, Comm. ACM, 12 (1969) 576-583.

[6] Karp, R.M., *Some applications of logical syntax to digital computer programming*, Thesis, Harvard University, 1959.

[7] Manna, Z., and J. Vuillemin, *Fixpoint approach to the theory of computation*, Comm. ACM, 15 (1972) 528-536.

[8] Scott, D., *Lattice theory, data types, and semantics*, in NYU Symposium on formal semantics, pp. 64-106, Princeton, 1972.

[9] Scott, D., and J.W. de Bakker, *A theory of programs*, Unpublished notes, IBM Seminar, Vienna, 1969.

PROCEDURES, FORMAL COMPUTATIONS AND MODELS

Andrzej Salwicki
Institute of Mathematical Machines, Warsaw University
00-901 Warszawa PKiN VIIIp. / POLAND

ABSTRACT

Starting from the logical point of view we conceive procedures as formulas of a formalized algorithmic language defining functions and/or relations. The notion of formal computation is introduced in a way resembling formal proofs. Computations may serve to extend the original interpretation of the language onto symbols defined by procedures. The main result is: if a system of procedures is consistent then the computed extension of a given interpretation is the smallest model of the system. From this the principle of recursion induction can be proved. A technique transforming any system of procedures to a consistent system of conditional recursive definitions is shown.

INTRODUCTION

We are interested in the semantics of procedures. At first we conceive procedures as a recipe of computing and since parameters can be transmitted in different ways this recipe can be understood variously. The notion of formal computation has been proposed in order to obtain a formalized tool for investigation of computations in the presence of procedures. The next step is to conceive procedures as axioms of an algorithmic theory. The question of models i.e. of interprtations arises in a natural way. Is the computed extension of original interpretation of the language a model of the system of procedures?

The answer is yes, if the system of procedures is consistent. Consider the class of all models of the system which are extensions of original interpretation of the language. It can be shown that the computed extension is the smallest in the class. What are other elements of the class which may be of interest for programmer? It seems that searching for the greatest effective model is natural. We are hoping that the construction making use of Gentzen-style diagrams gives the desired result.

§1. LANGUAGE, PROCEDURES, FORMAL COMPUTATIONS.

Let L denotes a formalized algorithmic language [4] . The well-formed expressions of L are of three disjoint sets:

T - terms i.e. formal counterparts of arithmetic expressions,

F - formulas i.e. formal counterparts of Boolean expressions.

FS - programs i.e. expressions built of formulas (F) and substitutions (S) by means of structured programming.

We recall that each FS-expression can be viewed as a program in an ALGOL-like language. Substitutions of the form

$$z_1 := \omega_1 \ \underline{\text{and}} \ \dots \ z_n := \omega_n$$

are the simplest programs. The variables $z_1 \dots z_n$ are either individual or propositional, expression ω_i is then term or open (quantifier-free) formula corresponding to the type of variable z_i $(i=1,\dots,n)$. Every substitution can be translated into a string of assignment instructions. We shal keep the substitutions since their simultaneous execution (first. the values of the expressions ω_i, $i = 1,\dots,n$, are computed; next. all the assignments are simulatneously executed) is more convenient in the treatment of procedures. If two programs P_1 and P_2 are the results of translation of two FS-expressions K_1 and K_2 then the FS-expression $\circ[K_1 \ K_2]$ has to be translated onto following program

$$\underline{\text{begin}} \ P_1 \ ; \ P_2 \ \underline{\text{end}}$$

Similarly, $\veebar[\alpha \ K_1 \ K_2]$ turns into: $\underline{\text{if}} \ \alpha \ \underline{\text{then}} \ P_1 \ \underline{\text{else}} \ P_2$

and $*[\alpha \ K_1]$ into: $\underline{\text{for}} \ i := i \ \underline{\text{while}} \ \neg\alpha \ \underline{\text{do}} \ P_1$

where the variable i does not occur in α or P_1.

We shall also use the notion of realization of a formalized language L in a non-empty set J and two-element Boolean algebra [3.4]

Let $\varphi_1 \dots \varphi_p$ and $\varrho_1 \dots \varrho_l$ be functors and predicates that do not belong to the language L. We shall assume the functor φ_j is m_j-ary $(j=1,\dots,p)$ and the predicate ϱ_i is n_i-ary $(i=1,\dots,l)$. Throughout this paper we shall assume that equality sign is in L. By L′ we shall denote the extension of L obtained by adding the functors $\varphi_1 \dots \varphi_p$ and the predicates $\varrho_1 \dots \varrho_l$ to the alphabet of L.

Let $K_1,\dots,K_l, M_1,\dots,M_p$ be programs i.e. FS-expressions, $\alpha_1 \dots \alpha_l$ - open formulas, $\tau_1 \dots \tau_p$ - terms of the language L′ such that free variables of formulas $K_i\alpha_i$ are $x_1,\dots,x_{n_i}$ (for i=1 ... l) and free variables of terms $M_j\tau_j$ are $x_1 \dots x_{m_j}$ (for j=1 ... p) then the following system of equations and equivalences

$$(*)\quad \begin{cases} \varphi_1(x_1 \dots x_{m_1}) = M_1\tau_1 \\ \dots\dots\dots\dots\dots\dots\dots \\ \varphi_p(x_1 \dots x_{m_p}) = M_p\tau_p \\ \varrho_1(x_1 \dots x_{n_1}) \Leftrightarrow K_1\alpha_1 \\ \dots\dots\dots\dots\dots\dots\dots \\ \varrho_l(x_1 \dots x_{n_l}) \Leftrightarrow K_l\alpha_l \end{cases}$$

will be called system of procedures defining notions $\varphi_1 \dots \varphi_p . \varrho_1 \dots \varrho_l$.

Note, that each procedure can be translated into an ALGOL-like programming language as follows: the equation

$$\varphi(x_1 \dots x_m) = M\tau$$

turns into following procedure:

```
real procedure φ(x1,...,xm); value x1,...,xm;
real x1,...,xm;
begin "the program M translated"; φ:=τ end of φ ;
```

Similarly, the equivalences of (*) -system can be translated into Boolean procedures.

Let R be a realization of language L in a nonempty set J and two-element Boolean algebra B_0. Given an expression $\omega \in$ L′ we shall compute its value at a valuation v in the realization R. Obviously, value of a term will be an element of the set J. value of a formula will be an element of the algebra B_0 of logical values truth and false. value of a program will be a valuation of variables.

We introduce the notion of computation. By a computation we shall understand a finite sequence of ordered triplets $\langle v, \omega, w \rangle$ where

- v - is a valuation of variables,
- ω - is an expression of the language L;
- w - is a value associated with the expression ω at the valuation v.

We assume that the realization R is proper for equality i.e. that the realization of binary predicate = is the identity relation.

We shall admit the following set of computing rules. Each rule has at least one triplet as a premise and exactly one triplet called conclusion or result.

$$(F)\quad \frac{\{\langle v, \tau_i, j_i \rangle\}_{i=1}^{n}}{\langle v, \varphi(\tau_1 \ldots \tau_n), j \rangle} \qquad \text{where } \varphi \text{ is an n-ary functor of L, } \varphi_R(j_1, \ldots, j_n) = j$$

$$(R)\quad \frac{\{\langle v, \tau_i, j_i \rangle\}_{i=1}^{n}}{\langle v, \varrho(\tau_1 \ldots \tau_n), w \rangle} \qquad \text{where } \varrho \text{ is an n-ary predicate of L, } \varrho_R(j_1, \ldots, j_n) = w$$

$$(D1)\quad \frac{\langle v, \alpha, \mathbb{0} \rangle \langle v, \beta, \mathbb{0} \rangle}{\langle v, (\alpha \vee \beta), \mathbb{0} \rangle} \qquad (D2)\quad \frac{\langle v, \alpha, \mathbb{1} \rangle}{\langle v, (\alpha \vee \beta), \mathbb{1} \rangle} \qquad (D3)\quad \frac{\langle v, \beta, \mathbb{1} \rangle}{\langle v, (\alpha \vee \beta), \mathbb{1} \rangle}$$

$$(N1)\quad \frac{\langle v, \alpha, \mathbb{0} \rangle}{\langle v, \neg\alpha, \mathbb{1} \rangle} \qquad (N2)\quad \frac{\langle v, \alpha, \mathbb{1} \rangle}{\langle v, \neg\alpha, \mathbb{0} \rangle}$$

$$(I1)\quad \frac{\langle v, \alpha, \mathbb{1} \rangle \langle v, \beta, \mathbb{0} \rangle}{\langle v, (\alpha \Rightarrow \beta), \mathbb{0} \rangle} \qquad (I2)\quad \frac{\langle v, \alpha, \mathbb{0} \rangle}{\langle v, (\alpha \Rightarrow \beta), \mathbb{1} \rangle} \qquad (I3)\quad \frac{\langle v, \beta, \mathbb{1} \rangle}{\langle v, (\alpha \Rightarrow \beta), \mathbb{1} \rangle}$$

$$(C1)\quad \frac{\langle v, \alpha, \mathbb{1} \rangle \langle v, \beta, \mathbb{1} \rangle}{\langle v, (\alpha \wedge \beta), \mathbb{1} \rangle} \qquad (C2)\quad \frac{\langle v, \alpha, \mathbb{0} \rangle}{\langle v, (\alpha \wedge \beta), \mathbb{0} \rangle} \qquad (C3)\quad \frac{\langle v, \beta, \mathbb{0} \rangle}{\langle v, (\alpha \wedge \beta), \mathbb{0} \rangle}$$

$$(P)\quad \frac{\{\langle v, \omega_i, w_i \rangle\}_{i=1}^{n}}{\langle v, [z_1 := \omega_1 \ \underline{\text{and}} \ \ldots \ z_n := \omega_n], v' \rangle} \qquad \text{where } v'(z) = \begin{cases} w_i & \text{if } z = z_i \\ v(z) & \text{otherwise} \end{cases}$$

$$(S)\quad \frac{\langle v, K, v' \rangle \langle v', M, v'' \rangle}{\langle v, \underline{\text{begin}}\ K ; M\ \underline{\text{end}}, v'' \rangle}$$

$$(B1)\quad \frac{\langle v, \alpha, \mathbb{1} \rangle \langle v, K, v' \rangle}{\langle v, \underline{\text{if}}\ \alpha\ \underline{\text{then}}\ K\ \underline{\text{else}}\ M, v' \rangle} \qquad (B2)\quad \frac{\langle v, \alpha, \mathbb{0} \rangle \langle v, M, v' \rangle}{\langle v, \underline{\text{if}}\ \alpha\ \underline{\text{then}}\ K\ \underline{\text{else}}\ M, v' \rangle}$$

$$(G1)\quad \frac{\langle v, \alpha, \mathbb{1} \rangle}{\langle v, \underline{\text{while}} \neg\alpha\ \underline{\text{do}}\ K, v \rangle}$$

$$(G2)\quad \frac{\langle v.\alpha.\mathbb{1}\rangle \langle v,K,v''\rangle \langle v'',\underline{\text{while}}\neg\alpha\ \underline{\text{do}}\ K,\ v'\rangle}{\langle v,\ \underline{\text{while}}\neg\alpha\ \underline{\text{do}}\ K,v'\rangle}$$

$$(K\tau)\quad \frac{\langle v,K,v'\rangle \langle v',\tau,j\rangle}{\langle v,K\tau,j\rangle} \qquad (K\alpha)\quad \frac{\langle v,K,v'\rangle\langle v'.\alpha,w\rangle}{\langle v,K\alpha,w\rangle}$$

$$(Fv)\quad \frac{\langle v,[x_1/\tau_1\ \dots\ x_n/\tau_n]M\tau,w\rangle}{\langle v,\varphi(\tau_1\dots\tau_n),w\rangle}$$

where φ is an n-ary functor defined by the procedure $\varphi(x_1\dots x_n) = M\tau$

$$(Rv)\quad \frac{\langle v,[x_1/\tau_1\ \dots\ x_n/\tau_n]K\alpha,w\rangle}{\langle v,\rho(\tau_1\dots\tau_n),w\rangle}$$

where ρ is an n-ary predicate defined by the procedure $\rho(x_1\dots x_n) \Leftrightarrow K\alpha$

Triplets of the form

$$\langle v,z,v(z)\rangle \qquad \text{or} \qquad \langle v.\varphi.\varphi_R\rangle$$

where v is a valuation, z - a variable, $v(z)$ - the value ofvariable z at the valuation v. φ - a zero-argument functor, φ_R - its realization i.e. a constant from the set J, will be called <u>elementary</u>.

Let ω be an expression of the language L′, v - a valuation of variables. By a formal computation of the value w of the expression ω at the valuation v with the use of the system (*) of procedures in the realization R, we shall understand any finite sequence of ordered triplets $\{\langle v_i,\ _i,w_i\rangle\}_{i=1}^{N_o}$ such that

1° the last element of the sequence is identical with $\langle v,\omega,w\rangle$

$$\langle v_{N_o},\omega_{N_o},w_{N_o}\rangle = \langle v,\omega\, w\rangle$$

2° for every $i \leq N_o$ either the triplet $\langle v_i,\omega_i,w_i\rangle$ is elementary either it is a result in a computing rule from some triplets among $\langle v_1,\omega_1,w_1\rangle$ ... $\langle v_{i-1},\omega_{i-1},w_{i-1}\rangle$ being premises in that rule.

In the sequel we shall use shorter form "a computation of a triplet $\langle v,\omega,w\rangle$".

Obviously, some triplets possess computations some other do not. Observe, that there are some expressions ω of L′ for which does not exist a valuation v nor a value w such that the triplet $\langle v,\omega,w\rangle$ has a computation. Moreover, some pairs of valuations and expressions of L have the same property.

Example 1.1
Let L be the language of arithmetic, R its realization in the set of nonnegative integers. Let the system (*) consists of one procedure

$f(n) = [\underline{if}\ n=0\ \underline{then}\ z:=1\ \underline{else}\ z:=n \times f(n-1)]\ z$

A computation of the triplet

$\langle v: \frac{x\ y\ u\ z}{2\ 2\ 0\ 0},\ \underline{while} \neg x < y\ \underline{do}\ [u:=x\ \underline{and}\ y:=y+1]\ x=y, \mathbb{0} \rangle$

is presented below. The elements of computation are consecutively numbered, the last item in every line contains a comment showing the origin of the triplet in line i.e. the name of the rule used and numbers of triplets-premises, letter e indicates elementary triplets. Every valuation occurring in computation is displayed once, all subsequent occurrences are denoted by the letter v with corresponding index.

1.	$\langle v: \frac{x\ y\ u\ z}{2\ 2\ 0\ 0},\ x.\ 2 \rangle$	(e) - elementary
2.	$\langle v,\ y.\ 2 \rangle$	(e)
3.	$\langle v,\ x < y, \mathbb{0} \rangle$	(R,1,2)
4.	$\langle v,\ x,\ 2 \rangle$	(e)
5.	$\langle v. y, 2 \rangle$	(e)
6.	$\langle v.\ 1,\ 1 \rangle$	(e)
7.	$\langle v,\ y+1,\ 3 \rangle$	(F,5,6)
8.	$\langle v,\ [u:=x\ \underline{and}\ y:=y+1],\ v_1: \frac{x\ y\ u\ z}{2\ 3\ 2\ 0} \rangle$	(P,4,7)
9.	$\langle v_1,\ x,\ 2 \rangle$	(e)
10.	$\langle v_1,\ y,\ 3 \rangle$	(e)
11.	$\langle v_1,\ x < y, \mathbb{1} \rangle$	(R,9,10)
12.	$\langle v_1,\ \underline{while} \neg x < y\ \underline{do}\ [u:=x\ \underline{and}\ y:=y+1],\ v_1 \rangle$	(G1,11)
13.	$\langle v,\ \underline{while} \neg x < y\ \underline{do}\ u:=x\ \underline{and}\ y:=y+1\ .\ v_1 \rangle$	(G2,3,8,12)
14.	$\langle v_1,\ x,\ 2 \rangle$	(e)
15.	$\langle v_1,\ y,\ 3 \rangle$	(e)
16.	$\langle v_1,\ x=y, \mathbb{0} \rangle$	(R,14,15)
17.	$\langle v,\ \underline{while} \neg x < y\ \underline{do}\ u:=x\ \underline{and}\ y:=y+1\ \ x=y, \mathbb{0} \rangle$	(Kα,13,16)

In fact this computation makes no use of the procedure. A computation of $\langle v: \frac{x\ y\ u\ z\ n}{2\ 3\ 2\ 2\ 5},\ f(1)\ .\ 1 \rangle$ will use the rule (Fv) as it will be seen from the following example.

Example 1.2

1. $\langle v\colon \frac{x\ y\ u\ z\ n}{2\ 3\ 2\ 2\ 5},\ 1,\ 1\rangle$ (e)
2. $\langle v,\ n:=1,\ v'\colon \frac{x\ y\ u\ z\ n}{2\ 3\ 2\ 2\ 1}\rangle$ (P,1)
3. $\langle v',\ 1,\ 1\rangle$ (e)
4. $\langle v'.\ n,\ 1\rangle$ (e)
5. $\langle v',\ n-1.\ 0\rangle$ (F,3,4)
6. $\langle v',\ n:=n-1,\ v_3\colon \frac{x\ y\ u\ z\ n}{2\ 3\ 2\ 2\ 0}\rangle$ (P,5)
7. $\langle v_3,\ n.0\rangle$ (e)
8. $\langle v_3,\ 0,\ 0\rangle$ (e)
9. $\langle v_3,\ n=0,\ \mathbb{1}\rangle$ (R,7,8)
10. $\langle v_3,\ 1,\ 1\rangle$ (e)
11. $\langle v_3,\ z:=1,\ v_4\colon \frac{x\ y\ u\ z\ n}{2\ 3\ 2\ 1\ 0}$ (P,10)
12. $\langle v_3,\ \underline{\text{if}}\ n=0\ \underline{\text{then}}\ z:=1\ \underline{\text{else}}\ z:=n\times f(n-1)\ .v_4\rangle$ (B1,9,11)
13. $\langle v_4,\ z,\ 1\rangle$ (e)
14. $\langle v_3,\lfloor\underline{\text{if}}\ n=0\ \underline{\text{then}}\ z:=1\ \underline{\text{else}}\ z:=n\times f(n-1)\rfloor\ z.1\rangle$ (Kτ,13,12)
15. $\langle v',\lfloor n:=n-1\rfloor\lfloor\underline{\text{if}}\ n=0\ \underline{\text{then}}\ z:=1\ \underline{\text{else}}\ z:=n\times f(n-1)\rfloor z,1\rangle$ (Kτ,6,14)
16. $\langle v',\ n.\ 1\rangle$ (e)
17. $\langle v',\ f(n-1).1\rangle$ (Fv,15)
18. $\langle v',\ n\times f(n-1),\ 1\rangle$ (F,16.17)
19. $\langle v',\ z:=n\times f(n-1),\ v_2\colon \frac{x\ y\ u\ z\ n}{2\ 3\ 2\ 1\ 1}\rangle$ (P,18)
20. $\langle v'.\ 0,\ 0\rangle$ (e)
21. $\langle v',\ n,\ 1\rangle$ (e)
22. $\langle v',\ n=0,\ \mathbb{0}\rangle$ (R,20,21)
23. $\langle v';\ \underline{\text{if}}\ n=0\ \underline{\text{then}}\ z:=1\ \underline{\text{else}}\ z:=n\times f(n-1),\ v_2\rangle$ (B2,22,19)
24. $\langle v_2,\ z.\ 1\rangle$ (e)
25. $\langle v',\ \underline{\text{if}}\ n=0\ \underline{\text{then}}\ z:=1\ \underline{\text{else}}\ z:=n\times f(n-1)\ \ z.1\rangle$ (Kτ 23.24)
26. $\langle v,\lfloor n:=1\rfloor\lfloor\underline{\text{if}}\ n=0\ \underline{\text{then}}\ z:=1\ \underline{\text{else}}\ z:=n\ f\ n-1\rfloor\ z,1\rangle$ (Kτ.2,25)
27. $\langle v,\ f(1).\ 1\rangle$ (Fv.26)

R e m a r k. Observe that the examples are effective due to the simplification we made when the notion of valuation was replaced by a finite sequence of those variables only that occur in (*) and/or in the expression ω.

We can replace rules (Fv) and (Rv) by the rules (Fn) and (Rn)

$$(\mathrm{Fn})\quad \frac{\langle v, \overline{[x_1/\tau_1 \ldots x_n/\tau_n]^{M\tau}}, w\rangle}{\langle v, \varphi(\tau_1 \ldots \tau_n), w\rangle}$$

where $\overline{[x_1/\tau_1 \ldots x_n/\tau_n]M\tau}$ denotes the expression - result of simultaneous substitution of terms $\tau_1 \ldots \tau_n$ for variables $x_1 \ldots x_n$ in the expression $M\tau$. This and the following rule can be applied only if the resulting expression belongs to the language L′.

$$(\mathrm{Rn})\quad \frac{\langle v, [x_1/\tau_1 \ldots x_n/\tau_n]^{K\alpha}, w\rangle}{\langle v, \varrho(\tau_1 \ldots \tau_n), w\rangle}$$

In this way we obtain the second notion of computation. A computation using rules (Fn) and (Rn) will be called "by name " computation. If it will be necessary we shall call computations of the first kind - "by value" computations. Obviously, one can introduce different mixed types of computations. The following

Example 1.3
asserts that notions of computation "by value" and computation "by name" are different. Let us consider the procedure

$$s(x,i) = [\underline{\text{begin}}\ i:=i+1\ ;\ z:=x\ \underline{\text{end}}]z$$

and the realization in the set of integers. For any valuation v computations of the term $s(n^3,n)$ shall give different results ,we obtain n^3 in the case of "by value" computations and $(n+1)^3$ in the case of "by name" computations.

A triplet may possess a "by name" computation and no "by value" computation as it can be seen from the

Example 1.4
Consider the procedure $f(x,y) = [\underline{\text{if}}\ x=0\ \underline{\text{then}}\ z:=2\ \underline{\text{else}}\ z:=f(x-1,f(x,y))]z$
The following triplet $\langle \frac{x\ y}{1\ 2}, f(x,y), 2\rangle$ possesses a computation "by name" and does not possess any "by value" computation.

§2. BASIC PROPERTIES OF COMPUTATIONS

The following lemma indicates that any two computations for a valuation v and an expression ω bring the same result w . even if they are different.

Lemma 2.1

If two triplets $\langle v,\omega,w_1\rangle$ and $\langle v,\omega,w_2\rangle$ possess computations then $w_1=w_2$.

P r o o f is by induction on the length of the computation of the triplet $\langle v,\omega,w_1\rangle$.

If there exists a computation of $\langle v,\omega,w_1\rangle$ of the length 1 i.e. the only triplet in it is elementary then obviously this triplet constitutes a computation of $\langle v,\omega,w_2\rangle$.

Let us assume the lemma true for all computations of the first triplet of the length $\leq k$. Consider a compuattion of the length k+1. Now, according to the last used rule in the computation we shall distinguish following cases:

a. Last used rule is

$$(F)\ \frac{\{\langle v,\tau_i,j_i\rangle\}_{i=1}^{n}}{\langle v,\varphi(\tau_1\ldots\tau_n),w_1\rangle} \quad \text{and } \varphi_R(j_1\ldots j_n)=w_1$$

then in the second computation

$$(F)\ \frac{\{\langle v,\tau_i,j_i'\rangle\}_{i=1}^{n}}{\langle v,\varphi(\tau_1\ldots\tau_n),w_2\rangle}$$

is the last used rule, too. This is so, since there is no other rule that could be used in order to compute the value of the term $\varphi(\tau_1\ldots\tau_n)$. if $\varphi\in L$. From the induction assumption we know that $j_i=j_i'$ $(i=1,\ldots,n)$

b. In the case of the rule (R) our reasoning is similar.

c. Let us assume that the last used rule in the first computation is

$$(D1)\ \frac{\langle v,\alpha,\mathbb{O}\rangle\ \langle v,\beta,\mathbb{O}\rangle}{\langle v,(\alpha\vee\beta),\mathbb{O}\rangle}$$

then it is easily seen that the second compuation can use neither the rule (D2) nor (D3) because computations of $\langle v,\alpha,\mathbb{O}\rangle$ and $\langle v,\beta,\mathbb{O}\rangle$ are of the length $\leq k$ and making use of the inductive assumption we obtain that there is no computation of $\langle v,\alpha,\mathbb{1}\rangle$ nor of $\langle v,\beta,\mathbb{1}\rangle$. Hence the second computation ends with (D1), too.

d. Similarly we discuss the case of the rule (D2)

$$(D2)\ \frac{\langle v,\alpha,\mathbb{1}\rangle}{\langle v,(\alpha\vee\beta),\mathbb{1}\rangle}$$

If the first computation ends with (D2) then the second can not apply the rule (D1) as the last in the computation. Both of remaining possibilities lead to desired conclusion.

e. The cases of rules (D3) - (C3) can be treated similarly.

f. The cases of rules (P)(Fv) (Rv) are similar to the case of (F) rule.

g. If the last used rule is

$$(S)\ \frac{\langle v,\ K,\ v_1'\rangle\langle v_1',\ M,\ w_1\rangle}{\langle v,\ \underline{\text{begin}}\ K\ ;\ M\ \underline{\text{end}},\ w_1\rangle}$$

then in the second computation the last used rule must be

$$(S)\ \frac{\langle v,\ K,\ v_2'\rangle\langle v_2',\ M,\ w_1\rangle}{\langle v,\ \underline{\text{begin}}\ K\ ;\ M\ \underline{\text{end}},\ w_2\rangle}$$

Now, we see that since triplets $\langle v,K,v_1'\rangle$ and $\langle v,K,v_2'\rangle$ both possess computations and the length of computation of $\langle v,K,v_1'\rangle$ is less than k, hence $v_1' = v_2'$, the equality of triplets $\langle v_1',M,w_1\rangle$ and $\langle v_2',M,w_2\rangle$ follows immediately.

h. Similarly we discuss all the remaining cases.

This lemma can be repeated for "by name" computations.

Lemma 2.1^n

If two triplets $\langle v,\omega,w_1\rangle$ and $\langle v,\omega,w_2\rangle$ possess computations "by name" then $w_1 = w_2$.

The following lemma shows that notion of formal computation is an extension of the notion of semantic of formalized languages.

Lemma 2.2

For every expression $\omega \in L$ if there exists a computation of $\langle v,\omega,w\rangle$ in the realization R then

$$\omega_R(v) = w$$

In the following three lemmas we assume the realization R to be total i.e. every operation φ_R associated with a functor φ is total in contrary to realizations by partial operations.

Lemma 2.3

For every term $\tau \in L$, every open formula $\alpha \in L$ and for every valuation v

a. a computation of $\langle v,\tau,w\rangle$ exists iff $\tau_R(v) = w$,

b. a computation of $\langle v,\alpha,w\rangle$ exists iff $\alpha_R(v) = w$.

Lemma 2.4

Let K be a program of the language L, v a valuation. If computation of $\langle v,K,v'\rangle$ does not exist for any v' then the valuation $K_R(v)$ is undefined.

Lemma 2.5

For every $\alpha \in F, \tau \in T, K \in FS$, if computation of $\langle v,K\tau,w\rangle$ does not exist for any w then the value $(K\tau)_R(v)$ is undefined. If computation of $\langle v,K\alpha,w\rangle$ does not exist for any w then the value $(K\alpha)_R(v)$ is $\mathbb{O}$.

Lemmas 2.3 - 2.5 show that computations can be taken as a basis for the semantics of quantifier-free expressions of formalized algorithmic languages instead of the notion of realization.

§3. AN EXAMPLE OF INCOSISTENT PROCEDURE

Making use of the notion of computation we can define the realization R^c an extension of the realization R putting

$$\varphi_{R^c} = \varphi_R \qquad \text{for } \varphi \in L$$

$$\varrho_{R^c} = \varrho_R \qquad \text{for } \varrho \in L$$

and admitting

$$\forall j_1,\dots,j_n \in J \quad \varphi_{R^c}(j_1\dots j_n) = \begin{cases} j & \text{if there exists a computation of } \langle v, \varphi(x_1\dots x_n), j\rangle \text{ where } v(x_i) = j_i \quad i = 1,\dots,n \\ \text{undefined} & \text{otherwise} \end{cases}$$

$$\forall j_1,\dots,j_m \in J \quad \varrho_{R^c}(j_1\dots j_m) = \begin{cases} \mathbb{1} & \text{if there exists a computation of } \langle v, \varrho(x_1\dots x_m), \mathbb{1}\rangle \text{ where } v(x_i) = j_i \quad i = 1,\dots,m \\ \mathbb{O} & \text{otherwise} \end{cases}$$

for the remaining i.e. defined by procedures functors and predicates.

One could expect that the realization R^c is a model for the system $(*)$. The following example shows that it is not the case.

Example 3.1

The system of procedures consists of one procedure

$$\varrho(x) \Leftrightarrow \neg\varrho(x)$$

Regardless of a given realization R its extension satisfies $\forall j \in J \; \varrho_{R^c}(j) = \mathbb{O}$. Coming back to our equivalence we see that ϱ_{R^c} is not a model for it. Obviously, this equivalence can not possess a model due to its inconsistency.

§4. THREE EXAMPLES ILLUSTRATING THE METHOD

Our method of eliminating inconsistencies will be best illustrated by the following examples.

Example 4.1

Let us consider the system of two procedures

$$E\varrho(x) \Leftrightarrow E\varrho(x) \qquad \text{where } E\varrho \text{ is a predicate}$$

$$\varrho(x) \Leftrightarrow \neg\varrho(x)$$

Obviously, $E\varrho_{R^c}(j) = \varrho_{R^c}(j) = \emptyset$ for every $j \in J$.

Consider the following two formulas

$$E\varrho(x) \Leftrightarrow E\varrho(x)$$

$$E\varrho(x) \Rightarrow (\varrho(x) = \neg\varrho(x))$$

Now, the realization R^c is a model of these two formulas. The procedure E "describes" in a sense a process of computing of the value of the procedure . The second implication is valid in R^c since no computation exists.

Before we describe the long general construction of halting formulas and halting procedures, two more examples may be useful in understanding the idea behind it.

Example 4.2

Let us consider the procedure

$$f(n) = [\underline{\text{if}}\ n=0\ \underline{\text{then}}\ z:=1\ \underline{\text{else}}\ z:=n\times f(n-1)]\, z$$

and the expressions

α_1: $f(2) = u$

α_2: $f(2) = u \vee x = y$

The realization is in the set of integers with the obvious meaning of the symbols 0,1, -,

First, we introduce a halting procedure Ef for the procedure f

$$Ef(n) = [\underline{\text{if}}\ n=0\ \underline{\text{then}}\ a:=\mathbb{1}\ \underline{\text{else}}\ a:=Ef(n-1)]\, a$$

Observe that a computation of $\langle v, Ef(n), \mathbb{1}\rangle$ exists iff there exists an integer $w \in N$ such that there exists a computation of $\langle v, f(n), w\rangle$

Let us define

$E^{\emptyset}(\alpha_1)$: $Ef(2)\ f(2) \neq u$

$E^{\mathbb{1}}(\alpha_1)$: $Ef(2)\ f(2) = u$

$E(\alpha_1)$: $E^{0}(\alpha_1) \vee E^{1}(\alpha_1) \Leftrightarrow Ef(2)$

$E^{0}(\alpha_2)$: $(Ef(2) \wedge f(2) \neq u) \wedge (x \neq y)$

$E^{1}(\alpha_2)$: $(Ef(2) \wedge f(2) = u) \vee (x = y)$

$E(\alpha_2)$: $E^{0}(\alpha_2) \vee E^{1}(\alpha_2) \quad = 1$

Observe that a computation of $\langle v, \alpha_1, 1 \rangle$ exists iff there exists a computation of $\langle v, E^{1}(\alpha_1), 1 \rangle$

In the construction given below we shall use procedures of specific form to replace programs occurring in procedures of the system The following example is intended to give the intuition. Let the construction

if α then ω else ω'

be an equivalent replacing the expression $\star[\alpha\ [z/\omega]\ [z/\omega']]z$ where $z \notin V(\alpha) \cup V(\omega) \cup V(\omega')$.

Example 4.3
Let us consider the following program

$$K: \star[x < y\ [u/x \quad y/y+1]]$$

Let us denote by s the substitution $[u/x \quad y/y+1]$ another equivalent denotation of it is u:=x and y:=y+1

We define the system of twelve procedures

$Eh_x^s(x,y,u) \Leftrightarrow 1$ $\qquad h_x^s(x,y,u) = x$

$Eh_y^s(x,y,u) \Leftrightarrow 1$ $\qquad h_y^s(x,y,u) = y+1$

$Eh_u^s(x,y,u) \Leftrightarrow 1$ $\qquad h_u^s(x,y,u) = x$

$Eh_x^K(x,y,u) \Leftrightarrow$ if $x<y$ then 1 else $Eh_x^K(x,y+1,x)$

$Eh_y^K(x,y,u) \Leftrightarrow$ if $x<y$ then 1 else $Eh_y^K(x,y+1,x)$

$Eh_u^K(x,y,u) \Leftrightarrow$ if $x<y$ then 1 else $Eh_u^K(x,y+1,x)$

Let $E(K)$ denote the formula $Eh_x^K(x,y,u) \wedge Eh_y^K(x,y,u) \wedge Eh_u^K(x,y,u)$.

$h_x^K(x,y,u) =$ if $E(K)$ then $\{$if $x<y$ then x else $h_x^K(x,y+1,x)\}$ else $h_x^K(x,y,u)$

$h_y^K(x,y,u) =$ if $E(K)$ then $\{$if $x<y$ then y else $h_y^K(x,y+1,x)\}$ else h_y^K x,y,u

$h_u^K(x,y,u) =$ if $E(K)$ then $\{$if $x<y$ then u else $h_u^K(x,y+1,x)\}$ else $h_u^K(x,y,u)$

Observe the following equivalences which hold for every variable x,y or u, for every valuation v and every value w:

1. conditions (i) and (ii) are equivalent

(i) there exists a computation of $\langle v, Kx, w \rangle$.

(ii) there exists a computation of $\langle v. h^K_x(x,y.u), w \rangle$,

2. conditions (iii) and (iv) are equivalent

(iii) there exists a computation of $v.Eh^K_x(x,y,u).\mathbb{1}\rangle$.

(iv) there exists a value w such that there exists a computation of $\langle v, Kx, w \rangle$,

3. conditions v and vi are equivalent

(v) the valuation $v' = K_R\, v$ is defined.

(vi) there exists a computation of $\langle v. E(K).\mathbb{1}\rangle$.

§5. HALTING FORMULAS AND PROCEDURES

We shall show that the method exemplified in the preceding section is general. A system (**) of procedures associated with the system (*) will be defined.

Four goals are to be achieved by one simultaneous definition

1^0 an extension L" of the language L′.

2^0 a mapping that associates with expressions of L" formulas denoted by $E(\omega)$, $E^{\Phi}(\omega)$, $E^{\mathbb{1}}(\omega)$.

3^0 a mapping which with every program that occurs in (*) associates a system of procedures that replace it.

4^0 a mapping which with every procedure of the system (*) associates its companion - halting procedure.

Every procedure of the system (*) is replaced by a system of new procedures. If the procedure

$$\varphi(x_1 \dots x_n) = M\tau$$

belongs to the system (*) then two procedures

$$\varphi(x_1 \dots x_n) = \tau\left(z_1/h^M_1(y_1 \dots y_m) \dots z_l/h^M_l(y_1 \dots y_m)\right)$$

$$E\varphi(x_1 \dots x_n) = E(M)$$

where $y_1, \dots, y_m$ are all the variables occurring in M, $z_1, \dots, z_l$ are all the variables of the term τ

as well as procedures $h^M_1, \dots, h^M_m$, $Eh^M_1, \dots, Eh^M_m$ associated with the program M and defined below, are inserted into the system (**). Observe that E, $Eh^M_1, \dots, Eh^M_m$ are new predicates when E(M) is a formula.

Definition of the mapping E.

With every term τ we associate a formula $E(\tau)$. With every formula α we associate two formulas $E^{\mathbb{0}}(\alpha)$ and $E^{\mathbb{1}}(\alpha)$, next we admit

$$E(\alpha) = E^{\mathbb{0}}(\alpha) \vee E^{\mathbb{1}}(\alpha)$$

All formulas considered here are quantifier-free.

$E(x) = \mathbb{1}$ where x is an individual variable

$E^{\mathbb{1}}(a) = a$ where a is a propositional variable,

$E^{\mathbb{0}}(a) = \neg a$

$E^{\mathbb{1}}(\mathbb{1}) = \mathbb{1} = E^{\mathbb{0}}(\mathbb{0})$

$E^{\mathbb{0}}(\mathbb{1}) = \mathbb{0} = E^{\mathbb{1}}(\mathbb{0})$

$$E(\varphi(\tau_1,\dots,\tau_n)) = \bigwedge_{i=1}^{n} E(\tau_i) \wedge E\varphi(\tau_1\dots\tau_n)$$

$$E^{\mathbb{0}}(\varrho(\tau_1\dots\tau_n)) = \bigwedge_{i=1}^{n} E(\tau_i) \wedge E\varrho(\tau_1\dots\tau_n) \wedge \neg\varrho(\tau_1\dots\tau_n)$$

$$E^{\mathbb{1}}(\varrho(\tau_1\dots\tau_n)) = \bigwedge_{i=1}^{n} E(\tau_i) \wedge E\varrho(\tau_1\dots\tau_n) \wedge \varrho(\tau_1\dots\tau_n)$$

R e m a r k 1. We assume

$$E\varphi(x_1 \dots x_n) = \mathbb{1} \quad , \quad E\varrho(x_1 \dots x_n) = \mathbb{1}$$

for every functor φ, for every predicate ϱ of the language L.

R e m a r k 2. It is possible to admit partial realization of functors i.e. to allow φ_R to be a partial operation in J. In the sequel such an assumption will be allowed only if there exists a predicate $E\varphi$ in L and its realization $E\varphi_R$ with the following property

$$\varphi_R(j_1 \dots j_n) \text{ is defined iff } E\varphi_R(j_1 \dots j_n) = \mathbb{1}$$

As an example we can take the division operation and the predicate $Ed(j_1, j_2) \overset{def}{=} \mathbb{1}$ iff $j_2 \neq 0$.

$E^{\mathbb{0}}(\alpha \vee \beta) = E^{\mathbb{0}}(\alpha) \wedge E^{\mathbb{0}}(\beta)$

$E^{\mathbb{1}}(\alpha \vee \beta) = E^{\mathbb{1}}(\alpha) \vee E^{\mathbb{1}}(\beta)$

$E^{\mathbb{0}}(\neg\alpha) = E^{\mathbb{1}}(\alpha)$

$E^{\mathbb{1}}(\neg\alpha) = E^{\mathbb{0}}(\alpha)$

$E^{\mathbb{0}}(\alpha \wedge \beta) = E^{\mathbb{0}}(\alpha) \vee E^{\mathbb{0}}(\beta)$

$E^{\mathbb{1}}(\alpha \wedge \beta) = E^{\mathbb{1}}(\alpha) \wedge E^{\mathbb{1}}(\beta)$

$E^{\mathbb{0}}(\alpha \Rightarrow \beta) = E^{\mathbb{1}}(\alpha) \wedge E^{\mathbb{0}}(\beta)$

$E^{\mathbb{1}}(\alpha \Rightarrow \beta) = E^{\mathbb{0}}(\alpha) \vee E^{\mathbb{1}}(\beta)$

With every program M we associate procedures $h_1^M \dots h_m^M$, $Eh_1^M \dots Eh_m^M$

where m is the number of variables of the program M. Definition of these procedures is by induction with respect to the length of the program M. Let us denote the set of all variables $z_1 \ldots z_m$ occurring in M by $\vec{z}$. By E(M) we shall denote the formula $\bigwedge_{i=1}^{m} Eh_i^M(\vec{z})$

Let s be a substitution

$$s: [z_1 := \omega_1 \text{ and } \ldots z_m := \omega_m]$$

where ω_i is a term or a formula corresponding to the type of variable z_i, then we put

$$h_i^s(\vec{z}) = \underline{\text{if}}\ E(s)\ \underline{\text{then}}\ \omega_i\ \underline{\text{else}}\ h_i^s(\vec{z})$$

$$Eh_i^s(\vec{z}) = E(\omega_i) \qquad i = 1 \ldots m.$$

Let us assume that procedures $f_1^K \ldots f_m^K$, $Ef_1^K \ldots Ef_m^K$ are associated with a program K and procedures $g_1^N \ldots g_m^N, Eg_1^N \ldots Eg_m^N$ are associated with a program N.

In the case when program M is of the form $\circ[K\ N]$ we define

$$h_i^M(\vec{z}) = \underline{\text{if}}\ E(M)\ \underline{\text{then}}\ g_i^N(z_1/f_1^K(\vec{z}) \ldots z_m/f_m^K(\vec{z}))\ \underline{\text{else}}\ h_i^M(\vec{z})$$

$$Eh_i^M(\vec{z}) = E(K) \wedge E(g_i^N(z_1/f_1^K(\vec{z}) \ldots z_m/f_m^K(\vec{z})))$$

When the program M is of the form $\veebar[\alpha\ K\ N]$, we define

$$h_i^M(\vec{z}) = \underline{\text{if}}\ E(M)\ \underline{\text{then}}\{\text{if}\ \alpha\ \underline{\text{then}}\ f_i^K(\vec{z})\ \underline{\text{else}}\ g_i^N(\vec{z})\}\ \underline{\text{else}}\ h_i^M(\vec{z})$$

$$Eh_i^M(\vec{z}) = \underline{\text{if}}\ E^{\mathbb{1}}(\alpha)\ \underline{\text{then}}\ Ef_i^K(\vec{z})\ \underline{\text{else}}\ Eg_i^N(\vec{z})$$

When the program M is of the form $*[\alpha\ K]$, we define

$$h_i^M(\vec{z}) = \underline{\text{if}}\ E(M)\ \underline{\text{then}}\{\underline{\text{if}}\ \alpha\ \underline{\text{then}}\ z_i\ \underline{\text{else}}\ h_i^M(z_1/f_1^K(\vec{z}) \ldots z_m/f_m^K(\vec{z}))\}\ \underline{\text{else}}\ h_i^M(\vec{z})$$

$$Eh_i^M(\vec{z}) = \underline{\text{if}}\ E^{\mathbb{1}}(\alpha)\ \underline{\text{then}}\ \mathbb{1}\ \underline{\text{else}}\ E(h_i^M(z_1/f_1^K(\vec{z}) \ldots z_m/f_m^K(\vec{z})))$$

To complete the definition of the mapping E we put

$$E(K\tau) = E(K) \wedge E(\tau(z_{i_1}/h_{i_1}^K(\vec{z}) \ldots z_{i_\tau}/h_i^K(\vec{z})))$$

where $V(\tau) = \{z_{i_1} \ldots z_{i_\tau}\}$

$$E^{\mathbb{0}}(K\alpha) = E(K) \wedge E^{\mathbb{0}}(\alpha(z_{i_1}/h_{i_1}^K(\vec{z}) \ldots z_{i_\alpha}/h_{i_\alpha}^K(\vec{z})))$$

$$E^{\mathbb{1}}(K\alpha) = E(K) \wedge E^{\mathbb{1}}(\alpha(z_{i_1}/h_{i_1}^K(\vec{z}) \ldots z_{i_\alpha}/h_{i_\alpha}^K(\vec{z})))$$

where $V(\alpha) = \{z_{i_1} \ldots z_{i_\alpha}\}$

Now, we define the system of procedures $(**)$ as containing all procedures replacing the procedures of the system $(*)$ and all procedures associated with all programs that occur in the procedures of the system $(*)$. (Compare with the examples of the preceding section.)

The extension L" of the language L′ is obtained by adding all newly defined functors and predicates which occur in $(**)$.

Theorem 5.1

1° For every expression $\omega \in L'$ a computation of $\langle v, \omega, w\rangle$ in the realization R with the use of the system $(*)$ exists iff there exists a computation of $\langle v, \omega, w\rangle$ in the realization R with the use of the system $(**)$.

2° If a computation of $\langle v, \omega, w\rangle$ in the realization R with the use of $(*)$ exists then there exists a compuation of $\langle v, E(\omega), \mathbb{1}\rangle$ and if there exists a compuattion of $\langle v, E(\omega), \mathbb{1}\rangle$ then for certain value w there exists a computation of $\langle v, \omega, w\rangle$.

§6. COMPUTED MODEL OF PROCEDURES

We define the realization R^c - computed extension of the realization R of the language L" in the set J and two-element Boolean algebra B_0 in a way described in §3 for L′.

With the system $(**)$ we associate the following system (w) of conditional recursive definitions (see examples 4.1 4.2)

1. every equivalence of the form

$$E\varphi(x_1 \dots x_n) \Leftrightarrow \omega \qquad \text{or} \qquad E\varrho(x_1 \dots x_m) = \omega'$$

which belongs to $(**)$ is an element of the system (w).

2. all remaining equalities and equivalences of the system $(**)$ are replaced by implications according to the following scheme

   a. if the equality $\varphi(x_1 \dots x_m) = K\tau$ belongs to $(**)$ then the implication

$$E\varphi(x_1 \dots x_m) \Rightarrow \{\varphi(x_1 \dots x_m) = K\tau\}$$

is an element of (w).

   b. if the equivalence $\varrho(x_1 \dots x_m) \Leftrightarrow M\alpha$ belongs to $(**)$ then the implication

$$E\varrho(x_1 \dots x_n) \Rightarrow \{\varrho(x_1 \dots x_n) \Leftrightarrow M\alpha\}$$

is an element of (w).

Theorem 6.1
The realization R^c is a model of the system (w) of conditional recursive definitions.

Making use of "by name" computations we can define another extension R^c_n of the realization R.

Theorem 6.2
The realization R^c_n is a model of the system (w).

§7. PRINCIPLE OF RECURSION INDUCTION

We have proved that R^c is a model of the system (w) in the set J and two-element Boolean algebra B_o. R^c is an extension of the realization R.

The example below shows that a system (w) can possess different models - extensions od R.

Example 7.1
Let (w) be the following system of two formulas

$$Ef(x,y) \Leftrightarrow \underline{if}\ x=0\ \underline{then}\ \mathbb{1}\ \underline{else}\ Ef(x-1,f(x,y)) \wedge Ef(x,y)$$

$$Ef(x,y) \Rightarrow \{ f(x,y) = \underline{if}\ x=0\ \underline{then}\ 2\ \underline{else}\ f(x-1,f(x,y)) \}$$

Let R be the realization in the set of real numbers with obvious meaning of the symbols 0,1,2 and -.

The realization R^c is as follows

$$Ef_{R^c}(j_1,j_2) = \begin{cases} \mathbb{1} & \text{when } j_1 = 0 \\ \mathbb{0} & \text{otherwise} \end{cases}$$

$$f_{R^c}(j_1,j_2) = \begin{cases} 2 & \text{when } j_1 = 0 \\ \text{undefined} & \text{otherwise} \end{cases}$$

It is not difficult to observe that the following extension R′ of R is also a model of (w)

$$Ef_{R'}(j_1,j_2) = \begin{matrix} \mathbb{1} & \text{when } j_1 \in \mathcal{N} \\ \mathbb{0} & \text{otherwise} \end{matrix}$$

$$f_{R'}(j_1,j_2) = \begin{cases} 2 & \text{when } j_1 \in \mathcal{N} \\ \text{undefined} & \text{otherwise} \end{cases}$$

In the sequel we shall consider the set of all extensions of the realization R which are models of (w). It will be denoted by $Ext_R^{(w)}$

The set $Ext_R^{(w)}$ is ordered by the inclusion as follows. We assume that $R' \leq R''$ if both are models of (w) and

a. for every predicate ϱ L

$\varrho_{R'} \subset \varrho_{R''}$ i.e. for all $j_1 \dots j_n \in J$
$\varrho_{R'}(j_1 \dots j_n) = \mathbb{1}$ implies $\varrho_{R''}(j_1 \dots j_n) = \mathbb{1}$

b. for every functor $\varphi \in L''$

$\varphi_{R'} \subset \varphi_{R''}$ i.e. for all $j_1 \dots j_m \in J$ if $\varphi_{R'}(j_1 \dots j_m)$ is defined and equal to j then $\varphi_{R''}(j_1 \dots j_m) = j$.

Theorem 7.1
The model R^c is the least of models of (w) in $Ext_R^{(w)}$.

The theorem 7.1 can be compared with the statements asserting that function computed by a procedure is the least fixed point of this procedure treated as a functional equation.

Theorem 7.2 (principle of recursion induction)
Let (*) be a consistent system of procedures. Let (*) contain only functional (not relational) procedures. We shall treat (*) as a system of functional equations. Every solution R′ of the system (*) (R′ is a model of (*)) with domain equal to the domain of computed solution R^c is equal to R^c.

Here, by the domain of a model R′ we obviously understand the family of sets

$$\{\mathrm{Dom}\,\varphi_{R'}\}_{\varphi \in \{\varphi_1 \dots \varphi\}}$$

where $$\mathrm{Dom}\,\varphi_{R'} \stackrel{def}{=} \{(j_1 \dots j_n) \in J^n : \varphi_{R'}(j_1 \dots j_n) \text{ is defined}\}$$

The following example shows that assumption about absence of relational procedures in (*) is essential.

Example 7.2
Let us consider the following relational procedure

$$\varrho(x,y,z) = \underline{if}\ x=0 \wedge z=2 \text{ then } \mathbb{1} \text{ else } \varrho(x-1,y,z) \wedge \varrho(x,y,z)$$

and two models R^c and R′ in the set of real numbers

$$\varrho_{R^c}(j_1,j_2,j_3) = \begin{cases} \mathbb{1} & \text{when } j_1 = 0 \text{ and } j_3 = 2 \\ \mathbb{0} & \text{otherwise} \end{cases}$$

$\varrho_{R'}(j_1, j_2, j_3) = 1\!\!1$ for all $j_1, j_2, j_3 \in$

Domains of R^c and R' are equal , models are different. This is caused by our definition of R^c realization. Standing on the ground of two-valued logic we put $\varrho_{R^c}(j_1 \dots j_n) = \mathbb{O}$ either if this value is computed or if no computation exists.

§8. FINAL REMARKS

It is not difficult to find greater or even maximal models of procedures. A natural question arises: how to find the greatest of effective models in $Ext_R^{(w)}$?

Another way to find a model of procedures is via Gentzen-style diagrams of formulas. We have no space here to give full details. The idea is as follows: 1° The Gentzen-style axiomatization of algorithmic logic of Mirkowska [2] is taken and enriched: 2° Each procedure is transformed to a scheme according to following example

$\varrho(\tau_1 \dots \tau_n) \Leftrightarrow K\alpha$ is transformed to

$$(Ra) \quad \frac{\Gamma', s\varrho(\tau_1 \dots \tau_n), \Gamma'' \rightarrow \Delta}{\Gamma', s[x_1/\tau_1 \dots x_n/\tau_n]K\alpha, \Gamma'' \rightarrow \Delta}$$

3° The diagram of the relational structure described by the realization R is used to modify the notion of fundamental sequent and also to generate further schenes.

NOTE: the notion of diagram of a formula differs of the notion of diagram of a relational system.

4° The notion of diagram of a formula is borrowed from [2]

Now, diagram of a formula of the form $\varphi(1,2) = u$ can be used in order to compute the value of the procedure $\varphi(x,y)$ at $(1,2)$. Namely, if in the diagramof $\varphi(1,2) = u$ it is possible to turn all non-fundamental sequents to fundamental ones by one simultaneous replacement of the variable u by a constant, say c, then the value of $\varphi(1,2)$ is assumed to be c.

It can be proved [5] that the realization R^D defined in that way is a model of a given system of procedures. A statement asserting that in certain circumstances the model R^D can be extended can be proved and we interpret this as an indication that R^D is the greatest of effectively constructible extensions of R - models of w .

From the example given by W.Dańko [1] follows that there are functions definable by procedures which are not programmable. the relational system in the example is not a constructive one. quite contrary in every constructive relational system (let us denote it by R) all recursively definable functions and relations i.e. R^c, R^c_n, R^D models of the system (w) are programmable in R. From this an analogon of Beth definability theorem can be proved:

Let all models of an algorithmic theory $T = \langle L,C,A \rangle$ are constructive relational systems. If a relation (a function) is implicitly definable in T by a system of procedures than it is programmable In T.

Another notion of computation closer to the computer practice can be introduced. We call these computations algolic [5]. It can be shown that in absence of procedures both notions describe the same. The situation changes however if procedures are introduced. An example shows that formal computations seem to be more advantageous than algolic ones. Also non-functional procedures are introduced first in algolic than in modified formal computations.

It is the author's belief that the studies of formal and algolic computations will allow new implementations of programming languages with procedures and will be of some help in rethinking of hardware.

REFERENCES

[1] Dańko,W. Not programmable function defined by a procedure. Bull.Acad.Pol.Sci. Ser.Math.Astr.Phys. 22 1974 587-594

[2] Mirkowska.G. On formalized systems of algorithmic logic. ibid. 21 1971 421-428

[3] Rasiowa.H.; Sikorski.R. Mathematics of metamathematics. PWN, Warszawa 1963

[4] Salwicki.A. Formalized algorithmic languages. Bull.acd .Pol. Sci. Ser.Math.Astr.Phys. 18 1970 227-232

[5] Salwicki,A. Programmability and recursiveness. an application of algorithmic logic to procedures. to appear in Dissert.Math.

Printed in the United States
By Bookmasters